HANDBOOKS

NORTH CAROLINA

JASON FRYE

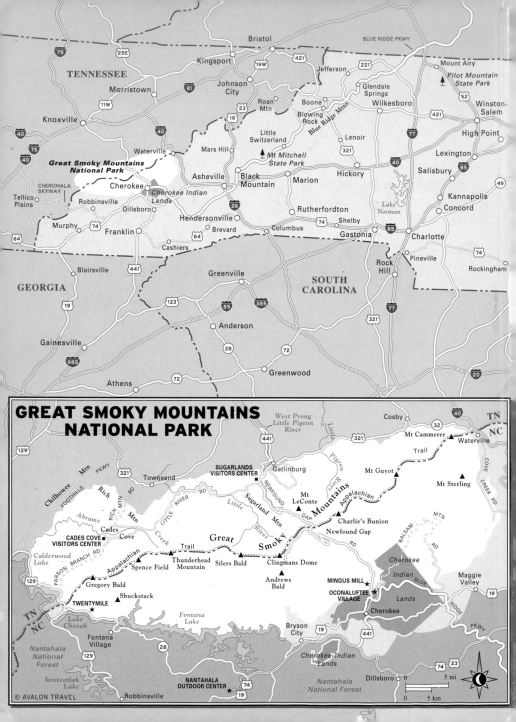

Contents

DISCOVER
North Carolina

North Carolina has a way of getting to you, and it happens in an instant. Pelicans flying in a line, skimming the wave tops, then rising and diving in their strange half-corkscrew and emerging from the ocean. The high, lonesome sound of a bluegrass fiddle calling across the mountain evening, joined by the pluck of a banjo. The heady scent of drying tobacco. No matter what it is that grabs you, you're hooked. You start looking for the gentle peaks of the Smoky Mountains around every corner, watching for the rise of the Blue Ridge on every horizon. You listen for surf crashing, frogs calling, or the wind rattling the heavy heads of sea oats every time you open your window. You find yourself picking a side in the great Tobacco Road basketball debate: Duke or UNC. North Carolina has worked its magic on you.

From the mountains to the sea, from the Outer Banks to Asheville, Charlotte to Chapel Hill, Wilmington to Winston-Salem, you'll find people as varied as the landscapes they inhabit, and histories as wild as the woods, creeks, rivers, and mountains. In the mountains, listen to a

blacksmith play his anvil like a musical instrument, making it "sing" with the hammer. In Greensboro, visit the spot where four brave young men fanned the flames of the Civil Rights movement. Meet communities like the Cherokee and Seagrove, in which traditional arts have been practiced for centuries and are still alive today.

I didn't grow up here, but I call North Carolina home all the same. Come for the pace and quality of life. Come for the barbecue, for the basketball, for the bluegrass. Come to add your own experiences to this contradictory, complex, captivating state. Come to live the state's motto, *Esse Quam Videri*—"to be, rather than to seem"—and let North Carolina's magic make a change in you.

Planning Your Trip

▶ WHERE TO GO

The Outer Banks

This stretch of shoreline is rich with ecological wonders, centuries-old traditions, and historical mysteries. Around Nags Head and the Cape Hatteras National Seashore, surfers and hang gliders ride the wind and waves. One of the first English settlements appeared and then disappeared on Roanoke Island and Blackbeard roamed these waters before losing his head near Ocracoke. Along the vast Pamlico and Albemarle Sounds, colonial towns and fishing villages stand sentinel along deep, still rivers. The Great Dismal Swamp is an eerie, unforgettable place for kayaking and canoeing.

Beaufort and the Crystal Coast

Quiet, comfortable beach towns line the Crystal Coast. Beaufort and New Bern, two of early North Carolina's most important cities, have some of the most stunning early architecture in the South. Morehead City is a hot spot for scuba diving the offshore wrecks in the Graveyard of Atlantic, and Cape Lookout National Seashore has 56 miles of undeveloped shoreline inhabited only by wild horses birds.

Wilmington and the Cape Fear Region

The towns surrounding the mouth of the Cape Fear River are year-round knockouts. The old port city of Wilmington is known for its antebellum homes and gardens as well as lively shops and restaurants. Topsail Island, Wrightsville Beach, and Kure and Carolina Beaches offer some of the most beautiful stretches of sand in the nation. Inland, the Waccamaw and Lumber Rivers creep through blackwater swamps while the Cape Fear River leads upstream to Fayetteville, a military hub.

Raleigh and the Triangle

College towns Raleigh, Durham, and Chapel Hill share a creative verve and intellectual vibe. Visitors enjoy rich music and literary scenes and volcanically exciting college sports. Come hungry and thirsty—fantastic restaurants, bars, and breweries await.

Winston-Salem and Central Carolina

Few visitors experience North Carolina's Piedmont in all its glory, but more should. At the southeastern edge, the Sandhills are a golfing mecca, with the famed Pinehurst Resort and one of the best-known courses in the world, and the nearby town of Seagrove is renowned for its pottery. The ancient, creepy Uwharrie Mountains shelter deep forests and mountain lakes. Greensboro and Winston-Salem house great galleries, museums, and

---

If You Have . . .

- **A Weekend:** Pick one special natural area to explore: the Outer Banks, beaches near Wilmington, the Blue Ridge Parkway, or the Great Smoky Mountains National Park.

- **5 Days:** Add a nearby city—Charlotte, the Triangle, Asheville, Winston-Salem, Greensboro, and Wilmington are all fantastic.

- **A Week:** Add a festival—check out www.visitnc.com or www.ncfestivals.com to find out what's happening during your visit.

- **10 Days:** Go camping—North Carolina's state parks preserve some spectacular natural environments, great hiking trails and boating spots, and wildlife-watching opportunities.

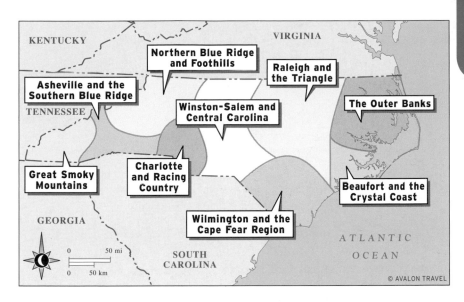

KENTUCKY

VIRGINIA

Northern Blue Ridge
and Foothills

Raleigh and
the Triangle

Asheville and the
Southern Blue Ridge

TENNESSEE

Winston-Salem and
Central Carolina

The Outer Banks

Great Smoky
Mountains

Charlotte
and Racing
Country

Beaufort and the
Crystal Coast

GEORGIA

Wilmington and the
Cape Fear Region

0   50 mi

0   50 km

SOUTH
CAROLINA

ATLANTIC

OCEAN

© AVALON TRAVEL

restaurants. Old Salem preserves the village built by 18th century religious pilgrims, and the Yadkin Valley, the heart of North Carolina's wine country, is nearby.

Charlotte and Racing Country

The Old South, New South, and Global South come together to make Charlotte unmatched in its cultural vitality. The diverse

restaurants alone show this: you'll find everything from fried chicken to *pho* to enchiladas. North of Charlotte is the epicenter of NASCAR at the Charlotte Motor Speedway. The surrounding towns are filled with fun shops and historic sites.

Northern Blue Ridge and Foothills

The Blue Ridge Parkway winds through

NASCAR racing in Charlotte

Blowing Rock

some of the South's most graceful mountain scenery. Friendly foothills towns like Mount Airy and Wilkesboro are rich with mountain music. Blowing Rock retains the feel of an elite mountain retreat from 100 years ago, while nearby college town Boone is progressive and eclectic. Yadkin Valley wineries wait for tasters, and outdoor recreation—hiking, skiing, and whitewater rafting—is abundant.

Asheville and the Southern Blue Ridge

Asheville boasts artistic wealth and deep creative passions. A top beer destination and one of the South's premier food cities, Asheville is filled with galleries, boutiques, and the general weirdness you expect from bigger cities. Its location between the Blue Ridge and Smokies gives easy access to the mountains, where recreation opportunities abound.

Great Smoky Mountains

Straddling the border with Tennessee, the Great Smoky Mountains National Park is a land of ridges, rocky rivers, virgin forests, and tumbling waterfalls. Visit appealing little towns like Dillsboro, Waynesville, and Sylva, as well as the tribal seat of the Eastern band of the Cherokee, a casino, and the first (and only) fly fishing trail in the U.S.

▶ WHEN TO GO

Spring debuts in the southeast as early as late February, then creeps into central North Carolina and up the coast, reaching the mountains a little later. Temperatures are a pretty consistent 60-70 degrees by mid-April. The weather's nice, but some regional events are so large that entire cities or corners of the state may be booked. April is the most challenging month, with Wilmington's Azalea Festival, Durham's

Full Frame Documentary Festival and North Wilkesboro's MerleFest.

Summer is the high season: beaches are jam-packed, traffic is slow in the mountains, and across the state you'll find festivals and events. Heat and humidity can be brutal, and the cooler mountains and coast draw the most visitors for this reason.

Autumn begins in the mountains and spreads across the state. Fall foliage accounts for the mountains' second high season, running from late September through early November; it's busiest in October, when cooler weather offers relief after sweltering September. Near the coast, fall doesn't begin until after hurricane season has passed, in early November. Water along the coast stays swimmably warm past Halloween most years.

Winter is milder here than in many parts of the country, but many businesses in the mountains and along the coast reduce their hours or close entirely. West of I-95, the Piedmont gets a few snow showers, and the coast gets one or two every couple of years. In the mountains, temperatures are much colder and snow falls a few times a year. You'll hear no complaints from skiers. If you plan to visit the beach or the deep mountains in January, book accommodations in advance.

▶ BEFORE YOU GO

Weather can change on a whim. It pays to layer, as temperatures in the 80s can drop into the 60s at night. Pack for chilly weather in the mountains, even in the summer. On the coast, it can be breezy and cool on the water even on warm days.

Cell phone signals are pretty consistent, but there are rural pockets on the extreme coast or in the deep mountains where cell service and 3G, 4G, and LTE connectivity is spotty.

Wilmington's Azalea Festival

An elk grazes in the Cataloochee Valley inside Great Smoky Mountains National Park.

The Best of North Carolina

From the mountains to the sea, North Carolina sweeps across some 560 miles of wildlands, woodlands, and wetlands. Explore towns and cities, shores and summits, Sandhills and Blue Ridge foothills, eating, drinking, and playing your way into nearly every corner of the state.

This day-by-day route takes you from the Great Smoky Mountains in the west to pristine beaches in the east, crossing through rural and metropolitan North Carolina along the way. You could easily reverse the route or start in Charlotte, Raleigh, or Winston-Salem. You need at least two weeks for this epic road trip, but each region stands as its own two- to five-day getaway, allowing you to discover the state on your own terms.

Adventure in the Great Smokies

Hiking, rafting, waterfalls, fly-fishing, sightseeing trains, and the western end of the North Carolina Barbecue Trail are just some of the things waiting around the next mountain curve.

The sun sets over the Smoky Mountains.

DAY 1

Begin your journey in the southwestern corner of the state in Murphy, a town surrounded by towering mountains. Stroll the Murphy River Walk and browse the antiques stores on your way to lunch at Herb's Pit Bar-B-Que, the western terminus of the North Carolina Barbecue Trail. Then, travel northeast to Robbinsville, about an hour away, and hop on the Cherohala Skyway, a 43-mile scenic highway that winds through the Smoky Mountains. Popular with sports-car and motorcycle enthusiasts, the curves and views are thrilling.

An hour east is the quaint railroad town of Bryson City. Take a half-day train excursion on the Great Smoky Mountains Railroad, and check in to a mountain cabin for the night.

DAY 2

Start your day in Bryson City white-water rafting the Nantahala River, then enjoy a riverside lunch at the Nantahala Outdoor Center. Take U.S. 74 southeast to Sylva for prime trout fishing on the Western North Carolina Fly Fishing Trail, or continue past Sylva on to Highway 107 for about an hour to view several waterfalls near the town of Cashiers. Sliding Rock, Silver Run Falls, and Whitewater Falls are beautiful year-round, but stunning in the fall. Reverse course and make the hour trip northwest to Cherokee and spend the night at Harrah's Cherokee Casino and Hotel.

DAY 3

Book a massage at Harrod's Mandara Spa or spend a few hours at the gaming tables. Next, admire Native American art at the Qualla Arts and Crafts Mutual, and visit the Museum of the Cherokee Indian across the street and the Oconaluftee Indian Village, just up the hill. During the summer months, catch an evening performance of *Unto These Hills*.

Great Smoky Mountains National Park is just a few minutes' drive from the town of Cherokee. Reserve a campsite, spend the night in the great outdoors, and prepare for hiking tomorrow.

DAY 4

Take the 30-mile Newfound Gap Road through the park into Gatlinburg, Tennessee, eat lunch, and head back to North Carolina. You're as likely to see a bear as a deer on this stunning scenic road, and you'll also pass a number of trailheads. Trails range from short jaunts to overnight hikes leading deep into the forest. The Alum Cave Trail and trails around Clingmans Dome—the highest point in the Smokies— are popular. The Appalachian Trail crosses Clingmans Dome, so take a stroll here if for no other reason than to say you've hiked on the AT. Beat a retreat back to your campsite or Harrah's and rest up; tomorrow, you're heading to Asheville.

Art and Beauty: Asheville and the Blue Ridge

In Asheville, you'll find streets lined with galleries, one of the nation's largest collections of art deco architecture, and a growing array of chefs, brewers, and mixologists. Farther north, around Boone and Blowing Rock, winter sports abound, but there's plenty to do year-round.

DAY 1

If you're leaving Cherokee, hop on the Blue Ridge Parkway. The first section takes about 30 minutes before you traverse unforgettable mountain passes en route to U.S. 19. From here, it's a 45-minute drive east to Asheville, not counting an essential stop at Maggie Valley's lauded Joey's Pancake House.

In Asheville, head directly to the Biltmore Estate. Tour the Biltmore Winery, watch the blacksmith at Antler Hill Village make music with the anvil, and find lunch at the Biltmore Bistro or Cedric's Tavern. Head downtown and check into Aloft, freshen up, and get ready to roam.

Eat across the street from Aloft at Barley's Taproom and Pizzeria, or at Wicked Weed Brewing one block away, then head to nearby Orange Peel for live music. Make one last stop at Aloft's hotel bar, W Xyz bar, for a nightcap on the patio.

on the Blue Ridge Parkway

The Barbecue Trail

Red Bridges Barbecue Lodge in Shelby

North Carolina is also known as the "Cradle of 'Cue," and we take our barbecue so seriously that old North Carolina families will tell you the four most important things in life are God, family, basketball, and barbecue. The **North Carolina Historic Barbecue Trail,** organized by the North Carolina Barbecue Society, features two dozen renowned barbecue pits and joints that serve true barbecue: cooked over live coals, never on a gas grill or in an electric oven.

Running from east to west, the trail starts in Ayden at the famed **Skylight Inn (p. 92),** where you'll sample eastern North Carolina-style barbecue. This is cooked whole-hog, most often pulled apart rather than chopped, and finished with a pepper-laced vinegar sauce that's clear, tart, and perfect (if you ask folks out east, anyway).

As you move westward, more restaurants add barbecue chicken and ribs to their menus rather than focusing on whole-hog cooking. The transition between eastern and western 'cue becomes apparent in the Piedmont. In

Lexington, home to the annual **Barbecue Festival (p. 232)** held in October, you find the Lexington Dip, a sauce that's somewhere between east and west: just vinegary enough to bring a tang to the pork, but ketchupy enough to thicken it a bit. The Lexington Dip is a bit of an anomaly, and it's hard to find outside the central corridor of North Carolina. For a good example, try **Smiley's Lexington BBQ (p. 232).**

Moving into the mountains, the style changes completely, and the sauce makes all the difference. It takes on a thicker consistency, more like a Kansas City mop (I'll have to watch my back next time I'm having 'cue in the mountains because of that remark) but without so much sweetness. They still use the vinegar of the eastern style, but in less copious amounts. Try **Red Bridges Barbecue Lodge (p. 270)** in Shelby for 'cue that's a cross between western and Lexington Dip. But for the full western North Carolina barbecue experience, you have to head to **Herb's Pit Bar-B-Que (p. 380)** in Murphy.

DAY 2

A few blocks away on Wall Street, breakfast awaits at Early Girl Eatery. Window shop at Malaprop's bookstore and Woolworth Walk art gallery, and don't sweat lunch: a food tour with Eating Asheville will fill you up and point you in a direction for dinner. Walk off your food tour at the Asheville Art Museum while you debate dinner at Cúrate, Cucina 24, or Table.

DAY 3

Eat breakfast at West Asheville's Biscuit Head (and don't skimp on the infused jams and syrups) before hitting the road. Travel east on I-40 for one hour until you reach Morganton. Peruse art galleries like Kalā, then grab lunch at Wisteria Southern Gastropub before heading north on Highway 181 until you reach the Blue Ridge Parkway (about 45 minutes). Slow your pace and follow the parkway past Grandfather Mountain and across the precariously perched Linn Cove Viaduct until you come to the town of Blowing Rock, about 40 minutes if you don't stop to take pictures.

In Blowing Rock, tour the antiques shops and galleries downtown, making your way to the Blowing Rock Art and History Museum, also home to the Blowing Rock Visitors Center. Sleep in a bed-and-breakfast in the heart of downtown.

DAY 4

Visit the namesake Blowing Rock before taking a short drive to Boone. Eat a late breakfast at Sunrise Grill and walk next door to River and Earth Adventures to schedule a guided hike, rafting trip, or caving expedition, then spend the afternoon exploring. Clean up at your bed-and-breakfast, then revisit Boone for dinner at Joy Bistro.

Racing Around Charlotte

In addition to its storied racing sights, Charlotte offers outstanding art museums, first-class dining, and professional sports galore. It's no wonder that its status as a must-visit Southern city seems to be written in stone.

DAY 1

If you're leaving Blowing Rock, drive two hours south along U.S. 321 through Hickory and some beautiful North Carolina countryside until you connect with I-85 outside Gastonia. Once you arrive in Charlotte, take a break from your windshield time at the NASCAR Hall of Fame in the heart of downtown. Great restaurants are located within a few blocks, or you can check into The Dunhill Hotel and explore nearby eateries like gourmet burger joint Cowbell Burger & Bar. After lunch, visit the Mint Museum's uptown location at the Levine Center for the Arts. Here you'll also find the Bechtler Museum of Modern Art, the Harvey B. Gantt Center for African-American Arts + Culture, and the John S. and James L. Knight Theatre, where you might catch a ballet or concert. Dinner at The King's Kitchen, a not-for-profit restaurant serving up fine Southern cuisine, is in order after a day of exploring.

DAY 2

Northeast of Charlotte in nearby Concord is the Charlotte Motor Speedway, a mecca for racing fans. Take a ride-along in a stock car or even take one for a spin yourself. After visiting the track, head across the street to the Concord Mills Mall or visit one of the many golf courses around town. The upscale Ballantyne Hotel Golf Club and affordable Charlotte Golf Links are good choices. Of course, if you're in Charlotte during sports season, take in a Panthers or Hornets game.

DAY 3

Carowinds, a few minutes south of downtown Charlotte, straddles the South Carolina state line and is home to an impressive collection of roller coasters, including the Dale Earnhardt-themed Intimidator. Get your thrills here, or spend the morning shopping in the elegant South Park neighborhood, home to the state's only Neiman Marcus. At the SouthPark Mall, keep an eye out for film stars or some of Charlotte's elite athletes. After shopping, enjoy a leisurely meal at Upstream.

Generations of Artistry

the North Carolina Pottery Center

SEAGROVE POTTERY

Seagrove is an amazing place, a community of artists whose passion for their work has been going strong for more than 200 years. The **North Carolina Pottery Center,** where you'll learn about the roots of this local industry and the families who have made it famous for generations, is a great starting point. Next, venture out into the town of Seagrove and nearby communities like **Whynot** and **Westmoore,** where you'll find dozens of working pottery studios to visit, each producing distinctive and lovely wares.

MORAVIAN ARTISANS

Up in **Winston-Salem,** the district of Old Salem preserves the history and handiwork of one of North Carolina's most interesting historic communities, that of the 18th- and 19th-century Unitas Fratrum, better known as the Moravians. These German and Swiss immigrants and their descendants were wonderful artisans, masters at creating everything from churches to chairs to cookies. At the **Museum of Early Southern Decorative Arts** in Old Salem, you can see the work of many early artisans from Salem and throughout the region.

FOLK ART IN THE MOUNTAINS

Hundreds of artists' studios throughout the Blue Ridge and Smoky Mountains are open to the public, and by driving down almost any major road you'll spot the shops of potters and quilters and carvers. To browse the work of many traditional artists in one place, visit the folk art galleries on the **Blue Ridge Parkway**—the **Folk Art Center** near Asheville and the **Moses Cone Manor** near Blowing Rock—and the **Qualla Arts and Crafts Mutual** in Cherokee, which represents many great artists of the Eastern Band of the Cherokee.

One unusual revival of the beautiful folk art of quilting is a series of nine **Quilt Trails of Western North Carolina,** which feature more than 200 painted "quilt blocks:" wood and paint re-creations of traditional quilt designs. Many hang on the sides of barns and outbuildings, adding to their special charm.

Wining and Dining in Winston-Salem

The Quaker village of Salem and the industry town of Winston merged to form one hard-working town that honors its past as it evolves into a city known for food, arts, and innovation. It's also the gateway to the Yadkin Valley Wine Trail, so come thirsty.

DAY 1

From Charlotte, drive an hour northeast on I-85 to Lexington, home of a tremendous Barbecue Festival each October. Take a tour of the wine-making process at Childress Vineyards and taste to your heart's content, then enjoy a meal onsite. Continue north on U.S. 52 for 30 minutes and check in to one of Winston-Salem's beautiful bed-and-breakfasts, such as the Shaffner House Bed and Breakfast or the possibly haunted Brookstown Inn. For dinner, try internationally inspired Southern dishes at Spring House Restaurant, Kitchen & Bar.

DAY 2

After breakfast at Mary's Gourmet Diner, hit the Yadkin Valley Wine Trail. Head west on U.S. 421 North for 45 minutes to Raffaldini Vineyards and Winery. Make a meal of their gourmet snack selection, then go to your next winery—Medaloni Cellars, Westbend Vineyards and Brewhouse, and Shelton Vineyards are all good options—working your way back east to Winston-Salem. Dinner at Mozelle's Fresh Southern Bistro and a bottle of wine from your tastings make a great end to the day.

DAY 3

After a day of decadence, enjoy some quiet in the colonial Quaker village of Old Salem. Take a self-guided tour through cobblestone streets and colonial homes before visiting the Museum of Early Southern Decorative Arts. Lunch at The Tavern in Old Salem features chicken pie, a recipe based on a dish eaten by the original inhabitants. Visit the Southeastern Center for Contemporary Art, then contrast the pieces there with those at the Reynolda House Museum of American Art. After a day of art and history, relax with a beer and pub food at Foothills Brewing Company downtown.

DAY 4

Travel east on I-40 to Greensboro to see one of the most important sites in Civil Rights history: the Woolworth's Lunch Counter, where a peaceful sit-in ignited the civil rights movement in North Carolina. The International Civil Rights Center and Museum is housed in the former F. W. Woolworth building where the protest took place. After exploring the museum, stop by Natty Greene's Pub to sample ales and IPAs and grab a bite to eat. Spend the afternoon exploring galleries and gardens, then eat dinner at Table 16.

College Town Antics in Raleigh and the Triangle

The Triangle—Raleigh, Durham, and Chapel Hill—is a hotbed of intellectual activity and home a number of major universities. It's a lively international scene with many ethnic and ethnic-fusion restaurants and a trio of fantastic museums in Raleigh, the state capital.

DAY 1

Chapel Hill, about an hour east of Greensboro, is home to the University of North Carolina. This progressive little college town is great to walk and filled with fun eateries. Walk around campus, cruise the streets, and pop into vintage shops, galleries, and boutiques. Thirsty? Point yourself toward The Crunkleton to sample an impressive selection of bourbon. Retire to The Carolina Inn, where you'll find dinner and a bed for the night.

DAY 2

Raleigh, a short drive east from Chapel Hill, is home to the North Carolina Museum of History, North Carolina Museum of Natural Sciences, and North Carolina Museum of Art. The History and Natural Sciences museums are downtown, right across from the capital, perfect for a morning visit. Head to the Museum of Art, not far from downtown, for lunch at Iris, the museum's top-notch restaurant. Splurge and spend the night at The Umstead Luxury Hotel and Spa, a few minutes northwest of downtown Raleigh. Dine there or at one of the great international restaurants downtown, such as Sitti, or try Beasley's Chicken + Honey.

DAY 3

Wake up early to hike or bike the miles of trails in William B. Umstead State Park, just outside the bustle of Raleigh. Drive 20 minutes northwest to Durham and take in some baseball if the Durham Bulls are playing. Downtown, stroll the storied Duke University campus or shop the markets and boutiques before heading to Fullsteam Brewery to find distinctly Southern beers and a rotating lineup of the Triangle's food trucks.

DAY 4

Travel 1.5 hours northeast along U.S. 64 and I-95 to the historic town of Halifax, birthplace of the documents that inspired the Declaration of Independence. Visit the museum and Colonial sites, then head south and east to the Sylvan Heights Waterfowl Center and Eco-Park in Scotland Neck. Continue south along U.S. 258 to U.S. 64 east, which you'll follow through wetlands and swamps until you reach the Croatan Sound and Roanoke Island, the gateway to the Outer Banks and North Carolina's coast. Check into a beachfront motel and get ready to put your toes in the sand.

Cruise the Coast

North Carolina has more than 300 miles of coastline stretching from Virginia to South Carolina. You'll find storied lighthouses, pristine beaches, pirate havens, and places you won't want to leave.

DAY 1

In Nags Head, grab breakfast at Sam & Omie's, an Outer Banks institution, and head to the beach for a brisk morning walk. Brush the sand off your feet, then start traveling north, past the huge sand dune known as Jockey's Ridge and the Wright Brothers

the Wright Brothers National Memorial

Mother Earth Brewing tap selections

National Memorial. Stop in the village of Duck to shop at beach boutiques and enjoy lunch on the sound at Aqua Restaurant and Spa. Check in to Sanderling Resort and Spa before continuing north to Corolla for a wild horse tour and a glimpse at some of the Outer Banks' oldest residents: a herd of wild mustangs known as the Banker ponies. Farther north, climb to the top of Currituck Beach Lighthouse, then head back to the Sanderling for a dip in the ocean and dinner at Kimball's Kitchen.

DAY 2
Head south to visit the Wright Brothers National Memorial. Make a first flight of your own with a hang gliding lesson at Jockey's Ridge State Park, or walk out on the dunes and watch others take to the sky. Head back across the sound to the north end of Roanoke Island and tour the Elizabethan Gardens or catch a performance of *The Lost Colony*, a seasonal outdoor drama. Continue south to Manteo to dine on the waterfront and claim a room at one of Manteo's quaint bed-and-breakfasts.

DAY 3
Cross back onto the mainland and take U.S. 264 south along the Pamlico Sound and through haunting marshlands. Passing through small towns and the Alligator River National Wildlife Refuge, you'll be in a desolate but verdant landscape. As you near civilization, follow Highways 102 and 11 south and west to Kinston. Tour Kinston's Mother Earth Brewing and consider a meal at Chef and the Farmer. From here, you're only 1.5 hours from Wrightsville Beach, your next stop. Take Highway 41 to I-40, then head south to Wilmington and Wrightsville Beach. Check in at a beachfront hotel and dine on the water at Oceanic or Dockside.

DAY 4
Soak up some morning sun at sandy Wrightsville Beach before heading to downtown Wilmington. Try lunch at Copper Penny or Front Street Brewery before browsing River to Sea Gallery or Barouke, shops housed in former shipping warehouses. Grab a craft beer at Cape Fear Wine and Beer or a cocktail at Manna. For dinner Circa 1922

offers fine dining, while Nikki's Restaurant and Sushi Bar caters to a college crowd.

DAY 5
Travel south along U.S. 17 to the southern end of Brunswick County, an hour from Wilmington, to find the Big Cats, a collection of five golf courses. After your round, head to the sea town of Calabash, home of the eponymous and world-famous style of fried seafood. Beck's, Ella's of Calabash, and Coleman's Original use original recipes and serve up heaping platters of golden flounder, scallops, and clams.

Best Scenic Drives

Down East on U.S. 70
U.S. 70 runs almost the entire length of North Carolina, from Asheville to Core Sound. The farthest-east section, a dogleg through Craven, Jones, and Carteret Counties, gives you a taste of life Down East. This is a great drive to take if you're staying in New Bern because you can pick up U.S. 70 there. Drive southeast through the Croatan National Forest, then east through seafood central—Morehead City. When you cross the bridge into the colonial port of Beaufort, leave U.S. 70 for a few blocks by turning right onto a side street. This takes you into historic downtown Beaufort and down to the waterfront along Front Street, where most of the attractions and 18th-century architecture are found.

From Beaufort, U.S. 70 winds up along Core Sound through fishing communities and marshes full of herons and egrets. Just past Stacy, you can either backtrack on U.S. 70 or proceed to the Cedar Island National Wildlife Refuge at the end of the peninsula and catch the Ocracoke Ferry at Cedar Island.

This drive is just over 70 miles. Driving quickly, it could be done in about 1.5 hours. But the point is to dawdle and enjoy the scenery and small towns, so it's more fun to set aside a whole day. It's an attractive drive any time of year, but old coastal cities like New Bern and Beaufort are most gorgeous in spring, especially late March and early April when the azaleas are in bloom.

Cherohala Skyway
On the opposite end of the state, the Cherohala Skyway was built for beauty. For 43 miles between Robbinsville and the town of Tellico Plains, Tennessee, the road winds along the top of the Smoky Mountains, sometimes at elevations well over 5,000 feet. The vistas are incredible, and the road is legendary for motorcyclists and pleasure trippers. Avoid the route in wintry weather, and fill your gas tank and stomach before leaving; there are no facilities other than restrooms along the way. You'll feel like you're in the wilderness on top of the world.

The prettiest times for this drive are summer and fall, but the road is often extremely crowded during leaf season. The Cherohala Skyway website (www.cherohala.com) lists current road conditions.

Blue Ridge Parkway
Running more than 450 miles between Shenandoah National Park in Virginia and Great Smoky Mountains National Park in North Carolina, the Blue Ridge Parkway is the mother of all scenic roads. It covers more than 200 miles in North Carolina, from Lowgap at the state line to Cherokee in the Smokies, and passes by many major destinations in western North Carolina, including Linville Falls, Mount Mitchell, and the Biltmore Estate. There are great places to stay on and near the parkway.

Traveling the parkway from the North Carolina line to Great Smoky Mountains National Park in one day requires a pretty rigorous schedule. Plan at least two days to enjoy sights along the way. Traffic on the parkway is always slow—the maximum

Historic Lighthouses

The Bodie Island Lighthouse opened to climbers for the first time in 2013.

Centuries of mariners have plied the waters off North Carolina's coast, harvesting its aquatic beasts, protecting or prowling the shore, and skirting or foundering on its dangerous shoals. As beautiful as North Carolina's lighthouses are, they were built to perform a service of life-and-death importance. Today, the historic lights—some still in operation—are popular destinations for visitors. Most are open for climbing and offer fantastic views. The following are some of North Carolina's favorites.

- Visitors willing to climb the 214 spiral steps to the top of **Currituck Beach Lighthouse (p. 33)** are treated to a dazzling view of Currituck Sound.
- Climb to the top of **Bodie Island Lighthouse (p. 52),** which overlooks Lighthouse Bay and the Atlantic Ocean. This striking structure has been sending its signal out to sea since 1872, but was closed to the public until 2013.
- **Cape Hatteras Lighthouse (p. 53),** the tallest brick lighthouse in the United States, has a black-and-white spiral exterior that makes it visible from miles away. Pay a small

admission price to climb all the way to the top.

- Whale oil originally powered the beam of **Ocracoke Lighthouse (p. 56),** the second-oldest working lighthouse in the United States. Because it's still on duty, visitors can't go inside, but there are lovely places to walk on the grounds.
- The black-and-white diamond-spangled **Cape Lookout Lighthouse (p. 106),** one of the most iconic symbols of North Carolina, has stood watch since 1859. The nearby keeper's quarters give an intriguing glimpse into the isolated and meditative life of the light keeper. While you're there, explore Cape Lookout's 56 miles of unspoiled beach, where you may have a close encounter with one of the Outer Banks' famous wild horses.
- Commissioned by Thomas Jefferson and built in 1817, **Old Baldy Lighthouse (p. 144)** is North Carolina's oldest lighthouse. From its strategic point on the southern coast of Bald Head Island, Old Baldy has seen has seen nearly two centuries of commerce, war, and peace.

The Blue Ridge Parkway is beautiful year round.

speed limit never exceeds 45 mph, and along many stretches driving that fast would be reckless. Traffic can be congested in summer, particularly on weekends, and during leaf season. In any season, drive slowly and be ready to hit the brakes. The twisty road can get incredibly foggy, and you never know when a deer or other beast will leap out of the trees.

Sections of the parkway sometimes close due to weather or other conditions. Snow and ice are considerations three seasons of the year; rockslides are also possible. To find out about current closures, visit www.nps.gov/blri or call 828/298-0398.

Highway 12: A Serene Seascape

Highway 12 traces the Outer Banks from the mainland onto the barrier islands and all the way up to the Virginia border. It's a 160-mile trip that shows you nearly every square inch of the Banks.

Start at Sealevel (technically on U.S. 70, but a great place to start a beachside drive) and connect with Highway 12. Take the ferry at Cedar Island across to Ocracoke, home to one of the state's oldest lighthouses, and the place where the pirate Blackbeard held an epic party before losing his head, literally, in a nearby inlet. Continue through scenery that's surreally beautiful and serene. Another ferry takes you to the village of Hatteras at the southern end of Hatteras Island, part of the Cape Hatteras National Seashore. This landscape is desolate and beautiful, although you'll find tiny villages along with a legion of surfers and kite-surfers. Crossing Oregon Inlet, you're approaching the touristed section of the Outer Banks and stellar options for food and lodging. You'll travel from Whalebone Junction into Nags Head and the dunes of Jockey's Ridge, then on to Kill Devil Hills, where the Wright Brothers took their first flight, and the towns of Duck and Corolla, where the paved highway ends. If you're adventurous and have a four-wheel-drive vehicle and beach driving experience, head north a few miles toward the Virginia border. A herd of wild horses (and not much else) lives here.

THE OUTER BANKS

The Outer Banks stand off the northeastern corner of North Carolina like a magnificent net. They catch all sorts of things: storms, shipwrecks, horses, history, and the hearts of visitors. This thin strip of islands stretches some 125 miles and an hour-long ferry ride from the Virginia border to the end of Ocracoke Island. Susceptible to profound change brought about by the grind of wind and waves and the force of single storms, the Outer Banks stand guard, protecting the inland and fragile marshland of the Inner Banks. A powerful hurricane can fill a centuries-old inlet in a night and open a new channel a few hundred yards away. As recently as 2012, Hatteras Island was again cut off from the rest of the Outer Banks as Hurricane Sandy washed out roads, damaged bridges, and filled roadways with several feet of sand. The landscape poses challenges to the life it supports, but those same challenges have created an adaptable and hardy group of plants, animals, and people.

Between the Outer Banks and the mainland in the Inner Banks is a collection of sounds known as the Albemarle-Pamlico Estuary. Many travelers ignore the sounds, giving them little more than a glance as they cross on a bridge or a ferry, but they play an enormously important role in the region. The Albemarle-Pamlico Estuary is the second-largest estuarine system in the country after Chesapeake Bay to the north, and it includes Albemarle, Pamlico, Core, Croatan, Roanoke, and Currituck Sounds. Covering more than 3,000 square miles, they drain more than 30,000 square miles and provide diverse marine and terrestrial

© JASON FRYE

HIGHLIGHTS

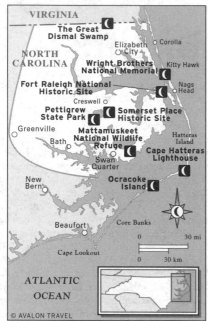

© AVALON TRAVEL

LOOK FOR ⬤ TO FIND RECOMMENDED SIGHTS, ACTIVITIES, DINING, AND LODGING.

⬤ **Wright Brothers National Memorial:** See where North Carolina earned the slogan "First in Flight" and view a replica of the famed *Wright Flyer* (page 30).

⬤ **Fort Raleigh National Historic Site:** See where the Lost Colony, the first English settlement in the New World, mysteriously disappeared in the 1580s (page 43).

⬤ **Cape Hatteras Lighthouse:** Climb to the top of this iconic lighthouse at the tip of Cape Hatteras in the nation's first National Seashore (page 53).

⬤ **Ocracoke Island:** On this remote island, you'll find a historic village that is the home to one of the country's most unique communities, along with the waters where Blackbeard met his fate and one of the oldest lighthouses in the nation (page 55).

⬤ **The Great Dismal Swamp:** This natural wonder, straddling the Virginia-North Carolina border, is an amazing place for canoeing, kayaking, bird-watching, and sightseeing (page 59).

⬤ **Somerset Place Historic Site:** The graceful architecture and exotic setting of this early plantation contrast with the tragic history of its involvement in slavery (page 68).

⬤ **Pettigrew State Park:** Lake Phelps, the centerpiece of Pettigrew State Park, is an attractive enigma, a body of shallow water with a deep history (page 68).

⬤ **Mattamuskeet National Wildlife Refuge:** The landmark lodge on Lake Mattamuskeet towers over a dramatic waterscape that attracts tens of thousands of migratory birds (page 72).

environments that shelter essential plant and animal life. The vast and beautiful marshlands and wide shallow sounds protect the mainland from storm surges and the Atlantic Ocean from toxins and sediment, all the while providing nursery grounds to countless fish and bird species.

Sheltered from the Atlantic, the Inner Banks are a much more accommodating (ecologically speaking) and familiar landscape than

the Outer Banks. Along the marshes and wetlands, hundreds of thousands of migratory birds shelter and rest on their annual journeys, while pocosins (a kind of bog) and maritime forests have nurtured innumerable generations of animals and people. This is where you'll find North Carolina's oldest towns—Bath, New Bern, and Edenton. Settlers established their roots here and the towns have survived for more than 300 years. In Washington County, a rural expanse of farms and wetlands, 4,000-year-old canoes pulled out of Lake Phelps stand witness to the region's unplumbed depths of history. Rivers flow from farther inland, with towns like Roanoke Rapids and Halifax that played a vital role in North Carolina's history and development from colony to state.

PLANNING YOUR TIME

Most visitors plan to come to the coast during late spring and summer, and the reasons are obvious: the beaches, restaurants and attractions that are only open in season, and numerous warm-weather festivals and goings-on. Summer is a great time to visit, but many prefer the shoulder seasons: early to mid-spring and early in the fall. During the fall, the water is still warm, most of the restaurants and attractions are still open, and the crowds are smaller. To many of us who live here, the solitude offered by a winter beach is hard to beat, and a growing number of visitors are coming to love the coast in the off-season as well.

As schools and colleges call students back and the summer season ends, eastern North Carolina's second busy season begins: the tobacco harvest. In rural areas, trucks laden with huge yellow-green tobacco leaves head for the curing barns. The smell of curing tobacco, and later the tight bales of golden leaves, is like none other, and once you smell it, you'll have a taste for fall in this part of the state. Early autumn also brings intermittent clouds of smoke as farmers and backyard-garden hobbyists clear their summer gardens and prepare the ground for cool-weather crops. Beds of lettuce and onions and patches of mustard greens and collards begin to appear alongside houses. Collards, which are at their most flavorful after a touch of fall frost, are a local favorite, although they're popular with North Carolina transplants and visitors searching for an authentic Southern dish. There's no end to the way folks here will prepare collards, but they either accent or mask their mustiness; either way, after a forkful, you'll go back for more. Cotton comes in late in the year and as the bolls ripen, the fields appear snow-covered and quite beautiful.

Spring and fall, and even the occasional winter warm spell, offer many ideal days for exploring eastern North Carolina's rivers, creeks, and swamps in a kayak, canoe, or stand-up paddleboard. Mild temperatures are comfortable enough for a day of paddling, and though the foliage is still green, the absence of summer's leafiness means you can see deeper into the landscape and spy on wildlife from a safe distance. Keep in mind, though, that you can see alligators or even snakes in late fall and throughout the winter. They're never far off, and an especially warm day will have them seeking out sunny patches for basking. If you go for a hike, wear boots, and don't wade or swim in fresh water. Keep an eye out for alligators if you're in, on, or around the water. Gators are hard to spot, especially if you've never looked for them, so watch for their nostrils and the bony ridges of their brow and dorsal spines just above the water's surface.

While the coast can be ideal to visit in the fall, remember that autumn is peak hurricane season in North Carolina. Surfers may love the waves before and after storms, but even people with lots of experience avoid hurricanes. These storms can be beautiful in their ferocity and violence, but anyone who's been through even a weak hurricane will tell you they're no joke. About a week before a fall visit, check the long-term forecasts and call to confirm the weather where you're staying. If authorities issue evacuation orders during your visit, don't hesitate, just pack up and head to safety on the mainland.

INFORMATION AND SERVICES

The **Aycock Brown Welcome Center** (Milepost 1, Kitty Hawk, 877/629-4386, www.outerbanks.org, 9am-5pm daily, closed Thanksgiving and Dec. 25) at Kitty Hawk and the **Outer Banks Welcome Center on Roanoke Island** (1 Visitors Center Circle, Manteo, 252/473-2138 or 877/629-4386, www.outerbanks.org, 9am-5pm daily, closed Thanksgiving and Dec. 25) are the main welcome centers in the Outer Banks, with smaller

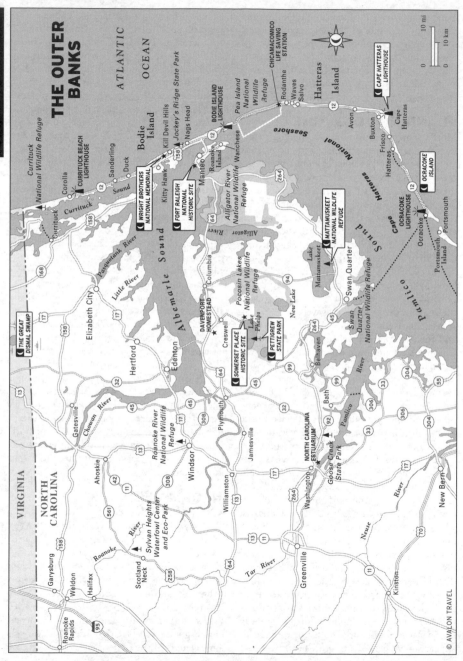

THE OUTER BANKS

PRONUNCIATION PRIMER

North Carolina is full of oddly pronounced place-names, and the farthest northeast corner is a good place to pause for a lesson in talking like a native. The Outer Banks are a garland of peculiar names as well as names that look straightforward but are in fact pronounced in unexpectedly quirky ways. If you make reference publicly to the town of Corolla and pronounce it like the Toyota, you'll be recognized right away as someone "from off." It's pronounced "ker-AH-luh." Similarly, Bodie Island, site of the striped lighthouse, is pronounced "body." That same pattern of pronouncing o as ah is repeated farther down the coast at Chicamacomico, which comes out "chick-uh-muh-CAH-muh-co." But just to keep you on your toes, the rule doesn't apply to Ocracoke, which is pronounced like the Southern vegetable and Southern drink: "O-kra-coke."

Farther south along the banks is the town of Rodanthe, pronounced "ro-DAN-thee." On Roanoke Island, Manteo might resemble a Spanish word but is in fact front-loaded, like so many Carolina words and names. It's pronounced "MAN-tee-oh" or "MAN-nee-oh." Next door is the town of Wanchese, pronounced like a pallid dairy product, "WAN-cheese." Inland, Cashie River is pronounced "cuh-SHY," Bertie County is "ber-TEE," and Chowan County is "chuh-WAHN." If you think the names around here are unusual, just wait until you get into the mountains.

welcome centers at Hatteras and Whalebone Junction.

Major hospitals include **The Outer Banks Hospital** (4800 S. Croatan Hwy., Milepost 14, Nags Head, 252/449-4500, www.theouterbankshospital.com) in Nags Head, **Albemarle Health** (1144 North Road St., Elizabeth City, 252/335-0531, www.albemarlehealth. org) in Elizabeth City, **Vidant Roanoke-Chowan Hospital** (500 S. Academy St., Ahoskie, 252/209-3000, www.vidanthealth. com) in Ahoskie, **Vidant Chowan Hospital** (211 Virginia Rd., Edenton, 252/482-8451, www.vidanthealth.com) in Edenton, **Vidant Beaufort Hospital** (628 E. 12th St.,

Washington, 252/975-4100, www.beaufortregionalhealthsystem.org) in Washington, **Vidant Bertie Hospital** (1403 S. King St., Windsor, 252/794-6600, www.vidanthealth. com) in Windsor, and **Halifax Regional Hospital** (250 Smith Church Rd., Roanoke Rapids, 252/535-8011, www.halifaxregional. us) in Roanoke Rapids. On Ocracoke, which is only accessible by air or water, nonemergency medical situations can be addressed by **Ocracoke Health Center** (305 Back Rd., 252/928-1511, after-hours 252/928-7425, www.ocracokeisland.com). Note that 911 emergency service is available on Ocracoke, as it is throughout the state.

Nags Head and Vicinity

Coral reefs anchor most barrier islands, lending them a bit of strength and permanence; not so on North Carolina's Outer Banks. Here, no reef helps shape the islands, and they're more like enormous sandbars, susceptible to the whims of the wind, the sea, and storms. But that's part of the beauty. These natural forces shape the land as well as its history and culture.

Jockey's Ridge, a 100-foot-high dune visible to sailors far out to sea, has been used as a navigational aide for hundreds of years. Legend has it that Nags Head earned its name because of these dunes and the passing ships. Islanders known as proggers (a shipwreck scavenger or land pirate) would lead a nag or mule along the beach and dune ridge, a lantern hung around

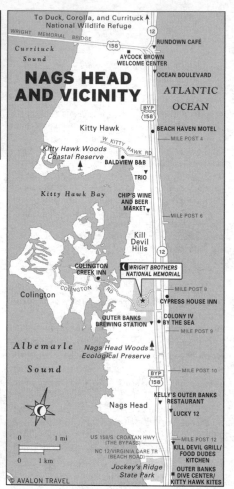

a NASA engineer and inventor of hang gliding. Today, thousands flock to the Wright Brothers Memorial to see where history was made, and even more visit Jockey's Ridge to watch hang gliders or even to take to the sky themselves. With kite-flying, kite-boarding, skydiving, parasailing, and even paragliding, flight enthusiasts love the Outer Banks. Add to this sailing, diving, surfing, paddling, hiking, bird-watching, and, of course, visits to beaches like Duck, which is lovely at sunset, and Corolla, where you can spot wild ponies, and it's obvious that the northern Outer Banks are among the most promising areas in North Carolina for outdoor adventure.

SIGHTS
◖ Wright Brothers National Memorial

In 1903, Orville and Wilbur Wright changed the world in just 12 seconds. Their first flight was short, but it was the culmination of more than three years of failed designs, tests, and travels between their Dayton, Ohio, home and Kitty Hawk, North Carolina, where they tested their gliders on Kill Devil Hill, then the tallest dune on the Outer Banks. A number of Banker families fed and housed them, built them hangars, and assisted with countless trial runs that helped make their experiment a success. On the morning of December 17, 1903, several local people were on hand to help that famous first powered flight get into the air. John Daniels, a lifesaver from a nearby station, took the iconic photo of the airplane lifting off. It was the only photograph he ever took. He was later quoted in a newspaper saying of the flight, "I didn't think it amounted to much." Even though he was unimpressed, the feat is honored at the **Wright Brothers National Memorial** (Milepost 7.5, U.S. 158, Kill Devil Hills, 252/441-7430, www.nps.gov, park daily year-round, visitors center 9am-5pm daily). Replica gliders, artifacts from the original flight, and tools the Wright brothers used to make their flight possible are on display. In the adjacent field a wooden runner and stone markers show their runway, takeoff point, and the spots where

its neck, luring ships into the shallows and shoals where they'd wreck, making their cargo easy pickings. Likewise, the shoals, shallows, and currents gave birth to the heroic members of the United States Lifesaving Service, predecessor to the Coast Guard, who braved many storms to save those shipwrecked.

The relentless wind on the Outer Banks lured Orville and Wilbur Wright to Kill Devil Hills, where they became the first people in history to take flight. It also drew Francis Rogallo,

© JASON FRYE

The Wright Brothers National Memorial stands tall over Kill Devil Hills.

their first four flights landed. Climb to the top of nearby Kill Devil Hill to the 60-foot monument honoring their achievement and marking the spot where they launched hundreds of gliders that preceded that first powered flight. At the foot of the hill, a life-size bronze sculpture of the *Wright Flyer* seconds after liftoff lets you get a sense of the excitement of the moment.

Jockey's Ridge State Park

Jockey's Ridge State Park (Milepost 12, U.S. 158, 252/441-7132, http://ncparks.gov, park 8am-6pm daily Nov.-Feb., 8am-8pm daily Mar.-May, 8am-9pm daily June-Aug., 8am-8pm daily Sept.-Oct., visitors center 9am-5pm daily Nov.-Feb., 9am-6pm daily Mar.-Oct.), contains 420 acres of recreational opportunities in an array of environments. With the big dune, which shifts between 80 and 100 feet high, the smaller dunes surrounding it, the maritime forest, and the sound, you can sand-board (think snowboarding at the beach), fly kites, hike, go for a swim, or even learn to hang glide.

Nags Head Woods Ecological Preserve

Adjacent to Jockey's Ridge, the Nature Conservancy maintains the 1,400-acre **Nags Head Woods Ecological Preserve** (701 W. Ocean Acres Dr., 1 mile from Milepost 9.5 on U.S. 158, 252/441-2525, www.nature.org, dawn-dusk daily year-round). The landscape includes deciduous maritime forest, dunes, wetlands, and interdune ponds, providing a compact look at the diverse environments found on the Outer Banks. It's a bird-watcher's paradise as more than 50 species nest here in season. Ruby-throated hummingbirds, green herons, and red-shouldered hawks are among the easiest to spot, but don't just look for winged wildlife; a number of land animals and reptiles, and even some unusual plants, call this place home. Five miles of public trails wind through the property, starting at the visitors center.

Kitty Hawk Woods Coastal Reserve

Kitty Hawk Woods Coastal Reserve (south of U.S. 158, Kitty Hawk, trail access from Woods Rd. and Birch Lane, off Treasure St., 252/261-8891, http://nccoastalreserve.net, dawn-dusk daily year-round), an 1,822-acre nature preserve maintained by the North Carolina Coastal Reserve, contains one of the largest remaining maritime forests in the Outer Banks. Maritime forests help barrier islands absorb the brunt of powerful storms, and Kitty Hawk Woods contains unusual examples of maritime swale ecosystems, swampy forest sheltered between coastal ridges. Hiking and birding opportunities are abundant, and exploring it from the water via canoe, kayak, or stand-up paddleboard is easy thanks to a put-in. Hunting is permitted in Kitty Hawk Woods, so exercise caution while hiking or paddling during the spring and fall hunting seasons.

Jennette's Pier

My family vacationed on the Outer Banks, and **Jennette's Pier** (7223 S. Virginia Dare Tr., Nags Head, 252/255-1501, www.jennettespier. net, 8am-5pm daily Dec.-Mar., 6am-midnight

© JASON FRYE

sandy trail at Jockey's Ridge State Park

daily Apr., 5am-midnight daily May-Aug., 6am-midnight daily Sept.-Nov., fishing $12, under age 13 $6, walk-on $2 donation) was a fixture on each trip. The then-wooden pier, originally built in 1939, was picturesque but fragile; the owners repaired it after each storm until 2003, when the North Carolina Aquariums bought the pier and Hurricane Isabel demolished 540 feet of the pier structure. Many thought it was the end of this beach-side institution, but a new 1,000-foot concrete pier was built. Now an educational and recreational platform managed by the North Carolina Aquarium, the new Jennette's Pier is a LEED Platinum-certified facility and a beautiful lasting structure. Staff here are friendly and accommodating, and during peak season, activities that include summer day camps and nighttime seashore explorations teach kids and adults alike about the ecology of the area.

Currituck Heritage Park

We've come to expect grand ostentatious beachside homes, but on the shore of Currituck Sound, you'll find what may be the original one on the Outer Banks: the **Whalehead Club** (1100 Club Rd., Corolla, 252/453-9040, www.whaleheadclub.org, 9am-5pm Mon.-Sat. summer, 11am-4pm Mon.-Sat. off-season). This art deco home was built in the 1920s as a summer cottage for Edward Collings Knight Jr., an industrialist whose wealth was made in railroads and sugar. The beautiful simple yellow house is the centerpiece of **Currituck Heritage Park,** where visitors can picnic, wade, launch from the boat ramp, or learn about the ghosts (yes, it's rumored to be haunted, and it's no wonder, with so many shipwrecks just off shore).

Next to the Whalehead Club is the **Outer Banks Center for Wildlife Education** (1160 Village Lane, Corolla, 252/453-0221, www.ncwildlife.org, 9am-4:30pm Mon.-Sat., donation). Exhibits focus on native birds, fish, and other creatures in Currituck Sound as well as a huge collection of antique decoys. These decoys represent an important folk-art tradition and way of life for many along the Carolina

© JASON FRYE

Jennette's Pier

coast. They're beautiful not just for their design but also for their utility. Naturalists put on a number of nature and art programs throughout the year; check the calendar on the website before you go to see what they have planned.

A favorite spot here is the **Currituck Beach Lighthouse** (1101 Corolla Village Rd., 252/453-4939, www.currituckbeachlight. com, 9am-5pm daily Mar.-Nov., $7, under age 8 free with an adult) and its grounds. Built in 1875, this 158-foot-tall redbrick lighthouse is open to ascend much of the year. As you climb the 214 steps to the top, think about the lighthouse keepers, who for years carried pails of lard, then later pails of kerosene, to the top to fuel the light. Once at the observation deck, take a moment to catch your breath and take in the scenery (and hold onto your hat; it can be windy). The Currituck light is a twin to the Bodie Island Lighthouse, 32 miles south. Upon its completion it lit the last "dark spot" on the North Carolina coast, making for safer navigation.

Corolla Wild Horse Museum

In the town of Corolla you'll find a museum dedicated to some of the more unexpected residents of the Outer Banks. The **Corolla Wild Horse Museum** (1129 Corolla Village Rd., Corolla, 252/453-8002, www.corollawild-horses.com) tells the history of the herd of horses that have lived on the Outer Banks from Corolla to Cape Lookout since the 1600s. The Corolla herd now lives in a preserve north of the town, and several guides offer tours to see the horses in their native habitat.

ENTERTAINMENT AND EVENTS

My favorite spot for wine and beer on the Outer Banks is **Trio** (308 N. Croatan Hwy., Milepost 4.5, 252/261-0277, http://obxtrio. com, 11am-11pm Mon.-Sat., noon-10pm Sun.). The trio the name refers to is wine, beer, and cheese, the passions of the four owners. The selection at Trio is focused and representative of different styles, nations, and grape varietals. Upstairs, North Carolina wine

© JASON FRYE

The distinctive redbrick Currituck Beach Lighthouse is the northernmost lighthouse in the state.

and beer tastings are complimentary and serve as a good introduction to drinks produced across the state. Other tastings include the Trio Passport (focusing on wine from different nations) as well as varietal- and style-specific tastings. Nearly two dozen beers are on tap, and self-serve wine vending stations give you the chance to try tasting-size samples or even full glasses of expensive, hard to find, or interesting wines. Trio serves a selection of small plates, including paninis, salads, cheese plates, and other nibbles that go well with a glass of whatever you're drinking.

Chip's Wine and Beer Market (Milepost 6, Croatan Hwy./U.S. 158, Kill Devil Hills, 252/449-8229, www.chipswinemarket.com) is exactly what its name says. More than 450 craft beers from regional, national, and international breweries along with 2,000-plus wines line the shelves—but don't worry, the knowledgeable staff can find a brew or a bottle that suits your taste. Chip's is also home of the Outer Banks

Wine University, offering everything from beginner classes to private tastings.

Food Festivals

As food-centered travel has gained momentum, four festivals taking advantage of this trend have emerged on the Outer Banks. Each draws visitors during the shoulder seasons and showcases something different about the area and its food.

In March, **Taste of the Beach** (www.obx-tasteofthebeach.com) features wine tastings, cooking classes by local chefs, cook-offs, dine-arounds, and more, hosted by more than 50 restaurants, breweries, wine shops, and food purveyors on the Banks. The four-day festival (there are plans to make it longer) culminates with the OBX Grand Tasting, where restaurants compete for the best overall dish, best local seafood dish, the Chefs Award, and the People's Choice Award. *Coastal Living* magazine named Taste of the Beach one of the top seafood and wine festivals in the country in 2008, and it has been on the list ever since.

The **Duck and Wine Festival** (www.duck-andwine.com), a one-day cook-off held in mid-late April, brings foodies together in the town of Duck to sample dishes that local chefs have created using, you guessed it, duck. The town of Duck shines again in mid-October for the **Duck Jazz Festival** (www.townofduck.com), a one-day festival that features talented national jazz artists and alfresco dining from some of Duck's best restaurants.

Mid-October is also the time for the **Outer Banks Seafood Festival** (www.outerbanksseafoodfestival.org). Although oyster roasts, clam bakes, shrimparoos, and other informal seafood celebrations have been the norm on the Outer Banks for more than a century, 2012 was the first year for this formal seafood festival. More than a dozen restaurants participate in the one-day event, and organizers plan to grow the festival into a marquee event.

Nightlife

One part beach dive bar, one part sports bar, **Lucky 12** (Milepost 12, S. Virginia Dare Tr./

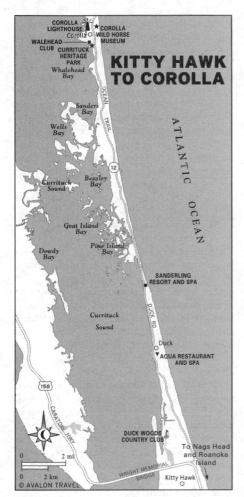

KITTY HAWK TO COROLLA

4:30pm-1am Sun.-Thurs., 4:30pm-2am Fri.-Sat., entrées around $22, tavern fare around $10) is a good bet for live music. Throughout the week karaoke and open-mike nights are the norm, but the weekend feature DJs and bands. With a tavern and a dining-room menu, it's easy to find the right thing to eat.

Ocean Boulevard (Milepost 2.5, N. Virginia Dare Tr./Hwy. 12, Kitty Hawk, 252/261-2546, www.obbistro.com, 5pm-9pm Mon.-Thurs., 5pm-1:30am Fri., 5pm-10pm Sat., 5pm-9pm Sun., entrées $21-31), an upscale but casual martini bar and bistro, features live music on Friday and Saturday during the season, and with the impressive drink menu, it's easy to see why the place is popular with locals and visitors.

Port O' Call Restaurant (Milepost 8.5, S. Virginia Dare Tr./Hwy. 12, Kill Devil Hills, 252/441-7484, http://obxportocall.com, call for hours, entrées $16-28) has been an Outer Banks fixture for more than 50 years. The menu features local seafood and a nice wine list, and live entertainment is available in the bar almost nightly throughout high season.

The Comedy Club (252/207-9950, www.comedyclubobx.com) is, well, a comedy club with two locations on the Outer Banks. Local, up-and-coming, and established comedians perform nightly in summer at the Comedy Club in the Ramada Plaza Hotel (Milepost 9.5, S. Virginia Dare Tr./Hwy. 12, Kill Devil Hills, showtimes vary), and Wednesday in summer at the Currituck Club (620 Currituck Clubhouse Dr., Corolla, showtimes vary). Both clubs serve cocktails and appetizers during the show.

SHOPPING

Much of the shopping on the Outer Banks is focused on beachy souvenir T-shirts and tchotchkes, or beach supplies like towels, boogie boards, and rash guards. There are too many of these mass-market beachwear clearing houses to list, but they're so prolific that they're easy to find. There are also some boutiques, carrying things like bathing suits, art, and jewelry.

Birthday Suits (2000 S. Croatan Hwy./U.S.

Hwy. 12, Nags Head, 252/255-5825, www.lucky12tavern.com, 11:30am-2am daily) is a hit with locals and visitors alike. With 20 beers on tap, another 90 in bottles or cans, a staggering 40-martini drink menu, and more than a dozen TVs, it's the kind of place to watch a game, hang out with friends, and order a pizza (served until 2am).

Kelly's Outer Banks Restaurant and Tavern (Milepost 10.5, U.S. 158, Nags Head, 252/441-4116, www.kellysrestaurant.com,

158, Milepost 10, Kill Devil Hills, 252/441-5338, http://birthday-suits.com, 10am-9pm daily summer, 10am-6pm daily spring, 10am-5pm daily fall) has been in the business of outfitting Bankers and visitors in the best bathing suits for more than 25 years. **Kitty Hawk Kites** (Milepost 12.5, S. Croatan Hwy./U.S. 158, Nags Head, 252/449-2210, www.kittyhawk.com, call for hours) carries swimwear and beach supplies as well as kites, toys, and an assortment of beach games and sports equipment.

In Duck, **Scarborough Faire** (1177 Duck Rd., Duck, 540/272-0974, www.scarborough-faireinducknc.com, hours vary, generally from 10am daily), has served the boutique shopping needs of visitors and residents for over 30 years. More than a dozen shops call Scarborough Faire home, including **Island Bookstore** (252/261-8981, www.islandbooksobx.com, 9am-7pm Mon.-Fri., 9am-6pm Sat.-Sun.), which carries a decent selection of best-sellers and books for kids and teens, and **The Mystic Jewel** (252/255-5515, http://themysticjewel.com, 10am-5pm Mon.-Sat., 11am-4pm Sun.), a jewelry store specializing in unusual stones and limited-edition jewelry pieces by artists from around the world; prices range $20 to around $400.

Fans of local art will want to take a look at **KDH Cooperative Gallery and Studios** (502 S. Croatan Hwy./U.S. 158, Milepost 8.5, Kill Devil Hills, 252/441-9888, www.kdhcoopera-tive.com, 10am-6pm Mon.-Sat.), where more than 40 artists, selected by a jury of their peers to be the best to hang and sell in the gallery, show oil, acrylic, and watercolor paintings, photography, ceramics, sculptures, and more; a few even keep working studios here, providing the opportunity to see them in action. Prices vary as wildly as the media and styles, but if you're an art lover, KDH Cooperative is a must-see.

SPORTS AND RECREATION
Kayaking and Stand-Up Paddleboarding

The Outer Banks combines two very different paddle-sport opportunities, kayaking and stand-up paddleboarding (SUP), in two very different environments—the challenge of ocean paddling and even surfing, and the leisurely drifting tours of salt marshes and creeks. **Kitty Hawk Kites** (Milepost 12.5, S. Croatan Hwy./U.S. 158, Nags Head, 252/449-2210, www.kittyhawk.com, kayak tours $35-55, SUP lessons $59) has locations up and down the Outer Banks where they offer kayak tours, SUP lessons and rentals, and a range of other recreational activities and equipment. *National Geographic Adventure* magazine called them one of the "best adventure travel companies on earth," and they have been in business since the early 1990s.

Kitty Hawk Kayak & Surf School (Milepost 1, N. Croatan Hwy./U.S. 158, Kitty Hawk, 252/261-0145, www.khkss.com, tours $40-60, kayak rentals $99 per week, SUP rentals $150 per week) teaches kayaking and SUP, rents equipment for paddling and surfing, and leads group and private tours, including overnighters. Many of the tours take you to seldom-seen marsh habitats and gorgeous creeks, and even back to the mainland to explore the waterways of the Alligator River National Wildlife Refuge.

Coastal Kayak Touring Company (reservations at North Beach Outfitters, 1240 Duck Rd., Duck, 252/441-3393, www.outerbankskayaktours.com, kayak tours $40-60, SUP tours $50-65) leads groups through some of the beautiful nature reserves on the Outer Banks, namely Kitty Hawk Woods Coastal Reserve and the Pine Island Audubon Sanctuary. Tours range 1.5 to 3 hours.

Outer Banks Stand-Up Paddle (1446 Duck Rd., Duck, 252/305-3639, www.outerbankssup.com, lessons $45-150, rentals from $145 per week) teaches SUP techniques from the basics to the challenge of SUP surfing. Introductory lessons on the sound give first-timers a feel for the board in shallow, wave-free water, where they can build confidence to try ocean-side SUPing on their own with a rented board or with an advanced lesson. The most advanced paddlers will definitely want to take advantage of the SUP surfing lessons.

© JASON FRYE

Kayak the vast sounds along the Outer Banks to experience the barrier islands in a unique way.

Diving

The **Outer Banks Dive Center** (3917 S. Croatan Hwy., 252/449-8349, www.obxdive.com) offers instruction and guided tours of wrecks off the coast of the Outer Banks. Guided wreck dives are only available April-November. All levels of divers are welcome.

Hiking and Tours

At **Jockey's Ridge State Park** (Milepost 12, U.S. 158, 252/441-7132, http://ncparks.gov, park 8am-6pm daily Nov.-Feb., 8am-8pm daily Mar.-May, 8am-9pm daily June-Aug., 8am-8pm daily Sept.-Oct., visitors center 9am-5pm daily Nov.-Feb., 9am-6pm daily Mar.-Oct.), explore the dunes at your own pace or follow one of the trails. The Soundside Nature Trail is about one mile long and takes you through maritime thickets and grassy dunes on a walk through a seldom-seen part of the park. Follow the Tracks in the Sand trail on its 1.5-mile course early in the morning to see undisturbed animal tracks left during the night. Remember,

the dunes can be considerably warmer and the sand can be downright hot, especially during the summer. Bring sunscreen, shoes, and plenty of water if you're trekking around this park.

The **Currituck Banks National Estuarine Preserve** (Hwy. 12, 252/261-8891, www.nccoastalreserve.net) protects some 1,000 acres of woods and water, extending far out into Currituck Sound. A short boardwalk runs from the parking lot to the sound, and a primitive trail runs 1.5 miles through the maritime forest.

You can hike in any park and most of the preserves on the Outer Banks, but nothing compares to seeing the Wild Horses in Corolla. The **Corolla Wild Horse Fund** (1129 Corolla Village Rd., Corolla, 252/453-8002, www.corollawildhorses.com, $45, $20 children) is a nonprofit group dedicated to preserving the herd and its environment, and they lead tours (3 times daily Mon.-Sat.). On the tour you'll ride along with herd managers and conservationists and get a glimpse into how they help

THE OUTER BANKS

keep the horses and their environment safe and healthy.

Back Country Outfitters and Guides (107-C Corolla Light Town Center, Corolla, 252/453-0877, http://outerbankstours.com, wild horse tours $49, $29 ages 3-12, Segway safari $124 over age 12) leads wild horse tours as well as backcountry Segway tours, kayak trips, and other off-road tours.

Surfing

North Carolina has a reputation among surfers for having some of the best waves on the East Coast, making this a top destination for experienced surfers and those new to the sport. **Kitty Hawk Kites** (Milepost 12.5, S. Croatan Hwy./U.S. 158, Nags Head, 252/449-2210, www.kittyhawk.com)provides lessons and board rentals. At **Island Revolution Surf Co. and Skate** (252/453-9484, www.island-revolution.com, group lessons $65 pp, private lessons $110), you can take private or group surf lessons, and more experienced surfers can opt to join the Surf Safari, where local surfers teach the finer points of reading local waves and breaks and show you some of the best surf spots on the island. **Farmdog Surf School** (2500 S. Virginia Dare Tr., Nags Head, 252/255-2233, http://farmdogsurfschool.com, $65) and **Corolla Surf Shop** (807 Ocean Tr., Corolla, 252/453-9283, www.corollasurfshop. com, $68) also offer lessons, rentals, and advice.

If you're a veteran surfer and you're bringing your own board, several online resources will help you find the best conditions and the perfect breaks. The websites of the Outer Banks District of the Eastern Surfing Association (www.outerbanksesa.com), OBXSurfInfo (www.obxsurfinfo.com), Surfline (www. surfline.com), and SwellInfo (www.swellinfo. com) will help you find the best places to suit up and drop in.

Hang Gliding

With all the wind on the Outer Banks, everyone thinks about flying a kite, but how about flying a hang glider? **Kitty Hawk Kites** (Milepost 12.5, S. Croatan Hwy./U.S. 158,

hang gliding off Jockey's Ridge

© JASON FRYE

Nags Head, 252/449-2210, www.kittyhawk. com, $99) offers dune hang gliding lessons that will give you a taste of the thrill of flight as you lift off over the face of dunes on Jockey's Ridge. More than 300,000 people have learned to hang glide here since the company's Hang Gliding Training Center opened in 1974. Learning to fly on the dunes is quite a thrill, but you can up the thrill factor and try a tandem flight that will have you and an instructor towed up to a mile high before being released to fly back to earth. If you want to pursue advanced certification through the United States Hang Gliding Association, you can do that on the dunes or on a tandem flight; you can even buy a glider and all the accessories you need to get started at the Kitty Hawk Kites retail store across the road from the school.

Golf

There are plenty of mini golf courses on the Outer Banks, but for the full-scale experience, only a handful of courses are open to the public. **Duck Woods Country Club** (50 S. Dogwood Tr., Southern Shores, 252/261-2609, www.duckwoodscc.com, greens fees vary by season, $115 summer) is a 6,000-plus-yard, par-72 course that's challenging but fun any time of year. **Sea Scape Golf Links** (300 Eckner St., Kitty Hawk, 252/261-2158, www.seascapegolf. com, greens fees $50-99) offers 18-hole, par-70 links-style play only a block from the ocean. Be warned, the wind can be a major factor when you play here; keep your ball low.

At another links-style course, the 18-hole, par-71 **Nags Head Golf Links** (5615 S. Seachase Dr., Nags Head, 252/389-9079, www.club-corp.com, greens fees $55-125), the wind is definitely in play; in fact, *Golf Digest* called this course "the longest 6,126 yards you'll ever play."

ACCOMMODATIONS

The **⊂ First Colony Inn** (6720 Virginia Dare Tr., Nags Head, 800/368-9390, www.first-colonyinn.com, $99-299, varies by season) is a wonderful 1932 beachfront hotel. This regional landmark has won historic preservation and landscaping awards for its 1988 renovation, which involved moving the entire building, in three pieces, three miles south of its original location. The pretty and luxurious guest rooms are surprisingly affordable.

In Duck, the **Sanderling Resort and Spa** (1461 Duck Rd., Duck, 855/412-7866, www. sanderling-resort.com, $299-539) reopened in May 2013 after a $6 million renovation. More than a face-lift, the renovation added guest rooms and an adults-only pool, revitalized the dining experience at the resort, created new event spaces, and upgraded the public spaces resort-wide. Kimball's Kitchen, the resort's main restaurant, serves a menu focused on local seafood and grass-fed steaks. The view of Currituck Sound is amazing from every seat in the house, and the restaurant's elegance, view, and level of service make it an experience like no other on the Outer Banks.

There are many bed-and-breakfasts, including the **Cypress Moon Inn** (1206 Harbor Court, Kitty Hawk, 877/905-5060, www.cy-pressmooninn.com, no children, $135-210, varies by season), a small but beautiful sound-side home featuring three guest rooms. The owners also have three cottages nearby that are perfect for secluded getaways.

The **Cypress House Inn** (Milepost 8, Beach Rd., Kill Devil Hills, 800/554-2764, www.cypresshouseinn.com, $99-219, varies by season) is only 125 yards from the ocean, and that, combined with its central location to Outer Banks attractions and undeniable charm, makes it a desirable B&B. Guests staying in each of the six guest rooms at the 1940s-style inn are treated to complimentary beach chairs and towels. **The Atlantic Street Inn** (Milepost 9.5, Kill Devil Hills, 252/305-0246, www.atlanticstreetinn.com, $69-159) offers similar treatment, with bicycles available for guest use; its six guest rooms can be reserved individually or, if you book far enough ahead, reserve the entire inn or the nearby beach house.

The **Colington Creek Inn** (1293 Colington Rd., Kill Devil Hills, 252/449-4124, www. colingtoncreekinn.com, no children or pets,

Sanderling Resort and Spa

$178-298, varies by season) has four guest rooms with water views of the sound and its namesake creek, along with porches perfect for morning coffee or an evening drink.

At the **Nags Head Beach Inn** (303 E. Admiral St., Nags Head, 252/441-8466, www.nagsheadbeachinn.com, $131-219), a converted beach club dating to the 1930s that's only steps from the beach, all the accoutrements that guest need—chairs, bicycles, body boards, and the like—are available for use. Quaint and comfortable, the Nags Head Beach Inn is one of several cottages known as the "Unpainted Aristocracy." Some of these cottages date back to the 1830s, but they all have common features—weatherworn shake siding and a yesteryear charm.

Throughout Kitty Hawk and Nags Head, you'll find a number of motels, ranging from chains to classic 1950s mom-and-pops. The **Surf Side Hotel** (6701 Virginia Dare Tr., Nags Head, 800/552-7873, www.surfsideobx.com, $79-299, varies by season) has simple, comfortable standard guest rooms and efficiencies in

a location only steps from the beach. At the **Blue Heron** (6811 Virginia Dare Tr., Nags Head, 252/441-7447, www.blueheronnc.com, $58-158, varies by season), every guest room faces the ocean, and for rainy days or off-season visits there is an indoor heated pool.

If you're looking for a motel with that classic beach-motel feel, three spots come to mind. The bargain **Sea Foam Motel** (7111 S. Virginia Dare Tr., Nags Head, 252/441-7320, www.seafoam.com, $68-149, varies by season) is a no-frills motel with a lot of wood paneling and a lot of retro charm. **Beach Haven Motel** (4104 N. Virginia Dare Tr., Kitty Hawk, 252/261-4785, www.beachhavenmotel.com, $77-189, varies by season) offers a little kitsch in the accommodations and even a grill and outdoor picnic area where you can cook your own fresh catch. The wood-paneled walls at **Outer Banks Motor Lodge** (1509 S. Virginia Dare Tr., Milepost 9.5, Kill Devil Hills, 877/625-6343, www.obxmotorlodge.com, $39-225, varies by season) are so tacky that they only add to the place's appeal.

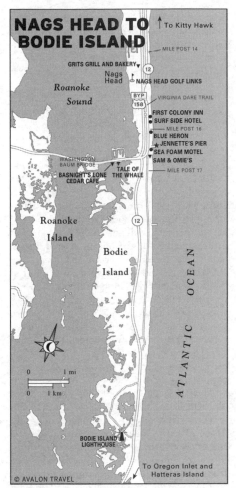

NAGS HEAD TO BODIE ISLAND

To Kitty Hawk

MILE POST 14

GRITS GRILL AND BAKERY

Nags Head

Roanoke Sound

NAGS HEAD GOLF LINKS

BYP 158

VIRGINIA DARE TRAIL

FIRST COLONY INN

SURF SIDE HOTEL

MILE POST 16

BLUE HERON

JENNETTE'S PIER

SEA FOAM MOTEL

WASHINGTON BAUM BRIDGE

SAM & OMIE'S

BASNIGHT'S LONE CEDAR CAFE

TALE OF THE WHALE

MILE POST 17

Roanoke Island

12

Bodie Island

ATLANTIC   OCEAN

0   1 mi

0   1 km

BODIE ISLAND LIGHTHOUSE

To Oregon Inlet and Hatteras Island

© AVALON TRAVEL

FOOD

When I first started visiting the Outer Banks, it seemed that every other restaurant was a seafood buffet. Today, buffets still abound but a number of notable independent restaurants have taken root, and the selection varies from pizza to burgers, gourmet and down home, along with barbecue, fine dining, and a decent representation of international cuisines.

The **Outer Banks Brewing Station** (Milepost 8.5, Croatan Hwy./U.S. 158, Kill Devil Hills, 252/449-2739, www.obbrewing. com, 11:30am-2am daily, entrées $15-31) is an innovative and interesting spot to eat, not just because the food is creative and the beers are adventurous, but because they're wind-powered. Founded by a group of friends who met in the Peace Corps, they combined their love of food, beer, and sustainability to create a hot spot on the Outer Banks' dining and nightlife scenes.

Sam & Omie's (7728 S. Virginia Dare Tr., Nags Head, 252/441-7366, www.samandomies.net, 7am-10pm daily Mar.-mid-Dec., breakfast $1.50-8, dinner $6-26) opened in the summer of 1937 as a place for charter fishing customers and guides to catch breakfast before heading out to sea. They still serve a hearty breakfast heavy on the classics—two eggs your way, pancakes, grits, and the like—but take a look at the specialties, such as crab benedict or the chef's special. Sam & Omie's also serves lunch and dinner, and, as you might expect, both menus emphasize seafood. Sure, you can get a burger, steak, or chicken breast, but why would you when you can get a clam dog, fried oysters, or the massive Whale of a Seafood Platter (which really is more food than one person should eat)?

Owens' Restaurant (Milepost 16.5, Beach Rd., Nags Head, 252/441-7309, www.owensrestaurant.com, 5pm-9pm daily, open later during summer, $20-38) opened in 1946 and has been in continuous operation by the same family ever since. A perennial Outer Banks favorite, Owens serves giant mixed seafood platters, their own version of cioppino and jambalaya, steaks, and more. At Owens' you'll find a treasure trove of photos and artifacts on display, telling the history of the family and the Outer Banks.

A favorite restaurant on the Outer Banks is **Aqua Restaurant and Spa** (1174 Duck Rd., Duck, 252/261-9700, http://restaurantsouterbanks.com, lunch 11:30am-3pm daily, dinner 5pm-9pm Sun.-Thurs., 5pm-10pm Fri.-Sat., lunch from $8.50, dinner entrées from $21). IT has an interesting concept, with a day spa upstairs and an excellent restaurant downstairs, creating flavorful food using community-sourced organic ingredients and natural meats that will, as the owner puts it, "nourish your body and spirit." Grab a table by the windows or on the deck (weather permitting) and enjoy views of the sound while you dine. The food is straightforward and familiar but flawlessly executed. Try the fresh-catch fish tacos or a salad topped with the catch of the day or crab cakes at lunch, and at dinner it's hard to go wrong with either the duck or the line-caught catch of the day. Vegetarian options are available at both lunch and dinner. Two must-orders are the cone of Aqua fries with truffles, shaved parmesan, and a secret dipping sauce; and the funnel cake, unlike any you've had elsewhere. Light, crispy, chewy, and flavorful even without the homemade ice cream or chocolate drizzle, it's a dessert to share, and one you'll come back for. Aqua also has an exceptionally well-curated wine menu and knowledgeable staff able to steer you toward a glass or bottle that will complement your meal perfectly.

Dining sound-side, especially near sunset, affords two memorable experiences in the food and the view. Another great place to dine on the water is on the causeway at **Tale of the Whale** (7575 S. Virginia Dare Tr., Nags Head, 252/441-7332, http://taleofthewhalenagshead.com, dinner only, hours vary seasonally, around $27). Order a pre-dinner cocktail and enjoy it on the pier that juts out into the Roanoke Sound, or sit and listen to local musicians at the pier-side gazebo. From the dining room, the water view is almost as good as the food. They've got a big menu with everything from off-the-boat fresh fish to grass-fed steaks, pastas, and even vegetarian options. A decent wine list and a creative cocktail menu round out the offerings.

I love a good breakfast place like **Grits Grill** (2000 S. Croatan Hwy., Milepost 14, Nags Head, 252/449-2888, www.gritsgrill.com, 6am-2pm daily, $5-13). The omelets are fluffy, the pancakes are stacked high, and the grits are some of the best I've eaten. Sit at the counter to watch the short-order cooks grill dunes

of shredded potatoes into submission as they make countless orders of hash browns. Grits Grill serves lunch—salads, baskets, and sandwiches, including the elusive Monte Cristo—and have breakfast available all day, so it's never hard to find something to eat.

Blue Moon Beach Grill (4104 S. Virginia Dare Tr., Nags Head, 252/261-2583, www.bluemoonbeachgrill.com, 11:30am-9pm daily, $12-25) is rapidly becoming a local favorite. Known for its seafood dishes, Blue Moon is also a popular place to grab a draft beer after work.

Tortuga's Lie (3016 S. Virginia Dare Tr., Nags Head, 252/441-7299, www.tortugaslie.com, 11:30am-10pm Sun.-Thurs., 11:30am-10:30pm Fri.-Sat., about $18) has a good and varied menu specializing in seafood, some of it local, cooked in Caribbean-inspired dishes, along with some good vegetarian options.

For casual and on-the-go chow options at Nags Head, try **Maxximuss Pizza** (5205 S. Croatan Hwy., Nags Head, 252/441-2377, www.nagsheadpizza.com, $6.50-27), which specializes in calzones, subs, and paninis in addition to pizza; **Yellow Submarine** (Milepost 14, U.S. 158 Bypass, Nags Head, 252/441-3511, http://yellowsubmarineobx.com, $7-20), a very casual subs-and-pizza shop.

The **Kill Devil Grill** (2008 S. Virginia Dare Tr., Kill Devil Hills, 252/449-8181, $13-20) serves hearty meals for brunch, lunch, and dinner. Entrées include excellent seafood and steaks. Vegetarians will find limited options, but meat eaters will be well satisfied. **Food Dudes Kitchen** (1216 S. Virginia Dare Tr., Kill Devil Hills, 252/441-7994, 11:30am-9pm Mon.-Sat., 11am-9pm Sun., $10-17) has great seafood, wraps, and sandwiches. **Rundown Café** (5218 N. Virginia Dare Tr., Kitty Hawk, 252/255-0026, 11:30am-late Mon.-Sat., noon-late Sun., $10-15) is a popular local affordable Caribbean-influenced fare.

One other interesting dining option is joining **Outer Banks Restaurant Tours** (252/722-2229, www.outerbanksrestauranttours.com, tours from $45) on a dine-around excursion in Kitty Hawk, Duck, or Corolla. Each tour consists of four to six stops at restaurants, wine shops, bakeries, and specialty food markets. Other tours include the Brews-Day Tuesday Beer Tour, winery tours, cooking classes, and dessert-only tours.

GETTING THERE AND AROUND

The closest major airport to this region is **Norfolk International Airport** (ORF, 2200 Norview Ave., Norfolk, VA, 757/857-3351, www.norfolkairport.com), approximately an hour from the northern Outer Banks. **Raleigh-Durham International Airport** (RDU, 2600 W. Terminal Blvd., Morrisville, 919/840-2123, www.rdu.com) is three to five hours' drive from most Outer Banks destinations.

Only two bridges exist between the mainland and the northern Outer Banks. U.S. 64/264 crosses over Roanoke Island to Whalebone, just south of Nags Head. Not too far north of there, U.S. 158 crosses from Point Harbor to Southern Shores. Highway 12 is the main road all along the northern Outer Banks.

Roanoke Island

The first nonnative residents of the Outer Banks, and perhaps the most famous, called Roanoke Island home for a brief time in the 1580s. These intrepid English colonists found the island protected from the brunt of storms by Albemarle, Roanoke, and Croatan Sounds and the mass of Bodie Island. They established Fort Raleigh, where Virginia Dare, the first European born on the new continent, came into the world. The community then vanished completely, known to history as the Lost Colony. No one knows what happened to them.

Visitors to Roanoke Island today will find what the colonists found: a beautiful, welcoming island ripe for exploration. The relative abundance of bed-and-breakfasts, restaurants, and shops make staying on Roanoke Island much easier than it was four centuries ago.

At the northern end of Roanoke Island the Fort Raleigh National Historic Site marks the last known location of the Lost Colony, and the nearby town of Manteo offers a day or two of dining and distractions. Most of the island's offerings for visitors are concentrated here, although a visit to the tiny town of Wanchese at the southern end of the island is worthwhile. Here, some of Dare County's oldest immigrant families continue to ply their ancestral trades of boatbuilding and fishing.

◖ FORT RALEIGH NATIONAL HISTORIC SITE

Fort Raleigh National Historic Site (1401 National Park Dr., Manteo, 252/473-2111, www.nps.gov, 9am-5pm daily, closed Dec. 25, free) includes much of the original site of the first English settlement in the New World. Archaeologists still conduct digs here, regularly unearthing new artifacts and assembling clues about the Lost Colony's fate, but sections of the earthworks associated with the original 1580s fort remain and have been preserved, making it easy to imagine the site as a working fort on the frontier of an unknown land. In the visitors center, which underwent an extensive renovation in early 2013, artifacts and interactive displays tell the story of the fort and the missing colonists, and of the freedman's colony—a colony of freed and displaced slaves established on the island during the Civil War. Two nature trails in the park allow you to explore the natural landscape and the site of a Civil War battle.

Within the National Historic Site, two of Manteo's most famous attractions operate autonomously. Nearly 60 years ago, **Elizabethan Gardens** (1411 National Park Dr., Manteo, 252/473-3234, http://elizabethangardens. org, 10am-4pm daily Dec.-Feb., 9am-5pm daily Mar., 9am-6pm daily Apr.-May, 9am-7pm daily June-Aug., 9am-6pm daily Sept.,

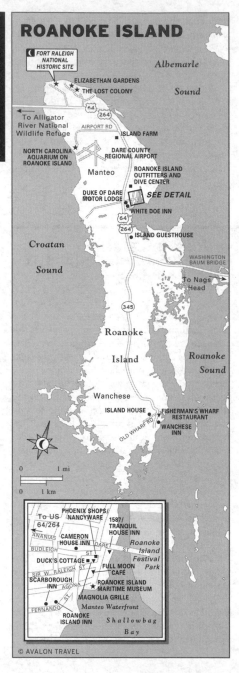

ROANOKE ISLAND

FORT RALEIGH NATIONAL HISTORIC SITE

Albemarle

ELIZABETHAN GARDENS
THE LOST COLONY

Sound

To Alligator River National Wildlife Refuge

AIRPORT RD

ISLAND FARM

NORTH CAROLINA AQUARIUM ON ROANOKE ISLAND

DARE COUNTY REGIONAL AIRPORT

Manteo

ROANOKE ISLAND OUTFITTERS AND DIVE CENTER

DUKE OF DARE MOTOR LODGE

SEE DETAIL

WHITE DOE INN

ISLAND GUESTHOUSE

WASHINGTON BAUM BRIDGE

Croatan

Sound

To Nags Head

345

Roanoke

Island

Roanoke
Sound

Wanchese

ISLAND HOUSE
FISHERMAN'S WHARF RESTAURANT
OLD WHARF RD
WANCHESE INN

0   1 mi
0   1 km

PHOENIX SHOPS/ NANCYWARE
To US 64/264
1587/ TRANQUIL HOUSE INN
ANANIAS
CAMERON HOUSE INN
DARE
Roanoke
BUDLEIGH
ST
Island
DUCK'S COTTAGE
ST
Festival
SIR W. RALEIGH
ST
FULL MOON CAFÉ
Park
SCARBOROUGH INN
AGONA
ROANOKE ISLAND MARITIME MUSEUM
MAGNOLIA GRILLE
FERNANDO
Manteo Waterfront
ROANOKE ISLAND INN
Shallowbag
Bay

© AVALON TRAVEL

9am-5pm daily Oct.-Nov., $9, $6 ages 6-17, under age 6 free, $3 pets) was conceived by the Garden Club of North Carolina as a permanent memorial to the settlers of Roanoke Island. As a tribute, they planted the types of gardens and plants that would have been common in the colonists' native England in the 16th century. There are many corners to explore in this 10.5 acre garden, and many treasures both natural and artificial to discover: an ancient live oak so huge that many believe it has been standing since the colonists' days; a sunken garden containing Renaissance-era statuary; a Shakespearian herb garden; an impressive display of camellias and azaleas; and a 19th-century statue of Virginia Dare. The statue was underwater off the coast of Spain for two years, was salvaged, and made it to Massachusetts, where it was nearly lost in a fire. It finally arrived in North Carolina in the 1920s, where modest residents, shocked by the statue's nudity, passed it around the state for years until it found a permanent home in Elizabethan Gardens.

Also within the park is the Waterside Theatre. North Carolina has a long history of outdoor performances celebrating regional heritage and history, and the best known of these is Roanoke Island's *The Lost Colony* (1409 National Park Dr., Manteo, 252/473-2127, http://thelostcolony.org, from $24). Playwright Paul Green was commissioned to write a drama about the colony in 1937 to celebrate the 350th anniversary of the birth of Virginia Dare. What he thought would be a single-season production has turned into a fixture, with performances every year since, except when extraordinary circumstances, like German U-boats prowling off the coast during World War II, interrupted the production schedule.

OTHER SIGHTS

The **Roanoke Island Maritime Museum** (104 Fernando St., Manteo, 252/475-1750, http://roanokeisland.com, hours vary, free) is a unique working boat shop and repository for artifacts that offer a look at local and regional maritime heritage. Traditional boat builders offer

© JASON FRYE

Elizabethan Gardens at Fort Raleigh National Historic Site

classes in boat building and handling at the George Washington Creef Boathouse, but visitors not enrolled in the classes are still welcome to come and observe. Also on the grounds is the **Roanoke Marshes Lighthouse.** The large lighthouses protecting the outer Atlantic coast are well known, but a number of smaller river and marsh lighthouses also once dotted the coast. This structure is a reconstruction of the square cottage-style lighthouse that was decommissioned in 1955.

Island Farm (1140 U.S. 64, Manteo, 252/473-6500, www.theislandfarm.com, 10am-4pm Wed.-Sat. Apr.-Nov., closed Thanksgiving Day, $6 adults, free under age 5) is a living-history site that transports you back to a Roanoke Island farm circa 1850. Reproduction outbuildings include the smokehouse, cookhouse, and slave house alongside the original farmhouse, built between 1845 and 1850. Period interpreters lead tours and talks that focus on the gardening, cooking, and day-to-day doings on a farm in the pre-Civil War Outer Banks.

The **North Carolina Aquarium on Roanoke Island** (374 Airport Rd., Manteo, 252/473-3494, www.ncaquariums.com, 9am-5pm daily year-round, closed Thanksgiving, Dec. 25, and Jan. 1, $8, $7 over age 61, $6 ages 3-12, free under age 3) is one of three state aquariums on the North Carolina coast. A great place for kids, the aquarium is home to all sorts of marine fauna and tells the aquatic story of North Carolina from the deep sea to freshwater tributaries. See river otters, alligators, freshwater fish, sharks, and more in traditional and touch-tank aquariums. Don't miss the daily dive shows in the huge 285,000-gallon Graveyard of the Atlantic tank. Displays in the aquarium detail the U.S. Lifesaving Service, and outside is the grave of Richard Etheridge, the first African American to captain a Lifesaving Station, on Pea Island, just south of the Bodie Island Lighthouse.

Roanoke Island Festival Park (across the water from downtown Manteo, 252/475-1500, http://roanokeisland.com) is a state-operated living-history site in Manteo. The highlight here is the *Elizabeth II,* a reconstruction of a 16th-century ship like those that brought Walter Raleigh, the members of the Lost Colony, and so many others to the New World. A museum, reconstructed settlement, and costumed interpreters help tell the story of the Roanoke colony, focusing more on their daily life than on their mysterious fate.

THE LOST COLONY

On July 4, 1584, an English expedition commissioned by Walter Raleigh dropped anchor in the sound near Hatteras Island. Within a couple of days, local Native Americans were coming and going from the English ships, making trades and some of the first offers of Southern hospitality. They got on famously, and when the English returned home to tell the court of the land they'd found, two indigenous Roanoke men, Manteo and Wanchese, came along as guests. It seems that Wanchese was a bit taciturn and found London not to his liking, but Manteo was amazed at what he saw and found the English to be all right.

A year later, a new expedition set out for Roanoke, this time with the intentions of establishing a permanent settlement. When they reached the Pamlico Sound, their bad luck began. Most of their food stores were soaked and ruined when seawater breeched the ship, so from the moment they set foot on land, they were dependent on the mercy of the indigenous inhabitants. Manteo and Wanchese went to Roanoke chief Wingina to discuss the colonists' plight. Wanchese was a man of superior insight, told Wingina of what he had seen, and begged Wingina to withhold help for the colonists. Manteo, however, pled their case well, and the colonists were made welcome.

The colonists grew dependent on the Roanoke people's generosity and had done very little to become self-sufficient by the time winter arrived. That's when a silver cup disappeared from the English compound. They believed the thief to be from a nearby Native American village, which they promptly burned to the ground. Wingina, worried for the fate of his people, shut down his assistance in hopes that the English would either starve or leave. They did neither, and instead killed the generous chief. Three weeks later an English supply ship arrived with reinforcements of soldiers, materiel, and food stores, only to find the colony totally deserted.

Another attempt at colonizing Roanoke was made, this time with families rather than rowdy gangs of single men. A young couple, Eleanor and Ananais Dare, were expecting a child, and soon after they landed on Roanoke, Virginia Dare, the first English child born in the New World, arrived. The situation with the Native Americans grew worse, though, and the Roanoke people, now under the leadership of Wanchese, were unwilling to aid the second wave of colonists. Manteo, ever the optimist and still friendly with the English, tried to enlist the help of his people, but they were facing lean times as well. John White, leader of the colonial expedition and grandfather to Virginia Dare, returned to England on what he planned to be a fast there-and-back voyage for supplies. It was three years before he returned, and when he did, he found no signs of the settlers—no bodies, no bones, no sign except the letters "CRO" carved on a tree and "CROATOAN" on a palisade stake.

And so began 400 years of mystery and speculation that will probably never be resolved. Some believe the English were killed, others that they were captured and sold into slavery to indigenous people farther inland, still others believe they left under the protection of nearby Native Americans known to be friendly, and then died off or assimilated into Indian society. Several communities in the South of uncertain or mixed racial heritage believe themselves to be descendants of the lost colonists, and some evidence suggests that this may be true. Although answers may never be found, the mystery hangs heavily over Roanoke Island and its two towns, Manteo and Wanchese.

© JASON FRYE

Island Farm, a living-history site

SPORTS AND RECREATION

Roanoke Island Outfitters and Dive Center
(312 U.S. 64, Manteo, 252/473-1356, www.
roanokeislandoutfittersanddivecenter.com)
is a one-stop shop for outdoor activities on
Roanoke Island. They rent out kayaks, stand-
up paddleboards, bicycles, and camping equipment and offer lessons and tours for kayaks and
paddleboards, even teaching scuba diving at all
levels. Experienced divers looking for a thrill
will want to take advantage of their spearfishing charters (they don't rent out spear guns, so
bring your own).

Spearfishing is just one way to catch a big
one on the Outer Banks. On Roanoke Island
it's easy to catch fish with a rod and a reel
thanks to a number of inshore and offshore
charters that are available year-round. The
Outer Banks Visitors Bureau (www.outer-
banks.org) has a comprehensive list of charters;
look under "Fishing" for operators and rates.

Daring travelers can take in the sights of
Roanoke Island and the Outer Banks from
9,000 feet with **Skydive OBX** (410 Airport Rd.,

Manteo, 252/678-5867, www.skydiveobx.com,
$249). Each tandem jump provides 30 seconds
of free fall at 120 mph and plenty of time to admire the view. Discounts are offered on same-
day second jumps.

TOURS

The ***Downeast Rover*** (sails from Manteo waterfront, 252/473-4866, www.downeastrover.
com, daytime cruises $30 adults, $15 ages 2-12,
sunset cruises $40) is a 55-foot reproduction
of a 19th-century schooner. Cruises last two
hours and depart three times daily at 11am,
2pm, and sunset. To see the Outer Banks from
the air, options include a World War II biplane
or a closed-cockpit Cessna through **OBX Air
Charters** (410 Airport Rd., Manteo, 252/256-
2322, www.outerbanksaircharters.com, $210
for up to 5 people).

The gardens and quaint waterfronts on
Roanoke Island are charming for adult visitors,
but not so much for kids; thankfully, two tours
fulfill the fun quotient for the young ones. On
Captain Johnny's Outer Banks Dolphin Tours

WATERMAN RICHARD ETHERIDGE

The Outer Banks is a land of firsts: one of the first English settlements in the nation, the first flight, and another first that transcended racial boundaries in the tumultuous years after the Civil War. Richard Etheridge, Keeper of the Pea Island Life-Saving Station, was born a slave on Roanoke Island in 1842 and became the first African American to command a Life-Saving crew, one made up entirely of African Americans.

Slavery on the Outer Banks was different than it was across most of the South. The absence of large plantations kept the numbers of slaves low, and the demands of the Banker lifestyle—scratching a farm out of the sand, subsistence fishing, crabbing, and foraging—kept slave owners and slaves in constant close company. The children of enslaved people often grew up alongside their slave-owning counterparts, and a few, like Etheridge, were rumored to have white fathers and received special treatment, even learning, as Etheridge did, to read and write. Etheridge worked alongside possible half brothers, fishing, farming, hunting, scavenging shipwrecks, and learning the finer points of being a waterman: how to read currents, swim, predict the weather, and navigate boats in breakers and under perilous conditions.

During the Civil War, one of the first Union victories occurred on Roanoke Island. General Ambrose Burnside freed the enslaved people here, established a massive freedman's colony (a sort of homestead for displaced and freed slaves), and recruited soldiers for the 36th U.S. Colored Troop, in which Etheridge enlisted. He saw action across North Carolina and Virginia, and after the war served in Texas in the Cavalry units that came to be known as the Buffalo Soldiers. He returned home a free man, married, and worked as a fisherman. In 1875 he joined the U.S. Life-Saving Service, precursor to the modern-day Coast Guard, serving as a Surfman at the Bodie Island Life-Saving Station.

As a Surfman, Etheridge served on a "checkerboard crew" made up of black and white Surfmen under the command of a white Keeper. He repeatedly garnered attention, not all of it positive, from his fellow Surfmen and superiors. By 1879 he was serving in another checkerboard crew at Pea Island station, and was promoted to Keeper after the white Keeper was fired. Despite the Emancipation Proclamation, the Union's victory in the war, Etheridge's possible parentage, and his expertise as a Surfman, he was not permitted to command white men; his command had to be formed entirely of black Surfmen. Only five months after taking command of the Pea Island station and becoming the first African American Keeper (and the first commander of the first all-African American crew), the smoldering racism of Jim Crow burned his station to the ground.

Etheridge served as Keeper for 21 years, never letting racism stand in the way of his duties as a member of the Life-Saving Service. In October 1896, in the midst of a storm so bad Etheridge had suspended the nightly beach patrols, the E. S. Newman grounded south of his station. The Pea Island crew leapt into action, but the waves were too high to launch their rescue surfboat. Two of his crew swam to the ship to secure a rescue line and made the trip back and forth nine times in order to rescue the passengers and crew, including the captain's three-year-old daughter. It was Etheridge's, and his crew's, finest moment.

Etheridge died of a fever in 1900. He's buried with his family in Manteo on Roanoke Island, outside the North Carolina Aquarium. In 1996 the Coast Guard posthumously awarded Keeper Etheridge and his crew the Gold Lifesaving Medal, the service's highest peacetime honor. In 2011 the Coast Guard launched a cutter named after Etheridge, extending their respect to this groundbreaking American hero.

(Manteo Waterfront, 252/473-1475, www.outerbankscruises.com, from $28, $18 children), you'll get up close to bottlenose dolphins in their native habitat and watch as they swim, leap, hunt, and sometimes even inspect the boat on each two-hour tour. Kids get the chance to transform themselves into pirates with **Pirate Adventures of the Outer Banks** (408 Queen Elizabeth Ave., Manteo, 252/473-2007, www.piratesobx.com, tours 9:30am, 11am, 12:30pm, 2pm, 3:30pm, and 5pm daily, $20, $12 under age 3). Aboard the *Sea Gypsy*, a 40-foot pirate ship replete with a water cannon and a costumed pirate crew, kids get the chance to dress like pirates with face-painted mustaches, beards, and fearsome scars, read a treasure map, hunt down an enemy pirate, engage in a water-cannon battle, find sunken treasure, and have a pirate party. These 1.25-hour tours sail six times daily, seven days a week, giving parents opportunities to take an hour to explore the Manteo waterfront.

If you don't mind a scare, take a 90-minute stroll through Manteo with **Ghost Tours of the OBX** (399 Queen Elizabeth Ave., Manteo, 252/573-1450, www.ghosttoursoftheobx.com, $13, $8 under age 11). Visit the village cemetery, look for the ghosts of pirates and lost sailors along the shore and waterfront, and learn about supernatural creatures in the surrounding woods on one of three chilling but kid-friendly tours.

ENTERTAINMENT AND EVENTS

Roanoke Island is a pretty tame place, with most of the events and activities of a family-oriented nature. To that end, on the first Friday of the month April-December, the town of Manteo celebrates **First Friday,** a free downtown festival. In addition to live music on the streets, many restaurants and shops feature their own musical acts, sales, and refreshments. The **Dare County Arts Council Gallery** (300 Queen Elizabeth Ave., Manteo, 252/473-5558, www.darearts.org, 10am-6pm Mon.-Fri., 10am-8pm 1st Fri., noon-4pm Sat.) always hosts a reception during First Friday

that showcases a new exhibit by a local or regional artist.

One of the best spots for nightlife is **Poor Richard's Sandwich Shop** (303 Queen Elizabeth Ave., Manteo, 252/473-3333, www.poorrichardsmanteo.com, dining room breakfast and lunch 8am-3pm Mon.-Sat., bar 5pm-2am Mon.-Sat., entrées around $6). During the summer season they have live entertainment in the bar most nights; they also serve one of the best breakfasts in town.

SHOPPING

Roanoke Island is a haven for artists, with many calling Manteo home. Downtown are several studios and galleries featuring local artists' paintings, drawings, pottery, and jewelry. A favorite is the pottery studio of Nancy Huse, **Nancyware** (402 Queen Elizabeth Ave., Manteo, 252/473-9400, www.nancywareobx.com, call for hours), where she shapes, glazes, and fires beautiful and functional pots, trivets, decorative pottery pieces, ornaments, and earrings. The small but impressive **Gallery 101** (101 Budleigh St., Manteo, 252/473-6656, www.gallery101mante.com, call for hours) has a mix of original watercolors, oils, acrylics, photographs, and other objets d'art for sale.

The **Phoenix Shops** (Budleigh St. and Queen Elizabeth Ave.) are home to an eclectic mix of boutiques, galleries, and home-goods stores. **Duck's Cottage Downtown Books** (105 Sir Walter Raleigh St., Manteo, 252/473-1056, www.duckscottage.com, 10am-5pm Mon.-Sat. summer, 10am-5pm Tues.-Sat. off-season) is a small but well-stocked bookstore, with more than just the best-sellers; there is quite a selection of books by local and regional authors. The staff are friendly and knowledgeable and can point out easy summer reads.

ACCOMMODATIONS

The **❰ White Doe Inn** (319 Sir Walter Raleigh St., Manteo, 800/473-6091, www.whitedoeinn.com, from $175 off-season, $350 summer) is one of North Carolina's premier inns. The 1910 Queen Anne is the largest house on the island and is listed on the National Register of Historic Places. Guest rooms are exquisitely furnished in turn-of-the-20th-century finery. Guests enjoy a four-course breakfast, evening sherry, espresso and cappuccino any time, and a 24-hour wine cellar. Spa services are available on-site, and you need only step out to the lawn to play croquet or boccie.

The **Roanoke Island Inn** (305 Fernando St., 877/473-5511, www.roanokeislandinn. com, $150-200) has been in the owner's family since the 1860s. It's a beautiful old place, with a big porch that overlooks the marsh. They also rent out a single cottage on a private island, five minutes away by boat, and a nice cypress-shingled bungalow in town. Another top hotel in Manteo is the **Tranquil House Inn** (405 Queen Elizabeth Ave., 800/458-7069, www.1587.com, $109-239). It's in a beautiful location, and downstairs is one of the best restaurants in town, 1587. The **Scarborough Inn** (524 U.S. 64, 252/473-3979, www.scarborough-inn.com, $75-125, varies by season) is a small hotel with 12 guest rooms and great rates. It's the sort of old-time hotel that's hard to find these days.

The **Cameron House Inn** (300 Budleigh St., Manteo, 800/279-8178, http://cameronhouse-inn.com, $130-210) is a cozy 1919 arts and crafts-style bungalow. All of the indoor guest rooms are furnished in a lovely and understated craftsman style, but the nicest guest room in the house is the porch, which has an outdoor fireplace, fans, and flowery trellises.

The **Island Guesthouse** (706 U.S. 64, 252/473-2434, www.theislandmotel.com, rooms from $60 off-season, from $85 summer, cottages from $125 off-season, from $200 summer, additional fee for pets) offers simple and comfortable lodgings with two double beds, air conditioning, and cable TV in each guest room. They also rent out three cute tiny cottages. Another affordable option is the **Duke of Dare Motor Lodge** (100 S. U.S. 64, 252/473-2175, from $42 summer), a 1960s motel that's not at all fancy but a fine budget choice.

The **Wanchese Inn** (85 Jovers Lane, Wanchese, 252/475-1166, www.wancheseinn. com, from $69 off-season, from $129 summer)

is a simple and inexpensive bed-and-breakfast in a nice Victorian house with modern guest rooms. There's a boat slip and on-site parking for a boat and trailer. The **Island House** (104 Old Wharf Rd., 866/473-5619, www.island-house-bb.com, $85-175) was built in the early 1900s for a local Coast Guardsman with wood cut from the property and nails forged on-site. It's very comfortable and quiet, and a big country breakfast is served every day.

FOOD

Located in the Tranquil House Inn with a great view of Shallowbag Bay, **🄲1587** (405 Queen Elizabeth Ave., 252/473-1587, www.1587.com, dinner entrées $17-42) is widely regarded as one of the best restaurants in this part of the state. The menu has hearty chops and seafood, with local ingredients in season; a full vegetarian menu is available, and the wine list is a mile long.

Basnight's Lone Cedar Café (Nags Head-Manteo Causeway, 252/441-5405, www. lonecedarcafe.com, dinner from 4:30pm daily, brunch 11am-3pm Sun., dinner entrées $14-32, brunch entrées $8-14) is a water-view bistro that specializes in local food—oysters from Hyde and Dare Counties, fresh-caught local fish, and North Carolina chicken, pork, and vegetables. It's one of the most popular restaurants on the Outer Banks, and they don't take reservations, so be sure to arrive early. The full bar is open until midnight.

The **Full Moon Café** (208 Queen Elizabeth St., 252/473-6666, www.thefullmooncafe.com, 11:30am-9pm daily summer, call for off-season hours, $10-30) is simple and affordable, specializing in quesadillas and enchiladas, wraps, sandwiches, a variety of seafood and chicken bakes, and quiches. Despite the seemingly conventional selection, the food is so good that the Full Moon has received glowing reviews from the *Washington Post* and the *New York Post*—quite a feat for a little café in Manteo. On the brewery side of Full Moon, they brew their own British- and Irish-style beers, and they carry a variety of other North Carolina brews. Ask for a taste or order a tasting flight before committing to a full pint; the bartenders will be happy to accommodate you and help you find a beer you'll enjoy.

The **Magnolia Grille** (408 Queen Elizabeth St., 252/475-9787, www.roanokeisland.net, 7am-8pm Tues.-Sat., 7am-4pm Sun.-Mon.) is a very inexpensive place for your three daily meals and snacks in between. They've got a great selection of breakfast omelets, burgers, salads, soups, and deli sandwiches, with nothing priced over $7.

In Wanchese, the Daniels family has been fishing the waters of the Outer Banks since the 1930s and cooking up their catch since 1974. **Fisherman's Wharf Restaurant** (4683 Mill Landing Rd., Wanchese, 252/473-6004, www.fishermanswharfobx.com, 11am-9pm Mon.-Sat., lunch entrées $9-25, dinner entrées $15-25) serves fresh seafood in traditional Banker preparations. The Fisherman's Fried Platter is a feast unto itself, with fresh flounder, shrimp, sea scallops, clam strips, and crab bites. The Scallop Cakes, a Daniels family original, are not to be missed.

Avenue Grille (207 Queen Elizabeth Ave., Manteo, 252/473-4800, www.avenueeventsobx.com, 11am-9pm Mon.-Sat. summer, call for hours off-season, lunch entrées $8-18, dinner entrées $11-28) serves modern coastal cuisine in a modern dining room overlooking the bay. Their slider trio includes a crab cake, an angus burger, and duck confit to give you a taste of how they treat fish, beef, and fowl, but their Tuna Oscar or crab cakes, both of which use locally-sourced seafood, steal the show.

GETTING THERE AND AROUND

Coming from the mainland, you first reach the town of Mann's Harbor on the inland side of the Croatan Sound; from there you have two choices to cross to Roanoke Island. If you take U.S. 64/264, to the north (left), you'll cross the sound to the north, arriving in Manteo. If you drive straight ahead at Mann's Harbor, you'll be on the U.S. 64/264 Bypass, which crosses to the middle of the island, south of Manteo. Proceed until you get to the main intersection with Highway 345, where you can turn left onto U.S. 64/264 to go to Manteo, or right onto Highway 345 to Wanchese.

To reach Roanoke Island from the Outer Banks, take U.S. 158 or Highway 12 to Whalebone Junction, south of Nags Head, and cross Roanoke Sound on the U.S. 64/264 bridge.

Cape Hatteras National Seashore

Most Americans recognize Cape Hatteras as a name often heard during hurricane season. Hatteras stretches farther south and east than any other part of the United States, jutting out into the Atlantic far enough to be a prime landmark for mariners, meteorologists, and storms.

Because of its position near the Gulf Stream, a treacherous zone of shifting sandbars called Diamond Shoals extends from the cape and it's pristine beaches to the warm Gulf Stream currents. Only two channels—Diamond Slough and Hatteras Slough—offer water deep enough for ships to traverse Diamond Shoals safely; ships that miss either slough end up shoaled on sandbars if they're lucky, and become one more

shipwreck in the Graveyard of the Atlantic if they are not so fortunate. Countless ships have gone down here over the centuries, including the 1837 wreck of the steamboat *Home* in which 90 passengers lost their lives. The wreck, which received considerable media attention, led Congress to pass the Steamboat Act, which established the requirement of one life vest per passenger on all vessels.

In 2003, Hurricane Isabel struck Hatteras Island, opening a 2,000-foot-wide channel where none had been before, separating the towns of Hatteras and Frisco, and causing major inconveniences for weeks. The inlet was filled in and the island remained intact for several years until Hurricane Sandy in 2012. Sandy washed out roads, deposited sand several feet deep across Highway 12, and wreaked general mayhem up and down the island, all without a direct hit. The destruction from these two hurricanes demonstrates the vulnerability of the Outer Banks.

BODIE ISLAND

You'll spot the horizontal black-and-white stripes of the 170-foot **Bodie Island Lighthouse** (6 miles south of Whalebone Junction, 252/473-2111, www.nps.gov/caha, lighthouse climbs $8 adults, $4 seniors and under age 12) from several miles away. The Bodie Light's huge Fresnel lens first beamed in 1872, but this is the third lighthouse to guard this stretch of coast from this location. The first iteration of the Bodie Light (pronounced "body") was built in the 1830s, but due to engineering errors and shifting sand it leaned like the Tower of Pisa and didn't last too long. The next one stood straight but proved such a tempting target for the Yankee Navy during the Civil War

that the Confederates blew it up themselves. The third light still stands, although a flock of geese nearly put it out of commission soon after its first lighting when they collided with and damaged the lens.

In 2013 the Bodie Island Lighthouse opened to the public for the first time after extensive renovations by the National Park Service. Ranger-led tours (daily late Apr.-early Oct.) take you on a strenuous climb up the lighthouse, but it is worth it for the view. Solid shoes are required to climb the lighthouse, so no heels, flip-flops, or bare feet.

The nearby Lighthouse Keeper's Cottage serves as a visitors center, and it is also the trailhead for self-guided nature trails to Roanoke Sound. These trails wind through beautiful marsh on the sound side of Bodie Island.

The **Oregon Inlet Campground** (Hwy. 12, 877/444-6777, www.recreation.gov, $20), operated by the National Park Service, offers camping behind the sand dunes, with cold-water showers, potable water, and restrooms.

HATTERAS ISLAND

As Cape Hatteras arches dramatically along the North Carolina coast, it shelters Pamlico Sound from the ocean like a giant cradling arm. The cape itself is the point of the elbow, an exposed and vulnerable spit of land that's nearly irresistible to passing hurricanes. Most of the island is included in Cape Hatteras National Seashore, the first of its kind in the country, although a handful of small towns— Rodanthe, Waves, Salvo, Avon, Buxton, Frisco, and the village of Hatteras—dot the coastline. For the most part Hatteras Island isn't much wider than the dune line and Highway 12, which makes for a great deal of dramatic scenery on all sides.

Chicamacomico Life Saving Station

Lifesaving operations are an important part of North Carolina's maritime heritage. Corps of brave men occupied remote stations along the coast, ready at a moment's notice to risk their lives to save foundering sailors in the

© JASON FRYE

Bodie Island Lighthouse

relentlessly dangerous waters off the Outer Banks. In Rodanthe, the **Chicamacomico Life Saving Station** (Milepost 39.5, Hwy. 12, Rodanthe, 252/987-1552, www.chicamacomico.net, 10am-5pm Mon.-Fri. Apr.-Nov., $6, $4 under age 17 and over age 62) preserves the original station building, a handsome gray-shingled 1874 building, the 1911 building that replaced it and which now houses a museum of fascinating artifacts from maritime rescue operations, and a complex of other buildings and exhibits depicting the lives of lifesavers and their families.

◖ Cape Hatteras Lighthouse

At 208 feet tall, **Cape Hatteras Lighthouse** (near Buxton, 252/473-2111, www.nps.gov/caha, 9am-4:30pm daily late Apr.-June and early Sept.-early Oct., 9am-5:30pm June-early Sept., $8, $4 children and seniors, children under 42 inches tall not permitted) is the tallest brick lighthouse in the United States, and its distinctive black-and-white spiral paint job makes it easy to see from miles away on land or sea. It was built in 1870 to protect ships at sea from coming upon the shoals unaware. It still stands and is open for climbing during the warm months. If you have a healthy heart, lungs, and knees and are not claustrophobic, get your ticket and start climbing. Tickets are sold on the premises beginning at 8:15am, and climbing tours run every 10 minutes starting at 9am. Winds at the top can be ferocious, so hold onto your hats, cameras, phones, and anything else you don't want to fly away.

Sports and Recreation

Pea Island National Wildlife Refuge (Hwy. 12, 10 miles south of Nags Head, 252/987-2394, www.fws.gov/peaisland) occupies the northern reach of Hatteras Island. Much of the island is covered by ponds, making this an exceptional place for watching migratory waterfowl. Two nature trails link some of the best bird-watching spots, including the 0.5-mile fully wheelchair-accessible North Pond Wildlife Trail. Viewing and photography blinds are scattered along the trails for extended observation.

© JASON FRYE

Cape Hatteras Lighthouse

The Outer Banks owe their existence to the volatile action of the tides. The same forces that created this habitable sandbar also make it an incredible place for water sports. **Canadian Hole,** a spot in the sound between Avon and Buxton, is one of the most famous windsurfing and sailboarding places in the world (and, of course, it's perfect for flying kites). The island is extraordinarily narrow at Canadian Hole, so it's easy to tote your board from the sound side over to the ocean for a change of scene.

It's important to know your skill level and choose activities accordingly. Beginners and experts alike can benefit from the guidance of serious water-sports instructors. **REAL** (25706 Hwy. 12, Waves, 866/732-5548, www.realkiteboarding.com) is the largest kite-surfing school in the world. They offer kite-surfing camps and classes in many aspects of the sport for all levels as well as surfing and stand-up paddleboarding lessons and rentals. **Outer Banks Kiting** (Avon, 252/305-6838, www.outerbankskiting.com) also has lessons and two-day camps and carries boarders out on charter excursions to find the best kite-surfing spots.

Among the ways to tour Hatteras, **Equine Adventures** (Frisco, 252/995-4897, www.equineadventures.com, tours from $30) leads two-hour horseback tours through the maritime forests and along the beaches of Cape Hatteras. With **Hatteras Parasail** (Hatteras, 252/986-2627, www.hatterasparasail.com, $65 parasail ride, $55 WaveRunner rental, $35 kayak tour, $275 per day boat rental) you can ride 400 feet in the air over the coast; go even higher with **Burrus Flightseeing Tours** (Frisco, 252/986-2679, www.outerbanksairtours.com, $45-80 pp).

Hatteras Watersports (Milepost 42.5, Hwy. 12, Salvo, 252/987-2306, www.hatteraswatersports.com) offers sailboat, Jet Ski, and kayak rentals as well as guided and self-guided kayak tours. Their location on shallow Pamlico Sound is a perfect spot to head out in any of their watercraft, even for novices.

Shopping

In a place this beautiful and inspiring, it's no surprise that you'll find a number of galleries showcasing the works of local and regional artists. The **Pea Island Art Gallery** (27766 Hwy. 12, Salvo, 252/987-2879, call for hours) has works from over 100 artists in a range of media in a gallery that's a replica of a 19th-century Lifesaving Station. **SeaWorthy Gallery** (58401 Hwy. 12, Hatteras, 252/986-6511, www.seaworthygallery.com, call for hours) carries pieces ranging from fun, cartoonish folk art representations of area wildlife to painstaking paintings of area landmarks, seascapes, and landscapes. **Blue Pelican Gallery** (57762 Hwy. 12, Hatteras, 252/986-2244, www.bluepelicangallery.com, call for hours) carries jewelry from local glassblowers, lockets filled with objects found on and inspired by the shore, jewelry, and a beautiful selection of yarn and supplies for knitting and other needle arts.

The indie **Buxton Village Books** (47918 Hwy. 12, Buxton, 252/995-4240, www.buxtonvillagebooks.com, 10am-5pm daily) carries a large selection of books about the Outer Banks and by regional authors, along with the latest in contemporary and Southern fiction. The staff are knowledgeable and can point you to beach reads or something deeper.

Accommodations

Among the lodging choices on Hatteras Island is the very fine **Inn on Pamlico Sound** (49684 Hwy. 12, Buxton, 866/726-5426, www.innonpamlicosound.com, $100-350, varies by season). The inn is right on the sound, with a private dock and easy waterfront access. The dozen suites are sumptuous and relaxing, many with their own decks or private porches. Another good choice is the **Cape Hatteras Bed and Breakfast** (49643 Old Lighthouse Rd., Buxton, 252/995-6004, www.capehatterasbandb.com, Apr.-late Nov., $120-210), which is only a few hundred feet from the ocean. Guests rave about the breakfast.

Simpler motel accommodations include the clean, comfortable, and pet-friendly **Cape Pines Motel** (47497 Hwy. 12, Buxton, 866/456-9983, www.capepinesmotel.com, $49-199, varies by season, pets $20); the

Outer Banks Motel (47000 Hwy. 12, Buxton, 252/995-5601 or 800/995-1233, www.outerbanksmotel.com, $69-365, varies by season), with both motel rooms and cottages; and the Avon Motel (Avon, 252/995-4123 or 252/995-5774, www.avonmotel.com, $39-140, varies by season, pets $10 per day), a pet-friendly motel that has been in business for more than 50 years.

CAMPING
Rodanthe Watersports and Campground (24170 Hwy. 12, 252/987-1431, www.watersportsandcampground.com, $19.25 for 2 people, $4.75 per additional adult, $3 children and dogs, add $4.75 for electrical hookup) has a campground on the sound for tents and RVs under 25 feet, with water and electrical hookups and hot showers.

The National Park Service operates two campgrounds in this stretch of the National Seashore: **Frisco Campground** (late Apr.-mid-Oct., $20), where you actually camp in the dunes, and **Cape Point Campground** (46700 Lighthouse Rd., Buxton, and 53415 Billy Mitchell Rd., Frisco, 877/444-6777, late-May-Aug., $20), with level campsites located behind the dunes. Both have cold showers, restrooms, and potable water. **Frisco Woods Campground** (Hwy. 12, Frisco, 800/948-3942, www.outerbanks.com/friscowoods, $30-90, varies by season) has a full spectrum of camping options, including no-utilities tent sites, RV sites with partial or full hookups, and one- and two-bedroom cabins. The campground has wireless Internet access, hot showers, and a coin laundry.

Cape Hatteras KOA (2509 Hwy. 12, Rodanthe, 252/987-2307 or 800/562-5268, www.koa.com, from $56) offers campsites, RV sites, and small cabins along with a pool, a play area for kids, a small commissary, and direct beach access.

Food
Dining options are limited on Hatteras Island, but there are plenty of places to eat. The **Restaurant at the Inn on Pamlico Sound** (Hwy. 12, Buxton, 252/995-7030, www.innonpamlicosound.com, 5pm-9pm daily, $25-35) is primarily for guests of the inn, but if you call in advance, you might be able to get a reservation for dinner, even if you're staying elsewhere. The chef likes to use fresh-caught seafood, sometimes caught by the guests themselves earlier in the day. Vegetarian fare and other special requests are available.

For breakfast, try the **Gingerbread House** (52715 Hwy. 12, Frisco, 252/995-5204, http://gbhbakery.com, breakfast 7am-11am, dinner 4:30pm-9pm Tues.-Sat., breakfast around $6, dinner around $18), which serves great baked goods made on the premises. In the evenings, try pan and hand-tossed pizza made using fresh dough; in addition to the usual toppings, they offer a whole-wheat crust and a number of specialty pies topped with local shrimp, clams, crab, or barbecued chicken. **StingWrays's Bar and Grill** (24394 Hwy. 12, Rodanthe, 252/987-1500, 4pm-11pm Mon.-Wed., 11am-11pm Thurs.-Sun. entrées $10-30) is a laid-back place with a great outdoor deck and great sunset views, along with a good selection of North Carolina beers on tap.

◖ OCRACOKE ISLAND
Ocracoke Island, one of the most geographically isolated places in the state, is the southernmost part of the Cape Hatteras National Seashore. Accessible only by water and air, this 16-mile-long island seems charmingly anchored in the past. Regular ferry service didn't start until 1960, as most residents were content to stay on their island, separate from the rest of the state, and they didn't have a paved highway until 1963. The natural beauty of the island is mostly intact, and some areas look much like they did in 1585 when the first English colonists ran aground. It may have been during their time on Ocracoke (called Wococon at the time) that the ancestors of today's wild ponies first set hoof on the Outer Banks. Theirs was not the last shipwreck at Ocracoke, nor was it the first; Spanish explorers reportedly ran aground here too, and it's possible the now-feral Banker ponies came from their ships. As

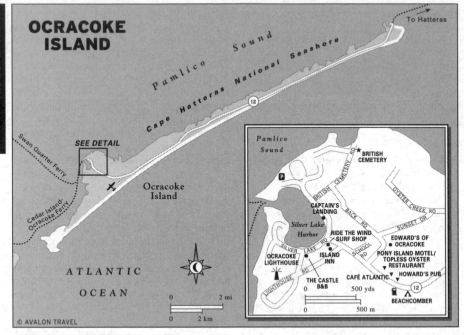

on the northern stretches of the Outer Banks, Ocracokers subsisted partially on the flotsam and goods that would wash up after shipwrecks, so wherever the wild horses came from, like other gifts from the sea they have become part of the island's history and lifestyle.

In some ways, Ocracoke is a little creepy. Its isolation has something to do with that, but so do its legends and ghosts. During the early 18th century, Ocracoke was a favorite haunt of the pirate Edward Teach, better known as Blackbeard. He lived here from time to time, married his 14th wife here, and died here. He met his fate in Teach's Hole, a spot just off the island, when a band of privateers (pirate hunters) hired by Virginia's Governor Spottswood finally cornered and killed him. According to legend, he didn't go down without a fight; it took five musket shots, more than 20 stab wounds, and a near beheading before his fight was over. Afterward, Spottswood's privateers took Blackbeard's head as a trophy and dumped his body overboard where, legend has

it, it swam around the ship seven times before going under.

All of **Ocracoke Village,** near the southern end of the island, is on the National Register of Historic Places. While the historical sites of the island are highly distinctive, the most unique thing about the island and its people is the culture that has developed over the centuries. Ocracokers have a "brogue" or dialect of their own, similar to those of other Outer Banks communities but distinctive and unique to the island.

Ocracoke Lighthouse

A lighthouse has stood on Ocracoke since at least 1798, but due to the constantly shifting sands, the inlet that it protected kept sneaking away. Barely 20 years after that first tower was built, it was almost a mile from the water. The current **Ocracoke Lighthouse** (Ocracoke Village, 888/493-3826) was built in 1823 and originally burned whale oil to power the beam. It is still in operation, the oldest continuously operating light in North Carolina and the second-oldest in the nation. Because it's on active duty, it is not publicly accessible, but a boardwalk nearby gives nice views.

British Cemetery

The **British Cemetery** (British Cemetery Rd.) is not, as one might suppose, a colonial graveyard but rather a vestige of World War II, when the Carolina coast was lousy with German U-boats. Many old-timers today remember catching a glimpse of a furtive German sub casing the beach. Defending the Outer Banks became a pressing concern, and on May 11, 1942, the HMS *Bedfordshire*, a British trawler sent to aid the U.S. Navy, was torpedoed by the German *U-558*. The *Bedfordshire* sank, killing all 37 men on board. Over the course of the next week, four bodies washed up on Ocracoke—those of Lieutenant Thomas Cunningham, Ordinary Telegraphist Stanley Craig, and two unidentified sailors. An island family donated a burial plot, where the four men lie today, memorialized with a plaque that bears a lovely verse by Rupert Brooke, a young World War I British sailor and poet who died of disease on his way to the battle of Gallipoli.

Sports and Recreation

Ride the Wind Surf Shop (486 Irvin Garrish Hwy., 252/928-6311, www.surfocracoke.com) gives individual and group surfing lessons for adults and children ($75 per hour for 1 person, $35 per hour each additional person), covering ocean safety and surfing etiquette in addition to board handling. A three-day surf camp for kids ages 9-17 ($85 per day, $200 per week) gives an even more in-depth tutorial. Ride the Wind also leads sunrise, sunset, and full-moon kayak tours ($35) around the marshes of Ocracoke. Kayak, stand-up paddleboard, surfboard, and boogie-board rentals ($12-55 per day, $28-150 per week) are available.

The *Windfall II* (departs from Community Store Dock, Ocracoke, 252/928-7245, www.schoonerwindfall.com), a beautiful 32-foot lazy jack schooner, sails out into the Pamlico Sound to visit Teach's Hole, where Blackbeard

was brought to justice, and conducts daily sunset cruises. The *Wilma Lee*, a 46-foot skipjack that can accommodate up to 42 passengers, also sails for pleasure cruises, sunset cruises, weddings at sea, and other private functions. Passengers are encouraged to try their hand at the wheel or trimming the sails.

Tradewinds Tackle (1094 Irvin Garrish Hwy., 252/928-5491, www.fishtradewinds. com) offers fishing tips and sells all the gear you'll need, including fishing licenses, to land a big one. The Ocracoke Island fishing experts at Tradewinds can tell you where to catch what and how, or they can simply send you to a good fishing guide. A comprehensive list of fishing charters and guides is available on the Ocracoke Village website (www.ocracokevillage.com).

Accommodations

The **Captain's Landing** (324 Hwy. 12, 252/928-1999, www.thecaptainslanding.com, from $280 summer, from $110 off-season), with a perch right on the harbor (called Silver Lake) looking toward the lighthouse, is a modern hotel owned by a descendant of Ocracoke's oldest families. Suites have 1.5 baths, full kitchens, comfortable sleeper sofas for extra guests, and decks with beautiful views. They also have a bright airy penthouse with two bedrooms, an office, a gourmet kitchen, and even a laundry room. The Captain's Cottage is a private two-bedroom house, also right on the water, with great decks and its own courtyard.

The **Pony Island Motel and Cottages** (785 Irvin Garrish Hwy., 252/928-4411 or 866/928-4411, www.ponyislandmotel.com, from $115 summer, from $60 off-season) has been in operation since the late 1950s and run by the same family for more than 40 years. It has regular and efficiency motel rooms and four cottages on the grounds. Clean guest rooms, a good location, and reasonable rates year-round make this a top choice on the island.

Edwards of Ocracoke (226 Old Beach Rd., 252/928-4801 or 800/254-1359, www.edwardsofocracoke.com, from $54 spring and fall, from $90 summer, weekly rentals $445-2,095) has several cozy bungalows typical of coastal

Carolina, referred to here as "vintage accommodations." The mid-20th-century vacation ambiance is pleasant, the cabins are clean and well-kept, and the rates are great. Private cottages are available, as are two homes perfect for larger groups traveling together.

The pet- and child-friendly **Island Inn** (25 Lighthouse Rd., 252/928-4351, www.ocracokeislandinn.com, from $49 off-season, from $89 summer) is on the National Register of Historic Places and bills itself as the oldest operating business on the Outer Banks. It was built in 1901, first used as an Oddfellows Hall, and later used as a barracks during World War II. The building is made of salvaged shipwreck wood, which everyone knows brings strange juju; add that to the 1950s murder of a caretaker and the discovery of colonial bones under the lobby, and it's a given that the place is considered haunted. The resident wraith is believed to be a woman, because she seems to enjoy checking out female guests' cosmetics and clothes, which will sometimes turn up in the morning in places other than where they were left the night before. No one has ever seen her, but her footsteps are sometimes heard in empty guest rooms, and odd happenings are attributed to her—most notably the unraveling of an entire roll of toilet paper in the presence of a terrified guest. Like many hotel ghosts, she is most active during the inn's less crowded seasons.

The Castle B&B (155 Silver Lake Rd., 252/928-3505 or 800/471-8848, www.thecastlebb.com, from $189 summer, from $139 off-season) is a beautiful home with well-appointed guest rooms, spectacular views, a pool, and, of course, breakfast. Get to breakfast early, when the biscuits are hot; they're legendary around these parts.

CAMPING

At **Ocracoke Campground** (4352 Irvin Garrish Hwy., Ocracoke, 252/928-6671, www.recreation.gov, $23), campsites are right by the beach and behind the dunes. Remember to bring extra-long stakes or sand anchors to stake your tent in the sand.

Beachcomber Campground (990 Irvin Garrish Hwy., 252/928-4031, www.ocracokecamping.com, tents from $31, RVs from $42) is open year-round and is conveniently located near both the Cape Hatteras National Seashore and Ocracoke Island's only gas station, perfect for those late-night munchies. Throughout the season they feature live music. There isn't a lot of shade, so it is more pleasant during the shoulder seasons, when the weather is milder.

Food

Ocracoke's **Café Atlantic** (1129 Irvin Garris Hwy., 252/928-4861, www.ocracokeisland.com, dinner daily, lunch Sun., $14-21) has a large and eclectic menu, with tastes venturing into Italian, Nuevo Latino, and local fare. Lunch and dinner choices may include a BLT, a crab cake (with Pamlico Sound crabmeat), or a *caciucco*, an Italian seafood stew. While many restaurants will accommodate vegetarians with a single pasta dish at the end of the list of entrées, Café Atlantic has several options without meat or seafood. There's also an extensive wine list.

Topless Oyster Restaurant (875 Irvin Garrish Hwy., 252/928-2800, 11am-2am daily, $10-30) serves, you guessed it, oysters on the half shell. Oysters purists will probably order them plain, but for those with an adventurous palate, several types of specialty oysters (topped with crab, ceviche, and the like) are available. Topless Oyster also serves burgers, ribs, barbecue, and more.

Howard's Pub & Raw Bar Restaurant (1175 Irvin Garrish Hwy., 252/928-4441, www.howardspub.com, 11am-10pm daily, entrées $15-26) serves steaks, burgers, salads, sandwiches, and a wide assortment of appetizers. Try the homemade hush puppies and the conch fritters; they'll get you ready for a memorable meal.

GETTING THERE AND AROUND

The northern part of Cape Hatteras National Seashore can be reached by car, following Highway 12 south from Nags Head. Along Highway 12 you'll go through the towns of Rodanthe, Waves, Salvo, and Avon, and then around the tip of the cape to Buxton, Frisco, and Hatteras, where the highway ends. From here, you have two choices: backtrack or take a ferry to Ocracoke.

Ocracoke can only be reached by ferry. The Hatteras-Ocracoke Ferry (800/368-8949, www.ncdot.gov/ferry, 1 hour, free) is the shortest route to Ocracoke. On some maps, Highway 12 is shown crossing from Ocracoke to Cedar Island, as if there were an impossibly long bridge over Pamlico Sound. In fact, that stretch is a ferry route too. The **Cedar Island-Ocracoke Ferry** (800/293-3779, www.ncdot.gov/ferry), a 2.25-hour ride, costs $15 one-way for a regular-size vehicle. There's also an **Ocracoke-Swan Quarter Ferry** (800/293-3779, 2.5 hours, $15 regular-size vehicle one-way).

Across the Sounds

Traditionally called the Albemarle, although today sometimes called the Inner Banks, the mainland portion of northeastern North Carolina is the heart and hearth of the state's colonial history, the site of its first colonial towns and earliest plantations, and the seat of power for the largely maritime economy.

Inland, early European Carolinians and Virginians named a region they thought of as a diseased and haunted wasteland "the Great Dismal Swamp." They planned to drain it and create more hospitable places to settle, and to a point they succeeded in doing so, but enough of the swamp remains today that it is recognized it as one of the state's prettiest places, valued by human visitors almost as much as by the bears and wolves that live there.

Early cities like Edenton and Bath were influential centers of commerce and government, and today they preserve some of the finest examples of colonial and early Federal architecture in the Southeast. Inland, along the Roanoke River, the small town of Halifax played a key role in American history; in a tavern in Halifax, representatives from North Carolina wrote and ratified the Halifax Accords, the first documents to denounce British rule over the colonies and to declare American independence. The Halifax Accords were read at the Continental Congress in Philadelphia, which led to the Declaration of Independence and the Revolutionary War.

The vast networks of rivers and creeks feeding the Roanoke River and other major waterways include some of the state's best places for inland canoeing and kayaking. Along the Albemarle Regional Canoe-Kayak Trail, a number of camping platforms allow paddlers to spend an unforgettable night listening to owls hoot and otters splash. The abundant water also irrigates the vast farms in this corner of the state, and if a small town has a restaurant, it'll be either a country kitchen or a fish shack. Either way, you'll get to sample the region's inland seafood traditions.

◖ THE GREAT DISMAL SWAMP

Thought of for centuries as an impediment to progress, the Great Dismal Swamp is now recognized for the national treasure that it is, and tens of thousands of its acres are protected. There are several points to access the interior of the Dismal Swamp. On U.S. 17 a few miles south of the Virginia-North Carolina border is the **Dismal Swamp Welcome Center** (2294 U.S. 17 N.) as well as the **Dismal Swamp Visitors Center** (2356 U.S. 17 N., South Mills, 877/771-8333, www.dismalswamp.com, 9am-5pm daily June-Oct., 9am-5pm Tues.-Sat. Nov.-May). Arriving by water, you'll find the Welcome Center at Mile 28 on the Intracoastal Waterway. You can tie up to the dock and spend the night, or wait for one of the four daily lock openings (8:30am, 11am, 1:30pm, and 3:30pm) to proceed. There are also picnic tables and grills, and restrooms open 24 hours.

Another area of the swamp to explore is

the **Great Dismal Swamp National Wildlife Refuge** (3100 Desert Rd., Suffolk, VA, 757/986-3705, www.fws.gov, dawn-dusk daily), which straddles the state line. Two main entrances are outside of Suffolk, Virginia, off White Marsh Road (Hwy. 642). These entrances, Washington Ditch and Jericho Lane, are open 6:30am-8pm daily April 1-September 30, and 6:30am-5pm daily October 1-March 31. In the middle of the refuge is Lake Drummond, an eerie 3,100-acre natural lake that's a wonderful place for canoeing. Contact refuge headquarters for directions on navigating the feeder ditch into Lake Drummond. You may see all sorts of wildlife in the swamp, including poisonous cottonmouths, canebrake rattlers, copperheads, and possibly even black bears. Controlled hunting is permitted on certain days in October-December, so if you visit in the fall, wear bright-colored clothing and contact refuge staff before your visit to find out about closures.

GATESVILLE

Near the town of Gatesville, west of South Mills on U.S. 158, is another gorgeous natural swamp area, **Merchant's Millpond State Park** (176 Millpond Rd., Gatesville, 252/357-1191, http://ncparks.gov, office 8am-4:30pm Mon.-Fri. except holidays, park 8am-6pm daily Nov.-Feb., 8am-8pm daily Mar.-May and Sept.-Oct., 8am-9pm daily June-Aug.). There is an amazing variety of wildlife, particularly among reptiles, with many species snakes (most are harmless) and turtles (harmless, except for the snappers), and despite the relatively northerly clime, alligators (most emphatically not harmless). Other denizens include salamanders, mink, and nutrias.

This is a great spot for canoeing or kayaking, with miles of beautiful blackwater backwaters. For those unfamiliar with blackwater, it looks like it sounds: black water. Tannins from decaying vegetation leech into the water, turning it a dark tea or coffee color and creating a beautiful, but eerie, effect. The park has canoe rentals ($5 1st hour, $3 per additional hour, $20 per day for campers). There are nine miles of

hiking trails, all classified as easy, but rangers strongly caution hikers to be careful to avoid ticks. Wear bug spray, tuck your pant legs into your socks, wear light-colored clothing to see the ticks better, and when you return, do a tick check by running your fingers over every inch of your body.

Merchant's Millpond has several campsites ($13-20): The family campground, near the park office, is easily accessible, accommodates tents and RVs, and has a washhouse with restrooms, showers, and drinking water. Off the park's Lassiter trail are five backpack campsites, where all supplies, including water, must be packed in; there is a pit toilet nearby. There are also two canoe camping areas accessed by canoe trails, with pit toilets; campers must bring water and other supplies.

ELIZABETH CITY

The **Museum of the Albemarle** (501 S. Water St., 252/335-1453, www.museumofthealbemarle.com, 10am-4pm Tues.-Sat.) covers the four centuries since the first English settlers arrived at Roanoke. Come to learn about the Lost Colonists, the pirates who swarmed the region, and the folkways of the Sound country.

To stay in Elizabeth City, the **Pond House Inn** (915 Rivershore Rd., 252/335-9834, www.thepondhouseinn.com, $99-165) is on the banks of the Pasquotank River. Each of the large guest rooms has its own fireplace in this pleasant 1940s house. The **Culpepper Inn** (609 W. Main St., 252/335-9235, www.culpepperinn.com, $110-135), just a few blocks from Albemarle Sound, has several comfortable guest rooms in the main house as well as cozy accommodations in a carriage house and a cottage.

There are also chain motels in the area, including the **Travelers Inn** (1211 N. Road St., 252/338-5451, www.travelersinn.webs.com, around $70) and **Econo Lodge** (510 S. Hughes Blvd., 252/338-4124, www.econolodge.com, around $70), both of which allow small pets, the **Holiday Inn Express** (306 S. Hughes Blvd., 252/338-8900, www.ihg.com, $75-125), and **Hampton Inn** (402 Halstead Blvd.,

252/333-1800, www.hamptoninn3.hilton.com, around $130).

Toyama Japanese Restaurant (218 N. Poindexter St., 252/338-5021, lunch 11am-2:30pm daily, dinner 4:30pm-10pm Mon.-Thurs., 4:30pm-11pm Fri.-Sun., entrées $8-20) has a fantastic reputation for quality sushi on a staggeringly lengthy menu. Don't worry if you're not a sushi fan; there's plenty on the menu that's not raw fish.

Cypress Creek Grill (113 Water St., 252/334-9915, www.cypresscreekgrill.com, 11am-9pm Mon.-Thurs., 11am-10pm Fri., 5pm-10pm Sat., entrées $11-27) is close to downtown and serves gulf-style seafood, Tex-Mex cuisine, and a few creole dishes. The owners are from Texas, and they've blended their native flavors with the local ingredients of eastern North Carolina to make for some tasty dining.

HERTFORD

If you're traveling between Edenton and Elizabeth City, don't miss Hertford, a pretty little Spanish moss-draped town on the Perquimans (per-KWIH-muns) River. The historic **Newbold-White House** (151 Newbold-White Rd., 252/426-7567, www.newbold-whitehouse.org, guided tours 10am-4pm Tues.-Sat. Apr.-Nov., $5 adults, $3 students) is the oldest brick house in North Carolina, built in 1730 by one of the region's early Quakers. The grounds include a seasonal herb garden and a 17th-century Quaker graveyard.

Stop in at **Woodard's Pharmacy** (101 N. Church St., 252/426-5527, 9am-6pm daily, under $10), an old-fashioned lunch counter and soda fountain in the heart of downtown, where you can grab a pimiento cheese sandwich and an ice cream cone. If you're making it an overnight, stay at **1812 on the Perquimans** (385 Old Neck Rd., 252/426-1812, $80-85), or at the **Beechtree Inn** (948 Pender Rd., 252/426-1593, www.beechtreeinn.net, $80-90), where guests stay in restored pre-Civil War cottages and children and pets are welcome. The **Beautiful Moon Café** (252/426-2500, www. beautiful-moon-cafe.com, 5:30pm-8pm Mon.-Thurs., 5:30pm-9pm Fri.-Sat., $12-19) is at the Beechtree Inn and serves a small, simple menu of steak, chicken, and some seafood.

EDENTON

Incorporated in 1722 but inhabited by colonists for 50 years before that, Edenton was not only North Carolina's first permanent settlement, it was also one of the most important colonial towns in the state. This beautiful waterside town served as the colonial capital until 1743, and the state's oldest courthouse, built in 1767, is still in use today.

Historic District

All of Edenton is lined with historic buildings, and several especially important sites are clustered within a few blocks of the waterfront. The easiest starting point for a walking tour is the headquarters of the **Edenton State Historic Site** (108 N. Broad St., 252/482-2637, www. nchistoricsites.org, 9am-5pm Tues.-Sat., guided tours $1-10), also referred to as the Edenton Visitors Center. The 1782 **Barker House** (505 S. Broad St., 252/482-7800, http://ehcnc.org, 10am-4pm daily), a stunning Lowcountry palazzo, was the home of Penelope Barker, an early revolutionary and organizer of the Edenton Tea Party. It's now the headquarters of the Edenton Historical Commission and the location of their bookstore. The 1758 **Cupola House** (408 S. Broad St., tickets and information at Edenton Visitors Center, 108 N. Broad St., 252/482-2637, www.cupolahouse.org, 9am-4:30pm daily) is a home of great architectural significance and a National Historic Landmark. Although much of the original interior woodwork was removed in 1918 and sold to the Brooklyn Museum in New York, where it remains, Cupola House has been meticulously restored inside and out and its colonial gardens recreated. Also a designated National Historic Landmark is the **Chowan County Courthouse** (117 E. King St., 252/482-2637, www.edenton.nchistoricsites.org, hours vary), a superb 1767 brick building in the Georgian style. It's the best-preserved colonial courthouse in the United States.

Downtown you'll find yourself surrounded

by beautiful examples of Jacobean, Georgian, Federal, and Victorian homes as well as a number of other important historical sites, including **St. Paul's Episcopal Church** (W. Church St. and N. Broad St., 252/482-3522, http://stpaulsedenton.org), the second-oldest church structure in the state, and **Colonial Waterfront Park** (Edenton waterfront, parking on W. Water St. and S. Broad St.), a stop on the Underground Railroad. African American workers would find sailors sympathetic to the cause of freeing slaves and arrange their passage on ships to a free state. Harriet Jacobs's description of her 1842 escape by sea from Edenton is one of the few existing written accounts. Learn more about her story at http://harrietjacobs.org or on a guided or self-guided walking tour (tours begin at the Edenton State Historic Site) that highlights her years in Edenton.

Sports and Recreation

Right on the water, Edenton is surrounded by miles of paddling trails (www.visitedenton.com), but there is only one kayak and canoe rental outfit, the **Edenton Town Harbor Dock Master** (Edenton Harbor, 252/482-2832, www.visitedenton.com, kayaks from $5 per hour, canoes $10 per hour).

The **Chowan Golf & Country Club** (1101 W. Sound Shore Dr., 252/482-3606, http://chowangolfandcountryclub.com, 18 holes, par 72, greens fees $25 with cart, $15 walking) is the only golf course around, and it's a friendly, very playable course with beautiful water views from a few holes. Rental clubs are available ($10).

Accommodations and Food

((The Pack House Inn (103 E. Albemarle St., 252/482-3641, www.thepackhouse.com, from $99) occupies three exceptional historic buildings: the 1900 grand Victorian mansion known as The Proprietor's; the 1915 Pack House, which started its life as a tobacco packing house on a nearby plantation; and the 1879 Tillie Bond House cottage. Each is artfully restored with soft and restful furnishings. A three-course breakfast, which features gluten-free and vegetarian selections if arranged

in advance, is served every morning in the Tillie Bond Dining Rooms. Lunch and dinner are also available at the Proprietor's Table Restaurant.

The **Granville Queen Inn** (108 S. Granville St., 866/482-8534, www.granvillequeen.com, $105-155) is a rather splendid early-20th-century mansion decorated in a variety of period styles. Breakfasts are as ornate and elegant as the house itself, featuring poached pears, potato tortillas, and crepes. Children are welcome most of the year, but there are occasions when their presence isn't appropriate; let the innkeepers know about any children in your party when making reservations.

WINDSOR

A small historic town on the Cashie (Cuh-SHY) River, Windsor is the seat of Bertie (Ber-TEE) County. Historic architecture, good food, and wetlands exploration are equally compelling reasons to visit this lesser-known treasure of the Albemarle region.

Sights

Hope Plantation (132 Hope House Rd., 252/794-3140, www.hopeplantation.org, visitors center 9am-4pm Mon.-Fri., 10am-4pm Mon.-Sat., 2pm-5pm Sun. Apr.-mid-Dec., 10am-4pm Sat., 2pm-5pm Sun. mid-Dec.-Mar. 31, $10, $8 seniors, $5 students and children) was built in 1803 for David Stone. Stone did not live to see his 50th birthday, but by the time of his death he had been governor of North Carolina, a U.S. senator and representative, a state senator, a Superior Court judge, and had been elected seven times to the State House. He graduated from Princeton and passed the bar when he was 20, fathered 11 children, and was one of the founders of the University of North Carolina. As busy as he was, he managed to oversee the construction of this impressive house. Characterized by a mixture of Georgian and Federal styles with significant twists of regional and individual aesthetics, Hope House is on the National Register of Historic Places. Also on the register and now on the grounds of the plantation is the brick-end, gambrel roof

King-Bazemore House, built in 1763 and also a significant example of its type. The **Roanoke-Cashie River Center** (112 W. Water St., Windsor, 252/794-2001, www.partnershipforthesounds.org, 10am-4pm Wed.-Fri., 10am-2pm Sat. Apr.-Oct., 10am-4pm Tues.-Fri. Nov.-Mar., $2, $1 children) has interpretive exhibits about this region's history and ecology. There is a canoe ramp outside where you can access the Cashie River, and canoe rentals ($10 per hour, $25 half-day, $35 full-day) are available.

Southeast of Windsor on the Cashie River, the **San Souci Ferry** (Woodard Rd. and Sans Souci Rd., 252/794-4277, 6:30am-6pm Mar. 16-Sept. 16, 6:45am-5pm Sept. 17-Mar. 15) operates, as it has for generations, by a cable and a honk of the horn. To cross the river, pull up to the bank and look for the ferry. If it's across the river, honk your horn and wait. The ferry operator will cross to you and pull you to the opposite bank. There's only room for two cars at a time, but it's a charming way to cut 20 miles off your journey.

Recreation
The headquarters of the **Roanoke River National Wildlife Refuge** (114 W. Water St., 252/794-3808, www.fws.gov/roanokeriver) is located in Windsor. The refuge stretches over nearly 21,000 acres in Bertie County, through the hardwood bottomlands and cypress-tupelo wetlands of the Roanoke River Valley, an environment that the Nature Conservancy calls "one of the last great places." The refuge is an exceptional place for bird-watching, with the largest inland heron rookery in North Carolina, a large population of bald eagles, and many wintering waterfowl and neotropical migratory species.

Food
Bunn's Bar-B-Q (127 N. King St., 252/794-2274, 9am-5pm Mon.-Tues., 9am-2pm Wed., 9am-5pm Thurs.-Fri., 9am-2pm Sat., from $5) is a barbecue and Brunswick stew joint of renown, an early gas station converted in 1938 to its present use. Service here is blazing fast,

primarily because there are just a few choices on the menu. Super-finely chopped barbecue is the specialty, and you get it with or without Brunswick stew, on a plate or a sandwich, with tart or creamy coleslaw and cornbread. It comes lightly sauced, the way the locals like it, but if you want more, or hotter, sauce, you'll find a bottle close at hand.

SCOTLAND NECK
In the little Halifax County community of Scotland Neck, west of Windsor, is the **Sylvan Heights Waterfowl Center and Eco-Park** (500 Sylvan Heights Park Way, off Lees Meadow Rd., 252/826-3186, www.shwpark.com, 9am-5pm Tues.-Sun. Apr.-Sept., 9am-4pm Tues.-Sun. Oct.-Mar., $9 adults, $5 ages 2-12, $7 over age 62, free under age 2), a center for the conservation of rare species of birds and home to the world's largest collection of waterfowl, comprising more than 1,000 birds of 170 different species. You'll see birds native to every continent except Antarctica; it gets a little hot here for penguins. A visit to Sylvan Heights is an unbeatable opportunity to get up close to birds you won't encounter elsewhere, as well as for wildlife photography—you won't even need your zoom lens.

HISTORIC HALIFAX AND ROANOKE RAPIDS
Sometimes the biggest things come from the smallest places. Less than 300 people call the tiny hamlet of Halifax home, but it is the birthplace of a nation, where the first official documents calling for independence from British rule were written. Once an important town due to its proximity to the river and trade routes, Halifax dwindled as nearby Roanoke Rapids rose in significance. Today, Halifax is not much more than a state historic site, with the vast majority of local shopping, dining, and infrastructure located in Roanoke Rapids.

In its heyday Roanoke Rapids was home to several textile mills, but, like so many other Southern towns, the mill jobs left and the town suffered. More recently a canal, once part of a complex series of locks allowing river traffic to

ROANOKE RIVER

After a long journey down from the Blue Ridge Mountains of Virginia, the waters of the Roanoke River cross into North Carolina just northwest of the town of Roanoke Rapids and travel another 130 miles before emptying into Albemarle Sound. The Roanoke River played a crucial role in the region's history as a major route for transportation and commerce in colonial times. It is also a river of tremendous ecological importance; its floodplain represents the Mid-Atlantic's largest and most pristine bottomland hardwood forest ecosystem. It's a region of beautifully primitive dark swamps and towering ancient trees.

More than 100,000 acres surrounding the river are preserved as wilderness. The **Roanoke River National Wildlife Refuge** (114 Water St., Windsor, 252/794-3808, www.fws.gov) comprises more than 20,000 acres in three separate tracts–Broadneck Swamp, Company Swamp, and Conine Island–between the towns of Hamilton and Windsor. Limited road access is available from U.S. 17 north of Windsor, but the best way to experience the refuge is by water. The Nature Conservancy also owns tens of thousands of acres of forests and wetlands along the river. These areas can be explored on field trips led by the North Carolina chapter of the **Nature Conservancy** (www.nature.org).

For a lover of river journeys by canoe or kayak, this is an irresistible place, and thanks to a network of area environmental and community organizations, it is increasingly a destination for paddlers. **Roanoke River Partners** (252/792-0070 or 252/724-0352, www.roanokeriverpartners.org) has designated a paddle trail through this wild region. They've also constructed more than a dozen camping platforms at locations along the river from Weldon, near the Virginia line, to Albemarle Sound. Every camping platform is different, but most are sturdy wooden decks over the cypress swamps or in the woods near the river on which campers can pitch their tents. Others are positively cushy screened houses in which campers can sleep protected from hovering bugs.

Reservations are required to use the platforms, and there's a lot to learn before you embark on a Roanoke River trip. For instance, do you know what to do if a bear pays a visit to your campsite? At some of the campsites, that information may come in handy. Read the information on the Roanoke River Partners website or call to find out more. Some stretches of the trail are best suited to experienced paddlers and campers. Novices can enjoy the river too by signing up for guided trips with conservation organizations such as the Nature Conservancy, paddle clubs such as the **Roanoke Paddle Club** (www.roanokeriver.com), or commercial river guides. Williamston-based **Roanoke Outdoor Adventures** (252/809-9488, http://roanokeoutdooradventures.com), for example, leads trips on many stretches of the Roanoke.

bypass the falls on the Roanoke River, has become a museum and a well-used walking and cycling trail.

Sights
The main attraction is **Historic Halifax** (25 St. David St., Halifax, 252/583-7191, www.nchistoricsites.org, 9am-5pm Tues.-Sat., free). Several colonial-era buildings still stand, including a prominent merchant's home and the Tap Room tavern, both from 1760, and the 1790 Eagle Tavern; there are also several early-19th-century buildings, including a home, an attorney's office, the clerk's office, and the jail. Tours (30 minutes) run throughout the day. On April 12 the Halifax Day celebration commemorates the date of the 1776 Halifax Resolves, which may have been signed in the Eagle Tavern. Events, speakers, tours, and usually costumed Colonial-era reenactors fill the day with the sights, sounds, smells, and activities that would have given the community so much energy so long ago.

In Roanoke Rapids, the **Roanoke Canal**

© JASON FRYE

Historic Halifax contains colonial buildings.

Museum and Trail (15 Jackson St. Ext., 252/537-2769, www.roanokecanal.com, museum 10am-4pm Tues.-Sat., trail dawn-dusk daily, museum $4, trail free) calls itself the world's longest museum as it included the 7.5-mile nature trail. At the trailhead, a museum tells the story of this 200-year-old canal, originally opened to allow river traffic to bypass the falls, and all its subsequent incarnations. In 1882 investors developed it into an early hydroelectric power source, and by 1900 two powerhouses were in full operation. The investors couldn't maintain it, and it was sold to a power company that operated it for several decades. In 1976 what remained of the canal was placed on the National Register of Historic Places. Learn about this in greater detail in the museum, which also provides an overall feel for the history of the Roanoke River Valley.

Sports and Recreation
The **Roanoke Canal Trail** (15 Jackson St. Ext, trailheads at Roanoke Rapids Lake, near Oakwood Ave., Roanoke Rapids; and Rockfish

THE HALIFAX RESOLVES

On April 12, 1776, in a bar in the tiny town of Halifax, one of the most important but little-known documents in the history of the United States was ratified. At the Sign of the Thistle tavern, 83 members of the Fourth Provincial Congress of North Carolina met in secret to write and unanimously ratify the Halifax Re- solves, the first official provincial action to declare independence from Great Britain. Three delegates from North Carolina delivered the Resolves to the Continental Congress in Philadelphia, and a few months later, word spread that the Declaration of Independence had been signed.

Dr., near U.S. 158/301, Weldon, dawn-dusk daily) runs for 7.5 miles along the tow path beside the 19th-century canal. Expect river views and secluded woodsy sections along the path; bring water and bug spray.

Every spring, anglers from around the country come to nearby Weldon to catch striped bass, known here as rockfish; as they travel up the river to spawn, the fishing is excellent. The Roanoke River's other fish species include shad, largemouth bass, and catfish. Outfitters can provide gear as well as the requisite fishing license. A comprehensive list of outfitters and guides is maintained by the **Halifax County Convention and Visitors Bureau** (www.visithalifax.com).

If kayaking is more your speed, **Roanoke River Partners** (www.roanokeriverpartners. org) maintains an index of outfitters and guides happy to help you with a solo or guided exploration of the river.

Shopping

At the western end of the Roanoke Canal Trail is **Riverside Mill** (200 Mill St., Weldon, 252/536-3100, www.riversidemill.net, 10am-6pm daily), an antiques mall and artisans gallery in a historic cotton mill. It's a fun place to explore because of the eclectic mix of local pottery, paintings, crafts, and antiques.

Along King Street in Halifax, you'll find a number of antiques stores that pop up for a year or two and are then replaced just as quickly by others. One of the permanent residents on this "antiques row" is **Ernie's Place** (18 King St., 252/583-2110, 9am-5pm Tues.-Sat.), a consignment shop that carries works by 30 or 40 local artisans.

Accommodations and Food

Most of the bed-and-breakfasts in the area are on the smaller side; the lone B&B in Roanoke Rapids is the charming **Twin Magnolias Bed & Breakfast** (302 Jackson St., Roanoke Rapids, 252/308-0019, $80), with just two guest rooms, a quaint garden, and a porch lined with chairs and tables that provide plenty of room to spread out.

Nearby Enfield, just a few miles south of Roanoke Rapids, is home to two B&Bs. **Bellamy Manor and Gardens Bed and Breakfast** (613 Glenview Rd., Enfield, 252/445-2234, www.manorbnb.com, $145) has four charming guest rooms in a beautiful home. Extensive gardens provide a place to walk and unwind, and if you're the sporting type, request a skeet-shooting outing when you make your reservation. The smaller **Healthsville Haven Bed and Breakfast** (25560 Hwy. 561, 252/445-5448, www.healthsvillehaven.com, from $70) has three guest rooms and serves breakfast in the dining room or on the deck, terrace, or garden (weather permitting), or even in your room if you're in the Executive Suite. The innkeepers are devoted to healthy eating and clean living to the point that if you want artificial sweetener for your coffee, you'll have to bring your own.

King Street Deli (20 S. King St., Halifax, 252/583-2112, 10am-2pm Mon.-Sat., around $8) specializes in rotisserie and fried chicken. The house-made potato chips are always good, and if you want fried pickles, this is the only place in town to get them. **Abner's Drive In** (93 Roanoke Ave., Roanoke Rapids, 252/519-1296, 6:30am-2:30pm daily, $7) may lack aesthetics but they serve a great breakfast; try the pancakes.

WILLIAMSTON AND VICINITY

Williamston is at the junction of U.S. 17 and U.S. 64. If you're passing through town, Williamston is a great place to stop for barbecue or a fresh seafood meal.

Sights

A little west of Williamston on U.S. 13/64 is the town of Robersonville and the **St. James Place Museum** (U.S. 64 and Outerbridge Rd., by appointment with Robersonville Public Library, 252/795-3591, year-round). A Primitive Baptist church built in 1910 and restored by a local preservationist and folk-art enthusiast, St. James Place is an unusual little museum that fans of Southern craft will not want to miss. A serious collection of traditional quilts is the main feature of the museum. Of the 100 on display, nearly half are African American quilts, which are much less likely to survive and find their way into museum collections than their counterpane counterparts made by white quilters. Getting a glimpse of the two traditions side by side is an education in parallel Southern aesthetics.

Also on U.S. 13/64 west of Williamston is **East Carolina Motor Speedway** (4918 U.S. 64, 252/385-2018, www.ecspeedway.com, pits from 3:30pm, grandstands from 5pm, green flag 7:30pm Sat., pits from 10am, practice noon, green flag 2:30pm Sun., usually Apr.-Oct., $24 pit access, $10 adults, $5 ages 6-12, free under age 6, no one under age 12 in the pits), a 0.4-mile hard-surface track featuring several divisions, including late-model stock, street stock, mini stock, and U-Car divisions. U-Cars are fun to watch; they are front-wheel-drive vehicles like Ford Escorts, Dodge Daytonas, and Toyota Tercels that have been upfitted with safety measures and race on short tracks. Drivers range in age from 14-50 and are divided into classes by age. Fast and fun, this racing division has been gaining more fans every year.

One of the oddest sights in eastern North Carolina may be **Deadwood** (2302 Ed's Grocery Rd., 252/792-8938, www.deadwoodnc.com, from 5pm Thurs.-Sat., noon-9pm Sun. year-round), a tiny amusement park with an Old West flair. The owner calls this 10-acre park as "a weird, out-of-hand backyard project" inspired by Dolly Parton's Dollywood in Tennessee. Amusements here include miniature golf, a miniature train ride, a kid-friendly roller coaster, and a murder-mystery dinner show (first Sat. of the month, $30), complete with pratfalls, a gunfight, and a hearty dinner. It's well worth the stop, even if all you do is play a round of mini golf and eat ice cream.

Food

Come to Williamston on an empty stomach: It has an assortment of old and very traditional eateries. The **C** **Sunny Side Oyster Bar** (1102 Washington St., 252/792-3416, www.sunnysideoysterbarnc.com, from 5:30pm Mon.-Sat., from 5pm Sun. Sept.-Apr., $6.50-25) is the best-known, a seasonal oyster joint open in the months whose names contain the letter *R*—that is, oyster season. It has been in business since 1935 and is a historic and gastronomic landmark. Oysters are steamed behind the restaurant and then hauled inside and shucked at the bar. Visit the restaurant's website to meet the shuckers. In eastern North Carolina, a good oyster shucker is as highly regarded as a good artist or athlete, and rightly so. The Sunny Side doesn't take reservations, and it soon fills to capacity, so come early.

Down the road a piece, **Martin Supply** (118 Washington St., 252/792-2123, 8am-5pm Mon.-Fri., 8am-1pm Sat.), an old general store, is a good place to buy local produce and preserves, honey, molasses, and hoop cheese, and a place to stock up on hunting, fishing, and sporting supplies. **Griffin's Quick Lunch** (204 Washington St., 252/792-0002, 6am-8:30pm Mon.-Fri., 6am-2pm Sat., under $10) is a popular old diner with good barbecue and a devoted following. Back on U.S. 64, **Shaw's Barbecue** (202 West Blvd., 252/792-5339, 6am-7pm Mon.-Sun., $3-8) serves eastern North Carolina-style barbecue, fried chicken, and all the fixin's. They're open early, so if you're passing through to or from the Outer Banks, stop in for a good greasy breakfast—two eggs over easy, bacon, grits, and toast.

East of Williamston at the intersection of U.S. 64 and Highway 171, a most unusual restaurant in the small Roanoke River town of Jamesville draws attention from all over the country. The **C** **Cypress Grill** (1520 Stewart St., off U.S. 64, 2nd Thurs. in Jan.-Apr., 11am-2pm and 5-8pm Mon.-Sat., under $10) is an unprepossessing wooden shack on the river, a survivor of the days when Jamesville made its living in the herring industry, dragging the fish out of the water with horse-drawn seines. Herring—breaded and seriously deep-fried, not pickled or sweet—is the main dish, although they also serve bass, flounder, perch, oysters, and catfish. The Cypress Grill is open for the a few months of the year and provides an intensely authentic small-town dining experience.

The Smokehouse Grill (252/792-8516, www.deadwoodnc.com, dinner from 5pm Thurs.-Sat., noon-9pm Sun., $9-23), in the Deadwood amusement park, serves steaks, ribs, chicken, and shrimp, and Tex-Mex specialties in a kitschy but charming Old West venue.

EAST ON U.S. 64

The eastern stretch of U.S. 64 runs along the Albemarle Sound between Williamston and the Outer Banks, passing through the towns of Plymouth, Creswell, and Columbia before it crosses to Roanoke Island. Here you'll encounter evidence of North Carolina's ancient past in old-growth forests, its recent past in the form of a plantation with a long and complex history of slavery, and its present in art galleries and abundant wildlife-watching and recreational opportunities.

Plymouth

Plymouth is an attractive little town on the Roanoke River with a rich maritime and military history. Most notably it was the site of the 1864 Battle of Plymouth, the second-largest Civil War battle in North Carolina, fought by more than 20,000 soldiers. At the **Roanoke River Lighthouse and Maritime Museum** (W. Water St., 252/217-2204, www.roanokeriverlighthouse.org, 11am-3pm Tues.-Sat. and by appointment, $3 adults, $2 students), visitors can explore a pretty replica of Plymouth's 1866 screw-pile lighthouse and, across the street in an old car dealership, the maritime museum, featuring artifacts and photographs from the region's water-faring heritage. On East Water Street is the **Port O'Plymouth Museum** (302 E. Water St., 252/793-1377, www.livinghistoryweekend.com, 9am-4pm Tues.-Sat., $3 adults, $2 students). This tiny museum is packed with Civil War artifacts, including a collection of beautiful pistols, telling the story of the Battle of Plymouth.

Davenport Homestead

West of Creswell is the **Davenport Homestead** (3 miles south from U.S. 64's exit 554 on Mt. Tabor Rd., 252/793-1377), a small 18th-century cabin built by Daniel Davenport, the first state senator from Washington County. In 1800 this diminutive homestead was home to 14 people—six members of the Davenport family and eight enslaved people. Visitors can take a self-guided tour of the Davenport Homestead, but for a closer look, ask Loretta Phelps, who lives across the road and is a Davenport descendant, to unlock the buildings and show you around.

❰ Somerset Place Historic Site

Somerset Place Historic Site (2572 Lake Shore Rd., Creswell, 252/797-4560, www.ah.dcr.state.nc.us, 9am-5pm Tues.-Sat., free) was one of North Carolina's largest and most profitable plantations for the 80 years leading up to the Civil War. In the late 18th and early 19th centuries, 80 Africa-born men, women, and children were brought to Somerset to labor in the fields. The grief and disorientation they experienced and the subsequent trials of the slaves, whose numbers grew to include more than 300 people, are told by the historian Dorothy Spruill Redford in the book *Somerset Homecoming*. Somerset is a significant historical place for many reasons, but the story of its African Americans makes it one of this state's most important historic sites.

Somerset Place is a lovely but eerie place to visit. The restored grounds and buildings, including the Collins family's house, the slave quarters, and several dependencies, are deafeningly quiet, and the huge cypress trees growing right up to the quarters and the mansion make it feel almost prehistoric. Visitors can walk around the estate at their leisure. A small bookshop on the grounds is a good source for books about North Carolina history in general and African American history in particular.

❰ Pettigrew State Park

Pettigrew State Park (2252 Lakeshore Rd., Creswell, 252/797-4475, http://ncparks.gov), on the banks of **Lake Phelps,** preserves an unusual ancient waterscape that's unlike anything

© JASON FRYE

Lake Phelps

else in the state. Archaeology reveals that there was a human presence here at least 10,000 years ago. The lake, which is five miles across and never more than nine feet deep, is only fed by rainfall and has yielded more than 30 ancient dugout canoes, some as old as 4,400 years and measuring more than 30 feet. The natural surroundings are ancient too, encompassing some of eastern North Carolina's only remaining old-growth forests. **Pungo Lake,** a smaller body of water within the park, is visited by 50,000 migrating snow geese over the course of the year, an unforgettable sight for wildlife watchers.

Visitors can camp at the family campground ($20), which has drive-in sites and access to restrooms and hot showers, or at primitive group campsites (from $13).

Art Galleries

Eastern North Carolina has always had a folk-art tradition. **Pocosin Arts** (Main St. and Water St., Columbia, 252/796-2787, www. pocosinarts.org, 10am-5pm Tues.-Sat.) has helped keep the tradition of arts and crafts

alive, teaching community classes in ceramics, fiber arts, sculpture, jewelry making, metalwork, and other media. The sales gallery has beautiful handmade items, and the main gallery displays many examples of folk art from eastern North Carolina.

Sports and Recreation

Palmetto-Peartree Preserve (entrance on Pot Licker Rd./Loop Rd./State Rd. 1220, east of Columbia, 252/796-0723 or 919/967-2223, www.palmettopeartree.org) is a 10,000-acre natural area, wrapped in 14 miles of shoreline along Albemarle Sound and Little Alligator Creek. Originally established as a sanctuary for the red cockaded woodpecker, this is a great location for bird-watching and spotting other wildlife, including alligators, wolves, bears, and bobcats, as well as hiking, cycling, and horseback riding along the old logging trails through the forest and canoeing and kayaking. The preserve's excellent paddle trail passes by Hidden Lake, a secluded cypress-swamp blackwater lake. There is an overnight camping platform at the lake, which can be used in the daytime without a permit for bird-watching and picnicking. To stay overnight, arrange for a permit through **Roanoke River Partners** (252/792-3790, www.roanokeriverpartners.org, $20 single campers, $10 pp multiple campers).

Once the southern edge of the Great Dismal Swamp, **Pocosin Lakes National Wildlife Refuge** (205 S. Ludington Dr., 6 miles south of Columbia, 252/796-3004, www.fws.gov/pocosinlakes) is an important haven for many species of animals, including migratory waterfowl and reintroduced red wolves. Five important bodies of water lie within the refuge: Pungo Lake, New Lake, the 16,600-acre Lake Phelps, and stretches of the Scuppernong and Alligator Rivers. All of these areas are good spots for observing migratory waterfowl, but Pungo Lake is special in the fall and winter, when snow geese and tundra swans visit in massive numbers—approaching 100,000—on their arctic journeys.

The landscape here was drastically altered by a tremendous wildfire in summer 2008, blanketing towns as far away as Raleigh with thick smoke. You can still observe some of the damage today, from burn marks on some of the larger trees to the growth patterns of the smaller trees, shrubs, and grasses. Wildfire is an important part of the natural cycle, however, and now is a unique opportunity to watch the regeneration of an ecosystem.

Also east of Columbia on U.S. 64 is the **Alligator River National Wildlife Refuge** (between Columbia and Roanoke Island, 252/473-1131, http://alligatorriver.fws.gov). The large refuge covers most of the peninsula bounded by the Alligator River to the west, Albemarle Sound to the north, Croatan Sound to the east, and Pamlico Sound to the southeast. This large swath of woods and pocosin represents one of the most important wildlife habitats in the state, home to over 200 species of birds as well as alligators, red wolves, and more black bears than anywhere in the coastal Mid-Atlantic. In the 1980s, red wolves were introduced into the Alligator River Refuge as they became extinct in the wild elsewhere in their original range. Rangers lead "howlings" (reservations required, $7), nighttime expeditions into the refuge to hear the wolves' calls. The Columbia-based **Red Wolf Coalition** (252/796-5600, http://redwolves.com) works to educate the public about the wolves in the hope of helping to establish free-ranging, self-sustaining red wolf populations at a number of sites.

There are many other ways to enjoy the Alligator River National Wildlife Refuge, including hiking, kayaking, and bird-watching. The refuge does not have a physical headquarters or traditional visitors center, but detailed directions and visitor information are available on the website.

WASHINGTON, BATH, AND BELHAVEN

North of the Pamlico River, as you head toward the Mattamuskeet National Wildlife Refuge and the Outer Banks, the towns of Washington, Bath, and Belhaven offer brief but beautiful diversions into the nature and history of the region.

North Carolina Estuarium

The **North Carolina Estuarium** (223 E. Water St., Washington, 252/948-0000, www.partnershipforthesounds.org, 10am-4pm Tues.-Sat., $4, $2 children, free under age 5) is a museum dedicated to both the natural and cultural history of the Tar-Pamlico River basin. In addition to the exhibits, which include live native animals, historic artifacts, a 0.75-mile boardwalk along the Pamlico River, and hands-on displays, the Estuarium operates pontoon-boat tours (10:30am Wed.-Sat., 1:30pm Wed.-Fri., reservations required, free).

Moss House

Located in the historic district a block from the river, the **Moss House** (129 Van Norden St., 252/975-3967, www.themosshouse.com, $125-145) dates to 1902 and is now a cozy bed-and-breakfast with airy guest rooms and delicious breakfasts, often including hot cross buns. An easy walk from the Moss House is **Bill's Hot Dogs** (109 Gladden St., 252/946-3343), a longtime local favorite for a quick snack. It's been around since 1928, so they've got their process down—you can only order when they ask for your order—and they know how to produce the dogs on the double.

Goose Creek State Park

Goose Creek State Park (2190 Camp Leach Rd., 252/923-2191, http://ncparks.gov, 8am-6pm daily Nov.-Feb., 8am-8pm daily Mar.-May and Sept.-Oct., 8am-9pm daily June-Aug., closed Dec. 25) is on the banks of the Pamlico River where Goose Creek joins it. It's an exotic environment of brackish marshes, freshwater swamps, and tall pine forests that are home to a variety of wildlife, including bears, a multitude of bird species, and lots of snakes. Eight miles of hiking trails as well as boardwalks and paddle trails traverse the hardwood swamp environment, and miles of shoreline and creek await exploration from a kayak or canoe (bring your own). Twelve primitive campsites (year-round, $13) are available, with access to toilets and water, including one campsite that is wheelchair-accessible.

Historic Bath

North Carolina's oldest town, Bath was chartered in 1705. The town has changed so little that even today it is mostly contained within the original boundaries laid out by the explorer John Lawson. For its first 70 years Bath enjoyed the spotlight as one of North Carolina's most important centers of trade and politics, home to governors, a refuge from the Indian wars, and frequently host to and victim of the pirate Blackbeard. Bath faded into obscurity as the town of Washington grew in the years after the Revolution, and today almost all of Bath is designated as **Historic Bath** (252/923-3971, www.nchistoricsites.org, visitors center and tours 9am-5pm Mon.-Sat., 1pm-5pm Sun. Apr.-Oct., 10am-4pm Tues.-Sat., 1pm-4pm Sun. Nov.-Mar., admission charged for the Palmer-Marsh and Bonner Houses). Important

sites on the tour of the village are the 1734 St. Thomas Church, the 1751 Palmer-Marsh House, the 1790 Van Der Veer House, and the 1830 Bonner House. Bath, like any self-respecting town of its age, has its fair share of legends, including a set of indelible hoof prints said to have been made by the devil's horse and "Teach's light"—the head of the pirate Blackbeard, often seen near his former home.

While in Bath, drop in at the **Old Town Country Kitchen** (436 Carteret St., 252/923-1840, 7am-8:30pm daily, under $12) for some country cooking and seafood. If you decide to stay the night, try the **Inn on Bath Creek** (116 S. Main St., 252/923-9571, www.innonbathcreek.com, 2-night minimum Fri.-Sat. Apr.-Nov., $130-225). This bed-and-breakfast, built on the site of the former Buzzard Hotel, fits in nicely with the old architecture of the historic town, but because it was built in 1999, it has modern conveniences to make your stay comfortable. Breakfast is big—think scratch-made blueberry pancakes, scrambled-egg wraps, and quiche along with the usual fruit, coffee, and pastries; vegetarian options are available.

Belhaven

Belying its innocuous name, **Belhaven Memorial Museum** (210 E. Main St., 919/943-6817, www.beaufort-county.com, 1pm-5pm Thurs.-Tues., free) is actually a very strange little institution that houses the collection of Miss Eva—Eva Blount Way, who died in 1962 at the age of 92—a most accomplished collector of oddities. In 1951 the local newspaper described her: "housewife, snake killer, curator, trapper, dramatic actress, philosopher, and preserver of all the riches of mankind, inadequately describes the most fascinating person you can imagine." Miss Eva kept among her earthly treasures a collection of pickled tumors (one weighs 10 pounds), a pickled one-eyed pig, a pickled two-headed kitten, cataracts (pickled), and three pickled human infants. There's also a dress that belonged to a 700-pound woman, a flea couple dressed in wedding togs, 30,000 buttons, and assorted snakes that Miss

Eva determined needed killing. It must have taken a very long time to carry everything over here, but Miss Eva's collection is now on public display, the core of the Belhaven Memorial Museum's collection.

Belhaven has an especially nice inn, the **Belhaven Water Street Bed and Breakfast** (567 E. Water St., 866/338-2825, www.belhavenwaterstreetbandb.com, $85-125). The guest rooms in this 100-year-old house face Pantego Creek and have their own fireplaces and private baths as well as wireless Internet access.

◖ MATTAMUSKEET NATIONAL WILDLIFE REFUGE

Near the tiny town of Swan Quarter, **Mattamuskeet National Wildlife Refuge** (856 Mattamuskeet Rd., off Hwy. 94, between Swan Quarter and Englehard, 252/926-4021, www.fws.gov/mattamuskeet) preserves one of North Carolina's most remarkable natural features as well as one of its most famous buildings. Lake Mattamuskeet, 18 miles long by 6 miles

wide, is the state's largest natural lake, and at an average of 1.5 feet deep—5 feet at its deepest point—it is a most unusual environment. The hundreds of thousands of waterfowl who rest here on their seasonal rounds make this a world-famous location for bird-watching and wildlife photography.

Old-timers in the area have fond memories of dancing at the **Lodge at Lake Mattamuskeet,** one of eastern North Carolina's most recognizable buildings. The huge structure was built in 1915 and at the time was the world's largest pumping station, moving over one million gallons of water per minute. In 1934 it was bought by the federal government along with the wildlife sanctuary, and the Civilian Conservation Corps transformed it into the lodge, a favorite gathering place for the next 40 years. Efforts have been made to return the lodge to its former glory, but with the economic downturn that began in 2008, state budget shortfalls have kept the project from getting the resources necessary to complete the restoration.

Hiking and biking trails thread through the

the Lodge at Lake Mattamuskeet

© JASON FRYE

refuge, but camping is not permitted. In hunting season, which runs during spring and autumn months, beware of hunters (wearing a bright color like safety orange isn't a bad idea) and keep an eye out as well for copperheads, cottonmouths, two kinds of rattlesnakes, and alligators. Bears and red wolves abound here as well.

Within the administration of the Mattamuskeet Refuge is the **Swan Quarter National Wildlife Refuge** (252/926-4021, www.fws.gov/swanquarter), located along the north shore of the Pamlico Sound, and accessible only by water. It is a gorgeous waterscape full of wildlife and worth exploring if you have the time and the means to get here.

While you're here, stop in one of the handful of roadside produce stands you'll pass and inquire about getting some Mattamuskeet onions. Much like the famed Vidalia onion, the Mattamuskeet onion has a sweet, distinctive flavor farmers and foodies swear is endemic to the region thanks to the makeup of the soil.

GETTING THERE AND AROUND

This remote corner of North Carolina is crossed by two major north-south routes, U.S. 17 and U.S. 168, both from Chesapeake, Virginia. U.S. 168 passes to the east through Currituck, and U.S. 17 is the westerly route, closest to the Dismal Swamp and Elizabeth City, passing through Edenton, Windsor, and Williamston. At Williamston, U.S. 17 meets U.S. 64, a major east-west route that leads to Plymouth, Creswell, and Columbia to the east.

If you continue south on U.S. 17 from Williamston, the next major town is Washington, where you can turn east on U.S. 264 to reach Bath and Belhaven. Alternately, you can reach U.S. 264 from the other direction, taking Highway 94 at Columbia and crossing Lake Mattamuskeet.

There is one state ferry route in this region, at the far northwest corner between Currituck and Knotts Island (877/287-7488, 45 minutes, six trips daily, free).

BEAUFORT AND THE CRYSTAL COAST

Long before you smell the ocean salt on the air, you can feel the ocean drawing near. The sky seems wider and it takes on a deeper shade of blue. Hardwoods and hills give way to towering pines and flat fields, and then more and more water—creeks, wetlands, and widening rivers. Somewhere between Kinston and New Bern, still an hour's drive from the beaches and sounds of Carteret County, you can sense the Atlantic.

Along the Crystal Coast, as North Carolina's central coast is known in tourism literature, you'll find New Bern and Beaufort, two old North Carolina towns that were centers of colonial commerce and access to the Atlantic. These two towns are beautifully preserved, with great examples of historic commercial and residential architecture dating as far back

as three centuries, including one home believed to have belonged to the dreaded pirate Blackbeard.

The Neuse River winds through pine forests, passing Kinston—a town with an unusual Civil War past and a food scene that's more than worth the visit—and widening as it enters the coastal plain, feeding the primeval forest, creeks, hidden lakes, and tiny towns in the Croatan National Forest. To the northeast, the Cedar Island National Wildlife Refuge is a vast swath of marshes, gradually easing into the Pamlico Sound, where Cape Lookout National Seashore shelters the mainland from storms. Along the seashore are miles of beach where the only occupants are wild horses, the Banker ponies, and the beautiful diamond-patterned Cape Lookout Lighthouse. You won't find

© JASON FRYE

HIGHLIGHTS

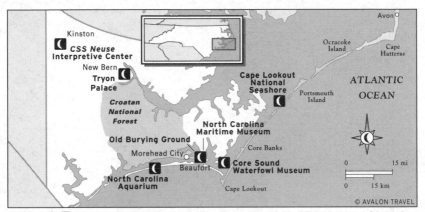

LOOK FOR **(** TO FIND RECOMMENDED SIGHTS, ACTIVITIES, DINING, AND LODGING.

(Tryon Palace: The splendid, and in its day controversial, seat of colonial government is reconstructed in New Bern's historic district, worthy of a day's leisurely exploration (page 79).

(CSS *Neuse* Interpretive Center: Far up the Neuse River a Confederate ironclad was built, fought, scuttled, and burned to prevent its capture. It stayed in the river for nearly a century before being salvaged for historic preservation. This museum tells its story, complete with the recovered hull (page 88).

(North Carolina Maritime Museum: North Carolina's seafaring heritage, ranging from pirate history to its fishing legacy to current maritime culture, is represented by fascinating exhibits and activities at this great museum (page 95).

(Beaufort's Old Burying Ground: One of the prettiest and most storied cemeteries in the South, this churchyard is home to the

"Little Girl Buried in a Barrel of Rum" and other fascinating residents (page 95).

(Core Sound Waterfowl Museum: Actually a museum about people rather than ducks, the Waterfowl Museum eloquently tells of the everyday lives of past generations of Down Easterners while bringing their descendants together to reforge community bonds (page 102).

(Cape Lookout National Seashore: The more than 50 miles of coastline along Core and Shackleford Banks, now home only to wild horses and turtle nests, were once also the home of Bankers who made their livings in the fishing, whaling, and shipping trades (page 104).

(North Carolina Aquarium: Sharks, jellies, otters, and their aquatic kin show their true beauty in underwater habitats at the aquarium. Hiking trails and boat tours lead to the watery world outdoors (page 107).

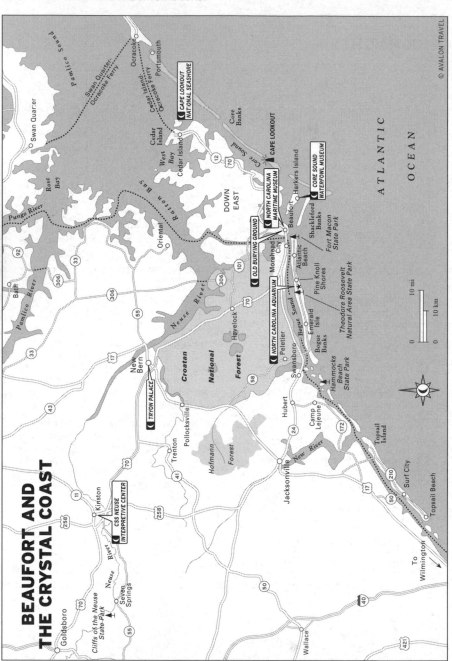

© AVALON TRAVEL

homes here. Portsmouth Village, a once-thriving whaling port washed away by a series of storms, is now nearly empty except for seagulls.

Sometimes people in North Carolina refer to any part of the coast, from Wilmington to Nags Head, as "Down East." In the truest sense of the term, Down East refers to northeast Carteret County, the area north of Beaufort. Here the islands, marshes, and towns bordering Core Sound are undergoing colossal cultural shifts as people from "up North" (meaning "anywhere but here") move into the area and local youth leave generations of family life for greener economic pastures. Changes in global trade and in the environment have made traditional maritime occupations like fishing and shrimping untenable. Nonetheless, Down Easterners work to preserve the treasure of their home, the Core Sound, with conservation and historic preservation as well as folkways education. Witness the Core Sound Waterfowl Museum on Harkers Island, where community members have assembled an interesting collection of family photos, quilts, baseball uniforms, oyster knives, net hooks, and other treasures to tell their story.

PLANNING YOUR TIME

Beach-season rules apply along the coastal areas and river towns, meaning that prices increase dramatically between Memorial Day in May and Labor Day in early September. Conversely, prices drop to rock bottom during the off-season. Visiting during shoulder seasons can mean warm water, empty beaches, and no waiting for restaurant tables, but your accommodations and dining choices can be limited, particularly in smaller towns.

When you visit, try the fresh local seafood. To ensure you're getting the best local catch, **North Carolina Sea Grant** (www.ncseagrant. org) provides downloadable cards and information on the seasonally fresh seafood caught in the area.

Across the Southeast, late summer and early autumn are hurricane season. The paths of hurricanes can be quite unpredictable, so if you're planning a week at the beach at this time of year, be aware that even if reports say a storm will dissipate over Cuba, that doesn't mean it won't turn into a hurricane and head for the Carolina coast. Chance are that you'll have sufficient warning before any major storm, but it's advisable to keep an eye on the weather forecast. A storm that stays offshore, even at some distance, can cause foul beach conditions; surfers love the big waves that precede a storm, but they know the danger of powerful tides, strong undertow, rip currents, and the general unpredictability that storms bring. Not unique to this region, the risk is the same anywhere on the North Carolina coast.

Barring storms, fall is a fabulous time to visit. Days and nights are still warm, the ocean is swimmable, and the crowds are smaller. Mild weather often holds through the end of October into November, but the water becomes chilly for swimming then, although air temperatures are still nice for strolling on the sand.

INFORMATION AND SERVICES

Hospitals in the area include **Carteret General Hospital** (3500 Arendell St., 252/808-6000, www.ccgh.org) in Morehead City, **Carolina East Medical Center** (2000 Neuse Blvd., 252/633-8111, www.carolinaeasthealth.com) in New Bern, **Vidant Duplin Hospital** (401 N. Main St., 910/296-0941, www.vidanthealth. com) in Kenansville, **Lenoir Memorial Hospital** (100 Airport Rd., 252/522-7000, www.lenoirmemorial.org) in Kinston, and **Wayne Memorial Hospital** (2700 Wayne Memorial Dr., 919/736-1110, www.wayne-health.org) in Goldsboro.

Extensive travel information is available from the **Crystal Coast Tourism Authority** (3409 Arendell St., 800/786-6962, www.crystalcoastnc.org) in Morehead City.

BEAUFORT

New Bern

New Bern's history attracts visitors, but the natural beauty of this artistic community keeps many of them returning year after year. Situated at the confluence of the Trent and Neuse Rivers, it's a prime spot for sightseeing and retirement living. Despite the attention it gets and the consequent traffic, New Bern has retained its charm and is still a small and enormously pleasant town. An important note: It's pronounced "NYEW-bern" or "NOO-bern," sometimes even like "neighbor," but never "New-BERN."

At the junction of two major highways, New Bern is easily reached by car. U.S. 17 passes through New Bern north-south, and U.S. 70 crosses east-west, with Beaufort and Morehead City to the east and Kinston to the west.

HISTORY

New Bern's early days were marked by tragedy. It was settled in 1710 by a community of Swiss and German colonists under the leadership of English surveyor John Lawson (author of the 1709 *A New Voyage to Carolina,* available today in reprint) and Swiss entrepreneur Christoph von Graffenried (from Bern, Switzerland). More than half of the settlers died en route to the New World, and those who made it alive suffered tremendous hardship in the first years. Lawson and Graffenried were both detained in 1711 by the indigenous Tuscarora people, whom the colonists had evicted from their land without compensation. Graffenried was released, according to some accounts because he wore such fancy clothes that the Tuscarora feared executing such a high-ranking official.

© JASON FRYE

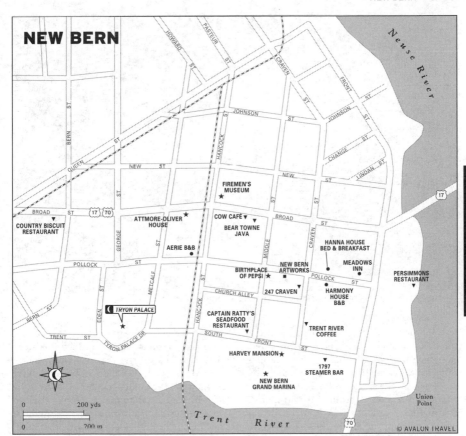

NEW BERN

HOWARD ST
PASTEUR ST
CRAVEN ST
FRONT ST

Neuse River

BERN ST
QUEEN ST
NEW ST
JOHNSON ST
HANCOCK ST
JOHNSON ST
CHANGE ST
LINDAN ST

FIREMEN'S MUSEUM ★

NEW ST

17

BROAD ST 17 70
COUNTRY BISCUIT RESTAURANT ▼
ATTMORE-OLIVER HOUSE ★
GEORGE ST
COW CAFÉ ▼ ▼
BEAR TOWNE JAVA
BROAD ST
HANNA HOUSE BED & BREAKFAST ●
POLLOCK ST
AERIE B&B ▼
METCALF ST
BIRTHPLACE OF PEPSI ★
NEW BERN ARTWORKS ■
CRAVEN ST
MEADOWS INN ●
PERSIMMONS RESTAURANT ▼
CHURCH ALLEY
247 CRAVEN
POLLOCK ST
HARMONY HOUSE B&B ●
TRYON PALACE ★
EDEN ST
HANCOCK ST
CAPTAIN RATTY'S SEADFOOD RESTAURANT ▼
BERN ST
TRENT ST
TRYON PALACE DR
SOUTH ST
FRONT ST
TRENT RIVER COFFEE ▼

HARVEY MANSION ★
1797 STEAMER BAR ▼
★ NEW BERN GRAND MARINA

Union Point

0 200 yds
0 200 m

Trent River

70

© AVALON TRAVEL

BEAUFORT

Lawson was tried and burned at the stake, and the conflict escalated into the Tuscarora War.

Despite early disasters, New Bern was on its feet again by the mid-18th century, when it was home to the colony's first newspaper and its first chartered academy. It also became North Carolina's capital, an era symbolized by the splendor of Tryon Palace, one of the most recognizable architectural landmarks the state.

During the Civil War, New Bern was captured early on by Ambrose Burnside's forces, and despite multiple Confederate attempts to retake the city, it remained a Union stronghold for the balance of the war. It became a center for African American resistance and political organization through the Reconstruction years, a story grippingly told in historian David Cecelski's book *The Waterman's Song*.

SIGHTS
Tryon Palace

Tryon Palace (529 S. Front St., 252/639-3500 or 800/767-1560, www.tryonpalace.org, 9am-5pm Mon.-Sat., noon-5pm Sun., last guided tour 4pm, gardens 9am-7pm Mon.-Sat., noon-7pm Sun. summer, museum shop 9am-5pm Mon.-Sat., noon-5pm Sun., full admission $20 adults, $10 schoolchildren, galleries and gardens only $12 adults, $4 children, gardens only $6 adults, $3 children) is a remarkable

BEAUFORT

© JASON FRYE

Tryon Palace is a re-creation of North Carolina's colonial capitol.

feat of historic re-creation, a reconstruction of the 1770 colonial capitol and governor's mansion done from the ground up. It was a magnificent project the first time around too, when Governor William Tryon bucked the preferences of Piedmont Carolinians and had the colonial government's new home built here on the coastal plain. He hired English architect John Hawks to design the complex, a Georgian house on an estate laid out in the Palladian style. The palace's first incarnation was short-lived, standing for a scant 25 years before burning down in 1798. As the new state had relocated its governmental operations to Raleigh, there was no need to rebuild the New Bern estate, but it was not forgotten. In the early 20th century a movement arose to rebuild Tryon Palace. By the 1950s both the funds and, incredibly, Hawks's original drawings and plans had been secured, and the palace was rebuilt over a period of seven years using the drawings as well the stables, the only original building not destroyed in the fire, as a model. Today, it is once again one of the most striking and recognizable buildings in the state.

Tryon Palace is open for tours year-round, and it hosts various lectures and living-history events throughout the year. One of the best times to visit is during the December holiday season, when the estate is decorated beautifully and a recreated **Jonkonnu,** a colonial African American celebration once seen throughout the Caribbean and Southeast, is celebrated. Also known by the name Junkanoo, John Canoe, and several other variations, enslaved Africans and African Americans would put on a Mardi Gras-like festival with deep African roots, parading through plantations with music and wearing outlandish costumes, some representing folk characters associated with the celebration. Like Mardi Gras, it was a sort of upside-down day, when the social order was temporarily inverted and enslaved people could boldly walk right onto the master's porch and demand gifts or money. Some slave owners got into the spirit of the celebration and played along with the remarkable pantomime. It was a tradition fraught with both joy and sorrow. Tryon Palace puts on a lively and enlightening re-creation.

© JASON FRYE

BEAUFORT

period gardens at Tryon Palace

Tryon's living-history interpreters do a wonderful job of enlightening visitors to certain aspects of colonial life, on a guided tour of the palace and on a walk through the nearby kitchen. In the kitchen, costumed interpreters show what was involved in running an 18th-century household, utilizing the nearby kitchen garden for most of what they cook with during the demonstrations. Lately the cooking demonstrations have expanded, pairing the beauty of the palace with the talents of a local chef to put on dinner events, including the on-site Savoring Spring event that makes use of the bounty of the kitchen garden.

At the Tryon Palace ticket office is the **North Carolina History Center,** a collection of galleries and exhibits that illustrate the history of the region and New Bern in particular. The **Pepsi Family Center** is a hit with kids, as interactive displays transport you back to 1835, when the region was busy producing valuable things like turpentine for the nation's young navy. Visitors interested in Jonkonnu will find enlightening exhibits on the festival, and art lovers will appreciate the best of the region in

the **Duffy Exhibit Gallery.** Admission to the Pepsi Family Center, Duffy Exhibit Gallery, and Regional History Museum are included in the admission cost for Tryon Palace.

Visiting Tryon Palace and its gardens along with the North Carolina History Center can fill an afternoon or even a full day. When you're done exploring, the surrounding neighborhood contains some wonderful old homes.

New Bern Firemen's Museum

The **New Bern Firemen's Museum** (408 Hancock St., 252/636-4087, www.newbernfiremuseum.com, 10am-4pm Mon.-Sat., $5 adults, $2.50 children, free under age 6) is a fun little museum for gearheads that has an antiquarian bent. The museum houses a collection of 19th- and early-20th-century fire wagons and trucks and chronicles the lively and contentious history of firefighting in New Bern. The city was the first in North Carolina and one of the first in the country to charter a fire department. After the Civil War, three fire companies operated in New Bern; one was founded before the war, one was founded after, and the third was a boys bucket brigade, a training program for junior firefighters. During Reconstruction, every fire became a competition among the companies, as residents would gather to see which would get to a blaze first—the "good old boys" (white Southerners) or the "carpetbaggers" (Northerners who came to the South during Reconstruction for economic opportunities).

Attmore-Oliver House

The beautiful 1790 **Attmore-Oliver House** (512 Pollock St., 252/638-8558, www.newbernhistorical.org, 10am-4pm Mon.-Fri., guided tours by appointment, free) is a historic house museum with exhibits about New Bern's Civil War history. It's also the headquarters of the New Bern Historical Society.

Birthplace of Pepsi

We often think of Coca-Cola as the quintessential Southern drink, but it was here in New Bern that Caleb Bradham, a drugstore owner, put together what he called Brad's Drink—later Pepsi-Cola. The Pepsi-Cola Bottling Company operates a soda fountain and gift shop at the location of Bradham's pharmacy, called the **Birthplace of Pepsi** (256 Middle St., 252/636-5898, www.pepsistore.com). A few Pepsi antiques sit in display cases, but the pièce de résistance is the mural showing the original recipe for a production batch of Brad's Drink.

ENTERTAINMENT AND EVENTS

New Bern's historic Harvey Mansion has a cozy old-fashioned pub in its cellar, the **1797 Steamer Bar** (221 S. Front St., 252/635-3232, 5pm-2am daily). As you might guess, the pub serves steamed seafood and other light fare. This basement bar is a rarity for houses of such an age; it was originally the house's kitchen, which in the 18th century was typically in a separate building because of the danger of fire. Today, it's a perfect hangout—the low ceiling, exposed beams, and copper-topped bar make it cozy. **Captain Ratty's Seafood Restaurant** (202-206 Middle St., 252/633-2088 or 800/633-5292, www.captainrattys.com, 11:30am-9:30pm Mon.-Fri., 8am-9:30pm Sat.) has a rooftop bar that's a popular gathering spot for locals and travelers alike, and the impressive wine list, combined with a few choice appetizers, make this a great place to watch the sun go down.

SHOPPING

Given its age, the fact that New Bern is a great place for antiques shopping comes as no surprise. Check out **New Bern Antiques** (1000 Greenleaf Cemetery Rd., 252/672-1890, www.new-bern-antiques.com, 9:30am-5:30pm Mon.-Sat., 1pm-5pm Sun.) and the adjacent **New Bern Flea Mall** (4109 U.S. 17 S., 252/636-1855, http://new-bern-flea-mall-complex.com, 10am-5pm Mon.-Sat.), with nearly 40,000 square feet of antiques, collectibles, and vendors. **Tom's Coins and Antiques** (244 Middle St., 252/633-0615, hours vary) carries an impressive array of antique coins and currency as well as a good selection of small mementos and antiques. There are also periodic antiques shows and even a salvaged antique architectural hardware show at the New Bern Convention Center (www.visitnewbern.com).

Tryon Palace is a fun shopping spot for history buffs and home-and-garden fanciers. The historical site's **Museum Shop** (Jones House, Eden St. and Pollock St., 252/514-4932, 9am-5pm Mon.-Sat., noon-5pm Sun.) has a nice variety of books about history and architecture as well as handicrafts and children's toys and games. In season, the **Garden Shop** (610 Pollock St., 252/514-4932, 10am-5pm Mon.-Sat., 1pm-5pm Sun.) sells special bulbs and plants grown in Tryon Palace's own greenhouse. Out of season you can still find a nice variety of gardening tools and accessories. A Shop Pass is available at the Museum Shop; it allows you to visit the shops at Tryon Palace without paying the entrance fee.

Strolling the streets of New Bern, you'll notice a number of art galleries. One of the best is **New Bern Artworks and Company** (323 Pollock St., 252/634-9002, www.newbernartworks.com, 10am-6pm Mon.-Fri., 10am-5pm

Sun.), a well-curated gallery and working studio with architecture almost as beautiful as the artwork. The gallery is in a former jewelry store and has the original antique cases and even the safe. This is a great stop for art and architecture buffs.

Carolina Creations Fine Art and Contemporary Craft Gallery (317-A Pollock St., 252/633-4369, www.carolinacreationsnewbern.com, 10am-6pm Mon.-Thurs., 10am-8pm Fri., 10am-6pm Sat., 11am-4pm Sun. springsummer, 10am-6pm Mon.-Sat., 11am-3pm Sun. winter) has a mix of fine arts and functional craft items. You'll find everything from turned wooden bowls to oil paintings and hand-forged menorahs.

SPORTS AND RECREATION

Right on the river and near miles of tributaries to explore by boat, it's no surprise that watersports dominate New Bern's outdoor offerings. Familiarize yourself with the area on a two-hour tour waterfront tour on the catamaran *Lookout Lady* (New Bern Grand Marina, 100 Middle St., Dock F, 252/728-7827, www. tournewbern.com, $25 adults, $15 children, sunset cruises $26 adults, $16 children). Tours pass Millionaire's Row, where author Nicholas Sparks has a home, and are narrated by knowledgeable local residents.

Head out on the water on your own aboard a kayak or stand-up paddleboard and discover New Bern by water. Kayakers will want to head to the Grand Marina, where **Captain Fins** (New Bern Grand Marina, 100 Middle St., Dock F, 252/876-2288, http://kayaknewbern.com, single kayaks $30 for 2 hours, $40 half-day, $55 full-day, double kayaks $40 for 2 hours, $55 half-day, $70 full-day) rents out kayaks and provides some guidance on where to go and what to see. For a self-propelled tour of New Bern's waterfront, join **Stand Up Outfitters** (244 Craven St., 252/514-0404, www.standupoutfitters.com, lessons from $45, tours from $60, rentals from $35 per day) on their Historic New Bern Tour. This 1.5-2 hour tour will give you a workout and unique views of this beautiful town.

Golfers visiting New Bern will want to check out **Harbour Pointe Golf Club** (1105 Barkentine Dr., 252/638-5338, www.harbourpointegolfclub.com, 18 holes, par 72, greens fees $38 for 18 holes, $25 for 9 holes, $28 midday, $15 twilight, $25 military, fees include cart). The course presents challenges but gives you plenty of opportunities to take strokes back. And the must-see hole is number 14, where the green's sweeping view of Broad Creek and the Neuse River can even take the sting out of a double bogey. The **Emerald Golf Club** (5000 Clubhouse Dr., 252/633-4440, www.emeraldgc.com, 18 holes, par 72, greens fees $56 for 18 holes, $34 for 9 holes, $40 after 11am, rates include cart) is a pretty course with wide fairways flanked by trees, bunkers, and water.

At **Carolina Colours Golf Club** (3300 Waterscape Way, 252/772-7022, www.carolinacoloursgolfclub.com, 18 holes, par 72, Tues.-Sun., greens fees $49 for 18 holes, $28 for 9 holes), the course winds through some heavily wooded terrain to reveal beautiful fairways that invite seasoned golfers to challenge bunker placements and shoot aggressively for the green, while allowing recreational golfers to play at a pace and level they're accustomed to. This is one of the prettiest public courses in the area.

ACCOMMODATIONS

The ◖**Aerie Bed and Breakfast** (509 Pollock St., 800/849-5553, www.aeriebedandbreakfast. com, $129-229) is the current incarnation of the 1880s Street-Ward residence. Each of its seven luxurious guest rooms are decorated with Victorian furniture reflecting the house's earliest era. There is a lovely courtyard for guests to enjoy, and the inn is only one block from Tryon Palace.

Pollock Street is lined with charming 19th-century houses decorated in classic bed-and-breakfast style. The **Harmony House Inn** (215 Pollock St., 800/636-3113, www.harmonyhouseinn.com, $109-175) has seven well-appointed guest rooms and three suites. Two of the suites feature king beds and two-person jetted tubs, while the third is more suited to a group that may want to spread out, with a queen bed and a separate living room that has a queen sleeper sofa.

At the **Hanna House Bed and Breakfast** (218 Pollock St., 252/635-3209 or 866/830-4371, http://hannahousenc.net, no children under age 6, $99-165), expect one of the best breakfasts you can get at a B&B. The owners take pride in their morning spread and offer a selection of dishes ranging from eggs en croûte, a variety of frittatas, and my favorite, stuffed french toast. Hanna House isn't all breakfast; each of the five guest rooms is comfortable and spacious for both single travelers and couples.

Also on Pollock Street, the **Meadows Inn** (212 Pollock St., 877/551-1776, www.meadowsinn-nc.com, $139-179) started as a humble four-room home, but was expanded in the late 19th century. You'll find six guest rooms and a two-bedroom third-floor suite, all furnished with a mix of antiques and modern conveniences. Because of its prime location, make reservations early.

Several motels can be found around New Bern as well, including **Holiday Inn Express** (3455 Martin Luther King Jr. Blvd., 252/638-8266, www.hiexpress.com, from around $100), and **Hampton Inn** (200 Hotel Dr., 252/637-2111, www.hamptoninn.com, from around $125).

Camping

New Bern's **KOA Campground** (1565 B St., 800/562-3341, www.newbernkoa.com, from $35) is on the other side of the Neuse River from town, right on the riverbank. Choices include 20-, 30-, 40-amp RV sites; "Kamping Kabins and Lodges"; and tent sites. Pets are allowed, and there is a dog park on-site. The campground has free wireless Internet access. Stop by the New Bern Convention Center's visitor information center before checking in, and pick up a KOA brochure for some valuable coupons.

FOOD

One of the top restaurants in New Bern also happens to have the best view. At **Persimmons**

Restaurant (100 Pollock St., 252/514-0033, www.persimmonsrestaurant.com, lunch 11am-2pm Tues.-Fri., 11am-4pm Sat. and Sun., dinner 5pm-9pm Tues.-Thurs. and Sun., 5pm-9:30pm Fri. and Sat.) you can take in the water views from a seat in the comfortable dining room our outside on the dockside deck. With two separate menus—one focused on fine dining, with walnut and whole-grain mustard-crusted red snapper or pan-roasted duck breast and wild-game sausage (dinner entrées $18-31), and the other on burgers, fish tacos, and other handhelds ($10-13), you'll be able to make your meal as refined or relaxed as you want.

For a down-home breakfast, the **Country Biscuit Restaurant** (809 Broad St., 252/638-5151, http://thecountrybiscuit.com, 5am-2pm Mon.-Fri., 5am-9pm Sat., dinner 4pm-9pm Wed.-Fri., breakfast $2-9, lunch and dinner $5-9), is popular, not surprisingly, for its biscuits. They say they serve "real food for real folks," and indeed, the food is simple, homey, and filling.

Moore's Olde Tyme Barbeque (3711 U.S. 17 S./Martin Luther King Jr. Blvd., 252/638-3937, www.mooresbarbeque.com, 10am-8pm Mon.-Thurs., 10am-8:30pm Fri.-Sat., $2.50-9) is a family business, in operation since 1945. They roast and smoke their own barbecue in a pit on-site, burning the wood that you'll see piled up by the shop. The menu is short and simple—pork barbecue, chicken, shrimp, fish, hush puppies, fries, and slaw—and the prices are lower than many fast-food joints. In addition to making some good 'cue, Moore's is a Guinness World Record holder for making the world's largest open barbecue sandwich with slaw, on July 4, 2010. Weighing in at more than half a ton, it was one big sandwich.

There are lots of good snack stops in New Bern to grab a bite or a cup of coffee before a day of touring on foot or on the water. The **Trent River Coffee Company** (208 Craven St., 252/514-2030, 7:30am-5pm Mon.-Fri., 8am-5pm Sat., 10am-5pm Sun.) is a casual coffee shop with good coffee in a cool old downtown storefront. It's sometimes patronized by well-behaved local dogs that lie patiently under the tables while their owners read the newspaper. This is a nice meeting place, and a shaded oasis in the summer heat.

Bear Towne Java (323 Middle St., 252/633-7900, www.beartownejava.com, 7am-6:30pm Mon.-Thurs., 7am-8pm Fri.-Sat., 7am-8pm Sun., meals $9) serves a robust cup of coffee, carries the traditional array of coffee-shop confections, and even serves a respectable lunch and dinner. Try The Florence Panini; it comes with smoked turkey, provolone, and a cherry pepper relish that's just the right balance of sweet and hot.

The **Cow Café** (319 Middle St., 252/672-9269, www.cowcafenewbern.com, 10am-7pm Mon.-Thurs., 10am-9pm Fri.-Sat., 11:30am-5pm Sun., around $7) is a pleasant downtown creamery and snack shop with some unusual and classic homemade ice cream flavors you can't find anywhere else in town. The fun logo and outrageous Holstein cow decor makes it hard to miss from a visual standpoint, and the ice cream makes it hard to miss flavor-wise.

The small but popular **247 Craven** (247 Craven St., 252/635-1879, www.247craven.com, 11am-2:30pm, 5pm-late Tues.-Sat., 11am-2:30pm Sun., lunch around $9, dinner $18-25, brunch around $9) makes one of the best burgers in New Bern, although the lunchtime fried green tomato BLT is a must. For dinner, the seared scallops Fra Diavolo is a crowd pleaser. They focus on local and seasonal ingredients, so the menu varies a little, but no matter the season it's worth a visit.

Sea Glass Café and Bakery (1803 S. Glenburnie Rd., 252/634-2327, http://seaglasscafe.com, 7:30am-3pm Mon.-Sun., around $8) is a local favorite for their pecan cranberry toast made with bread baked on-site and their scones. Open for breakfast and lunch, they put out food ranging from scrambled eggs to chicken salad on pecan cranberry bread to seared ahi tuna over salad. The place is small, but the food is worth the wait if there are no tables free when you arrive.

Croatan National Forest and Vicinity

A huge swath of swampy wilderness, the Croatan National Forest is all the land bounded by the Neuse, Trent, and White Oak Rivers and Bogue Sound, from New Bern to Morehead City and almost all the way to Jacksonville. Despite its size, Croatan is one of the lesser-known and least developed federal preserves in the state. All three nearby towns in Jones County, population just over 10,000, enjoy a similar atmosphere of sequestration, where barely traveled roads lead to dark expanses of forest and swamp as well as narrow old village streets.

CROATAN NATIONAL FOREST

Headquartered just off U.S. 70 south of New Bern, the **Croatan National Forest** (141 E. Fisher Ave., New Bern, 252/638-5628, www.fs.usda.gov) has few established amenities for visitors but has plenty of land and water trails to explore.

Hiking

The main hiking route is the **Neusiok Trail,** which begins at the Newport River Parking area and ends at the Pinecliff Recreation Area on the Neuse River. It traverses 20 miles of beach, salt marsh, swamp, pocosin, and pinewoods. The 1.4-mile **Cedar Point Tideland Trail** covers estuary marshes and woods, starting at the Cedar Point boat ramp near Cape Carteret. The 0.5-mile **Island Creek Forest Walk** passes through virgin hardwood forests and marl (compacted prehistoric shell) outcroppings.

Boating

The spectacular **Saltwater Adventure Trail** is a

BEAUFORT

JOHN LAWSON ON ALLIGATORS

Explorer John Lawson, in *A New Voyage to Carolina*, describes a 1709 encounter with an alligator on the Neuse River.

The Allegator is the same, as the Crocodile, and differs only in Name. They frequent the sides of Rivers, in the Banks of which they make their Dwellings a great way under Ground...Here it is, that this amphibious Monster dwells all the Winter, sleeping away his time till the Spring appears, when he comes from his Cave, and daily swims up and down the Streams...This Animal, in these Parts, sometimes exceeds seventeen Foot long. It is impossible to kill them with a Gun, unless you chance to hit them about the Eyes, which is a much softer Place, than the rest of their impenetrable Armour. They roar, and make a hideous Noise against bad Weather, and before they come out of their Dens in the Spring. I was pretty much frightened with one of these once, which happened thus: I had built a House about half a Mile from an Indian Town, on the Fork of the Neus-River, where I dwelt by my self, excepting a young Indian Fellow, and a Bull-Dog, that I had along with me. I had not then been so long a Sojourner in America, as to be thoroughly acquainted with this Creature. One of them had got his Nest directly under my House, which stood on pretty high Land, and by a Creek-side, in whose Banks his Entring-place was, his Den reaching the Ground directly on which my House stood. I was sitting alone by the Fire-side (about nine a Clock at Night, some time in March) the Indian Fellow being gone to Town, to see his Relations; so that there was no body in the House but my self and my Dog; when, all of a sudden, this ill-favour'd Neighbour of mine, set up such a Roaring, that he made the House shake about my Ears, and so continued, like a Bittern (but a hundred times louder, if possible), for four or five times. The Dog stared, as if he was frightened out of his Senses; nor indeed, could I imagine what it was, having never heard one of them before. Immediately I had another Lesson; and so a third. Being at that time amongst none but Savages, I began to suspect, that they were working some Piece of Conjuration under my House, to get away with my Goods.... At last, my Man came in, to whom when I had told the Story, he laugh'd at me, and presently undeceiv'd me, by telling me what it was that made that Noise.

newly designated water route, roughly 100 miles in length, that starts at Brice's Creek, south of New Bern, and winds north to the Neuse River; it follows the Neuse all the way to the crook at Harlowe, where it threads through the Harlowe Canal. The route then leads down to Beaufort and all the way through Bogue Sound, turning back inland on the White Oak River, and ending at Haywood Landing north of Swansboro. If you're up for the challenge, it's an incredible trip.

For boat rentals, not many outfitters serve the national forest. **White Oak River Outfitters** (U.S. 17, 1 mile south of Maysville, 910/743-2744, www.whiteoakrivercampground.com, single kayaks $30 half-day, $40 full-day, double kayaks $40 half-day, $50 full-day, canoes $40 half-day, $50 full-day) rents out canoes and kayaks, has a shuttle service that makes trips a lot easier, and offers guided tours on the White Oak River and other waters in the area.

Great Lake is a popular spot to explore via canoe, kayak, or small flat-bottomed boat.

© JASON FRYE

BEAUFORT

Waterways offer countless opportunities to get outdoors.

Surrounded by centuries-old cypress trees, it's easy to feel like you're in another world or another time. A handful of campsites lets you extend your stay, or just enjoy the day paddling around or fishing for crappie, perch, and bullhead, all easy catches.

The **Oyster Point Campground,** which is also the trailhead for the Neusiok Trail, offers a boat launch suitable for both motorized and paddle watercraft. It's easy to explore the marshy fringes of the forest from here, or head into one of the tributaries or winding marsh creeks nearby.

Camping

There are three developed campsites in the Croatan Forest. **Neuse River** (also called Flanners Beach, $10-15) has 41 sites with showers and flush toilets. **Cedar Point** ($15) has 40 campsites with electricity, showers, and flush toilets. **Fisher's Landing** (free) has nine sites and no facilities other than vault toilets. Primitive camping areas are at Great Lake, Catfish Lake, and Long Point.

TRENTON

A little way outside Croatan National Forest is the pretty village of Trenton. The Jones County seat's tiny historic business district is an appropriate focal point for this bucolic area. A Revolutionary-era millpond, presided over by a large wooden mill, is a good picnic spot. **Trenton Red and White** (372 NC Hwy. 52 N, 252/448-1134, 6am-10pm daily, under $10) is a grocery store with a great little deli where you can get all sorts of sandwiches, from your standard ham and cheese or turkey and cheese to thick-sliced bologna or even olive loaf.

KINSTON

In years past you wouldn't find Kinston on many must-see lists, but this formerly prosperous tobacco town has made quite a turnaround in recent years. A couple of locals have spearheaded renewal, opening a renowned restaurant and a brewery with a growing reputation for great craft beer and changing the face of downtown. Add to that a top-of-the-line museum dedicated to the town's Civil War history

BEAUFORT

KINSTON'S MUSICAL LEGACY

Music has always been a big deal here, and African American Kinstonians have made huge contributions to American jazz, R&B, funk, soul, and gospel. In the heyday of jazz, the top musicians—North Carolinians Thelonious Monk and John Coltrane, along with Louie Armstrong and others—would stop in Kinston and play for mixed crowds. It really wasn't until 1964 that Kinston was put on the music map, when James Brown met and hired a promising young drummer and college student, Melvin Parker, a native of Kinston, to play in his band. Melvin agreed, but only if James hired his brother, saxophonist Maceo Parker. The Parkers weren't the only Kinstonians to tour with Brown; bandleader Nat Jones, trombonist Levi Raspberry, trumpeter Dick Knight, and a number of other young musicians from the area made names for themselves and helped create the groundbreaking sound of funk. In fact, Maceo Parker joined Parliament-Funkadelic, the band of George Clinton, another North Carolina native, to further explore funk and influence generations of musicians.

In 2013, a groundbreaking for the African American Music Trail was held. The trail is the result of a partnership among the North Carolina Department of Cultural Resources, Kinston's Community Council for the Arts, and other local entities who have done a lot of hard work. It recognizes the contributions of African American musicians in Kinston and other points along the proposed trail. Construction is underway on the African American Music Trail Gateway Park in downtown Kinston, with plans for it to be a gathering spot for live music as well as a place honoring the depth of African American music in the state.

and a community that's passionate about preserving its past.

Sights

Like many towns that were once prosperous and suddenly experienced a downturn, Kinston is an architectural time capsule. Driving, or better, walking the several downtown blocks of **Queen Street,** the town's main artery, is an education in early-20th-century commercial architecture. The Hotel Kinston is the town's tallest building, an 11-story structure with a ground level that's a crazy blend of art deco and Moorish motifs. The 1914 post office is a big heavy beaux-arts beauty, and the Queen Street Methodist Church is turreted to within an inch of its life. The People's Bank building testifies to the heyday of early-20th-century African American commerce. With its many strange and daring experiments in building styles, Queen Street is a crazy quilt, but the buildings are beautifully complementary in their diversity. In the Herritage Street neighborhood, near the bend of the river, block after block of grand old houses stand in threadbare glory. On the

other side of town are shotgun houses, the icon of Southern folk housing, lining the alleys of the old working-class neighborhood. Shotgun houses are narrow, at most 12 feet wide, with a door at either end, and usually closely spaced.

ⓒ CSS *NEUSE* INTERPRETIVE CENTER

The remains of the Confederate ironclad gunboat CSS *Neuse* are on display in Kinston in a museum located near the spot where she was scuttled in 1865 to keep her out of the hands of the advancing Union Army. All that remains is the core of the 158- by 34-foot hull, but even in such deteriorated condition the *Neuse* is a striking feat of boatbuilding. At the **CSS *Neuse* Interpretive Center** (100 N. Queen St., 252/522-2107, 9am-5pm Tues.-Sat., free) you can see what remains of the hull, which sat in the river for more than 100 years before it was salvaged, first for profit, then for preservation. If you're lucky, one of the volunteers will be a Kinston old-timer who can tell you stories about using the *Neuse* as a diving board for summer swims. On display are artifacts recovered from the *Neuse,* including the ironclad's bell, cannonballs and shells, coal rakes, and other small items. Wall plaques tell the story of the ship's construction, demise, and eventual salvage, but the centerpiece is the overhead view of the ironclad's hull. Now outfitted with a ghostly shape showing the original form of the ship, it's an impressive sight.

For a full-scale look at the CSS *Neuse,* the **CSS Neuse II** (Herritage St. and Gordon St., 252/560-2150, www.cssneuseii.org, 9am-2pm Mon.-Fri., 9am-5pm Sat., 1pm-5pm Sun., free), a 158-foot facsimile of the gunboat. Climb aboard to feel how tight the quarters were and peer out the gun ports, then imagine sleeping, eating, and fighting on board.

MOTHER EARTH BREWING

Founded by a father-in-law, son-in-law duo, **Mother Earth Brewing** (311 N. Herritage St., 252/208-2437, www.motherearthbrewing.com,

brewery tours on the hour 9am-4pm Tues.-Fri., noon-7pm Sat., free, tap room 4pm-10pm Wed.-Fri., 1pm-9pm Sat.) has been making craft beer in Kinston since 2008. Since then they've added a popular Christmas seasonal beer, the Silent Night series, and explored new flavors. They've pushed into craft spirits and have a small production still in the brewery, but the focus is beer. Brewery tours are free, but as it is a working brewery, some days the tours may be crowded, limited to certain areas, or canceled altogether. Tours start and end in the **Mother Earth Brewing Tap Room,** solar-powered and serving up the best Mother Earth brews. A mix of original art, exposed brick walls, sleek modern lines, and contemporary lighting make this room one of a kind. Cozy up to the bar or grab a pint to take to a nearby table or to the patio out back. No matter where you chose to enjoy the beer, enjoy it you will.

BEAUFORT

BATTLE FOR KINSTON AND THE CSS *NEUSE*

In early December 1862, Confederate forces in Kinston manned the earthen fortifications that ringed the city in anticipation of an attack by advancing Union forces. General John G. Foster was leading nearly 10,000 infantry, 640 cavalry, and 40 pieces of artillery with the intention of taking the city and controlling traffic on the Neuse River. Despite being grossly outnumbered—the Confederates numbered somewhere around 2,400—the Confederates mounted an effective, but unimpressive, resistance against probing Union forces. On the second and final day of the battle, the Union soldiers swarmed Confederate positions, overwhelming them and driving them back across the river. Retreating troops, acting on order, burned the bridge across the Neuse and, in the confusion of retreat and burning, left some 400 of their comrades on the Union side of the river. To make matters worse, Confederate artillery began shelling Union positions, including their own trapped troops. By the next day, the Union had secured what remained of the bridge, looted the town, and captured some 400 shell-shocked Confederate soldiers.

That wasn't the end of Kinston's role in the Civil War. In 1863 the CSS *Neuse,* an ironclad gunboat 158 feet long, 34 feet wide, and armored in eight inches of oak and iron plate, was launched with the intention of controlling the river and the lands around it. It was an impressive sight at its launch, but the inexperienced men on board quickly ran it aground, where it sat mired in river mud for nearly a month before it could be refloated. By then, the ground-support troops assigned to it had been reallocated, and the ironclad stayed in Kinston, acting more as a floating fortification and gun emplacement than a proper naval weapon. In March 1865, Union forces were once again attacking Kinston and were once more successful. Confederate troops packed the *Neuse* with explosives, set it on fire, and fled. The ensuing explosion breeched the hull, and the fire burned to the waterline. The wreck stayed in the river for almost 100 years before being raised for historic preservation, and many residents of Kinston remember fishing around the hull or climbing on the deck to dive off into the river.

© JASON FRYE

Mother Earth Brewing is a big brewery for a small town.

I'm fond of the Dark Cloud Dunkel and Old Neighborhood Oatmeal Porter, but the *kölsch, witbier,* and IPA are popular.

Entertainment and Events

Kinston is fortunate to have a great local arts engine, the **Kinston Community Council for the Arts** (KCCA, 400 N. Queen St., 252/527-2517, www.kinstoncca.com, 10am-6pm Tues.-Fri., 10am-2pm Sat.), which has the kind of energy and artistic vision one would expect to find in a much larger city. It occupies an old storefront on Queen Street, remodeled into a gorgeous gallery and studio space. In addition to the many community events hosted here, KCCA has consistently innovative exhibits in the main gallery, including avant-garde photography and collage art and a recent exhibition of dozens of custom motorcycles.

Every spring, typically the last weekend in April, barbecue enthusiasts flock to Kinston for the **BBQ Festival on the Neuse** (252/560-2693, www.bbqfestivalontheneuse.com). This four-day festival features competitions pitting barbecue teams against one another in categories such as showmanship, quality, and sauce. During the festival, downtown hosts fair food, smoke from a dozen barbecue cookers, carnival rides, concerts, a wine garden, and beer from Mother Earth Brewing. Many artists come for the opening day's Plein Air Paint Out, a competitive painting event whose winner is the image for next year's festival poster. The Art Fest event invites artists and nonartists alike to make some art inspired by the festival; it's a hit with kids as well as adults who shake off their artistic inhibitions. With concerts, fireworks, and heaping plates of 'cue, there's plenty to do, see, and eat.

Sports and Recreation

In 2013 a new water park, **Lions Water Adventure** (2602 W. Vernon Ave., 252/939-1330, www.lionswateradventure.com, 11:30am-5:30pm Mon.-Sat., 12:30pm-5:30pm Sun., $10 pp, $54 for 6), opened in Kinston, with three three-story high slides—the zebra slide, a twisty tube ride; the lion slide, a straightforward waterslide with a decent drop at the end; and the low-splash slide. There's a 5,000-square-foot kiddie lagoon, a lazy river longer than a football field, a lap pool, and a heated therapeutic pool. They serve food, mainly kid-friendly bites and snacks, but the water park is close enough to town that you can head out for a real meal with little effort.

In Kinston you can enjoy disc golf or a traditional round. At the **Barnet Disc Golf Course** (100 Sand Clay Rd., 252/939-3332, http://kinstondiscgolf.com, dawn-dusk daily, 18 holes, par 67, free), you'll need to bring your own discs, but this fun course layout rewards aggressive but accurate players. For a traditional day on the course, **Falling Creek Country Club** (2359 Falling Creek Rd., 252/522-1828, www.fallingcreekgolf.com, 18 holes, par 71, greens fees $18 Mon.-Fri., $23 Sat.-Sun. and holidays, cart fee $15) is a good option for all skill levels. The course features some narrow fairways, a handful of crooked doglegs, and long par-3s, but it's forgiving enough on other holes to make up for missing the green a time or two.

Accommodations

There's only one bed-and-breakfast in town, but you'll find several chain motels just outside the downtown area. **The Bentley** (117 W. Capitola Ave., 252/523-2337, www.bentleybedandbreakfast.com, $139-159) has four beautiful guest rooms and 13 acres of gardens, lawns, and woods to walk. The house and grounds are large enough to host lavish events like weddings and receptions but has a luxe homey feel you don't find in many places. As for hotels, the **Hampton Inn** (1382 U.S. 258 S., 252/523-1400, www.hamptoninn.com, around $110) is convenient and comfortable, and the staff are especially nice.

Food

Kinston's reputation as a food town has been on the rise lately, thanks in large part to a trio of locals—chef Vivian Howard Knight and brewery owners Stephen Hill and Trent Mooring. They collectively opened a renowned restaurant, a top-notch brewery and tap room, and

an oyster bar. And though they may be the best known, they're not the only food options in town.

Chef and the Farmer (120 W. Gordon St., 252/208-2433, www.chefandthefarmer.com, 5:30pm-9:30pm Tues.-Thurs., 5:30pm-10:30pm Fri.-Sat., entrées $12-30), from chef-owner Vivian Howard Knight, elevates the simple Southern food she grew up eating on a farm not far from here into true fine-dining dishes that have been recognized by the James Beard Foundation. The menu changes with the local crops and catch, but a few staples remain, including the wood-fired-oven pizzas, massive burgers, and Pimp My Grits menu (where you can get your grits topped with a variety of interesting cheeses, meats, and veggies). Whether you're there for a multicourse affair (the desserts are fantastic) or just a burger at the kitchen counter, you'll leave full and happy.

Queen Street Deli (117 S. Queen St., 252/527-1900, www.queenstreetdeli.com, 7:30am-4pm Mon.-Thurs., breakfast from $2, lunch around $8) bakes vegan and non-vegan cookies and makes great sandwiches for breakfast and lunch. The Queen's Chicken Salad comes with toasted pecans and cranberries and is a filling sandwich. Their take on the BLT is called Prides Pimento, another good option made with pimento cheese, sliced tomatoes, and bacon.

The entrepreneurial owners of Mother Earth Brewing and Chef and the Farmer have opened **The Boiler Room** (108 W. North St., 252/208-2433, 4:30pm-midnight Tues.-Sat., around $12), an oyster bar, raw bar, and gourmet burger joint so named because of the massive boiler standing in the dining room. The Boiler Room represents the efforts of lifelong-locals Vivian Howard Knight and Stephen Hill to revitalize downtown by leveraging the popularity of their other businesses and serving up some delicious seafood and burgers.

Ginger 108 (108 W. North St., 252/208-2663, www.ginger108.com, 11am-2pm, 5pm-midnight Tues.-Fri., 1pm-midnight Sat., entrées around $22) brings fine Asian Fusion dining to Kinston. The chef uses Taiwanese

BEAUFORT

BEAUFORT

© JASON FRYE

North Carolina, the Cradle of 'Cue

flair but leaves no ingredient—global or local—unexplored. The miso-butter poached sea bass, or any fish special, for that matter, is a must.

I'd be remiss if I didn't mention that the North Carolina Barbecue Trail's eastern terminus is in Ayden, just a short drive from Kinston. Here the world-famous **Skylight Inn** (4618 S. Lee St., Ayden, 252/746-4113, www.skylightinnbbq.com, 10am-7pm Mon.-Sat., under $10) serves eastern North Carolina-style barbecue done up in the traditional manner: chopped and served with a vinegary sauce that brings out the flavor in the pork like no other sauce can. This family has been cooking 'cue since 1830, so they know their way around a hog; their current location has been here since 1947.

SEVEN SPRINGS

Seven Springs is an attractive historic little town about 30 minutes' drive southwest of Kinston. It's the site of **Cliffs of the Neuse State Park**

(240 Park Entrance Rd., 919/778-6234, http://ncparks.gov, office 8am-5pm Mon.-Fri., park 8am-6pm daily Nov.-Feb., 8am-8pm daily Apr.-May, 8am-9pm daily June-Aug., 8am-8pm daily Sept.-Oct.), a highly unusual blend of environments, including high red bluffs overlooking the Neuse River, hardwood and pine forests, and cypress swamps. Hiking trails follow the cliff line through Spanish moss-draped forests. Boating and swimming (10am-5:45pm daily late May-early Sept.) are permitted at the park's artificial lake during the summer; swimming is allowed only when a lifeguard is on duty. Boats must be rented—no private watercraft are permitted.

Family camping ($20/night) is available year-round. There is a washhouse with hot showers and electricity, and several water stations are located in the campsite. Note that unless you have a medical emergency, when you're camping you must stay inside the park from the time the gates close until 8am the next morning—so no slipping out for a late supper.

Beaufort and Vicinity

The small waterside town of Beaufort has unusual problems stemming from its geography—there's also a Beaufort in South Carolina—and the idiosyncrasies of regional Southern dialects, in that it's also pronounced differently. This Beaufort is pronounced in the French way, "BO-fert," while the name of town in South Carolina is pronounced "BYEW-fert." Pronunciation notwithstanding, Beaufort is a beautiful little town. The third-oldest colonial settlement in North Carolina, it matches its elders, Bath and New Bern, in the charm department. Once North Carolina's window to the world, Beaufort was a surprisingly cosmopolitan place that would often receive news from London or Barbados sooner than from other colonies. Today, you'll find the streets crowded with old homes, many built in that double-porch, steep-sided roof style that shows off early cultural ties to the Caribbean.

It was long rumored that the pirate Blackbeard ran his ship aground in the inlet here, which is plausible because he did frequent Beaufort, and his pirate base at Ocracoke Island isn't far away. In the late 1990s the rumor was proved to be true: In Beaufort Inlet the *Queen Anne's Revenge,* the French slave ship that Blackbeard captured in 1717 and made into the flagship of his dreaded fleet, sat mired in nearly three centuries of silt. Blackbeard had increased his ship's arsenal to 40 cannons, a fact that helped confirm the identity of the wreck. A few months after he ran his flagship aground, Blackbeard himself was killed at Ocracoke after putting up a tremendous fight with privateers (pirate hunters) sent from Virginia. In the intervening time between the shipwreck and its discovery, incredible artifacts from the *Queen Anne's Revenge* washed up on the shores here, a number of which are

BEAUFORT

Spanish moss drips from the trees in Beaufort.

© JASON FRYE

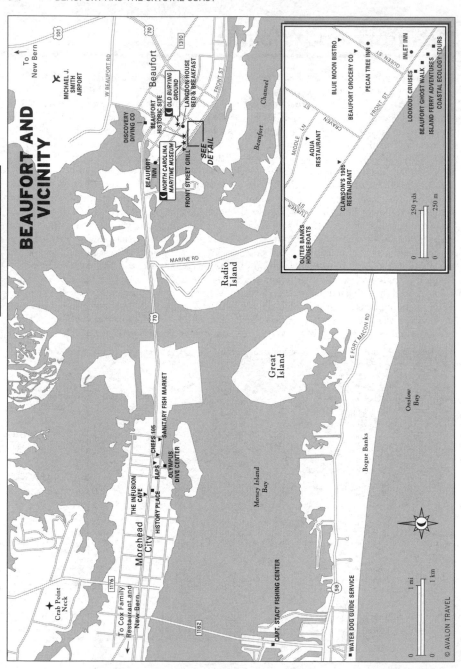

BEAUFORT

BEAUFORT AND VICINITY

101
To New Bern
70
1310
W BEAUFORT RD
MICHAEL J. SMITH AIRPORT
DISCOVERY DIVING CO
Beaufort
BEAUFORT HISTORIC SITE
OLD BURYING GROUND
LANGDON HOUSE BED & BREAKFAST
FRONT ST
BEAUFORT INN
NORTH CAROLINA MARITIME MUSEUM
FRONT STREET GRILL
SEE DETAIL
Beaufort Channel
MARINE RD
Radio Island
70
Great Island
E FORT MACON RD
SANITARY FISH MARKET
CHEFS 105
RAPS
THE INFUSION CAFE
HISTORY PLACE
OLYMPUS DIVE CENTER
Morehead City
Money Island Bay
Onslow Bay
Bogue Banks
1176
Crab Point Neck
To Cox Family Restaurant and New Bern
58
CAPT. STACY FISHING CENTER
WATER DOG GUIDE SERVICE
1182

0   1 mi
0   1 km

© AVALON TRAVEL

Detail inset:
BLUE MOON BISTRO
BEAUFORT GROCERY CO
PECAN TREE INN
INLET INN
QUEEN ST
FRONT ST
LOOKOUT CRUISES
BEAUFORT GHOST WALK
ISLAND FERRY ADVENTURES
COASTAL ECOLOGY TOURS
CRAVEN ST
MIDDLE LN
AQUA RESTAURANT
CLAWSON'S 1905 RESTAURANT
TURNER ST
OUTER BANKS HOUSEBOATS

0   250 yds
0   250 m

on display at the North Carolina Maritime Museum.

From the Maritime Museum, a short walk leads to Beaufort's cafés, boutiques, antiques shops, restaurants, and dock. Across the waterway you can see Carrot Island, home to a herd of wild horses, one of the few remaining in eastern North Carolina. You can also catch a ride on a ferry or tour boat to Cape Lookout National Seashore, where the stunning Cape Lookout Lighthouse has guarded the coast for more than 150 years. Or simply tour the marshes for a close-up glimpse of the area's wildlife.

SIGHTS
◖ North Carolina Maritime Museum

The **North Carolina Maritime Museum at Beaufort** (315 Front St., 252/728-7317, www.ncmaritimemuseums.com, 9am-5pm Mon.-Fri., 10am-5pm Sat., 1pm-5pm Sun., free) is among the best museums in the state and one three state maritime museums; the others are in Southport and on Roanoke Island. Even if you don't think you're interested in boatbuilding or maritime history, you'll get caught up in the exhibits here. Historic watercraft, reconstructions, and models of boats are on display, well presented in rich historical and cultural context. The display of artifacts and weapons recovered from Blackbeard's *Queen Anne's Revenge* wows visitors. There's also a lot about the state's fishing history, including related occupations, such as the highly complex skill of net-hanging. Far from being limited to the few species caught by today's fisheries, early North Carolinians did big business hunting sea turtles, porpoises, and whales.

Across the street from the museum's main building, perched on the dock, is the **Harvey W. Smith Watercraft Center.** For many generations North Carolina mariners had an international reputation as expert shipbuilders, and even today some builders continue to construct large seaworthy vessels in their own backyards. This has always been done "by the rack of the eye," as locals say, meaning that builders use traditional knowledge handed down through the generations rather than modern industrial methods. Their exceptional expertise is beautifully demonstrated by the craft in the museum and by boats still working the waters today. At the Watercraft Center is a workspace for builders of full-size and model boats, and it teaches a vast array of classes in both traditional skills and mechanized boat-building methods.

◖ Old Burying Ground

One of the most beautiful places in North Carolina is Beaufort's **Old Burying Ground** (Anne St., daily dawn-dusk), a picturesque cemetery that's quite small by the standards of some old Carolina towns and crowded with 18th- and 19th-century headstones. Huge old live oaks, Spanish moss, wisteria, and resurrection ferns, which unfurl and turn green after a rainstorm, give the Burying Ground an irresistibly Gothic feel. Many of the headstones reflect the maritime heritage of the town, including a sea captain whose epitaph reads,

> The form that fills this silent grave
> Once tossed on ocean's rolling wave
> But in a port securely fast
> He's dropped his anchor here at last.

Captain Otway Burns, an early privateer who spent much time in Beaufort, is buried here; his grave is easy to spot as it is topped by a canon from his ship, the *Snap Dragon*. Nearby is another of the graveyard's famous burials, the "Little Girl Buried in a Barrel of Rum." This unfortunate waif is said to have died at sea and been placed in a cask of rum to preserve her body for burial on land. Visitors often bring toys and trinkets to leave on her grave, which is marked by a simple wooden plank. Though hers is the most gaudily festooned, you'll see evidence of this old tradition of funerary gifts on other graves here as well—in this cemetery, most often coins and shells. This is a tradition found throughout the coastal South and the Caribbean, with roots tracing back to Africa. Feel free to add to her haul of goodies, but beliefs hold that it's not karmically advisable to tamper with those already here.

Beaufort Historic Site

The **Beaufort Historic Site** (130 Turner St., 252/728-5225, www.beauforthistoricsite.org, 9:30am-5pm Mon.-Sat. Mar.-Nov., 10am-4pm Mon.-Sat. Dec.-Feb., $8 adults, $4 children) recreates life in late-18th- and early-19th-century Beaufort in several restored historic buildings. The 1770s "jump and a half" (1.5-story) Leffers Cottage reflects middle-class life in its day; a merchant, whaler, or, as in this case, a schoolmaster would have lived it. The Josiah Bell and John Manson Houses, both from the 1820s, reflect the graceful Caribbean-influenced architecture so prevalent in the early days of the coastal South. A restored apothecary shop, a 1790s wooden courthouse, and a haunted 1820s jail that was used into the 1950s are among the other important structures. There are tours led by costumed interpreters as well as driving tours of the old town in double-decker buses.

SPORTS AND RECREATION

Diving

North Carolina's coast is a surprisingly good place for scuba diving. The **Discovery Diving Company** (414 Orange St., 252/728-2265, www.discoverydiving.com, $65-110 per excursion) leads half-day and full-day scuba trips to explore the reefs and dozens of fascinating shipwrecks near Beaufort.

Cruises and Tours

Coastal Ecology Tours (252/241-6866, www.goodfortunesails.com) runs tours of the Cape Lookout National Seashore and other island locations in the area on the *Good Fortune,* as well as a variety of half-day, full-day, overnight, and short trips to snorkel, shell, kayak, and bird-watch, along with cruises to Morehead City restaurants and other educational and fun trips. Prices range from $180 pp for a 2.5-hour dolphin-watching tour to $600 plus meals for an off-season overnight boat rental.

Island Ferry Adventures (610 Front St.,

252/728-7555, www.islandferryadventures. com, $13-18 adults, $5-8 children) runs dolphin-watching tours, trips to collect shells at Cape Lookout, and trips to see the wild ponies of Shackleford Banks. **Lookout Cruises** (600 Front St., 252/504-7245, www.lookoutcruises. com, $25-70 adults, $15-30 under age 13) carries sightseers on lovely catamaran rides in the Beaufort and Core Sound region, out to Cape Lookout, and on morning dolphin-watching trips.

Port City Tour Company leads a **Beaufort Ghost Walk** (601 Front St., 252/772-9925, http://pctourco.com, $15) through town. Highlights include supposedly haunted homes, tales of Blackbeard and other ghost pirates, ghost ships, mysterious murders, and more. Many people report taking photos in the cemetery and seeing ghostly figures, orbs, and other unexplained phenomena in the resulting images.

Take a **Wild Horse and Shelling Safari** (610 Front St., 252/772-9925, http://pctourco.com, $25 adults, $15 children) with Port City Tour Company. On the safari you'll make the journey over to Shackelford, a medium-size barrier island home to wild horses, crabs, and not much more. The shelling is incredible and the beaches pristine, but the real treat is the horses. The herd here is small, but they're active and for the most part easy to spot. Be careful around the horses as they are feral; listen to your safari guide, who knows how to stay safe with them.

ACCOMMODATIONS

◖ Outer Banks Houseboats (324 Front St., 252/728-4129, www.outerbankshouseboats. com) will rent you your own floating vacation home, drive it to a scenic spot for you, anchor it, and then come and check in on you every day during your stay. You'll have a skiff for your own use, but you may just want to lie on the deck all day and soak up the peacefulness. Rates run from $1,200 per weekend for the smaller houseboat to $3,000 per week for the luxury boat, with plenty of rental options in between.

BLACKBEARD AND BONNET: THE BOYS OF 1718

In the 18th century the Carolina coast was crawling with the vermin of the high seas: pirates. For the most part they hung out around South Carolina's Charleston Harbor, like a bunch of rowdies on a frat-house balcony causing headaches for passersby. Some liked to venture up the coast into the inlets and sounds of North Carolina. The most famous pirate visitors were **Blackbeard,** whose real name was Edward Teach, and **Stede Bonnet,** the so-called "Gentleman Pirate." They did most of their misbehaving here in 1718 and enjoyed a short-lived but spectacular rise to notoriety.

Blackbeard is said never to have killed anyone except in self-defense, but clearly he didn't need to kill to reinforce his reputation. He was a huge man with a beard that covered most of his face, and his hair is usually depicted as twisted into ferocious dreadlocks. He wore a bright red coat and festooned himself with every weapon he could carry; as if all that didn't make him scary enough, he liked to wear burning cannon fuses tucked under the brim of his hat and even in his beard. He caused trouble from the Bahamas to Virginia, taking ships, treasure, and child brides at will.

Poor Stede Bonnet. With a name like that, he should have known better than to try to make a living intimidating people. He is said to have been something of a fancy-pants, a man with wealth, education, and a nagging wife. To get away from his spouse, he bought a ship, hired a crew, and set sail for a life of crime. Though never quite as tough as Blackbeard, with whom he was briefly partners, Bonnet caused enough trouble along the Southern coast that the leaders of Charleston saw to it that he was captured and hanged. Meanwhile, Virginia's leaders had also had it with Blackbeard's interference in coastal commerce, and Governor Spottswood dispatched a team to kill him. This they did at Ocracoke, but it wasn't easy; even after they shot, stabbed, and beheaded Blackbeard, his body is said to have taunted them by swimming laps around the ship before finally giving up the ghost.

In recent years, Blackbeard has surfaced again. In 1996, a ship was found off the North Carolina coast that was identified as Blackbeard's flagship, *Queen Anne's Revenge.* All manner of intriguing artifacts have been brought up from the ocean floor: cannons and blunderbuss parts, early hand grenades, even a penis syringe supposed to have been used by syphilitic pirates to inject themselves with mercury. During one standoff in Charleston Harbor, Blackbeard and his men took hostages to ransom for medical supplies; perhaps this explains why they were so desperate. To view artifacts and learn more about Blackbeard, Stede Bonnet, and their low-down ways, visit the North Carolina Maritime Museum in Beaufort, where you'll find relics from the *Queen Anne's Revenge.* A number of underwater archaeological expeditions have been mounted and are ongoing to recover artifacts from the wreck. In early 2013 two cannons were raised and are undergoing preservation treatment. Keep up with the status of the digs and research into the wreck at the **Queen Anne's Revenge Project** (www.qaronline.org).

The **Beaufort Inn** (101 Ann St., 252/728-2600, www.beaufort-inn.com, $119-279 summer) is a large hotel on Gallants Channel, along one side of the colonial district. It's an easy walk to the main downtown attractions, and the hotel's outdoor hot tub and balconies have great views, making it tempting to stay in as well. The **Pecan Tree Inn** (116 Queen St., 800/728-7871, www.pecantree.com, $130-189 summer) is such a grand establishment that the town threw a parade in honor of the laying of its cornerstone in 1866. The house is still splendid, as are the 5,000-square-foot gardens. The **Inlet Inn** (601 Front St., 800/554-5466, www.inlet-inn.com, $130-170 summer) has one of the best locations in town, right on the water, near the docks where many of the ferry and tour boats land. If you're planning to go dolphin-watching or hop the ferry to Cape Lookout, you can get ready at a leisurely pace and just step outside to the docks. Even in high season, prices are quite reasonable.

Catty-corner to the Old Burying Grounds is the **Langdon House Bed and Breakfast** (135 Craven St., 252/728-5499, www.langdonhouse. com, $137-238). One of the oldest buildings in town, this gorgeous house was built in the 1730s on a foundation of English ballast stones, creating a unique look. Unlike most other B&Bs, Langdon House allows guests to customize their breakfast (and overall room rate) by selecting from options that range from coffee and tea only to the two-course Hallmark Breakfast, which includes fresh fruit, waffles, French toast, omelets, and more; it's quite a production.

FOOD

For generations, local families have plied the waters off Beaufort to earn a living and catch fish for their families. To ensure residents and visitors dine at eateries utilizing locally caught seafood when possible, Carteret Catch (http:// carteretcatch.org) provides a list of such restaurants. Not only does this help the local fishing industry, it allows chefs to provide the best and freshest seafood possible, meaning your dinner tastes even better.

Among the Beaufort eateries certified by Carteret Catch is the **Blue Moon Bistro** (119 Queen St., 252/728-5800, www.bluemoonbistro.biz, 5:30pm-late Tues.-Sat., $13-29). Blue Moon Bistro makes what they'd like to eat themselves. To that end, you'll find lasagna and *udon* noodle bowls on the menu alongside local shrimp risotto and steak. The wine list is a little short on wines by the glass, and the plating is always interesting. You'll find the dining room warm and inviting, a good place to spend your dinner hour.

Clawson's 1905 Restaurant (425 Front St., 252/728-2133, www.clawsonsrestaurant. com, 11:30am-9pm Mon.-Sat., noon-8pm Sun., $15-30) was a grocery store long before it was a restaurant. Starting in 1905, Clawson's sold canned goods, fresh produce, and freshly baked bread until the Great Depression forced it to close in 1934. Now a restaurant, it serves

everything from burgers to ribs, but the specialty is seafood. It's hard to beat their lump crab cakes or fried seafood plate, but one standout dish is the mahimahi, grilled and served over tortellini with sweet peas and a champagne dill sauce.

Aqua Restaurant (114 Middle Lane, 252/728-7777, www.aquaexperience.com, dinner 6pm Tues.-Sat., small plates $8-14, big plates $23-28) uses local seafood in a number of their dishes, including a fresh catch tostada, shrimp and grits, and bouillabaisse. Along with local seafood, they also use locally and regionally sourced produce and meats. The menu changes frequently, but structurally it's always tapas, small plates, salads, and big plates. With a number of vegetarian and gluten-free items, the menu is amenable to most dietary needs.

If you're traveling with a cooler and want to buy some local seafood to take home, try the **Fishtowne Seafood Center** (100 Wellons Dr., 252/728-6644, www.fishtowneseafood.com, 9am-6pm Mon.-Sat.). Fresh fish selections include flounder, grouper, speckled trout, red snapper, trigger fish, redfish (or drum), spots, tuna, and black bass. Include in that mix the fresh shrimp, clams, oysters (in season), and crabs and you have a great mix of seafood. The website lists what is seasonally available.

Beaufort Grocery (117 Queen St., 252/728-3899, www.beaufortgrocery.com, lunch and dinner Wed.-Mon., brunch Sun., $23-33), despite its humble name, is a sophisticated little eatery. At lunch it serves salads and crusty sandwiches along with Damn Good Gumbo and specialty soups. In the evening the café atmosphere gives way to that of a more formal gourmet dining room. For starters, the ahi tuna napoleon is both beautiful and delicious, and Aunt Marion's Apple and Onion Salad makes an interesting plate to share. Some of the best entrées include Thai chicken curry; duck two ways (seared and leg confit); and whole rack of lamb, served with a chèvre and mint *gremolata*. Try the cheesecake for dessert.

The waterfront **Front Street Grill** (300

THE CHANGING FISHING INDUSTRY

Despite its more than 300 miles of coastline and 300 years of fishing traditions, North Carolina's fishing industry has been on a steady decline for the last 50 years. At one time you couldn't find anything but local seafood in supermarkets and restaurants, but today, it's rare to see "local catch" posted outside a handful of small fishmongers up and down the coast. Ask people in the fishing industry what the problem is, and they'll tell you it's overregulation and the imposition of unrealistic catch limits. Ask environmentalists, and they'll tell you it's overfishing and decades of poor harvest practices. The truth probably lies somewhere in between, but whatever the reason, you can sit in a dockside restaurant in North Carolina, watch a fishing boat unload its catch, and dine on shrimp raised in Thailand or fish caught in South America. Like the textile industry, which was big business in the state for a long while but fell off as globalization became the norm, North Carolina's commercial fisheries have suffered tremendous losses at the hands of globalized trade. There are groups dedicated to promoting the interests of local fisheries before it's too late to recover and enjoy anything caught commercially in North Carolina. **Carteret Catch** (in Carteret County, www.carteretcatch.org), **Brunswick Catch** (in Brunswick County), and a number of other groups promote local fishing and the restaurants that serve locally caught seafood. While visiting the Crystal Coast, take a look at the Carteret Catch website to find local restaurants and fish markets that buy local seafood from people who live and work in the community rather than from international wholesalers.

As recently as 15 years ago, the shores and riverbanks of eastern North Carolina were dotted with fish houses. Often these were small family-run operations and were the best place in the world for seafood lovers. These ramshackle restaurants bought the catch right off the boat and cleaned, cooked, and served it within minutes. Today, things are different; the old-fashioned seafood house is in danger of extinction. Declines in popular fish and shellfish populations have hit North Carolina's fishing business hard, and at the same time, coastal real estate values have skyrocketed, making property taxes unaffordable for generations-old restaurants or worth more to a developer as a waterfront lot. Either way, it's a death knell.

This book will steer you toward some of the few remaining fish houses and seafood restaurants that serve catches fresh from the local docks. Traditional seafood houses may serve dishes you're unfamiliar with, but give them a try—you may love what you find, and paying a visit to one of these mom-and-pops helps support a way of life that's critically endangered.

BEAUFORT

Front St., 252/728-4956, www.frontstreetgrillatstillwater.com, 11:30am-2:30pm, 5:30pm-9:30pm Tues.-Sat., brunch 1130am-2:30pm Sun., lunch $9-16, dinner $15-25, brunch $10-17) is popular with boaters drifting through the area as well as diners who arrive by land. The emphasis is on seafood and fresh regional ingredients, and the fried oysters are a must. Front Street Grill's wine list is not extensive but is well stocked, and they have repeatedly won *Wine Spectator* magazine's Award of Excellence. If you're looking for a place where you can sit overlooking the water while you enjoy a fine glass of wine and some excellent food, this is it.

MOREHEAD CITY

Giovanni da Verrazzano may have been the first European to set foot in present-day Morehead City when he sailed into Bogue Inlet. It wasn't until the mid-19th century that the town came into being, built as the terminus of the North Carolina Railroad to connect the state's overland commerce to the sea. Despite its late start, Morehead City has been a busy place. During the Civil War it was the site of major encampments by both armies. A series of horrible hurricanes in the 1890s, culminating in 1899's San Ciriaco Hurricane, brought hundreds of refugees from the towns along what is now the Cape Lookout National Seashore. They settled in a neighborhood that they called Promise Land, and many of their descendants are still here. The Atlantic and North Carolina Railroad operated a large hotel here in the 1880s, ushering in Morehead's role as a tourism spot, and the bridge to the Bogue Banks a few decades later increased holiday traffic considerably.

Morehead is also an official state port, one of the best deepwater harbors on the Atlantic Coast. This mixture of tourism and gritty commerce gives Morehead City a likeable, real-life feel missing in many coastal towns today.

Sights

Morehead City's history is on display at **The History Place** (1008 Arendell St., 252/247-7533, www.thehistoryplace.org, 10am-4pm Tues.-Sat.). There are many interesting and eye-catching historical artifacts on display, but the most striking exhibit is that of a carriage, clothes, and other items pertaining to Morehead City's Emeline Piggott, considered a heroine by the Confederacy. She was a busy woman all through the Civil War, working as a nurse, a spy, and a smuggler. The day she was captured, they found 30 pounds of contraband hidden in her skirts, including Union troop movement plans, a collection of gloves, several dozen skeins of silk, needles, toothbrushes, a pair of boots, and five pounds of candy.

Entertainment and Events

Seafood is a serious art in Morehead City. The enormous **North Carolina Seafood Festival** (252/726-6273, www.ncseafoodfestival.org), the state's second-largest, takes place here every October. The city's streets shut down and some 150,000 visitors descend on the waterfront. Festivities kick off with a blessing of the fleet, followed by music, fireworks, competitions such as the flounder toss, and, of course, loads of food.

If you're in the area on the right weekend in November, you'll not want to deprive yourself of the gluttonous splendor of the **Mill Creek Oyster Festival** (Mill Creek Volunteer Fire Department, 2370 Mill Creek Rd., Mill Creek, 252/247-4777). Food is the focus of this

small-town fete, a benefit for the local volunteer fire department, and the meals are cooked by local experts. Choose from all-you-can-eat roasted oysters, fried shrimp, and fried spot (a local fish considered a delicacy by locals and a cult classic by foodies), all in mass quantities. Many of the oysters may not be local these days, but the cooking is very local—an authentic taste of one of North Carolina's best culinary traditions. You'll find Mill Creek and this extraordinary gastronomic event northwest of Morehead City on the Newport River.

Sports and Recreation

Many of this region's most important historic and natural sites are underwater. From Morehead City's **Olympus Dive Center** (713 Shepard St., 252/726-9432, www.olympusdiving.com, 6am-8pm daily June-Sept., 9am-6pm Mon.-Sat. Oct.-May, lessons from $340, charters from $70), scuba divers of all levels of experience can take charter trips to dozens of natural and artificial reefs that teem with fish, including the ferocious-looking but not terribly dangerous eight-foot-long sand tiger shark. This is the Graveyard of the Atlantic, so there are at least as many shipwrecks to choose from, including an 18th-century schooner, a luxury liner, a German U-boat, and many Allied commercial and military ships that fell victim to the U-boats that infested this coast during World War II.

Anglers love this part of the coast for its inshore and offshore fishing; find an up-to-date list of Morehead City charter boats at www.downtownmoreheadcity.com. Just over the bridge from Morehead City, **Captain Stacy Fishing Center** (416 Atlantic Beach Causeway, Atlantic Beach, 252/247-7501 or 800/533-9417, www.captstacy.com, from $55 adults, $45 children) has been hauling in big fish off the coast for decades. Charter options include a nighttime shark fishing expedition where they regularly catch tiger, sand, and black-tip sharks. Full-day and half-day bottom-fishing excursions take you offshore into deep water where you can expect to catch black sea bass, spottail porgies, triggerfish, red snapper, and other good eating fish. Serious anglers may want to join one of the overnighters April to November; these trips include a two-day bag limit and have a reputation for bringing in loads of fish. Captain Stacy's can accommodate private charters as well, and most importantly they can point you to the fish.

Inshore fishing has its own fans, and **Water Dog Guide Service** (252/728-7907 or 919/423-6310, www.waterdogguideservice.com, tours from $325) knows where to find the fish, including speckled trout, flounder, and red drum, in the sounds, marshes, and creeks. They also fish at near-shore wrecks and reefs for bluefish, mahimahi, and Spanish mackerel. Check their website to see what's biting and plan a trip around the red drum spawn, when red drum invade the marsh in huge numbers. Or try something different and join them for a duck hunt.

Crystal Coast Ecotours (252/808-3354, www.crystalcoastecotours.com, $100 per hour, $275 half-day, $375 full-day) is run by a marine biologist with a passion for introducing people to the world of the marshes, creeks, barrier islands, and waterways where she makes her home. Tours lead you to secluded barrier islands, the Cape Lookout National Seashore, and even into near-ocean waters so you can explore the area by birding, dolphin watching, shelling, snorkeling, and watching wild horses.

Food

The 🅒 **Sanitary Fish Market** (501 Evans St., 252/247-3111, www.sanitaryfishmarket.com, from 11:30am daily, $13-31) is not only the most widely known eatery in Morehead City, it's probably its best-known institution. The rather odd name reflects its 1930s origins as a seafood market that was bound by its lease and its fastidious landlord to be kept as clean as possible. Today, it's a huge family seafood restaurant. Long lines in season and on weekends demonstrate its popularity. Of particular note are its famous hush puppies, which have a well-deserved reputation as some of the best in the state, and the monstrous Famous Deluxe Shore Dinner—soup, fried fish, shrimp, oysters, scallops, soft shelled crab, fries, and, of

course, hush puppies. Be sure to buy a Sanitary T-shirt on the way out; it'll help you blend in elsewhere in the state.

Chefs 105 (105 S. 7th St., 252/240-1105, www.chefs105.com.com, 5pm Wed.-Fri., 11am Sat.-Sun., $10-35) sits on the Morehead City waterfront and serves everything from burgers to Steak Oskar. Their seafood is largely fried, but they have a steam bar where you can get clams, shrimp, crab legs, and oysters by the dozen, pound, cluster, or peck. They don't take reservations, so if you want dinner, expect a little wait during summer, or get here early.

El's Drive-In (3706 Arendell St., 252/726-3002, 10:30am-10pm daily, around $7), a tiny place across from Carteret Community College, seems like it has been around almost as long as the town. It's most famous for its shrimp burgers but serves all sorts of fried delights. It's a hit among locals and road-food fans, but most everyone agrees that the shakes are great, as are the onion rings. Be forewarned: It's car-side service and the place is mobbed with gulls at times; they'll swoop down and grab a French fry before you can get it in the car. As fun as they are to watch, it's not a good idea to feed the birds.

The **Bistro-by-the-Sea** (4031 Arendell St., 252/247-2777, www.bistro-by-the-sea.com, 5pm-9:30pm Tues.-Thurs., 5pm-10pm Fri.-Sat., entrées $10-25) participates in Carteret Catch, a program that ensures that fresh locally caught seafood graces the tables of Carteret County. They serve a number of seafood dishes, but don't just stick to the sea; they also serve steaks, prime rib, and even fresh calf liver. Most interesting, though, are the small plates, with items such as a half-slab of baby back ribs, baked oysters, or a Japanese bento box.

For an old-fashioned luncheon or afternoon tea, visit the tiny five-table tearoom at **The Infusion Café** (1012 Arendell St., 252/240-2800,, 10am-5pm Tues.-Thurs., 10am-9pm Fri., 11am-3pm Sat., under $10). In addition to the many teas, you can order scones, desserts, dainty quiches, and sandwiches. They serve a formal tea 2pm-4pm Monday-Friday with reservations required at least a day in advance.

(**Cox Family Restaurant** (4109 Arendell St., 252/726-6961, 6am-9pm Mon.-Sat., 6am-8pm Sun., around $8) also has served down-home cooking for many years and is known for its friendly staff and coterie of local regulars. The food here is simple—it is home cooking, after all—but well done. At breakfast, no matter what you get, order a side of home fries; you won't be disappointed.

Raps Grill and Bar (709 Arendell St., 252/240-1213, www.rapsgrillandbar.com, 11am-10pm Mon.-Thurs., 11am-10:30pm Fri.-Sat., bar open later, $10-20) serves a lot of what you'd expect—wings, mozzarella sticks, loaded cheese fries—but then expands into unexpected territory with fried pickles, crab cakes, and fried green tomatoes—and that's just the appetizers. Like other restaurants along the Crystal Coast, they serve version of fried seafood, but they like to bring in a Tex-Mex influence, serving fajitas, iron skillets (think fajitas without the tortillas), and fish tacos.

HARKERS ISLAND

The Core Sound region stretches east-northeast from Beaufort, many miles up to the Pamlico Sound. Filled with birds and boats and not much else, it's a hauntingly beautiful landscape. Like much of the North Carolina coast, the marshes and pocosins serve as way stations for countless flocks of migratory birds as they migrate, regularly adding greatly to the year-round bird population. Fishing has always been a way of life here, but so has hunting, particularly hunting waterfowl. In earlier generations, and to a lesser extent today, men who earned a living fishing most of the year had sideline businesses hunting birds. They ate the birds they shot, sold the feathers for women's hats, trained bird dogs, and worked as birding outfitters to visiting hunters. Consequentially, many Down Easterners became expert decoy carvers. The beautifully carved decoys started as functional pieces, but today most are produced as art for art's sake; either way, the tradition survives.

Woodworking on a much grander scale has defined the culture of the people of Harkers Island, as it is home to generations of boat builders whose creations are as elegant as they are reliable. Keep an eye out as you drive through; you may see boats under construction in backyards and garages—not canoes or dinghies, but full-size fishing boats.

To get to Harkers Island, follow U.S. 70 east from Beaufort around the dogleg that skirts the North River. East of the town of Otway, you'll see Harkers Island Road; go right and head south toward Straits. Straits Road will take you through the town of Straits, and then across a bridge over the Straits themselves, finally ending up on Harkers Island.

(Core Sound Waterfowl Museum

The **Core Sound Waterfowl Museum** (1785 Island Rd., 252/728-1500, www.coresound. com, 10am-5pm Mon.-Sat., 2pm-5pm Sun., $5), which occupies a beautiful modern building on Shell Point next to the Cape Lookout National Seashore headquarters, is a community-wide labor of love. The museum is home to exhibits crafted by members of the communities it represents, depicting the Down East maritime life through decoys, nets, and other tools of the trades as well as everyday household objects, beautiful quilts, and other utilitarian folk arts. This is a sophisticated modern institution, but its community roots are evident in touching details like the index-card labels, written in the careful script of elderly women, explaining what certain objects are, what they were used for, and who made them. For instance, just as Piedmont textile workers made and treasured their loom hooks, folks down here took pride in the hooks that they made to assist in the perennial off-season work of hanging nets. Baseball uniforms on display represent an era when one town's team might have to travel by ferry to its opponent's field. The museum hosts Core Sound Community Nights on the second Tuesday of every month. These get-togethers are a taste of the old home days when families and long-lost friends reunite over home-cooked food to reminisce about community history and talk about their hopes and concerns for the future.

The museum's gift shop has a nice selection of books and other items related to Down East culture. Be sure to pick up a copy of *Island Born and Bred: A Collection of Harkers Island Food, Fun, Fact and Fiction* by the Harkers Island United Methodist Women. This cookbook has become a regional classic for its wonderful blend of authentic family recipes and community stories. You might also be able to find a Core Sound Christmas Tree, made by Harvey and Sons in nearby Davis. This old family fishery has made a hit in recent years manufacturing small Christmas trees out of recycled crab pots. It's a fun, playful item, but it carries significant messages about the past and future of the Core Sound region.

Core Sound Decoy Carvers Guild

Twenty years ago, over a pot of stewed clams, some decoy-carving friends Down East decided to found the **Core Sound Decoy Carvers Guild** (1575 Harkers Island Rd., 252/838-8818, www.decoyguild.com, call for hours). The guild is open to the public and gives demonstrations, competitions, and classes for grown-ups and children; the museum shop is a nice place to browse.

Events

The Core Sound Decoy Carvers Guild also hosts the **Core Sound Decoy Festival,** usually held in the early winter. Several thousand people come to this annual event—more than the number of permanent residents on Harkers Island—to buy, swap, and teach the art of making decoys.

Food

Captain's Choice Restaurant (977 Island Rd., 252/728-7122, 10am-9pm Tues.-Thurs., 7am-9pm Fri.-Sun., closed Mon., breakfast $2-10, lunch and dinner $6-25) is a great place to try traditional Down East chowder. Usually made of clams but sometimes with other shellfish or fish, chowder in Carteret County is a point of pride. The point is the flavor of the seafood itself, which must be extremely fresh and not hidden behind lots of milk and spices. Captain's Choice serves chowder in the old-time way—with dumplings.

Fish Hook Grill (980 Island Rd., 252/728-1790, www.fishhookgrill.com, 11am-9pm Mon.-Sat., 11am-3pm Sun., $6-26) is a small-town restaurant serving big portions of seafood, burgers, and more. They're known locally for their chowder, crab cakes, potato salad, hushpuppies, fried oysters, coleslaw, and, well, just about everything on the menu. Check to see if Miss Faye, the owner and operator, is here when you visit; if she is, stop by and say hello. She's as friendly as the food is good.

VILLAGE OF CEDAR ISLAND

For a beautiful afternoon's drive, head back to the mainland and follow U.S. 70 north. You'll go through some tiny communities—Williston, Davis, Stacy—and if you keep bearing north on Highway 12 when U.S. 70 heads south to the town of Atlantic, you'll eventually reach the tip of the peninsula and the village of Cedar Island. This little fishing town has the amazing ambience of being at the end of the earth. From the peninsula's shore you can barely see land across the sounds. The ferry to Ocracoke departs from Cedar Island, a two-hour-plus ride across Pamlico Sound to get there. The beach here is absolutely gorgeous, and horses roam on it; they're not the famous wild horses of the Outer Banks, but they move around freely as if they were.

A spectacular location for bird-watching is the **Cedar Island National Wildlife Refuge** (U.S. 70, east of Atlantic, 252/926-4021, www.fws.gov/cedarisland). Nearly all of its 14,500 acres are brackish marshland, and it's often visited in season by redhead ducks, buffleheads, surf scoters, and many other species. While there are trails for hiking and cycling, this refuge is primarily intended as a haven for the birds.

Accommodations and Food

◖ **The Driftwood Motel** (3575 Cedar Island Rd., 252/225-4861, www.clis.com, $85) is a simple motel in an incredible location, and since the ferry leaves from its parking lot, it's the place to stay if you're coming from or going to Ocracoke. There's also camping (tents $25,

BEAUFORT

RVs $30) here with electricity, water, and sewer hookups.

The Driftwood's **Pirate's Chest Restaurant** (3575 Cedar Island Rd., 252/225-4861, 5pm-8:30pm Thurs., 5pm-9:30pm Fri. and Sat., noon-8pm Sun., around $18) is the only restaurant on Cedar Island, so it's a good thing that it's a good one. Local seafood is the specialty, and many dishes can be adapted for vegetarians. Their Cream of Crab Soup is an interesting take on the she-crab soup you'll find served in Virginia and Maryland.

GETTING THERE AND AROUND
By Car
One of the state's main east-west routes, U.S. 70 provides easy access to most of the destinations in this chapter. From Raleigh to Beaufort is a little over 150 miles, but keep in mind that long stretches of the highway are in commercial areas with plenty of traffic and red lights. U.S. 70 continues past Beaufort, snaking up along Core Sound through little Down East towns like Otway and Davis, finally ending in the town of Atlantic. At Sea Level, Highway 12 branches to the north, across the Cedar Island Wildlife Refuge and ending at the Cedar Island-Ocracoke Ferry.

Down south, to reach the Bogue Banks (Atlantic Beach, Emerald Isle, and neighboring beaches) by road, bridges cross Bogue Sound on Highway 58 at both Morehead City and Cedar Point (not to be confused with Cedar Island).

By Ferry
Inland, a 20-minute free passenger and vehicle ferry (800/339-9156, pets allowed) crosses the Neuse River between Cherry Branch (near Cherry Point) and Minesott Beach in Pamlico County every 30 minutes.

Lower Outer Banks

The southern stretch of the Outer Banks of North Carolina contain some of the region's most diverse destinations. Core and Shackleford Banks lie within Cape Lookout National Seashore, the fifth national seashore established in the country and the second in North Carolina (Cape Hatteras National Seashore to the north was the first in the country). It's a wild place, a maritime environment populated by birds, herds of wild horses, and not a single human. The towns of Bogue Banks—Atlantic Beach, Salter Path, Pine Knoll Shores, Indian Beach, and Emerald Isle—are classic beach towns with clusters of motels and restaurants and even a few towel shops and miniature golf courses. Both areas are great fun; Cape Lookout especially so for ecotours and history, and Bogue Banks for those looking for a day on the beach followed by an evening chowing down on good fried seafood.

◖ CAPE LOOKOUT NATIONAL SEASHORE
Cape Lookout National Seashore (1800 Islands Rd., Harkers Island, 252/728-2250, www.nps.gov/calo) is an otherworldly place: 56 miles of beach stretched out across four barrier islands, a long tape of sand seemingly so vulnerable to nature that it's hard to believe there were ever any towns on its banks. There were: Cape Lookout was settled in the early 1700s, and people in the towns of the south Core Banks made their living in fisheries that might seem brutal to today's seafood eaters—whaling and catching dolphins and sea turtles, among the more mundane species. Portsmouth, at the north end of the park across the water from Ocracoke, was a busy port of great importance to the early economy of North Carolina. Portsmouth declined slowly, but catastrophe rained down all at once on the people of the southerly Shackleford Banks, who were driven out of their own long-established communities to start new lives on

the mainland when a series of terrible hurricanes decimated the islands in the 1890s.

Islands often support unique ecosystems. Among the dunes, small patches of maritime forest fight for each drop of fresh water, while ghost forests of trees that were defeated by advancing saltwater look on resignedly. Along the endless beach, loggerhead turtles come ashore to lay their eggs, and in the waters just off the strand, three other species of sea turtles are sometimes seen. Wild horses roam the beaches and dunes, and dolphins frequent both the ocean and sound sides of the islands. Other mammals, though, are all of the small and scrappy variety: raccoons, rodents, otters, and rabbits. Like all of coastal North Carolina, it's a great place for bird-watching as it's located in a heavily traveled migratory flyway. Pets are allowed if they're on a leash. The wild ponies on Shackleford Banks can pose a threat to dogs that get among them, and the dogs can frighten the horses, so be careful not to let them mingle.

Portsmouth Village

Portsmouth Village, at the northern tip of the Cape Lookout National Seashore, is a peaceful but eerie place. The village looks much as it did 100 years ago, the handsome houses and churches all tidy and in good repair, but with the exception of caretakers and summer volunteers, no one has lived here in nearly 50 years. In 1970 the last two residents moved away from what had once been a town of 700 people and one of the most important shipping ports in North Carolina. Founded before the Revolution, Portsmouth was a lightering station, a port where huge seagoing ships that had traveled across the ocean would stop and have their cargo removed for transport across the shallow sounds in smaller boats. There is a visitors center located at Portsmouth, open varying hours April-October, where you can learn about the village before embarking on a stroll to explore the quiet streets.

In its busy history, Portsmouth was captured by the British during the War of 1812 and by Union troops in the Civil War, underscoring its strategic importance. By the time of the Civil War, though, its utility as a way station was already declining. An 1846 hurricane opened a new inlet at Hatteras, which quickly became a busy shipping channel. After abolition, the town's lightering trade was no longer profitable without enslaved people to perform much of the labor. The fishing and lifesaving businesses kept the town afloat for a few more generations, but Portsmouth was never the same.

Once a year, an unusual thing happens when boatloads of people arrive on shore, the church bell rings, and the sound of hymns being sung comes through the open church doors. At the Portsmouth Homecoming, descendants of the people who lived here come from all over the state and the rest of the country to pay tribute to their ancestral home. They have an old-time dinner on the grounds and then tour the little village together. It's like a family reunion with the town itself the matriarch. The rest of the year, Portsmouth receives visitors and National Park Service caretakers, but one senses that it's already looking forward to the next spring when its children will come home again.

Shackleford Banks

The once-busy villages of Diamond City and Shackleford Banks are like Portsmouth in that, although they have not been occupied for many years, the descendants of the people who lived here retain a profound attachment to their ancestors' homes. Diamond City and nearby communities met a spectacular end. The hurricane season of 1899 culminated in the San Ciriaco Hurricane, a disastrous storm that destroyed homes and forests, killed livestock, flooded gardens with saltwater, and washed the Shackleford dead out of their graves. The Bankers saw the writing on the wall and moved to the mainland en masse, carrying as much of their property as would fit on boats. Some actually floated their houses across Core Sound. Harkers Island absorbed most of the refugee population, and many also went to Morehead City; their traditions are still an important part of Down East culture. Daily and weekly programs held at the Light Station Pavilion and the porch of the Keepers Quarters during the

BEAUFORT

summer months teach visitors about the natural and human history of Cape Lookout, including what day-to-day life was like for the keeper of the lighthouse and the keeper's family.

Descendants of the Bankers feel a deep spiritual bond to their ancestors' home, and for many years they would return frequently, occupying fish camps that they constructed along the beach. When the federal government bought the Banks, it was made known that the fish camps would soon be off-limits to their deedless owners. The outcry and bitterness that ensued reflected the depth of the Core Sounders' love of their ancestral grounds. The National Park Service may have thought that the fish camps were ephemeral and purely recreational structures, but to the campers, the Banks was still home, even if they had been born on the mainland and had never lived here for longer than a fishing season. Retaining their sense of righteous, if not legal, ownership, many burned down their own fish camps rather than let the government take them down.

Cape Lookout Lighthouse

By the time you arrive at the 1859 **Cape Lookout Lighthouse** (252/728-2250, www.nps.gov/calo, visitors center and Keeper's Quarters Museum 9am-5pm daily Apr.-Nov., lighthouse climbs 10am-3:45pm Wed.-Sat. early May-mid-Sept., $8 adults, $4 seniors and under age 13), you will have seen it portrayed on dozens of brochures, menus, signs, and souvenirs. With its striking diamond pattern, it looks like a rattlesnake standing at attention. This 163-foot-tall lighthouse was first lit in 1859. Like the other lighthouses along the coast, it's built of brick. At its base, the walls are nine feet thick, narrowing to two feet at the top. The present lighthouse isn't the first to guard this section of the coast; originally a lighthouse was built only a few yards away, but it was plagued with problems and replaced by the current structure.

Accommodations

There are cabins to rent on Cape Lookout, but you must reserve well in advance to obtain one. On **Long Point, Great Island, and Morris Marina** (877/444-6777, www.nps.gov/calo, reservations www.recreation.gov, Apr.-Nov. $73-170) you can rent cabins with hot and cold water, gas stoves, and furniture, but in some cases visitors must bring their own generators for lighting as well as linens and utensils. Rentals are not available December-March, and before you make a reservation, remember that with no air-conditioning, it can get quite hot in these cabins; fall or spring are more comfortable than summer.

CAMPING

Camping is permitted within Cape Lookout National Seashore. There are no designated campsites or camping amenities, and everything you bring must be carried back out when you leave. Campers can stay for up to 14 days, and large groups (25 or more campers) require special permits. The National Park Service website for Cape Lookout (www.nps.gov/calo) has full details on camping regulations and permits.

Getting There

Except for the visitors center at Harkers Island, Cape Lookout National Seashore can only be reached by ferry. Portsmouth, at the northern end of the park, is a short ferry ride from Ocracoke, but Ocracoke is a very long ferry ride from Cedar Island. The **Cedar Island-Ocracoke Ferry** (800/293-3779) is part of the state ferry system, and costs $15 one-way for regular-size vehicles (pets allowed). It takes 2.25 hours to cross Pamlico Sound, but the ride is fun, and embarking from Cedar Island feels like sailing off the edge of the earth. The **Ocracoke-Portsmouth Ferry** is a passenger-only commercial route, licensed to Captain Rudy Austin of **Austin Boat Tours** (252/928-4361 or 252/928-5431, www.portsmouthnc.com, $20 pp, 3-person minimum, daily as weather permits). Call to ensure a seat. Most ferries operate April-November, with some exceptions.

Commercial ferries cross every day from mainland Carteret County to the southern parts of the national seashore. There is generally a ferry route between Davis and Great Island, but service can be variable; check the Cape Lookout National Seashore website (www.nps.gov/calo) for updates.

From Harkers Island, passenger ferries to Cape Lookout Lighthouse and Shackleford Banks include **Harkers Island Fishing Center** (252/728-3907, http://harkersmarina.com, $15 adults, $10 children, $6 pets) and **Local Yokel** (516 Island Rd., 252/728-2759, www.tourcapelookout.com, $15 adults, $10 children).

From Beaufort, passenger ferries include **Outer Banks Ferry Service** (326 Front St., 252/728-4129, www.outerbanksferry.com, $15 adults, $8 children), which goes to both Shackleford Banks and to Cape Lookout Lighthouse; **Island Ferry Adventures at Barbour's Marina** (610 Front St., 252/728-6181, www.islandferryadventures.com, $15 adults, $8 children) does as well. Morehead City's passenger-only **Waterfront Ferry Service** (201 S. 6th St., 252/503-1955, www.crystalcoastferry.com, $15 adults, $8 children) goes to Shackleford Banks too. On-leash pets are generally allowed, but call ahead to confirm with the ferry operator.

BOGUE BANKS

The beaches of Bogue Banks are popular, but they have a typically North Carolinian laid-back feel, a quieter atmosphere than the fun-fun-fun neon jungles of beaches elsewhere. The major attractions, Fort Macon State Park and the North Carolina Aquarium at Pine Knoll Shores, are a bit more cerebral than, say, amusement parks and bikini contests. In the surfing, boating, bars, and restaurants, and the beach itself, there's also a bustle of activity to keep things hopping. Bogue, by the way, rhymes with "rogue."

C North Carolina Aquarium

The **North Carolina Aquarium at Pine Knoll Shores** (1 Roosevelt Blvd., Pine Knoll Shores, 800/832-3474, www.ncaquariums.com, 9am-5pm daily, 9am-9pm Thurs. July, $8 adults, $7 seniors and under age 13, free under age 3)

is one of the state's three great coastal aquariums. Here at Pine Knoll Shores, exhibit highlights include a 300,000-gallon aquarium in which sharks and other aquatic beasts go about their business in and around a replica German U-Boat (plenty of originals lie right off the coast and form homes for reef creatures); a "jelly gallery" (they really can be beautiful); a tank filled with the beautiful but dangerous nonnative lionfish; a pair of river otters; and many other wonderful animals and habitats.

Trails from the parking lot lead into the maritime forests of the 568-acre **Theodore Roosevelt Natural Area** (1 Roosevelt Dr., Atlantic Beach, 252/726-3775), where network of trails takes your through secluded marshes, on a high dune ridge, and under a coastal forest canopy, providing plenty of opportunities for bird-watching and wildlife viewing. The trails close at 4:30pm, so get an early start.

Fort Macon State Park

At the eastern tip of Atlantic Beach is **Fort Macon State Park** (2300 E. Fort Macon Rd., 252/726-3775, http://ncparks.gov, visitors center 9am-6pm daily, fort 9am-5:30pm daily, bathhouse area 8am-5:30pm Nov.-Feb., 8am-8pm Mar.-Oct., swimming area 10am-5:45pm daily May-Sept. as staffing allows). The central feature of the park is Fort Macon, an 1820s federal fort that was a Confederate garrison for one year during the Civil War. Guided tours are offered, and there are exhibits inside the casemates. For such a stern and martial building, some of the interior spaces are surprisingly pretty. The park has 1.5 miles of beach, perfect for fishing, swimming, sunbathing, or simply strolling. At different times throughout the year, the park is filled with costumed Civil War reenactors.

Sports and Recreation

The ocean side of Bogue Banks offers plenty of public beach access. In each of the towns—Atlantic Beach, Pine Knoll Shores, Salter Path, Indian Beach, and Emerald Isle—are parking lots, some free and some paid. The beach at **Fort Macon** is bounded by the ocean, Bogue

Sound, and Beaufort Inlet. Because there's a Coast Guard station on the Sound side and a jetty along the Inlet, swimming is permitted only along one stretch of the ocean beach. A concession stand and bathhouse are located at the swimming beach.

Atlantic Beach Surf Shop (515 W. Fort Macon Rd., Atlantic Beach, 252/646-4944, www.absurfshop.com) gives individual ($50 per hour) and group ($40 per hour, call for reservations) surfing lessons on the beach at Pine Knoll Shores in the morning and early afternoon. This is a great place to learn because the south-facing beach catches some big long-riding swells, especially when the wind's right.

Barrier Island Kayaks (160 Cedar Point Rd., Swansboro, 252/393-6457, www.barrierislandkayaks.com) offers custom trips, excursions to Bear Island at the southern edge of this region, eco-adventures focused on wandering marsh creeks and viewing wildlife up close, and trips out to the Cape Lookout National Seashore. They also rent out kayaks and stand-up paddleboards ($30 for 2 hours, $40 half-day, $55 full-day, $35 additional days).

Lookout Adventures (208 Arendell St., 252/515-0356, http://lookoutadventures.com) has a long list of boat charters ($195-675), including a private dolphin cruise, sunset fishing excursions, and daylong fishing or sightseeing trips to Cape Lookout and surrounding islands. Their combo-day package brings together the best of fishing (a half-day in their personal fishing hot spots) and sightseeing as you cruise the marshes and waterways and learn about the ecology of the Cape Lookout area.

Reef Gander Tours (Atlantic Beach, 252/725-4444, www.reefgandertours.com, call for rates) has been exploring the waters around Carteret County, Cape Lookout, and Atlantic Beach for more than 25 years. Customized tours include hitting the best fishing spots, exploring the barrier islands or marsh creeks, shelling, and swimming on one of the barrier islands.

At **Dragonfly Parasail** (Anchorage Marina, 571 E. Fort Macon Rd., 252/422-5500, www.dragonflyparasail.com, $65-75, observers $10-20), you can join the 100,000 other people who've taken a flight over the beautiful waters off Atlantic Beach. Decide before you go up if you want to get wet; if you do, they'll slow the boat and let you drift down from more than 400 feet until you touch the water, and then pull you back into the air. It's kid-friendly and provides spectacular views.

If fishing's your thing, **Pelagic Sportfishing** (212 Smith St., 252/904-3361, www.pelagicsportfishing.com, fishing $400-1,700, cruising $100 per hour) has 31-foot and 61-foot boats at Atlantic Beach for half-day and full-day charters for tuna, mahimahi, and redfish. Sunset cruises and sightseeing tours are also offered.

Accommodations

The **Atlantis Lodge** (123 Salter Path Rd., Atlantic Beach, 252/726-5168 or 800/682-7057, www.atlantislodge.com, $55-280) is an old established family-run motel. It has simple and reasonably priced efficiencies in a great beachfront location; the hotel's private boardwalk puts you on the beach in two minutes. Well-behaved pets are welcome for an additional fee. The **Clamdigger Inn** (511 Salter Path Rd., Atlantic Beach, 252/247-4155 or 800/338-1533, http://clamdiggerinn.com, $49-255) is another reliable option with all-oceanfront guest rooms. You'll find beach chairs and umbrellas to use as well as a game room, a poolside bar, and wireless Internet access. Pets are not allowed. The **Windjammer Inn** (103 Salter Path Rd., Atlantic Beach, 252/247-7123 or 800/233-6466, www.windjammerinn.com, $169-205) is another simple, comfortable motel with decent rates through the high season and great rates (under $100) in the off-season.

Food

The **Channel Marker** (718 Atlantic Beach Causeway, Atlantic Beach, 252/247-2344, 11am-late daily, $14-37) is a fancier alternative to some of the old-timey fried seafood joints on Bogue Banks. They offer shrimp nine ways, including with grits (classic), steamed (peel and eat—classic), blackened, panned in butter, scampi, fried calabash-style, and broiled in garlic-herb butter. Channel Marker gives you a break from the ubiquitous fried seafood with a selection of broiled seafood; the flounder is especially good broiled, as are the bay scallops. Try the crab cakes with mango chutney, or the Greek shrimp salad. The extensive wine list has wines from the Biltmore Estate in Asheville.

ℂ White Swan Bar-B-Q and Chicken (2500-A W. Fort Macon Rd., Atlantic Beach, 252/726-9607, www.whiteswanbarbeque. com, 7am-2pm Mon.-Sat., around $8) has been serving the Carolina trinity of barbecue, coleslaw, and hush puppies since 1960, using a 70-year-old top-secret recipe. This is a "whole hog" barbecue joint, meaning they cook whole hogs, not just shoulders or butts, giving it a richer flavor and providing the pit master and assistants plenty of meat, bark (that crispy outer rind of good barbecue), and juices to work with when assembling your plate. They also flip a mean egg for breakfast.

The **ℂ Big Oak Drive-In and Bar-B-Q** (1167 Salter Path Rd., 252/247-2588, www.bigoakdrivein.com, 11am-3pm Tues.-Thurs. and Sun., 11am-8pm Fri. and Sat., around $6) is a classic beach drive-in: a little red, white, and blue-striped building with a walk-up counter and drive-up spaces. They're best known for their shrimp burgers ($5), a fried affair slathered with Big Oak's signature red sauce, coleslaw, and tartar sauce. Then there are the scallop burgers, oyster burgers, clam burgers, hamburgers, and barbecue, all cheap and made for snacking on the beach.

Frost Seafood House (1300 Salter Path Rd., Salter Path, 252/247-3202, www.frost-seafoodhouse.com, 4:30pm-9:30pm Mon.-Thurs., 7am-9pm Fri. and Sat., breakfast around $7, dinner around $22) began in 1954 as a gas station and quickly became the restaurant that it is today. The Frost family catches its own shrimp and buys much of its other seafood locally. Be sure to request a taste of the "ching-a-ling" sauce. Another community institution is the **Crab Shack** (140 Shore Dr., Salter Path, 252/247-3444, www.thecrabshacksalterpath.com, daily from 11am, $16-38), behind the Methodist Church in Salter Path. Operated by the Guthries—a family name that dates back to the early colonists in this area—the restaurant was wiped out in 2005 by Hurricane Ophelia but has since been rebuilt.

BEAUFORT

WILMINGTON AND THE CAPE FEAR REGION

In 1524, Giovanni da Verrazzano, the first known European explorer to arrive in the Cape Fear Region, wrote in a letter to the king of France that the land was "as pleasant and delectable to behold as is possible to imagine." With barrier islands that contain the largest intact piece of maritime forest in the state, beautiful beaches, miles of river, marsh, and creek to explore, and the rising Sandhills and hardwood forests inland, the southeastern corner of North Carolina is a natural beauty.

As enthusiasm for the New World built in Europe, the influence of England, Spain, and France profoundly changed the cultural and physical landscapes of the Caribbean and the southern Atlantic coast of North America. Towns and forts sprung up where Native Americans once lived among the trees, built by enslaved Africans for their European masters. Wilmington shares this legacy with other cities in the Atlantic-Caribbean region such as Havana, Nassau, New Orleans, Savannah, and Charleston. The architecture of these cities shows European influence, and the culture—language, food, and folkways—shows the influence of Africans.

The Lumbee people, Native Americans historically and spiritually tied to the black-water Lumber River, now make their home in Pembroke. They are the largest indigenous community east of the Mississippi River, though their name is not widely known. This is due in part to the fact that they've been denied federal status, a complex and contentious issue that continues to cast a shadow for members of the community. They don't have a reservation,

© JASON FRYE

HIGHLIGHTS

LOOK FOR **◖** TO FIND RECOMMENDED SIGHTS, ACTIVITIES, DINING, AND LODGING.

◖ Wilmington's Historic District: Downtown reflects its glory days of commerce and high society in the state's largest 19th-century historic district, a gorgeous collection of antebellum and late-Victorian townhouses and commercial buildings, including many beautiful Southern iterations of the Italianate craze that preceded the Civil War (page 117).

◖ Wrightsville Beach: North Carolina has many wonderful beaches, but few can compare with Wrightsville for its pretty strand, easy public access, clear waters, and overall beauty (page 119).

◖ Hammocks Beach State Park: One of the wildest and least disturbed Atlantic coast beaches, accessible only by boat, Bear Island is a popular stopover for migrating waterfowl and turtles (page 137).

◖ Southport: From this picturesque fishing town you can see the oldest and newest lighthouses in North Carolina, enjoy dinner on the water with the locals, and celebrate your independence at the state's official Fourth of July celebration (page 141).

◖ Zip-Lining: Soaring through the trees at ZipQuest in Fayetteville provides thrills and an unusual look at pine and hardwood forests (page 155).

and for centuries have lived a rural existence with deeply rooted Christianity. Their little-known history can be explored in and around Pembroke.

Between Wilmington and Lumberton the landscape of the state's southeast corner becomes a waterscape comprising blackwater creeks and seductive, even eerie swamps, bays, marshes, and rivers. It's the world's only native habitat of the Venus flytrap. Many visitors wrinkle their noses at the marsh's distinctive smell as the tide recedes and the mudflats are exposed, but to locals the mingled scent of marsh and salt water is the scent of home. The cypress knees, tannic creeks, marsh birds, and occasional alligator make this region pleasant and delectable to behold, an experience that is enhanced by staying a little longer.

The greatest draw is the water: the beautiful beaches of Brunswick, New Hanover, Pender, and Onslow Counties and the well-known Wrightsville and Topsail beaches as

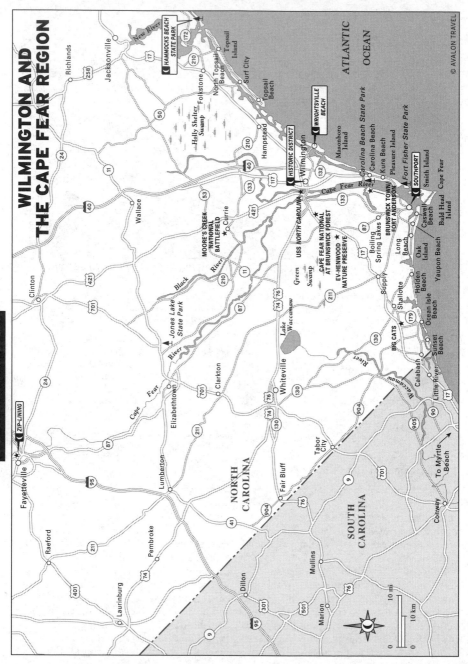

WILMINGTON AND THE CAPE FEAR REGION

© AVALON TRAVEL

well as other hidden gems just north of bustling Myrtle Beach, South Carolina. You can find the same mini golf and beach-towel vendors peppering the beach towns of North Carolina, but the state's coast mostly seems downright bucolic compared to its southern neighbor.

Inland, the landscape changes but the water is no less important. At the edge of this region is Fayetteville, with a long history that includes Revolutionary War standoffs, Civil War battles, and links to the Cape Fear River. At Fayetteville the marshes give way to rolling hills with a mix of pines and hardwoods. Home to Fort Bragg, Fayetteville has a large military presence and history, dating to the colonial era when immigrant Scots called these hills home.

PLANNING YOUR TIME

There's a lot to do in the Cape Fear region, and depending on your interests, a wide range of choices for a home base. Wilmington is the obvious choice: Centrally located on the coast, it's minutes from Wrightsville, Kure, and Carolina Beaches and only a little farther from Topsail and the beaches of Brunswick County. Fayetteville and Raleigh are only a couple of hours away, making day trips a possibility. The town of Wilmington is full of activities and sights, and you'll want a day or two to explore this historic river city. For inland adventures in the region, Fayetteville offers a good selection of motels, and it's still a reasonable drive to the coast for a day at the beach.

HISTORY

Giovanni da Verrazzano's 1524 visit started a land race that took two centuries to take off. Lucas Vásquez de Ayllón and his crew, which possibly included the first enslaved Africans brought to what is now the United States, walked the shores here in 1526 scouting for resources and settlement sites before their shipwreck in South Carolina. In the 1660s explores from the Massachusetts Bay Colony visited and either didn't like what they found or wanted others to think it was undesirable land, at the end of their short trip they left a sign at the end of the cape that read, in essence, "Don't bother; nothing to see here."

The next summer a settlement appeared on the banks of the river, but it failed as colonists, citing the humidity, hurricanes, and bugs, among other things, abandoned it. It wasn't until 1726 that European settlement took hold in the region. Maurice Moore and his brother Roger established their family's domain at Brunswick Town and Orton Plantation, 0.5 miles north. Today, only ruins remain at Brunswick Town in the form of ballast-stone house foundations and the brick walls of an Anglican church, but Orton Plantation still stands and is once again owned by Moore descendants. The machinations of the Moores and Brunswick Town residents led to the demise of the indigenous Cape Fear people. Many of them were driven off, and the remainder were rounded up and later murdered.

Brunswick Town was an important port, as the only inland deepwater access on the river, but it was soon eclipsed by Wilmington to the north once dredging technology allowed the shoals between the two towns to be cleared. As Brunswick Town declined, the Revolution heated up, and the small port town played important roles in defying George III's taxes and harrying General Cornwallis and his troops as they raided the area. At the same time, the large population of Scottish immigrants around Fayetteville grew even larger, making their living in the forests preparing tar, pitch, and turpentine for naval stores.

In the lower Cape Fear Region, especially present-day Brunswick, New Hanover, Bladen, and Onslow Counties, the concentration of enslaved laborers was significantly larger than in many other parts of the state. The naval stores industry demanded workers, as did the large rice and indigo plantations, including Orton, that once dominated the local agricultural industry. The same was true along the coasts of South Carolina, Georgia, and parts of northern Florida, where many of the slaves had been taken from the same part of Africa. These large communities of African born and first-generation American-born people shared ideas, memories, and culture, which became what is known today as Gullah or Geechee culture. Most prominent around Charleston and Savannah, the Gullah dialect and cultural influence still exist in and around Wilmington. The dialect is reminiscent of English as spoken in the Caribbean, and cultural traditions still in evidence include the cuisine, heavy with gumbo, peanuts, and okra; and folklore, in which houses are painted bright blue to keep bad luck away, and bottle trees are used to capture evil spirits.

Another cultural group in the Cape Fear region is the indigenous Lumbee people. Also called the Croatan Indians, Pembroke Indians, and Indians of Robeson County, they're they largest indigenous community in the eastern United States. During the time of slavery and the Civil War they were called "free people of color," and they had no right to vote or to bear arms. The Lumbee people have a long history of resistance and defending their land. Most famously, in the 19th century the Lowry (sometimes spelled Lowrie) Band of outlaws defined the Lumbee cause for future generations. Another transformative moment in Lumbee history was a 1958 armed conflict near Maxton. Ku Klux Klan grand wizard "Catfish" Cole and about 40 other armed Klansmen held a rally at Hayes Pond. Fed up with a recent wave of vicious intimidation at the hands of the Klan, 1,500 armed Lumbee people showed up at the rally and shot out the lone electric light. No one was killed in the exchange of gunfire, and the Klansmen fled. The confrontation was reported around the country, energizing the cause of Native American civil rights.

In the late 20th and early 21st century, southeastern North Carolina's role as a military center expanded. Fort Bragg in Fayetteville is one of the country's largest Army installations and home to thousands of the soldiers who were stationed in Iraq and Afghanistan; the base continues to grow. Nearby Pope Air Field is the home of the 440th Airlift Wing, and there is a major Marine Corps presence nearby at Camp Lejeune in Jacksonville. Numerous museums in Fayetteville and Jacksonville tell the history of the military in southeastern North Carolina.

Perhaps most important in the region's recent history is the booming film industry. Wilmington is the center of cinematography in North Carolina, as evidenced by a 50-acre studio lot, the largest outside Los Angeles. Productions such as *Iron Man 3, Dawson's Creek,* and innumerable TV pilots and independent features have been filmed in the region, along with production offices and set pieces for productions like *The Hunger Games* and *Homeland.*

INFORMATION AND SERVICES

Area hospitals include two in Wilmington, **Cape Fear Hospital** (5301 Wrightsville Ave., Wilmington, 910/452-8100, www.nhrmc. org) and the **New Hanover Regional Medical Center** (2131 S. 17th St., Wilmington, 910/343-7000, www.nhrmc.org); two in Brunswick County, **Brunswick Novant Medical Center** (240 Hospital Dr. NE, Lockwoods Folly, 910/721-1000, www.brunswicknovant.org) and **Dosher Memorial Hospital** (924 N. Howe St., Southport, 910/457-3800, www.dosher.org); in Onslow County, **Onslow Memorial Hospital** (317 Western Blvd., Jacksonville, 910/577-2345, www.onslow.org); in Pender County, **Pender Memorial Hospital** (507 E. Fremont St., Burgaw, 910/259-5451, www.nhrmc.org); and Fayetteville's **Cape Fear Valley Medical Center** (1638 Owen Dr., Fayetteville, 910/615-4000, www.capefearvalley.com). Myrtle Beach, South Carolina, has the **Grand Strand Regional Medical Center** (809 82nd Pkwy., Myrtle Beach, SC, 843/692-1000, www.grandstrandmed.com), not far from the southernmost communities in Brunswick County. In an emergency, of course, call 911.

More information on dining, attractions, and lodging is available through local convention and visitors bureaus: the **Wilmington and Beaches CVB** (505 Nutt St., Unit A, Wilmington, 877/406-2356, www.wilmingtonandbeaches.com, 8:30am-5pm Mon.-Fri., 9am-4pm Sat., 1pm-4pm Sun.), **Brunswick**

County Tourism Development Authority (20 Referendum Dr., Bldg. G, 800/795-7263, www.ncbrunswick.com), and the **Fayetteville**

Area CVB (245 Person St., Fayetteville, 800/255-8217, www.visitfayettevillenc.com, 8am-5pm Mon.-Fri.).

Wilmington

In some ways, Wilmington is a town where time has stood still. During the Civil War, General Sherman's fiery march that razed so many Southern towns missed Wilmington. For most of the 20th century the economy moved in fits and starts with long slumps, standstills, and short boom periods. Surviving the Civil War combined with a slow economy provided Wilmington's architecture with an unexpected benefit: historic preservation. Much of the downtown remains a museum of beautiful buildings dating to the town's first heyday, and that historic appeal accounts for much of its popularity as a destination today.

Things are looking up for Wilmington economically, in part because of the burgeoning film industry. It's not uncommon to see film crews at downtown locations or to run into film stars at local eateries.

HISTORY

Founded in the early 1730s, Wilmington went through a short identity crisis as New Carthage, New Liverpool, and New Town before settling on Wilmington in 1739. Early on it was a deepwater port and quickly became a bustling shipping center for the export of lumber, rice, and naval stores, including turpentine and tar tapped from longleaf pine trees and lumber for ships' keels and ribbing from live oak branches. Wilmington's reputation and commerce grew. By 1769 the town had grown from a collection of wharves, warehouses, and homes into a respectable colonial city, included on a map drawn by acclaimed French cartographer C. J. Sauthier. By 1840 the city was booming, one of the largest in the state, and positioned as the southern terminus of the Wilmington and Weldon Railroad (the 161-mile track was the longest in the world at the time).

During the Civil War the Wilmington and Weldon Railroad line was an essential Confederate artery for trade and troop transport. The Union navy attempted a blockade of the Cape Fear River and inlets up and down the coast, but Wilmington's port was a hive of blockade runners bringing in arms, food, medicine, and materials from Europe and the Caribbean. In January 1865 the Union took nearby Fort Fisher, the key gun emplacement guarding the river's mouth, and Wilmington soon fell. It was a crushing blow to the failing Confederacy. Continued commerce at the port allowed Wilmington to thrive during the Civil War and Reconstruction, unlike many towns in the South; by 1890 the population hit 20,000, making it the largest city in North Carolina.

Political tensions ran high during Reconstruction, and there were conflicts between whites and blacks, Democrats and Republicans, and staunch Confederate supporters and carpetbaggers (Northerners who came to South for economic opportunities) and copperheads (their Southern supporters). In 1898 the only successful coup d'état on American soil took place in the Wilmington Race Riot. White Democrats loyal to the long-dead Confederacy threatened to overthrow the city government if their candidate lost. He did, and two days after the election, a mob of white Democrats and their supporters overthrew the city's Republican government, destroyed the city's African American newspaper, the *Daily Record,* and killed at least 22 African American citizens.

In the early 20th century, North Carolina's power center shifted from the agriculture and shipping at coastal towns like Wilmington to the textile mills and manufacturing of the Piedmont region. Charlotte surpassed

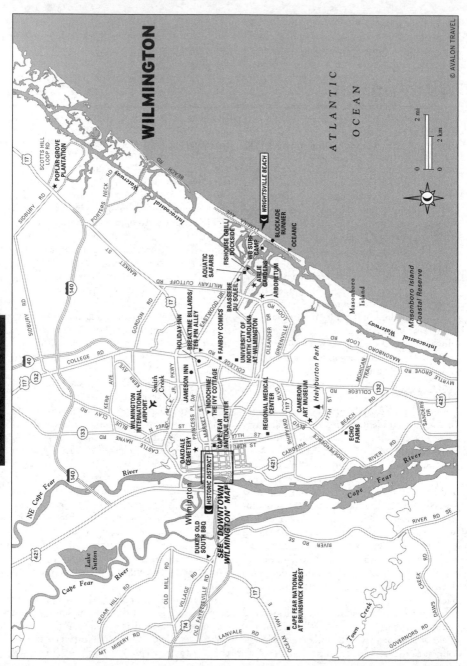

WILMINGTON

ATLANTIC OCEAN

© AVALON TRAVEL

WILMINGTON AND CAPE FEAR

Wilmington in population, interstate highways joined larger cities to the rest of the nation, and economically Wilmington stood still. In 1960 the Atlantic Coast Line Railroad relocated its headquarters to Florida, and the city experienced several decades of decline After I-40 was completed, connecting Wilmington to the rest of the country, the tourism industry began to rise. Wilmington and surrounding towns had a real estate boom in the late 1990s that lasted for several years. At the same time, the film industry grew, boosting the local economy and influencing local culture. Like most of the country, Wilmington was hit hard by the end of the real estate bubble in 2006, and the city is still climbing out from under the wreckage of that widespread economic collapse. There are signs of growth, however, thanks to the University of North Carolina, the tourism and film industries, and the resilience of the people.

SIGHTS
◖ Historic District

Comprising more than 200 blocks, Wilmington's historic district is among the largest in North Carolina. You'll find shady tree-lined streets and a gorgeous collection of antebellum and late Victorian homes, mansions, and commercial buildings. Wilmington is home to the state's largest 19th-century historic district, which includes beautiful examples of pre-Civil War Italianate architecture as well as influences from the French and English Caribbean. Until 1910, Wilmington was the state's most populous city; the earlier boom and subsequent decline are reflected in the architecture, as the city lacks the fine examples of early-20th-century buildings found in cities like Asheville and Charlotte.

The **Bellamy Mansion** (503 Market St., 910/251-3700, www.bellamymansion.org, tours hourly 10am-5pm Tues.-Sat., 1pm-5pm Sun., $10 adults, $4 under age 12) is a superb example of Wilmington's late-antebellum mansions. This porticoed, four-story, 22-room home shows both Greek Revival and Italianate architectural influences and stands as one of the most beautiful Southern city homes of its era. Just two months before North Carolina seceded from the Union in 1861, planter and physician

Bellamy Mansion

© JASON FRYE

WILMINGTON AND CAPE FEAR

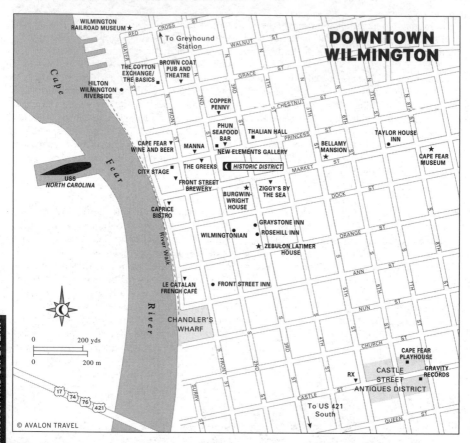

DOWNTOWN WILMINGTON

WILMINGTON RAILROAD MUSEUM ★

To Greyhound Station

THE COTTON EXCHANGE/THE BASICS

BROWN COAT PUB AND THEATRE

HILTON WILMINGTON RIVERSIDE

COPPER PENNY

PHUN SEAFOOD BAR

THALIAN HALL

TAYLOR HOUSE INN

CAPE FEAR WINE AND BEER

MANNA

NEW ELEMENTS GALLERY

BELLAMY MANSION ★

CAPE FEAR MUSEUM ★

THE GREEKS   HISTORIC DISTRICT

CITY STAGE

USS NORTH CAROLINA

FRONT STREET BREWERY

BURGWIN-WRIGHT HOUSE ★

ZIGGY'S BY THE SEA

CAPRICE BISTRO

GRAYSTONE INN

WILMINGTONIAN   ROSEHILL INN

ZEBULON LATIMER HOUSE ★

LE CATALAN FRENCH CAFÉ

FRONT STREET INN

CHANDLER'S WHARF

0   200 yds
0   200 m

CAPE FEAR PLAYHOUSE

RX   CASTLE STREET

GRAVITY RECORDS

CASTLE STREET ANTIQUES DISTRICT

To US 421 South

17 74 76 421

John Bellamy and his family moved into their city home, where they lived until the fall of Fort Fisher and the ensuing fall of Wilmington to the Union. After the war, Bellamy traveled to Washington to ask President Andrew Johnson, a fellow North Carolinian, for a pardon, and used his pardon to recover the home from federal ownership.

In addition to the mansion, another significant building stands on the property: the slave quarters. This two-story brick building is a rare surviving example of urban dwellings for enslaved people, and the interior, which remained largely unchanged through the years, is an important part of the historical record of slavery in the South.

The **Burgwin-Wright House** (224 Market St., 910/762-0570, www.burgwinwrighthouse.com, tours 10am-4pm Tues.-Sat. Feb.-Dec., $10 adults, $5 ages 5-12) is older than the Bellamy Mansion by nearly a century, but it has an oddly similar history. John Burgwin ("ber-GWIN"), a planter and treasurer of the North Carolina colony, built the home in 1770 atop the city's early jail. Soon after, British forces commandeered the home as their headquarters during the Revolutionary War. In 1781, General Cornwallis, then on the last leg of his campaign before falling into George Washington's trap that signaled the end of British occupation, took the house as his headquarters. Joshua Grainger Wright purchased the house in 1799, and it served as a residence until 1937, when the National Society of the Colonial Dames of America purchased the home because of its historic significance.

Like the Bellamy Mansion, the Burgwin-Wright House is a version of the classic white-columned, magnolia-shaded Southern home of the wealthy merchant-planter class, but it's not overly ostentatious. Seven terraced gardens filled with native plants and those grown in the 18th century surround the house; through the years, restoration efforts have helped preserve many original garden structures, including walls, paths, steps, and gates.

Another beautiful home in Wilmington's historic district is the **Zebulon Latimer House** (126 S. 3rd St., 910/762-0492, www.hslcf.org, tours 10am and 3pm Mon.-Fri., hourly 10am-3pm Sat., $10 adults, $5 ages 5-12). Merchant Zebulon Latimer built this home in 1852, and it housed three generations of Latimers, until

1963 when it became a museum and the head-quarters of the Lower Cape Fear Historical Society. In its day the Latimer House was a little more fashion-forward, architecturally speaking, than its neighbors; delicate cast-iron cornices and porch railings speak to both the Italianate and emerging Victorian influences. Also located on the grounds are a two-story brick dwelling for slaves and gardens planted with period-authentic plants.

A **three-house ticket** ($24) to tour the Bellamy Mansion, the Latimer House, and the Burgwin-Wright House is available at the first house you visit; it will save you several dollars if you plan to spend the day touring the historic district. Join the **Historic Wilmington Guided Walking Tour** (910/762-0492, 10am Sat., reservations recommended, $10), departing from the Latimer House.

Just three blocks from the Latimer House is the **Wilmington Riverwalk,** a mile-long riverside promenade that stretches the length of downtown Wilmington, overlooking the Cape Fear River and the battleship USS *North Carolina*. Most of the boutiques, dining, and nightlife in Wilmington are on the Riverwalk or a block from it. A **Visitors Information Booth** (Market St.) or friendly locals can steer you in the right direction.

Wrightsville Beach

A few miles east of Wilmington is one of the nicest beaches on the Carolina coast: **Wrightsville Beach.** Wide and easily accessible, it is one of the most visitor- and family-friendly beaches you'll find. Wrightsville benefits from the proximity of the Gulf Stream; here the warm ocean current sweeping up the Atlantic seaboard lies only 30-40 miles offshore, which means warmer waters that are colored more like the Caribbean.

A number of lodging and rental choices along the beach make it an easy place to stay, and numerous public beach access points (www.towb.org), some of which are disabled-accessible, and some with showers or restrooms, line Lumina Avenue. The largest public parking lot, with 99 spaces, disabled access, showers, and restrooms,

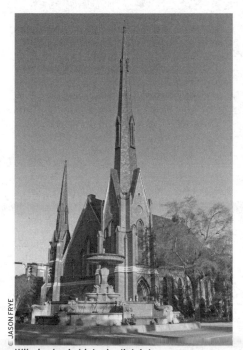

JASON FRYE

Wilmington's historic district

WILMINGTON AND CAPE FEAR

Wilmington Riverwalk

© JASON FRYE

is a Beach Access 4 (2398 N. Lumina Ave.). Beach Access 36 (650 S. Lumina Ave.) has 86 parking spaces, disabled access, showers, and restrooms. On busy days the parking lots can fill up, but trekking from one access point to the next will often yield a spot. To avoid the rush, plan to park before 9am, when you'll be able to grab a spot in most of the lots or on the street.

Historic Sights Around Wilmington

POPLAR GROVE PLANTATION
North of the city, about halfway between Wilmington and Topsail Island, is **Poplar Grove Plantation** (10200 U.S. 17 N., 910/686-9518, www.poplargrove.com, 9am-5pm Mon.-Sat., noon-5pm Sun., $10 adults, $9 seniors and military, $5 ages 6-15, $7 self-guided tour). This antebellum peanut plantation preserves the homestead of a successful farming family, including the beautiful main house, a restored tenant farmer's cabin, a blacksmith's shop, and a barn. A 67-acre nature preserve with an extensive network of hiking trails winds through

coastal forests and wetlands, and a **Farmers Market** (8am-1pm Wed. Apr.-Nov.) shows off the bounty of the area's agriculture.

MOORE'S CREEK NATIONAL BATTLEFIELD
In Wilmington and the surrounding area are a number of significant military sites, most dating to the Revolutionary War and the Civil War. About 20 miles northwest of Wilmington, outside the town of Currie, near Burgaw, is the **Moore's Creek National Battlefield** (40 Patriots Hall Dr., Currie, 910/283-5591, www.nps.gov/mocr, 9am-5pm daily, closed Thanksgiving, Dec. 25, and Jan. 1). The site commemorates the brief but bloody battle of February 1776 between Loyalist Scottish highlanders, kilted and piping and brandishing broadswords, and Patriot colonists. The Patriots fired on the Scotsmen with cannons and muskets as they crossed a bridge over Moore's Creek. Some 30 Loyalists died in the attack, and the remainder scattered into the surrounding swamps and woods. The battle marked an important moment in the

WELCOME TO "HOLLYWOOD EAST"

It all started with a little girl who played with fire. From the ashes of the 1984 feature film *Firestarter*, an adaptation of Stephen King's novel of the same name, Wilmington's film industry grew and North Carolina became a film-friendly state. Wilmington is known as "Hollywood East" for good reason: since that first film, hundreds of films, television programs, reality shows, and music videos have been shot here, and EUE/ScreenGems Studios maintains 10 soundstages on a 50-acre studio lot, the largest outside Los Angeles. Some of the most notable films and television shows shot in Wilmington include:

- *Firestarter*
- *Blue Velvet*
- *Maximum Overdrive*
- *Trick or Treat*
- *Weekend at Bernie's*
- *Teenage Mutant Ninja Turtles*
- *Super Mario Brothers*
- *Billy Bathgate*
- *The Crow*
- *I Know What You Did Last Summer*
- *Summer Catch*

- *Domestic Disturbance*
- *Divine Secrets of the Ya-Ya Sisterhood*
- *Safe Haven*
- *Iron Man 3*
- *Dawson's Creek*
- *One Tree Hill*
- *Eastbound and Down*
- *Revolution*
- *Under the Dome*

Filmed elsewhere in the state, you may have seen:

- *Bull Durham*
- *Cold Mountain*
- *Days of Thunder*
- *The Last of the Mohicans*
- *The Hunger Games*
- *Hannibal*
- *The Green Mile*
- *Evil Dead II*
- *Homeland*
- *Banshee*

Revolutionary War, as the Scottish Loyalists were unable to join General Cornwallis's army in Southport and mount an attack on Patriots nearby. It also marks an important moment in Scottish military history, as the battle was the last major broadsword charge in Scottish history, led by the last Scottish clan army.

USS *NORTH CAROLINA*

Don't be alarmed if you notice a battleship across the Cape Fear River from Wilmington; it's the **USS *North Carolina*** (1 Battleship Rd., Eagles Island, 910/251-5797, www.battleshipnc.com, 8am-8pm daily late May-early Sept., 8am-5pm daily early Sept.-late May, $12 adults, $10 seniors and active or retired military, $6 ages 6-11, free under 5), a decommissioned World War II warship that now serves as a museum and memorial to North Carolinians who died in World War II. This hulking gray colossus participated in every major naval offensive in the Pacific, earning 15 battle stars, and was falsely reported to have sunk six times.

Tours are self-guided and start with a short film providing an overview of the museum, then proceed onto the one-acre deck of the battleship. Nine levels of the battleship are open to explore, including the 16-inch gun turrets on the deck, the bridge, crew quarters, ship's hospital, kitchens, and the magazine, where munitions were stored. It gets tight belowdecks and stairways are quite steep, so visitors prone to claustrophobia and those unable to traverse steep steps may want to stay topside.

© JASON FRYE

Wrightsville Beach

The hallways and quarters below are dark, narrow, and surprisingly deep; from the heart of the ship, it takes more than a few minutes to find your way back to the deck. Crowds can make this more constricting, but nothing like it would have been in the balmy Pacific with 2,000 sailors aboard.

The USS *North Carolina* is also one of North Carolina's most famous haunted houses—reputedly home to several ghosts, seen and heard by staff and visitors alike. The SyFy Channel has featured the ship on various ghost-hunting and paranormal shows, and it has been the subject of extensive investigations. Check out **Haunted NC** (www.hauntednc.com) to hear some chilling and unexplained voices recorded by investigators.

OAKDALE CEMETERY

By the mid-19th century, Wilmington was experiencing growing pains as the bustling shipping and railroad center of North Carolina. The city's old cemeteries were becoming overcrowded with former residents, and **Oakdale Cemetery** (520 N. 15th St., 910/762-5682, www.oakdalecemetery.org, 8am-5pm daily year-round) was founded some distance from downtown to ease the graveyard congestion. Designed in the park-like style of graveyards popular at the time, it was soon filled with superb examples of funerary art—weeping angels, obelisks, willow trees—set off against the natural beauty of the place. Separate sections were reserved for Jewish burials and for victims of the 1862 yellow fever epidemic. Oakdale's website has an interesting guide to Victorian grave art symbolism.

Museums

CAPE FEAR MUSEUM

The **Cape Fear Museum** (814 Market St., 910/798-4350, www.capefearmuseum.com, 9am-5pm Tues.-Sat., 1pm-5pm Sun., $7 adults, $6 seniors, military, and college students, $4 ages 3-17) has exhibits showing the history and ecology of Wilmington and the region, including locally important historical perspectives and the fossil skeleton of a giant ground sloth unearthed in town.

CAMERON ART MUSEUM

The **Cameron Art Museum** (3201 S. 17th St., 910/395-5999, www.cameronartmuseum.com, 10am-5pm Tues.-Wed. and Fri.-Sun., 10am-9pm Thurs., closed July 4, Thanksgiving, Dec. 25, and Jan. 1, $8 adults, $5 seniors, military, and students, $3 ages 2-12) is one of the major art museums in North Carolina. This 42,000-square-foot facility includes a permanent collection of art in a range of styles and media, with an emphasis on North Carolina artists. Artists represented include masters like Mary Cassatt and Utagawa Hiroshige, and North Carolina artists like Claude Howell and Minnie Evans. Special exhibits change throughout the year.

WILMINGTON RAILROAD MUSEUM

The **Wilmington Railroad Museum** (505 Nutt St., 910/763-2634, www.wilmingtonrailroadmuseum.org, hours vary, generally 10am-4pm Mon.-Sat., $8.50 adults, $7.50 seniors and military, $4.50 ages 2-12) sheds light on a largely forgotten part of Wilmington's history: its role as a railroad town. In 1840, Wilmington became the southern terminus for the world's longest continuous rail line, The Wilmington and Weldon (W&W) Railroad, which was an important supply line during the Civil War and one of the reasons Wilmington became a priority target for federal troops. In 1900 the Atlantic Coast Line Railroad absorbed W&W and kept its headquarters in Wilmington until the 1960s, when it moved its offices and employees to Florida, devastating the city's economy for years. On display at the museum are a number of railroad artifacts, including timetables, tools, and locomotives. A classic locomotive, steam engine number 250, has been lovingly restored and maintained and now greets visitors as they enter the museum.

Gardens and Parks

AIRLIE GARDENS

Airlie Gardens (300 Airlie Rd., 910/798-7700, www.airliegardens.org, 9am-5pm daily, closed Thanksgiving Day, Dec. 24-25, Jan. 1,

$5 adults, $3 ages 6-12), a formal garden park dating to 1901, features more than 50,000 azaleas, several miles of walking trails, and grassy areas perfect for picnics and park concerts, including the Summer Concert Series (1st and 3rd Fri. May-Sept., call for hours). Highlights of Airlie Gardens include the Airlie Oak, a massive live oak believed to be 500 years old, and the Minnie Evans Sculpture Garden and Bottle Chapel. Evans, a visionary African American artist whose mystical work is among the best examples of outsider art, was the gatekeeper here for 25 of her 95 years; examples of her work can also be seen at the Cameron Art Museum. Most of the paths and walkways comply with federal disabled-access rules, but for visitors not mobile enough to walk the gardens, trams are available; the tram schedule is listed on the website.

BLUETHENTHAL WILDFLOWER PRESERVE

On the campus of the University of North Carolina Wilmington, you'll find the **Bluethenthal Wildflower Preserve** (601 S. College Rd., University of North Carolina Wilmington campus, located behind the Fisher University Union on Price Dr., 910/962-3000, http://uncw.edu/physicalplant/arboretum/bluethenthal.htm, dawn-dusk daily, free), a small nature preserve with a rich bed of wildflowers and, more importantly, carnivorous plants like the venus fly trap. It's a lovely walk any time of year, though a little buggy if the wind is still. You'll bump into a number of professors and contemplative students.

HALYBURTON PARK

There are a number of parks in and around Wilmington, but many visitors stop by **Halyburton Park** (4099 S. 17th St., 910/341-0075, www.halyburtonpark.com, grounds dawn-dusk daily, nature center 9am-5pm Mon.-Sat.) for the natural landscape made for walking and biking. A 1.3-mile disabled-accessible trail encircles the 58-acre park, while the interior is a spiderweb of trails, both of which

ANOLES OF CAROLINA

© JASON FRYE

anole, dewlap extended

While you're in the Wilmington area, you'll almost certainly run across a few anoles. These tiny bright-green lizards skitter up and down trees and walls and dash along railings–impossibly fast and improbably green. You may hear locals call them "chameleons" because anoles can change their color from bright green to dirt brown as a way to camouflage themselves against the background and guard against predators. If you watch them long enough, you'll see a fascinating courtship and territorial dominance ritual: a male anole will spread his forelegs wide and do several "push-ups," then puff out his little crescent-shaped dewlap, the scarlet pouch beneath the chin. When you see one do this, keep still and keep watching; they often repeat the act several times.

Explorer John Lawson was quite taken with them, as he describes in his 1709 *A New Voyage to Carolina:*

Green lizards are very harmless and beautiful, having a little Bladder under their Throat, which they fill with Wind, and evacuate the same at Pleasure. They are of a most glorious Green, and very tame. They resort to the Walls of Houses in the Summer Season, and stand gazing on a Man, without any Concern or Fear. There are several other Colours of these Lizards, but none so beautiful as the green ones are.

© JASON FRYE

Thalian Hall

provide a glimpse of the Sandhills, Carolina bays (elliptical, often boggy, depressions in the ground), and longleaf pine and oak forest that once dominated the area's landscape.

NEW HANOVER COUNTY ARBORETUM

The **New Hanover County Arboretum** (6206 Oleander Dr., 910/798-7660, dawn-dusk daily) is another popular spot for a stroll or a picnic. The five-acre gardens are also home to a Cooperative Extension horticulture laboratory. Most of the gardens comprise native plants and showcase the floral variety of the area.

ENTERTAINMENT AND EVENTS
Performing Arts

Thalian Hall (310 Chestnut St., 800/523-2820, www.thalianhall.com), the only surviving theater designed by prominent architect John Montague Trimble, has been in near-continuous operation since it opened in 1858. Once serving as the city hall, a library, and an opera house, at the time of its construction it could seat one-tenth of the population of Wilmington, North Carolina's largest city. In its heyday, Thalian Hall was an important stop for theater troupes, productions, and artists touring the country, and today it serves as a major arts venue in the region, hosting a variety of musical acts, ballet, children's theater, and art-house and limited-release films. The resident theatre company, the **Thalian Association** (910/251-1788, www.thalian. org), can trace its roots back to 1788 and is North Carolina's official community theater company.

A number of other theater groups call Thalian Hall home. In 2015 the **Opera House Theatre Company** (910/762-4234, www.operahousetheatrecompany.net) will celebrate its 30th anniversary. Opera House has produced

WILMINGTON AND CAPE FEAR

annual big-name musicals and dramas as well as works by important North Carolinians and other Southern playwrights at Thalian Hall. **Stageworks Youth Theatre** (910/538-8378, www.stageworksyouth.org), a community company comprising actors ages 10 to 17, also calls Thalian Hall home. Stageworks puts on serious dramas, comedies, and musicals and regularly partners with **Cape Fear Shakespeare on the Green** (910/399-2878, www.capefearshakespeare.org) to put on plays by the Bard at Thalian Hall and at Greenfield Lake Amphitheatre.

Being an artsy town with a flair for stage and screen performances, it's no surprise to learn that a lot of theater is produced "off Thalian," as it were. **Big Dawg Productions** (910/367-5237, www.bigdawgproductions.org) puts on several plays each year at their 50-seat Cape Fear Playhouse (613 Castle St.). Plays range from classical to contemporary works. They also host the **New Play Festival** each year, a celebration of first-time productions authored by playwrights under the age of 18. The festival is approaching its 20th anniversary and has seen many works that premiered here go on to wider audiences and acclaim.

City Stage (21 N. Front St., 5th Fl., 910/264-2602, www.citystagenc.com), puts on a number of performances, ranging from edgy musicals like *Hedwig and the Angry Inch* and *The Rocky Horror Picture Show* to comedies and dramas, in a building once owned by Dennis Hopper. Nearby, **Brown Coat Pub and Theatre** (111 Grace St., 910/341-0001, www.browncoattheatre.com, 10pm-2am Mon.-Wed., 7pm-2am Thurs.-Sat., 4pm-2am Sun.) stages all sorts of productions, including musical comedies, Shakespeare, and contemporary plays. They also host a number of other live performance events, including poetry nights, independent and local film screenings, and a live weekly sitcom.

Festivals

Wilmington plays host to a number of small festivals throughout the year, but the crown jewel is the **Azalea Festival** (910/794-4650, www.ncazaleafestival.org), held at venues around the city each April, hopefully coinciding with the blooming of the namesake flowering shrubs. Tours of azalea-laden historic and contemporary homes and gardens draw many visitors, but the street fair, which takes over much of Water Street and a good portion of Front Street, draws many more. With over 200 arts and crafts vendors, countless food vendors, a dedicated children's area, and four stages of entertainment from national and local acts, the street fair is quite a party. Garden tours and the street fair only scratch the surface of what the Azalea Festival has to offer; a parade, a circus, dance competitions, gospel concerts, boxing matches, and fireworks round out Azalea Festival events. And like any self-respecting Southern town, it crowns royalty—in this case, the North Carolina Azalea Festival Queen, a Princess, the Queen's Court, a phalanx of cadets from The Citadel, and 100 Azalea Belles. The Azalea Festival draws more than 300,000 visitors annually, so book accommodations and make dinner reservations well in advance. If you decide to visit the area on a weekend trip in early April, be prepared to find Wilmington far more bustling than normal.

Each October, **Riverfest** (910/452-6862, www.wilmingtonriverfest.com) takes over part of downtown for a street fair that includes art shows; art, crafts, and food vendors; and car shows. It's smaller than the Azalea Festival, but many downtown venues coordinate concerts and events with Riverfest, making downtown more vibrant for the weekend.

What would a film town be without a film festival? The **Cucalorus Film Festival** (910/343-5995, www.cucalorus.org) celebrates independent films and filmmakers each November. About 150 films from national and international indie filmmakers are shown, along with panels featuring filmmakers, writers, and actors, at Thalian Hall and other venues around town. In a short time Cucalorus has garnered the attention of major film-industry publications and has been called "one of the 25 coolest film festivals."

© JASON FRYE

The Azalea Festival in Wilmington draws more than 300,000 visitors annually.

In the town of Hampstead, between Wilmington and Topsail Island, the annual **North Carolina Spot Festival** (www.ncspotfestival.com) celebrates the spot, a small fish that's a traditional staple of coastal Carolina. For more than 50 years, hundreds of people have gathered here at the end of September to deep-fry and gobble up spot. The festival features art and crafts vendors, a pageant, concerts, and fireworks, but the fun is in eating spot.

Burgaw, a tiny town 30 minutes north of Wilmington, is home to the **North Carolina Blueberry Festival** (www.ncblueberryfestival.com) each June. Live music, food vendors, and loads of products featuring blueberries—soap, barbecue sauce, ice cream, muffins—make up this festival. Along with the Spot Festival, the Blueberry Festival is a great small-town festival experience.

Nightlife

Ziggy's By The Sea (208 Market St., 910/769-4096, http://ziggysbythesea.com, box office noon-5pm Mon.-Fri., doors generally open

around 8 p.m. with shows starting shortly thereafter, cash only, credit card users should purchase online) hosts live music in a renovated building in the historic district.

Craft beer fans will want to pull up a barstool at **Cape Fear Wine and Beer** (139 N. Front St., 910/763-3377, www.capefearwineandbeer.net, 4pm-2am Mon.-Wed., 1pm-2am Thurs.-Sun.), a spot that's more punk than trendy, but one that welcomes beer lovers of any ilk. The bartenders know their brews and can guide you to one you like from their vast collection of bottled and draft beers. You'll find rare microbrews, meads, and barley wines from around the world, but you'll also find a strong emphasis on the best North Carolina beers. Throughout the week, Cape Fear Wine and Beer runs specials on beer flights, chair massages, and North Carolina beer, among others. Get here early and spend a little time talking to the bartender to find your perfect brew. Don't be shy about asking for a sample pour of a draft beer if you're unsure.

Just down the street, **Front Street Brewery**

(9 N. Front St., 910/251-1935, www.frontstreetbrewery.com, 11:30am-midnight daily) serves lunch and dinner, and as good as the pulled-chicken nachos are, the best part about Front Street Brewery is the *kölsch*, IPA, pilsner, and seasonal beers brewed on-site; you can tour the brewery and get a sample to wet your whistle 3pm-5pm every afternoon.

On the other end of town, **Satellite Bar and Lounge** (120 Greenfield St., www.satellitebarandlounge.com, 4pm-2am Mon.-Sat., 2pm-2am Sun.) draws a diverse hip crowd to this former industrial space. The rustic decor matches the large selection of bottled and canned beer, and an outdoor seating area allows the bar, which can get crowded, to breathe. Local food trucks swing by on a rotating basis to serve grub to the late-night crowd, and on Sunday, the Satellite Bluegrass Band treats patrons to an extended and lively bluegrass jam session. Satellite is on the outskirts of Wilmington, bordering some less than savory neighborhoods, so it's best to call a cab or bring a designated driver.

Breaktime Billiards/Ten Pin Alley (127 S. College Rd., 910/452-5455, www.breaktimetenpin.com, billiards and bowling 11am-2am daily, lounge 6pm-2am Mon.-Fri., 11am-2am Sat.-Sun.) is a 30,000-square-foot entertainment palace, with 24 billiard tables and one regulation-size snooker table, 24 bowling lanes and skee-ball, and between them the Lucky Strike Lounge, a full bar and snack shop with all manner of video games and which hosts soft-tip dart and foosball tournaments. Put in an order for a meal and a beer or cocktail, and the staff will bring it to you if you're in the middle of a game.

SHOPPING
Shopping Centers
The group of buildings known as **The Cotton Exchange** (Front St. and Grace St., 910/343-9896, www.shopcottonexchange.com, 10am-5:30pm Mon.-Sat., noon-4pm Sun.) has housed a variety of businesses in 150 years of continuous operation: the largest flour and hominy mill in the south, a printing company, a Chinese laundry, a "mariners saloon" (where they served more refreshment than just beer), and, of course, a cotton exchange. Today, dozens of boutiques and restaurants call these historic buildings home. **Caravan Beads** (O'Brien Building, 910/343-3000) has an impressive selection of beads and beading materials; **Down to Earth** (O'Brien Building, 910/251-0041) carries essential oils and will make custom blends in-house for you; and **Occasions—Just Write** (O'Brien Building, 910/343-9033) is a great shop for writers and stationery lovers.

Near Wrightsville Beach, the boutique shops and restaurants of **Lumina Station** (1900 Eastwood Rd., 910/256-0900, www.luminastation.com, 10am-6pm Mon.-Sat.) can keep shoppers busy for an afternoon. Some of Wilmington's nicest boutiques call Lumina Station home, including **Island Passage** (Suite 8, 910/256-0407, www.islandpassageclothing.com), specializing in women's wear; **Ziabird** (Suite 9, 910/208-9650, www.ziabird.com), which carries beautiful jewelry and accessories from local designers; and **Airlie Moon** (1908 Eastwood Rd., 910/256-0655, www.airliemoon.com), a purveyor of chic coastal home goods,.

Mayfaire Town Center (6861 Main St., 910/256-5131, www.mayfairetown.com, 10am-9pm Mon.-Sat., noon-6 Sun.) is a Main Street-meets-the mall shopping center, with a familiar range of shops, but one of my favorites is **Brilliant Sky Toys** (910/509-3353, www.wilmingtontoystores.com), a store packed with toys, games, and puzzles for kids. The 16-screen movie theater, wide selection of shops to browse, and numerous restaurants in Mayfaire make it an easy place to spend part of a day shopping, dining, and taking in a movie, alone or in a group.

Antiques and Consignment Stores
On Castle Street, along the southern edge of the historic district, an expanding group of antiques shops, restaurants, and stores, all

clustered in a three- or four-block stretch, have emerged in recent years. **Michael Moore Antiques** (539 Castle St., 910/763-0300, 10am-6pm Mon.-Sat. 1pm-6pm Sun.) carries a collection of pristine furniture, as do many of the antiques stores in the area. Be sure to stop in **Maggy's Antiques and Collectibles** (507 Castle St., 910/343-5200, 10am-5pm Tues.-Sat., 1pm-5pm Sun.), which occupies an old church building, and **Castle Corner Antiques** (555 Castle St., 910/815-6788, 10am-5pm Mon.-Sat., 1pm-5pm Sun.).

In the riverfront area, **Silk Road Antiques** (103 S. Front St., 910/343-1718, 10:30am-5pm Mon.-Sat., 10:30am-4pm Sun.) and **Antiques of Old Wilmington** (25 S. Front St., 910/763-6011, 10am-6pm daily in summer, 10am-5pm daily in winter) are only a block apart, one block from the Riverwalk, and surrounded by great restaurants and coffee shops.

On Market Street, heading away from downtown, you'll find **Cape Fear Antique Center** (1606 Market St., 910/763-1837, 10am-5:30pm Mon.-Sat., noon-5pm Sun.), an antiques shop that specializes in vintage home furnishings, from bedroom and dining room furniture to desks and armoires. They also have a nice selection of antique jewelry.

A little farther up Market Street, **The Ivy Cottage** (3020, 3030, 3100 Market St., 910/815-0907, www.threecottages.com, 10am-5pm Mon.-Fri., 10am-6pm Sat., 12am-5pm Sun.) occupies a trio of buildings and an overflow warehouse, all filled with antiques and consignment furniture. In Cottage 2, you'll find antique jewelry as well as an extensive collection of crystal stemware and decanters; I found my favorite decanter in Cottage 2. At Cottage 3, you'll find more beachy, shabby-chic furniture and home goods, while Cottage 1 carries more armoires, dressers, and knickknacks. It's worth a stop to snoop and explore; you never know what you'll find.

Books and Comics

Wilmington has an active and vibrant literary culture. The University of North Carolina Wilmington is home to a creative writing program of growing renown, and the town several good bookstores. **McAllister & Solomon** (4402-1 Wrightsville Ave., 910/350-0189, www.mcallisterandsolomon.com, 10am-6pm Mon.-Sat.) stocks over 20,000 used and rare books and is quite a treat to explore if you're a bibliophile. Nearby, **Pomegranate Books** (4418 Park Ave., 910/452-1107, www.pombooks.net, 10am-6pm Mon.-Sat.) hosts readings by local writers and boasts a good selection of literary work by local and regional authors. **Two Sisters Bookery** (318 Nutt St., Cotton Exchange, 910/762-4444, www.twosistersbookery.com, 10am-5:30pm Mon.-Sat., noon-4pm Sun.) carries books covering all genres and subject matters and is a great place to pick up a best-seller. **Old Books on Front Street** (249 N. Front St., 910/762-6657, www.oldbooksonfrontst.com, 9am-9pm Mon.-Sat., noon-9pm Sun.) is a used bookstore with nearly two miles of books on their floor-to-ceiling shelves. Knowledgeable staff and extensive selection make this a must-stop for book lovers.

Fanboy Comics (419 S. College Rd., University Landing, 910/452-7828, www.fanboycomics.biz, 11am-7pm Mon.-Tues., 10am-9pm Wed., 11am-7pm Thurs.-Sat.) specializes in buying and selling Silver and Bronze Age super-hero comics, a period beginning in the 1950s and ending, at least in terms of Fanboy's stock, around 1977. The owner and staff know their comics and can point out the finer details of this era's stories and art, such as the character development of the heroes and various stylistic innovations. There are also contemporary comics and books about comic book characters, art, and storytelling.

Galleries and Art Studios

New Elements Art Gallery (201 Princess St., 910/343-8997, www.newelementsgallery.com, 11am-6pm Tues.-Sat.) has been showcasing works by local and regional artists since 1985. Featuring contemporary art in a wide range of styles and media, New Elements remains an influential gallery today, and openings are well attended. With art that includes the avant-garde, classical plein air oil paintings, and wire or ceramic sculptures, they always have something you'll want to take home.

Between Wilmington and Wrightsville is **The Gallery at Racine** (203 Racine Dr., 910/452-2073, www.galleryatracine.com, 11am-5pm Tues.-Fri., 10am-5pm Sat.-Sun.), a huge gallery with works ranging in price from $8 to $150,000 and ranging in style from folk art to fine blown glass. The gallery features only local and regional artists and is an excellent way to get a feel for a broad spectrum of the area's arts scene.

Perhaps the most interesting art studio in Wilmington is **Acme Art Studios** (711 N. 5th Ave., 910/232-0027, www.acme-art-studios.com). This shared space is home to a dozen or more artists working in media such as oils, tintype photography, sculpture, and printmaking. Open to the public only for Wilmington's Fourth Friday Gallery Crawl (910/343-0998, http://artscouncilofwilmington.org, 6pm-9pm fourth Friday of each month) and exhibit openings, the work coming out of Acme is some of the best in the region.

Barouke (119 S. Water St. in the Old City Market, 910/762-4999, www.barouke.com, 10am-6pm Sun.-Thurs., 10am-9pm Fri. and Sat.) carries handcrafted works by master woodworkers, including hand-turned pens and vases, clocks, decorative bowls, boxes, games, kitchen accessories, and more. Most everything is finished in such a way as to allow the wood's natural beauty to show through.

River to Sea Gallery (225 S. Water St., in Chandler's Wharf, 910/763-3380, www.rivertoseagallery.com, 10am-5pm Mon.-Sat., 1pm-4pm Sun.) carries works from around three dozen local artists. You'll find serious art photography and plein air paintings alongside whimsical ceramic and knit pieces and illustrative art.

Music

With the advent of digital music, most of Wilmington's music stores are gone, but

Gravity Records (612 Castle St., 910/343-1000, 9am-6pm Mon.-Sat., noon-6pm Sun.), has held on, carving out a niche for itself by stocking LPs and CDs by the most relevant contemporary artists. If you want to know what to listen to next, the staff at Gravity Records can turn you on to it. They've got a huge stock of vinyl as well as an impressive selection of new and used CDs.

SPORTS AND RECREATION
Masonboro Island

Just a few minutes' boat ride or a 30-minute paddleboard or kayak ride from Wrightsville Beach brings you to Masonboro Island. Masonboro is an 8.5-mile-long undeveloped barrier island that is fantastic for shelling, birding, surfing, and camping. Get here via your own boat, kayak, or paddleboard, or catch a lift with **Wrightsville Beach Scenic Tours** (275 Waynick Blvd., Wrightsville Beach, 910/200-4002, www.wrightsvillebeachscenictours.com, water taxi $20), docking across the street from the Blockade Runner and offering a shuttle to and from the island three times daily Monday-Saturday during summer. The boat leaves Wrightsville Beach at 9am, 12:30pm, and 2pm, and departs Masonboro at 11:30am, 2:30pm, and 5pm. If you go over, you'll be there for a while, so pack a cooler with plenty of water, and remember your sunscreen. Wrightsville Beach Scenic Tours also offers a number of other tours for adults and for families, including birding tours ($35) in and around Masonboro Island, shelling tours, pirate tours ($30 adults, $20 kids), and sunset tours ($25).

In Wilmington you can tour the Cape Fear River with **Wilmington Water Tours** (212 S. Water St., Cape Fear Riverwalk, 910/338-3134, www.wilmingtonwatertours.net, $10-35 adults, $5-16.50 kids). From the comfort of the 46-foot catamaran *Wilmington* you can learn more about the Cape Fear River, its tributaries, and the history of the surrounding land. Bring your binoculars and a zoom lens for your camera because you'll spot ospreys, eagles, and other birds on your trip.

Surfing

East Coast surfers love Wrightsville Beach because the waves are consistent and the surf is fun year-round. If you've never tried hanging 10, join one of the many surf camps in the area and they'll have you in the water and riding a wave in no time. **WB Surf Camp** (222 Causeway Dr., 910/256-7873, www.wbsurfcamp.com, camps from $200-600, more for overnight or travel camps) is one of the largest surfing schools in the area, with a large number of classes, including one-day, week-long, kids-only, teens-only, women-only, and family camps. **Crystal South Surf Camp** (Public Access 39, Wrightsville Beach, 910/465-9638, www.crystalsouthsurfcamp.com) offers individual five-day instruction for all ages ($265).

Kayaking and Stand-Up Paddleboarding

With miles of winding marsh creeks around Masonboro Island and lining the shores of the Intracoastal Waterway, there's no shortage of areas to explore by kayak or stand-up paddleboard. Several outfitters lead tours, provide lessons, and rent out all the gear you'll need to get on the water. **Hook, Line and Paddle** (435 Eastwood Rd., 910/792-6945; 275 Waynick Blvd., 910/685-1983, www.hooklineandpaddle.com, fishing kayaks $50 half day to $155 weekly, single kayaks $40 half day to $130 weekly, double kayaks $60 half day to $160 weekly, tours $45-75, fishing guide $175 for 5 hours) leads group tours around Wrightsville Beach and Masonboro Island and has a variety of kayaks for rent, including fishing kayaks, sit-in and sit-on kayaks, and double kayaks. **Mahanaim Adventures** (910/547-8252, www.mahanaimadventures.com, from $55 for half day and $90 for full day, $150 and up for overnight trips) offers kayak trips on the rivers and in the swamps and creeks inland from the area's beaches. **Town Creek, Three Sisters Swamp,** and **Black River** expeditions are fun and take you into parts of the coastal landscape you'd otherwise never see.

© JASON FRYE

Blackwater creeks like Town Creek are great for kayaking.

For a different type of paddling experience, try stand-up paddleboarding. Stand-up paddleboards resemble oversize surfboards that you propel with a long paddle, and they can take you anywhere a kayak can go. **Wrightsville SUP** (275 Waynick Blvd., 910/378-9283, www.wrightsvillesup.com, lessons $80 for two hour instructional tour, $20/hour rentals, $15/hour for return customers) rents out paddleboards and provides lessons, as does Hook, Line and Paddle (rentals $60/half day to $160/week). It looks difficult at first, but once you get the hang of it, you'll gain confidence quickly.

Diving

The warm, clear water along North Carolina's coast beckons divers from the world over, and the abundance of shipwrecks, ledges, and natural formations off the coast of Wrightsville Beach make it an ideal location for diving. **Aquatic Safaris** (7220 Wrightsville Ave., Suite A, 910/392-4386, www.aquaticsafaris.com, 9am-7pm Mon.-Fri., 6:30am-6pm Sat., 6:30am-5pm Sun. summer, 10am-6pm Mon.-Fri., 10am-5pm Sat., noon-4pm Sun. off-season, beginner open water classes $295, rental gear $10-50, charters $50-145) has been getting divers in the water since 1988, visiting sites from 3 to 59 miles offshore in water as shallow as 25 feet or as deep as 130 feet. They rent out gear, give classes that will have beginners in open water in as few as three days, and provide charter services to two dozen offshore sites.

Evolve Freediving (910/358-4300, www.evolvefreediving.com, introductory freediving $350) offers an entirely different undersea experience. In free diving, all you have is a mask, fins, a wetsuit, and a deep breath, because you dive without an air tank. Husband and wife duo Ren and Ashley Chapman (she holds multiple world records for free dives, including diving 266 and 269 feet deep on a single breath) teach courses that will have novices holding their breath for more than two minutes and diving up to 66 feet in a couple of days. This is not a sport for the faint of heart, but it is exciting and challenging.

Golf

One of the best things about the Wilmington region is the weather, perfect for both the beach and the golf course. In the winter the weather is mild enough to play anytime, and in the summer the courses are immaculate, and it doesn't get all that hot on the greens. Hit the links at **Beau Rivage** (649 Rivage Promenade, 910/392-9021, www.beaurivagegolf.com, 18 holes, par 72, greens fees $20-60), just south of Wilmington, halfway to Kure Beach; it's a lovely and reasonably priced course with challenging holes. Risk-taking players will enjoy taking shots over water hazards on several holes, including one par 3 that will put your ball in the drink if you don't land it just right.

Echo Farms (4114 Echo Farms Rd., 910/791-9318, www.echofarmsnc.com, 18 holes, par 72, greens fees $19-40), also south of Wilmington, is another fun fast-paced course. The Donald Ross-designed **Wilmington Municipal Golf Course** (311 S. Wallace Ave., 910/791-0558, 18 holes, par 71, greens fees $7-26) features forgiving fairways and on more than one hole raises the classic question "Can I carry that bunker?" North of Wilmington, **Castle Bay** (107 Links Court, 910/270-1978, www.castlebaycc.com, 18 holes, par 72, greens fees $35-39 Mon.-Thurs., $42-48 Fri.-Sun., includes cart) offers a different round of golf. As a Scottish links-style course, it's level, open, and full of deep bunkers, water, and waste areas. The wind can be a factor here, but it's a beautiful course where you can play a round unlike any other in the area.

Spectator Sports

Wilmington has its own professional basketball team, the **Wilmington Sea Dawgs** (910/791-6523, www.goseadawgs.com), part of the Tobacco Road Basketball League. They play downtown in the Schwartz Center at Cape Fear Community College (601 N. Front St.). In baseball, the **Wilmington Sharks** (910/343-5621, www.wilmingtonsharks.com, reserved seats $8 adults, $7 seniors, military, and ages 1-12, general admission $6 adults, $5 seniors, military, and ages 6-12, free under age

6) play in the Coastal Plain League. Home games are played at Legion Sports Complex (2131 Carolina Beach Rd.). Also playing at the Legion Sports Complex are the **Wilmington Hammerheads** (910/777-2111, www.wilmingtonhammerheads.com, $12 adults, $10 seniors, $8 children), a professional soccer team in the United Soccer Leagues Pro division.

Each summer in early July, rugby teams from around the world descend on Wilmington for the **Cape Fear Sevens Tournament** (http://fear7s.com), a stripped-down, fast-paced form of rugby that showcases the best in speed, tackles, and ball handling, it's a fun, free event that serves to introduce newcomers to the sport and give rugby fans a charge. In the past it has been held at Ogden Park (7069 Market St.), but check the website for the date and location of this two-day tournament.

ACCOMMODATIONS
Bed-and-Breakfasts
Wilmington's Historic District is large and filled with historic bed-and-breakfasts. Check with the **Wilmington and Beaches Convention and Visitors Bureau** (www.wilmingtonandbeaches.com) for a comprehensive listing of area lodging.

◖ **Front Street Inn** (215 S. Front St., 800/336-8184, www.frontstreetinn.com, $139-239) is a tiny boutique B&B only a block from the Riverwalk and a short stroll to a number of notable restaurants and charming shops. It occupies an old Salvation Army building and offers bright, airy guest rooms in a great location. The **Wilmingtonian** (101 S. 2nd St., 800/525-0909, www.thewilmingtonian.com, $155-175) is a three-building complex closer to the heart of downtown offering beautiful guest rooms and locally roasted coffee with breakfast. The **Rosehill Inn Bed and Breakfast** (114 S. 3rd St., 800/815-0250, www.rosehill.com, $139-199) occupies a gorgeous 1848 home only three blocks from the river. The flowery high-B&B-style decor suits the house.

The **Taylor House Inn** (14 N. 7th St., 800/382-9982, www.taylorhousebb.com, $125-250) is in a newer home that dates to 1905.

Despite this relative novelty it's a pretty but not ostentatious building, unlike some of the homes nearby. The famous **Graystone Inn** (100 S. 3rd St., 888/763-4773, www.graystoneinn.com, $159-379) was built in the same year as the Taylor House Inn but with a very different aesthetic. Solid stone and castle-like, the Graystone has beautiful guest rooms in a beautiful home only blocks from good restaurants, shopping, and nightlife. **Angie's B&B** (1704 Market St., 901/762-5790, www.angiesbandb.com, $139-179) is just out of downtown in a more residential but no less charming section of Wilmington. The home and grounds are owned by local restaurateurs, and the breakfast they deliver is out of this world.

Hotels
An upscale place to stay is the **Hilton Wilmington Riverside** (301 N. Water St., 910/763-5900, www.wilmingtonhilton.com, rooms from $169), located right on the river so that many of the guest rooms have stunning river views; others enjoy a beautiful cityscape. The Riverwalk is right out the door, putting the restaurants and nightlife of downtown Wilmington only a short walk away, along with the on-site Ruth's Chris Steakhouse.

At Wrightsville Beach, it's hard to beat the **Blockade Runner** (275 Waynick Blvd., 800/541-1161, www.blockade-runner.com, $169-479). From the outside it looks like any other 1960s hotel, but inside it's chic, stylish, and comfortable. Every guest room has a great view—the Atlantic Ocean and sunrise on one side, the Intracoastal Waterway and sunsets on the other—and with several adventure outfitters operating in the hotel, recreation options abound. The hotel restaurant, East, is a hidden gem in Wilmington's dining scene.

There are plenty of more affordable options available just a couple of miles out of downtown. The **Holiday Inn** (5032 Market St., 866/893-2703, wilmingtonhi.com, $97) on Market Street is clean, comfortable, close to downtown, and minutes from the beach. The **Jameson Inn** (5102 Dunlea Court, 910/452-5660, www.jamesoninns.com, from $77) is another affordable option, although it can be hard to find. From Market Street, turn onto New Centre Drive and look for the sign across the street from Target.

FOOD
French
For a town of its size, Wilmington has a surprising number of good restaurants. Downtown, **Caprice Bistro** (10 Market St., 910/815-0810, www.capricebistro.com, 5pm-10pm Sun.-Thurs., 5pm-11pm Fri.-Sat., bar until 2am daily, entrées $14-24) serves some delicious traditional French cuisine and has an extensive wine list. Upstairs, an intimate bar lined with sofas and a scattering of tables serves a limited menu but is one of the more relaxed places to grab a quick bite and a drink downtown. This is one of the best restaurants downtown.

Just a few blocks away on the Riverwalk, **Le Catalan French Café** (224 S. Water St., 910/815-0200, www.lecatalan.com, lunch and dinner from 11:30am Tues.-Sat., $5-15) serves small plates of classic French food such as quiches, cassoulet, and a well-known chocolate mousse. As good as the food is at Le Catalan, the location and the view are even better. Situated right on the Riverwalk, their outdoor seating area is the perfect place to enjoy the sunset and a glass of wine.

One of the best restaurants in Wilmington is **Ⅽ Brasserie du Soleil** (1908 Eastwood Rd., 910/256-2226, www.brasseriedusoleil.com, lunch 11:30am-5pm Mon.-Sat., dinner 5pm-10pm Sun.-Thurs., dinner 5pm-11pm Fri.-Sat., entrées $12-32), a brasserie-style French restaurant that utilizes the best ingredients from local, regional, and small-farm sources to create food that will keep you coming back. Personal favorites include the duck and flounder for dinner, and the burgers—three sliders made of either lamb, short ribs, or salmon—or a build-your-own-salad for lunch. For dessert, the mini chocolate pots de crème (served in a shot glass) is the way to go. When the weather's nice, enjoy your meal at one of the outdoor tables.

Italian
Two good Italian restaurants in Wilmington are **Terrazzo Trattoria** (1319 Military Cutoff Rd., 910/509-9400, www.terrazzatrattoria. com, dinner from 5pm Mon. and Sat., lunch and dinner 11:30am-10pm Tues.-Fri., entrées $10-30) and **Osteria Cicchetti** (1125-K Military Cutoff Rd., 910/256-7476, www.osteria-cicchetti.com, lunch 11:30am-4pm Mon.-Fri., dinner from 5pm daily, entrées $11-21). They're both popular and can get crowded even on weeknights, so reservations are recommended, especially in summer. Terrazzo's veal margherita, linguini filleto de pomodoro, or neapolitan pizza are good choices for dinner. At Osteria Cicchetti, or OC as it's known to regulars, the pizzas are rustic and a perfect starter (try the Soprano or the Parma); for pasta, the linguini with clams or spaghetti cicchetti, with meatballs and sausage, make great meals.

Seafood
Near Wrightsville Beach, **Fishouse Grill** (1410 Airlie Rd., 910/256-3693, www.thefishhousegrill.com, lunch and dinner from 11:30am daily, entrées $6-18) and **Dockside** (1308 Airlie Rd., 910/256-2752, www.thedockside.com, 11am-9pm daily, entrées $7-24), two restaurants only steps apart on the Intracoastal Waterway, deliver good food and great views. At Fishouse, the food is a little more casual, with a menu that focuses on burgers and sandwiches; Dockside focuses more on seafood, and their elevated deck gives you a bird's-eye view of passing boats while you dine.

On Wrightsville Beach proper, **Oceanic** (703 S. Lumina Ave., 910/256-5551, www.oceanicrestaurant.com, 11am-11pm Mon.-Sat., 10am-10pm Sun., entrées $8-32) serves seafood with fine fusion preparations and stunning ocean views. The restaurant is in an old pier house with a good portion of the restored Crystal Pier jutting out into the ocean. Tables on the pier are ideal when the weather is nice, but they go fast, so make a reservation or come early if you want to dine on the deck.

Southern and Barbecue

Downtown at the Cotton Exchange, **The Basics** (319 N. Front St., 910/343-1050, www.thebasicswilmington.com, 8am-9pm Mon.-Thurs., 8am-10pm Fri., 10am-10pm Sat., 10am-4pm Sun., entrées $10-18) serves up classic Southern comfort food, including lunch, dinner, and Sunday brunch. If breakfast is what you're craving, look no further than the **Dixie Grill** (116 Market St., 910/762-7280, 8am-3pm Mon.-Sat., 8am-2pm Sun., $4-13). This old-fashioned diner is a fixture for locals and visitors alike, and on the weekend there can be a wait; it's worth it. For gussied-up Southern food, head to **Rx** (421 Castle St., 910/399-3080, www.rxwilmington. com, 11:30am-10pm Tues.-Thurs. and Sun., 11:30am-1am Fri.-Sat., entrées around $25). Their cast iron skillet-fried chicken is hard to beat, and their innovative takes on classic Southern dishes will make you look at the region's cuisine in a new light.

What's a visit to North Carolina without barbecue? Fortunately, two great barbecue restaurants near downtown serve up eastern North Carolina 'cue (a style that relies on a thin, spicy, vinegar-based sauce) and all the fixin's, buffet style. **Casey's Buffet Barbecue and Home Cookin'** (5559 Oleander Dr., 910/798-2913, lunch Tues.-Sat., dinner Wed.-Sun., under $10), in Wilmington, delivers a feast of barbecue, Brunswick stew, fried chicken, okra, collard greens, and more. Adventurous non-Southerners will want to try chitterlings (pronounced "CHIT-lins," but you already knew that) and chicken gizzards; Casey's is a rare opportunity to try these Southern and soul food staples. Just across the Cape Fear River in the town of Leland, 【 **Duke's Old South BBQ** (318 Village Rd., Leland, 910/833-8321, www. dukesoldsouthbbq.com, 11am-9pm Wed.-Sat., 11am-3pm Sun., buffet $9) serves both eastern North Carolina and South Carolina (known for a sweeter, often mustard-based sauce) 'cue, fried chicken, and some great 'nanner pudding. Duke's barbecue is some of the best in the area, take it from me: I'm a certified North Carolina barbecue judge.

Eclectic American

Wilmington native Keith Rhodes, a James Beard Award semifinalist and a *Top Chef* contender, owns two restaurants in Wilmington, both of which serve his "Viet-South" cuisine, a fusion of Vietnamese flavors and Southern ingredients and techniques. **Catch** (6623 Market St., 910/799-3847, www.catchwilmington.com, lunch 11:30am-2pm Tues.-Fri., dinner from 5:30pm Mon.-Sat., entrées around $28), his flagship restaurant, is more formal than **Phun Seafood Bar** (215 Princess St., 910/762-2841, www.phunrestaurant.com, lunch 11:30am-2:30pm Mon.-Fri., dinner 5pm-10pm Wed.-Sat., entrées around $22), but both restaurants use locally caught seafood and other fresh local ingredients. At Catch, you can't go wrong with anything served alongside Rhodes's grits, and at Phun, the duck noodle bowl is a hit.

Down the street from Phun is **Manna** (123 Princess St., 910/763-5252, www.mannaavenue.com, dinner from 5:30pm Tues.-Sun., entrées around $28), an innovative restaurant that also focuses on local seasonal ingredients. Their menu is playful, with dishes like Snapper John MD and Iron Chef: Bobby Filet, but the food is seriously good. One of the few bars in Wilmington where making a cocktail is treated as an art, this is definitely a restaurant where you'll want to show up early and enjoy a drink at the bar. Reservations are advised.

Across the street from Manna, 【 **The Greeks** (124 Princess St., 910/343-6933, www. the-greeks.com, 10am-3pm Mon., 10am-9pm Tues.-Sun., entrées around $9) offers a completely different dining experience: a diner serving classic Greek dishes. The Authentic, a pork gyro loaded with tomato, onion, french fries, and mustard, is a dish the owner grew up eating in Greece and is a popular choice. But if you love falafel, theirs is the best in town, hands down.

One block over, the **Copper Penny** (109 Chestnut St., 910/762-1373, www.copperpennync.com, lunch and dinner from 11am Mon.-Sat., from noon Sun., entrées $10-15) serves traditional pub grub in a traditional pub atmosphere. It can get crowded and loud, especially on game days, but the food, especially their cheesesteak, chicken wings, and fish-and-chips, make any wait worth it.

Circa 1922 (8 N. Front St., 910/762-1922, www.circa1922.com, 5pm-10pm Sun.-Thurs., 5pm-11pm Fri.-Sat., brunch 10am-3pm Sun., entrées $13-21, 3-course prix fixe $23), an eclectic restaurant serving tapas-style small plates as well as traditional entrées, has a menu driven by seasonal availability. The small plates naturally encourage sharing, making this a great downtown place to grab an intimate meal with friends.

Flaming Amy's Burrito Barn (4002 Oleander Dr., 910/799-2919, www.flamingamysburritobarn.com, 11am-10pm daily) is, in their own words, "Hot, fast, cheap, and easy." They've got a long menu with 20 specialty burritos (Greek, Philly steak, Thai), eight fresh salsas, and bottled and on-tap beers. It's inexpensive—you can eat well for under $10, drinks included. Frequent special promotions include Tattoo Tuesdays: if you show the cashier your tattoo, they discount your meal by 10 percent.

CAM Café (3201 S. 17th St., 910/777-2363, www.camcafe.org, 11am-3pm Tues.-Sat., dinner 5pm-9pm Thurs., lunch $12 and under, dinner around $15) is one of the best spots in town for lunch. Housed inside the Cameron Art Museum, the CAM Café offers an upscale lunch that features everything from fish tacos to vegetarian and even vegan options. The menu, which changes frequently, is often inspired by the art museum's current special exhibits.

Asian

Where Catch and Phun take Asian cuisine and blend it with Southern food culture, a number of Asian restaurants in Wilmington stay true to their roots. **Indochine** (7 Wayne Dr., at Market St., 910/251-9229, www.indochinewilmington.com, lunch 11am-2pm Tues.-Fri., noon-3pm Sat., dinner 5pm-10pm daily, entrées $11-20) serves an expansive menu of Thai and Vietnamese dishes as well as a number of vegetarian options. Entrées are huge, so

sharing is encouraged, but even then, be prepared for leftovers. **Big Thai 2** (1319 Military Cutoff Rd., 910/256-6588, www.bigthaiwilmington.com, lunch 11am-2:30pm Mon.-Sat., dinner 5pm-9:30pm Mon.-Thurs., 5pm-10pm Fri.-Sat., noon-9:30pm Sun., entrées around $14) has delicious and authentic pad thai and massaman curry, and their coconut cake is a great way to end the meal.

Blue Asia (341 S. College Rd., 910/799-0002, www.blueasia.info, 11am-10pm Mon.-Wed., 11am-10:30pm Thurs.-Sat., noon-10pm Sun., entrées around $15) serves pan-Asian cuisine but focuses primarily on Japanese and Chinese dishes. Sushi lovers will appreciate the all-you-can-eat sushi lunch and dinner.

Nikki's Restaurant and Sushi Bar (16 S. Front St., 910/772-9151, www.nikkissushibar.com, 11am-10pm Mon.-Thurs., 11am-11pm Fri. and Sat., noon-10pm Sun., $5-25) is a longtime downtown Wilmington favorite. Serving up sushi, a wide selection of vegetarian dishes, bento boxes and other Asian-inspired plates, Nikki's has built a reputation for good food and cold sake.

NORTH OF WILMINGTON
Topsail Island

If you want to say it like a local, Topsail is pronounced "TOP-sel," so called because legend has it that pirates once hid behind the island and only their topsails were visible to passing ships. There are three towns on Topsail Island—Topsail Beach, North Topsail Beach, and Surf City. All are popular beach destinations and are less commercial than many beach communities but still have enough beach shops and souvenir shacks to keep that beach town charm. A swing bridge spans the Intracoastal Waterway at Surf City, and it opens on the hour for passing ships (expect traffic backups when it opens). At the north end of the island, a tall bridge between Sneads Ferry and North Topsail Beach eliminates the traffic backups from passing ships and provides an unheralded view of the 26-mile-long island and the marshes around it.

Among Topsail's claims to fame is its

importance in the conservation of sea turtles. The **Karen Beasley Sea Turtle Rescue and Rehabilitation Center** (822 Carolina Ave., Topsail Beach, www.seaturtlehospital. org, visiting hours 2pm-4pm Mon.-Tues. and Thurs.-Sat. June-Aug.) treats sea turtles that have been injured by sharks or boats, or that have fallen ill or become stranded. Its 24 enormous tubs, which look something like the vats at a brewery, provide safe places for the animals to recover from their injuries and recoup their strength before being released back into the ocean. Hospital staff also patrol the full shoreline of Topsail Island every morning in the summertime, before the crowds arrive, to identify and protect any new clutches of eggs that were laid overnight. Founder Jean Beasley has been featured as a Hero of the Year on the Animal Planet TV channel. Unlike most wildlife rehabilitation centers, this hospital allows visitors.

Topsail has an interesting history of naval warfare, starting with pirates—Blackbeard was known to haunt these waters—through World War II, when the island was a proving ground for Navy missiles. The **Missiles and More Museum** (720 Channel Blvd., 910/328-8663, www.missilesandmoremuseum.org, 2-4pm Mon.-Fri. in Apr., May, Sept., and Oct., 2pm-4pm Mon.-Sat. from the second week of May-first week of Sept., free, donations accepted) commemorates the island's naval history, paying special attention to Operation Bumblebee. Operation Bumblebee led to major advancements in missile technology and the development of jet engines, which were later used in supersonic jet design. The fascinating exhibits include real warheads left over from the tests, including one that washed up on the beach 50 years after it was fired. A rare color film from a 1940s missile test over the island gives visitors a strange look back in this island's history.

One of the best places to eat on the island is the **Beach Shop and Grill** (701 S. Anderson Blvd, 910/328-6501, www.beachshopandgrill. com, 8am-9pm Thurs.-Sat., 8am-2pm Sun., entrées around $22), an island fixture since 1952 when it served burgers and hot dogs as

Warren's Soda Shop. Now it serves sophisticated cuisine that plays with local ingredients and Southern food traditions, with some great dishes for breakfast, lunch, and dinner.

Jacksonville

Jacksonville is best known as the home of **Camp Lejeune,** a massive Marine Corps installation that dates to 1941. Lejeune is the home base of the II Marine Expeditionary Force and MARSOC, the Marine Corps division of U.S. Special Operations Command. The base's nearly 250 square miles include extensive beaches where service members receive training in amphibious assault skills.

Camp Johnson, a satellite installation of Camp Lejeune, used to be known as Montford Point and was the home of the famous African American Montford Point Marines, the first African Americans to serve in the United States Marine Corps. Their history, a crucial chapter in the integration of the U.S. Armed Forces, is paid tribute at the **Montford Point Marine Museum** (Bldg. 101, East Wing, Camp Gilbert Johnson, 910/450-1340, www.montfordpointmarines.com, 11am-2pm and 4pm-7pm Tues. and Thurs., 11am-4pm Sat., free, donations accepted).

ⓒ Hammocks Beach State Park

At the appealing little fishing town of Swansboro you'll find the mainland side of **Hammocks Beach State Park** (1572 Hammocks Beach Rd., 910/326-4881, http:// ncparks.gov, 8am-6pm daily Sept.-May, 8am-7pm daily June-Aug.). Most of the park lies on the other side of a maze of marshes on Bear and Huggins Islands. These wild, totally undeveloped islands are important havens for migratory waterfowl and nesting loggerhead sea turtles. Bear Island is 3.5 miles long and less than 1 mile wide, surrounded by the Atlantic Ocean, Intracoastal Waterway, Bogue and Bear Inlets, and wild salt marshes. Much of the island is covered by sandy beaches and dunes. A great place to swim, Bear Island has a bathhouse complex with a snack bar, restrooms, and outdoor showers. Huggins Island, by contrast, is significantly smaller and covered in ecologically significant maritime forest and lowland marshes. Two paddle trails, one just over 2.5 miles long and the other 6 miles long, weave through the marshes that surround the islands. Camping is permitted on Bear Island in reserved and first-come, first-served sites near the beach and inlet, with restrooms and showers available nearby ($13/day).

A private boat or **passenger ferry** (910/326-4881, http://ncparks.gov, $5 adults, $3 seniors and children) are the only ways to reach the islands. The ferry's schedule varies by the day of the week and the season, but generally departs from the mainland and the islands every 30 to 60 minutes from mid-morning until late afternoon; ferries don't run every day in the off-season. Check the website for current ferry times.

GETTING THERE AND AROUND

Wilmington is the eastern terminus of I-40, more than 300 miles east of Asheville and approximately 120 miles south and east of Raleigh. The Cape Fear region is also crossed by a major north-south route, U.S. 17, the old Kings Highway of colonial times. Wilmington is roughly equidistant along U.S. 17 between Jacksonville to the north and Myrtle Beach, South Carolina, to the south; both cities are about an hour's drive.

Wilmington International Airport (ILM, 1740 Airport Blvd., Wilmington, 910/341-4125, www.flyilm.com) serves the region with flights to and from East Coast cities. For a wider selection of routes, it may be worthwhile to consider flying into Myrtle Beach or Raleigh and renting a car. Driving to Wilmington from the Myrtle Beach airport, add another 30 to 60 minutes to get through Myrtle Beach traffic, particularly in summer, as the airport is on the southern edge of town. Driving from Raleigh-Durham International Airport takes at least 2.25 hours. There is no passenger train service to Wilmington.

Wave Transit (910/343-0106, www.wave-transit.com), Wilmington's public transportation system, operates buses throughout the metropolitan area and trolleys in the historic district. Fares are a low $2 one-way. If you're planning on exploring outside the city, you'll need a car.

The Southern Coast

From the beaches of Brunswick and New Hanover County to the swampy subtropical fringes of land behind the dunes, this little corner of the state is special, one of the most beautiful parts of North Carolina. Extending south from Wrightsville Beach, a series of barrier islands and quiet low-key beaches stretches to the South Carolina border. Starting with Pleasure Island, which comprises Kure and Carolina Beach, and ending with the Brunswick Island, including Oak Island, Holden Beach, Sunset Beach, and Ocean Isle, these beaches are family-friendly places where you're more likely to find rental homes than high-rise hotels.

You'll see some distinctive wildlife here, including the ubiquitous green anole, called "chameleons" by many locals. These tiny lizards, normally bright lime green, are able to fade to brown. They're everywhere—skittering up porch columns and along balcony railings, peering around corners, and hiding in the fronds of palmetto trees. The males put on a big show by puffing out their strawberry-colored dewlaps. Generations of Lowcountry children have spent thousands of hours trying to catch them, usually with next to no success. If you catch them from the front, they'll bite (albeit harmlessly), and if you catch them from behind, they'll ditch their writhing tails while the rest of them keeps running. From a respectful distance, they're amusing companions on your outdoor sojourns in this region.

This is also the part of the state where you'll find the largest population of alligators. Unlike their tiny cousins, the anoles, which threaten but can't back it up, alligators have the potential to be deadly. All along river and creek banks and in bays and swamps, you'll see their scaly hulks basking in the sun. If you're in a kayak, a canoe, or on a paddleboard, you may mistake them for a log until you see their eyes and nostrils poking out of the water. Be careful and be aware of where you, children, and pets step when hiking, and avoid swimming in fresh water in places where alligators are prone to lurk. All that said, alligators are thrilling to see and generally will vacate the area if you come too close.

If you're in the area during the early part of summer, you could see a sea turtle dragging herself into the dunes to lay a clutch of eggs. Huge loggerhead sea turtles, tiny Kemp's ridley sea turtles, greens, and even the occasional leatherback make their nests along the beaches here. Nesting season runs from mid-May through August, although August nestings are rare, and they hatch between 60 and 90 days later, depending on the species. Organizations such as the **Bald Head Island Conservancy** (700 Federal Rd., Bald Head Island, 910/457-0089, www.bhic.org) on Bald Head Island help protect nests and educate area residents and visitors on issues relevant to protecting sea turtles.

In certain highly specialized environments, mainly in and around Carolina bays, which have both moistness and nutrient-poor soil, the Venus flytrap and other carnivorous plants thrive. The flytrap and some of its cousins are endangered, but in this region—and nowhere else in the world—you'll have plenty of opportunities to see them growing wild.

KURE BEACH

Kure is a two-syllable name, pronounced "KYUR-ee" like the physicist Marie Curie, not like "curry." This is a small beach community without the neon lights and towel shops of larger beaches. Most of the buildings on the island are houses, both rentals for vacationers and the homes of Kure Beach's year-round residents, although a few motels and hotels are scattered through the community. The beach

itself, like all North Carolina ocean beaches, is public.

Carolina Beach State Park

Just to the north of Kure is **Carolina Beach State Park** (1010 State Park Rd., off U.S. 421, Carolina Beach, 910/458-8206, http://ncparks.gov, grounds 8am-5pm daily, facility hours vary). Of all the state parks in the coastal region, this may be the one with the greatest ecological diversity. Within its boundaries are coastal pine and oak forests, pocosins between the dunes, saltwater marshes, a 50-foot sand dune known as Sugarloaf Dune, and limesink ponds. Of the limesink ponds, one is a deep cypress swamp, one is a natural garden of water lilies, and one is an ephemeral pond that dries into a swampy field every year, an ideal home for carnivorous plants. You'll see Venus flytraps and their ferocious cousins, but resist the urge to dig them up, pick them, or tempt them with your fingertips. Sort of like stinging insects that die after delivering their payload, the flytraps' traps can wither and fall off once they're sprung.

The park has 83 drive-in and walk-in campsites (year-round except Dec. 24-25, $20, $15 over age 62), each with a grill and a picnic table. Two are wheelchair-accessible, and restrooms and hot showers are nearby.

Fort Fisher State Park

At the southern end of Kure Beach is **Fort Fisher State Park** (1000 Loggerhead Rd., off U.S. 421, 910/458-5798, http://ncparks.gov, 8am-9pm daily June-Aug., 8am-8pm daily Mar.-May and Sept.-Oct., 8am-6pm daily Nov.-Feb.), with six miles of beautiful beach; it's a less crowded and less commercial alternative to the other beaches of the area. A lifeguard is on duty 10am-5:45pm daily late May-early Sept. The park also includes a 1.1-mile hiking trail that winds through marshes and along the sound, ending at an observation deck where visitors can watch wildlife.

Fort Fisher is also a significant historic site, a Civil War earthwork stronghold designed to withstand massive assault. Modeled in

© JASON FRYE

Flip flops pile up like sand dunes at the beach.

part on the Crimean War's Malakhoff Tower, Fort Fisher's construction was an epic saga as hundreds of Confederate soldiers, enslaved African Americans, and conscripted indigenous Lumbee people were brought here to build what became the Confederacy's largest fort. After the fall of Norfolk in 1862, Wilmington became the most important open port in the South, a vital harbor for blockade-runners and military vessels. Fort Fisher held until nearly the end of the war. On December 24, 1864, U.S. General Benjamin "The Beast" Butler attacked the fort with 1,000 troops but was repulsed; his retreat led to him being relieved of his command. A few weeks later, in January 1865, Fort Fisher was finally taken, but it required a Union force of 9,000 troops and 56 ships in what was the largest amphibious assault by Americans until World War II. Without its defenses at Fort Fisher, Wilmington soon fell, hastening the end of the war, which came just three months later. Due to the final assault by the Union forces and 150 years of wind, tides, and hurricanes, not much of the massive earthworks survive, but the remains of this vital Civil War site are preserved in an oddly peaceful and pretty seaside park that contains a restored gun emplacement and a visitors center with interpretive exhibits.

The **North Carolina Aquarium at Fort Fisher** (900 Loggerhead Rd., 910/458-8257, www.ncaquariums.com, 9am-5pm daily year-round except Thanksgiving, Dec. 24, and Jan. 1, $8 adults, $7 seniors, $6 ages 3-12) is one of three aquariums operated by the state; this is a beautiful facility that shows all manner of marinelife native to North Carolina waters. The aquarium follows the path of the Cape Fear River from its headwaters to the ocean. Along the way you'll meet Luna, an albino alligator; have the opportunity to touch horseshoe crabs, sea stars, and even bamboo sharks; and see a variety of sharks, fish, eels, and rays in a two-story 235,000-gallon aquarium. Dive shows and daily feedings complement the exhibits. It's hard to miss the Megalodon exhibit, dedicated to the huge prehistoric shark—it was bigger than a school bus—with teeth the size of dinner plates and a jaw eight feet across. Fortunately, all that remains are fossil relics of this two-million-year-old animal, many of which are found at dive sites nearby in less than 100 feet of water. Pose for a picture behind the massive set of jaws as proof of the ultimate fish story.

Accommodations

The beaches of the Carolinas used to be lined with boardinghouses, the old-time choice in lodging for generations. They were a precursor to today's bed-and-breakfasts, cozy family homes where visitors dined together with the hosts and were treated like houseguests. Hurricane Hazel razed countless boardinghouses when it pummeled the coast in 1954, ushering in the epoch of the family motel. The **Beacon House** (715 Carolina Beach Ave. N., 877/232-2666, www.beaconhouse-innb-b.com, some pets allowed in cottages, $139 summer) at Carolina Beach, just north of Kure, is a rare survivor. The early-1950s boardinghouse has the typical upstairs and downstairs porches and dark wood paneling indoors, along with nearby cottages. You'll be treated to a lodging experience from a long-gone era.

Food

Seafood is a staple all along Kure and Carolina Beaches. **Shuckin' Shack Oyster Bar** (6a N. Lake Park Blvd., 910/458-7380, www.pleasureislandoysterbar.com, 11am-2am Mon.-Sat., noon-2am Sun., entrées from $10) is a friendly oyster bar that serves fresh seafood, including oysters by the bucket. You can shuck your own (don't be ashamed to ask for a tutorial if you've never used a shucking knife) or enjoy oysters on the half shell, but we recommend shucking your own and enjoying a steamed oyster on a saltine cracker with a dash of hot sauce. **Ocean Grill and Tiki Bar** (1211 S. Lake Park Blvd., 910/458-2000, www.oceangrilltiki.com, 5pm-9pm Mon.-Thurs., 11am-9pm Fri.-Sun., entrées $10-24) serves fried, grilled, and steamed seafood and has great views from the

dining room and outdoor tiki bar, where you can hear live music on weekends throughout the summer.

Freddie's Restaurant (111 K Ave., Kure Beach, 910/458-5979, www.freddiesrestaurant.com, from 5pm daily, entrées $12-25) in Kure Beach has a big menu and serves even bigger portions. With seafood, pasta, and a good specialty pork chop menu, it's not hard to find something to eat. Watch the tables around you for guidance about whether you want individual entrées or to share. **Pop's Diner** (104 N. Lake Park Blvd., 910/458-7377, 11am-10pm Sun.-Thurs., 11am-3am Fri. and Sat., $1-10) serves classic diner food in a 1950s-style diner. With checkerboard tiles, a stainless steel front, and red vinyl booths, they help keep a piece of the golden age of beach towns alive. If you're lucky, you may see the owner in one of his Elvis Presley jumpsuits.

After dinner, stop by **Britt's Donuts** (11 Boardwalk), a Carolina Beach institution since 1939. They use a secret recipe for their doughnut batter, and they come out salty, sweet, airy, crispy, and perfect. Pull up a seat at the bar and order half a dozen to enjoy.

◖ SOUTHPORT

Without a doubt, Southport is one of North Carolina's most picturesque coastal towns. The Cape Fear River, Intracoastal Waterway, and Atlantic Ocean meet here, and the water is almost always crowded with watercraft of all sizes and shapes: sailboats, shrimpers, anglers out for the day, huge cargo ships headed upriver to Wilmington, yachts, kayaks, and deep sea fishing boats. The town's history is rooted in the water, and there are still several multigenerational fishing and shrimping families around. River pilots who know the shoals and tides like no one else operate out of Southport, heading offshore in speedy boats to the container ships and tankers making their way to Wilmington; they help navigate the cumbersome ships through the currents and the channel and guide them safely to the port and back out to sea, just as people from local families have for 200-plus years. Throughout the town, historic buildings, including Fort Johnson, a British fort built in 1745, line the oak-shaded streets. The Old Smithville Burying Ground, a community cemetery dating to before the founding of the town, is a beautiful spot, and many of the headstones are inscribed with epitaphs for sea captains and their widows. Stop in at the **Fort Johnston-Southport Museum and Visitors Center** (203 E. Bay St., 910/457-7927, 10am-4pm Mon.-Sat., 1pm-4pm Sun., free) for more information on the town, although Southport is small enough to explore and discover on your own. While you're at the visitors center, ask about the history of four of the town's street names: Lord, Howe, Dry, and I Am.

Sights

The **North Carolina Maritime Museum at Southport** (204 E. Moore St., 910/457-0003, www.ncmaritimemuseums.com, 9am-5pm Tues.-Sat., free) tells the story of Southport as a maritime town in some detail. The pirate Blackbeard and his compatriot Stede Bonnet prowled these waters, and Stede Bonnet was captured on the river about a mile from the museum, then sent to Charleston, where he was hanged for his crimes. The museum sheds some light on their exploits. Other displays include a 2,000-year-old Native American canoe fragment, information on the blockade of the river during the Civil War, and many artifacts brought up from nearby shipwrecks.

Given the beauty of the town and its proximity to Wilmington, it's no surprise that Southport has been the star, location-wise, of several television shows and films. *Safe Haven*, an adaptation of North Carolina literary son Nicholas Sparks's novel of the same name, takes place here; one reviewer called the movie "an extended infomercial for the lulling charms of Southport." Since the movie's 2012 debut, a steady stream of fans has been touring its locations. **Southport Tours** (910/750-1951, $10) and **Southport Fun Tours** (608/334-0619, www.southportfuntours.com, $10 adults, $5 seniors and under age 12) both offer film and town-history tours.

Festivals

Southport has its share of fairs and festivals throughout the year, but they all pale in comparison to the **North Carolina 4th of July Festival** (800/457-6964, www.nc4thofjuly. com), the official Independence day celebration for the state. Some 50,000 people attend the parade, the festival park and street fair, and the fireworks in the evening. Launched from a barge on the river, the fireworks are a special treat as they reflect on the water. Perhaps the most moving of the events is the naturalization ceremony for new Americans as they declare their loyalty and enjoy their first 4th of July celebration.

Golf

In the vicinity of Southport, golfers will find several courses that are both challenging and beautiful. On Oak Island, the **Oak Island Golf Club's** (928 Caswell Beach Rd., Oak Island, 800/278-5275, www.oakislandgolf. com, 18 holes, par 72, greens fees from $45) is a 6,720-yard George Cobb-designed course that provides the serenity of a golf course with occasional ocean views and ocean breezes. In Boiling Spring Lakes, you can walk or ride **The Lakes Country Club** (591 S. Shore Dr., Boiling Spring Lakes, 910/845-2625, www.thelakes-countryclub.com, 18 holes, par 72, greens fees from $25), the oldest golf course in Brunswick County.

Shopping

There are a number of cute boutiques, antiques stores, and kid's shops in Southport, but our favorites are **Ocean Outfitters** (121 E. Moore St., 910/457-0433, www.oceanoutfitters.com, 10am-5:30pm Mon.-Fri., 10am-6pm Sat., 11am-4pm Sun. summer, 10am-5pm Mon.-Sat., 11am-4pm Sun. winter), a sportswear outfitter that carries clothing perfect for the local climate, and **Cat on a Whisk** (600-C N. Howe St., 910/454-4451, www.catonawhisk. com, 10am-5pm Mon.-Sat.), a kitchen store with knowledgeable staff, a fantastic selection of gadgets and cookware, and a friendly cat or two.

Accommodations

Lois Jane's Riverview Inn (106 W. Bay St., 910/457-6701, www.loisjanes.com, $120-180) is a Victorian waterfront home built by the innkeeper's grandfather. The guest rooms are comfortably furnished, bright and not froufrou; the Queen Deluxe Street, a cottage behind the inn, has its own kitchen and separate entrance. The front porch of the inn has a wonderful view of the harbor. At the same location the **Riverside Motel** (106 W. Bay St., 910/457-6986, $85-105) has a front porch with a fantastic panorama of the shipping channel. Another affordable option is the **Inn at River Oaks** (512 N. Howe St., 910/457-1100, www.theinnatriveroaks.com, $80-110, lower off-season), a motel-style inn with very simple suites.

At Oak Island, west of Southport, **Captain's Cove Motel** (6401 E. Oak Island Dr., Oak Island, 910/278-6026, www.captainscovemotel.net, $90) is a long-established family motel one block from the beach. The **Island Resort and Inn** (500 Ocean Dr., Oak Island, 910/278-5644, www.islandresortandinn.com, $132-220) is a beachfront property with standard motel rooms and one- and two-bedroom apartment suites. The **Ocean Crest Motel** (1417 E. Beach Dr., Oak Island, 910/278-3333, www.ocean-crest-motel.com, $105-330) is a large condo-style motel, also right on the beach.

One unusual bed-and-breakfast is the **Frying Pan Shoals Light Tower** (offshore, 704/907-0399, www.fptower.com, $300-500). Located some 30 miles offshore at the end of Frying Pan Shoals, this former light tower (think of a lighthouse on an oil derrick) has been converted to a bed-and-breakfast that caters to the adventurous set. You have to take a boat or a helicopter from Southport to reach the B&B, which can be booked when you book your room. The restoration project at Frying Pan Shoals is vast and ongoing, and often the owners will have "working getaways" when guests will pitch in to repair, restore, or reopen some part of the structure. Naturally, every guest room has water views, and deep-sea fishing and diving opportunities are literally right under your feet; the tower stands in 50 feet of water.

Food

For a town this size, Southport has a surprising number of good restaurants. I love to dine on the water at **Yacht Basin Provision Company**

© JASON FRYE

Yacht Basin Provision Company in Southport

(130 Yacht Basin Dr., 910/457-0654, 11am-9pm daily, entrées around $10), shortened to "Provision Company" by locals, to enjoy a plate of peel-and-eat shrimp or a grouper sandwich. **Frying Pan** (319 W. Bay St., 910/363-4382, 4pm-10pm daily, entrées around $18) is a restaurant that serves fried seafood and local delicacies from a dining room elevated 18 feet off the ground, offering commanding water views. Both restaurants get very crowded in summer, with two-hour waits at Provision for lunch around July 4; you can wait for your table at **Old American Fish Factory** (150 Yacht Basin Dr., 910/457-9870, www.oldamericanfish. com), an open-air bar featured in *Safe Haven* and other film and TV shot in Southport. The views are incredible as the deck extends out over the water. During the highest tides, your feet can get wet. Try not to drop anything; it may fall through the cracks in the deck into the river below.

Moore Street Market (130 E. Moore St., 910/363-4208, 7am-4pm daily, $1-10), a small coffee shop and deli, makes a good lunch and serves the best cup of coffee in town. Its central location is steps from antiques shops and historic sites in Southport. Dinner is always good at **Ports of Call Bistro and Market** (116 N. Howe St., 910/457-4544, www.portsofcallbistro.com, lunch 11:30am-2pm Tues.-Sat., dinner 5pm-9pm Tues.-Sat., brunch 10am-2pm Sun., entrées $17-33), a Mediterranean-inspired restaurant serving both tapas and entrée-size portions. Their menu changes seasonally and always features local seafood.

BALD HEAD ISLAND

Two miles off the coast of Southport is Bald Head Island. From the mainland you can see the most prominent feature, Old Baldy, the oldest lighthouse in North Carolina, standing tall above the trees. Accessible only by a 20-minute ferry ride or private boat, the island is limited to golf carts, bicycles, and pedestrians; the only larger vehicles are emergency services and those for deliveries or construction. Combined with the largest intact section of maritime forest in North Carolina, Bald Head Island seems like it's a world away.

Sights
Old Baldy was commissioned by Thomas Jefferson and built in 1817. You can climb to the top of the 109-foot lighthouse with admission to the **Smith Island Museum** (101 Lighthouse Wynd, 910/457-7481 www.old-baldy.org, 10am-4pm Tues.-Sat., 11am-4pm Sun., $5 adults, $3 ages 3-12). The museum, housed in the former lighthouse keeper's cottage, tells the story of Old Baldy and the other lighthouses that have stood on the island. The **Old Baldy Foundation** (910/457-5003, tours 10am Mon.-Sat., $57, $47 under 12, price includes ferry passage to and from Bald Head Island) also conducts historic tours that reveal the long and surprising history of the island.

Sports and Recreation
There are 14 miles of beaches to explore on Bald Head Island, several hundred acres of maritime forest with marked trails, miles of creeks that wind through the marsh behind the island, and ample opportunities to explore with one of the island's outfitters. **Riverside Adventure Company** (910/457-4944, www.riversideadventure.webly.com, rentals from $45, tours from $55) conducts guided kayak tours, nature hikes, sailing cruises, and surfing lessons from their storefront on the harbor. Riverside also runs other tours such as ghost walks and kids camps through the summer. If you want to try stand-up paddleboarding on the marsh or ocean, **Coastal Urge** (12B Maritime Way, 800/383-4443, www.rentals.coastalurge. com) supplies all the gear and lessons you need to get on the water.

The **Bald Head Island Conservancy** (700 Federal Rd., 910/457-0089, www.bhic.org, tours around $50 for off-island guests and $20 for on island guests, off-island ticket includes

© JASON FRYE

early morning on Bald Head Island

round trip ferry fare, dates and times vary, call or check the website for weekly schedule), a group dedicated to preserving the flora and fauna of the island, leads kayak tours, birding walks, kids camps, and, in the summer, turtle walks, giving Conservancy members (you can join while you're here) the chance to see a sea turtle make her nest.

Accommodations

Most of the houses on Bald Head Island are rental homes, ranging from one-bedroom cottages to massive beachside homes ideal for family reunions. Rentals are available through Bald Head Island Limited (www.baldheadisland. com) and Tiffany's Rentals (www.tiffanysrentals.com); rates range from $2,000 to $12,000 per week. One bed-and-breakfast, **The Marsh Harbour Inn** (21 Keelson Row, 910/454-0451, www.marshharbourinn.com, $275-575), operates here. With beautiful harbor and marsh views, free use of golf carts for guests, and membership privileges to the private Bald

Head Island Club, this is a great option for visitors not in a large group.

Food

There are only a few places to eat on the island, but fortunately they're good. In the harbor, **Delphina Family Eatery and Pub** (10 Marina Wynd, 910/457-1222, www.delphinacantina.webs.com, 11am-11pm daily, $6-15) and **Sandpiper Sweets and Ice Cream** (located inside Delphina at 10 Maritime Wynd, 7am-4:30pm Sun.-Thurs., 7am-9:30pm Fri.-Sat., under $10) are great options for families. **Mojo's on the Harbour** (16 Marina Wynd, 910/457-7217, www.mojosontheharbor.com, 11:30am-9pm Sun.-Tues., 11:30am-10pm Wed.-Thurs., 11:30am-11pm Fri.-Sat., $13-32) has harbor-side dining with beautiful sunset views.

The **Maritime Market Café** (8 Maritime Way, 910/457-7450, www.maritimemarketbhi. com, breakfast 8am-10:30am daily, lunch 11am-3pm daily), attached to a full-service

© JASON FRYE

kayaking Bald Head Island's marsh creeks

grocery store, serves breakfast and lunch that includes standard options and daily specials.

OCEAN ISLE

Ocean Isle is the next-to-most-southerly beach in North Carolina, separated from South Carolina only by Bird Island and the town of Calabash. In October, Ocean Isle is the site of the **North Carolina Oyster Festival** (www.ncoysterfestival.com), a huge event that's been happening for nearly 30 years. In addition to an oyster stew cook-off, a surfing competition, and entertainment, this event features the North Carolina Oyster Shucking Competition. Oyster shucking is not as picayune a skill as it might sound. In the not-that-long-ago days when North Carolina's seafood industry was ascendant, workers—most often African American women—lined up on either side of long work tables in countless oyster houses along the coast and the creeks, opening and cutting out thousands of oysters a day. A complex occupational culture was at work in those factories, with its own vocabulary, stories, and

songs. The speed at which these women worked was a source of collective and individual pride, and the fastest shuckers enjoyed quite a bit of prestige among their colleagues. High-speed shucking is a skill that's well remembered by many Carolinians who might now be working at Wal-Mart rather than in the old dockside shacks and warehouses.

SOUTH ALONG U.S. 17

U.S. 17 is an old colonial road; its original name, still used in some places, is the King's Highway. George Washington passed this way on his 1791 Southern tour, staying with the prominent planters in the area and leaving in his wake the proverbial legends about where he lay his head of an evening. Today, the King's Highway, following roughly its original course, is still the main thoroughfare through Brunswick County into South Carolina.

Brunswick Town and Fort Anderson

Near Orton is the **Brunswick Town-Fort**

Anderson State Historic Site (8884 St. Philip's Rd. SE, Winnabow, 910/371-6613, www.nchistoricsites.org, 9am-5pm Tues.-Sat., free, donations accepted), the site of what was a bustling little port town in the early and mid-1700s. In its brief life, Brunswick saw quite a bit of action. It was attacked in 1748 by a Spanish ship that, to residents' delight, blew up in the river. One of that ship's cannons was dragged out of the river and is on display. In 1765 the town's refusal to observe royal tax stamps was a successful precursor to the Boston Tea Party eight years later. But by the end of the Revolutionary War, Brunswick Town was gone, burned by the British but also made obsolete by the growth of Wilmington.

Today, nothing remains of the colonial port except the lovely ruins of the 1754 **St. Philip's Anglican Church** and some building foundations uncovered by archaeologists. During the Civil War, Fort Anderson was built on this site; some of its walls also survive. It was a series of sand earthworks that were part of the crucial defenses of the Cape Fear, protecting the blockade-runners who came and went from Wilmington. A visitors center at the historic site tells the story of this significant stretch of riverbank, and the grounds, with the town's foundations exposed and interpreted, are an intriguing vestige of a forgotten community.

Perhaps the most interesting artifact on display at the visitors center at Brunswick Town is the Fort Anderson battle flag that Confederate soldiers flew over the fort during their final battle. Once the fort fell, the flag was captured by a regiment from Illinois, who gave it to their commander, who gave it to the Illinois governor, who gave it to Abraham Lincoln in a ceremony at the National Hotel, the same National Hotel where John Wilkes Booth lived, that was reportedly witnessed by Booth. A number of Civil War and Lincoln scholars believe that this moment, when Lincoln received the battle flag, was when Booth's plan changed from kidnapping to assassinating the President.

Nature Preserves

The Nature Conservancy's **Green Swamp Preserve** (Hwy. 211, 5.5 miles north of Supply, regional office 910/395-5000, www.nature. org) contains more than 17,000 acres of some of North Carolina's most precious coastal ecosystems, the longleaf pine savanna and evergreen shrub pocosin. Hiking is allowed in the preserve, but the paths are primitive. It's important to stay on the trails and not dive into the wilds because this is an intensely fragile ecosystem. In this preserve are communities of rare carnivorous plants, including the monstrous little pink-mawed Venus flytrap, four kinds of pitcher plant, and sticky-fingered sundew. It's also a habitat for the rare red-cockaded woodpecker, which is partial to diseased old-growth longleaf pines as a place to call home.

The Nature Conservancy maintains another nature preserve nearby, the **Boiling Spring Lakes Preserve** (Hwy. 87, Boiling Spring Lakes, regional office 910/395-5000, www. nature.org), with a trail that begins at the Community Center. Brunswick County contains the state's greatest concentration of rare plant species and the most diverse plant communities anywhere on the East Coast north of Florida. This preserve is owned by the Plant Conservation Program and includes over half the acreage of the town of Boiling Spring Lakes. The ecosystem is made up of Carolina bays, pocosins, and longleaf pine forests. Like the Green Swamp Preserve, many of the species are dependent on periodic fires in order to propagate and survive. The Nature Conservancy does controlled burns at both sites to maintain this rare habitat.

The University of North Carolina Wilmington maintains a 174-acre nature preserve in Brunswick County, the **Ev-Henwood Nature Preserve** (6150 Rock Crek Road NE, near Town Creek, www.uncw.edu, dawn-dusk daily). Ev-Henwood (pronounced like "heaven wood" without the initial "h") is named after the surnames of the former owner's grandparents: Evans and Henry. The property had been owned by the family since 1799 and was the site of turpentine stills, tar kilns, and a working farm. Now several miles of hiking trails wind through the property past barns and

© JASON FRYE

Decide on a kayak route — into or out of the marsh?

home sites, across fields, beside the beautiful and eerie blackwater Town Creek, and through longleaf pine woods. Pick up a trail map at the parking lot and head out for a few hours in the woods. Bring water, bug spray, and your camera; if you're quiet enough, you may see otters playing in Town Creek or deer in the woods at the edge of a field.

Golf

Brunswick County is a golf mecca, where more than 30 championship courses appeal to all skill levels and playing styles. The website **Brunswick Islands** (www.ncbrunswick. com) maintains a list of golf courses, among them the notable **Cape Fear National at Brunswick Forest** (1281 Cape Fear National Dr., Brunswick Forest, 910/383-3283, www. capefearnational.com, greens fees from $47), named one of the "Top 18 Course Openings in the World 2010" by *Links* magazine when it opened, the course is beautifully maintained and fun to play from any tee. **Crow Creek** (240 Hickman Rd. NW, Calabash, 910/287-3081,

www.crowcreek.com, greens fees from $60), is almost on the South Carolina state line. About 45 minutes south of Wilmington, the **Big Cats** (351 Ocean Ridge Pkwy. SW, 800/233-1801, www.bigcatsgolf.com, greens fees $82-140) is at Ocean Ridge Plantation with five stunning courses—Tiger's Eye, Leopard's Chase, Panther's Run, Lion's Paw and Jaguar's Lair.

Calabash and Vicinity

The tiny fishing village of Calabash, just above the South Carolina state line, was founded in the early 18th century as Pea Landing, a shipping point for the local peanut crop. Local legend holds that calabash gourds were used as dippers in the town drinking water supply, explaining the town's 1873 renaming. Others hold that the crooked marsh creek that leads to the sea inspired the name. Either way, Calabash is home to some world-famous seafood.

In the early 1940s, Lucy High Coleman began frying fish for the local fisheries workers in a kettle of oil by the dock. Later she used a tent, which in turn became a lean-to

© JASON FRYE

on the dock after a day of fishing

and eventually a full-fledged restaurant, The Original, which was, well, the original Calabash-style seafood restaurant. Calabash-style seafood is marked by its light crispy batter and the freshness of the seafood, and Coleman's descendants carry on the family tradition at several restaurants in town. Locals like to say that like champagne, which can only come from one region in France, or bourbon, only distilled in Kentucky, you can only get Calabash seafood in Calabash; everything else is just an imitation.

Coleman's Original Calabash Restaurant (9931 Nance St., 910/579-6875, 4pm-9pm daily, $10-30) is on the site of the original venue, and its yesteryear kitsch is undeniably charming. Just up the street is **Ella's of Calabash** (1148 River Rd., 910/579-6728, www.ellasofcalabash.com, 11am-9pm daily, entrées around $14); Ella was Lucy's sister. **Beck's Restaurant** (1014 River Road, 910/579-6776, www.becksrestaurant.com, 11am-9pm daily, $5-19) rounds out the offerings of the original three Calabash restaurants.

All of these restaurants are run by descendants of Lucy High Coleman, but that's only part of her seafood legacy. In the 1940s, Calabash was little more than a dot on the map until Jimmy Durante, the comedian, big band leader, and radio personality, spent the night in town. Lucy High Coleman's descendants will tell you that Durante sampled the food and asked to meet the chef, who introduced herself as "Mrs. Calabash." He was so enamored with her, the food, and the town that he began to sign off his radio program with the famous line "Good night, Mrs. Calabash, wherever you are."

Indigo Farms (1542 Hickman Rd. NW, 910/287-6794, www.indigofarmsmarket.com, 9am-5pm Mon.-Sat., longer hours in summer), three miles north of the South Carolina line in Calabash, is a superb farm market, selling all manner of produce, preserves, and baked goods. They also have corn mazes and farm activities in the fall.

Sunset Beach, the southernmost of the Brunswick County beaches, is a wonderfully small place, a cozy town that until 2008 could only be reached via a one-lane pontoon bridge. One of the area's most popular restaurants is located just on the inland side of the bridge to Sunset Beach: **Twin Lakes Seafood Restaurant** (102 Sunset Blvd., Sunset Beach, 910/579-6373, http://twinlakesseafood.com) was built almost 40 years ago by Clarice and Ronnie Holden, both natives of the area. Clarice was born into a cooking family— she's the daughter of Lucy High Coleman—so she knows her way around a restaurant. Twin Lakes serves fresh, locally caught seafood, fried Calabash-style or broiled. In-season and on weekends, expect long lines.

In the nearby town of Shallotte (pronounced "Shuh-LOTE"), **Holden Brothers Farm Market** (5600 Ocean Hwy. W., 910/579-4500, 8am-6pm daily March-Memorial Day, 8am-7pm daily Memorial Day-Labor Day, 8am-6pm Labor Day-Dec. 25, closed Dec. 26-Mar.) is a popular source for local produce. The peaches in season are wonderful, and the variety of homemade canned goods and pickles are worth the trip.

GETTING THERE AND AROUND

The Brunswick County beaches like Holden, Ocean Isle, and Sunset are easily accessed on U.S. 17. The beaches and islands along the cape, due south of Wilmington, are not as close to U.S. 17. They can be reached by taking U.S. 76 south from Wilmington, then turning onto Highway 133 (closest to Wilmington), Highway 87, or Highway 211 (closer to the South Carolina border), or by ferry from Southport.

The **Southport-Fort Fisher Ferry** (Ferry Rd. SE, Southport, 800/368-8969 or 800/293-3779, from Southport 5:30am-7:45pm daily summer, 5:30am-6:15pm daily winter, from Fort Fisher 6:15am-8:30pm daily summer, 6:15am-7pm daily winter, $1 pedestrians, $2 bicycles, $3 motorcycles, cars $5, longer vehicles $15) is popular as a sightseeing jaunt as well as a means to get across the river. It's a 30-minute crossing; most departures are 45 minutes apart. Pets are permitted if leashed or in a vehicle, and there are restrooms on all ferries.

A small airport near Oak Island, **Cape Fear Regional Jetport** (4019 Long Beach Rd., Oak Island, 910/457-6534, www.capefearjetport.com), has no scheduled passenger service but is suitable for small private aircraft.

Inland from Wilmington

Driving inland from the Wilmington area, you first pass through a lush world of wetlands distinguished by the peculiar Carolina bays. Not necessarily bodies of water, as the name would suggest, bays are actually ovoid depressions in the earth of unknown and much-debated origin. They are often water-filled, but by definition are fed by rainwater rather than creeks or groundwater. They create unique environments and are often surrounded by bay laurel trees (hence the name), and home to a variety of carnivorous plants.

The next zone, bounded by the Waccamaw and Lumber Rivers, largely comprises farmland and small towns. For generations this was prime tobacco country, and that heritage is still very much evident in towns like Whiteville, where old tobacco warehouses line the railroad tracks. Culturally, this area—mostly in Columbus County and extending into Robeson County to the west and Brunswick County to the east—is linked with Horry, Marion, and Dillon Counties in South Carolina, with many of the same family names still found on both sides of the state line.

The area around the Lumber River, especially in Robeson County, is home to the Lumbee people, Native Americans with a long history of steadfast resistance to oppression and a heritage of devotion to faith and family. If you turn on the radio while driving through the area, you'll hear Lumbee gospel programming and get a sense of the cadences of Lumbee English. The characteristics that distinguish it from the speech of local whites and African Americans are subtle, but idiosyncratic pronunciation and grammar, which include subvariations among different Lumbee families and towns, make it one of the state's most distinctive dialects.

At the edge of the region is Fayetteville. From its early days as the center of Cape Fear Scottish settlement to its current role as one of the most important military communities in the United States, Fayetteville has always been a significant city.

ALONG U.S. 74

A short distance inland from Calabash, the countryside is threaded by the Waccamaw River, a gorgeous dark channel full of cypress knees and dangerous reptiles. The name is pronounced "WAW-cuh-MAW," with more emphasis on the first syllable than on the third. It winds its way down from Lake Waccamaw through a swampy portion of North Carolina

THE LEGEND OF HENRY BERRY LOWRY

In several pockets across the South, the Civil War didn't end the day General Robert E. Lee surrendered, but instead smoldered on in terrible local violence. One such place was the Lumbee community of Robeson County in the days of the famous Lowry Band.

Then as now, Lowry (also spelled Lowrie) was a prominent name in among the indigenous Lumbee people. During the Civil War, Allen Lowry led a band of men who hid out in the swamps, eluding conscription into the backbreaking corps of slave laborers who were forced to build earthworks to defend Wilmington and nearby gun emplacements. When the war ended, violence against the Lumbees escalated, and the Lowry Band retaliated, attacking the plantations of their wartime persecutors. Allen Lowry and his oldest son were captured in 1865 and killed. The youngest son, Henry Berry Lowry, inherited the mantle of leadership.

For the next several years, long after the end of the Civil War, the Lowry Band, now led by Henry Berry, was pursued relentlessly. Arrested and imprisoned, Lowry and his band escaped incarceration in Lumberton and Wilmington. Between 1868 and 1872 the state and federal governments tried everything from putting a bounty on Lowry's head to sending in a federal artillery battalion in an effort to capture Lowry. After an 11-month campaign of unsuccessful pursuit, the federal soldiers gave up. Soon afterward, the Lowry Band emerged from the swamps, raided Lumberton, and made off with a large amount of money. This was the end of the Lowry Band as one by one its members were killed in 1872—except, perhaps, Henry Berry. It's unknown whether he died, went back into hiding, or left the area altogether. As befits a legend, he seems to have simply disappeared.

Henry Berry Lowry is a source of fierce pride for modern Lumbee people, a symbol of their resistance and resilience. For many years, members of the community performed the outdoor drama *Strike at the Wind*, which tells the story of the Lowry Band. Funding for the play dried up, but the story lives on in oral and written histories and in the 2001 novel *Nowhere Else on Earth* by Josephine Humphreys.

and crossing Horry County, South Carolina (unofficial motto: "The *H* is Silent"), before joining the Pee Dee and Lumber Rivers in South Carolina to empty into Winyah Bay at the colonial port of Georgetown. Through the little toenail of North Carolina that the Waccamaw crosses, it parallels the much longer Lumber River, surrounding rural Columbus County and part of Robeson County in an environment of deep subtropical wetlands.

Sights

Pembroke is the principal town of the Lumbee people, and at the center of life here is the University of North Carolina at Pembroke (UNCP). Founded in 1887 as the Indian Normal School, UNCP's population is now only about one-quarter Native American, but it's still an important site in the history of North Carolina's indigenous people. The

Museum of the Native American Resource Center (Old Main, UNCP, University Rd., Pembroke, 910/521-6282, www.uncp.edu, 8am-5pm Mon.-Sat., free) is on campus, occupying Old Main, a 1923 building that's a source of pride for Pembroke. The Resource Center has a small but very good collection of artifacts and contemporary art by Native Americans from across the country.

Laurinburg's **John Blue House** (13040 X-Way Rd., Laurinburg, 910/276-2495, grounds open daily, house and grounds tours 10am-noon and 1pm-4pm Tues.-Sat., free, donations accepted) is a spectacle of Victorian design, a polygonal house built entirely of heart pine harvested from the surrounding property and done up like a wedding cake with endless decorative devices. John Blue, the builder and original owner, was an inventor of machinery used in the processing of cotton. A pre-Civil War cotton gin stands on the property, used today for educational demonstrations throughout the year. In October this is the site of the **John Blue Cotton Festival** (www.johnbluecottonfestival.com), which showcases not only the ingenuity of the home's famous resident and the process of ginning cotton, but also lots of local and regional musicians and other artists.

Entertainment and Events

Several of the state's big agricultural festivals are held in this area. If you're in the little town of Fair Bluff in late July, you might be lucky enough to witness the coronation of the newest Watermelon Queen. The **North Carolina Watermelon Festival** (910/949-6845, www.fairbluff.com) began as an annual competition between two friends, local farmers whose watermelons grew to over 100 pounds. The competition expanded into this festival that celebrates watermelon-growing throughout the state; a new court of watermelon royalty is crowned every year.

In Tabor City, there's a famous **Yam Festival** (910/377-3012 www.ncyamfestival.com) in late October, during which the tiny town's population sometimes quadruples. Yam partisans crown their own royal court during this festival. When spring rolls around, Chadbourn holds its annual **Strawberry Festival** (910/654-3518, www.ncstrawberryfestival.com), at which the coronation of the Strawberry Queen takes place. If this seems a strange sort of royalty, bear in mind that across the state line in South Carolina, they have a Little Miss Hell Hole Swamp competition.

Sports and Recreation

Several beautiful state parks line the Waccamaw and Lumber Rivers. **Lake Waccamaw State Park** (1866 State Park Dr., Lake Waccamaw, 910/646-4748, http://ncparks.gov, office 8am-5pm daily, park 8am-6pm daily Nov.-Feb., 8am-8pm daily Mar.-May and Sept.-Oct., 8am-9pm daily June-Aug.) encompasses the 9,000-acre lake. The lake is technically a Carolina bay, large, oval depressions in the ground, many

of which are boggy and filled with water but which are named for the bay trees that typically grow around them. Lake Waccamaw has geological and hydrological characteristics that make it unique even within the odd category of Carolina bays. Because of its proximity to a large limestone deposit, the water is more neutral than its usually very acidic cousins, and so it supports a greater diversity of life. There are several aquatic creatures that live only in Lake Waccamaw, including the Waccamaw fatmucket and the silverside (a mollusk and a fish, respectively). The park draws boaters and paddlers, but the only launches are outside the grounds. Primitive campsites ($9) are available in the park.

North of Whiteville on U.S. 701 is Elizabethtown, home to **Jones Lake State Park** (4117 Hwy. 242, Elizabethtown, 910/588-4550, http://ncparks.gov, office 8am-5pm Mon.-Fri., park 8am-6pm Nov.-Feb., 8am-8pm Mar.-May and Sept.-Oct., 8am-9pm June-Aug.). You can boat on Jones Lake either in your own craft (no motors over 10 hp) or in canoes or paddleboats ($5 per hour, $3 per additional hour) rented from the park. The lake is also great for swimming ($5 over age 12, $4 ages 3-12) from late May to early September, with shallow cool water and a sandy beach. A concession stand and a bathhouse are at the beach, and camping (call for rates) is available in a wooded area with drinking water and restrooms nearby.

Singletary Lake State Park (6707 Hwy. 53 E., Kelly, 910/669-2928, http://ncparks.gov, 8am-5pm daily), north of Lake Waccamaw in Kelly, has one of the largest of the Carolina bays, the 572-acre Singletary Lake, which lies within Bladen Lakes State Forest. There is no individual camping allowed, although there are facilities for large groups, including the entrancingly named Camp Ipecac, named for the purgative herb that grows here, that date from the Civilian Conservation Corps (CCC) era. There is a nice one-mile hiking trail, the CCC-Carolina Bay Loop Trail, and a 500-foot pier extending over the bay. Some of the cypress trees in the park are believed to have been saplings when the first English colonists came to Roanoke Island.

Lumber River State Park (2819 Princess Ann Rd., Orrum, 910/628-4564, http://ncparks. gov) has 115 miles of waterways with numerous put-ins for canoes and kayaks. Referred to as both the Lumber River and Lumbee River, and farther upstream as Drowning Creek, the river traverses both the coastal plain region and the eastern edge of the Sandhills. Camping ($13) is available at unimproved walk-in and canoe-in sites at group sites.

Yogi Bear's Jellystone Park (626 Richard Wright Rd., Tabor City, 877/668-8586, www. taborcityjellystone.com, RVs $31-67/night, tents $28-54/night, cabins $104-200/night, yurts $64-109/night) is a popular campground with RV and tent spaces, rental cabins, and yurts. The facilities are clean and well maintained, and there are tons of children's activities on-site. Some of the camping is in wooded areas, but for the most part expect direct sun.

Food

If you pass through Tabor City, have a meal at the ◖ **Todd House** (102 Live Oak St., Tabor City, 910/653-3778, www.todd-house. com, 11am-8pm Mon.-Fri., 11am-3pm Sun., under $10), which has been serving fine country cooking since 1923. The Todds are one of the oldest families in the tobacco-growing area along the state line, and the first in the restaurant business was Mary Todd, who cooked meals for visiting tobacco buyers. Through her daughter's time and subsequent owners the Todd House has continued to serve famously good barbecue, fried chicken, and other down-home specialties.

There's a take-out counter in Whiteville that chowhounds will drive an hour out of their way to reach because it's said to have the best burgers around. Next to the railroad tracks, **Ward's Grill** (706 S. Madison St., Whiteville, 910/642-2004, 7am-2pm Mon.-Thurs., 7am-1pm Wed., 7am-12pm first two Sat. of the month) has no seating, just a walk-up counter. Its burgers are famous, as are its chili dogs.

In Lumberton, try **Fuller's Old-Fashion BBQ**

(3201 Roberts Ave., Lumberton, 910/738-8694, www.fullersbbq.com, 11am-9pm Mon.-Sat., 11am-4pm Sun., lunch buffet $7, dinner buffet $9.50, Sun. buffet $11.25). Fuller's has a great reputation for its barbecue, but it also makes all sorts of country specialties like chicken gizzards, chitterlings, and a 12-layer cake.

Getting There and Around

This section of southeastern North Carolina is bisected by I-95, the largest highway on the East Coast. I-95 passes near Fayetteville and Lumberton. Major east-west routes include U.S. 74, which crosses Cape Fear at Wilmington and proceeds through Lake Waccamaw and Whiteville to pass just south of Lumberton and Pembroke to Laurinburg. Highway 87 goes through Elizabethtown, where you can choose to branch off onto Highway 211 to Lumberton, or bear north on Highway 87 to Fayetteville. Highway 87 and Highway 211 are quite rural and beautiful, especially in the spring, when azaleas are in bloom and the country is greening up for summer, as well as in the fall, when cotton fields will make you do a double take, thinking you just sped past a field of snow. Take your time on these roads and be ready to pull off to take photos of farmhouses, fields, and other pastoral scenes.

FAYETTEVILLE

Fayetteville is North Carolina's sixth-largest city, and in its own quiet way has always been one of the state's most powerful engines of growth and change. In the early 1700s it became a hub for settlement by Scottish immigrants, who helped build it into a major commercial center. From the 1818 initiation of steamboat travel between Fayetteville and Wilmington along Cape Fear—initially a voyage of six days—to the building of Plank Road, which was a huge boon to intrastate commerce, Fayetteville was well connected to commercial resources in the Carolinas.

At a national level, Fayetteville serves as the location of two high-level military installations. Fort Bragg is home to the XVIII Airborne

Corps, the 82nd Airborne, the Delta Force, and the John F. Kennedy Special Warfare Center and School. It's also home to many military families, and the community has a vibrant international community. Pope Air Field, home of the 440th Airlift Wing, is nearby.

Sights

The **Museum of the Cape Fear Regional Complex** (801 Arsenal Ave., 910/486-1330, http://ncmuseumofhistory.org, 10am-5pm Tues.-Sat., 1pm-5pm Sun., free) has three components, each telling different stories of Fayetteville's history. The museum has exhibits on the history and prehistory of the region, including its vital role in developing transportation in the state, as well as its military role. There is an 1897 house museum, the **Poe House,** which belonged to an Edgar Allen Poe—not the writer Edgar Allan Poe this one was a brickyard owner. The third section is the 4.5-acre **Arsenal Park,** site of a federal arms magazine built in 1836, claimed by the Confederacy in 1861, and destroyed by General Sherman in 1865.

The **Airborne and Special Operations Museum** (100 Bragg Blvd., 910/643-2766, www.asomf.org, 10am-5pm Tues.-Sat., noon-5pm Sun., noon-5pm federal holiday Mon., free, theater $4, motion simulator $5) is an impressive facility that presents the history of Special Ops paratroopers, from the first jump in 1940 to the divisions' present-day roles abroad in peacekeeping missions and war. In the museum's theater you can watch a film of what it looks like when a paratrooper makes a jump, and the 24-seat Pitch, Roll, and Yaw Vista-Dome Motion Simulator makes the experience even more exciting.

The **JFK Special Warfare Museum** (Ardennes St. and Marion St., Bldg. D-2502, Fort Bragg, 910/432-4272, www.jfkwebstore.com) tells the story of unconventional U.S. military projects, including Special Ops and Psychological Ops. The museum focuses on the Vietnam War era but chronicles warfare from colonial times to the present. Note that ID is required to enter the base.

Looking farther back in time, the **Fayetteville Independent Light Infantry**

Armory and Museum (210 Burgess St., 910/433-1612, by appointment, free) displays artifacts from the history of the Fayetteville Independent Light Infantry (FILI). FILI is still active, dedicated as North Carolina's official historic military command, which is a ceremonial duty. In its active-duty days, which began in 1793, FILI had some exciting times, particularly during the Civil War. In addition to military artifacts, the museum also exhibits a carriage in which the Marquis de Lafayette was shown around Fayetteville—the only one of the towns bearing his name that he actually visited.

The 79-acre **Cape Fear Botanical Garden** (536 N. Eastern Blvd., 910/486-0221, www.capefearbg.org, 10am-5pm Mon.-Sat., noon-5pm Sun., closed Sun. mid-Dec.-Feb., $8 adults, $2.50 ages 6-12, free under age 6, free 1st Sat. of every month and all of Apr.) is one of the loveliest horticultural sites in North Carolina. The camellia and azalea gardens are spectacular sights in the early spring, but the variety of plantings and environments represented makes the whole park a delight. Along the banks of the Paw Paw River and Cross Creek, visitors will find dozens of garden environments, including lily gardens, hosta gardens, woods, a bog, and an 1880s farmhouse garden. This is the prettiest place in Fayetteville and a fantastic spot for a picnic lunch on a long road trip down I-95.

Cross Creek Cemetery (N. Cool Spring St. and Grove St., 800/255-8217, dawn-dusk daily) is an attractive and sad spot, the resting place of many Scottish men and women who crossed the ocean to settle Cape Fear. People of other ethnicities and times are buried here, but the oldest section of the cemetery is the most poignant, where one stone after another commemorates early Scots colonists. The cemetery was founded in 1785, and the wall along the southern boundary is believed to be the oldest piece of construction still standing in Fayetteville.

Sports and Recreation

In Fayetteville you can attend a dizzying array of sporting events, from drag races to ice hockey. The **Fayetteville Fire Antz**

(1900 Coliseum Dr., 910/321-0123, www. fireantzhockey.com, from $14 adults, $5 children) are an ice hockey team in the Southern Professional Hockey League, unusual for this warm climate. The **Fayetteville Swamp Dogs** (910/426-5900, www.goswampdogs.com, from $5), a baseball team in the Coastal Plains League, play home games at the J. P. Riddle Stadium (2823 Legion Rd.).

The **Rogue Rollergirls** (www.roguerollergirls.com) is an up-and-coming all-female flat-track Roller Derby team participating in this fun fringe sport that had its heyday in the 1970s. In basketball, the **Fayetteville Crossover** (910/977-2954, http://crossover.trblproball.com) plays in the Tobacco Road Basketball League. An indoor football team, the **Cape Fear Heroes** (910/323-1100, www.capefearheroes.com, from $10), play home games at the Crown Center (1960 Coliseum Dr.).

There are two motorsports venues in Fayetteville: **Fayetteville Motor Sports Park** (4480 Doc Bennett Rd., 910/484-3677, www.fayettevillemotorsportspark.com) host drag races, and **Fayetteville Motor Speedway** (3704 Doc Bennett Rd., 910/223-7223, www.

thenewfayettevillemotorspeedway.com, around $20) hosts a variety of stock car races.

GOLF

The Sandhills of North Carolina are dotted with great golf courses, and the countryside around Fayetteville is no exception: **Anderson Creek Golf Club** (125 Whispering Pines Dr., Spring Lake, 910/814-2115, www.andersoncreekgolf.com, 18 holes, par 72, greens fees from $28), **Bayonet at Puppy Creek** (349 S. Parker Church Rd., Raeford, 888/229-6638, www.bayonetgolf.com, greens fees from $30), **Cypress Lakes** (2126 Cypress Lakes Rd., Hope Mills, 910/483-0359, www.cypresslakesnc.com, greens fees from $30), and **Gates Four Golf and Country Club** (6775 Irongate Dr., Fayetteville, 910/425-2176, www.gatesfour.com, greens fees from $45) all offer great golf; call at least 48 hours ahead for the best chance of getting a tee time in summer, although short-notice reservations may be possible.

◖ ZIP-LINING

If you want outdoor adventure, **ZipQuest** (533 Carvers Falls Rd., 910/488-8787, www.

ZipQuest's gear

zipquest.com, 9am-5pm Mon.-Sat., 10am-5pm Sun., $85) gives you a different sort of outdoor experience: flying through the trees on a zip line. The tour takes you over Carver's Creek and even 20-foot Carver's Falls, the only waterfall in the area. At the end of the run, you have the opportunity to get on the Swingshot, a swing that flies out over a four-story drop into the ravine below. Both the zip-line tour and Swingshot are exciting but not for the faint of heart.

INDOOR SKYDIVING

Paraclete XP SkyVenture (190 Paraclete Dr., Raeford, 888/475-9386, www.paracletexp.com, from $63) offers one of the most thrilling experiences you can have in the area: indoor skydiving. After a brief flight school, you'll step into a vertical wind tunnel with an instructor and take your first flight. If you show a little aptitude, they'll let you fly on your own (don't worry, they're never more than a couple of feet away) and even take you soaring to the top of the 51-foot tower, then rushing back down, giving you a real taste of what it's like to free fall. If you're lucky, you'll see the Golden Knights, the U.S. Army's parachute team, practicing aerial maneuvers, or maybe get to fly with world-class and even world-champion competitive skydivers, or see one of Paraclete's teams practice their wild aerial ballet.

Entertainment and Events

The **Cameo Theatre** (225 Hay St., 910/486-6633, www.cameoarthouse.com) is a cool old early-20th-century movie house, originally known as the New Dixie. Today it is "Fayetteville's alternative cinematic experience," a place for independent and art-house movies.

Cape Fear Regional Theatre (1209 Hay St., 910/323-4233, www.cfrt.org) began in 1962 as a tiny company with a bunch of borrowed equipment. Today it is a major regional theater with a wide reputation. Putting on several major productions each season and specializing

in popular musicals, it draws actors and directors from around the country but maintains its heart here in the Fayetteville arts community. The **Gilbert Theater** (116 Green St., entrance on Bow St. above Fascinate-U Museum, 910/678-7186, www.gilberttheater.com, around $10) is a small company that puts on a variety of productions throughout the year, with emphasis on classic drama and multicultural offerings.

Fayetteville's late-April **Dogwood Festival** (www.faydogwoodfestival.com) features rock, pop, and beach-music bands; a dog show; a recycled art show; a "hogs and rags spring rally;" and the selection and coronation of Miss, Teen Miss, Young Miss, and Junior Miss Dogwood Festival. In September, the **International Folk Festival** (www.theartscouncil.com) celebrates the many cultures that make up this community through food, music, art, and other cultural expressions.

Accommodations and Food

Fayetteville's lodging options are mostly chain motels, a multitude of which can be found at the Fayetteville exits along I-95. The chains have reasonable rates, but if you'd like to stay somewhere with more personality, Wilmington and Raleigh are both easily accessible. In town, **Gloria & Edgar's B&B** (3423 Dunn Rd., 910/484-6827, $80-125) is a four-bedroom bed-and-breakfast featuring private bathrooms and a spacious, sunny porch perfect for breakfast, afternoon tea, or a nightcap.

Likewise, the city's dining choices tend toward the highway chain restaurants, with some exceptions: ◖ **Hilltop House** (1240 Fort Bragg Rd., 910/484-6699, www.hilltophousenc.com, lunch 11am-2pm Tues.-Fri. and Sun., dinner 5pm-9pm Tues.-Thurs., 5pm-10pm Fri. and Sun., brunch 10:30am-2:30pm Sun., closed Sat., $20-33) serves hearty fare in an elegant setting, and was recognized in 2007 with a *Wine Spectator* magazine Award for Excellence—not surprising, given that the

Hilltop House has a wine list of more than 100 bottles.

Beer lovers will prefer the **Mash House** (4150 Sycamore Dairy Rd., 910/867-9223, www.themashhouse.com, 4pm-11pm Mon.-Thurs., 4-midnight Fri., noon-midnight Sat., noon-10pm Sun., $8-16), which has a good variety of pizzas and sandwiches as well as heartier entrées and a selection of good home-made brews, or **Huske Hardware House** (405 Hay St., 910/437-9905, www.huskehardware.com, 11am-10pm Mon.-Tues., 11am-midnight Wed.-Thurs., 11am-2am Fri.-Sat., 11am-9pm Sun., entrées $10-30), a gastropub serving great food and even better beer. For a taste of Fayetteville's international cuisine, try **Sherefe** (114 Gillespie St., 910/630-3040, www.sherefe.net, 11am-9pm Mon.-Thurs., 11am-10pm Fri.-Sat., entrées $14-26), a Mediterranean restaurant. The friendly staff can point out something good, and get the Mediterranean Trio (hummus, baba ghanoush, and meze) to share.

Information and Services
Cape Fear Valley Health Services (1638 Owen Dr., 910/615-4000, www.capefearvalley. com) is a large hospital complex with full services, including acute care and a major cardiac care program.

The website of the **Fayetteville Area Convention and Visitors Bureau** (245 Person St., 800/255-8217, www.visitfayettevillenc. com, 8am-5pm Mon.-Fri.) is an excellent source of visitor information for the city. You'll find not only the basics but also detailed driving tours and extensive historical information.

Getting There and Around
Fayetteville Regional Airport (FAY, 400 Airport Rd., 910/433-1160, www.flyfay. com) has daily flights to Charlotte (US Airways), Atlanta (Delta), and Washington DC (United and US Airways). **Amtrak** (472 Hay St., 800/872-7245, www.amtrak.com, 10am-5:45pm and 10pm-5:45am daily) runs the *Silver Meteor* between New York City and Miami and the *Palmetto* between New York City and Savannah, Georgia; each train stops in Fayetteville once daily in each direction.

Fayetteville is near I-95; it is easily reached via Highway 24 from Jacksonville, Warsaw, and Clinton, and via Highway 87 from points south.

WILMINGTON AND CAPE FEAR

RALEIGH AND THE TRIANGLE

The Triangle is a term long used to describe the Raleigh-Durham-Chapel Hill area. It once referred to the three major universities here, the University of North Carolina at Chapel Hill, Duke University in Durham, and North Carolina State University at Raleigh. A map or aerial photo of the region shows that these three cities are a uniform urban mass, but lumping them together overlooks the unique personality, quirks, and scene of each.

That said, there is a spirit that unites the communities of the Triangle. The intense concentration of colleges and universities—there are more than a dozen, including several prominent historically African American universities—results in a well-educated population with shared interests and sensibilities. By some counts, there are more PhDs per capita in the Triangle than anywhere in the country, partly due to the booming local biotech, pharmaceutical, and high-tech industries.

The Triangle has a deeply liberal bent, much to the frustration and befuddlement of many in this red state. Archconservative U.S. Senator Jesse Helms once remarked that there was no need to build a zoo in North Carolina; we could simply put a fence around Chapel Hill and achieve the same purpose. Gibes aside, Chapel Hill is a menagerie of all walks of humanity, making it the epicenter of progressive politics in the state, most intensely concentrated in the left-wing town of Carrboro, which elected North Carolina's first openly gay mayor. Carrboro was also the state's first community to extend domestic partnership benefits of to same-sex couples.

HIGHLIGHTS

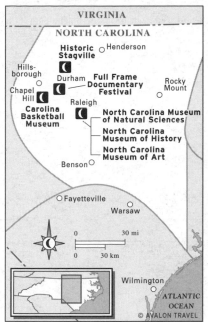

LOOK FOR **◖** TO FIND RECOMMENDED SIGHTS, ACTIVITIES, DINING, AND LODGING.

◖ North Carolina Museum of Natural Sciences: Get breathtakingly close to massive whale and dinosaur skeletons and discover the many ecosystems of the state in this excellent nature museum (page 161).

◖ North Carolina Museum of History: North Carolina boasts centuries of remarkable history, literature, art, and sports, and there's no better place to explore it than here (page 161).

◖ North Carolina Museum of Art: Amazingly varied collections encompass art from ancient Greece, Egypt, and the Americas as well as Judaica, pop art, and famous 18th- and 19th-century American and European artists (page 162).

◖ Historic Stagville: One of the South's largest enslaved populations lived and worked on this plantation immediately prior to the Civil War. The story of their community is preserved here (page 180).

◖ Full Frame Documentary Festival: This annual Durham shindig has become a festival of international importance, where new documentary work premieres and icons of the genre mingle with fans (page 181).

◖ Carolina Basketball Museum: Few sports fans would dispute that the University of North Carolina's basketball program has one of the greatest, if not the greatest, collegiate athletic traditions in American sports. On the UNC campus, this new museum celebrates the pride of Chapel Hill (page 189).

The Triangle is an area with deep roots in the arts, mostly of the literary and musical variety. Writers like David Sedaris and Charles Kuralt have called this area home, and it ranks with New Orleans and Oxford, Mississippi, as one of the literary capitals of the South. It seems that every writer in North Carolina is obliged to give a reading or a lecture or lead a workshop in Raleigh, Durham, Chapel Hill, or a satellite community. The music scene is just as lively, with Chapel Hill, the most collegiate of the local college towns, as its center.

Acts like the Squirrel Nut Zippers, Corrosion of Conformity, Southern Culture on the Skids, Ben Folds Five, and Chatham County Line hail from here, and that's just Chapel Hill. Genres are widely flung, and you'll find everything from great chamber groups and orchestras to modern-day jug bands, dubstep DJs, and a rich bluegrass and alt-country scene.

PLANNING YOUR TIME

The area covered in this chapter is best approached as three destinations. From east to

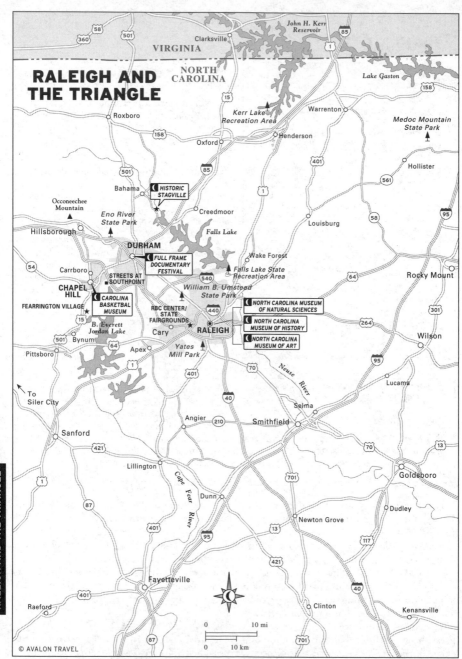

© AVALON TRAVEL

west, Wilson and other towns east of I-95 are an hour or less driving from Raleigh, and this region merits at least a day on its own. Raleigh and its suburbs such as Zebulon, Cary, and Wake Forest, all radiating from the Beltline (the I-440 ring road), call for another full day. Durham and Chapel Hill are only nine miles apart, so together they are the third region of this chapter. Carrboro is so closely linked to Chapel Hill—it's actually difficult to tell exactly which block of Franklin Street or Main Street demarcates their city boundary—that

they're treated here as one entity. Hillsborough is an easy drive from both Chapel Hill and Durham, and Pittsboro is about 20 minutes south of Chapel Hill.

If you decide to choose one town in the Triangle to stay in while exploring the wider area during the day, Durham is the most centrally located of the three cities. But I-40 and U.S. 70 link the whole Triangle area quite efficiently, and there are few points in the Triangle that are more than 30 minutes' drive from any other point.

Raleigh and Vicinity

The first time I heard of Raleigh was on *The Andy Griffith Show*. Any time trouble found Mayberry, it either came from "up North" or from Raleigh. Even though many of Andy's observations of life in North Carolina are accurate, his assertion that Raleigh is a hive of citified depravity is just wrong. It is a great city, home to a number of universities and the state government (granted, many would agree that involves its own kind of depravity). Raleigh is one of the sparks that helps power the cultural engine of North Carolina.

North Carolina State University is here, along with two historically African American universities, Shaw and Saint Augustine's, and two small but well-known women's colleges, Peace and Meredith. The North Carolina Museum of History is excellent, as are the Natural Sciences Museum and the North Carolina Museum of Art. There are a number of music and art festivals as well as the must-see event of the year, the State Fair.

SIGHTS
€ North Carolina Museum of Natural Sciences
The **North Carolina Museum of Natural Sciences** (Bicentennial Plaza, 11 W. Jones St., 919/707-9800, www.naturalsciences.org, 9am-5pm Mon.-Wed. and Fri.-Sat., noon-5pm Sun., 9am-9pm Thurs. and the 1st Fri.

of the month, free) hosts national traveling exhibitions and is home to excellent permanent exhibits. "Mountains to the Sea" is a re-creation of the regional environments of the state, populated with live and mounted animals and plants. Stars of "Prehistoric North Carolina" include the world's only publicly displayed skeleton of an *Acrocanthosaurus*, a 38-foot, 4.5-ton predatory dinosaur, and the remains of "Willo," a 66-million-year-old small vegetarian dinosaur whose fossilized heart is a rare boon to paleontology. The whales whose skeletons hang in the Coastal Carolina exhibit are celebrities, each with its own interesting story, including "Trouble," a sperm whale who washed up at Wrightsville Beach in 1928, and "Mayflower," a right whale killed in a legendary 1874 struggle with Carolina whalers off Shackleford Banks. In 2012 an 80,000-square-foot expansion called the Nature Research Center opened. Here visitors can watch scientists conduct research and experiments in the "Window on Research" areas. A three-story multimedia space provides plenty of room to show films, clips, and presentations. Other exhibits in this wing include displays on aquatics, astronomy, microbiology, and genetics.

€ North Carolina Museum of History
Also on Bicentennial Plaza is the **North**

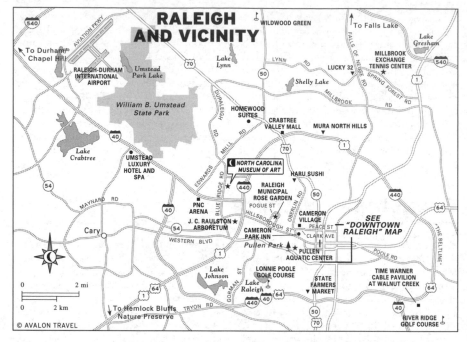

RALEIGH AND THE TRIANGLE

Carolina Museum of History (5 E. Edenton St., 919/807-7900, http://ncmuseumofhistory.org, 9am-5pm Mon.-Sat., noon-5pm Sun., free), where visitors learn about the history of the state's contributions to the military, from the Revolutionary War to the Iraq War; about the musicians and genres that make this state one of the wellsprings of American music; about the handicrafts, including pottery, textiles, and furniture, created by centuries of renowned artisans; and about medicine in North Carolina, from traditional African American root medicine and Native American herbal treatments to the pharmaceutical and medical technology businesses that draw patients and researchers from around the world. You can also see a uniform worn by Harlem Globetrotter and Wilmington native Meadowlark Lemon and a stock car driven by Carolina legend Richard Petty. The Museum of History hosts concerts and many educational events throughout the year.

◖ North Carolina Museum of Art

The **North Carolina Museum of Art** (2110 Blue Ridge Rd., 919/839-6262, http://ncartmuseum.org, 10am-5pm Tues.-Thurs. and Sat.-Sun., 10am-9pm Fri., free) is just outside the Beltline. Its collections include masterpieces from many eras and regions of the world, including ancient Egyptian, Greek, Roman, and pre-Columbian American art and the work of Botticelli, Giotto, Raphael, Monet, Georgia O'Keeffe, Thomas Hart Benton, and many more. The gallery is also home to one of the nation's two Jewish ceremonial art collections and to collections of 19th- and 20th-century African art. Perhaps most impressive is the collection of sculptures by the French master Auguste Rodin.

A 160-acre outdoor gallery has miles of trails looping through it from one enormous outdoor art installation to the next. These include a metal tree that's so organic that many visitors ask if the artist painted a real tree or wrapped one in foil. Throughout the park are

© CHRIS ADAMCZYK

the Nature Research Center at the North Carolina Museum of Natural Sciences

opportunities to interact with the art pieces and the environment. A couple of the trails lead to the large outdoor amphitheater, which hosts concerts and film screenings during summer and fall.

Historic Homes

The 1770s **Joel Lane Museum House** (St. Mary's St. and W. Hargett St., 919/833-3431, www.joellane.org, 10am-2pm Wed.-Fri., 1pm-4pm Sat. Mar.-mid-Dec., $5 adults, $4 seniors, $3 students) is Wake County's oldest extant home. Costumed docents lead tours of the house and period gardens. The 1799 **Haywood Hall** (211 New Bern Place, 919/832-8357, http://haywoodhall.org, call for hours, free) is another of Raleigh's oldest buildings. Built for the state's first elected treasurer and his family, it features a historic doll collection. A fee is charged for tours of the house and gardens.

Mordecai Historic Park (Mimosa St. and Wake Forest Rd., 919/857-4364, www.raleighnc.gov, grounds dawn-dusk daily, hourly house tours 9am-4pm Tues.-Sat., 1pm-4pm

Sun., 1-hour tours $5 adults, $3 seniors and ages 7-17, 30-minute tours $3 adults, $2 seniors and ages 7-17) includes a plantation house dating from the late-18th and early-19th centuries. It has restored dependencies and other buildings, including the birthplace of President Andrew Johnson.

More historic homes can be seen in Raleigh's historic **Oakwood Neighborhood,** listed on the National Register of Historic Places. Structures mostly date from the late-19th century in this neighborhood, bounded by Franklin, Watauga, Linden, Jones, and Person Streets, and self-guided walking- and driving-tour brochures can be picked up at the Capital Area Visitor Information center inside the Museum of History on Bicentennial Plaza.

Other Sights

The **North Carolina State Capitol** (1 E. Edenton St., 919/733-4994, www.ncstatecapitol.org, 9am-5pm Mon.-Sat., tours 11am and 2pm Sat., free), built in the 1830s, is a Greek Revival structure that has been restored to its

RALEIGH AND THE TRIANGLE

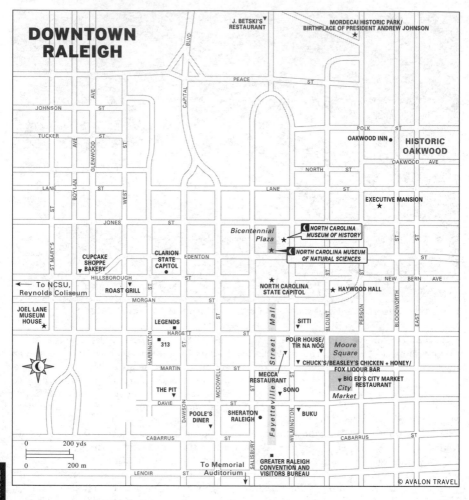

DOWNTOWN RALEIGH

J. BETSKI'S ▼
RESTAURANT

MORDECAI HISTORIC PARK/
BIRTHPLACE OF PRESIDENT ANDREW JOHNSON ★

PEACE ST

JOHNSON AVE ST

TUCKER ST AVE GLENWOOD ST

POLK ST
OAKWOOD INN ●   **HISTORIC OAKWOOD**
OAKWOOD AVE

NORTH ST

LANE BOYLAN ST WEST ST

LANE ST

EXECUTIVE MANSION ★

JONES ST

Bicentennial
Plaza ★
★
▶ ◖ NORTH CAROLINA MUSEUM OF HISTORY
▶ ◖ NORTH CAROLINA MUSEUM OF NATURAL SCIENCES

ST ST

ST MARY'S

CUPCAKE SHOPPE
▼ BAKERY

CLARION
STATE
CAPITOL ●

EDENTON

ST

HILLSBOROUGH ST
←— To NCSU,
Reynolds Coliseum   ▼ ROAST GRILL

★
NORTH CAROLINA
STATE CAPITOL   ★ HAYWOOD HALL

NEW BERN AVE

MORGAN ST

JOEL LANE
MUSEUM
HOUSE ★

LEGENDS ■

HARGETT ST

Street Mall

SITTI ▼

BLOUNT PERSON BLOODWORTH EAST

■ 313 ST
HARRINGTON

POUR HOUSE/
TÍR NA NÓG ▼

Moore
Square

MARTIN ST

MCDOWELL

▼ CHUCK'S/BEASLEY'S CHICKEN + HONEY/
FOX LIQUOR BAR

THE PIT

MECCA
RESTAURANT ▼

▼ SONO

▼ BIG ED'S CITY MARKET RESTAURANT
City Market

DAVIE ST

Fayetteville

DAWSON

POOLE'S
DINER ▼

SHERATON
RALEIGH ▼

▼ BUKU

WILMINGTON

CABARRUS ST

CABARRUS ST

0   200 yds
0   200 m

SALISBURY

LENOIR ST

To Memorial
Auditorium ▼

GREATER RALEIGH
CONVENTION AND
VISITORS BUREAU ■

© AVALON TRAVEL

antebellum appearance. Be alert when you visit the library; this is where the capitol's many reported ghosts are allegedly most active. Guided tours last approximately 45 minutes.

The **Executive Mansion** (200 N. Blount St., 919/807-7950), built in the 1890s, is a lovely example of Victorian architecture, once described by President Franklin D. Roosevelt as possessing "the most beautiful governor's residence interior in America." Tours are available, but the hours vary according to state functions—it is still the home of the governor. It's necessary to be with an official tour group; phone for more information.

The **J. C. Raulston Arboretum** (4415 Beryl Rd., across from Capitol City Lumber Company, 919/515-3132, www.ncsu.edu, 8am-8pm daily Apr.-Oct., 8am-5pm daily Nov.-Mar., free) is a public garden focused on the development of ornamental plants suitable to the Southern climate. You can visit highly specialized areas devoted to white flowers, roses,

COURTESY OF THE RALEIGH CONVENTION & VISITORS BUREAU/VISITRALEIGH.COM

the Rodin collection at the North Carolina Museum of Art

and border plants; the 300- by 18-foot perennial border may cause some serious yard envy. The **Raleigh Municipal Rose Garden** (301 Pogue St., near North Carolina State University, 919/821-4579) is home to over 1,000 roses of 60 varieties. Carolina roses are blessed with an extra-long growing season, and the Municipal Rose Garden also features bulbs and other ornamental plants, so a visit to the garden is special any time of year. Another place for a scenic walk is **Historic Yates Mill County Park** (4620 Lake Wheeler Rd., 919/856-6675, www.wakegov.com, 8am-sunset daily), a few miles south of downtown. The gristmill that presides over the millrace is nearly 200 years old. Hiking trails encircle the millpond.

A favorite place to visit in Raleigh is the **State Farmers Market** (1201 Agricultural St., 919/733-7417, www.ncagr.gov, 5am-6pm Mon.-Sat., 8am-6pm Sun., free), where you'll find the best produce, finest meats, and all sorts of arts, crafts, candies, baked goods, bedding plants, garden plants, pots, and pretty things. A 30,000-square foot-pavilion where most of the

farmers set up to sell their wares is the central focal point, but the Market Shoppes, at around half the size, are where you'll find candy, baked goods, and other assorted North Carolina gifts, notions, soaps, and lotions.

ENTERTAINMENT AND EVENTS
Performing Arts
The **North Carolina Symphony** (919/733-2750, www.ncsymphony.org), a full-time 65-member orchestra under the direction of conductors Grant Llewellyn and William Henry Curry, tours throughout the state and beyond. Its home venue is the wonderful Meymandi Concert Hall at **Duke Energy Center** (2 E. South St., 919/996-8700, www.dukeenergycenterraleigh.com). The **North Carolina Opera** (919/792-3850, www.ncopera.org) has its home stage at Memorial Auditorium, also in the Duke Energy Center. The opera's rehearsals, held at a nearby church, are sometimes open to the public—see their website for details.

RALEIGH AND THE TRIANGLE

© CHRIS ADAMCZYK

the Executive Mansion, home of the governor of North Carolina

The **Time Warner Cable Music Pavilion at Walnut Creek** (3801 Rock Quarry Rd., 888/494-3902) is a top local music venue, attracting top pop and country acts. Given the stature of the artists who play here, concerts can sell out quickly. The **Lincoln Theatre** (126 E. Cabarrus St., 919/821-4111, www.lincolntheatre.com, all ages) is another important local performing arts institution where major rock, blues, jazz, and other bands fill the schedule.

In the heart of downtown, the **Red Hat Amphitheater** (500 S. McDowell St., 919/996-8800, www.redhatamphitheater.com) has room for around 5,500 concertgoers and draws big names; Widespread Panic, The National, and Bob Dylan have played here. Major headliners sell out quickly at this relatively small venue, so check their schedule ahead of time.

Nightlife

The best place to find out what's going on at Triangle-area clubs on any given night of the week is the *Independent Weekly,* a free newspaper that's available at restaurants and shops throughout the region. By state law, establishments that serve liquor and make no more than 30 percent of their revenue from food must be private-membership clubs, but every club has ways of getting first-time visitors through the doors. Some clubs must be joined a few days in advance, while others accept applications with nominal dues at the door. Raleigh's popular nightspots are dance clubs, lots of live-music venues, and gay clubs with great drag events.

Fox Liquor Bar (237 S. Wilmington St., 919/322-0128, www.ac-restaurants.com, 5pm-2am daily) serves the best cocktails in all of Raleigh, hands down. The mixologists here aren't just bartenders; they're artists who take pride in the cocktails they create. The menu explains each cocktail down to the shape of the glass it's served in and the shape of the ice that goes in it. You'll find a lot of bourbon, rye, and gin but little vodka used in their classic, reimagined, and newly minted drinks, along with a number of house-made and exotic bitters.

The **Pour House Music Hall** (224 S. Blount St., 919/821-1120, www.

© CHRIS ADAMCZYK

Historic Yates Mill County Park

thepourhousemusichall.com, tickets by phone noon-5pm Tues.-Fri., doors 8pm Sun.-Thurs., 9pm Fri and Sat.) is a great venue with alternative country, rock and roll, bluegrass, and all sorts of other bands on the schedule. Visitors must print the membership form from the website, fill it out, and bring it to the door with $1. For Irish ambience, visit **Tír Na Nóg Irish Pub and Restaurant** (218 S. Blount St., 919/833-7795, www.tirnanogirishpub.com, 11am-1am daily, $11-30) and get the fish-and-chips, or the **Hibernian Restaurant and Bar** (8021 Falls of Neuse Rd., 919/803-1609, www.hibernianpub. com, 11am-2am daily, $7-15).

Legends (330 W. Hargett St., 919/831-8888, www.legends-club.com, 5pm-2am Sun.-Thurs., 5pm-2:30am Fri., 5pm-3am Sat.) is one of the most popular gay and lesbian clubs in the state, a fun bar that is also ground-zero for the area's pageant circuit. Call for membership details. Nearby are two other popular gay nightspots: **313** (313 Hargett St., 919/755-9599, http://313raleigh.com, 9pm-late Tues.-Sat., over age 17), where you can see some great

female impersonators, and **Flex Club** (2 S. West St., 929/832-8855, www.flex-club.com, from 8pm Mon.-Sat., from 2pm Sun., membership $15), which is primarily a men's bar.

For Latin dancing and delicious Spanish food, try the **Jibarra** (327 W. Davie St., Suite 102, 919/755-0556, www.jibarra.net, 5pm-10pm Tues.-Thurs., 5pm-11pm Fri., noon-11pm Sat., 11pm-9pm Sun., open late the 2nd and 4th Sat. of the month, $9-24). **Berkeley Café** (217 W. Martin St., 919/821-0777, www. berkeleycafe.net, call for hours) serves both lunch and dinner and stays open late with music by well-known rock-and-roll and alternative bands.

Players' Retreat (105 Oberlin Rd., 919/755-9589, www.playersretreat.net, 11am-2am daily) has been a favorite Raleigh bar since 1951. Great places to watch Atlantic Coast Conference college sports are **Mitch's Tavern** (2426 Hillsborough St., 919/821-7771, http://mitchstavern.com, 11am-2am Mon.-Sat., 5pm-midnight Sun., under $10) and **Sammy's Tap and Grill** (2235 Avent Ferry Rd.,

fresh produce at the State Farmers Market

919/755-3880, www.sammysncsu.com, 11am-2am daily, around $10), if you can find a seat. Other choices for sports bars include **Skybox Grill and Bar** (3415 Wake Forest Rd., 919/878-4917, www.theskyboxgrillandbar.com, 11am-2am Mon.-Sat., noon-midnight Sun., $9-20) and two locations of the **Carolina Ale House** (512 Creekside Dr., 919/835-2222; 4512 Falls of Neuse Rd., 919/431-0001, www.carolinaalehouse.com, 11am-2am daily, $11-30).

Goodnight's Comedy Club (861 W. Morgan St., 919/828-5233, www.goodnightscomedy.com, showtimes and prices vary) has a national reputation as a great place to see major and emerging stand-up comedians. **Comedy Worx** (431 Peace St., 919/829-0822, www.comedyworx.com, 8pm and 10pm Fri.-Sat., matinee 4pm Sat., $6-12) is a venue for competitive improv in which the audience decides what the performers will do and who does it best.

Festivals and Events

The 10-day **North Carolina State Fair** (1025 Blue Ridge Rd., 919/821-7400, www.

ncstatefair.org), held each October, is the nation's largest agricultural fair, with an annual attendance of about 800,000. Plan on going back several times to take it all in: livestock and produce competitions, big-name bluegrass concerts, carnival rides, fighter-jet flyovers, and lots of deep-fried food.

Raleigh ends the year right with the celebration of **First Night** (919/832-8699, www.firstnightraleigh.com, $12, $9 in advance). From dusk until midnight, when the Raleigh Acorn drops (Raleigh is known as the City of Oaks), downtown stays open on New Year's Eve for a night of home-grown jazz, rock-and-roll, traditional, country, and blues music at a variety of wonderful venues. First Night also features art exhibits, dance competitions, magic shows, clowns, comedians, circus acrobats, yoga, flue choirs, and fashion shows. The atmosphere is romantic and elegant for adults, but there is a great deal of fun for children as well. The downtown streets, still twinkly with Christmas lights, are closed off to allow for relaxed pedestrian traffic. The First Night Tram offers

COURTESY OF THE RALEIGH CONVENTION & VISITORS BUREAU/VISITRALEIGH.COM

the North Carolina State Fair

comfortable transportation among the venues for those who prefer to ride.

Raleigh has two fantastic events for music lovers. The annual **Hopscotch Music Fest** (various venues, http://hopscotchmusicfest.com, 3-day pass $125, day pass $65, single events $40) brings more than 150 bands into downtown Raleigh for a three-day extravaganza. Expect street parties, outdoor and indoor concerts, impromptu jams, odd collaborations, and all sorts of nuttiness at this early-September gathering. In late September, the **Wide Open Bluegrass Festival** (Red Hat Amphitheatre, Raleigh Convention Center, City Plaza, 615/256-3222, http://bluegrassfanfest.org, passes $40-140 adults, $30-70 under age 15), the official fan festival for the International Bluegrass Music Association (IBMA), has a number of top-shelf bluegrass musicians playing around town in front of crowds large and small. The IBMA and the festival will be in Raleigh at least through 2015 for the festival and the organization's annual awards ceremony, bringing in acts like Steve Martin, Steep Canyon Rangers, Sam Bush, Bela Fleck, Del McCoury, The Infamous Stringdusters, and more musicians than you could shake a fiddle bow at.

May's **Out! Raleigh** (Fayetteville St., downtown Raleigh, 919/832-4484, www.outraleigh.org), a family-friendly festival celebrating the LGBT community, is a young festival—the first was held in 2011—but one that's growing as Raleigh and the Triangle continue to grow as LGBT-friendly. The first year saw 6,000 attendees, and in 2012 there were over 10,000. The one-day event features a number of activities for kids as well as concerts and speakers.

SHOPPING

Cameron Village (Oberlin Rd. between Hillsborough St. and Wade Ave., 919/821-1350, www.shopcameronvillage.com) was one of the earliest shopping centers in the Southeast, a planned commercial neighborhood built on the grounds of the old Cameron plantation in the late 1940s. Their motto was, "Shop as you please, with the greatest of ease, in

COURTESY OF THE RALEIGH CONVENTION & VISITORS BUREAU/VISITRALEIGH.COM

the biggest acorn in Raleigh, the City of Oaks

the wonderful Cameron Village!" The complex opened with three stores, but today there are nearly 100. It tends toward independent boutiques and high-end chains and is a fun place to splurge. Some of the notable shops are **Great Outdoor Provision Company** (2017 Cameron St., 919/833-1741, http://greatoutdoorprovision.com, 10am-9pm Mon.-Fri., 9am-6pm Sat., noon-6pm Sun.), an favorite outdoor-gear retailer; **Ivy & Leo** (2010 Cameron St., 919/821-7899, 10am-7pm Mon.-Sat., noon-5pm Sun.), a fun boutique that brings in top styles, much to the delight of Raleigh's fashionistas; **Uniquities** (450 Daniels St., 919/832-1234, www.uniquities.com, 10am-7pm Mon.-Sat., noon-6pm Sun.), a great women's clothing boutique; and the **Junior League Bargain Box** (401 Woodburn Ave., 919/833-7587, www.bargainboxraleigh.org, 10am-6pm Mon.-Sat.), a nice thrift shop.

The 1914 **City Market** (214 E. Martin St., 919/821-8023, www.citymarketraleigh.com) complex is another collection of nifty little shops and restaurants in a historic setting.

Crabtree Valley Mall (Glenwood Ave./U.S. 70 at I-440, 919/787-8993, www.crabtree-valley-mall.com, 10am-9pm Mon.-Sat., noon-7pm Sun.) is the main conventional shopping mall in Raleigh. **North Hills** (4321 Lassiter Mill Rd., at North Hills Ave., 919/881-1146, www.northhillsraleigh.com, 8am-11pm daily) is a popular outdoor shopping center with a variety of shops and restaurants, a small green space for kids to play, and a movie theater. There's an REI, the popular outdoor outfitter and gear shop; a number of clothing boutiques and jewelers; several good restaurants; a Starbucks; and a Ben and Jerry's ice cream shop. Park underground for an easy spot out of the weather.

SPORTS AND RECREATION
Outdoor Recreation
Between Raleigh and Durham, **William B. Umstead State Park** (8801 Glenwood Ave., 919/571-4170, http://ncparks.gov, 8am-8pm daily Mar.-Apr. and Sept.-Oct., 8am-9pm daily May.-Aug., 8am-6pm daily Nov.-Feb., closed Dec. 25, visitors center 8am-5pm daily) offers 20 miles of hiking trails, boat rentals ($5 per hour, $3 per additional hour), and mountain bike trails. For an easy hike, try Sal's Branch Trail, a 2.7-mile trip that usually takes about an hour to complete; the trailhead is right behind the visitors center. There are also 13 miles of equestrian-friendly trails. Horses are not permitted on hiking trails, but hikers and cyclists often interact with equestrian enthusiasts at trailheads and on certain multiuse paths. The deep forest and creek banks feature flora normally found at higher elevations, including mountain laurel, and are frequented by a variety of wildlife. The Crabtree Creek entrance, where you'll find the visitors center, is 10 miles northwest of Raleigh along U.S. 70.

If your canoe or kayak is already strapped onto your car and all you need is a place to put in, try the **Neuse River Canoe Trail.** Over a stretch of 17 miles of the Neuse are five different launches, beginning at the Falls Lake Dam. Visit the City of Raleigh (www.raleighnc.gov) website for downloadable maps of the river. Raleigh also has a wonderful series

RALEIGH AND THE TRIANGLE

of hiking trails in the **Capital Area Greenway Trail System** (919/996-4776, www.raleighnc. gov for maps). Currently there are around 100 miles of trails in the city. They're not all interconnected, but plans are to join them to make a huge interconnected urban trail system. Pets, bicyclists, skaters, and skateboarders are all welcome on the Greenway Trail System.

There are several parks around Raleigh, but one that stands out is the wildly popular **Pullen Park** (520 Ashe Ave., 919/996-6468, www.raleighnc.gov, grounds and playground dawndusk daily, free, some activities charge fees), North Carolina's first public park, dating from 1887. The **Amusement Center** (10am-9pm daily July-Sept., hours vary in other months) has a spectacular Gustav A. Dentzel Carousel from 1911, listed on the National Register of Historic Places, as well as a miniature train, a small lake with pedal-boat rentals, and picnic shelters galore. Rides are only $1.

GOLF

At North Carolina State University, the **Lonnie Poole Golf Course** (1509 Main Campus Dr., 919/833-3338, www.lonniepoolegolfcourse.com, 18 holes, par 72, tee-time reservation required, made up to one week in advance, greens fees Mon.-Thurs. $49, $35 after 3pm, $25 replays, Fri.-Sun. and holidays $75, $45 after 3pm, $35 replays) is simply spectacular. A superb layout by Arnold Palmer includes views of the Raleigh skyline while offering a challenging but playable course. Be warned, though, that the first hole is a monster (578 yards from championship tees, par 5), requiring a long carry to a narrow, bunker-guarded fairway. This is the home course for the university's Wolfpack men's and women's golf teams, and a working research project for students in the College of Agriculture and Life Sciences (they're studying turf grass and storm water) and students in the Professional Golf Management Program.

Wildwood Green Golf Club (3000 Ballybunion Way, 919/846-8376, www.wildwoodgreennc.com, 18 holes, par 70, greens fees Mon.-Thurs. $30-47, Fri. before $30-55,

Sat.-Sun. and holidays $32-66, discounts over age 60 and under age 18) has four sets of tees that help even the distance between experienced and novice golfers. Generously wide fairways on most holes help beginners build some confidence and reward aggressive players who try long drives and green-seeking second shots. It's a pretty course with a little water throughout, but nothing too intimidating.

At **River Ridge Golf Club** (3224 Auburn-Knightdale Rd., 919/661-8374, www.golfriverridge.com, 18 holes, par 72 men, par 71 women, greens fees Mon.-Thurs before 3pm $45, Fri. before 3pm $52, Sat.-Sun. before 3pm $62, 3pm-5pm $30, after 5pm $22 daily), they like to brag that you'll get "private club golf course conditions at a daily-fee price." From what I've seen, they're right. There's not a lot of water on the course, but there is some elevation change, causing you to club up or down, depending on your position, the wind, and the slope of the course.

Indoor Recreation

Millbrook Exchange Tennis Center (1905 Spring Forest Rd., 919/872-4128, www.raleighnc.gov, 8:30am-9:30pm Mon.-Fri., 8:30am-6pm Sat.-Sun. summer, 9am-6pm Mon.-Fri., 10am-4pm Sat.-Sun. winter) has 23 public hard-surface courts, a pro shop, and many other amenities. The **Pullen Aquatic Center** (410 Ashe Ave., 919/831-6197, open swim 12:30pm-8pm Mon.-Fri., 12:30pm-7pm Sat., 1pm-6pm Sun., lap swimming 5:30am-8pm Mon.-Fri., 6am-7pm Sat., 1pm-6pm Sun., diving boards 12:30pm-5pm Mon.-Fri., 12:30pm-7pm Sat., 1pm-6pm Sun.) has an Olympic-size pool, dedicated lap-swim lanes, diving boards, and extensive programs. Several area skating facilities are available for ice, roller, and in-line skating, including the **Raleigh IcePlex** (2601 Raleigh Blvd., 919/878-9002, www.iceplex.com, public skating Mon.-Sat., call for hours).

Spectator Sports

North Carolina State University is the southern terminus of Tobacco Road, the zone of legendary college sports traditions in the Atlantic Coast Conference. Although the rivalry between the University of North Carolina and Duke may score more media attention, North Carolina State University's **Wolfpack Athletics** (www.gopack.com) are worthwhile. Men's basketball games take place at the 20,000-seat **PNC Arena** (1400 Edwards Mill Rd., 919/861-2300, www.thepncarena.com), and football is next door at **Carter-Finley Stadium** (4600 Trinity Rd., 919/834-4000). Women's basketball and other Wolfpack sporting events take place at **Reynolds Coliseum** (E. Dunn Ave., 919/865-1510) and **Doak Field** (1081 Varsity Dr., 919/865-1510).

During ice hockey season, PNC Arena is home to the **Carolina Hurricanes** (http://hurricanes.nhl.com). North Carolina may seem an unlikely place for a National Hockey League franchise, but the Canes proved themselves in the 2005-2006 season, beating the Edmonton Oilers to win the Stanley Cup. Tickets can be purchased in person at the Time Warner Cable Box Office inside PNC Arena (1400 Edwards Mill Rd., no phone sales) or through Ticketmaster (www.ticketmaster.com).

We North Carolinians love our "sports entertainment," and for those who don't enjoy wrestling, there's Roller Derby. Women's Roller Derby is making a comeback nationwide, and the cities of the Carolinas are blessed with some bruisers. Raleigh-based **Carolina Rollergirls** (www.carolinarollergirls.com) is a Women's Flat Track Derby Association league that currently comprises three teams: the Debutante Brawlers, the Trauma Queens, and the Carolina Rollergirls All Stars. Derbies take place at the State Fairgrounds at Dorton Arena (1025 Blue Ridge Blvd., 919/821-7400). Tickets are available in Raleigh from **Schoolkids Records** (2114 Hillsborough St., 919/821-7766, www.schoolkidsrecords.com, 10am-9pm Mon.-Sat. and noon-7pm Sun.) and other enlightened establishments.

ACCOMMODATIONS

Although many other cities in North Carolina have small nonchain and boutique hotels,

Raleigh is still catching up. There are dozens of chain motels around the city, concentrated near the airport and downtown, and at various exits off I-40 and U.S. 70. For individualized service, your best choice in Raleigh is a bed-and-breakfast. Raleigh's best-known B&B is the ◖ **Oakwood Inn** (411 N. Bloodworth St., 919/832-9712, www.oakwoodinnbb.com, from $120). Housed in the 1871 Raynor-Stronach House, it's listed in the National Register of Historic Places and is one of only 4 of the original 11 houses remaining in the historic Oakwood neighborhood. The innkeepers have won a slew of awards for the inn's excellence and their hospitality. **Cameron Park Inn** (211 Groveland Ave., 919/835-2171 or 888/257-2171, www.cameronparkinn.com, from $149) is a 1916 home in the Cameron Park historic district, located in the North Carolina State-Cameron Village area. The wide porch and lush English garden are mellow retreats after a day in the city.

If you don't need to stay inside the city limits and are craving some pampering, ◖**Umstead Luxury Hotel and Spa** (100 Woodland Pond, Cary, 919/447-4000 or 866/877-4141, www.theumstead.com, from $279) in Cary has a 14,000-square-foot spa with a large menu of services: 10 different specialized massages; facial, manicure, and pedicure choices; milk, mineral, and aromatherapy baths; and a long list of body therapies and Asian body-care rituals. There's also a three-acre lake on the property, a 24-hour fitness center, and an outdoor heated pool. Guests have tee privileges at the Prestonwood Country Club, about 10 minutes away.

Downtown chain choices tend to be more expensive than chain lodgings beyond the I-440 Beltline, many of which are near the airport on I-40. The **Clarion State Capitol** (320 Hillsborough St., 919/832-0501, www.raleigh-clarion.com, from $85) gets mixed reviews, but the location is convenient to the downtown sights. The **Sheraton Raleigh** (421 S. Salisbury St., 919/457-1365, from $149) is also in the heart of the city, and the **Double Tree by Hilton Hotel Raleigh Brownstone-University**

(1707 Hillsborough St., 919/828-0811, www. brownstonehotel.com, from $125) is convenient to both downtown and North Carolina State University. Outside the Beltline, try the **Hampton Inn** (111 Hampton Woods Lane, 919/233-1798, www.hamptoninn.com, from $115) or **Homewood Suites** (5400 Homewood Banks Dr., 919/785-1131, www.homewoodsuites.com, from $115).

FOOD
Eclectic American

Raleigh has a lot of very good restaurants, and one of the chefs on the scene is Ashley Christensen. Since opening her first restaurant, **Poole's Diner** (426 S. McDowell St., 919/832-4477, www.ac-restaurants.com, dinner 5:30pm-midnight daily, $12-30) in 2007, she has garnered all sorts of media attention, appearing on *Iron Chef America,* getting write-ups in major food magazines, and racking up several James Beard Award nominations for "Best Chef: Southeast." The menu at Poole's changes daily, but it's always loaded with fine North Carolina produce, seafood, meats, and cheeses.

In addition to Pooles, Christensen also owns a trio of eateries in a former downtown Piggly Wiggly grocery store: **Chuck's** (237 S. Wilmington St., 919/322-0126, www.ac-restaurants.com, 11:30am-10pm Sun.-Wed., 11:30am-midnight Thurs.-Sat., $5-10), a burgers-and-fries place with a couple of salads. It's wildly popular and can get crowded late on the weekend. **Beasley's Chicken + Honey** (237 S. Wilmington St., 919/322-0127, www.ac-restaurants.com, 11:30am-10pm Sun.-Wed., 11:30am-midnight Thurs.-Sat., $7-13) makes some fabulous fried chicken, but the biscuits are crazy good and the fried chicken, waffles, and honey are worth waiting in line for. Purists will want the quarter fried chicken, but those with a nose for unusual, but still classic, Southern dishes will want the fried chicken served over a waffle, smothered in honey. The sides are all updates to traditional Southern supper side dishes, and the mac and cheese custard is particularly good. **Fox Liquor Bar**

(237 S. Wilmington St., 919/322-0128, www.ac-restaurants.com) is downstairs (the entrance is around the corner) and serves unparalleled craft cocktails. Christensen is planning to expand, adding at least two more eateries in 2013 and 2014.

It's not unusual for a major museum to have a small café or snack bar tucked away between galleries, but the North Carolina Museum of Art has a café that's a destination in itself, that diners visit even if they don't plan to see the exhibits. **Iris** (North Carolina Museum of Art, 2110 Blue Ridge Rd., 919/664-6838, www.ncartmuseum.org, lunch 11:30am-2pm Tues.-Sat., 10:30am-2:30pm Sun., dinner 5:30pm-8:30pm Fri., $10-22) has seasonal fare with a menu that changes with the availability of produce. Chef Andy Hicks delivers international dishes such as seared scallops in a light red curry lemongrass broth along with down-home flavors like pork barbecue with purple slaw and beer-battered onion rings.

Lilly's Pizza (1813 Glenwood Ave., 919/833-0226, www.lillyspizza.com, 11am-10pm Sun.-Thurs., 11am-11pm Fri.-Sat., $7-22) is a locally owned, one-of-a-kind parlor that's been around for more than 15 years. They use lots of organic local ingredients, even in the homemade crusts. You can choose favorite ingredients for a custom pie or have an equally tasty calzone, stromboli, or lasagna. **Hayes Barton Café and Dessertery** (2000 Fairiew Rd., 919/856-8551, http://hayesbartoncafe.com, lunch 11:30am-2pm Tues.-Sat., dinner 6pm-9pm Wed.-Thurs., 6pm-9:30pm Fri.-Sat., $7-20) also serves up a good burger and plenty of other choices, but the real treat at this 1940s-themed restaurant is the long list of cakes and pies.

Asian

Waraji Japanese Restaurant (5910 Duraleigh Rd., 919/783-1883, www.warajijapaneserestaurant.com, lunch 11:30am-2pm Mon.-Fri., noon-2pm Sun., dinner 5:30pm-9:30pm Mon.-Thurs., 5:30pm-10:30pm Fri.-Sat., 5pm-9pm Sun., $10-40) occupies a very spare storefront in a strip mall, belying the uniqueness of this very serious sushi restaurant. Dozens of traditional and imaginative specialty rolls are served, along with tempura, *udon*, and other Japanese entrées. **Mura North Hills** (North Hill Mall, 4121 Main at North Hills St., 919/781-7887, www.muranorthhills.com, 11am-10pm Mon.-Thurs., 11am-11pm Fri.-Sat., 4pm-10pm Sun., $20-70) is known for fine Asian-fusion and has won accolades for its sushi and steak. Sushi, hibachi-style meals, bento boxes, and entrées like crispy duck breast and yellowfin tuna are on the menu. An ever-popular sushi spot is **Haru Sushi** (2603-155 Glenwood Ave., 919/235-0589, www.harusushiusa.com, lunch 11:30am-2:30pm Mon.-Fri., dinner 5pm-10pm Mon.-Fri., 5pm-11pm Sat., 5pm-9pm Sun., $10-20), located in Glenwood Village. **Sono** (319 Fayetteville St., Suite 101, 919/521-5328, www.sonoraleigh.com, lunch 11am-2pm Mon.-Fri., dinner 5pm-10pm Sun.-Thurs., 5pm-11pm Fri.-Sat., $10-60), makes many original sushi rolls as well as bento and noodle dishes along with a seven-course meal.

Sawasdee Thai Restaurant (3601 Capital Blvd., Suite 107, 919/781-7599, http://sawasdeeraleigh.com, lunch 11:30am-2:30pm Mon.-Fri., dinner 5pm-9pm Mon.-Thurs., 5pm-9:30pm Fri., noon-10pm Sat., noon-9pm Sun.; 6204 Glenwood Ave., 919/781-7599, lunch 11:30am-2:30pm Mon.-Fri., dinner 5pm-9:30pm Mon.-Thurs., 5pm-10:30pm Fri., noon-10:30pm Sat., noon-9:30pm Sun., under $20) has a promising system for identifying the relative hotness of its food; it uses the scale of "spicy," "extra spicy," and "make you cry." Many vegetarians have discovered that Thai dishes have hidden animal products, such as oyster or fish sauce, but Sawasdee is happy to make vegetarian dishes.

European

J. Betski's Restaurant (10 W. Franklin St., Suite 120, 919/833-7999, www.jbetskis.com, lunch 11:30am-2pm Tues.-Fri., 11:30am-2:30pm Sat., dinner 5:30pm-10pm Tues.-Sat., $10-26) gets high praise in these parts for traditional German and Polish cuisine, including great pierogi and kielbasa, rich strudel and gingerbread desserts, and a wide selection of German wines and beers. **518 West** (518 W. Jones St., 919/829-2518, www.518west.com, 11:30am-9:30pm Mon.-Thurs., 1:30am-10:30pm Fri.-Sat., 10:30am-2pm and 5pm-9pm Sun., $9-25) serves fresh pasta, wood-fired pizza, and many standard and special Italian dishes, including vegetarian choices. Diners with picky children will be relieved to spot hot dogs and french fries on the kids menu. A fine option for Italian is **Vivace** (4209 Lassiter Mill Rd., Suite 115, 919/787-7747, www.vivaceraleigh.com, 11am-10pm Mon.-Thurs., 11am-11pm Fri.-Sat., 11am-9pm Sun., $10-30), which has a dining room as stylish as the food is delicious. The wine list is unbelievable.

Middle Eastern

◖ **Sitti** (137 S. Wilmington St., 919/239-4070, www.sitti-raleigh.com, 11am-10pm Mon.-Thurs., 11am-midnight Fri.-Sat., 11am-9pm Sun., $12-25) derives its name from the affectionate Lebanese nickname for grandmothers, and this Lebanese restaurant draws from Lebanese family traditions. Chef Ghassan Jarrouj prepares old family recipes as well as specialties he has developed over his 30-year career, which included jobs as chef for three U.S. ambassadors to Lebanon. The menu includes kebabs, hearty stews, and special chef's creations such as pan-seared sea bass.

More than 30 years ago, **Neomonde Baking Company** (3817 Beryl Rd., 919/828-1628, www.neomonde.com, 10am-9pm Mon.-Sun., under $10) was founded in Raleigh by four brothers who had just emigrated from Lebanon. The superior quality of the baked-on-site bread is because the brothers grew up in a family that made bread from scratch—starting not with the flour but with planting a wheat field. Many favorite and less familiar Middle Eastern snacks and sandwiches are on the menu.

Southern

Big Ed of **Big Ed's City Market Restaurant** (220 Wolfe St., 919/836-9909, 7am-2pm Mon.-Fri., 7am-noon Sat., 8am-1pm Sun., lunch about $10, cash only) has made some remarkable claims about his food over the years—asserting that a Big Ed's breakfast will make a tadpole slap a whale, and that the biscuits alone will empower a poodle to pull a freight train. It's not certain that those exact hypotheses have been put to the test, but the crowds at Big Ed's for breakfast and lunch suggest that the claims might not be purely rhetorical. The joint specializes in pork—bacon, country ham, barbecue—and in-season regional vegetables. If you visit for breakfast, you'll be able to order the classic Southern breakfast: ham, grits, and biscuits with red-eye gravy. Now you're in North Carolina.

Greek American restaurateur families have had a strong influence on Southern cuisine for more than a century, often opening the first restaurants in small towns and mastering the arts of frying chicken and boiling greens. Raleigh's **Mecca Restaurant** (13 E. Martin St., 919/832-5714, www.mecca-restaurant. com, 7:30am-midnight Mon.-Wed., 7:30am-2am Thurs.-Sat., $6-18) was opened in 1930 by the Dombalis family and has become so popular with state government bureaucrats that when it celebrated its 75th anniversary, the whole city celebrated Mecca Restaurant Day. At the Mecca's lunch counter you can order any Southern classic you can think of, including eastern North Carolina barbecue and fried trout as well as their popular hamburgers. There's also assorted Mediterranean fare.

Another such case is the Poniros family's **Roast Grill** (7 S. West St., 919/832-8292, www.roastgrill.com, 11am-4pm Mon.-Sat., under $5), which has been serving hot dogs since 1940. You can get a hot dog blackened to your specifications, chili, a glass-bottle Coke or beer, pound cake, and baklava, and that's all—unless the Christmas parade is going by outside, in which case you may also have hot chocolate or coffee. Whatever you do, don't ask for condiments; they admonish customers with "A word of warning: We do not serve french fries, potato chips, ketchup, cheese, kraut, pickles, relish, or mayonnaise. We feel them to be terribly unnecessary and truly demeaning to the passions of a great hot dog connoisseur."

It may sound Spartan, but Raleigh diners have been coming back for almost 70 years.

Barbecue fans will want to make reservations for **The Pit** (328 W. Davie St., 919/890-4500, www.thepit-raleigh.com, 11am-10pm Mon.-Thurs., 11am-11pm Fri.-Sat., 11am-9pm Sun., $12-22). Only a block or so from the heart of downtown, The Pit cooks whole hogs over wood coals and serves eastern North Carolina style 'cue as well as western style, Texas-style beef brisket, baby-back and spare ribs, barbecue chicken and turkey, and fried chicken. Make a reservation; this place gets packed. If it's just one or two of you, and you're feeling a little adventurous, ask to sit at The Piggy, a kitchen-window counter that puts you in the midst of the action.

Eclectic International
Buku (110 E. Davie St., 919/834-6963, http:// bukuraleigh.com, 11am-late daily, $7-30) serves street food from many cultures. Chef William D'Auvray stresses that this is not "fusion" food; each dish is prepared in a way that's faithful to its culinary tradition. The result is a menu that offers dishes as varied as Indian *paneer,* Lebanese *fattoush,* Colombian arepas, and Vietnamese crepes. There are also a number of gluten-free dishes available.

Food Trucks
Augmenting all of Raleigh's fantastic restaurants are a fleet of food trucks. Events like the **Downtown Raleigh Food Truck Rodeo** (http:// downtownraleighfoodtruckrodeo.com), held throughout the year on Fayetteville Street, bring as many as 50 food trucks from across the triangle into one street-party smorgasbord. Attending the rodeo will give you a feel for the vibrancy of Raleigh's foodie hordes and let you sample some of the best food trucks; you'll know them by their long lines.

Only Burger (919/937-9377, http://onlyburger.com, $5-10) serves burgers exclusively, including the specialty Fried Green Tomato Burger, served with a fried green tomato, a fried egg, and homemade pimento cheese. **Chirba Chirba** (www.chirbachirba.

com, under $10) serves Chinese dumplings, steam buns, and dim sum dishes. **Porchetta** (919/727-6750, www.porchettardu.com, $6-10), pronounced "Por-KET-ah," is a pork enthusiast's dream. The menu is all pig, all the time, with dishes like shaved roasted pork on ciabatta with a variety of toppings, from apple-horseradish slaw to provolone and grain mustard. **Local in Motion** (www.boxcarrfarms.com, $2.50-12) is a food truck based out of a local organic and sustainable farm. The menu's ever-changing, but they always serve things you won't anticipate, like breakfast and even brunch fare; offerings have included french toast, eggs benedict, cubano sandwiches, and squash soup.

Bakeries

Raleigh has its very own cupcake boutique, the **Cupcake Shoppe Bakery** (104 Glenwood Ave., 919/821-4223, http://thecupcakeshopperaleigh.com, 10am-8pm Mon.-Thurs., 10am-11pm Fri.-Sat. $3 per cupcake, mixed dozen $33). They bake fresh batches daily in at least a dozen flavors, including basic chocolate and vanilla with chocolate and vanilla icing, red velvet with cream cheese icing, and dark chocolate with espresso buttercream icing. A nice touch is that the shop is open late on the weekend, allowing for quick satisfaction of cravings after dinner and a movie.

Balcazar Bakery (4020 Capital Blvd., Suite 104, 919/878-5120, http://balcazarbakery.com, 4pm-9:15pm Mon., 9am-9pm Tues.-Sat., 10am-8pm Sun., $3-20), specializing in baked delicacies from Latin America such as shakes, pastries, wedding cakes, and breads.

INFORMATION AND SERVICES

The main hospital in Raleigh is **WakeMed** (3000 New Bern Ave., 919/350-8900), although Rex Healthcare and Duke Health also operate hospitals. If you have an emergency, call 911. There is at least one 24-hour pharmacy, **CVS** (3914 Capital Blvd., 919/876-0817).

Visitor information can be found at the

Greater Raleigh Convention and Visitors Bureau (Bank of America Plaza, 421 Fayetteville St., 800/849-8499, www.visitraleigh.com), the **Greater Raleigh Chamber of Commerce** (800 S. Salisbury St., 919/664-7000, www.raleighchamber.org), and the state **Department of Tourism** (301 N. Wilmington St., 1st Fl., 800/847-4862, www.visitnc.com). For international travelers who need to exchange currency, Raleigh-Durham Airport has **TRAVELEX outlets** (919/840-0366, 7am-8pm daily Terminal 2 Ticketing Lobby, 2pm-5:30pm daily Terminal 2 Baggage Claim).

GETTING THERE AND AROUND

I-40 and U.S. 70 are the main highways to and through town. The Raleigh Beltline, I-440, forms a ring around the city, with I-40, U.S. 70, and U.S. 64 radiating outward. I-40 is the quickest route west to Chapel Hill and east to I-95. I-40 and U.S. 70 are both good routes to Durham. U.S. 64 goes to Wilson, and on the other side of the city joins U.S. 1 headed southeast toward Sanford and the Sandhills.

Raleigh-Durham International Airport (RDU, 2400 John Brantley Blvd., Morrisville, 919/840-2123, www.rdu.com) is the primary airport in the Triangle, and one of the main airports in the state. It's located 15 minutes' drive northwest of Raleigh along I-40 and is a hub for most major national airlines. **Amtrak** (800/872-7245, www.amtrak.com) has stations in Raleigh (320 W. Cabarrus St., Raleigh) and in neighboring Cary (211 N. Academy St., Cary) served by several trains daily on regional routes and long-haul trains between New York City and Miami.

Raleigh's **CAT** (Capital Area Transit, 919/485-7433, www.raleighnc.gov) system runs buses all over the city, both inside and outside the Beltline, and connects to major transportation hubs. Many taxi and car services are available, including **Yellow Cab** (919/677-0000, http://rduyellowcab.com), **Alliance Concierge** (919/815-6953), and **Blue Diamond Limousines and Sedans** (919/772-9595, www.bluediamondlimo.com).

RALEIGH SUBURBS

Raleigh is girded by extensive suburbs and old towns that have become bedroom communities, including Apex, Zebulon, Fuquay-Varina, and Cary—home to many of the new arrivals who work in the tech sector. The small town of **Wake Forest** in northern Wake County is the original home of Wake Forest University, which is now located 100 miles west in Winston-Salem. Wake Forest is an attractive town with pretty historic architecture—including the pre-1820 **Calvin Jones House** (440 N. Main St., Wake Forest, 919/556-2911, www.wakeforestbirthplace.org, tours 9am-4:30pm Tues.-Fri. and 2pm-5pm Sun., free) as well as cafés, shops, and **Falls Lake State Recreation Area** (13304 Creedmoor Rd., Wake Forest, 919/676-1027, http://ncparks.gov). At Falls Lake, you'll find 13 miles of mountain biking trails, several miles of hiking trails, fishing, and swimming at Sandling Beach and Beaverdam.

Zebulon, just east of Raleigh, is the home of the **Carolina Mudcats** (www.gomudcats.com), a double-A minor-league baseball team affiliated with the Florida Marlins major-league team. The Mudcats' **Five County Stadium** (1501 Hwy. 39, Zebulon, 919/269-2287, www.gomudcats.com) is a great place to watch serious baseball in an affordable, cozy small-town setting.

Cary, southwest of Raleigh, is in many ways the quintessence of the suburban growth experienced in the this region in the last couple of decades. It's also a historical place; you can explore the old **Page-Walker Hotel** (119 Ambassador Loop, Cary, 919/460-4963, www.friendsofpagewalker.org, 10am-9:30pm Mon.-Thurs., 10am-5pm Fri., 10am-1pm Sat., free, donations accepted), now a local heritage museum. You can also catch a **Carolina Railhawks** (http://carolinarailhawks.com) pro soccer game, and try *chum-chum* or *sandesh* at the **Mithai House of Indian Desserts** (744-F E. Chatham St., Cary, 919/469-9651, www.mithaius.com, 11:30am-5:30pm Mon., 11am-9pm Tues.-Sun.). For a good Southern-inspired lunch or supper, visit **Lucky 32** (7307 Tryon Rd., between U.S. 1/64 and Kildaire Farm, Cary, 919/233-1632, www.lucky32.com, 10am-9pm Mon., 11:15am-10pm Tues.-Thurs., 11:15am-11pm Fri.-Sat., 10am-9pm Sun., brunch until 3pm Sat.-Sun., lunch $10-16, dinner $10-28, brunch $9-13).

Cary's **Booth Amphitheatre** (8003 Regency Pkwy., 919/462-2025, http://boothamphitheatre.com) hosts a number of concerts, movies, and events throughout the year in a beautiful lakeside facility. I was impressed not only with the size and arrangement of the place but with the food options, the outstanding concessions, and the beer selection. Check their website for upcoming concerts and events.

Durham

Home of Duke University and North Carolina Central University (called "Central"), Durham hosts several major arts festivals, most notably the Full-Frame Documentary Festival and the American Dance Festival, that bring in tens of thousands of visitors every year. Duke University's famous Blue Devils are one of the nation's dominant college basketball teams, and Central's Eagles are a football powerhouse. There's a great deal of literary activity here too, with a wide variety of bookstores.

Formerly abuzz with cigarette-rolling factories, Durham has met the demise of the tobacco industry, to which it owes its existence, gracefully. Many of the long brick warehouses, formerly factories for Lorillard and Winston and American Tobacco, have been transformed into attractive restaurants and public venues. The American Tobacco Historic District ensures that the city's smoky origins won't be forgotten.

Durham is also an important center of urban African American heritage. In the early 20th century it was called the capital of the

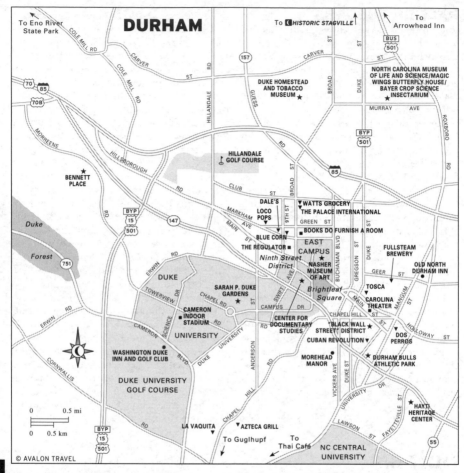

DURHAM

black middle class. North Carolina Central University is a historically African American school, and though it's often overshadowed by nearby Duke, the University of North Carolina, and North Carolina State, it is one of the state's major educational institutions. Next to Central's campus is Hayti, a neighborhood where African Americans maintained a bustling commercial district during the era of segregation. Blind Boy Fuller, Reverend Gary Davis, and other Carolina blues legends did stints here as street performers, and a historical marker next to the Hayti Heritage Center commemorates their time in Durham.

DUKE UNIVERSITY

Duke University is often considered a sort of Southern Ivy League school, and the reputation is deserved, as its students are among the academic elite in the country. The architecture of the Duke campus—much of it designed by turn-of-the-20th-century African American architect Julian Abele—is done up in dark Gothic stonework and feels like it could be in the Northeast. Originally called Trinity

© JASON FRYE

Signs around town reveal Durham's tobacco past.

College and located in Randolph County, it came to Durham and became Duke University under the patronage of the Duke family, tobacco barons who were responsible for, among other things, the university's early policy of enrolling women. It continues to be a leading light in the world of academia.

Duke's **Center for Documentary Studies** (CDS, 1317 W. Pettigrew St., 919/660-3663, http://documentarystudies.duke.edu, gallery 9am-7pm Mon.-Thurs., 9am-5pm Fri., 11am-4pm Sat., 1pm-5pm Sun.) is an invaluable resource for artists, documentarians, and educators throughout the region as well as a fascinating place to visit when you're in town. Occupying the Lyndhurst House, a handsome old home on Pettigrew Street within easy walking distance of the 9th Street shops and restaurants, CDS includes a gallery, teaching facilities, and extensive darkrooms and labs. The gallery showcases documentary screenings and cutting-edge photography and multimedia work and makes a fun stop for anyone intrigued by today's documentary renaissance.

The Nasher Museum of Art (2001 Campus Dr., 919/684-5135, www.nasher.duke.edu, 10am-5pm Tues.-Wed. and Fri.-Sat., 10am-9pm Thurs., noon-5pm Sun., $5 adults, $4 seniors, $3 students and under age 16) is home to extensive collections of ancient and medieval art, including one of the largest collections of pre-Columbian Latin American art in the United States. The building is a stunningly modern creation by architect Rafael Viñoly. Adjoining the grounds of the Nasher are the **Sarah P. Duke Gardens** (420 Anderson St., 919/684-3698, http://gardens.duke.edu, 8am-dusk daily, free), 55 acres of some of the finest landscaping and horticultural arts to be seen in the Southeast.

Duke also has a fantastic music and performance series, **Duke Performances** (919/660-3356, http://dukeperformances.duke.edu), which brings in 60-70 performers each year. Music includes string quartets, rock bands, bluegrass groups, and folk music from around the world as well as theater performances and

RALEIGH AND THE TRIANGLE

dance. Events take place at various venues on campus and in town.

NORTH CAROLINA CENTRAL UNIVERSITY

North Carolina Central University was founded in 1910, the first public liberal arts college for African Americans in the United States. Still a predominantly black institution, Central is one of the state's great universities, rivaling Duke, its much larger neighbor, in significance. The **North Carolina Central University Art Museum** (Lawson St., between Fine Arts Bldg. and Music Bldg., NCCU campus, 919/530-6211, www.nccu.edu, 9am-5pm Tues.-Fri., 2pm-4pm Sun., free) specializes in the work of 19th- and 20th-century African American artists. The collections include work by such prominent masters as Romare Bearden, Jacob Lawrence, Henry Ossawa Tanner, and Minnie Evans. Inside the William Jones Building on Central's campus is a display of Durham's **Woolworth Lunch Counter,** site of a 1960 sit-in attended by Martin Luther King Jr. that signaled a sea-change in the civil rights movement.

AFRICAN AMERICAN HERITAGE SIGHTS

Sites of importance in African American history are found throughout Durham. **St. Joseph's Performance Hall** and the **Hayti Heritage Center** (804 Old Fayetteville St., 919/683-1709, www.hayti.org, 10am-5pm Mon.-Fri., 10am-3pm Sat.) celebrate the historic African American community of Hayti—pronounced "HAY-tye," to rhyme with "necktie." The former St. Joseph's AME Church sanctuary is a special venue for the performing arts in Durham, and the Heritage Center houses an art gallery, a dance studio, and a community meeting space. Also on Fayetteville Street is **White Rock Baptist Church** (3400 Fayetteville St., 919/683-1649, www.whiterockbaptist-church.org.whsites.net), home of a congregation founded in 1866. Martin Luther King Jr. spoke here in 1960 after participating in the Woolworth sit-in.

The neoclassical revival-style **Mechanics and Farmers Bank Building** (116 W. Parrish St., 919/687-7803, 9am-5pm Mon.-Thurs., 9am-6pm Fri.) stands at the heart of a downtown district known in the early 20th century as **Black Wall Street.** Mechanics and Farmers Bank and "the Mutual" were the flagships of Durham's African American commercial establishment. The history of the Mutual, the **North Carolina Mutual Life Insurance Company** (411 W. Chapel Hill St., 919/682-9201, www.ncmutuallife.com), is chronicled in the Heritage Room at its modern-day location on West Chapel Hill Street.

ℂ Historic Stagville

About 15 minutes' drive north of downtown Durham, **Historic Stagville** (5828 Old Oxford Hwy., 919/620-0120, www.stagville.org, 10am-4pm Tues.-Sat., hourly tours 10am-3pm most days) preserves part of what was a staggeringly large plantation system. In 1860 the Cameron-Bennehan family's holdings totaled nearly 30,000 acres, and the 900 enslaved African Americans who worked the land were one of the South's largest slave communities. Historic Stagville includes 71 acres of the original plantations, with several notable vernacular structures that include a two-story timber-frame slave quarters, a massive hipped-roof barn built in 1860, and the late-18th-century Bennehan plantation house. Interpretation of the Stagville site acknowledges the central role that enslaved African Americans played here and tries to reconstruct, through documentary evidence, archaeology, and folklore, what life may have been like for the slaves. One of the main events on Stagville's calendar is its **Juneteenth Celebration,** an event celebrated in parts of the South for generations that marks the emancipation of enslaved African Americans at the end of the Civil War. Stagville's Juneteenth features music, food, crafts, and interpretation by costumed guides.

OTHER SIGHTS

A different side of 19th-century Durham life is presented at the **Duke Homestead and**

Tobacco Museum (2828 Duke Homestead Rd., 919/477-5498, www.dukehomestead. org, usually 9am-5pm Tues.-Sat., free). Here the patriarch of Durham's tobacco industry, Washington Duke, began his career as a humble tobacco farmer. Discovering the popularity of bright-leaf tobacco among Union soldiers at the end of the Civil War, he began processing large quantities of it, at one point wrapping the product in labels that read, ironically, "Pro Bono Publico." This was the beginning of North Carolina's quick rise to the top of the world tobacco market, an economy that transformed the state and built the city of Durham. The Duke Homestead displays and demonstrates period techniques in tobacco culture throughout the year.

Bennett Place (4409 Bennett Memorial Rd., 919/383-4345, www.bennettplacehistoricsite.com, 9am-5pm Tues.-Sat., free) is a historic site that commemorates the meeting of Confederate General Joseph Johnston and Union General William Tecumseh Sherman in April 1865. In the last days of the Civil War, when Jefferson Davis was fleeing south to Georgia and Abraham Lincoln was dead, Johnston and Sherman held a series of negotiations here that led to the surrender of all the Confederate forces in the Carolinas, Georgia, and Florida.

The **North Carolina Museum of Life and Science** (433 Murray Ave., 919/220-5429, http://lifeandscience.org, 10am-5pm Mon.-Sat., noon-5pm Sun., $14 adults, $11 over age 64 and military, $10 ages 3-12), home of the Magic Wings Butterfly House and the Bayer Crop Science Insectarium, is the perfect place for children who enjoy meeting strange bugs, climbing inside tornadoes, and taking a trip on a locomotive to see red wolves. Grayson's Café, inside the museum, is open until 4pm daily.

For the truly adventurous, there is no better way to see Durham than in the open air. Pilot Mike Ratty takes one or two passengers at a time for **sightseeing flights** (www. carolinabarnstormers.com, fall-spring, $125 for 25 minutes, $225 per hour) in a 1940s biplane. The price is steep but the experience is unforgettable.

ENTERTAINMENT AND EVENTS

🎬 Full Frame Documentary Festival

April brings the **Full Frame Documentary Festival** (919/687-4100, www.fullframefest. org, films $15, opening-night party and awards barbecue $25, some screenings and talks free), identified by the *New York Times* as the premier documentary film festival in the country before it was even in its 10th year. Venues around downtown host screenings, workshops, panels, and soirees where documentary fans and aspiring filmmakers can mingle with the glitterati of the genre.

Other Festivals

February's **Black Diaspora Film Festival** (919/683-1709, www.hayti.org, free) takes place at the Hayti Heritage Center (804 Old Fayetteville St.). Films about African and African American experiences are screened and discussed in a stimulating event. The **Grady Tate Jazz Festival** (www.nccu.edu) takes place in April at North Carolina Central University. The state was home to jazz legends such as Thelonious Monk and John Coltrane, and Central has a widely respected jazz program, so it's only fitting that Durham should host this prestigious event.

For six weeks every summer, Durham is the site of the **American Dance Festival** (919/684-6402, www.americandancefestival.org), an internationally known event where the world's best choreographers often premiere new work. Durhamites and the visitors who come from around the world are one step ahead of audiences in New York. One of the region's most popular music festivals is the **Festival for the Eno** (919/620-9099, www.enoriver.org), which takes place every 4th of July weekend. The festival is held on the banks of the Eno River, so you can listen to the performances from the comfort of your inner tube while floating in the river. In addition to showcasing dozens of excellent world, folk, and bluegrass bands, the Festival for the Eno is a great place for browsing the work of many of North Carolina's craftspeople. The beautiful images used to promote each year's festival are collected by festivalgoers in the Triangle.

August's **North Carolina Gay and Lesbian Film Festival** (919/560-3030, www.carolinatheatre.org, screenings $10, 10-film pass around $85) is the second-largest such event in the Southeast. Approximately 10,000 visitors attend the festival every year to watch new work by up-and-coming LGBT filmmakers at Durham's Carolina Theater (309 W. Morgan St.). The **Bull Durham Blues Festival** (804 Old Fayetteville St., 919/683-1709, www.hayti.org/blues) is put on by the Hayti Heritage Association in September. Now more than 20 years old, the festival brings modern blues artists from around the region and around the world to celebrate Durham's history as a gathering place for some of the greatest Piedmont-style blues musicians. The oldest old-timers still remember Reverend Gary Davis, Blind Boy Fuller, and other important figures in early blues busking on the street corners of Durham when the tobacco markets were in full swing.

Nightlife

The **All People's Grill** (6122 Guess Rd., 919/620-9591) has been serving Southern soul food and great blues music for generations. While gobbling up on-the-money collard greens and fried chicken, you can hear some of the top blues artists of this region, many of them on the roster of the Music Maker Relief Foundation (www.musicmaker.org), a regional organization that promotes blues musicians to ensure that they are able to make a living playing and to pass on their art. Nowadays the grill is only open for special events, so call for details on upcoming shows.

Bingo parlors dot the landscape, but Durham is one of the few places where you can be part of the craze that is **Drag Bingo** (NC State Fairgrounds, Holshouser Bldg., 1025 Blue Ridge Blvd., Raleigh, www.dragbingo.com, doors open 5:30pm, games at 7pm, $20).

Once a month, tickets go on sale and sell out fast for a bingo event to benefit area HIV/AIDS services. It's an incredibly fun scene—a mixture of gay and straight, folks in drag and in everyday attire, covetable prizes, a little bit of raunchy humor, and a lot of money raised for a great cause.

James Joyce Irish Pub (912 W. Main St., 919/683-3022, www.jamesjoyceirishpub.com, 11:30am-2am Mon.-Sat., 10am-2am Sun.) is a favorite local bar, established by a Durhamite originally from County Kerry. Here you can drink a pint while listening to live music or watching Duke basketball, rugby, or football (in this place, that means soccer).

One of the best places to grab a beer in Durham is ◖ **Fullsteam Brewery** (726 Rigsbee Ave., 919/682-2337, www.fullsteam.ag, 4pm-midnight Mon.-Thurs., 4pm-2am Fri., noon-2am Sat., noon-midnight Sun.). This fun and funky hangout celebrates two great things: Southern farmers and beer. The brews all incorporate Southern heirloom grains, botanicals, and locally-foraged goods like persimmons for some creative and flavorful beers. They have a number of beers sold year-round, ranging from Carver Sweet Potato beer, the Working Man's Lunch (a rich beer that's malty, chocolaty, and has notes of vanilla), and the namesake Fullsteam Southern Lager. Seasonal beers include a hickory-smoked porter, a basil saison, and an IPA laden with lemon thyme and bronze fennel. Many of the local food trucks stop by to feed the hungry crowds, and events like trivia, yoga, discussions on theology, chair massages, craft nights, belly dancers, music, and mystery movie night keep this place hopping (pun intended).

SHOPPING
Malls and Shopping Districts
Brightleaf Square (905 W. Main St., 919/682-9229, www.historicbrightleaf.com) is handsome circa-1900 American Tobacco Company warehouses that are no longer hives of cigarette rolling but have evolved into the flagship of Durham's post-tobacco industry revitalization.

Over a dozen restaurants now occupy the old industrial bays, side-by-side with diverse and interesting retailers.

The **Streets at Southpoint** (6910 Fayetteville Rd., at I-40, 919/572-8808, www.streetsatsouthpoint.com, 10am-9pm Mon.-Sat., noon-7pm Sun.) is a traditional shopping mall with movie theaters and a food court, but it's huge, with one million square feet of retail and restaurant space. In addition to the usual anchor department stores and mall chains, Southpoint features a nice selection of upscale clothing shops and has one of only three **Apple Stores** in North Carolina, along with a wide range of food that goes well beyond the traditional mall food court.

The core of the **9th Street District** of Durham, adjacent to the Duke campus, are the blocks between Main Street and Hillsborough Road/Markham Avenue. You'll find many small and very good eateries and an eclectic mix of shops that include several good bookstores and a pair of vintage boutiques worth peeking into.

Books

The Regulator (720 9th St., 919/286-2700, www.regulatorbookshop.com, 10am-9pm Mon.-Sat., noon-6pm Sun.) is one of the Triangle area's favorite bookshops. It hosts readings by important authors from around the world and has a periodicals section that carries an eccentric selection of literary journals and homemade zines. **Wentworth and Leggett Rare Books and Prints** (Brightleaf Square, 905 W. Main St., 919/688-5311, www.wentworth-leggettbooks.com, 11am-7pm Mon.-Sat. Jan.-Oct., call for hours Sun. and Nov.-Dec.) is an antiquarian book dealer also specializing in old prints, maps, postcards, and magazines. Other good area bookstores are **Books Do Furnish a Room** (1809 W. Markham Ave., 919/286-1076, www.booksdofurnisharoom.com, 10am-6pm most days) for new books, and the Durham branch of **Nice Price Books** (811 Broad St., 919/416-1066, http://nicepricebooksandrecords.com, 10am-9pm Mon.-Sat., noon-6pm Sun.) for used books and music.

SPORTS AND RECREATION
Hiking, Cycling, and Water Sports

Durham is loaded with choices for hikers, joggers, and bikers. The Eno River is surrounded by thousands of acres of parkland, much of which is marked for hiking. **Eno River State Park** (6101 Cole Mill. Rd., 919/383-1686, http://ncparks.gov, hours vary for river access points, call or check the website), northwest of Durham, offers hiking, canoeing through Class I-III rapids, and camping in the beautiful and wild river valley. The **Eno River Association** (www.enoriver.org) has more information on sites and ways to enjoy the river. **Frog Hollow Canoe and Kayak** (919/416-1200, www.froghollowoutdoors.com, 9am-4pm Tues.-Sat., 10am-4pm Sun. Mar.-mid-Dec., noon-4pm Wed.-Sat. mid-Dec.-Feb., tours by reservation only, from $25) rents out boats and guides tours. Their guides can take you on moonlight paddles and other trips down various rivers in the area, and even paddling and camping.

The **American Tobacco Trail** (www.triangletrails.org) comprises 12 miles of walking, hiking, and cycling trails throughout Durham, including some through downtown. The trail will eventually be 22 miles long. The **Carolina Tarwheels** (919/687-5066, www.tarwheels.org), a weekend cycling club, welcomes newcomers and visitors.

Golf

Golfers have several good public courses to choose from. **Hillandale Golf Course** (1600 Hillandale Rd., 919/286-4211 or 800/367-2582, www.hillandalegolf.com, 18 holes, par 71, greens fees Mon.-Fri. about $21, cart $9-13, Sat.-Sun. about $25, cart $9-16) has relatively few bunkers and almost no water hazards, making for a course where long drivers and aggressive players can score some eagles. The course record is 59, and with its player-friendly design, if you're on top of your game, you may be able to shave a stroke or two off that.

Lakeshore Golf Course (4621 Lumley Rd., 919/596-2401, www.lakeshoregc.com, 18 holes, par 73, greens fees Mon.-Fri. $19 walking, $34 riding, Sat.-Sun. and holidays $42, discounts for seniors, under age 17, military, late play, 9 holes) has a number of water hazards to contend with. On the front nine, if you hit your drive to the left on number 1, you're in the water, and on number 6, a creek guards the front of the green—but this is nothing compared to the back nine, where you'll find some hellish water hazards, including creeks, lakes, and number 15, almost completely surrounded by water. This is a beautiful but at times brutal course.

The **Duke University Golf Club** (3001 Cameron Blvd., 919/681-2288, http://golf. duke.edu, 18 holes, par 72, greens fees Mon.-Thurs. $55, Fri.-Sun. $100, discounts for seniors and late play) underwent renovations in 2013 and has come back more beautiful and playable than ever. With numerous doglegs and narrowing fairways, this course can be a challenge for novice golfers. Number 13, a short par 4, demands proper ball placement or you'll end up in the pond in front of you or in one of two creeks, guarded by trees, on either side of the fairway.

Indoor Recreation

Play billiards, foosball, shuffleboard, and darts at **The Green Room** (1108 Broad St., 919/286-2359, www.greenroomdurham.com, 5pm-2am daily). They've got 100 brands of beer, including a decent selection of microbrews and craft brews, in bottles and cans. **XTreme Kombat** (7460 Hwy. 98/Wake Forest Rd., 919/596-6100, www.xtremekombat.com, 10am-6pm Sat.-Sun., by appointment Mon.-Fri., paintball from $45, Airsoft from $25, laser tag $370 for eight players) is a paintball, Airsoft, laser tag, and combat-scenario extravaganza. Seven fields of play offer different challenges to paintball and shooting-sport enthusiasts.

Spectator Sports

Thanks to the exploits of a demon and a smoke-snorting steer, Durham is probably even better known for its sports than its history as a tobacco dynamo. The NCAA Division 1 **Duke Blue Devils** embody the gold standard in college basketball and excel in many other sports.

Their history is chronicled in the **Duke Sports Hall of Fame** (Towerview Rd., 919/613-7500, 9am-5pm Mon.-Fri., free), inside Cameron Indoor Stadium. Coach Mike Krzyzewski—that's pronounced "shuh-SHEV-skee," and don't mispronounce it, but you can call him Coach K—has shepherded the men's basketball team since 1980, leading them to a phenomenal number of championships. His resemblance to the Duke mascot, a blue-clad horned demon, is equally phenomenal. Duke has turned out some of the greatest basketball players of the last 20 years, including Grant Hill, Christian Laettner, and J. J. Reddick.

Not surprisingly, it is extremely difficult to come by Duke basketball tickets. Duke students are famous for living in tents for months on end outside Cameron Indoor Stadium, waiting to buy tickets and then to snag good standing-room spots in the courtside student section of the arena. If you're on campus in season, take a look at their tent city, known as Krzyzewskiville. If you're lucky enough to get into a game, you'll have the treat—or trauma, depending on your loyalties—of seeing the "Cameron Crazies" in the flesh. These Duke fans, often half naked and painted blue like Pictish warriors, are known for their creative, funny, and sometimes edgy chants and heckles.

The **Durham Bulls** (Durham Bulls Athletic Park, 409 Blackwell St., 919/687-6500, www.durhambulls.com)—yes, of "Bull Durham" fame—are one of the nation's most recognizable minor-league baseball teams. They are the Triple-A farm team for the Tampa Bay Devil Rays, so you're likely to see big-league players here rehabbing from injury and rookies on the brink of making it big. The ballpark, designed by the architect who built Baltimore's Camden Yards, is comfortable and fun. A big wooden bull peers down from the end of the third-base line, and when a Bull hits a home run, the bull's eyes light up red, his tail flaps, and smoke billows from his nostrils.

ACCOMMODATIONS

The most upscale place to stay in Durham is the **Washington Duke Inn and Golf Club**

SCORING COLLEGE BASKETBALL TICKETS

If you're visiting the Triangle during college basketball season and are hoping to catch a game in person, you can count on not being able to buy tickets at the box office. The 20,000-seat "Dean Dome," UNC's Dean E. Smith Center, routinely sells out for men's basketball in-conference games, and the PNC Arena, the 20,000-seat NC State men's basketball home court, often does as well. Duke plays at the comparatively small Cameron Indoor Stadium, and its 9,000 seats are the hardest of all to obtain tickets for. Tickets for women's basketball games, which at UNC and NC State are played on older, smaller courts, are much less difficult to come by, although the Atlantic Coast Conference (ACC) division games sometimes sell out, and the Duke-versus-UNC women's games always do. The most prized and scarce treasure of all is a ticket to the Duke-versus-UNC men's basketball game. Unless a current student of one of the schools really likes you or you're a major benefactor with a classroom building named in your honor, your chances of paying face value for a ticket are slim to none.

During basketball season, tickets appear on eBay, Craigslist, and ticket-scalping websites. Really good tickets will probably go on the auction block well in advance of the game and are fought over fiercely. If you wait until the day of a game, there's a chance of finding a seller who has just that day decided not to use his or her own tickets and wants to get rid of them fast; to win these, you've got to stay alert and act fast. Prices vary from game to game, and for a minor out-of-conference game played early in the season, you should be able to get a reasonably good ticket for $10-20 above face value and without much difficulty, if the game sells out at all. For a sold-out game between ACC teams, prices go up steeply; expect to pay three or more times the face value for a seat at an in-conference game of minor importance. For an important ACC game, the worst seats in the house could be over $100, and good seats $200-300 or more. If you want to go to a UNC-versus-Duke game, seats up in the rafters will be in the hundreds, and a good seat could easily set you back over $1,000.

Ticket scalping is illegal in North Carolina, and it's also pretty common. On game day, the scalpers are the people hanging around outside the arena or on nearby street corners holding signs that say "Need Tickets." Technically, they probably will buy tickets if you're selling, but "Need Tickets" is code for "I have tickets." If you buy from a scalper, be firm in your negotiations. If you ask for courtside seats for $20, you'll only get laughter and lose your bargaining position, but if you start not too far below the bounds of reason, they'll talk business. Be willing to turn down a best offer; there's another scalper just a few steps away. If you don't mind missing the first few minutes of the game, you'll find that prices start going down at tip-off.

For hard-core basketball fans, the research, haggling, and expense are a small price to pay for a chance to attend an ACC game. There's nothing like watching your favorite team warm up, seeing Crazy Towel Guy do his thing at Cameron Indoor Stadium, or being in the same room with 10,000 people who know all the words to the fight song.

(3001 Cameron Blvd., 800/443-3853, www.washingtondukeinn.com, from $200). Located on the grounds of the Duke University Golf Course on the Duke campus, the guest rooms and suites are sunny and plush, with the option of bunk beds for families traveling with kids. Babysitting services can be arranged by the concierge. Also convenient to the Duke campus, the **University Inn** (502 Elf St.,

919/286-3817 or 800/313-3585, www.universityinnduke.com, from $90, lower for extended visits) is a basic motel that's a good value in a good location.

Durham's most celebrated bed-and-breakfast is the C **Arrowhead Inn** (106 Mason Rd., 800/528-2207, www.arrowheadinn.com, from $150), a AAA Four Diamond awardee on a Revolutionary-era plantation about 15 minutes from downtown. All of the luxurious guest rooms have their own fireplaces, and several have two-person whirlpool tubs. On the inn's grounds are a garden cottage with a whirlpool tub and two-person steam shower, along with a rather fabulous log cabin with a sleeping loft and spa-like bath appointments. The **Old North Durham Inn** (922 N. Mangum St., 919/683-1885, www.bbonline. com, from $125) is a pretty house on one of the old primary roads in the city. It has been cited by the Durham Historic Preservation Society for its excellent renovation. Guests receive free tickets to Durham Bulls games and can look out their bedroom windows across the street at the home where much of *Bull Durham* was filmed. Also downtown is **Morehead Manor** (914 Vickers Ave., 888/437-6333, www.more-headmanor.com, from $145), a late-20th-century house built for a tobacco executive, in easy walking distance from many downtown attractions. The **Eno Cottage Guest House** (2800 Old Oxford Rd., 919/236-3879, www.enocottage.com, from $125) is 10 minutes' drive outside downtown Durham on a 50-acre working horse farm. Within walking distance of the Eno River and some federal game lands, there are plenty of outdoor activities here.

There are many chain motels around the city, including **La Quinta** (4414 Durham-Chapel Hill Blvd., 919/401-9660, www.lq.com, from $85, pets allowed), **Holiday Inn Express** (2516 Guess Rd., 919/313-3244, www.ihg.com, from $95), **Hampton Inn** (1524 N. Gregson St., 919/688-8882, http://hamptoninn3.hilton. com, from $115, pets allowed), and **Quality Inn and Suites** (3710 Hillsborough Rd., 919/382-3388, www.qualityinn.com, from about $70, pets allowed).

FOOD
Eclectic American

(Watts Grocery (1116 Broad St., 919/416-5040, www.wattsgrocery.com, 11:30am-2:30pm and 5:30pm-10pm daily, brunch 11am-2:30pm Sat. and Sun., entrées $18-23), located in the Watts neighborhood of Durham, near the Duke campus, is the restaurant of Amy Tornquist, a master Southern chef. The menu features locally grown produce in season, North Carolina seafood, and local artisanal cheeses. The menu features many gourmet variations on classic North Carolina dishes and is bound to please any fan of Southern food.

The **(Cosmic Cantina** (1920 Perry St., 919/286-1875, 11am-4am daily, under $10), a casual take-out or seat-yourself joint in the middle of the 9th Street neighborhood near the Duke campus, serves the best burritos you'll find just about anywhere. Folks who love it swear that eating at the Cantina is a life-changing experience. The award-winning restaurant **Nana's** (2514 University Dr., 919/493-8545, www.nanasdurham.com, from 5pm Mon.-Sat., $18-30) is presided over by chef Scott Howell, a North Carolina native. The fare is hearty but elegant, and the wine list has won *Wine Spectator* magazine's Award of Excellence. Vegetarian options are few, but carnivores will be well satisfied.

The **Blue Note Grill** (4125 Durham-Chapel Hill Blvd., 919/401-1979, www.thebluenotegrill.com, 11am-10pm Mon. and Wed.-Thurs., 11am-11pm Tues., 11am-midnight Fri., 4pm-midnight Sat., noon-8pm Sun., $8-23) is a blues bar with a barbecue problem. In all seriousness, this restaurant is a fine place to see blues, jazz, and bluegrass acts while you eat some fantastic ribs. The menu features ribs, barbecue, burritos, some well-regarded burgers that include a patty melt, and late-night bar bites like wings and assorted fried snacks.

African

The Palace International (1104 Broad St., 919/416-4922, www.thepalaceinternational. com, 11am-9pm Tues.-Thurs., 11am-10pm Fri., 4pm-10pm Sat., 11am-4pm Sun., entrées $10-17), hosted by Kenyan American proprietors, serves East and West African specialties. The menu features tilapia, goat curry, and oxtails, among many other entrées, but vegetarians will also find delicious and filling meals.

Asian

The **(Thai Café** (2501 University Dr.,

919/493-9794, www.thaicafenc.com, 11:30am-3pm and 5pm-10pm daily, $10-20) is the sort of restaurant whose regulars might visit a dozen times before they'll try a second item on the menu because whatever they tried on that first visit was so good they've been craving it since. Classic Thai offerings include pad thai, *tom yum,* and *pad prik*—all delicious—but the real masterpieces here are the curries. You can choose yellow, green, panang, and massaman curries with meat, seafood, tofu, or vegetables. One warning: "Not spicy" at Thai Café means incredibly spicy. If you want mild food, make a special point of it to the server.

On 9th Street, convenient to Duke, is an Indian restaurant with the rather unlikely name of **Dale's** (811 9th St., 919/286-1760, www.dalesindiancuisine.net, lunch 11am-3pm Mon.-Fri., lunch buffet 11am-2:30pm Mon.-Fri., brunch noon-3pm Sat.-Sun., dinner 5pm-10pm daily, under $20), with a delicious à la carte menu, but most customers opt for the quick buffet, which includes dal, masalas, and *palak paneer,* among other items.

Latin American

A new star of Durham's food scene is **Dos Perros** (200 N. Mangum St., 919/956-2750, http://dosperrosrestaurant.com, lunch 11:30am-2:30pm Mon.-Fri., dinner 5pm-10pm Mon.-Sat., 4pm-9pm Sun., entrées $14-20), located in the heart of downtown and serving three meals. Try the pork roasted in banana leaves or the spice-rubbed grouper; there are also good vegetarian entrées. **Cuban Revolution** (318 Blackwell St., 919/687-4300, www.thecubanrevolution.com, 11am-midnight Sun.-Thurs., 11am-2am Fri.-Sat., entrées $12-20) is another new arrival. Decorated with portraits of revolutionaries and trappings of circa-1959 Cuba, this restaurant serves classic Cuban dishes like *ropa vieja* and Cuban sandwiches as well as new inventions like the shrimp and maduro kebab. **Blue Corn** (716 9th St., 919/286-9600, http://bluecorncafedurham.com, 11:30am-9pm Mon.-Thurs., 11:30am-9:30pm Fri.-Sat.) is an award-winning pan-Latin restaurant. The menu includes Mexican favorites like fajitas and quesadillas, Cuban specialties like *picadillo,* and plenty of vegetarian choices.

Durham is busting out with wonderful Mexican restaurants and taco stands as the number of Mexican immigrants in the area swells. A local favorite is **🎔 La Vaquita** (2700 Chapel Hill Rd., 919/402-0209, http://lavaquitanc.com, 10am-9:30pm daily, $5-10), a little building with an outdoor walk-up counter and a huge fiberglass cow on the roof (it wears a Santa hat in the Christmas season), has a huge menu for a place with such limited kitchen space. It's authentic and has many kinds of tacos, stews, tamales, ribs, and *barbacoa.* The **Azteca Grill** (1929 Chapel Hill Rd., 919/403-2530), gets the best authenticity recommendation from its clientele: At lunch hour the dining room fills with Mexican workers, clearly happy to find a taste of home in North Carolina.

Wildly popular in hot weather, **Loco Pops** (2600 Hillsborough Rd., 919/286-3500, www.ilovelocopops.com, noon-9pm daily, under $5) has several locations in the Triangle where it vends *paletas,* Mexican-style popsicles. They come in crazy flavors—ginger cantaloupe, mango chili, cucumber chili, tamarind—as well as a few more-familiar choices. *Paletas* are a favorite after-school or after-work treat, and the line at Loco Pops often stretches out the door.

European

Best known as a bakery and patisserie, **🎔 Guglhupf** (2706 Durham-Chapel Hill Blvd., 919/401-2600, www.guglhupf.com, breakfast 8am-11am Tues.-Fri., lunch 11am-4:30pm Tues.-Fri., dinner 5:30pm-9:30pm Tues.-Thurs., 5:30pm-10pm Fri.-Sat., brunch 8am-4:30pm Sat., 9am-3pm Sun., dessert 3pm-5pm Sun., $8-24) is also a wonderful café. Guglhupf's founder is from southern Germany, and the menu is based on that cuisine, with forays into other continental and American styles. Even if you don't have time for a full sit-down meal, stop in for dessert or to pick up a pastry or artisanal bread for the road.

For a top-notch Italian meal, try **Tosca** (604 W. Morgan St., 919/680-6333, www.

bluecorn-tosca.com, lunch 11:30am-2:30pm Mon.-Fri., dinner 5:30pm-10:30pm Mon.-Sat., entrées $16-30). The owners of Blue Corn have another winner with Tosca, a restaurant serving delicious Southern and central Italian specialties with a wine list that has received special recognition from *Wine Spectator* magazine.

Food Trucks

Durham has a lively food-truck scene, with many congregating around campus but even more making regular stops at places like Fullsteam Brewery. **Captain Poncho's Tacos!** (919/697-2237, www.captainponchos.com, $2-8) makes tacos, quesadillas, burritos, and even *sopes*. It's cheap, delicious, and has both gluten-free and vegetarian options. The playfully named **Sympathy for the Deli** (www.sympathyforthedeli.com, $6.50-8.50) makes some serious sandwiches. In addition to standard deli sandwiches like a pastrami on rye or a turkey reuben, they have the "French Dipless," which comes on an au jus-soaked baguette, as well as a roasted beet sandwich and, when tomatoes are in season, a grilled caprese sandwich. **American Meltdown** (516/317-8395, http://americanmeltdown.org, $6-9) is a grilled-cheese truck, so you can get your fix of Phish Summer Tour parking-lot grilled-cheese anytime. Sandwiches here are finely crafted and bring together diverse ingredients and playful names. Try the Scarborough Fare, a grilled cheese with a Simon and Garfunkel twist—a generous spread of pureed parsley, sage, rosemary, and thyme; The Hangover, homemade pimento cheese, salsa verde, and a fried egg; or the Pigs 'N' Figs, with speck, local goat cheese, black mission figs, and a balsamic reduction

on fresh sourdough. You can always just get a plain grilled-cheese—melty cheddar on rustic bread, grilled to crisp perfection—it never disappoints.

INFORMATION AND SERVICES

Duke University Medical Center (2301 Erwin Rd., 919/684-8111, www.dukehealth. org) is the main hospital in Durham. **Duke Regional Hospital** (3643 N. Roxboro Rd., 919/470-4000) is also operated by Duke Health Systems. **Walgreens** (6405 Fayetteville St., 919/544-6430) is a 24-hour pharmacy.

Information for travelers is available from the **Durham Convention and Visitors Bureau** (101 E. Morgan St., 919/687-0288, www.durham-nc.com). The *Durham Herald-Sun* is the primary Durham-specific newspaper, although many people also read the Raleigh *News & Observer*. The *Independent Weekly* is a popular weekly cultural newspaper, available free throughout the region.

GETTING THERE AND AROUND

The Triangle's extensive network of buses and shuttles is run by **Triangle Transit** (www.triangletransit.org). The Raleigh-Durham Airport is 10-20 minutes from Durham by cab or shuttle bus. **Amtrak** (800/872-7245, www.amtrak.com) runs the New York City-Charlotte *Carolinian* once daily in each direction and Raleigh-Charlotte *Piedmont* trains twice daily in each direction; both stop at Durham Station (601 W. Main St., 7am-9pm daily), in the heart of downtown. The New York City-Miami *Silver Star* stops at Raleigh's Amtrak Station.

Chapel Hill, Carrboro, and Vicinity

The third corner of the Triangle is Chapel Hill and Carrboro. To many people in North Carolina this is hallowed ground because of the Dean Smith Center, where the University of North Carolina Tar Heels play basketball. Even for nonfans, Chapel Hill is a very cool college town. The University of North Carolina (UNC) is the heart of the town, and the 60,000 residents, many of whom are UNC alumni, maintain a stimulating community with fertile ground for the arts and culture. Music is ubiquitous here. On a weekend tour of the clubs you may well hear a future legend. Singer James Taylor, legendary blues guitarist Elizabeth Cotton, and the Squirrel Nut Zippers are among the many Chapel Hill-Carrboro natives who have gone on to wider fame.

SIGHTS

University of North Carolina

The UNC campus comprises a couple of beautiful quads surrounded by many outlying complexes; the quads date to 1789, the oldest state university in the country. Massive poplar trees on the quads make the campus an indulgent shady hideaway during the 100-degree weather of a central Carolina summer. Elegantly unpretentious federal-style buildings were dorms and classrooms for 18th- and 19th-century students; today, they're home to undergraduates. Guided tours of the historic sites on campus depart from the **UNC Visitors Center** (250 E. Franklin St., 919/962-1630, www.unc.edu, 1:30pm Mon.-Fri.). You can also pick up a brochure and walk through campus at your own pace. It is a beautiful campus, especially when classes are in session and it comes alive with the vibrancy unique to college campuses.

The 1851 **Old Playmakers Theater** (E. Cameron Ave. on campus), was built by Alexander Jackson Davis and was originally intended to be a library and a ballroom; in the 1920s, the University converted the building to a theater. At **Kenan Football Stadium**

(Bell Tower Dr., off South Rd., 919/966-2575, www.goheels.com), the **Charlie Justice Hall of Honors** (8am-5pm Mon.-Fri. and 3 hours before home games, free) chronicles the doughty deeds of UNC's football program.

The **Ackland Art Museum** (Franklin St. and Columbia St., 919/966-5736, www.ackland.org, 10am-5pm Wed. and Fri.-Sat., 10am-8pm Thurs., 1pm-5pm Sun., free), at the heart of the UNC campus, has a collection of European sculpture and painting spanning centuries along with an acclaimed collection of Asian art. The **North Carolina Collection Gallery** (200 South Rd., 919/962-1172, www.lib.unc.edu, 9am-5pm Mon.-Fri., 9am-1pm Sat. 1pm-5pm Sun., free), on the ground floor of Wilson Library, is a cozy museum that will capture the fancy of any Southern history enthusiast.

Carolina Basketball Museum

While on the UNC campus, visit the **Carolina Basketball Museum** (Ernie Williamson Athletic Center, 450 Skipper Bowles Dr., 919/962-6000, www.goheels.com, 10am-4pm Mon.-Fri., 9am-1pm Sat., free), a new addition to the roster of campus attractions. This multimillion-dollar 8,000-square-foot hagiological shrine holds mementos from a century of Carolina basketball. On a reproduction of the Heels' court, footprints and even players' actual shoes mark the spots from which some of the program's most memorable baskets were launched. There's a lot of video and interactive content, but the item most likely to please the Tar Heel faithful is a letter from Duke University basketball coach Mike Krzyzewski to a high school player from Wilmington, expressing his regret that the young man had chosen to attend UNC rather than Duke; the addressee was the later famous Michael Jordan.

Other Museums

Across Franklin Street from the main quad is **Kidzu** (123 E. Franklin St., Suite B,

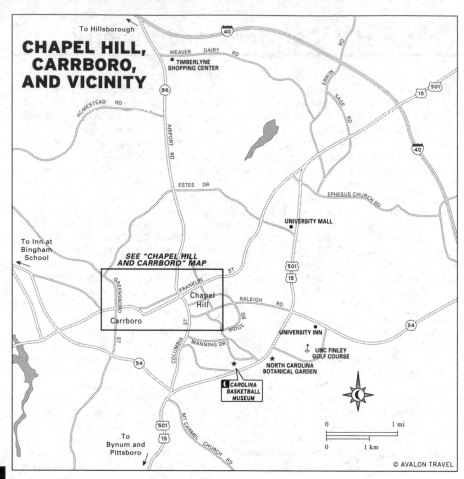

CHAPEL HILL,
CARRBORO,
AND VICINITY

© AVALON TRAVEL

919/933-1455, www.kidzuchildrensmuseum. org, 10am-5pm Tues.-Sat., 1pm-5pm Sun., $5 over age 2, $2 age 1, free Sun.), a children's museum that features imaginative interactive exhibits for kids to explore, as well as a fun gift shop. The **Chapel Hill Museum** (523 E. Franklin St., 919/967-1400, www.chapelhillmuseum.org, 10am-4pm Wed.-Sat., 1pm-4pm Sun., free), just down the hill from campus, is a small museum that documents the town's heritage and hosts exhibits by local artists. It has a good selection of North Carolina pottery on display, and the gift shop carries the work of local authors and artists.

Nostalgic College Spots

Every college town has a few emblematic hangouts that are charged with nostalgia for generations of alumni. At UNC, these icons are the **Carolina Coffee Shop** (138 E. Franklin St., 919/942-6875, www.thecarolinacoffeeshop.com, 9am-2am Tues. and Thurs.-Sat., 9am-10pm Wed., 9am-2pm Sun., lunch and dinner around $8, coffee from $2). A dark soporific retreat, it has been the site of thousands of first dates over the years, and a place to have an afternoon breakfast if you've been studying all night or to inhale a sandwich

© JASON FRYE

The UNC Chapel Hill campus is quiet in summertime.

before heading across the street to a movie. At night, the liquor license kicks in and it becomes a busy bar.

Across the street is **Sutton's Drug Store** (159 E. Franklin St., 919/942-5161, 7am-4:30pm Mon.-Sat., 9am-3pm Sun., under $10), a Chapel Hill institution for more than 90 years and a good place to catch a glimpse of members of the basketball team, who often stop here between classes. An old-time small-town drugstore, Sutton's has a greasy-spoon burger-and-fries lunch counter and a tiny prescription window at the back staffed by a benevolent druggist, who knows everyone's name and probably knew their parents too. Along the walls you'll see snapshots of customers eating at the counter or posing under the front awning. Look closely and you'll find some sports legends.

Weaver Street Market

Weaver Street Market (101 E. Weaver St., 919/929-0010, www.weaverstreetmarket. coop, 7:30am-10pm daily) is the community hub of the politically liberal, artistically active, and often quite eccentric residents of Carrboro. Weaver Street Market is an organic foods co-op with a small dining area—it's too plain to be called a café—inside and on the front lawn. On nice days the lawn is jammed with families and college students eating locally grown food grown in nearby Pittsboro and Hillsborough, where there's an organic farm or creamery wherever there's an open patch of land. Diners listen to local bluegrass, old-time mountain music, punk, or perhaps Hare Krishna musicians. You'll probably see some tai chi or hula-hooping going on too. Weaver Street Market on a crowded day demonstrates what a peculiar and congenial community this is.

Botanical Gardens

UNC's **North Carolina Botanical Garden** (Old Mason Farm Rd., off U.S. 15/501/Hwy. 54, 919/962-0522, http://ncbg.unc.edu, 8am-5pm Mon.-Fri., 9am-5pm Sat., 1pm-5pm Sun., $5 deposit for keycard granting access

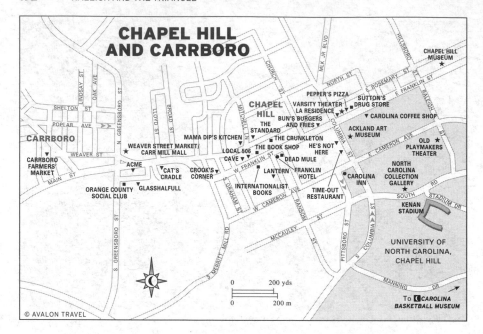

CHAPEL HILL
AND CARRBORO

© AVALON TRAVEL

to multiple gardens) is the Southeast's largest botanical garden. The 800 acres contain beautiful hiking trails, an herb garden, an aquatic plant area, and a carnivorous plant garden. On the campus, **Coker Arboretum** (E. Cameron St. and Raleigh St., dawn-dusk daily, free) is much smaller, but it's also a beautiful retreat. The five landscaped acres are most beautiful in the spring, when students will make detours on their way to class just to pass through the amazing 300-foot-long arbor of purple wisteria.

ENTERTAINMENT AND EVENTS
Movies
Like any good college town, Chapel Hill has several movie theaters, including small theaters that show independent films. The **Varsity Theater** (123 E. Franklin St., 919/967-8665, www.varsityonfranklin.com) is on the edge of campus, and the **Chelsea** (1129 Weaver Dairy Rd., 919/968-3005, www.thechelseatheater.com) and the **Regal Timberlyne 6** (120 Banks

Dr., 919/933-8666, www.regmovies.com) are in the Timberlyne shopping center, north of town along Highway 86 (Columbia St./Martin Luther King Jr. Blvd.). The **Lumina Theater** (620 Market St., 919/969-8049, www.thelumina.com) is located in Southern Village, a development south of Chapel Hill on U.S. 15/501. The Lumina screens movies outdoors on summer evenings.

Nightlife
LIVE MUSIC
Chapel Hill-Carrboro is one of the best places in the Southeast to hear live music, and several small top-notch clubs are legendary venues where major artists get their start and return again and again. The best-known and serious about good music is the **Cat's Cradle** (300 E. Main St., Carrboro, 919/967-9053, www.catscradle.com), with a big dark room with a stage at the front, a few benches, lots of standing and dancing room, and a small room in the back with a pool table and a beer counter. The artists who play the Cat's Cradle are leading lights

in rock-and-roll, Americana, alt-country, and world music, and the audience comes to hear the music. Shows sell out quickly. The **Cave** (452½ W. Franklin St., Chapel Hill, 919/968-9308, http://caverntavern.com, no advance tickets) and **Local 506** (506 W. Franklin St., Chapel Hill, 919/942-5506, www.local506.com) are also important local venues, tending toward pop, rock, and punk. Note that to attend shows at Local 506, you must first join the club ($3), which you can do at the door.

PRIVATE CLUBS

Bars and pubs tend to be either beer-and-wine bars or private clubs. They're not being elitist; it has to do with obtaining a liquor license. To serve liquor, if a business doesn't make more than 30 percent of its revenue from food, it must be a members-only club that charges annual dues. The three-day advance-purchase rule applies to most such watering holes. Favorite members-only bars include the **Dead Mule** (303 W. Franklin St., Chapel Hill, 919/969-7659, 3pm-2am daily, membership $25 1st year, $5 renewal), a hangout for grad students and literary types in a little house set back from the road on Franklin Street, and the **Orange County Social Club** (108 E. Main St., Carrboro, 919/933-0669, www.orangecountysocialclub. com, 4pm-2am daily, membership $10) in Carrboro, a hip and noisy bar frequented by students. New members must submit a written application and the fee before a membership card is issued.

Without a doubt, one of the coolest private clubs in Chapel Hill is **The Crunkleton** (320 W. Franklin St., 919/969-1125, http://thecrunkleton.com, 4pm-2am daily, membership $5-150), a serious bar with Mission-style furniture in warm wood tones that makes it feel anachronistic, along with a classic menu filled with vintage and a few reimagined cocktails served by bow tie-wearing bartenders. There are more than 300 distilled spirits, with an impressive collection of bourbons, and a dozen beers on tap.

BEER AND WINE BARS

If you want to go out for a drink but haven't planned your barhopping three days in advance, you still have options. The **West End Wine Bar** (450 W. Franklin St., Chapel Hill, 919/967-7599, www.westendwinebar.com, 5pm-1am Sun.-Thurs., 5pm-2am Fri.-Sat.) has a great rooftop patio, over 100 by-the-glass wines, and lots of "boutique beers." **He's Not Here** (112½ W. Franklin St., Chapel Hill, 919/942-7939, http://hesnotherenc.com, 4pm-2am Mon.-Wed. and Sun., 2pm-2am Thurs.-Sat.) has been a hot spot since 1975. There's good live rock and roll with a low cover charge. **Caffe Driade** (1215-A E. Franklin St., Chapel Hill, 919/942-2333, www.caffedriade.com, 7am-11pm Mon.-Thurs., 7am-midnight Fri.-Sat., 7:30am-11pm Sun.), an elegant little coffee shop in the woods off East Franklin Street, serves wine and beer as well as caffeine and pastries, and in the warm months they have live outdoor music on Wednesday, Friday, and Saturday evening.

SHOPPING
Malls and Shopping Districts

University Mall (919/945-1900, www.universitymallnc.com, 10am-9pm Mon.-Sat., 1pm-6pm Sun.), on Estes Drive between Franklin Street and Fordham Boulevard (U.S. 15/501), is gradually changing from being a small 1970s-style mall to a collection of upscale boutiques and commercial art galleries. There are still a few fast-food counters and a discount shoe outlet or two, but these shops are being replaced by jewelry and lingerie stores. Stop in at **Wentworth & Sloan Jewelers** (919/942-2253, www.wentworthandsloan.com, 10am-7pm Mon.-Sat.) for an impressive and always changing collection of estate and heirloom jewelry. University Mall is anchored at its southern terminus by **A Southern Season** (877/929-7133, www.southernseason.com, 8am-8pm Mon.-Thurs., 8am-9pm Fri.-Sat., 10am-7pm Sun.), probably the region's most famous specialty foods seller, with a strong emphasis on local and regional delicacies and a wide variety of gourmet foods and fine cookware. Check out the hot sauce and chocolate sections. Southern Season operates a small café, popular for weekend brunches.

Behind Weaver Street Market, **Carr Mill Mall** (Weaver St. and Greensboro St., Carrboro, 919/942-8669, http://carrmillmall.com) in Carrboro is an early example of what has become an important entrepreneurial movement in North Carolina: the transformation of obsolete but historic industrial buildings, particularly old textile mills, into stylish retail space. This 1898 cotton-mill building houses some small specialty shops. **Ali Cat** (919/932-3954, 10am-6pm Mon.-Sat., 10am-3pm Sun.) is a children's toy store specializing in high-quality educational games. **The Bead Store** (919/933-9439, www.carrmillbeadstore.com, 10am-6pm Mon.-Wed. and Fri.-Sat., 10am-7pm Thurs.) is a bead shop that has a highly varied selection of high-quality materials, and offers frequent classes and good customer service.

Wootini (101 Lloyd St., 919/933-6061, http://wootini.com, noon-7pm Tues.-Thurs., noon-8pm Fri.-Sat., noon-6pm Sun.), at the other end of Carr Mill Mall is a toy store for grown-ups. No, not that kind of toys: Wootini is a "purveyor of three-dimensional art." Specializing in plush and wind-up art toys and the work of offbeat cartoonists and pop artists, the store's concept, like Carrboro, it's strange and charming.

Two residential developments, Meadowmont and Southern Village, both planned communities, feature "Main Street" areas dotted with stores and cafés. The shops at **Meadowmont,** on Highway 54 (Raleigh Rd.) south of the UNC campus, are a good place to find handmade jewelry, upscale apparel, and luxury cosmetics. On Market Street in **Southern Village,** on U.S. 15/501 south of Chapel Hill, you'll find garden and home accessory shops, a satellite branch of Weaver Street Market, a pet-friendly bookstore, and a farmers market (evening Thurs. summer).

Books

Along Franklin Street, which becomes Carrboro's Main Street a few blocks west of campus, you'll find the usual college-town mix of textbook exchanges, all-night convenience stores, and purveyors of sustainably crafted fair-trade bongs (water pipes). There are also a handful of chichi women's clothing shops, trendy vintage-wear boutiques, and some great bookstores. Among the best is **The Book Shop** (400 W. Franklin St., 919/942-5178, www.bookshopinc.com, 11am-9pm Mon.-Fri., 11am-6pm Sat., 1pm-5pm Sun.), a wonderful used and rare book dealer where you can find a $5 paperback classic or a $1,000 first edition. **Internationalist Books** (405 W. Franklin St., 919/942-1740, www.internationalistbooks.org, noon-9pm Mon.-Sat., noon-6pm Sun.) is the area's best-known source for far-left political and philosophical literature; it's a hangout for progressive activists.

SPORTS AND RECREATION
Golf

One of the finest courses in the area is the Tom Fazio-designed **UNC Finley Golf Course** (Finley Golf Course Rd., Chapel Hill, 919/962-2349, www.uncfinley.com, 18 holes, par 72, greens fees Mon.-Thurs. $45, Fri.-Sun. $73, discounts for students, alumni, and late play, carts $18). The first hole has a 240-yard carry over water and another 30 yards to the fairway. Few have the prowess to play from the back tees, which make this course considerably more difficult. For the most part, the fairways are wide and allow for some miscues, but if you keep the ball in play, you'll be rewarded with a number of birdie opportunities.

Spectator Sports

Tar Heel Athletics (www.goheels.com) are the beloved UNC sports teams. The most successful have been the men's basketball team: six-time NCAA Champions, coached for many years by the legendary Dean Smith and now by fellow Hall of Famer Roy Williams, and college home court to all-time great basketball players Michael Jordan, James Worthy, and Lennie Rosenbluth. The men play at the Dean Smith Center (Skipper Bowles Rd.), a great glowing stadium that seats more than 20,000. UNC women's basketball is coached

NORTH CAROLINA FICTION

Chapel Hill has long been one of the literary capitals of the South, the heart of a state that has produced many great writers. A selection of some of the best work by North Carolina writers or about North Carolina, past and present:

- Sheila Adams: *My Old True Love; Come and Go With Me*

- Doris Betts: *Souls Raised from the Dead; Beasts of the Southern Wilds; Heading West; The Gentle Insurrection*

- Wendy Brenner: *Phone Calls from the Dead; Large Animals in Everyday Life*

- Fred Chappell: *I Am One of You Forever; Brighten the Corner Where You Are; Look Back All the Green Valley; Farewell, I'm Bound to Leave You*

- Charles W. Chestnut: *Stories, Novels, and Essays; The Conjure Woman*

- Clyde Edgerton: *Raney; Walking Across Egypt; The Bible Salesman; Killer Diller*

- Charles Frazier: *Cold Mountain; Thirteen Moons*

- Kaye Gibbons: *Ellen Foster; A Virtuous Woman; Charms for the Easy Life; Divining Women*

- Alan Gurganus: *The Oldest Living Confederate Widow Tells All; White People; Plays Well with Others*

- Josephine Humphries: *Nowhere Else on Earth*

- Randall Kenan: *Let the Dead Bury Their Dead; A Visitation of Spirits*

- Rebecca Lee: *Bobcat and Other Stories; The City Is a Rising Tide*

- Margaret Maron: *Uncommon Clay; Bloody Kin*

- Jill McCorkle: *The Cheer Leader; Final Vinyl Days; Crash Diet; Tending to Virginia*

- Robert Morgan: *Gap Creek; The Truest Pleasure; This Rock*

- Reynolds Price: *A Long and Happy Life; Kate Vaiden; Blue Calhoun*

- Lee Smith: *On Agate Hill; Devil's Dream; Oral History; Me and My Baby View the Eclipse*

- Max Steele: *The Hat of My Mother; The Cat and the Coffee Drinkers; Where She Brushed Her Hair; The Goblins Must Go Barefoot*

- Thomas Wolfe: *You Can't Go Home Again; Look Homeward, Angel; Of Time and the River*

by Sylvia Hatchell, a member of the Women's Basketball Hall of Fame, and they play at historic Carmichael Auditorium in the heart of campus, except when they play Duke University, their biggest game of the year, when they move to the much larger Smith Center. Coach Butch Davis leads the football team, whose home field is the 1927 Kenan Stadium on the UNC campus. The baseball team plays at Boshamer Stadium, off Manning Drive in the southern part of campus near the Medical School. Other UNC sports achievers include soccer's Mia Hamm, golfer Davis Love III, and track star Marion Jones.

Getting tickets to UNC men's basketball games is exceedingly difficult, but football and women's basketball games are somewhat easier to attend. Try the main ticket office (800/722-4335, www.goheels.com).

ACCOMMODATIONS

A favorite inn for people in the entire state is ⊄ **The Carolina Inn** (211 Pittsboro St., 800/962-8519, www.carolinainn.com, from $160) has been a landmark on the UNC campus since it first opened in 1924. It's the place where visiting dignitaries are hosted, where the most important faculty functions take place, where lucky couples get married, and where old alumni couples celebrate their milestone anniversaries. It is at the center of campus, between the original quads and the modern medical school complexes and not far from the Dean Smith Center. The inn will be completely booked far in advance for homecoming weekends, big basketball and football games, and other campus events. The inn's restaurant, **Carolina CrossRoads** (919/918-2735, $20-36), serves three elegant meals a day by chef Jimmy Reale, a believer in creative cuisine from local ingredients. Afternoon tea (2:30pm-4:30pm Mon.-Sat., except holidays, $20-30) at the Carolina Inn is a popular treat; reservations are recommended.

The **Franklin Hotel** (311 W. Franklin St., 866/831-5999, www.franklinhotelnc.com, from $200) is a boutique hotel in a great location on Franklin Street near the boundary of Chapel Hill and Carrboro. The furnishings are elegant and the beds extremely comfortable. Guest rooms have great modern touches such as flat-screen LCD HDTVs and iPod docks.

The **C Inn at Bingham School** (Hwy. 54 and Mebane Oaks Rd., near Saxapahaw, 800/566-5583, www.chapel-hill-inn.com, rooms $150, cottage $195) is a 200-year-old home, originally the residence of the headmaster of the preparatory academy that operated here in the 18th and 19th centuries. The house is in sweeping countryside near the little town of Saxapahaw, about 20 minutes' drive outside Chapel Hill. Innkeepers Francois and Christina Deprez are renowned hosts and chefs whose talents shine in this beautiful setting.

Chapel Hill also has a handful of motels where guest rooms usually run in the $80-140 range. The **Days Inn** (1312 N. Fordham Blvd./U.S. 15/501, 919/929-3090, www.daysinn.com), **Holiday Inn** (1301 N. Fordham Blvd./U.S. 15/501, 919/929-2171, www.hichapelhill.com), and **Hampton Inn** (6121 Farrington Rd., 919/403-8700, www.hamptoninn.com) are all in convenient and safe neighborhoods. None is within walking distance of the UNC campus, a brief car ride or free bus trip.

FOOD
Southern and Soul

C Crook's Corner (610 W. Franklin St., 919/929-7643, www.crookscorner.com, dinner 5:30pm Tues.-Sun., brunch 10:30am-2pm Sun., $10-25) is one of the most influential restaurants in the South. It was the late Bill Eliot, its first chef, who put this restaurant on the culinary map with, among other brilliant creations, his now world-famous shrimp-and-grits recipe. It's now led by chef Bill Smith, a native Tar Heel with simple yet exquisite recipes, including watermelon and tomato salad, honeysuckle sorbet, and some of the best fried green tomatoes you'll ever find; Crook's Corner continues to be a great innovator in Southern cuisine. Their Atlantic Beach Pie got a pretty strong endorsement on NPR as "that pie that elicits the 'oh, my God' response."

Just a few blocks from Crook's Corner is another legendary Carolina chef's restaurant, **Mama Dip's Kitchen** (408 W. Rosemary St., 919/942-5837, www.mamadips.com, 8am-9:30pm Mon.-Sat., 8am-9pm Sun., under $20). Proprietress Mildred Council, Mama Dip herself, has been cooking since she was nine years old, and if you grew up in the South, you'll recognize at first bite the comfort-food recipes of a Southern matriarch. Dip's is known for its fried chicken and its vegetables. In soul food, the vegetable sides are not an afterthought but an art in their own right. Vegetarians, be sure to ask your server which vegetable dishes are vegetarian; in the old-time way, Dip's greens and beans sometimes contain a zest of fatback.

Time-Out Restaurant (133 W. Franklin St., 919/929-2425, 24 hours daily, around $10) is known for being the only 24-hour restaurant in town as well as being a hangout for star athletes past and present. The highlight of the menu is the Chicken Cheddar Biscuit, made fresh around the clock; the biscuit is split open, lined with fried chicken, and then topped with cheddar cheese.

Eclectic American

La Residence (202 W. Rosemary St., 919/967-2506, www.laresidencedining.com, dinner 6pm-8pm Tues.-Sun., lunch 11am-1:30pm Fri., late-night 9pm-2am Tues. and Thurs.-Sat., $20-28) has been a Chapel Hill favorite for more than 35 years, with an elegant continental-inspired menu created by chef Stephen Amos and delicious desserts by pastry chef Jill Lazarus. Carrboro's **Glasshalfull** (106 S. Greensboro St., Carrboro, 919/967-9784, http://glasshalfullcarrboro.com, lunch 11:30am-2:30pm Mon.-Fri., dinner 5pm-10pm Mon.-Sat., late-night from 10pm Fri.-Sat., $10-30) is equal parts restaurant and wine bar. The menu of contemporary American fare makes use of local ingredients and offers vegetarians plenty of good choices.

Spotted Dog (111 E. Main St., Carrboro, 919/933-1117, http://thespotteddogrestaurant. com, lunch 11:30am-5pm and dinner 5pm-10pm Tues.-Sun., late night menu until midnight Fri.-Sat. under $15) is a boisterous and noisy place, especially Friday-Saturday nights when it fills with students. There is often a wait, but Spotted Dog's location in a wedge-shaped block in the middle of Carrboro is a very pleasant place to hang out on a warm evening. The food is terrific, with great burgers and sandwiches, plenty of creative meat and seafood dishes, and a great selection of artfully crafted vegetarian and vegan creations.

A special treat for Triangle diners is **Sage** (Timberlyne Shopping Center, 1129 Weaver Dairy Rd., Chapel Hill, 919/968-9266, http://sagevegcafe.com, around $14), a vegetarian and vegan restaurant that draws at least as many omnivores as hard-core veggies. The proprietress is originally from Iran, where she learned to cook, and Sage's beautiful dishes are a fusion of classic Persian cooking and modern vegetarian haute cuisine. Also in the Timberlyne Shopping Center, a few doors down from Sage, is **Margaret's Cantina** (Timberlyne Shopping Center, 1129 Weaver Dairy Rd., 919/942-4745, www.margaretscantina.com, lunch 11:30am-2:30pm Mon.-Fri., dinner 5pm-9:30pm Mon.-Thurs., 5pm-10pm Fri.-Sat., under $15). This popular Southwestern café uses as many fresh, local, and organic ingredients as possible, and the results are divine. Don't miss the sweet potato and black bean burrito.

Acme (110 E. Main St., Carrboro, 919/929-2263, http://acmecarrboro.com, dinner at 5:30pm daily, brunch 10am-2pm Sun., under $30) is one of the best restaurants in town, according to *Bon Appétit* magazine, which named it one of the country's 50 best neighborhood restaurants in 2012. The menu is seasonal with an undeniable Southern influence, even if they do call their fries "frites." They host the annual Acme Tomato Festival during peak tomato season; it's billed as a "deep-fried, cross-eyed, absolutely tomato-fied belly flop into the juicy heart of summer," and all the menu items are showcases of this humble summer fruit, including chutneys, salsas, relishes, garnishes, toppings, stuffings, salads, steaks, and fried chicken.

Buns Burgers & Fries (107 N. Columbia St., 919/240-4746, www.bunsofchapelhill. com, 11am-10pm Mon.-Thurs., 11am-3am Fri.-Sat., 11am-9pm Sun., $5-9) has one of the best names and logos I've run across. This place serves "the best flippin' burgers in town"; walk in, choose your burger (Angus beef, fresh ground turkey, or homemade veggie), decide whether it's a single, double, or triple patty, add your toppings, and they cook it to order. They also have a grilled salmon sandwich, french fries, sweet-potato fries, and a small selection of bottled beer.

The Standard (403 W. Rosemary St., 919/918-3932, http://thestandardchapelhill. com, 5pm-2am daily, around $11) is a bar-pizza place with gourmet food, fresh and local ingredients, mostly craft beer, and knowledgeable staff. Their specialty pizzas include a duck confit pie complete with bacon blueberry jam, blue cheese, homemade mozzarella, pearl onions, duck confit, and arugula; The Standard has roasted garlic olive oil, shredded mozzarella, parmesan, pork sausage, and ricotta. Their burger selection is equally stellar, with a chicken parm sandwich, a pork belly confit (pork belly, pickled fennel and apple slaw, and cranberry sweet-and-sour hoisin sauce), and fish tacos.

Asian

Lantern (423 W. Franklin St., 919/969-8846, http://lanternrestaurant.com, 5:30pm-10pm Mon.-Sat., bar until 2am Mon.-Sat., $20-30) was named one of the country's top 50 restaurants by *Gourmet* magazine, and chef Angrea Reusing was named the Best Chef: Southeast

2011 by the James Beard Foundation. The pan-Asian menu draws from fresh locally raised meats and North Carolina-caught seafood. The meals may be exotic, but the ingredients are down-home. Try the Tea and Spice Smoked Poulet Rouge Chicken or the Seafood Hotpot, both dishes that show off the creativity of the kitchen while allowing the fresh ingredients to take their own place.

Local Fare
The **Carrboro Farmers Market** (301 W. Main St., http://carrborofarmersmarket.com, 7am-noon Sat., 3:30pm-6:30pm Wed.) is a bustling festive scene featuring local organic produce in abundance as well as gorgeous cut flowers, artisanal cheeses, and charmingly cuckoo lawn art.

The Chapel Hill area is blessed with a local dairy that supplies residents with old-fashioned bottled milk and fantastic ice cream. To sample Mapleview Ice Cream, you have an option beyond the freezer aisle of the grocery store: At the Carrboro **Maple View Ice Cream and Country Store** (6900 Rocky Ridge Rd., 919/960-5535, www.mapleviewfarm.com, noon-8pm Sun.-Thurs., noon-9pm Fri.-Sat.), you can pick up some ice cream and check out the farm while you eat it on the front porch.

GETTING THERE AND AROUND
Chapel Hill is accessed via I-40 and Highway 85; U.S. 15/501 runs through Chapel Hill from Durham to the northeast toward Pittsboro to the southwest.

HILLSBOROUGH
The beautiful little town of Hillsborough, home to a large number of authors, artists, and overflow Chapel Hillians, figured prominently in North Carolina history. Now on the National Register of Historic Places, Hillsborough was the site of an early trading path along the Eno River used by the indigenous Occaneechi people and later by European settlers. It was also the site of the Constitutional Convention of 1788 in which North Carolinians rejected the Constitution.

And legend holds that Daniel Boone departed from here for Kentucky in 1776.

Historic Downtown
The **Alexander Dickson House** (150 E. King St.) was built in the 1790s, a Quaker-plan house that would be headquarters to General Joseph Johnston during the Civil War. Today it's the **Orange County Visitors Center** (919/732-7741, www.historichillsborough.org, 9am-4pm Mon.-Fri., 10am-4pm Sat., noon-4pm Sun.), where you can pick up local information before visiting the medicinal garden and beginning your tour.

The **Burwell School** (319 N. Churton St., 919/732-7451, www.burwellschool.org, 11am-4pm Wed.-Sat., 1pm-4pm Sun., free, donations accepted) has had several interesting lives. For its first 20 years, 1837-1857, the handsome old building was one of the state's earliest girls schools. During the Civil War, the Collins family, owners of Somerset Plantation in Creswell, sheltered here. A young enslaved woman named Elizabeth Hobbes Keckly grew up here, and she went on to become Mary Todd Lincoln's dressmaker and author of an insightful book about the first lady. Docent- and self-guided tours are available.

The **Old Orange County Courthouse** (N. Churton and E. King Streets, open 9am-5pm Mon.-Fri., free, building still used for Judicial business), now the county judicial building, is a pretty 1844 Greek Revival, just what one hopes for in a small Southern county seat. At the corner of Cameron and East King Streets, a historical marker identifies the spot where six Regulators were hanged in 1771 after they refused Governor Tryon's order to declare loyalty to the crown.

Just east of downtown, **Ayr Mount Historic Site** (376 St. Mary's Rd., 919/732-6886, hours vary, tours $6) preserves an important 1815 home built by a Scottish merchant. Tours begin on the hour and lead visitors through the fine federal-style house. A walking trail called the Poets Walk traverses scenic parts of the 265-acre property; it's free and open every day.

Shopping

The Shops at Daniel Boone, an old strip-mall development off I-40's exit 261, is home to a cluster of antiques shops. The one called simply **Antique Mall** (387 Ja Max Dr., 919/732-8882) is the largest and has the most compelling selection of goods, but several shops surrounding it are also fun places to visit.

Recreation

Occoneechee Mountain State Natural Area (625 Virginia Cates Rd., Durham, 919/383-1686, http://ncparks.gov, office 8am-4:30pm Mon.-Thurs., 8am-8pm Fri., 9am-6pm Sat. Mar.-Oct., 8am-4:30pm Mon.-Fri., 12pm-4pm Sat.-Sun. Nov., 8am-4:30pm Mon.-Fri. Dec.-Feb., park 8am-6pm daily Nov.-Feb., 8am-8pm daily Mar.-Apr., 8am-9pm daily May-Aug., 8am-8pm daily Sept.-Oct.) is located in Orange County, although it has a Durham address. It is a monadnock environment—an isolated rock knob—and one of the most diverse ecological areas in the Triangle. At 867 feet, Occoneechee Mountain hosts species of flora and fauna that are otherwise found only in the mountain ranges 100 miles west. The hiking trails are steep and rather strenuous, but the views and deep-mountain feeling of the knob make the exercise a pleasure.

The **Occoneechee Golf Club** (1500 Lawrence Rd., 919/732-3435, www.occoneechee.com, 18 holes, par 71, greens fees Mon.-Fri. $20-34, Sat.-Sun. and holidays $26-40, discounts for seniors, juniors, walking, and 9-hole rounds) is a fun, playable course. Number 5, one of the toughest holes, has a severe dogleg left around 200 yards out; drive it short and you'll have to lay up to get around the corner. Number 6 is a short par 4 with a green that's well guarded by water on the front and left.

Food

The **Village Diner** (600 W. King St., 919/732-7032, 7:30am-2:30pm Mon.-Wed. and Sun., 7:30am-7:30pm Thurs.-Fri., 7:30am-noon Sat., under $10) is Hillsborough's longest-operating restaurant, a buffet-style country kitchen that serves fried chicken, barbecue, seafood, and a mean banana pudding.

Hillsborough BBQ Company (236 S. Nash St., Hillsborough, 919/735-4647, http://hillsboroughbbq.com, 11am-9pm Tues.-Thurs., 11am-10pm Fri.-Sat., noon-8pm Sun., $7-15) cooks barbecue over live coals, the way it's meant to be done. You can order plates of brisket, turkey breast, ribs, chopped 'cue, a barbecue sandwich, and even a black-eyed pea po'boy; you can also order in bulk and pay for your barbecue by the pound.

Antonia's (101 N. Churton St., 919/643-7722, www.antoniashillsborough.com, lunch 11:30am-2:30pm Thurs.-Sat., dinner 5pm-9pm Tues.-Thurs., 5pm-9:30pm Fri.-Sat., brunch 10:30am-2:30pm Sun., lunch $8-11, dinner $10-29, brunch $9-22) serves regional Italian cuisine and uses some beautiful fresh ingredients to bring the dishes to life. Try the Tagliata, grilled beef tenderloin served over arugula, roasted tomatoes, grilled eggplant, and zucchini; or go with any of the pasta dishes, all fresh and outstanding.

FEARRINGTON VILLAGE

Between Chapel Hill and Pittsboro on U.S. 15/501, Fearrington Village is a recently developed planned community that is worth exploring. Built on the grounds of an old dairy farm, Fearrington has adopted as its mascots a herd of belted Galloway cattle—beautiful stout beasts with white-belted black hides. From U.S. 15/501, if you don't spot the signs for Fearrington, you'll certainly notice the cows.

Events

Adding to the appeal of Fearrington Village are its activities and events: readings by prominent authors, concerts and square dances, antiques shows, and the popular annual **Folk Art Show** (919/542-2121, www.fearrington.com) in February. The Folk Art Show runs more to outsider or visionary art, technically speaking, than folk art, but it's still an exciting event.

Accommodations and Food

The center of the action is **LＣ Fearrington**

House (2000 Fearrington Village Center, 919/542-2121, www.fearrington.com, from $275), an extremely luxurious inn that earns awards and accolades from all quarters. It's the only inn in North Carolina to receive both the AAA Five Diamond Award and Exxon Mobil's Five Star Award. Impossibly plush guest rooms feature canopied feather beds, restful colors and lighting, beautiful pine floorboards salvaged from an antique building in England, and vases of fresh flowers. Rates are steep but the inn offers several weekend package options that are good bargains, combining luxury guest rooms, three-course dinners, English teatime, and gift cards for the shops.

The **Fearrington House Restaurant** (2000 Fearrington Village Center, 919/542-2121, www.fearrington.com, 6pm-9pm Wed.-Sat., 6pm-8pm Sun., 3-course prix fixe $89, 4-course $99) is no less exceptional than the inn. The restaurant, which occupies the 1927 farmhouse original to the property, has won major awards and recognitions, having been named one of *Travel + Leisure* magazine's three best U.S. restaurants in their World's Best Service Awards, one of *National Geographic Traveler*'s 10 Best Destination Restaurants, and *Gourmet* magazine's Best Farm-to-Table Restaurant for Special Occasions. The prix-fixe menu includes incredible seasonal dishes like yellow pepper soup, "62 Degree Egg," red pepper confit, foie gras, smoked sweetbreads, lemon-oil poached tuna, and seared North Carolina redfish with crispy egg yolk and mint velouté. The chef is creative, but not so much as to mask the individual flavors in each dish, so you're in for a treat.

JORDAN LAKE

Jordan Lake State Recreation Area (280 State Park Rd., Apex, 919/362-0586, http://ncparks.gov, office 8am-5pm daily, park 8am-6pm daily Nov.-Feb., 8am-8pm daily Mar.-Apr., 8am-9pm daily May-Aug., 8am-8pm daily Sept.-Oct.) is located west of Fearrington Village, Bynum, and Pittsboro, with the park office across the lake on U.S. 64 outside Apex. The 14,000-acre reservoir is surrounded by nine recreation areas. It's a popular area for many kinds of boating, including sailing, windsurfing, and waterskiing. Nearby **Crosswinds Marina** (565 Farrington Rd., Apex, 919/387-7011, www.crosswindsboating.com) rents out fishing and pontoon boats. There are four sandy beaches available for daytime visitors, and another four are accessible to campers. Jordan Lake also has more than 1,000 campsites for tenting and RV camping, most with restrooms and running water nearby ($13-48/day).

BYNUM

Between Fearrington Village and Pittsboro, just off U.S. 15/501, is the mill village of Bynum, today little more than a small residential community but in earlier generations a bustling mill town with several stores, a movie theater, and the mill where most of the residents worked. The mill closed in the 1970s, but many Bynumites remained in the community, joined over the years by younger people drawn to the area by UNC and Chapel Hill-Durham.

For nearly a decade now, the community of Bynum has hosted the **Bynum Front Porch Music Series** (www.bynumfrontporch.org), concerts (evening Fri., 10am-2pm 2nd and 4th Sat., May-Sept.) held on the front porch of the **Bynum General Store** (950 Bynum Rd.). The series features blues, bluegrass, rock, and rockabilly. It's a great opportunity to sample this area's rich musical offerings.

If you spend any time in Bynum, you'll notice that almost every yard has at least one peculiar animal sculpture hewn from rough logs and often festooned with tennis-ball or funeral-flower eyes. These beasts are the work of visionary "outsider" artist Clyde Jones, a resident of Bynum. Jones's animals are highly prized in the world of visionary art, and some pieces appear in the permanent collection of the Visionary Arts Museum in Baltimore. Once a year the residents of Chatham County hold a festival to celebrate the work of Bynum's most famous resident: **Clydefest** (919/542-0394, www.chathamarts.org, $7 adults, $3 under age 12) takes place in mid-late April at the Bynum Ball Field. There are plenty of games and activities for children, festivities in Jones's honor, bands from all over the region, and great local food.

PITTSBORO

Pittsboro is 30 minutes' drive south of Chapel Hill on U.S. 15/501, an easy afternoon trip if you're staying in the Triangle. This small county seat is laid out like a wheel, with the 1881 courthouse at the hub and its antiques shops and cafés radiating out in all directions.

Carnivore Preservation Trust

Founded in 1981 by a geneticist from the University of North Carolina, the **Carnivore Preservation Trust** (1940 Hanks Chapel Rd., 919/542-4684, www.carolinatigerrescue.org, tours 10am and 1pm Sat.-Sun., sunset Sat. Apr.-Oct., $17 adults, $10 children, sunset tours $26.50) had, as its original mission, the breeding of endangered wild cats. It soon became apparent that there was also an overwhelming need to create a safe haven for big cats that were abused or abandoned as illegal pets or in the entertainment industry, or that had lived at zoos that had closed. Among the dozens of cats living here today are a pair of tigers who were found as cubs walking along a highway near Charlotte; a tiger seized at a traffic stop (he was the passenger); a tiger rescued from an owner who tried to have him declawed and defanged; several other tigers and many leopards, jaguars, serval cats, ocelots, kinkajous, caracals, and binturongs.

On the tour of the Carnivore Preservation Trust you'll meet many of the big cats, some from just a few feet away. Visitors can expect tours to last approximately two hours and to involve a lot of walking, as it's a large property. The paths are not equipped for strollers or wheelchairs. You'll see the greatest number of cats during the warm-weather sunset tours,

when the animals are likely to be prowling around in the evening shade.

Shopping

The Chatham County Courthouse sits in an island in the center of Pittsboro, and the blocks that radiate out from it form a tiny but very interesting shopping district. A couple of blocks up from the courthouse are the offices of the **Chatham Arts Council** (45 West St., Suite 104, 919/542-0394, www.chathamarts.org). They have a nice little museum shop in front, which sells art from a variety of disciplines by some of Chatham County's amazingly creative folks.

Food

The **Pittsboro Roadhouse and General Store** (39 West St., 919/542-2432, www.pittsbororoadhouse.com, 11am-9pm Mon.-Thurs., 11am-10pm Fri.-Sat., brunch 10:30am-3pm 1st Sun. of the month, lunch $6-14, dinner $9-25, brunch around $8) is a casual and comfortable place to get a really good meal. Specialties include burgers, which come in ground beef, ground turkey, and a "vegan veggie" burger. Dinner features pasta dishes, salmon, tilapia, shrimp, turkey meatloaf, and steaks. The Roadhouse is also a favorite live-music venue in the area.

SILER CITY

Locavores in central North Carolina are fans of the goat cheese made at Celebrity Dairy, a beautiful farm. The **Inn at Celebrity Dairy** (144 Celebrity Dairy Way, Siler City, 877/742-5167, www.celebritydairy.com, rooms $100-165, tours 11:30am Tues.-Thurs., lunch and tours $15, goat milking at 6am and 6pm daily, free) allows visitors to experience the farm's peaceful atmosphere. This is a heavenly spot for animal lovers. The stars of the farm are the goats, but there are also llamas, turkeys, peacocks, and pigs. If you visit in the springtime, you may have a chance to see brand-new goat kids.

Sandy Lowlands

Between the Triangle and the beaches are a band of towns and cities that were once important in North Carolina's tobacco economy. Their roles have changed as that industry wanes, but towns like Wilson and its neighbors continue to be culturally vital, architecturally interesting, and full of good places to browse for antiques and to gobble up barbecue.

HENDERSON

Henderson is about 45 minutes northeast of Durham, near the Virginia state line. **Kerr Lake State Recreation Area** (6254 Satterwhite Point Rd., Henderson, 252/438-7791, http://ncparks.gov, office 8am-6pm daily, park 8am-6pm daily Nov.-Feb., 8am-8pm daily Mar.-Apr. and Sept.-Oct., 8am-9pm daily May-Aug.), outside Henderson, includes a 50,000-acre artificial lake and 800 miles of woods along the lakeshore straddling the state line.

Boating, including sailing, is the main activity. There are numerous public boat ramps, some available 24 hours daily, and two commercial marinas. It's also a great place to swim, but be aware that there are no lifeguards. The park offers many, many campsites, both drive-in and walk-in, some right along the shores of the lake. Visit the park's website to scout out the best camping locations and to read about the complicated fee schedule. To help you sound more like a native, in these parts Kerr is pronounced "car."

HOLLISTER

About 80 minutes' drive northeast of Raleigh, the small town of Hollister is the site of **Medoc Mountain State Park** (1541 Medoc State Park Rd., Hollister, 252/586-6588, http://ncparks.gov, office 8am-5pm daily, park 8am-6pm Nov.-Feb., 8am-8pm Mar.-May and Sept.-Oct., 8am-9pm June-Aug.). The park has more than 10 miles of hiking trails through loblolly pine and hardwood forests and alongside creeks and swamps. Should you happen to be traveling with your horse, you can enjoy 10 miles of bridle trails. There is also fine canoeing along Little Fishing Creek, ideal for beginning paddlers. Contact the park ahead of time to check on water levels; at times the creek can be swollen and less placid. Canoe rentals ($5 for the 1st hour, $3 per additional hour) are available in the park. There are 34 campsites ($20-48) for tents and trailers, 12 with electrical hookup.

WILSON
Sights

A peculiar little stone building on Nash Street East houses an unusual and interesting museum, the **Oliver Nestus Freeman Roundhouse African-American Museum** (1202 Nash St. E., 252/296-3056, 9am-4pm Tues.-Sat., free, donations accepted). The Roundhouse is not a railroad roundhouse but rather a three-room circular building made of stones, saplings, and a mix of strange materials like cola bottles and marbles—with a dinosaur sculpture out front. The museum celebrates the creativity of its builder, Nestus Freeman, as well as the contributions of generations of African Americans in Wilson.

Entertainment and Events

The **Arts Council of Wilson** (124 Nash St. SW, 252/291-4329, www.wilsonarts.com) hosts a great annual event, the spring **Theater of the American South** (www.theateroftheamericansouth.org). The heart of each year's festival is two repertory productions by prominent Southern playwrights, but it also hosts demonstrations by celebrity Southern chefs held in the homes of hospitable Wilson citizens, gospel concerts, garden parties, and more fun. Plays take place at the **Edna Boykin Cultural Center** (108 W. Nash St., 252/234-6161), a fantastic restored 1919 vaudeville theater.

Sports and Recreation

Wilson's baseball park, Fleming Stadium,

was built in 1939 by the Works Projects Administration. The **Wilson Tobs** (300 Stadium St., 252/291-8627, www.wilsontobs. com, $9, box seats $10, games 7pm Mon.-Sat., 6pm Sun.), a Coastal Plain minor-league baseball team, have been playing at Fleming Stadium since that year. The stadium is also home of the **North Carolina Baseball Museum** (252/296-3048, http://ncbaseballmuseum. com, 10am-4pm Thurs.-Sat., 1pm-5pm Sun., free, donations accepted), which honors North Carolina baseball greats including Negro League star and Rocky Mount native Buck Leonard, Hertford native "Catfish" Hunter, and Roxboro's Enos "Country" Slaughter.

ANGIER

For many years, farmer Marvin Johnson of Angier was famous in these parts for two things: his elderly pet alligator, whom he hand-fed hot dogs, and his **Gourd Museum** (289 N. Raleigh Ave., 919/639-8571, dawn-dusk daily, free). The alligator was called home many years ago, but the Gourd Museum is still going strong. Johnson's collection contains hundreds of painted and carved gourds—this is a popular craft in North Carolina—including a great many gourd animals, gourd hats, a gourd that looks like Benjamin Franklin, and a scene of the Last Supper in which all the figures are made out of gourd seeds. Marvin Johnson died, and his nephew now maintains the collection. The museum, housed in a small building on family property, is unlocked in the morning and locked up again at night, so stop by and walk right in.

SELMA

The small town of Selma, located east of Raleigh at the junction of I-95 and U.S. 70, is packed with antiques shops. Among the best and largest is **TWM's Antique Mall** (112 S. Pollock St./U.S. 301, 919/965-6699, www. twmsantiquemall.com), which is one of those rambling antiques shops with seemingly endless rooms, each filled with the booths of many dealers, crammed with furniture and china and books and toys. Another huge emporium is the **Selma Cotton Mills** (1105 W. Anderson St., 919/868-8014, www.visitselma.org, 10am-5pm Fri., 9am-5pm Sat.-Sun.), a weekends-only warehouse full of antiques and secondhand items.

LILLINGTON

Lillington is almost due south of Raleigh, located on U.S. 401. West of town you'll find **Raven Rock State Park** (3009 Raven Rock Rd., Lillington, 919/893-4888, http://ncparks. gov, office 8am-5pm daily, park 8am-6pm daily Nov.-Feb., 8am-8pm daily Mar.-May and Sept.-Oct., 8am-9pm daily June-Aug.), named for a high rock outcropping that towers over this upper reach of the Cape Fear River. The Cape Fear Canoe Trail runs through the park, although there are no access points within the park. Contact Raven Rock to find out about the nearest put-ins. Beautiful hiking trails loop up and down and around the rock. Camping is available ($13/day), both hike-in and, if you're traveling the Cape Fear Canoe Trail, canoe-in. Contact the park office for reservations.

WINSTON-SALEM AND CENTRAL CAROLINA

If you tell people "I'm going to North Carolina," they will probably picture a beach scene or a mountain sunset. Although neither of those apply to Winston-Salem and other Piedmont cities, they still make excellent getaway destinations that rival the state's better-known regions. The geography here is a lovely transition from the foothills of the Blue Ridge Mountains down into the true Piedmont and Sandhills. This is the heart of North Carolina's wine country, with great restaurants, art galleries, and lively arts communities. You'll also find engaging history, including religious and Civil Rights landmarks.

This part of North Carolina is bounded by Raleigh and the Triangle to the northeast, and to the southeast the Sandhills, a band of deep pine woods and sandy soil thought by some geologists to be the remnants of prehistoric sand dunes. To the south and southwest, Charlotte and it's creeping band of suburbs dominate the landscape, while the western, northwestern, and northern edges of this region are made up of the hills, forests, and valleys of the foothills of the Blue Ridge.

The two largest cities in this region—Winston-Salem and Greensboro—are close kin in both geographic terms and in their origins but different enough in their distinct flavors. Winston-Salem was once two towns. Salem traces its roots to the Moravians, a sect of Central European religious migrants who traveled down the Great Wagon Road in the 18th century from Pennsylvania. After traveling

HIGHLIGHTS

© AVALON TRAVEL

LOOK FOR [TO FIND RECOMMENDED SIGHTS, ACTIVITIES, DINING, AND LODGING.

[Old Salem: Craftspeople and historic interpreters bring this 18th- and 19th-century religious community to life in the beautiful restored Moravian village of Salem (page 207).

[International Civil Rights Center and Museum: This museum tells the story of the fight for integration and justice in North Carolina, a lesser-known but crucial front in the Civil Rights Movement (page 222).

[Barbecue Festival: Every October, the town of Lexington fills with smoke as dozens of barbecue pit masters descend on the town for the annual Barbecue Festival, which draws more than 150,000 hungry barbecue enthusiasts (page 232).

[North Carolina Zoo: Drive through rolling countryside and wander among traditional exhibits to see elephants, alligators, and many more exciting creatures you wouldn't expect to encounter in the Carolina Piedmont (page 233).

[Liberty Antiques Festival: Held twice a year, this event is a favorite among antiques collectors throughout the Southeast. From the finest of antique Southern furniture to baseball cards, tobacco tags, and other fun doodads, enthusiasts of old stuff will find treasures (page 234).

[North Carolina Pottery Center: The tiny town of Seagrove is home to a generations-old tradition of folk pottery. Start your visit at the Pottery Center and then explore the 100-plus studios tucked along the lovely country roads surrounding Seagrove (page 234).

[Uwharrie National Forest: This hauntingly pretty and ecologically unique outcropping of low mountains is unfamiliar even to most North Carolinians. Hiding under the canopy of forest are many miles of hiking trails and mysterious back roads (page 235).

through the Shenandoah Valley and into these Carolina hills, they established a hard-working town known for its integrity and education and the skills of its craftspeople. Greensboro has religious roots as well: a community of the quietest of Christians, the Quakers, was integral in the town's early days. Known for their abolitionist and pacifist beliefs, the Quakers

had a difficult time in the 18th- and 19th-century South as slavery and war raged around them. The struggles of racial equality continued through the Civil Rights movement of the 1960s, when the town played a key role in advancing equality for African Americans. Today, many Moravians and Quakers still practice their faith in this part of North Carolina.

WINSTON-SALEM

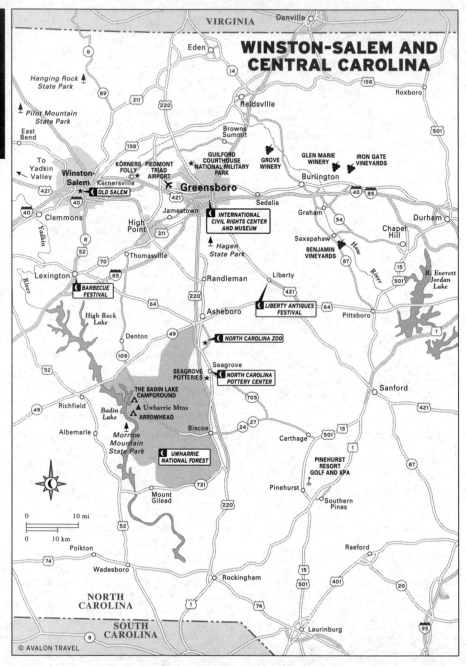

VIRGINIA
Danville
Eden
WINSTON-SALEM AND CENTRAL CAROLINA
Roxboro
Hanging Rock State Park
Pilot Mountain State Park
East Bend
Reidsville
Browns Summit
To Yadkin Valley
KÖRNERS FOLLY
PIEDMONT TRIAD AIRPORT
GUILFORD COURTHOUSE NATIONAL MILITARY PARK
GROVE WINERY
GLEN MARIE WINERY
IRON GATE VINEYARDS
Winston-Salem
Kernersville
OLD SALEM
Greensboro
Burlington
Sedalia
Clemmons
Jamestown
INTERNATIONAL CIVIL RIGHTS CENTER AND MUSEUM
Graham
Durham
Chapel Hill
High Point
Saxapahaw
BENJAMIN VINEYARDS
Thomasville
Hagen State Park
B. Everett Jordan Lake
Lexington
BARBECUE FESTIVAL
Randleman
Liberty
Asheboro
LIBERTY ANTIQUES FESTIVAL
Pittsboro
High Rock Lake
Denton
NORTH CAROLINA ZOO
Seagrove
SEAGROVE POTTERIES
NORTH CAROLINA POTTERY CENTER
Sanford
THE BADIN LAKE CAMPGROUND
Richfield
Badin Lake
Uwharrie Mtns
ARROWHEAD
Albemarle
Biscoe
Carthage
Morrow Mountain State Park
UWHARRIE NATIONAL FOREST
PINEHURST RESORT GOLF AND SPA
Mount Gilead
Pinehurst
Southern Pines
0 10 mi
0 10 km
Polkton
Raeford
Wadesboro
Rockingham
NORTH CAROLINA
SOUTH CAROLINA
Laurinburg
© AVALON TRAVEL

Winston-Salem and Greensboro are also home to several distinguished universities and colleges, including Wake Forest University in Winston, the University of North Carolina at Greensboro, North Carolina Agricultural and Technical State University, and Guilford College. Both cities have active arts scenes with visual artists, opera, ballet, and all kinds of music.

Located just about in the center of the state, the Uwharrie Mountains are one of North Carolina's biggest secrets. They rise out of the flatlands and rolling hills to form a beautiful and eerie cluster of high hills laden with hiking trails and campsites. At the edge of the Uwharrie Mountains is a tiny landlocked town called Seagrove, legendary for its pottery; it seems that everyone here throws clay and has at least a garage ceramics studio. More than 100 studios turn out highly prized ceramic work, some using patterns and methods passed down for generations. As you move closer to Fayetteville, to the southeast, you'll find Sothern Pines and Pinehurst, location of some of the world's best golf courses, some of which have hosted major professional golf events like the U.S. Open.

PLANNING YOUR TIME

This is a large region with a lot to see, so plan on devoting more than just a day or two to exploring. The golf towns of the Sandhills are clustered in the southeast corner of the region and are an easy drive from Raleigh and Wilmington. The Seagrove potteries and Uwharrie Mountains are most easily accessed from U.S. 220, which also takes you past the North Carolina Zoo. Winston-Salem and Greensboro are less than 30 minutes apart by road, but it's easy to spend a weekend or more in each.

For the eastern and western regions of the state, summer is the busiest time and the high season for prices and traffic; not so here. The heat and humidity of July and August send many residents fleeing to the coast or retreating to the mountains. In the Southern Pines and Pinehurst area, the season for visitors peaks in the spring. Between March and May temperatures are in the 60°F to 80°F range, beautiful and comfortable for golf. If you're planning to visit the Sandhills for golf, make your tee times and book your room and dinner reservations well in advance. In summer it's easier to book a tee time, but the heat makes it unpleasant or even dangerous on the links.

Winston-Salem

In the mid-18th century, the Unitas Fratrum, better known as the Moravians, established the town of Salem. These Protestant migrants moved from Europe to Pennsylvania and eventually into the hills of North Carolina, bringing with them some of the sensibilities and folk traditions of the Pennsylvania Dutch. Known for excellent and unostentatious craftsmanship, their strong religious faith, and community bonds, the Moravians were a unique cultural enclave in early North Carolina. Today, more than 20,000 North Carolinians belong to the Unitas Fratrum, keeping alive their religion and folk traditions, which include sacred brass bands and highly sought-after baked goods.

The Winston part of Winston-Salem was founded as Forsyth County's seat, and throughout the 19th and 20th centuries it boomed as an industrial and trading hub, powered by what appeared to be an endless stream of tobacco and textile money. Although the textile mills are mostly gone from North Carolina, and the tobacco industry is dying a slow death, Winston-Salem thrives as a banking center and the home of Wake Forest University and Winston-Salem State University.

SIGHTS
◖ Old Salem

Nestled in the center of a modern city, **Old**

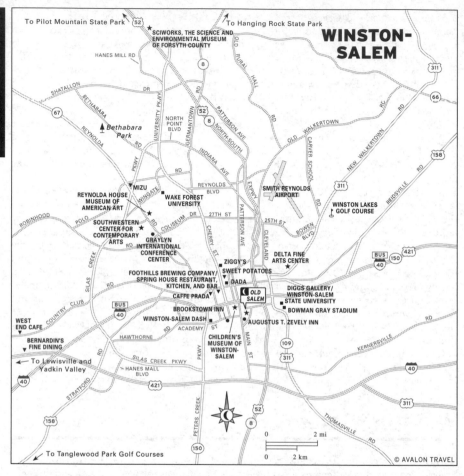

Salem (600 S. Main St., 336/721-7300, www. oldsalem.org, museum and gardens 9:30am-4pm Tues.-Sat., 1pm-4:30pm Sun., $21 adults, $10 children, Sun. $16 adults, $8 children) was once a bustling independent village that was home to the industrious Moravians. Throughout the second half of the 18th century and the 19th century, the German-speaking Unitas Fratrum produced beautiful and functional ceramics, furniture, tools, and other goods for themselves and their neighbors. This era is recreated today in the streets and homes of the old village, where it's common to see costumed interpreters carrying on the Moravian ways and making expertly crafted goods as prized today as they were essential 150 years ago.

Old Salem is home to two museums that are both worth examining, along with a beautiful garden to tour. The **Museum of Early Southern Decorative Arts** (924 S. Main St., 336/721-6140, www.mesda.org, 10am-5pm Tues.-Sat., 1pm-5pm Sun., $10 adults, $7 ages 6-17) tells the story of the early South through the objects made by a diverse range of craftspeople: early Jamestown residents, African

American decorative artists, and makers of furniture, ceramics, silver work, and textiles. There are several guided tours to choose from, including two focusing on the contributions of African Americans and an overview of the South through its objects (both 45 minutes, $10 adults, $7 ages 6-17). Longer tours include the museum's Expanded Tour (2 hours, $30) and the Private Study Tour ($25), tailored to meet your specific interests.

At each of the dozen or so gardens spread out around the village of Old Salem, you'll find the heirloom fruits, vegetables, and ornamental plants that the original Moravian inhabitants would have planted. One of the most impressive is the **Single Brothers Garden,** now only a fraction of its original 700 acres, laid out in squares on a series of terraces descending the slope behind the house, where a variety of vegetables and grains are grown, including corn, peas, winter wheat, lettuce, turnips, cabbage, and okra. Another garden of note is the **Miksch Garden,** a fine example of a household garden where crops like peas, leeks, garlic, lettuce, spinach, potatoes, and other commonly used crops are planted in raised beds. Many of the crops, as with other gardens around the village, are allowed to go to seed, meaning to grow beyond their culinary use, produce flowers, and produce the seeds that will be next year's crops. Costumed interpreters in the garden talk about the crops, gardening practices, and even break character to talk about the differences in gardening then and now; inside the house, more interpreters demonstrate some of the cooking and other household chores of the day.

As you walk through the streets of the old village, you'll pass dozens of historic buildings that house the workshops of many kinds of artisans and that hold significance in the history of this religious community. Among these are the **Single Brothers' House** and **Single Sisters' House,** the 18th-century dormitories in which "choirs," groups of young unmarried Moravian men and women, lived and worked. The **Salem Tavern** is an impressive old lodge where George Washington stayed on his 1791 tour of the

South. The **Vierling House** (463 Church St. SE), home of the Berlin-trained doctor who came to be Salem's town physician in 1790, is a fascinating repository of early medical and pharmaceutical goods. **Winkler Bakery** (521 S. Main St., 336/721-7302) was run by Swiss-born Christian Winkler and his descendants for over 120 years, and their wood-burning ovens are still turning out Moravian delicacies today (grab a tin of gingersnaps or Moravian cookies for the road).

While you're in Old Salem, visit one of the most important sites for African Americans and abolitionists in the state, **St. Philips African Moravian Church** (911 S. Church St.). This the oldest African American church still standing in North Carolina and one of the oldest in the nation. In the church in 1865 a Union Cavalry chaplain announced emancipation to the enslaved people in and around Salem.

Salem is a beautiful place for a morning or evening walk, when the light comes through the trees and dapples the cobblestone streets with sun and shadow, but it pales in comparison to the stark beauty of **God's Acre** (S. Church St. and Cemetery St.), the traditional name given to Moravian graveyards. Seeing this striking graveyard for the first time, you'll notice that all of the gravestones are the same—white marble of nearly uniform dimensions, all facing east—reflecting the emphasis Moravians place on equality of the souls of the faithful after death.

While you're in Salem, try some traditional Moravian dishes at **The Tavern in Old Salem** (736 S. Main St., 336/722-1227, http://thetaverninoldsalem.ws, 11am-9pm Tues.-Sat., 11am-3pm Sun., lunch $8.50-11, dinner $13-29), built in 1816 as an annex to the historic 1784 tavern next door. Here you can enjoy dishes inspired by Moravian delicacies from the 18th and 19th centuries. Every dish uses locally farmed food, and they serve a small selection of craft beer. Dinner is served by candlelight. One of my favorite dishes is the hearty and delicious Tavern Chicken Pie: Not exactly chicken pot pie, not exactly not chicken pot pie, it's shredded chicken wrapped in a pie shell,

God's Acre: a sacred, serene place

baked, topped with chicken gravy, and served with mashed potatoes and green beans.

Museums

Winston-Salem earned the nickname "The City of Arts and Innovation" partly thanks to the 1949 establishment of the nation's first local arts council. Since then, the city has continued to be a hive of artists and art collectors, and there are a number of museums dedicated to the arts, exploring history, and for children.

Winston-Salem's many art museums represent various places and centuries. **The Southeastern Center for Contemporary Art** (750 Marguerite Dr., 336/725-1904, www.secca.org, 10am-5pm Tues.-Wed. and Fri.-Sat., 10am-8pm Thurs., 1pm-5pm Sun., donation) hosts changing exhibits of modern work in a variety of media. Exhibits rotate every few months; one gallery may show avant-garde short films one month, and the next display photorealistic paintings or giant yarn sculptures.

The **Reynolda House Museum of American Art** (2250 Reynolda Rd., 336/758-5150, www. reynoldahouse.org, 9:30am-4pm Tues.-Sat., 1:30pm-4:30pm Sun., $14 adults, free under age 18, students, and military) has a distinguished collection of American masterpieces from colonial times through the present day in the beautiful 1917 home of R. J. and Katharine Reynolds, of the R. J. Reynolds Tobacco Company. The **Diggs Gallery** (601 S. Martin Luther King Dr., 336/750-2458, www.wssu.edu, 11am-5pm Tues.-Sat., free) at Winston-Salem State University, has excellent permanent and changing exhibitions of work by African and African American artists from North Carolina and the Southeast, with some pieces from influential artist from outside the area. **Delta Fine Arts Center** (2611 New Walkertown Rd., 336/722-2625, www.delta-artscenter.org, 10am-5pm Tues.-Fri., 11am-3pm Sat., free) also promotes African American visual and performing artists.

SciWorks (400 W. Hanes Mill Rd., 336/767-6730, www.sciworks.org, 10am-5pm Mon.-Sat., noon-5pm Sun., $11 adults, $9 over age

© JASON FRYE

Southeastern Center for Contemporary Art

61, $9 age 4-19, free under age 4), the Science and Environmental Museum of Forsyth County, was named one of the top 25 science museums by *Parents* magazine. Children can pet horseshoe crabs, play a floor piano with their feet, brush giant teeth, and learn about physics and biology. There's 25,000 square feet of exhibits, a 17-acre science and environmental studies park with nature trails and picnic spaces, and a planetarium. Also fun for kids is the **Children's Museum of Winston-Salem** (390 S. Liberty St., 336/723-9111, www.childrensmuseumofws.org, 9am-4pm Mon.-Fri., 10am-5pm Sat., 1pm-5pm Sun. June-Aug., 9am-4pm Tues.-Fri., 10am-5pm Sat., 1pm-5pm Sun. Sept.-May, $7, $5 over age 62). Kids love to climb the giant beanstalk in the lobby, which ascends all the way to the second floor. Other exhibits include a space with oversize building blocks, an enchanted forest, an educational garden open in warm weather, and a gallery filled with giant alphabet sculptures and activities.

A very different kind of gallery is the **Winston Cup Museum** (1355 N. Martin Luther King Dr., 336/724-4557, www.winstoncupmuseum.com, 10am-5pm Tues.-Sat., $8 adults, $4 ages 5-12, free under age 5), which chronicles R. J. Reynolds's 33-year sponsorship of NASCAR (there can be no more Carolinian combination than cigarettes and stock cars). Here you'll see cars driven by Dale Senior and Dale Junior (as the Earnhardts are known in these parts), drivers' helmets, winners' payout checks, and other great racing memorabilia. It's an interesting museum even for nonfans.

Historic Bethabara Park

In northern Winston-Salem, **Bethabara Park** (2147 Bethabara Rd., 336/924-8191, www.cityofws.org, guided tours 10:30am-4:30pm Tues.-Fri., 1:30pm-4:30pm Sat.-Sun. Apr.-Dec., $4 adults, $1 children) explores an even earlier period of Moravian settlement than at Salem. Bethabara was the first foothold of the Moravians in North Carolina: In the fall of 1753 a group of 15 Moravian men came down the Great Wagon Road from Pennsylvania, through the Shenandoah Valley of Virginia,

ART-O-MATS: A WINSTON-SALEM ORIGINAL

The City of Arts and Innovation was built with tobacco money, so it's fitting that a local artist has rescued and retrofitted several old-school cigarette vending machines—you know the ones, metal boxes with chrome knobs that you'd pull, and the cigarette pack would fall into the glamorous tray below—and placed them around town. Instead of putting in money and getting back a pack of smokes, once you pull the knob, original art falls out. Sure, it's a small piece of art (roughly the size of a cigarette pack), but it's cool, and so is the experience of buying it. Look for Art-O-Mats near the Reynolda House Museum of American Art, the Garage bar, and a few other spots around town (www.artomat. org).

and into the North Carolina Piedmont to begin construction of a village at the northwestern edge of the 100,000-acre tract of land that the church had bought and named Wachovia. The 15 original settlers and the other Moravians who would soon join them constructed a sturdy, attractive little village in just a few years.

During its first two decades of existence, Bethabara was a busy place. The Moravians' reputation as craftspeople drew settlers from the surrounding hills to buy their wares. The village's location on the Great Wagon Road was also an important factor in its growth. During the French and Indian War in the 1750s, Bethabara became a stockade, an enclosed safe haven not only for the Moravians but for an even greater number of non-Moravian neighbors. It was touched by war again in 1771, when General Cornwallis and his troops ransacked the town and stole livestock.

By the late 1760s, construction of Salem was underway, and the population of Bethabara gradually began to decline. The village mill and distillery remained in operation for some decades, but by the early 19th century, Bethabara had become a small farming community, and Salem, to the south, became the Moravian metropolis.

Körner's Folly

One of the weirdest places you can visit in North Carolina **Körner's Folly** (413 S. Main St., 336/996-7922, www.kornersfolly.org, 10am-4pm Thurs.-Sat., 1pm-4pm Sun., $10 adults, $6 ages 6-16, free under age 6), located east of Winston-Salem in Kernersville. The seven-level house with 22 rooms of insanely ornate moldings and eccentric architectural contraptions fits all the requirements of a classic Victorian monstrosity. But it's no monstrosity; its peculiarities make it awkwardly beautiful. In its late-1870s infancy, Körner's Folly was intended not as a home but a display of designer Jule Körner's architectural innovations, a showroom for his clients to tour and experience the architectural elements he was proposing. Gradually it also became Körner's home. His wife created an exquisite children's theater in the high-ceilinged attic, well worth a visit on its own.

Yadkin Valley Wine Trail

The Yadkin Valley is North Carolina's own little Napa Valley, a great place to spend a weekend touring and tasting some surprisingly good French- and Italian-style wines. There are close to 40 wineries in the 1.4-million-acre Yadkin Valley American Viticultural Area, the first in North Carolina, all within a short drive of Winston-Salem, and every year one or two new vineyards are added to the roster. Among the vineyards near Winston-Salem you'll find tasting rooms in barns, sleek modern buildings, and even Tuscan-style villas, all overlooking acres of vines in their orderly rows. You'll find winemakers who are still happy to take a minute or two to speak to visitors, answering questions or explaining steps of the wine-making process. Yes, it's a little strange to drink a glass

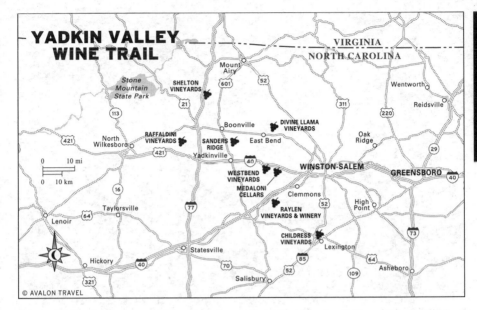

YADKIN VALLEY
WINE TRAIL

© AVALON TRAVEL

of impeccable chardonnay and hear the winemaker describe his grapes in a loving Southern accent, but you get used to it.

Among the best vineyards in the Yadkin Valley is **Childress Vineyards** (1000 Childress Vineyard Rd., Lexington, 336/236-9463, www.childressvineyards.com, tours noon and 3pm Mon.-Fri., on the hour noon-4pm Sat.-Sun., tasting room 10am-5pm Mon.-Sat., noon-5pm Sun.), owned by an unexpected wine fan, former NASCAR driver and NASCAR team owner Richard Childress. Childress Vineyards has more than 100 acres of grapes planted in a dozen varietals, including merlot and viognier, on land that resembles Burgundy in many ways. In their 35,000-square-foot production facility, you'll have plenty of opportunities to taste their wines. The viognier, cabernet franc, and Meritage red blend are especially good, as is the Three; its name refers to the blend of three grapes used to make this crisp white as well as the legendary Dale Earnhardt, who drove a NASCAR race car painted with the number 3 for Richard Childress for many years. Here you'll also find **The Bistro** (11am-3pm daily, sandwiches and entrées $9-16, 3-course prix

fixe $20, with wine $25), serving the Childress family's favorite sandwiches as well as entrées that include flatbread pizza, shrimp and grits, and gnocchi.

Medaloni Cellars (9125 Shallowford Rd., Lewisville, 336/946-1490, noon-sunset Sat.-Sun.) is a newcomer to the viticultural scene in the Yadkin Valley, established in 2011, but it's already getting noticed for their drinkable and accessible wines. This small winery produces only about 600 cases a year and are best known for their whites, including their Nude Chardonnay, an unoaked chardonnay that's great for sultry summer gatherings. They also have three cabins ($150-175) to rent on the property, two of which are woodsy and very private, the third of which is adjacent to the tasting room but still has a good deal of private space.

The oldest winery in Yadkin County, **Westbend Vineyards and Brewhouse** (5394 Williams Rd., Lewisville, 336/945-5032, www.westbendvineyards.com, 11am-5pm Tues.-Thurs., 11am-8pm Fri.-Sat., noon-5pm Sun.) still produces some great wine and now even brews some tasty beer. It started as an

© JASON FRYE

Medaloni Cellars tasting room

experiment in 1972 when a Winston-Salem businessman decided to go against expert opinions and attempt to grow French wine grapes. His first planting of cabernet sauvignon, merlot, and chardonnay grapes were successful and it has been operating ever since. With close to 20 bottles to choose from, including merlots, chardonnays, and ice wines, you'll have your work cut out for you in their tasting room. Their brewery has a smaller selection, with four to six beers on tap at any given time.

Other vineyards worth a visit include **Divine Llama Vineyards** (5349 Macedonia Rd., East Bend, 336/699-2525, www.divinellamavineyards.com, noon-5pm Fri.-Sat., 1pm-5pm Sun. Mar.-Dec., 1pm-5pm Sat.-Sun. Jan.-Feb.), where you'll find a couple of odd varietals and a llama; **RayLen Vineyards & Winery** (3577 U.S. 158, Mocksville, 336/998-3100, www.raylenvineyards.com, 11am-6pm Mon.-Sat., tastings $6-10), home to a number of award-winning wines; and **Sanders Ridge** (3200 Round Hill Rd, Boonville, 336/677-1700, www.sandersridge.com, noon-6pm Mon.-Sat.,

noon-5pm Sun.), one of the few wineries in these parts to make anything with the muscadine, a grape native to North Carolina, along with a couple of tasty fruit-based blends.

ENTERTAINMENT AND EVENTS
Performing Arts

The **Piedmont Opera** (336/725-7101, www.piedmontopera.org, $15-80) is a 30-year-old company that presents several operas each season, with a special emphasis on classic Italian opera. Now more than 60 years old, the **Winston-Salem Symphony's** (336/725-1035, www.wssymphony.org, $15-62) performance schedule includes a variety of baroque, pop, and other music.

The **University of North Carolina School of the Arts** (tickets and most performances at Stevens Center, 405 W. 4th St., 336/721-1945, www.uncsa.edu, box office 11am-6pm Mon.-Fri., $15 adults, $13 students and seniors) is one of the top performing arts schools in the world, in fact their School of Drama was named by

The Hollywood Reporter as the seventh-best in the world. The School of the Arts puts on a variety of performances throughout the year, including films, dance performances, plays, and concerts, but perhaps their most anticipated performance of the year is December's brief run of *The Nutcracker.*

Nightlife

The Garage (110 W. 7th St., 336/777-1127, www.the-garage.ws, 6pm-midnight Tues.-Thurs., 6pm-2am Fri.-Sat.) has a knack for identifying future stars in alternative rock and roll, Americana, blues, and alternative country music, and for booking great established acts. Any show you hear at the Garage is bound to be good. For good craft cocktails in a surprising dive-bar setting, **Single Brothers** (627 N. Trade St., 336/602-2657, 4pm-2am Mon.-Sat., 2pm-midnight Sun.) is the place to pull up a barstool. This is a hip, energetic bar with loyal local patrons and bartenders who know their way around a cocktail shaker.

The first time I came to Winston-Salem, it was to go to **C Ziggy's** (170 W. 9th St., 336/722-5000, http://ziggyrock.net, box office 11am-5pm Mon.-Fri., club 6pm-2am daily), a then-legendary concert venue. I've seen everything from heavy metal and electronica shows to bluegrass at Ziggy's, and they still book an eclectic mix of artists and styles, retaining their position as the place to see live music in Winston-Salem.

Events

The **1st Friday Gallery Hop** (336/734-1864, www.dadaws.org) takes place on the first Friday evening of every month in the Downtown Arts District Association (DADA) neighborhood along 6th, Trade, and Liberty Streets. Throughout the district, art galleries, craft studios, and shops are open well into the evening, with neighborhood restaurants and bars staying open even later for the event.

Starting at midnight and lasting into the early hours of Easter Sunday every year, roving brass bands play throughout the city in a tradition that the Moravians of Salem practiced 200 years ago and that remains an important part of Easter worship. The bands' rounds, as they're called, always begin with Bach's "Sleepers, Wake," a composition that was brand-new when the first Moravian band was organized in Saxony. Some bands play in Old Salem, but others get on buses and spread throughout the city, waking Winston-Salem to the news of Easter morning.

April brings the **RiverRun Film Festival** (336/724-1502, www.riverrunfilm.com, regular screenings $10, multiple-event pass $100), one of the largest film festivals in the Southeast. It is a great opportunity to see the work of both established and emerging filmmakers and to attend workshops and panels about the art and business of filmmaking.

In June, at the **North Carolina Wine Festival** (www.ncwinefestival.com, $25 advance tickets, $30 at the gate, $15 designated driver, free under age 12), you can sample prize wines from dozens of vineyards across the state, including the famously fertile Yadkin Valley, short drive from Winston-Salem. The festival is held just outside the city in Clemmons, which is southwest of Winston-Salem on I-40. June also brings the **Twin City Ribfest** (336/707-9188, http://twincityribfest.com, $7 adults, free under age 13), a competition that has been around for more than a decade and that continues to draw competition rib-cooking teams from all over. The four-day event features concerts day and night, a marketplace where you'll find more barbecue sauce than you can shake a rib at, rides for kids, and, of course, something good to eat.

The end of July and beginning of August is time for the **National Black Theater Festival** (336/723-2266, www.nbtf.org, prices vary). The six-day gathering includes classic and modern dramas as well as poetry slams and many other events. The *New York Times* reviewed 1989's inaugural festival, attended by 10,000 people, as "one of the most historic and culturally significant events in the history of black theater and American theatre in general." It now draws 60,000 visitors annually.

In August, one of Winston-Salem's newest

events, **Dr. Brownstone's Sweet Summer LuvLuv Festival** (450 N. Spring St., 336/293-4797, http://springhousenc.com) takes place at Spring House Restaurant, Kitchen & Bar, where chef Tim Grandinetti, a.k.a. Dr. Brownstone (ask him yourself), brings in an all-star lineup of chefs to his restaurant for five days of grilling goodness. Each night features incredible tasting menus that are masterfully paired with wine, craft cocktails, and North Carolina microbrews.

November's **Piedmont Craftsmen's Fair** (Benton Convention Center, 336/725-1516, www.piedmontcraftsmen.org, $7 adults, $6 seniors and students, free under age 12, $11 weekend pass) has been held in Winston-Salem for more than 40 years. This large gathering of artists and art lovers celebrates craft in media such as fiber, clay, and metal and demonstrates how innovation and tradition are interwoven to make North Carolina one of the world's great craft centers. If you miss the fair, don't worry; they have the **Piedmont Craftsmen Gallery** (601 N. Trade St., 10:30am-5pm Tues.-Fri., 11am-4pm Sat.), open year-round.

SHOPPING

The Downtown Arts District, referred to as **DADA** (www.dadaws.org), is a neighborhood of galleries and boutiques located downtown along 5th, 6th, and Trade Streets. There are over a dozen commercial galleries, including the **Piedmont Craftsmen** (601 N. Trade St., 336/725-1516, www.piedmontcraftsmen.org, 10:30am-5pm Tues.-Fri., 11am-4pm Sat.), which has a beautiful showroom with the work of hundreds of North Carolina's finest studio potters, fiber artists, jewelry designers, and craftspeople in many other media. Several restaurants, bars, and coffee shops are located in DADA. The **Reynolda Village Shops** (2201 Reynolda Rd., 336/758-5584, www.reynolda-village.com), near the historic Reynolda House and museum, is a cluster of specialty stores and boutiques full of unique jewelry, clothing, books, antiques, home goods, and gardening gifts.

For those who like early Americana, **Old Salem** (www.oldsalem.org, most shops 9:30am-5pm Tues.-Sat., 1pm-5:30pm Sun.) has fun shops as well as historical sites to visit. **T. Bagge: Merchant** (Main St., 336/721-7387, www.oldsalem.org) is the primary outlet for the work of Old Salem's own craftspeople, where you can buy beautifully made Moravian household wares and toys as well as great books for adults and children. At the **Winkler Bakery** (521 S. Main St., 336/721-7302, www.old-salem.com/winkler-bakery.html, 10am-5pm Mon.-Sat., 1pm-5pm Sun.), bread and the famous Moravian cookies are made in the old-time way. The **Horton Museum Center Store** (924 S. Main St., 336/721-7360, www.oldsalem.org, 10am-5pm Tues.-Sat., 1pm-5pm Sun.) is also a great place to find Old Salem's wonderful in-house products, with an extensive selection of books about early Southern arts and crafts, including the work of master furniture makers from North Carolina.

SPORTS AND RECREATION
Spectator Sports

Wake Forest University is the fourth school in the famous Tobacco Road athletic rivalry and a worthy competitor to its nemeses in the Triangle: Duke, the University of North Carolina, and North Carolina State. The jewels in the crown of **Demon Deacon Athletics** (499 Deacon Blvd., 888/758-3322 or 336/758-3322, www.wakeforestsports.com) are Wake's Atlantic Coast Conference Division I football and basketball teams. Football coach Jim Grobe has led the Deacons to four bowl games in seven years, and he's entering the 2013 season only four wins behind the school record. The basketball program has produced such notables as Billy Packer and the 5-foot, 3-inch Muggsy Bogues, now both famous sports broadcasters, as well as Tim Duncan, Randolph Childress, and Chris Paul. The women's field hockey team is consistently among the nation's most successful, winning three consecutive NCAA championships in the early 2000s, and the golf program is the athletic alma mater of Arnold Palmer, Curtis Strange, Lanny Wadkins, Scott Hoch, and Jay Haas. As is the case at its Tobacco Road counterparts, obtaining a ticket to see a Wake Forest football or basketball game can be quite difficult. The Single-A farm team of the Chicago White Sox baseball team plays here in the Piedmont. The **Winston-Salem Dash** (926 Brookstown Ave., 336/714-2287, www.milb. com, $10-20) draw a fun, fervent fan base, making this a great place to spend an afternoon or an evening, or both if it's a double header.

NASCAR
NASCAR racing at **Bowman Gray Stadium** (1250 S. Martin Luther King Dr., 336/723-1819, www.bowmangrayracing.com, gates open 6pm, races at 8pm, $10 adults, $1 ages 6-11, free under age 6) is not only a classic Carolina experience—weekly races have been run here for 50 years—but is also a less daunting experience than race events at the massive stadiums elsewhere in the state: Lowe's Speedway in Concord can accommodate over 200,000 spectators, but Bowman Gray seats a cozy 17,000. It's also as inexpensive as a minor-league baseball game, making this an ideal place for your first NASCAR experience. Weekly races include modified, street stock, sportsman, and stadium stock car events.

Golf
Winston Lakes Golf Course (3535 Winston Lake Rd., 333/727-2703, www.cityofws.org, 18 holes, par 71, Mon.-Fri. $15, Sat.-Sun. and holidays $20, discounts for seniors, juniors, and late play, carts $9-13) doesn't have many hazards—only 22 sand traps and few water hazards, although a creek guards the green on number 5. A number of holes here are drivers' dreams, as they're nearly arrow-straight, and you can really blast one down the fairly fairways. The par-4 number 10 is a great birdie opportunity, as is the monster 544-yard par-5 number 14.

Sporting Clays
Friendship Sporting Clays (4805 Siloam Rd., 336/699-8694, www.yadkinwines.com, 9am-6pm Wed.-Sat., 1am-6pm Sun., by

appointment for groups of 8 or more) in East Bend, a little town northwest of Winston-Salem on Highway 67, halfway to Elkin, is a "golf with a shotgun" course in a beautiful rural landscape. If you don't tote a gun, don't worry and don't be intimidated, you can rent one and can sign up for special one-on-one instruction.

ACCOMMODATIONS
A cotton mill built in the 1830s is home to the **Brookstown Inn** (200 Brookstown Ave., 336/725-1120, www.brookstowninn.com, from $95) has been renovated and transformed into a luxurious hotel, with beautiful exposed brick walls, huge guest rooms, and Wi-Fi. Guests enjoy wine and cheese in the evenings and milk and cookies at night. The Brookstown Inn is within walking distance of Old Salem, and taking a stroll there and back in the morning is a great way to start your day.

Augustus T. Zevely Inn (803 S. Main St., Old Salem, 800/928-9299, www.winstonsalembandb.com, $105-250, children not allowed) is the only B&B in Old Salem. The beautiful 1830s house is furnished in original and reproduction Moravian furniture, with special features peppered throughout, such as steam baths in some guest rooms, heated brick tile floors in others, and working cooking fireplaces. Each of the 12 guest rooms has a view of the old village or the house's period gardens. Add to this a quiet, beautiful neighborhood, an easy drive to great restaurants, and private baths.

Shaffner House Bed and Breakfast (150 S. Marshall St., 336/777-0052, www.shaffnerhouse.com, $139-269) was originally the home of a cofounder of the Wachovia Loan and Trust Company, and being a banker's home, no detail was spared. The home dates to 1909 and is rich with beautiful woodwork and fixtures. There are nine guest rooms, including a large suite.

The **Graylyn International Conference Center** (1900 Reynolda Rd., 800/472-9596, www.graylyn.com, $229-419) is a spectacular historic home and onetime residence of the Bowman Gray family. Gray was the son of a Wachovia Loan and Trust Company cofounder but left his banking job to become president of R. J. Reynolds Tobacco Company. The home was completed in 1932 and is the second-largest personal residence in North Carolina, at around 45,000 square feet. It has been everything from a private residence to a mental hospital renowned for its "experimental treatments." Now owned by Wake Forest University, it's a stunning high-end hotel and conference center.

Like all of North Carolina's major cities, Winston-Salem has a lot of chain motels. A pair of good bets are in the Twin City Quarter (425 N. Cherry St., 336/397-3614, www.twincityquarter.com) downtown: The **Marriott** (336/725-3500, $109-289) and **Embassy Suites** (336/724-2300, from $139) are adjacent to one another and to the Benton Convention Center. The downtown arts district is right around the corner, and many restaurants and bars are only steps away. More moderately priced chains include **La Quinta** (2020 Griffith Rd., 336/765-8777, www.lq.com, pets allowed, from $65), the **Holiday Inn Express** (2520 Peters Creek Pkwy., 336/788-1980, www.

ihg.com, from $100), and **Hampton Inn** (309 Summit Square Court, 336/377-3000, www.hamptoninn.com, from $110).

FOOD
Southern
🄲 **Sweet Potatoes** (529 N. Trade St., 336/727-4844, www.sweetpotatoes.ws, lunch 11am-3pm Tues.-Sat., dinner 5pm-10pm Tues.-Sat., brunch 10:30am-3pm Sun., $12-21), a much-acclaimed Southern-style gourmet restaurant, is more formally known as "Sweet Potatoes (Well Shut My Mouth!)—a Restaurant." Everything here is an expertly crafted version of Southern favorites and regional delicacies. Fried green tomatoes, Gullah shrimp, house-fried pork cracklin's, and some of the best fried chicken you'll find anywhere. Add some fine cocktails, and you have a restaurant where you'll need reservations.

Eclectic American
🄲 **Spring House Restaurant, Kitchen & Bar** (450 N. Spring St., 336/293-4797, http://springhousenc.com, 11am-3pm Mon.-Fri.,

Spring House Restaurant, Kitchen & Bar

© JASON FRYE

4pm-10pm Tues.-Sat., lunch $8-15, dinner $18-26) is a farm-to-fork restaurant led by an exuberant and creative chef, Tim Grandinetti. The menu here is playful, with items like shrimp corn dogs, the General Tso's Crispy Veal Sweetbreads, chicken-fried foie gras, and slow-cooked Kobe beef cheeks. The cocktails are out of sight, and the bartender will pair your drink with your meal. The Tasting Menu, a four-course or more prix-fixe menu, gives the chef a chance to show off and deliver a bevy of delicious small plates to your table. There's also the Chef's Table, which gives you a palate-expanding meal experience, and the five-course Whole-Animal Snout-to-Tail Extravaganza, a meal experience so big and so awe-inspiring that it takes 10 days to prepare for and requires six guests.

There's no better place for breakfast in Winston-Salem than ◖**Mary's Gourmet Diner** (723 Trade St., 336/723-7239, www.breakfastofcourse.com, 8am-3pm Mon.-Sat., 10am-2pm Sun., dinner 8pm-10pm 1st Fri. of the month for the First Friday Gallery Hop, $1-15). This place has soul; the food and the staff show it, as do the walls, adorned with hundreds of art pieces that include a huge mural and portraits of the staff as culinary warriors. On the menu are eggs, bacon, and grits in combinations, along with many vegetarian-friendly dishes. For something different, try the Mendoza Benedict, a bowl of grits topped with steamed spinach, poached eggs, and hollandaise; no matter what you order, you have to try a biscuit. They're huge, so you may want to share it.

◖**Mozelle's Fresh Southern Bistro** (878 W. 4th St., 336/703-5400, http://mozelles.com, lunch 11am-2pm Mon.-Fri., dinner 5pm-9pm Mon.-Thurs., 5pm-10pm Fri., brunch and regular menu 11am-10pm Sat., 11am-9pm Sun., lunch $8-14, dinner $12-30, brunch $9-13) is a cozy place with fantastic food. Try the fried goat cheese salad or The Leaf, a salad with an okra-bourbon vinaigrette, for starters, then move on to the shrimp and grits, scallops, or the pimento cheeseburger. When the weather is nice, sit at one of the tables outside.

Bernardin's Fine Dining (373 Jonestown

Rd., 336/725-6666, www.bernardinsfinedining.com, lunch 11:30am-2pm Mon.-Fri., dinner 5pm-late Mon.-Sat., $19-30) is one of the most lauded restaurants in Winston. In fact, the *Greensboro News and Record* labeled it "the Triad's only five-star restaurant." Chef Freddy Lee honed his skills at several prominent New York City restaurants before moving south and opening Bernardin's with his brother Terry. Seafood and hearty cuts of beef and veal dominate the menu. The wine list is extensive, and the desserts alone are worth a visit. Bernardin's doesn't offer vegetarian options, but carnivores will be satisfied.

The **West End Cafe** (926 W. 4th St., 336/723-4774, www.westendcafe.com, 11am-10pm Mon.-Fri., noon-10pm Sat., $11-24), in Winston's West End neighborhood, has been in business for almost 30 years. The "casual elegant" bistro makes great sandwiches—dozens of hoagies, grinders, stuffed pitas, and burgers. Dinner entrées range from homey burritos and rib eyes to exotic fare such as the sautéed skate wing. **Caffe Prada** (390 N. Broad St., 336/793-2468, www.caffeprada.com, 5pm-10pm Fri., noon-10pm Sat., 1pm-5pm Sun., under $10) in the West End serves a nice variety of coffee, wine, and beer. It's best known for its gelato, made on-site.

West End restaurant **The Old Fourth Street Filling Station** (871 W. 4th St., 336/724-7600, www.theoldfourthstreetfillingstation.com, 11am-9pm Mon.-Tues., 11am-10pm Wed.-Thurs., 11am-11pm Fri.-Sat., 10am-9pm Sun., entrées $15-28) is a hip, well-established eatery with a loyal following. Located in an old gas station with patio dining, the restaurant serves brunch, lunch, and dinner. Their signature dish is shrimp and grits, with the grits are served in a "cake" form, not loose as is usual, making for an interesting texture in this dish; and they claim to serve Winston's best calamari. The Filling Station has a full bar.

Foothills Brewing Company (638 W. 4th St., 336/777-3348, www.foothillsbrewing.com, 11am-2am daily, entrées $10-22) is a craft brewery, restaurant, and gathering place in the heart of downtown. They keep nine beers on tap at all times with another two to four seasonal and special brews. A few menu items stand out, including the ale-battered fish-and-chips, bacon-wrapped trout stuffed with Granny Smith apples, and Paul's Spicy Ostrich Burger (which is lean and spicy). A buzz begins and a line starts to form each fall when they announce the release of their Sexual Chocolate Imperial Stout. It sells out quickly, and restaurants and bars are known to keep a keg or two in reserve to bust out in the middle of winter when supplies have seemingly been exhausted, much to the joy of Foothills fans.

Asian

Mizu (3374 Robinhood Rd., 336/774-9797, http://mizuwinstonsalem.com, 11am-9:30pm Sun.-Thurs., 11am-10:30pm Fri.-Sat., lunch $7-15, dinner $11-50) serves Japanese cuisine and a variety of curries and noodle dishes along with some great sushi. They serve an assortment of specialty rolls as well as very fresh sashimi and *nigiri*. You'll find the presentations almost over the top, but just enough to be fun.

Bakeries

Winston-Salem has a reputation for fine baked goods and sweets. Ask any granny within 200 miles if she'll share her Moravian cookies with you at Christmastime, and she'll get as stingy as Scrooge. Krispy Kreme doughnuts also originated here, and you can find them in grocery stores around town. Nothing beats a fresh Krispy Kreme doughnut, so look for the "hot" sign and grab some fresh ones at either location of **Krispy Kreme** (259 S. Stratford Rd., 336/724-2484; 1814 Ivy Ave., 336/499-5478, 6am-11pm daily, drive through open 24 hours).

It seems that many things the early Moravians made, from furniture to music, was lovely. Among the best-loved Moravian arts is baking, a tradition carried on by, among others, **Salem Baking Company** (www.salembaking.com) and **Dewey's** (3121 Indiana Ave., 2820 Reynolda Rd., 336/724-0559, 10am-7pm Mon.-Thurs., 10am-9pm Fri.-Sat., noon-7pm Sun.; 262 Stratford Rd., 336/725-8321 or 800/274-2994, 7:30am-9pm Mon.-Thurs.,

7:30am-10pm Fri.-Sat., 10am-9pm Sun., www.deweys.com). At its locations in Winston-Salem and elsewhere in the state, you'll find heavenly Moravian cookies: a thin spiced wafer that is a popular export around Christmastime. In business since 1930, Dewey's Bakery produces a long list of variations on the basic Moravian cookie as well as cheese straws—another classic Southern snack—and shortbread.

INFORMATION AND SERVICES

Winston-Salem's main emergency hospital is **Wake Forest University Baptist Medical Center** (Medical Center Blvd., 336/716-2011, www.wakehealth.edu), located off Business I-40 between Cloverdale Avenue and Hawthorne Road. **Carolina Veterinary Specialists** (1600 Hanes Mall Blvd., 336/896-0902, www.carolinavet.com), a 24-hour emergency veterinary hospital, is located off I-40 just west of U.S. 421.

The *Winston-Salem Journal* (www.journalnow.com) is the city's main newspaper. The **Winston-Salem Visitors Center** (200 Brookstown Ave., 866/728-4200, www.visitwinstonsalem.com, 8:30am-5pm Mon.-Fri. mid-Nov.-Mar., 8:30am-5pm Mon.-Fri., 10am-4pm Sat. Apr.-mid-Nov.) and its website provide extensive travel information.

GETTING THERE AND AROUND

Winston-Salem is on I-40, North Carolina's largest east-west highway. It is about 20 minutes' drive from Greensboro, about 2 hours from Raleigh, and about 1.5 hours from Charlotte.

Piedmont Triad International Airport (GSO, 1000 Ted Johnson Pkwy., Greensboro, 336/665-5666, www.flyfrompti.com), commonly called "PTI," is nearby on the northwest side of Greensboro, with many daily scheduled flights to U.S. cities. **Winston-Salem Transit Authority** (336/727-2648, www.wstransit.com), the city's bus system, is connected to that of Greensboro via Piedmont Area Regional Transit's **Express Bus** (336/662-0002, www.partnc.org).

Greensboro and Vicinity

Greensboro may be more densely packed with colleges and universities than any town in the state. It's the home of the University of North Carolina Greensboro; North Carolina Agricultural and Technical State University (A&T); Guilford College, a small Quaker school; and Bennett College, a historically black women's college often called the "Vassar of the South." As befits a college town, Greensboro has a lively arts and music scene and a creative, engaged population.

Greensboro has a surprisingly urban feel for its size, partly due to its ethnic diversity; with such a mix of people, it feels like a larger city. In the 1970s and 1980s a significant number of Southeast Asian refugees settled here, making this an important population center for the Hmong people and the Montagnard

people. There is also a significant population of African immigrants and a growing population of Latin Americans. Mix in the long-established African American population, the Quaker traditions still carried on today, a handful of Native Americans, and college students of various backgrounds, and you have a culturally rich city.

SIGHTS
Historic Parks

When discussing the Revolutionary War, the battles that come to most people's minds are probably in the Mid-Atlantic region and New England. In truth, much of that war was fought in the South, and some of the major turning points occurred in North Carolina. The **Guilford Courthouse National Military**

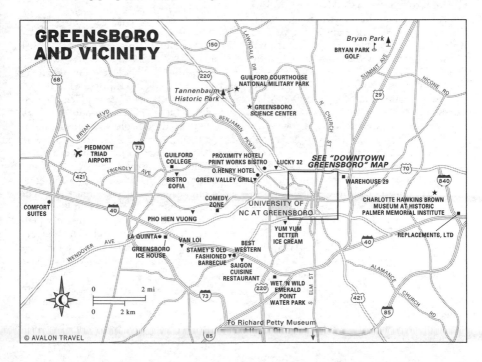

Park (2332 New Garden Rd., 336/288-1776, www.nps.gov/guco, 8:30am-5pm daily, free) commemorates the battle of Guilford Courthouse, when 1,900 British troops led by General Cornwallis routed 4,500 Patriots under General Nathaniel Greene. It proved to be a Pyrrhic victory, however, as Cornwallis's army was severely hobbled by the action. A 2.5-mile self-guided tour, which can be driven, hiked, or biked, stops at the essential spots on the battlefield.

Close by the battlefield is **Tannenbaum Historic Park** (2200 New Garden Rd., 336/545-5315, http://colonial.museum.com, 10am-4pm Tues.-Sat., free), where the Colonial Heritage Center and the 18th-century log Hoskins House display the life of the Carolina yeoman around the time of the Revolution.

International Civil Rights Center and Museum

Greensboro, the home of North Carolina A&T, a prominent historically black university, has played an important role in African American history. The **International Civil Rights Center and Museum** (134 S. Elm St., 800/748-7116, www.sitinmovement.org, 9am-6pm Mon.-Thurs., 9am-7pm Fri.-Sat. Apr.-Sept., 10am-6pm Mon.-Sat. Oct.-Mar., adults $10, students and seniors $8, ages 6-12 $6), is housed in Greensboro's old downtown Woolworth's building, the site of the famous 1960 lunch-counter sit-in that galvanized North Carolina's civil rights movement. That whites-only counter is the touchstone for this museum's exploration of the civil rights movement. The four men who staged the sit-in—David Richmond, Franklin McCain, Jibreel Khazan, and Joseph McNeil—are honored on the A&T campus with the **A&T Four Statue** (1601 E. Market St., http://docsouth.unc.edu).

In addition to the historic lunch counter, the museum has extensive exhibitions about life in the South in the Jim Crow era, and the struggles and successes of the civil rights movement. All tours are guided and begin every 30 minutes.

Charlotte Hawkins Brown Museum

A short distance outside the city in the crossroads town of Sedalia is the **Charlotte Hawkins Brown Museum at Historic Palmer Memorial Institute** (6136 Burlington Rd./U.S. 70, near Rock Creek Dairy Rd., Sedalia, 336/449-4846, www.nchistoricsites.org/chb, 9am-5pm Tues.-Sat., 1pm-5pm Sun., free). The Palmer Memorial Institute (PMI), founded by Brown, was a prestigious prep school for African Americans from 1902 to 1971. A walking tour through campus tells of the history of the PMI and its many extant buildings. Canary Cottage, where Charlotte Hawkins Brown lived and hosted salon-like gatherings for her students, has been restored to evoke the era of Brown's residence. In the Carrie Stone Teachers Cottage, visitors will find exhibits about the history of education for African Americans in North Carolina and can watch a 15-minute film about Charlotte Brown and her legacy.

Other Museums

The **Greensboro Science Center** (4301 Lawndale Dr., 336/288-3769, www.natsci.org, 9am-5pm daily, closed Thanksgiving and Dec. 25, $12.50 adults, $11.50 ages 3-13 and seniors) is a great place for kids and adults. Outside, the **Animal Discovery** (10am-4pm daily) displays live tigers, meerkats, alligators, crocodiles, and other wild animals. Inside are science exhibits and the **OmniSphere Theater** (shows on the hour noon-4pm daily, $3-5), showing 3-D digital shows on the domed planetarium ceiling. The newest addition, the **SciQuarium** (9am-5pm daily), is North Carolina's first inland aquarium, revealing the world under the waves to a new group of kids and adults. You can see African Penguins here, and who doesn't love penguins?

For children under age 10, the **Greensboro Children's Museum** (220 N. Church St., 336/574-2898, www.gcmuseum.com, 9am-5pm Tues.-Thurs. and Sat., 9am-8pm Fri., 1pm-5pm Sun., $8 adults and children, $7

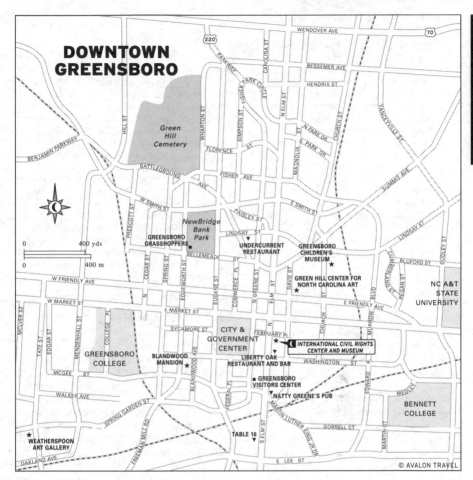

DOWNTOWN
GREENSBORO

© AVALON TRAVEL

seniors) features a pretend town with a Main Street where children can shop for groceries, bake and deliver pizza, put on a play with costumes and props, learn how houses are built, and scale a rock-climbing wall.

The **Green Hill Center for North Carolina Art** (200 N. Davie St., 336/333-7460, www.greenhillnc.org, 10am-5pm Tues.-Sat., free) presents exhibits of work by North Carolina artists. Much attention is given folk art traditions, and the state is also rich with formal studio artists, some of the best of whom are represented here. **ArtQuest** (200 N. Davie

St., 336/333-7460, www.greenhillcenter. org, 12:30pm-5pm Tues.-Sat., $5), an interactive children's museum in the Green Hill Center, teaches kids to appreciate the visual arts through hands-on studio experiences.

The **Weatherspoon Art Museum** (Spring Garden St. and Tate St., 336/334-5770, http://weatherspoon.uncg.edu, 10am-5pm Tues.-Wed. and Fri., 10am-9pm Thurs., 1pm-5pm Sat.-Sun., free), on the campus of UNC-Greensboro, has been dedicated to modern art since the early 1940s and has assembled a collection that includes works by Willem de

CHARLOTTE HAWKINS BROWN

In 1901, Charlotte Hawkins bravely left her home in Massachusetts to return to her birth state of North Carolina. At age 18 she was returning to the state where her grandparents had been enslaved to work as a schoolteacher in Sedalia, near Greensboro. Within a year of arriving, she'd raised the money for, founded, and opened her own school for young African Americans. She named it in honor of Alice Freeman Palmer, her mentor and the first female president of Wellesley College. The Palmer Institute graduated its first class in 1905, and for the next 66 years enjoyed a reputation for matriculating highly motivated young men and women who went on in remarkable numbers to advanced degrees and prestigious careers.

Charlotte Hawkins Brown, her married name, demanded excellence from her students' scholarly pursuits but also in their social graces. She taught her students etiquette, elocution, and all of the arts of courtesy usually taught in finishing schools limited to affluent whites. In 1944, Brown wrote a bible of etiquette called *The Correct Thing to Do, to Say, to Wear*. She became a leading figure in African American education, not only as the headmistress of the prestigious academy but as a speaker who traveled the world promoting a comprehensive approach to education.

Canary Cottage, the house where Brown lived, is one of the many buildings preserved on the campus of the Palmer Memorial Institute in Sedalia, now known as the Charlotte Hawkins Brown Museum.

Kooning, Andy Warhol, Cindy Sherman, and many other well-known 20th-century artists. This is the best collection of modern art in North Carolina and one of the best in the Southeast.

Blandwood Mansion

Blandwood Mansion (447 W. Washington St., 336/272-5003, www.blandwood.org, 11am-2pm Tues.-Sat., 2pm-5pm Sun. early-Jan.-Dec., $8 adults, $5 under age 12, $7 seniors) was built in 1790 as a farmhouse before the city appeared. In the 1840s its famous resident was Governor John Motley Morehead, the "Father of Modern North Carolina," whose efforts to institute humane treatment of the mentally ill, prisoners, and children with disabilities as well as to modernize the state's schools and transportation infrastructure made him an important historical figure. In 1844, Morehead engaged Alexander Jackson Davis, the architect largely responsible for the Gothic Revival style in U.S. architecture, to redo Blandwood Mansion; the result is the Italianate villa you see today.

ENTERTAINMENT AND EVENTS

Nightlife

Greensboro is a college town several times over, so there's a lot of late-night mischief to enjoy. Popular pubs include the **Rhinoceros Club** (315 S. Greene St., 336/272-9305, www.rhinoclub.com, 4pm-2am); **Natty Greene's Pub** (345 S. Elm St., 336/274-1373, www.nattygreenes.com, bar 11am-midnight Mon.-Wed., 11am-2am Thurs.-Sat., noon-midnight Sun., dining room 11am-11pm Mon.-Sat., 11am-10pm Sun.), home of some tasty, hoppy microbrews that are well-liked; and the cigar-and-drinks bar **Churchill's on Elm** (213 S. Elm St., 336/275-6367, www.churchillscigarlounge.com, 4:30pm-9pm Tues.-Wed., 4:30pm-midnight Thurs.-Sat.).

Warehouse 29 (1011 Arnold St., 336/333-9333, www.w29.com, 10pm-3am Fri.-Sun.) is a rather spectacular place, a hot spot for gay nightlife in this region for more than 15 years. In addition to great dancing, drinks, and shows—"from pageants and contests to fan dances and go-go boys"—Warehouse 29 has a huge outdoor patio (they brag that it's the biggest in the state) that features a sand volleyball court. A more low-key gay bar is **Club Q** (708 W. Market St., 336/272-2587, www.theqlounge.com, 8pm-2:30am Mon.-Fri., 9pm-2:30am Sat., 6pm-2:30am Sun.). It has a more traditional neighborhood-pub ambience, with trivia and theme music nights, and is a good place to catch up with friends over martinis.

If you're looking for a laugh, Greensboro has two comedy clubs. The **Comedy Zone** (1126 S. Holden Rd., 336/333-1034, http://thecomedyzone.com, from 8pm Fri.-Sat., $8.50 Fri., $9.50 Sat.) is a traditional comedy club with the occasional major headliner. **The Idiot Box** (348 S. Elm St., 336/274-2699, www.idiotboxers.com, $10) is the home of an improv, sketch, and stand-up comedy group that performs every weekend and even holds workshops in stand-up comedy.

Performing Arts

The **Greensboro Symphony Orchestra** (336/335-5456, ext. 224, www.greensborosymphony.org, $22-38, students $5-10) was created in the 1920s as a student orchestra at Greensboro Women's College, now the University of North Carolina at Greensboro. It grew to be a beloved institution in the wider community and a highly successful regional orchestra; performances are at various venues in town. Today's incarnation is conducted by Azerbaijani violinist Dmitry Sitkovetsky. The **Greensboro Opera** (336/273-9472, www.greensbooropera.org, $15-40) has been turning out wonderful performances of classical and modern opera for more than 30 years at various venues. Special productions have included guest appearances by stars such as Kathleen Battle. Each season at various venues, the **Greensboro Ballet** (336/333-7480, www.greensboroballet.org, call for prices) presents several major productions starring both longtime professional dancers and talented up-and-coming students. The School of the Greensboro Ballet, an affiliated institution, is one of only a handful of nonprofit ballet schools in the country and mints great dancers.

SHOPPING

Featured in a memorable early scene in the 2006 movie *Junebug*, **Replacements Ltd.** (1089 Knox Rd., off I-85 exit 132, 800/737-5223, www.replacements.com, 9am-7pm daily) is an incredible place to shop as well as simply to gawk. Replacements is five football fields of retail and behind-the-scenes space dedicated to what is surely the world's largest collection of tableware and flatware. This is much more than a plate outlet; it began in the 1970s as a small china collection in a North Carolina state auditor's attic and has grown so much that today it has an inventory of 11 million pieces in 250,000 patterns. If you want to replace your great-grandmother's 1865 baby spoon that you accidentally mangled in the garbage disposal, Replacements is at your service. If you cracked your granny's Fiestaware butter crock last time you visited and are praying she hasn't noticed yet, you can probably find its twin here before the jig is up. And, of course, if you want to buy a beautiful silver service for a bride or some brand-new designer stoneware for your own home, you've found the right place.

An unusual shopping experience can be had a Greensboro's first international shopping mall, **Fanta City International Shopping Center** (4925 W. Market St., between Market St. and Friendly Ave., 336/235-2300, 10am-9:30pm Mon.-Sat., noon-6pm Sun.), where you'll find four dozen shops offering international wares such as home goods, art, and food. It's a one-of-a-kind shopping day.

Greensboro Farmers Curb Market (501 Yanceyville St., 336/373-2402, http://gsofarmersmarket.org, 7am-noon Sat., 7am-11am and 3:30pm-6:30pm Wed.) is more than just a farmers market; it's a chance to make a connection with a farmer, craftsperson, or artisanal food maker. You can pick up steak, fresh eggs, cheese and assorted dairy products, seasonal produce, birdhouses, potted plants, fresh-cut flowers, and even soap, jewelry, and pottery. If you're hungry, just stop in for a bite; several food vendors are usually set up.

SPORTS AND RECREATION
Spectator Sports

The **Greensboro Grasshoppers** (336/268-2255, http://greensboro.grasshoppers.milb.com, $9 premium seats, $6 lawn) baseball team, a Single-A affiliate of the Miami Marlins, play at NewBridge Bank Park (408 Bellemeade St.), a field that has been graced by all-star pitcher Dontrelle Willis and catcher Paul Lo Duca.

Just north of Greensboro, in the town of Browns Summit, is the home field of the **Carolina Dynamo** (Bryan Park, 6105 Townsend Rd., Browns Summit, 336/669-0841, www.carolinadynamo.com, $7, $5 under age 19, $10 premium seats), a professional team in the Premier Development League of the United Soccer League. League champions twice in the 1990s and first-place regular-season finishers several times in the last decade, the Dynamo are a training ground for soccer's rising stars.

For more than 50 years, central Carolinians have been enjoying the roar and burning-rubber fumes of the race-track experience at the **Piedmont Dragway** (6750 Holts Store Rd., Julian, 336/449-7411, http://piedmontdragway.com, prices vary), located between Greensboro and Burlington, six miles from I-85 exit 132. All manner of wheeled motor vehicles tear around this 0.1-mile track, and you can catch an event almost any time of year.

Golf

Bryan Park (6275 Bryan Park Rd., 336/375-2200, www.bryanpark.com, 36 holes, greens fees $32-36 Mon.-Thurs., $35-39 Fri., $40-45 Sat.-Sun. and holidays, discounts for seniors and late play, cart $15) has two full courses, the par-72 Champions Course and the par-72 Players Course. Both are beautiful, and Champions is riddled with 97 sand traps and seven holes that border Lake Townsend. Open since 1990, it has received accolades that include being rated the 12th most affordable course in the country. The Players Course, a George Cobb design from 1974, is no less sandy, with 79 bunkers and eight lakes scattered around the course.

Jamestown Park Golf (7041 East Fork Rd., Jamestown, 336/454-4912, www.jamestownparkgolf.com, 18 holes, par 72, 11am-7pm Mon., 8am-7pm Tues.-Sun. Mar.-Oct., 8am-5pm daily Nov.-Feb., greens fees 18 holes $18 Mon.-Thurs., $23 Fri.-Sun. and holidays, cart $12, pull cart $2, 9 holes $12 Mon. Thurs., $12 Fri.-Sun. and holidays, cart $8, pull cart $1, discounts for seniors and juniors) is a pretty course, but the pace of play here can get a little slow.

Other Recreation

Greensboro's **Wet 'N Wild Emerald Point Water Park** (3910 S. Holden Rd., 336/852-9721, www.emeraldpointe.com, from 10am daily May-Sept., close varies, $36, $25 under 48 inches tall, $25 over age 60) offers more water rides than you could try in a full weekend. The central attraction is the two-million-gallon Thunder Bay wave pool, which features 84-foot-wide tsunami waves, and there are also five-story slides and riptide pools for the most intrepid swimmers, lazy rivers and shallow pools for those who prefer to relax, and many other adventures.

Piedmont's only year-round ice rink is the **Greensboro Ice House** (6119 Landmark Center Blvd., 336/852-1515, www.greensboroice.com, call for prices and hours). You can ice skate at a leisurely glide, practice figure skating, and even play pick-up hockey. The Ice House provides free Wi-Fi.

ACCOMMODATIONS

The high-style luxury boutique **Proximity Hotel** (704 Green Valley Rd., 336/379-8200, www.proximityhotel.com, from $189), opened in late 2007 with remarkable green architectural practices that have won awards and high praise, including the highest "Eco-Getaways" rating in *Outside* magazine. Solar panels on the roof, huge windows in each guest room that actually open, recycled building materials, and many other green features mean that the Proximity reduces energy and water use by almost half that a comparable hotel. The interior is beautiful and chic, and guest rooms are comfortable, brightly lit with natural light, and full of modern amenities.

The **◖ O.Henry Hotel** (624 Green Valley Rd., 336/854-2000, www.ohenryhotel.com, from $209), named for the Greensboro-born author of "Gift of the Magi," is a 1920s-style luxury hotel. The more than 130 oversize guest rooms feature nine-foot ceilings, neighbor-silencing double walls, comfy beds, terrazzo showers and huge bathtubs, and, like the Proximity, windows that open. The O.Henry's own London taxi will carry you to and from the airport free of charge.

There are plenty of motels in and around Greensboro. A particularly good deal is the **Red Roof Inn** (615 Regional Rd. S., 336/271-2636, www.redroof.com, from $45). Although the low rates might cause suspicion, the service and facilities are fine, at one-third the cost of many other area lodging choices. Other options are **La Quinta** (1201 Lanada Rd., 336/316-0100, www.lq.com, from $70, pets allowed), **Best Western** (2006 Veasley St., 336/294-9100, www.bestwestern.com, from $110), and **Comfort Suites** (7619 Thorndike Rd., 336/882-6666, www.comfortsuites.com, from $90, pets allowed).

Camping
Southeast of Greensboro in the town of Pleasant Garden, **Hagan-Stone Park** (5920 Hagan-Stone Park Rd., Pleasant Garden, 336/641-2090, http://haganstone.guilford-parks.com, tent camping $15 up to 5 people, RV camping $20 up to 5 people, additional campers $3 pp) offers pleasant individual campsites with tent pads, fire rings, lantern poles, and picnic tables. Restrooms and showers are nearby. RV sites, which can also be rented by tent campers who need an electric hookup, have a picnic table and 30-amp or 50-amp electricity and share water with the neighboring site. There are no sewer connections. Trails, a public pool, a pond, and a historic one-room schoolhouse are all within the park's boundaries. Reservations can be made online or by phone.

FOOD
Southern
Lucky 32 (1421 Westover Terrace, 336/370-0707, www.lucky32.com, 11:15am-9pm Mon., 11:15am-10pm Tues.-Thurs., 11:15am-11pm Fri.-Sat., 10am-9pm Sun., $10-26), just off Wendover Avenue, has been a Greensboro staple for 20 years. The menu features creative renditions of classic Southern fare. Standouts include chicken and dumplings, cornmeal-crusted catfish, and pulled pork on johnnycakes.

Stamey's Old Fashioned Barbecue (2206 High Point Rd., 336/299-9888, 10am-9pm Mon.-Sat.; 2812 Battleground Ave./U.S. 220, 336/288-9275, 11am-9pm Mon.-Sat., www.stameys.com, under $10) has been around in one form or another for almost 70 years. The Lexington-style barbecue is pit-fired over hickory wood for as much as 10 hours—old-time quality that's kept customers coming back for generations. I had my first taste of Lexington Dip here hours before a Bob Dylan concert, and even though the show was amazing, all I could think about was the 'cue.

Eclectic American
Table 16 (600 S. Elm St., 336/279-8525, www.table16restaurant.com, dinner 5:30pm-9:30pm Tues.-Sat., $15-50) is one of Greensboro's best restaurants. The menu blends New World cuisine with European culinary discipline, resulting in such creations as honeyed salmon and kumquats, tilefish and country ham, and striped bass with fried apples. The menu changes frequently, but no matter what's on it, expect high execution and the best ingredients.

The **◖ Liberty Oak Restaurant and Bar** (100-D W. Washington St., 336/273-7057, www.libertyoakrestaurant.com, 11am-9pm Mon.-Wed., 11am-10pm Thurs.-Sat., 11am-8pm Sun., $12-28) is credited with having started a culinary revolution in Greensboro, a fad for casual restaurants serving New American gourmet cuisine. Specialties include many seafood creations, duck confit, slow-roasted pork, and fried oysters. Originally a wine shop, Liberty Oak has a wine list a mile long, with some nice single-malt scotches and special-blend martinis thrown in for good measure.

Undercurrent Restaurant (327 Battleground Ave., 336/370-1266, http://undercurrentrestaurant.com, lunch 11:30pm-2pm Mon.-Fri., dinner 5:30pm-9pm Mon.-Wed., 5:30pm-9:30pm Thurs.-Sat., $15-28) provides great food with a focus on supporting local and regional farms, fishers, and ranchers. The beer menu is somewhat limited, but the wine list is more extensive. The dinner menu is made up of small and large plates as well as main courses, with creative and flavorful dishes like crab cakes and duck breast.

Big Burger Spot (3750-A Battleground Ave., 336/617-3777, www.bigburgerspot.com, 11am-9pm Sun.-Thurs., 11am-10pm Fri.-Sat., $2-12) was a unanimous winner when I polled friends about burgers in Greensboro, and for good reason; the burgers here are enormous. There are 11 to choose from, topped with everything from slaw to pesto mayonnaise to chili. You can get your burger Almost Big, Big, or Colossal, and the Colossal really is that: There's a $4 surcharge for this monstrosity, which has double the meat and double the toppings. And that's just the burgers. Check out their french-fry menu, with 10 specialty fries to choose from, including ones smothered with nacho toppings and ones drizzled with white truffle oil and Parmesan cheese.

Marisol (5834 High Point Rd., 336/852-3303, www.themarisol.com, 5:45pm-9:30pm Tues.-Sat., $14-38) offers a food experience that would be hard to recreate. The short printed menu is accompanied by an ever-evolving verbal menu. Ingredients are fresh, seasonal, and the best the chef can get. Enjoy everything from an amuse-bouche (it means mouth amusement, and it's a small bite served before the meal that sets the tone for what you can expect) when you take your seat to Parisian gnocchi to some of the freshest seafood around, all with interesting flavor combinations and preparations.

European

The award-winning **Print Works Bistro** (702 Green Valley Rd., 336/379-0699, www.printworksbistro.com, breakfast 6:30am-11am Mon.-Fri., lunch 11:15am-4pm Mon.-Fri., dinner 4pm-10:30pm Sun.-Thurs., 4pm-11pm Fri.-Sat., brunch 7:30am-4pm Sat.-Sun., bar until 11:30pm Mon.-Thurs., 1am Fri.-Sat., 11pm Sun., breakfast $5-14, lunch $6-14, dinner $11-30, brunch $10-15) is located at the Proximity Hotel and shares its clean, green aesthetic. The menu here is French bistro fare, so expect duck confit, chicken paillard, and *croque madame* for dinner, lunch, and brunch, and french toast and smoked salmon for breakfast.

Adjacent to the O.Henry Hotel and in the same restaurant family as Print Works is **Green Valley Grill** (622 Green Valley Rd., 336/854-2015, www.greenvalleygrill.com, 11:15am-10:30pm Mon.-Thurs., 11:15am-11pm Fri.-Sat., 9am-10pm Sun., brunch until 4pm Sun., $18-32), open every day of the year. The menu spans many European traditions, featuring dishes such as moussaka and Moroccan spiced fish. Green Valley Grill's wine list wins *Wine Spectator* magazine's Award of Excellence every year, with over 100 choices, including 50 by-the-glass selections.

Asian

Greensboro has a long-established Vietnamese community and a wealth of Vietnamese restaurants. A favorite of local diners is **Saigon Cuisine Restaurant** (4205 High Point Rd., 336/294-9286, lunch 11am-2pm Mon.-Sat., dinner 5pm-9pm Mon.-Thurs., 5pm-9:30pm Fri.-Sat., around $12), where some of the best dishes are the grilled pork over vermicelli and the flounder in hot chili basil sauce.

Pho Hien Vuong (4109-A Spring Garden Rd., 336/294-5551, 11am-9:30pm daily, $8-12) has both Vietnamese and Thai food with several vegetarian options. **Van Loi** (3829-D High Point Rd., 336/855-5688, 10am-10pm Wed.-Mon., around $12) serves good *pho* and Vietnamese sandwiches, but customers rave about the duck. Van Loi is popular with the local Vietnamese population.

Snacks

Yum Yum Better Ice Cream (1219 Spring Garden St., 336/272-8284, 10am-5:30pm Mon. and Sat., 10am-10pm Tues.-Fri., under $10) began in 1906 as a pushcart operation, when a young man named Wisdom Aydelette, who had been working to support his family since he was in the third grade, started peddling ice cream. "W. B." gradually expanded his operations, first graduating from pushcart to mule and wagon and eventually becoming a full-fledged brick-and-mortar ice cream shop. He also began selling hot dogs, which quickly matched the ice cream in popularity. Today, the Aydelettes still runs Yum Yum, selling ice cream and hot dogs that draw crowds.

INFORMATION AND SERVICES

The **Greensboro Visitors Center** (317 S. Greene St., 800/344-2282, www.visitgreensboronc.org, 8:30am-5:30pm Mon.-Fri., 9am-4pm Sat., and 1pm-5pm Sun.), downtown, across from the Carolina Theater, is open seven days a week. Greensboro has several hospitals, the largest of which is **Moses H. Cone Memorial Hospital** (1200 N. Elm St., 336/832-7000, www.conehealth.com). Should your pet have an emergency, you can go to the **After Hours Veterinary Emergency Clinic** (5505 W. Friendly Ave., 336/851-1990, www.ahvec.com).

GETTING THERE AND AROUND

Greensboro is connected to North Carolina's other cities by two of the state's major highways, I-40 and I-85. **Piedmont Triad International Airport** (GSO, 1000 Ted Johnson Pkwy., 336/665-5666, www.flyfrompti.com), commonly called "PTI," is on the northwest side of town, with many daily scheduled flights to U.S. cities. Once daily in each direction, Greensboro is a stop on **Amtrak's** (800/872-7245, www.amtrak.com) New York-New Orleans *Crescent* line and the New York City-Charlotte *Carolinian*. Regional Raleigh-Charlotte *Piedmont* trains stop twice daily in each direction. Trains stop at the **Greensboro**

Amtrak Station (236 E. Washington St., 24 hours daily). **Greensboro Transit Authority** (336/335-6499, www.greensboro-nc.gov), the local bus system, is connected to its counterpart in Winston-Salem by Piedmont Area Regional Transit's **Express Bus** (336/662-0002, www.partnc.org).

NORTH OF GREENSBORO

Venture north of Greensboro and you'll be in that proverbial place people refer to as "off the beaten path." This beautiful part of North Carolina isn't often explored by visitors, but there are some interesting historical spots and river activities, in addition to great country drives.

Eden

Well north of Greensboro is the small town of Eden, near the Virginia state line, home of **Troublesome Creek Outfitters** (413-B Church St., Eden, 336/627-6215, www.troublesomecreek.com, store 10am-6pm Fri.-Sat., trips 8am-5pm daily, call for prices), a full-service river outfitter that provides both rentals and guided trips along the beautiful nearby Mayo, Dan, and Smith Rivers. They've partnered with Three Rivers, a guide service, to expand their trip offers and have since started to offer overnight trips along the coast as well as river races and white-water canoeing and kayaking.

Eden's most famous resident was the banjo player Charlie Poole, a leading light in the earliest years of recorded country music whose playing is still idolized and emulated. Poole lived fast and died young in 1931; he is buried here in Eden. Every June the town hosts the **Charlie Poole Music Festival** (Eden Fairgrounds, 336/623-1043, www.charliepoole.com), a weekend of concerts and contests showcasing the traditional music of the North Carolina Piedmont, with special emphasis on the legacy of Poole and his band, the North Carolina Ramblers. It's a great opportunity to hear some of the region's greatest old-time bands in a less intense setting than at the region's megafestivals.

Milton

Northeast of Yanceyville, near the Virginia state line, the tiny town of Milton preserves much of the historic architecture of its circa-1800 heyday. In the 1820s and 1830s Milton was home to cabinetmaker Thomas Day, a free African American craftsman whose furniture can be seen in museums throughout the region. His workshop at Yellow-Union Tavern is undergoing renovation and will eventually open to the public. Day's woodwork is seen in the beautiful pews of **Milton Presbyterian Church** (66 Broad St.), which is open to visitors. It is said that Day donated his work to the church with the understanding that he and his wife, Acquilla, would be permitted to sit in a pew in the main chapel rather than in the slave gallery above.

BURLINGTON AND ALAMANCE COUNTY

One of North Carolina's early railroad towns, Burlington was an economic center in the Piedmont through much of the 19th and 20th centuries. The much smaller town of Graham, a short distance southeast of Burlington, is the seat of largely rural Alamance County. The county is crossed from east to west by the unpretty I-85, but roughly north to south it is crossed by the lovely Haw River, a rocky channel that's an area favorite for canoeing, kayaking, and tubing.

Sights

Alamance Battleground (5803 S. Hwy. 62, 336/227-4785, www.nchistoricsites.org, 9am-5pm Tues.-Sat., donation), south of Burlington, marks the spot where the War of the Regulation ended. On this battleground in 1771, Governor Tryon's colonial militia quashed an uprising by a band of backcountry settlers, the Regulators, who had banded together in protest of corruption in the colonial administration. On the grounds, a visitors center presents the history of the uprising, and a log house connected to the family of one of the Regulators is restored to period condition.

Haw River Wine Trail

The **Haw River Wine Trail** (www.hawriverwinetrail.com) is a lovely day's excursion for the oenophile. Tracing 50 miles along the Haw River, the trail leads to four wineries in the graceful hills of the northern Piedmont. **Benjamin Vineyards and Winery** (6516 Whitney Rd., Graham, 336/376-1080, www.benjaminvineyards.com, noon-5pm Thurs.-Sun.) planted its first vines in 2002, so it's a young winery. They have a range of dry white and red wines, including oaked and unoaked chardonnay as well as chambourcin, which is quickly becoming a favorite grape across North Carolina. They also have a few sweeter wines made from the native Muscadine grapes; be forewarned, these are sweet, fruit-forward wines that some will love and others will turn their noses up at, but everyone should try them at least once.

Grove Winery (7360 Brooks Bridge Rd., Gibsonville, 336/584-4060, http://grovewinery.com, noon-6pm daily, tasting $5) in Gibsonville produces over a dozen award-winning wines, and they allow volunteers to help crush grapes on Saturday in season. **Glen Marie Winery** (1838 Johnson Rd., Burlington, 336/578-3938, www.glenmariewinery.com, noon-6pm Thurs.-Sun.) is located on Mebane-Graham Lake in Burlington and has an extensive list of prizewinning wines. **Iron Gate Vineyards** (2540 Lynch Store Rd., Mebane, 919/304-9463, irongatevineyards.com, noon-6pm Mon.-Sat., 1pm-6pm Sun., tasting $5) has won a great many awards, including gold medals in the Mid-Atlantic Southeastern Wine Competition for its chambourcin and Dixie Dawn wines.

Shopping

Until just a few years ago there wasn't much shopping in Burlington and Alamance County; most travelers would zip through this part of the state without stopping. The arrival of two malls changed that. **Alamance Crossing** (1080 Piper Lane, 336/584-8157, www.alamancecrossing.com, most shops 10am-9pm Mon.-Sat., noon-6pm Sun.) has Barnes and

Noble (in case you need another copy of your well-worn Moon Handbook), Dick's Sporting Goods, a couple of large department stores, and the shops you'd expect in an outdoor shopping center of the faux-downtown sort. **Tanger Outlets** (4000 Arrowhead Blvd., 919/304-1520, www.tangeroutlet.com, 9am-9pm Mon.-Sat., 11am-7pm Sun.) is home to a familiar cast of outlet characters: Coach, J. Crew, Nike, and Saks Fifth Avenue Off 5th. It's a good place to grab a quick bite and a few minutes of shopping.

Sports and Recreation

No Carolina textile town would be complete without a serious baseball team, and Burlington is home to the **Burlington Royals** (1450 Graham St., 336/222-0223, www.milb.com, $6, $4 children and seniors, $8 reserved), a rookie-level affiliate of the Kansas City Royals. They play at Burlington Athletic Stadium (1450 Graham St.), convenient to I-40/I-85.

The Haw River, great for flat-water canoeing, rafting, wafting, and tubing, runs through Alamance County. The **Haw River Trail** (www.hawrivertrail.org) has designated access areas all along the river. Among the outfitters who run the Haw is the **Haw River Canoe and Kayak Company** (Saxapahaw, 336/260-6465, www.hawrivercanoe.com, rentals), which leads half-day and full-day guided paddles ($20-75) along different waterways in the Triangle and Triad regions and also rents out canoes, kayaks, and stand-up paddleboards ($30-60). Some of their trips provide excitement through some Class I-II rapids.

JAMESTOWN

There are many sites in this part of the state that are important to the history of Southern Quakers. **Mendenhall Plantation** (603 W. Main St., 336/454-3819, www.mendenhall-plantation.org, 11am-3pm Tues.-Fri., 1pm-4pm Sat., 2pm-4pm most Sun., $4 adults, $2 children, students, and seniors, cash or check only), built in 1811, is a beautiful plantation house located in what is now the center of Jamestown, southwest of Greensboro and about two-thirds

of the way to High Point. The plantation is a significant example of the folk architecture of early German Americans, both in the simple Quaker aesthetic of the house and in its "bank barn," a traditional German livestock barn built into a hillside. The Mendenhalls were abolitionists, which was typical of Quakers but rarer in the South. On the estate is one of only a very few surviving false-bottomed wagons, in which enslaved people were hidden during their journey to freedom on the Underground Railroad.

HIGH POINT

High Point is on I-85, 20 miles southwest of Greensboro and roughly the same distance southeast of Winston-Salem.

North Carolina has contributed a surprising number of greats to the world of jazz—most famously John Coltrane from High Point, Thelonious Monk from Rocky Mount, and Maceo Parker from Kinston. A **Statue of John Coltrane** with his horn presides over the intersection of Commerce Avenue and Hamilton Street, near the home on Underhill Street where he grew up.

Also on Hamilton Street is the **World's Largest Chest of Drawers** (508 Hamilton St.). The 40-foot-tall Goddard block-front chest, a tribute to the city's furniture industry, has huge socks dangling out one of the drawers in recognition of the local hosiery mills. It was built in 1926 by the High Point Chamber of Commerce, which was unable to resist the temptation to designate the chest of drawers the High Point Bureau of Information. A furniture mall in nearby Jamestown cheekily constructed an 80-foot highboy, built into the side of the mall rather than freestanding like the Hamilton Street bureau, but if you want to be really technical about it, it's actually the larger of the two. To maintain primacy as well as accuracy, High Point's bureau is sometimes referred to as the "World's Largest Goddard Block-Front Chest." In a similar vein you could also take a side trip to see Thomasville's World's Largest Duncan Phyfe Chair or the World's Largest Coffee Pot in Winston-Salem.

Accommodations

The **J. H. Adams Inn** (1108 N. Main St., 888/256-1289, www.jhadamsinn.com, from $109), a 1918 Italianate villa listed on the National Register of Historic Places, operates as a small luxury hotel. Seven guest rooms are located in the house, while the rest of the bedrooms and suites are located in a modern addition. The Adams Inn is a hotel rather than a bed-and-breakfast, but the attentive staff and special touches like an evening glass of wine combine the best of both lodging styles.

Food

Kepley's Pit-Cooked Barbecue (1304 N. Main St., 336/884-1021, www.kepleysbarbecue.com, 8:30am-8:30pm Mon.-Sat., $9 per pound) is the oldest restaurant in High Point still operating in the same spot. The Burleson family, proprietors, make the barbecue themselves in an eastern-Carolina style rather than that typical of nearby Lexington; such things can start arguments in these parts unless someone sets down a plate of 'cue in front of the combatants. They also serve 'slaw, hush puppies, and chili in this classic barbecue joint, the kind that uses paper placemats printed with block ads for local funeral homes and laundries. If you're coming at lunch hour, expect a crowd.

LEXINGTON
Food

The Piedmont town of Lexington is a veritable mecca for Southern chowhounds, especially those following the religion of 'cue. Billing itself as the "Barbecue Capital of the World," Lexington is known as the epicenter of North Carolina's western barbecue tradition. Known locally as "honeymonk," Lexington barbecue comes from the pork shoulder rather than the whole-hog meat, and also unlike in the east, the sauce usually has a dose of ketchup in it. This is blasphemy to easterners, just as their vinegar-heavy sauce is regarded around these parts.

Foodies will argue endlessly about which barbecue purveyor in the Lexington area is the best, but an oft-cited favorite is **Lexington No. 1** (100 Smokehouse Lane, 10 U.S. 29/70

S., 704/249-9814, www.lexbbq.com, under $10). In this friendly homey eatery, the barbecue is slow-cooked over wood coals, the way it should be. The hush puppies, a category of food that can inspire nearly as much partisan debate as barbecue, are also quite special. For some reason there's also a hamburger on the menu; skip it, get a chopped plate and a Cheerwine, and enjoy.

Speedy's (1317 Winston Rd., 336/248-2410, http://speedysbbqinc.com, 10:30am-9pm Mon.-Sat., under $12) has plentiful good food along with waitstaff who will bring it right to the curb for you, old-time drive-in style. Curb-service barbecue? A reputation for extra-large portions? Get a car-seat cover and a bib and sign me up. **The Barbecue Center** (900 N. Main St., 336/248-4633, www.barbecuecenter.com, 6am-9pm Mon.-Wed., 6am-9:30pm Thurs.-Sat., $4-14) serves pit-cooked 'cue, barbecue chicken (Wed.-Sat.), and exclusively red slaw. If you want to feed an army, you can do it here with the Tailgate, a dozen or more plates of 'cue. The menu is priced so you can eat yourself into a barbecue coma if you want.

Smiley's Lexington Barbecue (917 Winston Rd., 336/248-4528, 6am-9pm Tues.-Sun., closed Mon., under $12), one of the acclaimed stops on the North Carolina Barbecue Trail, specializes in the Lexington Dip sauce, a mix of Eastern vinegar and sweeter Western tomato sauce.

After a visit to one of Lexington's barbecue joints, make your way to **The Candy Factory** (15 N. Main St., 336/249-6770, www.thecandyfactory.net, 10am-5:30pm Mon.-Thurs., 10am-7:30pm Fri., 10am-4pm Sat.), a third-generation candy-making business housed in a 1907 old-time hardware store with beautiful creaky old floors. Lining the shop are barrels of candy—both the store's own Red Bird brand, and hundreds of classic candies that you may not have thought of since childhood.

◖ Barbecue Festival

October is officially Barbeque Month here in Davidson County, and late in the month every year, up to 100,000 people descend on Lexington for the **Barbecue Festival** (336/956-1880, www.barbecuefestival.com). Lexington No. 1, Speedy's, and a host of other local honeymonkeries provide the eats, while concerts, contests (lumberjacks anyone?), and children's activities fill the city. It's your chance to sample the full array of Carolina 'cue in one place. Considering that more than 15,000 pounds of barbecue are served each day, there's plenty of each style to go around. Word of advice: consider keeping your favorite style a little close to the vest. There are some folks here who take their 'cue seriously.

The Sandhills

In the center of the state, far from the major highways, you'll find an area known as the Sandhills. This is a part of the state that's often forgotten by travelers and travel writers alike, aside from those with a penchant for golf. Here you'll find placid countryside and tiny towns where it seems that every inhabitant is an artist. You'll find savannas trampled by elephants and zebras; mysterious, hidden, and haunted mountains; and towns called Whynot and Climax. The centerpiece of the Sandhills and actually the geographic center of North Carolina is the town of Seagrove, population 250, where a distinctive style of folk pottery is nearing its third century of tradition and innovation. The Uwharrie Mountains, a strange upthrust of deep hills and dark forests, are nearby. Asheboro, the largest town in the Sandhills with a whopping 25,000 residents, is home of the North Carolina Zoo and one of the state's most important culinary contributions: Cheerwine. Let's not forget golf: Pinehurst is known the world over for its famed golf course, but this resort town offers more than just a day on the links; a number of great galleries and restaurants can be found here too.

ASHEBORO AND VICINITY
◖ North Carolina Zoo
The **North Carolina Zoo** (Zoo Pkwy., 800/488-0444, www.nczoo.org, 9am-5pm daily Apr.-Oct., 9am-4pm daily Nov.-Mar., $12 adults, $10 students and over age 62, $8 ages 2-12) sprawls over more than 500 acres of Purgatory Mountain at the edge of the Uwharries. Elephants, zebras, polar bears, alligators, and many more live on large expanses of land planted and landscaped to approximate their native habitats. There are also five miles of hiking trails, from parking lots at each end of the zoo, that provide a great way to see the animals from a different vantage point. Trails are wheelchair-accessible, and for those who don't want to walk long distances, buses and trams run from exhibit to exhibit within the park (but you still have to get out of the vehicle to see the animals). This acclaimed zoo is operated by the state of North Carolina.

Other Sights and Activities
At the **North Carolina Aviation Museum** (2222-G Pilots View Rd., 336/625-0170, www.ncairmuseum.org, 10am-4pm Mon.-Fri., 10am-5pm Sat., 1pm-5pm Sun., $12 adults, $10 over age 59, $8 ages 6-18, students, and military, free under age 5), World War II through Vietnam-era fighter aircraft gleam in restored splendor. After touring the two hangars where the airplanes and other military memorabilia are housed, check out the gift shop, a model plane lover's dream. Be forewarned: This space isn't air conditioned, so a summertime visit may be a little on the warm side.

The **Asheboro Copperheads** (McCrary Stadium, Southway Rd., off McCrary St., 336/460-7018, www.teamcopperhead.com, $5 adults, $4 seniors and children, free under age 5, $6 reserved seats) baseball team, part of the Coastal Plain League, are a summer team of college players from schools in North Carolina and across the nation whose alumni include at least two current big-league pitchers.

€ Liberty Antiques Festival

Just outside Liberty, located between Asheboro and I-85, is a twice-yearly antiques fair that draws crowds from all over the Southeast. At the **Liberty Antiques Festival** (2855 Pike Farm Rd., Staley, 336/622-3041 or 800/626-2672, www.libertyantiquesfestival.com, $7), held over a three-day weekend in late April and again in late September, hundreds of vendors set up shop in a farm field, creating a huge outdoor antiques mall that offers many happy hours of browsing. Since it's in the open air, come prepared for bad weather and mud. There's huge variety among the dealers' wares, but overall the theme leans toward rustic Southern, including some fine early Southern furniture, museum-quality folk pottery, and other highly sought-after folk art collectibles, in a full range of prices.

SEAGROVE

The Carolina Sandhills are home to a generations-old pottery industry known as the Seagrove tradition, which still thrives today. The little crossroads town of Seagrove is built over beds of clay that were perfectly suited to the needs of 18th- and 19th-century Carolina potters. Several families of potters settled in this region, and drawing from the readily available excellent red and gray clays, were soon supplying much of the rest of the state with jugs, crocks, plates, and other utilitarian wares. The pottery that their descendants make today is much more decorative than the earlier style, combining beauty and function. Within just a few miles of Seagrove town and in little nearby communities such as Whynot and Westmoore are the shops and studios of over 100 potters. Many are families that have been here for generations—the Luck, Teague, Owen, Owens, Craven, and Chriscoe clans, to name just a few—and learned their art directly from family elders. Other potters have been drawn to the region because of its pottery tradition and have learned the techniques of the local old masters. The pottery made by all these Seagrove artists is among the most collectible of Southern folk art.

€ North Carolina Pottery Center

The **North Carolina Pottery Center** (233 East Ave., 336/873-8430, www.ncpotterycenter.com, 10am-4pm Tues.-Sat., $2 adults, $1 students) is the ideal place to start your tour of Seagrove. The primary focus of the Pottery Center is to preserve and present the work of Seagrove-area potters, but you'll also see representative work from the state's several other distinctive pottery traditions. The permanent exhibit and rotating shows introduce visitors to such late master artists as M. L. Owens, A. R. Cole, and Dorothy and Walter Auman, all in a beautiful airy building designed to echo the lines of a barn. There's also a nice little gift shop. On your way out the door, pick up a map of area potteries. There are dozens, each uniquely appealing, each representing a different facet of the tradition, and you'll need a map to help you choose which ones to visit.

Pottery Studios

Ben Owen Pottery (2199 Hwy. 705, 910/464-2261, www.benowenpottery.com, 10am-5pm Tues.-Sat. Feb.-June and mid-July-Dec.), three miles south of the Pottery Center on Highway 705, called "The Pottery Highway," is the studio and showroom of Ben Owen III, who learned the art from his grandfather, also a renowned area potter. Incorporating elements of Asian ceramics into his native Seagrove tradition, Owen has made a name for himself in the fine-arts world. Much of his work is positively monumental: massive vases and jars, many glazed in the brilliant red for which the family is famous. A small museum attached to the shop shows some of his father's and grandfather's beautiful work.

David and Mary Farrell of **Westmoore Pottery** (4622 Busbee Rd., Westmoore, 910/464-3700, www.westmoorepottery.com, 9am-5pm Mon.-Tues. and Thurs.-Sat.) were attracted to Seagrove by its pottery tradition and are now part of the community. The Farrells specialize in recreating historical ceramics, primarily North Carolina styles. Their work is so accurate that it appears in historic houses throughout the United States, at Old Salem and Colonial Williamsburg, and has been featured in many movies, including *Amistad* and *Cold Mountain*.

Luck's Ware (1606 Adams Rd., Seagrove, 336/879-3261, www.lucksware.com, 9am-5pm Mon.-Fri.) is the workshop of Sid Luck and his sons Matt and Jason, today's representatives of a generations-old family tradition. Sid fires his pots in a groundhog kiln—an old-timey Carolina form with a long, arched brick tunnel, part of which is usually subterranean. Some of the bricks with which the Lucks built their groundhog kiln came from Sid's great-grandfather's own kiln.

My favorite pottery from Seagrove comes out of **Johnston and Gentithes Studios** (249 E. Main St., 336/873-9176, www.johnstonandgentithes.com, 10am-5pm Mon.-Sat.); the pottery from this ceramic-arts duo is playful, artistic, and beautiful. With designs that are modern but inspired by primitive and ancient art, there's something to love in every part of their gallery. They make tiles, sculptures in often playful animal shapes and glazed with intricate patterns, bowls, and vases.

Shopping

One other shop in Seagrove with wares that rival the gleaming pottery in beauty is **Seagrove Orchids** (3451 Brower Mill Rd., 336/879-6677, www.seagroveorchids.com, 10am-5pm Tues.-Sat. and by appointment, blooms $18-40) is a wonderful place to visit even if your hobbies don't include exotic horticulture. There are over 220 kinds of orchids in the greenhouses here, from rare species to affordable plants for beginners. They're ready with tips and tricks that will help you set down roots in the orchid world. Seagrove Orchids even propagates new hybrid varieties of its own.

Accommodations

The **Duck Smith House** (465 N. Broad St., 336/873-7099 or 888/869-9018, www.ducksmithhouse.com, from $145), a farmhouse built in 1914, is a classic Southern bed-and-breakfast, with a large wraparound porch and a hearty country breakfast. The location is perfect for

a weekend of pottery shopping, and the four beautiful guest rooms are large enough to accommodate you and the pottery you'll buy.

UWHARRIE MOUNTAINS

The Uwharrie Mountains are strange and beautiful, a range of hills covered in deep rocky woods and dotted with small quiet towns with names like Ether and Troy. Peaks of this range, one of the oldest in North America, once soared to 20,000 feet, but the millennia have worn them down until the highest mountain now stands at just over 1,000 feet. Lakes, hiking trails, and history are cached in these mountains.

Uwharrie National Forest

The trail system of the **Uwharrie National Forest** has been compared to the Appalachian Trail. Although the Uwharrie Mountains are significantly lower than the Blue Ridge Mountains and the Smokies, they do shelter delicate mountain ecosystems closely related to those of the Appalachians. There are nearly 67 miles of trails in the forest, but two major trails, the Uwharrie National Recreational Trail and the Dutchman's Creek Trail, run through the park. Both begin 10 miles west of Troy, with parking at Highway 24/27. The 10-mile Dutchman's Creek trail loops with the 20-mile Uwharrie Trail, which ends 2 miles east of Ophir at Highway 1306. The hikes are somewhat strenuous—these are mountains, after all—and travel through pretty and somewhat spooky terrain: rocky woods with old homesteads and graveyards, and even some abandoned gold mines nearby. The Denson's Creek Trail is short—a 2.3-mile loop or a 0.7-mile short loop—and easy. Pick up the trail two miles east of Troy on Highway 24/27 behind the District Office.

Two large campgrounds are located near Badin Lake at the western edge of the park. **Arrowhead Campground** (Forest Rd. 597B, off Mullinix Rd./Rd. 1154, 910/576-6391, reservations 877/444-6777, www.fs.usda.gov, $6, with electricity $9, double sites $12, with electricity $18) has 48 sites with picnic tables and tent pads, 33 of which have electrical hook-ups. There are spigots for drinking water, and a bathhouse with hot showers, flush toilets, and a laundry sink. The Arrowhead Campground is 0.5 miles from Badin Lake. **The Badin Lake Campground** (Forest Rd. 576, off Hwy. 109, 910/576-6391, reservations 877/444-6777, $6-12), which has 34 sites, is directly on the lake. Each site has a picnic table, a grill, and a tent pad. Water spigots and chemical toilets are nearby. Several smaller sites throughout the park are accessible for tent camping, and one, Canebrake Horse Camp near Badin Lake, is for people traveling with their horses.

Morrow Mountain State Park

Located catty-corner to Badin and Albemarle, **Morrow Mountain State Park** (49104 Morrow Mountain Rd., Albemarle, 704/982-4402, http://ncparks.gov, 8am-6pm daily Nov.-Feb., 8am-8pm Mar.-May and Sept.-Oct., 8am-9pm June-Aug.) preserves one of the Uwharries' highest peaks, the 936-foot Morrow Mountain. Within the park, visitors can go boating on Lake Tillery or on the Pee Dee River, with rowboat and canoe rentals available in the spring and summer. More than 15 miles of trails snake up and down the mountains. Cabins are available for rent ($446 weekly summer, $88 nightly with a 2-night minimum off-season). There are also over 100 campsites ($12-48) with water, restrooms, and showers nearby, but no electricity. There's also a swimming pool ($5 over age 12, $4 ages 3-12) and boat rentals ($5 first hour, $3 per additional hour) on the lake. Visitors can also check out the exhibit hall (10am-5pm daily) to learn about the ecology and Native American heritage of the region, and to visit the restored 1870s home and infirmary of the first physician to venture into these parts.

Denton

The annual **Southeast Old Threshers' Reunion** (Denton Farm Park, 1072 Cranford Rd., Denton, 336/859-2755, www.farmpark.com, $14 adults, $6 under age 12) takes place in Denton, southwest of Asheboro and just to the north of the Uwharries. The gathering, usually held around the 4th of July, celebrates the old ways of farming that were replaced by tractors and other motorized equipment. At the Reunion, farmers who have kept the traditional methods alive gather to show off the strength of their draft horses in pulling competitions, horse-powered equipment demonstrations, and other feats of strength and skill. There's also plenty of music and food.

The second weekend in May brings countless bluegrass musicians and fans to the **Doyle Lawson and Quicksilver's Bluegrass Festival** (Denton Farm Park, 1072 Cranford Rd., Denton, 336/859-2755, www.farmpark.com, 3-day pass $75-85, 2-day pass $60-65, 1-day pass $30-35, half price ages 15-17, free under age 15). This three-day bluegrass jamboree has more than a dozen artists and groups descending on the park to celebrate the music they love.

If you'd like a taste of Lexington-style barbecue, a good bet is **Troutman's BBQ** (18466 S. Hwy. 109, 336/859-2206, around $12), a local landmark for many years. On the weekend you can get barbecue chicken if you're not in the mood for pork, but nothing beats a chopped plate with a side of hush puppies and red slaw.

Mount Gilead

The **Town Creek Indian Mound** (509 Town Creek Mound Rd., Mount Gilead, 910/439-6802, www.nchistoricsites.org, 9am-5pm Tues.-Sat., free) is an extraordinary archaeological site, the remains and reconstruction of a center of ancient indigenous Pee Dee culture. The mound itself was the location of three successive structures, including an earthen lodge and a temple. Over 500 people were buried at this site, and the remains of a mortuary were excavated nearby. Today, in addition to the mound, visitors can see reconstructions of two temples and the mortuary. The visitors center includes displays of artifacts and interpretive exhibits about the site's history.

INFORMATION AND SERVICES

Asheboro is the population center of Randolph County, where you'll find plenty of affordable chain motels and a fast food jungle clustered along U.S. 64. This is also a center for area medical services. The **Asheboro/Randolph County Chamber of Commerce** (317 E. Dixie Dr., 336/626-2626, http://chamber.asheboro.com) can fix you up with all the logistical information you need as you venture into the Sandhills.

GETTING THERE AND AROUND

U.S. 220, which runs from Greensboro almost to the South Carolina border, is the only major artery in this region, which has no major airports or rail lines. Charlotte, Greensboro, and Raleigh-Durham airports are all within one or two hours' drive.

Southern Pines and Pinehurst

Flip through the old postcards at any antiques shop in the Carolinas and you're likely to come across turn-of-the-century images of the Southern Pines region of the North Carolina Sandhills. The area's development kicked into high gear in the 1890s, when Bostonian James Tufts constructed the Pinehurst Resort with money made in the soda fountain industry. He commissioned Frederick Law Olmstead, the prolific landscape designer of New York's Central Park and Asheville's Biltmore Estate, to design a village, which he named Pinehurst. The first hotel opened in 1895, followed by the Pinehurst golf course (now called Pinehurst No. 1) in 1898, and the famed Pinehurst No. 2 course in 1907. The area quickly became a haven for Northern snowbirds. Postcards from that early era are clearly geared to a Northern audience, portraying the early spring blossoms that cover the Sandhills while New York, Chicago, and Milwaukee are still buried in snow, or showing rustic cabins and rural African Americans driving oxcarts or playing the banjo—holdovers from the stereotyped Victorian notions of the Old South, appealing to urbanites in search of a change of pace. The origins of the early visitors are also evident on streets signs in Southern Pines, where many of the roads are named for Northeastern and Midwestern states.

Today, this whole section of Moore County, anchored by the two picturesque towns of Pinehurst and Southern Pines, is a sea of golf courses and still a magnet for snowbirds and halfbacks (Northerners who retired to Florida,

found it too hot, and came halfway back to North Carolina). Primarily known for golf, the Pinehurst area has hosted the U.S. Open, the U.S. Women's Open, and the USGA National Championship. The spring months are exceptionally pretty, and the weather is usually warm but not dangerously hot as it is in high summer, so between March and May hotels and restaurants fill completely and golf courses can be booked solid. The key to having a good golf vacation in the springtime is planning well in advance. Golf packages are key here; by bundling lodging and greens fees, you can save money and hassles.

SHOPPING

Towns in this area may have been built around golf, but that's not all they offer; there are a surprising array of artists and a number of galleries displaying their wares. The **Artists League of the Sandhills** (129 Exchange St., Aberdeen, 910/944-3979, www.artistleague.org, noon-3pm Mon.-Sat.) is a group of some 200 Sandhills artists in all media. Not all have space in the studio-gallery, but more than three dozen painters, jewelry makers, printmakers, and other artists do. On any given day you'll find several artists working on pieces alone or collaboratively. Most of the work is for sale.

Knitters and those with a flair for fiber arts will want to stop by **Bella Filati** (277 NE Broad St., 910/692-3528, www.bellafilati.com, 10am-5pm Mon.-Tues. and Thurs.-Sat., 10am-7pm Wed.), a premium yarn shop in Southern Pines. They carry everything a knitter would need, from books and patterns to wools and yarns of all sorts. On Wednesday and Saturday they have a social knitting group, so stop in with your latest project or get started on something new. **Gentlemen's Corner** (1 Chinquapin Rd., Village Square, Pinehurst, 910/295-2011, http://thegcorner.com, 10am-6pm Mon.-Sat., 1pm-5pm Sun.), a high-fashion men's boutique, carries all the resort wear you'll need to spend a week at Pinehurst. They carry some high-end brands like Peter Millar, Carrot & Gibbs, and Kroon.

The Country Bookshop (140 NW Broad St., Southern Pines, 910/692-3211, http://thecountrybookshop.biz, 10am-6pm Mon.-Sat., 1pm-4pm Sun.) carries a great selection of books, including many about golf, but even more by local and regional authors of particular local interest. They also have well-stocked sections devoted to young-adult and children's literature.

River Jack Outdoor Trading Company (181 NE Broad St., Southern Pines, 910/692-5225, www.riverjack.com, 10am-6pm Mon.-Fri., 10am-5pm Sat.) carries everything you need for an outdoor adventure—tents, boots, trail-running shoes, kayaks, canoes, rock-climbing gear, and all the technical outdoor clothing you'd ever need. Their selection of outdoor shoes, and fashionable shoes by outdoor companies like Teva and Merrill, is quite good. The staff can provide recommendations on gear or on nearby hiking, biking, or kayaking routes.

SPORTS AND RECREATION
Golf
One of the most famous golf centers in the world, there are more than 40 major courses in the area around Southern Pines, Pinehurst, and Aberdeen. The **Pinehurst Resort** (80 Carolina Vista Dr., Pinehurst, 855/235-8507, www.pinehurst.com, call for greens fees) comprises eight major courses designed by some of the great golf course architects of the last century: Donald Ross, Ellis Maples, George and Tom Fazio, and Rees Jones. **Pine Needles** (1005 Midland Rd., Southern Pines, 910/692-7111, www.pineneedles-midpines.com, greens

fees $75-235) incorporates the Pine Needles (18 holes, par 71) and Mid-Pines (18 holes, par 72) courses, both Donald Ross creations. The **Talamore Golf Resort** (48 Talamore Dr., Southern Pines, 800/552-6292, www.talamoregolfresort.com) has 36 holes of top-level golf to play. The Resort Course (18 holes, par 71, greens fees $60-125) was designed by Rees Jones, and if you visit at the right time, you might be treated to the able caddying services of the Talamore llamas. The second course was designed by Arnold Palmer. The Mid South Course (18 holes, par 72, greens fees $60-125) has more than 11 acres of bunkers, making ball placement more important here than at most courses. The signature number 14 is especially bunker-riddled, so make sure you have your sand wedge; more importantly, make sure you know how to use it.

Other courses in the area were designed by Jack Nicklaus, Jack Nicklaus II, Dan Maples, Gary Player, and other leading lights of golf course architecture. Information about all of them can be found at the **Home of American Golf** (www.homeofgolf.com).

Hiking and Walking
Weymouth Woods-Sandhills Nature Preserve (1024 Fort Bragg Rd., Southern Pines, 910/692-2167, http://ncparks.gov, park 8am-6pm daily Nov.-Feb., 8am-8pm daily Mar.-Oct., museum 9am-5pm daily) comprises nearly 900 acres that are home to red-cockaded woodpeckers, fox squirrels, and other natives of the longleaf pine barrens. Most of the preserve is a limited-use area subject to periodic prescribed burning, but several trails, most one mile or shorter, let visitors explore the woods and swamps without too much commitment.

Another nice spot for walking is the **Horticultural Garden** (3395 Airport Rd., Pinehurst, 910/695-3882, http://sandhillshorticulturalgardens.com, dawn-dusk daily) at Sandhills Community College. A full acre of the property is dedicated to a formal English garden, while other areas show off plants of the woodlands and wetlands as well as collections of roses, holly, and conifers.

ACCOMMODATIONS
Resorts

A separate entity from the town of Pinehurst, the (**Pinehurst Resort** (80 Carolina Vista Dr., 855/235-8507, www.pinehurst.com), which opened in 1895, is the world's second-largest golf resort and also has three inns. The **Carolina** (from $263), built in 1901 and listed on the National Register of Historic Places, is a grand hotel in the Edwardian style, with long piazzas and lush lawns. The 1895 **Holly Inn** (from $235) was the first hotel built at the resort and is a smaller, cozier, more club-like inn. The third inn, the **Manor** (from $171), is the smallest and most laid-back of the accommodations.

The **Pinehurst Golf Academy** (one week from $2,305, weekend from $1,758) gives weekend and week-long classes for beginners and experienced players taught on Pinehurst 1, 3, and 5, with a stay at the Carolina included in the fee. Also on the grounds is the four-star **Spa at Pinehurst** ($50-200), with a long menu of skin and body-care therapies. The **Pinehurst Tennis Club** (courts 8:30am-8pm daily, $12-15 guests, $18-21 nonguests) is regarded as a top tennis resort nationally, with a high-quality pro shop and adult tennis camps. Golf, spa, and tennis packages can significantly reduce the overall cost of a stay at the Pinehurst, but surcharges for amenities might still apply.

Inns

The **Pine Crest Inn** (50 Dogwood Rd., Pinehurst, 910/295-6121, www.pinecrest-innpinehurst.com, $94-124) was owned for many years by Donald Ross, the golf course designer who helped make the Pinehurst Resort famous. Operated for the last 40 years by the Barrett family, the Pine Crest is a favorite for golfers and vacationers as well as for local diners who come to the Pine Crest Inn Restaurant and Mr. B's Lounge. The **Magnolia Inn** (Magnolia Rd. and Chinquapin Rd., Pinehurst, 910/295-6900, www.themagnoliainn.com, $125-200), built in 1896,

© JASON FRYE

the Holly Inn at Pinehurst Resort

is in a great downtown location. Guests are just steps from local shopping and restaurants and very close to the best area golfing. **The Inn at Eagle Springs** (1813 Samarcand Rd., Eagle Springs, 910/673-2722, http://innateaglesprings.com, from $75), 20 minutes west of Pinehurst, is quiet, quaint, and budget-friendly. Its location just outside of Pinehurst makes it a good base for golfing and for trips to Seagrove, the zoo in Asheboro, and other Sandhills destinations.

FOOD

Some of the best places to dine in the Pinehurst area are at the Pinehurst Resort (855/235-8507). The **Carolina Dining Room** (Carolina Inn, Pinehurst, breakfast 6am-10am daily, dinner 6:30pm-9pm daily, $22-50, resort wear required for breakfast, dinner jacket required for evening dining) is the resort's most formal dining room, serving fine chops and steak presented with the chef's suggestions for wine accompaniment. The breakfast buffet here is legendary. At the **1895 Restaurant** (Holly Inn, Pinehurst, 6:30pm-9:30pm Wed.-Sun., $24-36), the menu changes with some regularity, but the signature cider-brined grilled pork chop is a constant; other entrées include some version of shrimp and grits, a play on a land-and-sea duo, lamb, and steaks. The **Tavern** (The Manor, Pinehurst, lunch 11:30am-5pm daily, dinner 5pm-10pm daily, lunch $11-15, dinner $11-29) serves lighter café fare with entrée soups and sandwiches as well as an array of pasta dishes. Seven other restaurants, cafés,

and tea shops are scattered throughout the Pinehurst Resort, offering everything from snacks to bar bites.

At the **Magnolia Inn** (Magnolia Rd. and Chinaquapin Rd., Pinehurst, 800/526-5562, www.themagnoliainn.com, $12-30), you'll find some well-prepared food. The menu is steak-heavy, although seafood makes an appearance. One of the more interesting sandwiches is the grilled flat-iron steak sandwich, which comes out tender and smothered in cheese and caramelized onions; think of it as their take on Philly cheesesteak.

Ten-Ya Japanese Cuisine and Sushi (70 Market Square, Pinehurst, 910/255-1085, www.ten-ya.com, lunch 11:30am-2pm Tues.-Fri., noon-2:30 Sat., dinner 5:30pm-9pm Tues.-Wed. and Sun., 5:30pm-10pm Fri.-Sat., lunch $10, dinner $17-31, sushi $3-15) serves traditional bento boxes, hibachi-style meals, curries, and sushi in an intimate setting on Pinehurst's village square.

GETTING THERE AND AROUND

Southern Pines and Pinehurst are most easily reached by U.S. 15/501 south from Chapel Hill and U.S. 1 south from Raleigh. The area can also easily be reached from Fayetteville, just a short drive to the east. The area also has **Moore County Airport** (SOP, 7825 Aviation Dr., Carthage, 910/692-3212, www.moorecountyairport.com), open to private aircraft but currently with no scheduled passenger flights.

CHARLOTTE AND RACING COUNTRY

Charlotte is one of the most diverse cities in the Southeast, and one of the most perplexing to old-school North Carolinians for its juxtapositions. Charlotte's downtown is taller and more tightly filled with bankers than any other city in the state, but the countryside around the city is still filled with farmers. Two major sports franchises and the booming NASCAR scene have brought an influx of millionaires, but with them come the hordes of dreamers, up-and-comers, and wannabes. Besides that, the money NASCAR brings in has its roots in moonshining, and what's more of a surprise than a millionaire moonshiner? There's a worldliness in Charlotte not found elsewhere in North Carolina. Immigrants from Africa, Latin America, Southeast Asia, and India have brought their food, religions, holidays, languages, and customs with them, adding to the flavor of the city. Some folks don't know what to make of this, but they accept it all the same; that's Southern hospitality showing through.

More than anything, Charlotte is still a Southern city, where you may pay big-city prices for a meal but on your way out the door your waitress will tell you, "Y'all come back and see us soon, OK, hon'?" And even in the modern downtown banking neighborhood you'll still find men opening doors for women with a kindly "After you, ma'am."

The area just north and northeast of Charlotte is the epicenter for North Carolina's auto-racing industry and culture. Many NASCAR teams call the area around Mooresville, Concord, and Kannapolis home,

CHARLOTTE

HIGHLIGHTS

© Mint Museum: In downtown Charlotte, the two fantastic branches of the Mint Museum have galleries filled with art spanning the centuries and the world (page 244).

© Levine Museum of the New South: This museum tells the complicated and sometimes painful story of the post-Civil War South, and Charlotte in particular, in ways that are both respectful and innovative (page 248).

© U.S. National Whitewater Center: Home to the U.S. Olympic canoe and kayak teams, this facility is also designed for use by first-time paddlers as well as hikers, climbers, and other adventure-sports enthusiasts (page 254).

© Charlotte Motor Speedway: This Concord stadium seats well over 150,000 fans around a 1.5-mile track. It's a spectacular sight even when there's not a race (page 266).

© Textile Heritage Center: One of the best small museums in North Carolina, Cooleemee's Textile Heritage Center celebrates the incredibly rich heritage of "mill hill" communities of Southern textile workers (page 268).

LOOK FOR **©** TO FIND RECOMMENDED SIGHTS, ACTIVITIES, DINING, AND LODGING.

with their shops and headquarters in old textile mills and state-of-the-art garages. The huge storied Lowes Motor Speedway is here, and rarely a day goes by without the roar of race cars hurtling around the track. The sound is unmistakable and, around these parts, familiar.

PLANNING YOUR TIME

To get a good feel for Charlotte, spend at least a long weekend. Lodging is plentiful although more expensive than in much of the rest of North Carolina. Uptown hotels are within easy walking distance or a short cab ride from major

museums, sports complexes, and performance venues. Lodging in the Myers Park, Dilworth, and Plaza-Milwood neighborhoods are a quick hop from Uptown but have a less urban pace. There's a great deal to do in the Plaza-Milwood area—good cafés, fun shopping, and easy access to NoDa (the North Davidson neighborhood). Motels along I-85 to the north of Charlotte, particularly in the Concord Mills area, are not far from the city and are also convenient to the destinations in Kannapolis, Mooresville, Salisbury, and Spencer.

Charlotte sprawls, but it's fairly easy to get

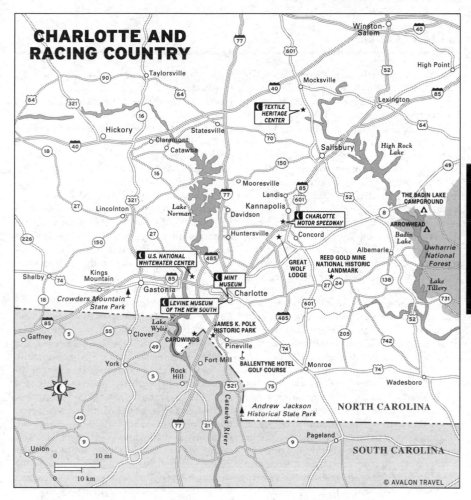

CHARLOTTE

from place to place in a short amount of time—if you're not on the road at rush hour. When traveling to the city, though, it's a good idea to check ahead to see if there will be any major sporting events during your visit. The Hornets (professional basketball) and Panthers (professional football) stadia are both downtown, so expect heavier traffic right before and right after games. Lowe's Motor Speedway, a few miles north of the city in Concord, can hold more than 200,000 people, so you can imagine the state of traffic and hotel room availability during race weeks. Other events, like concerts by major acts and sports tournaments, can also sell out hotels in areas of the city and cause gridlock.

Charlotte

Charlotte has often been a boomtown. In the late 18th century it was a midsize county seat, not much bigger than Salisbury or Hillsborough, but the end of the century brought the first boom. A farm boy discovered a beautiful, lumpy 17-pound rock in the creek in 1799. For years the family used his find as a doorstop until a visitor identified the mysterious rock as gold. The ensuing gold rush brought Charlotte and the frontier lands around it into the spotlight.

When railroad lines began to stretch across the Carolina backcountry, concerted efforts to court railroad decision-makers resulted in several important lines passing through Charlotte, and soon the town was a giant in the regional economy. Cotton farmers throughout the Piedmont brought their crops to Charlotte, and brokers funneled the raw cotton to Charleston. These early ties to South Carolina could be the origin of the subtle but pervasive sense that Charlotte is somehow part of South Carolina.

Economically adventurous, Charlotte rebounded quickly after the Civil War, encouraging Northern and foreign investment and business; this drew the disapprobation of people in other parts of North Carolina, but it laid the groundwork for greater prosperity. Textile mill money enriched the city through the early 20th century. In more recent years, Charlotte has become the second-largest banking center in the United States after New York City. Bank of America, Wachovia, and other locally based giants brought waves of newcomers to the Queen City. Today, North Carolina's booming film industry has found Charlotte, and television series that include *Homeland* as well as numerous commercials are filmed here.

SIGHTS
C Mint Museum
The **Mint Museum** (704/337-2000, www.mintmuseum.org, 11am-9pm Wed., 11am-6pm Thurs.-Sat., 1pm-5pm Sun., $10 adults,

$8 students and over age 64, $5 ages 5-17, free under age 5, free to all 5pm-9pm Wed.), North Carolina's oldest art museum, comprises two spectacular museums with diverse collections. At the **Mint Museum Randolph** (2730 Randolph Rd.), housed in an 1836 building originally home to a branch of the United States Mint, are galleries filled with art of the ancient Americas, European and African art, fashion, and decorative arts. The second location, the **Mint Museum Uptown** (at Levine Center for the Arts, 500 S. Tryon St.), is home to the internationally recognized Craft + Design collection, as well as wonderful collections of contemporary, American, and European art.

Other Art Museums
At the southern edge of Uptown Charlotte, the **Levine Center for the Arts** (www.levinecenterarts.org, 48-hour pass $20, www.carolinatix.org) is a bustling hive of artists, performers, and their patrons. Along with the Mint Museum, the Levine Center comprises three other institutions: The **Bechtler Museum of Modern Art** (420 S. Tryon St., 704/353-9200, www.bechtler.org, 10am-5pm Mon. and Wed.-Sat., noon-5pm Sun., $8 adults, $6 over age 64, students, and educators, $4 ages 11-18, free under age 11) has more than 1,400 works by 20th-century artists in its collection, including works by Andy Warhol, Max Ernst, Alexander Calder, Pablo Picasso, and Alberto Giacometti. The building itself is a work of art, with a four-story glass atrium extending through the core of the museum. Housed in the **Harvey B. Gantt Center for African-American Arts + Culture** (551 S. Tryon St., 704/547-3700, www.ganttcenter.org, 10am-5pm Tues.-Sat., 1pm-5pm Sun., $8 adults, $6 over age 62, students, educators, and military, free under age 6) are fine examples of the arts, crafts, and cultural contributions African Americans have made to American culture, visual art, theater, literature, film, music, and dance. The **John**

Firebird, by artist Niki de Saint Phalle, in front of the Bechtler Museum of Modern Art

COURTESY OF BECHTLER MUSEUM OF MODERN ART/PHOTO BY GARY O'BRIEN

CHARLOTTE

N. Tryon St.) and the Charlotte-Mecklenburg Police Headquarters (601 E. Trade St.).

NASCAR Hall of Fame

The **NASCAR Hall of Fame** (400 E. Martin Luther King Jr. Blvd., 704/654-4400 or 888/902-6463, www.nascarhall.com, 10am-6pm daily, $20 adults, $18 over age 59 and military, $13 ages 5-12) is a 150,000-square-foot interactive attraction that explores the heroes, heritage, and history of NASCAR. One of the most interesting exhibits is the Glory Road showcase of 18 historic cars and 40 current and historic tracks, including a banked racetrack. The Hall of Honor, where NASCAR Hall of Fame inductees are celebrated, also includes a number of race-driven cars and driver-worn helmets, gloves, suits, and other equipment.

History Museums and Sites

The **Charlotte Museum of History** (3500 Shamrock Dr., 704/568-1774, www.charlottemuseum.org, 10am-5pm Tues.-Sun., free) and the 1774 **Hezekiah Alexander Homesite**, the oldest structure in Mecklenburg County, tell the story of Charlotte's history. A self-guided recorded cell-phone tour (704/237-1998) is available.

On a busy block of North Tryon Street just outside Uptown is **Historic Rosedale Plantation** (3427 N. Tryon St., 704/335-0325, www.historicrosedale.org, tours 1:30pm and 3pm Thurs.-Sun., $10 adults, $8 over age 64 and ages 4-18), a graceful 1830s house. Twenty enslaved African Americans worked the surrounding 911 acres, most of which are now under strip malls and parking lots. Early plantation life is also represented at **Historic Latta Plantation** (5225 Sample Rd., Huntersville, 704/875-2312, www.lattaplantation.org, 10am-5pm Tues.-Sat., 1pm-5pm Sun., house tours on the hour, $7 adults, $6 students, over age 62, and military, $5 ages 6-18, free under age 6), a circa-1800 cotton farm that presents living history events year-round to demonstrate life in the late 18th and early 19th century. It also sits alongside a 1,300-acre nature preserve, an

S. and James L. Knight Theatre (430 S. Tryon St., www.charlottecultureguide.com) is the home stage to the North Carolina Dance Theatre, and it often features performances by the Charlotte Symphony and Opera Carolina. Touring Broadway productions and other musicians also stop here regularly.

The **Light Factory** (345 N. College St., 704/333-9755, www.lightfactory.org, 9am-6pm Mon.-Sat., 1pm-6pm Sun., free) is a gallery of modern photography and film. It hosts traveling exhibitions and offers classes and workshops. **Public art installations** are scattered throughout Uptown. A walking-tour brochure is available from the Arts and Science Council (www.artsandscience.org). Among the most notable North Carolinian artists whose work is on display are Charlotte-born Harlem Renaissance painter Romare Bearden, whose 1989 mural *Before Dawn* is at the main public library (310 N. Tryon St.), and celebrated fresco artist Ben Long, whose frescoes include those at the Bank of America Corporate Center (100

CHARLOTTE

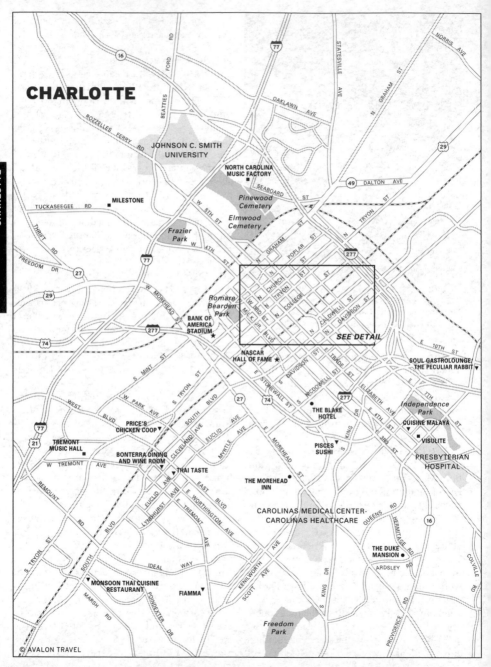

CHARLOTTE

JOHNSON C. SMITH UNIVERSITY

NORTH CAROLINA MUSIC FACTORY ■

MILESTONE ■

TUCKASEEGEE RD

Pinewood Cemetery

Elmwood Cemetery

Frazier Park

Romare Bearden Park

BANK OF AMERICA STADIUM ★

NASCAR HALL OF FAME ★

SEE DETAIL

SOUL GASTROLOUNGE/ THE PECULIAR RABBIT ■

PRICE'S CHICKEN COOP ▼

TREMONT MUSIC HALL ■

BONTERRA DINING AND WINE ROOM ▼

THAI TASTE ▼

THE BLAKE HOTEL ■

PISCES SUSHI ▼

THE MOREHEAD INN ●

Independence Park

CUISINE MALAYA ▼

VISULITE ■

PRESBYTERIAN HOSPITAL

CAROLINAS MEDICAL CENTER- CAROLINAS HEALTHCARE

THE DUKE MANSION ●

MONSOON THAI CUISINE RESTAURANT ▼

FIAMMA ▼

Freedom Park

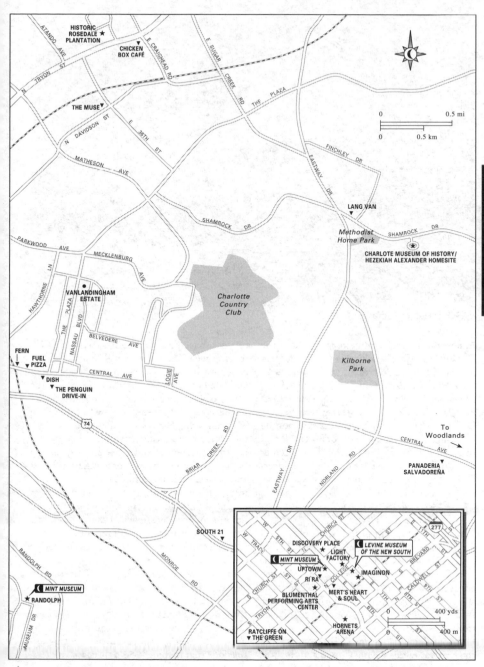

CHARLOTTE

HISTORIC ROSEDALE PLANTATION ★
CHICKEN BOX CAFÉ ▼
ATANDO AVE
N TRYON ST
E CRAIGHEAD RD
E SUGAR CREEK RD
THE PLAZA
THE MUSE ▼
N DAVIDSON ST
E 36TH ST
MATHESON AVE
FINCHLEY DR
EASTWAY DR

0   0.5 mi
0   0.5 km

SHAMROCK DR
LANG VAN ▼
Methodist Home Park
SHAMROCK DR
CHARLOTE MUSEUM OF HISTORY/ HEZEKIAH ALEXANDER HOMESITE ★

PARKWOOD AVE
MECKLENBURG AVE
HAWTHORNE LN
THE PLAZA
NASSAU BLVD
VANLANDINGHAM ESTATE ●
Charlotte Country Club
BELVEDERE AVE
FERN ▼
FUEL PIZZA ▼
CENTRAL AVE
LOGIE AVE
Kilborne Park
DISH ▼
THE PENGUIN DRIVE-IN ▼

74

BRIAR CREEK RD
CHURCH RD
EASTWAY DR
NORLAND RD
CENTRAL AVE
To Woodlands →
PANADERIA SALVADOREÑA ▼

SOUTH 21 ▼
W TRAC
MONROE RD
RANDOLPH RD
MINT MUSEUM ☾
RANDOLPH ★
MUSEUM DR
S TRYON

DISCOVERY PLACE ★
CHURCH ST
5TH ST
6TH ST
7TH ST
BREVARD ST
CALDWELL ST
277
MINT MUSEUM ☾
LIGHT FACTORY ★
LEVINE MUSEUM OF THE NEW SOUTH ☾
UPTOWN ★
RI RA ★
N COLLEGE ST
IMAGINON ★
W 5TH ST
S CHURCH ST
MERT'S HEART & SOUL ★
BLUMENTHAL PERFORMING ARTS CENTER ★
7TH ST
8TH ST
RATCLIFFE ON THE GREEN ▼
HORNETS ARENA ★

0   400 yds
0   400 m

NASCAR Hall of Fame

important haven for migratory birds and the home of the Carolina Raptor Center. A farm of a similar era is recreated at the **James K. Polk Historic Site** (12031 Lancaster Hwy., Pineville, 704/889-7145, www.nchistoricsites. org, 9am-5pm Tues.-Sat., free), where the 11th U.S. president was born. Visitors can tour log buildings that date to the era of his childhood (not original to the site); at the visitors center you can learn about Polk and the often overlooked significance of his presidency.

◖ Levine Museum of the New South

The **Levine Museum of the New South** (200 E. 7th St., 704/333-1887, www.museumofthenewsouth.org, 10am-5pm Mon.-Sat., noon-5pm Sun., $8 adults, $6 over age 61, students, educators, and military, $5 ages 6-18) tells the story, in its permanent exhibit called *Cotton Fields to Skyscrapers,* of the South's emergence from the devastation of the Civil War and the rancor of Reconstruction. The exhibit includes the postwar reign of King Cotton and the lives of the tobacco and textile industries that for so long were the staples of North Carolina's economy. Interwoven are stories of segregation and the civil rights movement, as well as the waves of globalization and immigration that are defining today's newer New South. Often in daring ways, changing exhibits address head-on issues of community, race, nationality, stereotyping, religion, and other fascinating and extremely complex aspects of Southern life past and present. The museum has a busy programming schedule, including the "Taste of the New South" series, which presents new regional food ways introduced by renowned chefs from across the Southeast, as well as walking tours and historical lectures related to the culture and future of Charlotte.

If you are curious about the Charlottean culture (that's pronounced "shar-le-TEE-en," by the way), you'll enjoy the Levine Museum's **New South for the New Southerner** series (around $10, reservations required). Led by museum historian Tom Hanchett, with guest speakers that include local politicians, writers,

CHARLOTTE

COURTESY OF CRVA

exhibits at the Levine Museum of the New South

religious leaders, and other community experts, the evening salon will teach you the quirks and charms of Charlotte in a fun social setting while you sample local wine and hors d'oeuvres.

Museums and Activities for Kids

Discovery Place (301 N. Tryon St., 704/372-6261, www.discoveryplace.org, 9am-5pm Mon.-Fri., 10am-6pm Sat., noon-5pm Sun., $12 adults, $10 children, IMAX theater $5 pp) is an interactive museum with an indoor rainforest, an IMAX theater, and preserved human body parts. Discovery Place also operates the **Charlotte Nature Museum** (1658 Sterling Rd., 704/372-6261, www.charlotte-naturemuseum.org) next to Freedom Park; it is home to live animals and a walk-through butterfly pavilion. **ImaginOn** (300 E. 7th St., 704/416-4600, www.imaginon.org, 9am-9pm Mon.-Thurs., 9am-6pm Fri.-Sat., 1pm-6pm Sun.) is a major Uptown arts complex for children and teens. It has theaters, libraries, a story lab, and a teen center.

SHOPPING
SouthPark Mall

The huge **SouthPark Mall** (4400 Sharon Rd., 704/364-4411, www.simon.com, 10am-9pm Mon.-Sat., 12:30pm-6pm Sun.) has more than 150 stores, including high-end retailers like **Tiffany & Co.** (704/365-7773), **Burberry** (704/365-3310), **7 For All Mankind** (704/365-1583), and **Louis Vuitton** (704/366-6622). You'll also find the **Apple Store** (704/364-2205), one of just three in the state. Even if you aren't buying, it's fun to window shop and watch for some of Charlotte's elite pro sports talent, as many of them have been spotted shopping here.

Phillips Place

Phillips Place (6700 Phillips Place Court, 704/556-0896, www.phillipsplace.info, 10am-7pm daily) is a premier outdoor shopping center in the South Park neighborhood. You'll find exclusive shops like **Granville** (704/799-6967) an interesting collection of 18th and 19th century French and English antiques; **Kla** (704/643-7800), a hot boutique carrying the most current men's and women's fashions; **Orvis** (704/571-6100, www.orvis. com), the famed fly-fishing and country lifestyle outfitter; and **Taylor Richards & Conger** (704/366-9092, www.trcstyle.com), an exclusive boutique that was named to *Esquire* magazine's Gold Standard list as one of America's top retailers.

There's good food, with **Upstream** (704/556-7730, www.harpersgroup.com, 11:30am-10pm Mon.-Thurs., 11:30am-11pm Fri.-Sat., 10:30am-10pm Sun., brunch 10:30am-2:30pm Sun., $23-39), a restaurant specializing in fresh fish. They have fantastic raw oysters, and a few of those paired with one of the larger appetizers, like the Black Iron Mussel Pot, can do for dinner. If you want something to grab and take with you for later, try **Dean & Deluca** (704/643-6868, www.deandeluca.com, 7am-9pm Mon.-Thurs., 7am-10pm Fri.-Sat., 8am-9pm Sun.), the renowned European-style market filled with fresh bread, a wide selection of cheeses, cases of prepared gourmet food, and an espresso bar.

Capitol

The chic clothing boutique **Capitol** (4010 Sharon Rd., 704/366-0388, www.capitolcharlotte.com, 10am-6pm Mon.-Sat.) was called "the finest boutique in America" by Isaac Mizrahi, and all of the press it has received in recent backs him up. They've been covered in *Elle, Garden & Gun, Veranda,* and the *New York Times.* They carry some exclusive brands like Alexander McQueen and Proenza Schouler as well as a number of designers whose work is as elegant as it is cutting-edge.

Meyer's Park

In the Meyer's Park neighborhood are stores as diverse as the folks who live here. **Reid's Fine Foods** (2823 Selwyn Ave., 704/377-1312, www.reids.com, 9am-8pm Mon.-Tues., 9am-9pm Wed., 9am-10pm Thurs.-Sat., 11am-7pm Sun.) is more than a neighborhood grocery store; they're invested in providing their neighbors and customers with superior meats, wines,

regional food, and service. They hold cooking classes and tasting programs, their butcher is top-notch, the wine selection is insane, and they have a great deal of prepared foods you just need to heat to eat.

The Pink Hanger (2935 Providence Rd., 704/366-7272, www.pinkhangeronline.com, 10am-7pm Mon.-Thurs., 11am-6pm Fri.-Sat., 1pm-5pm Sun.) is a fashion-forward boutique offering personalized service and reasonable prices. Their collection of dresses, jewelry, and accessories is well edited, and many pieces within their collection can work with one another. They've been recognized by *Charlotte* magazine for several years, winning superlatives like Best Cocktail Dress, Best Party Dress, and Best New Women's Boutique.

Lotus (111 Metropolitan Ave., Suite 140, 704/335-8884, www.lotuslook.com, 10am-8pm Mon.-Thurs., 10am-9pm Fri.-Sat., 1pm-6pm Sun.) believes that fashion isn't about cost; it's about creating a unique look. The store full of dresses, denim, jewelry, shoes, and tops, and it has what a discerning shopper need to create a unique look. The owners named the boutique after the flower, saying that just as the flower blooms, so does the self-confidence of their customers when they see how great they look in the clothing here.

Circa Interiors & Antiques (2321 Crescent Ave., 704/332-1688, 9am-5pm Mon.-Fri., 10am-3pm Sat.) sells antiques and fabulous home furnishings. The owners are the authors of the book *The Welcoming House: The Art of Living Graciously,* and everything in their shop encourages gracious, stylish living. Taking a look around the welcoming shop will give you some ideas for your own place, even if you don't leave with anything more than inspiration.

ENTERTAINMENT AND EVENTS

Performing Arts

Among the city's several excellent theater companies are **Theatre Charlotte** (501 Queens Rd., 704/376-3777, www.theatrecharlotte.org), which has been in business since the 1920s; the **Actor's Theatre of Charlotte** (650 E.

BEYOND BANKTOWN

Charlotteans and visitors alike often refer to the Queen City as Banktown, a name meant to conjure images of spotless sidewalks and shining office towers, a nine-to-five corporate culture with little room for the arts or nonconformity. But there's more to Charlotte than the Bank of America tower, sometimes called the Taj McColl, for the bank's former CEO, Hugh McColl. I happen to think that Uptown, with its sparkly skyscrapers and stampede of suits, is kind of cool—a little bit like Washington DC's K Street in a more tropical clime. But we do a disservice to Charlotte and to ourselves as travelers if we overlook the beautiful variety of people who live here. In addition to the suggestions in this chapter, these websites along with publications you can pick up in Banktown will illustrate what's happening outside the tower's shadow.

· **Creative Loafing** (http://clclt.com): This free weekly paper, which you can find all over the city, does a good job covering the arts, food, politics, and everything else that makes Charlotte hum. The website is as good a resource as the print edition.

· **Weird Charlotte** (www.weirdcharlotte. com): With the motto "Keep Charlotte weird? Make Charlotte weird!" it's an online compendium of "current weirdness," "historic weirdness," "random acts of weirdness," and "weirdos" in this fine city.

Stonewall St., 704/342-2251, www.actorstheatrecharlotte.org), a company specializing in contemporary drama; the **Carolina Actors Studio Theatre** (2424 N. Davidson St., Suite 113, 704/455-8542, www.nccast.com), for experiential art; and the **Children's Theatre of Charlotte** (www.ctcharlotte.org, 704/973-2800), which has its home at the ImaginOn arts complex (300 E. 7th St.).

The **Blumenthal Performing Arts Center** (130 N. Tryon St., 704/372-1000, www.blumenthalcenter.org) in Uptown is the home theater of the **Charlotte Symphony** (www.charlottesymphony.org), which has been in existence for nearly 80 years. These days, under the direction of Christof Perick and conductor Alan Yamamoto, it puts together seasons of baroque, romantic, and modern classical music as well as a series of pops-style concerts with guest artists. Almost 40 years old, **North Carolina Dance Theater** (704/372-1000, www.ncdance.org) is another venerable institution in Charlotte's arts scene. They perform full-length classical ballets and modern works, and tour widely, and their *Nutcracker* has become a Charlotte holiday-season staple. **Opera Carolina** (301 S. Tryon St., Suite 1550, 704/335-7177, www.operacarolina.org),

at 60 years old, is the leading opera company in the Carolinas. They produce four major operas each year, as well as an annual run of *Amahl and the Night Visitors* at Christmastime. **Charlotte Concerts** (704/527-6680, www.charlotteconcerts.org) has been bringing artists of international renown to the people of Charlotte since the 1930s, when the likes of Nelson Eddy and José Iturbi performed here, and more recently when Joshua Bell and the Russian National Ballet, among many others, have appeared. Each year's concert schedule is spectacular.

Festivals

Each May, race fans take over several blocks of Uptown for **Speed Street** (704/455-5555, www.600festival.com). For three days entertainers, race drivers, and thousands of enthusiasts celebrate the area's auto racing industry. Autograph sessions throughout the festival bring participants in close contact with racing royalty. Summer's **Charlotte Pride Festival** (http://charlottepride.org) is the city's celebration of its LGBT residents and businesses. The two-day festival features a parade, comedy and dance performers, musicians, and all sorts of goings on at local LGBT-owned and supportive

COURTESY OF CRVA

The North Carolina Music Factory draws large crowds.

businesses. Charlotte is an incredible city for foodies, and one way to learn the culinary ropes in a short time is to come to the early-June **Taste of Charlotte** (704/262-9847, www.tasteofcharlotte.com). Dozens of area restaurants make samples of their art available, from haute European masterpieces to soul food favorites, plus plenty of international flavors from this wonderfully diverse community.

Charlotte's rapidly expanding population of immigrants has filled the city's entertainment calendar with dozens of festivals and holidays from around the world. Spring's annual **Asian Festival** (704/540-6808, www.charlottedragonboat.com) features dragon-boat races on Ramsey Creek in Cornelius. Early September brings the **Yiasou Greek Festival** (Holy Trinity Greek Orthodox Cathedral, 600 East Blvd., 704/334-4771, www.yiasoufestival.org, $3), which celebrates one of the South's long-established Greek communities. October's **Latin American Festival** (704/531-3848, www.latinamericancoalition.org) celebrates the South's largest group of recent immigrants.

Nightlife

The **North Carolina Music Factory** (1000 Seaboard St., 704/987-0612, http://ncmusicfactory.com) is a huge complex of clubs and theaters on the northeast side of Uptown. Its venues range from the 5,000-seat Uptown Amphitheater to Butter, a new nightclub with top national DJs. Visit the website to find out about upcoming acts and for a map of the factory; it helps to get your bearings before you go. **Tremont Music Hall** (400 W. Tremont Ave., 704/343-9494, www.tremontmusichall.com) has a capacity of around 1,000 and hosts national acts in rock, punk, hardcore, ska, and metal. The smaller venue on the site, the Casbah, holds 400 people and often hosts regional and local acts. The **Visulite** (1625 Elizabeth Ave., 704/358-9200, www.visulite.com) is another major venue hosting major rock-and-roll, reggae, and world bands.

The **Milestone** (3400 Tuckaseegee Rd., www.themilestoneclub.com) has been hosting underground and up-and-coming bands since 1969; it was a major landmark for punk music in the South in the 1980s. Artists who've made appearances in the club's history run the gamut from R.E.M. to Hasil Adkins and Fugazi. Today's lineups are just as inspired. A popular Latin dance club, **Skandalo's** (5317 E. Independence Blvd., 704/535-4383) has great salsa, reggaeton, and other tropical music, and provides salsa dancing lessons. **Coyote Joe's** (4621 Wilkinson Blvd., 704/399-4946, www. coyote-joes.com) is a huge country dance hall and honky-tonk that hosts top Nashville artists. **Puckett's Farm Equipment** (2740 W. Sugar Creek Rd., 704/597-8230, www.puckettsfarm. com) is a smaller country juke joint with regular bluegrass and rockabilly shows.

There are several significant rock-and-roll clubs in Charlotte as well. The **Double Door Inn** (1218 Charlottetown Ave./Independence Blvd., 704/376-1446, http://doubledoorinn. com) calls itself "Charlotte's home of the blues." They've brought the glitterati of blues, roots, and roots-rock music to Charlotte for nearly four decades. The **Neighborhood Theatre** (511 E. 36th St., 704/942-7997, www.neighbor-hoodtheatre.com, all ages) in the NoDa (North Davidson) neighborhood is a place where artists already high on the charts, or new artists starting to make the climb to stardom, appear when they're in Charlotte. Visitors of all ages are admitted to most shows. NoDa also has a folk club, **The Evening Muse** (3227 N. Davidson St., 704/376-3737, www.theeveningmuse. com, 6pm-1am Mon., 7pm-1am Wed.-Thurs., 7pm-2am Fri.-Sat.). This is an intimate listening room with a penchant for booking great acts, and music fans of all ages are admitted. **Amos' Southend** (1423 S. Tryon St., 704/377-6874, www.amossouthend.com) also attracts some prestigious acts to play in its cool warehouse-style space. **Ri Ra** (208 N. Tryon St., 704/333-5554, www.rira.com) is an Uptown Irish pub, constructed from a Victorian Dublin pub that the owners disassembled and shipped to Charlotte. It serves traditional British Isles pub fare, and hosts all sorts of music and pub games.

Charlotte has a number of gay bars, ranging from casual martini lounges to 180-beats-per-minute dance clubs. Two popular venues are **The Woodshed Lounge** (4000 Queen City Dr., 704/394-1712, www.woodshedlounge.com, 5pm-2:30am daily), a bar where members of Charlotte's bear and leather communities come together. Something's going on here every night, including free pool, a light dinner buffet, karaoke, and theme nights. Another popular bar is **The Scorpio** (2301 Freedom Dr., 704/373-9124, www.thescorpio.com, 10pm-2:30am Wed. and Fri.-Sun.), Charlotte's longest-running nightclub that caters to the LGBT community; they've been around since 1968. Expect female impersonators, drag revues, dance parties, and drink specials. This is an upbeat, energetic spot.

SPORTS AND RECREATION
City Parks
In Charlotte, a lot of emphasis is placed on community and on neighborhood pride. One of the reasons is the amazing city park system and green space in and among nearly every neighborhood and throughout Mecklenburg County. There are 210 parks in the county on more than 17,600 acres of land; in addition there are 37 miles of developed greenway trails and 150 miles of undeveloped trails. Once you notice them, you'll start to find parks everywhere you look.

There are many activities, classes, sports in Charlotte's parks. **Romare Bearden Park** (300 S. Church St.), one of the newest parks, is home to a number of fitness programs, concerts, art and photography classes, and festivals small and large throughout the year. Its proximity to Bank of America Stadium, where the Carolina Panthers professional football team plays home games, ensures that this park has many visitors in addition to the regular neighborhood users. **Frazier Park** (1201 W. 4th St.) has a soccer and flag football field, two full basketball courts, a pair of tennis courts, playgrounds, a dog park, and is on one of the many greenways that crisscross the city. There's also a community garden where neighbors can rent 150-square-foot plots and raise vegetables or flowers.

North of downtown but still in the Beltline,

Hornets Nest Park (6301 Beatties Ford Rd., 704/336-8869), which has the best or perhaps the scariest name, is full of activities. In this 140-acre playground, you'll find four lighted softball fields, a disc golf course, a dozen tennis courts, shelters, a lake to fish in, playgrounds, horseshoe pits, and picnic shelters. The pièce de résistance is the **BMX bicycle track** (704/398-2711 or 704/226-8420), the site of BMX competitions every Saturday. Open practice sessions and clinics will help you sharpen your skills and give you time to attack the course at your own pace.

Other parks, like **Druid Hills Park** (2801 Lucena St.) and **Little Peoples Park** (1120 Harrill St.), with a playground for kids age 12 and under, are less intense and have playgrounds, picnic areas, and open space where you can spread out to relax, play, and enjoy the outdoors. You can find more information on the parks, activity schedules, and detailed maps at the Charlotte-Mecklenburg (http://charmeck.org) official website or by calling 704/432-4280.

Golf

It's no surprise that Charlotte, with professional athletes and big business types, has some fabulous golf courses. What may surprise you is that not all of them are behind country club gates but are in fact public courses.

The **Ballantyne Hotel Golf Club** (10000 Ballantyne Commons Pkwy., 704/248-4383, www.theballantynehotel.com, 18 holes, par 71, greens fees from $65, cart fees $14) has a number of challenges for seasoned and novice golfers: With water features on half of the holes, and in play on a good number of those, you may lose a ball or two if you miss the narrow, but playable, fairways. At the **Renaissance Park Golf Club** (1525 W. Tyvola Rd., 704/357-3373, www.charlottepublicgolf.com, 18 holes, par 72, greens fees Mon.-Thurs. $42, Fri. $44, Sat.-Sun. and holidays $50, discounts for juniors, seniors, late play, and 9 holes, carts $9.50) the pace of play can be a little on the slow side, but the payoff is a day on a beautiful course. The back nine

is more challenging, with a number of blind shots leading to the green.

The "Old Course" at Sunset Hills (800 Radio Rd., 704/399-0980, www.charlottepublicgolf.com, 18 holes, par 72, greens fees Mon.-Thurs. $31, Fri. $32, Sat.-Sun. and holidays $36.50, discounts for juniors, seniors, late play, and 9 holes, carts $9.50) is an enjoyable course where the fairways are wide and the hazards fairly placed. Novice golfers will find a number of confidence-building holes here, and more seasoned players will find plenty of opportunities for aggressive shots. The nine-hole **Dr. Charles L. Sifford Golf Course at Revolution Park** (1225 Remount Rd., 704/333-3949, www.charlottepublicgolf.com, 9 holes, par 36, greens fees $18-25) is a fun little course to walk for a quick nine or 18 holes. As with almost all nine-hole courses, this is a great one to learn on as it's designed to play quickly, but it presents you with all the challenges of a traditional 18-hole course.

The Scottish links-style golf course at **Charlotte Golf Links** (11500 Providence Rd., 704/846-7990, www.charlottegolflinks.com, 18 holes, par 71, greens fees Mon.-Thurs. $42, Fri. $52, Sat.-Sun. and holidays $62, discounts for juniors, seniors, students, military, late play) offers a different experience than other Charlotte-area courses. The subtle rolling of the Piedmont is the star, as are the thickets of grass that is so key to links-style courses. Just stay in the fairway and you'll be fine.

◖ U.S. National Whitewater Center

The U.S. National Whitewater Center (820 Hawfield Rd., 704/391-3900, www.usnwc.org, land activities $20, flat-water $25, all-access $54 adults, $44 under age 10), which opened in 2007, features "the world's only multichannel recirculating white-water river"—that is, a complex of artificial rapids—designed for training athletes at the Olympic level; it is the home of the U.S. Olympic canoe and kayak team. Visitors can try white-water rafting, kayaking, stand-up paddleboarding, and white-water kayaking. The center's 300 acres also

COURTESY OF CRVA

roller coaster at Carowinds

feature mountain biking trails and a climbing center.

Carowinds

The state's only big amusement park straddles the North Carolina-South Carolina state line just south of Charlotte. **Carowinds** (14523 Carowinds Blvd., 704/588-2600, www.carowinds.com, 10am-10pm daily summer, call for off-season hours, tickets $47 online, $57 at the gate, parking $15) has 13 coasters, including The Intimidator, the Dale Earnhardt-themed coaster that's currently the tallest, fastest, and longest coaster in the Southeast. They also have a wooden coaster called, unfortunately, the Hurler (don't eat a foot-long hot dog before hopping on this one), and another called the Carolina Goldrusher that's a little more tame (and presumably hot dog safe). On the Thunder Road coaster you'll cross over the state line, which runs through the park. There's also a water park called Boomerang Bay; it has some awesome slides, pools, and splash parks. The fascinating Dinosaurs Alive! exhibit brings

dinosaurs to life with highly detailed animatronics. The exhibits are based on actual fossil evidence and were made with help from leading paleontologists to ensure their accuracy.

Spectator Sports

The Carolinas' only professional basketball team, the NBA **Charlotte Hornets** (704/262-2287, www.nba.com), play in the massive Hornets Arena (333 E. Trade St.) in Uptown. The Hornets attract a statewide following by recruiting talent from the ranks of the University of North Carolina Tar Heel basketball alums. The roster perpetually includes one of the stars from the Heels teams, and Carolina legends Phil Ford and Buzz Peterson are part of the team's administration. Charlotte is also home to the Carolinas' only professional football team, the NFL **Carolina Panthers** (704/358-7800, www.panthers.com), who play at the Bank of America Stadium (9800 S. Mint St.) at the edge of Uptown. Fans twirling their growl towels cheered them on to regional titles in 1996 and 2003.

The Chicago White Sox baseball team Triple-A affiliate is the **Charlotte Knights** (704/357-8071, www.charlotteknights.com), whose home field (2280 Deerfield Dr., Fort Mill, SC) is just over the state line in South Carolina. As with any AAA team, there's a good chance of seeing a major-leaguer rehabbing from injury or brushing up on his skills, or a young turk about to break into a big-league career. A professional ice hockey team, the ECHL **Charlotte Checkers** (www.gocheckers.com, 704/342-4423), play at the Hornets Arena.

Each spring, the PGA Tour stops in Charlotte for some great golf at **The Wells Fargo Championship** (www.wellsfargochampionship.com) at the prestigious **Quail Hollow Club** (3700 Gleneagles Rd., 704/552-1800, www.quailhollowclub.com). The purse that comes with wining this tournament draws top-name talent from the PGA. Besides the opportunity to see golf idols swing a club, the event provides a rare look at this pristine course at one of the most exclusive clubs in Charlotte.

ACCOMMODATIONS

When it comes to the languid elegance of the Old South, **The Duke Mansion** (400 Hermitage Rd., 704/714-4400, www.dukemansion.com, from $200) is close to heaven. The circa-1915 mansion in Charlotte's lovely Myers Park neighborhood was home to North Carolina royalty, the Duke family, including the young Doris Duke. The downstairs foyer and gallery were clearly designed for entertaining high society, but the bedrooms—most restored to reflect the Duke family's tastes around 1930—are simple and comfortable, and some of the en suite baths still have their original tubs and tiles. In a wonderful Southern tradition, most guest rooms open onto sleeping porches, which are worth more than the room rates. You'll receive first-rate service, and the culinary team will present you with a splendid breakfast. Bring a book to read in the gardens, and keep an eye out for two friendly black cats. If you visit while the magnolias are blooming, you'll never want to leave.

The **VanLandingham Estate** (2010 The Plaza, 704/334-8909 or 888/524-2020, www.vanlandinghamestate.com, from $99), built in 1913, provides a glimpse of the affluent infancy of the neighborhood known as Plaza-Midwood. A streetcar ran down the middle of The Plaza, and wealthy families established five and six acre estates in what was then a bucolic suburb. Plaza-Midwood now feels very close to the center of the city, and the lots have long since been subdivided, but it is still a charming enclave of early 20th-century craftsman-style bungalows. The VanLandingham is an architectural marriage of the best arts-and-crafts design elements and aesthetics individually tailored to the tastes of the builders, early textile magnates Ralph and Susie Harwood VanLandingham. The staff take good care of guests, the grounds are beautiful, and Uptown is only a few minutes away.

The Dunhill Hotel (237 N. Tryon St., 704/332-4141, www.dunhillhotel.com, rooms from $149-329) has been a luxurious stopover for visitors since 1929. Though the 10-story hotel opened early in the 20th century, renovations have brought it up to modern standards. With cozy, upscale rooms inside and a bevy of great dining options only steps away, this hotel is the ideal culmination of location and comfort.

The Blake Hotel (555 S. McDowell St., 704/372-4100, www.blakehotelnc.com, from $109) is a slick, modern hotel with more than 600 guest rooms and suites. Remodeled in early 2012, it still feels new, cool, and almost exclusive. Situated in downtown Charlotte's busy business district, it's just a few minutes to nearby bustling nightlife and shopping. When *Southern Living* magazine says of a bed-and-breakfast, "expect to be spoiled rotten," y'all better listen up. At **The Morehead Inn** (1122 E. Morehead St., 704/376-3357, www.moreheadinn.com, from $139), a cozy 1917 home that's well guarded by azaleas and other beautiful flowering plants in the gardens, pampering's what you get. With well-appointed guest rooms and the comfort of the house, you won't want to leave to explore Charlotte.

About 20 minutes from downtown Charlotte, the **Davidson Village Inn** (117 Depot St., Davidson, 800/892-0796, www.davidsoninn. com, from $145) is tucked away on a cozy side street in this tiny college town. The guest rooms are nicely appointed, the staff are helpful, and the breakfast is bountiful. This is a pleasant alternative to staying in the city.

By North Carolina standards, lodging is expensive in Charlotte. It's pretty hard to find a good place to stay for under $100, and extremely difficult to find a decent low-cost room near Uptown. However, there are more choices as you head out of town. The **Microtel Inn and Suites** (1111 W. Sugar Creek Rd., 704/598-2882, www.microtelinn.com, from about $79) is located in the northeast part of the city, near the UNC-Charlotte campus. On the opposite side of town, the **Best Western Sterling Hotel and Suites** (242 E. Woodlawn Rd., 704/525-5454, http://book.bestwestern.com, from $69) is not too far from the airport.

FOOD

Charlotte is the eatingest place: There are so many good new restaurants opening every week that it's hard to keep up, but for reviews of the newest venues, with lots of interesting cultural observation, check out Tricia Childress's column in *Creative Loafing* (http://clclt.com), a free paper found at many area businesses, and Helen Schwab's and Kathleen Purvis's food writing in the *Charlotte Observer* (www.charlotteobserver.com).

Southern and Soul

Price's Chicken Coop (1614 Camden Rd., 704/333-9866, www.priceschickencoop.com, 10am-6pm Tues.-Sat., under $11) is one of Charlotte's favorite chicken places, a take-out counter where you can buy a box of deep-fried chicken, perch, shrimp, or liver and gizzards. What can I say about this fried chicken that hasn't been said? It's nearly perfect: moist, crispy, a little salty but not too salty, and as Southern as sweet tea. You can also buy it by the gallon.

Charlotte's not short on fried chicken. At the **Chicken Box Café** (3726 N. Tryon St., 704/566-6000, www.chickenboxcafe.com, 11am-8pm daily, $6-20), the food is undeniably rustic soul food. Since 1978 they've been serving Charlotte fried and barbecue chicken, neck bones (yes, chicken necks, where the meat is surprisingly tender and flavorful), turkey wings, trotters (that's pigs' feet to Yankees), ox tail, and even chitterlings (an acquired taste). **Mert's Heart & Soul** (214 N. College St., 704/342-4222, http://mertscharlotte.com, 11am-9:30pm Mon.-Thurs., 11am-11:30pm Fri., 9am-11:30pm Sat.-Sun., brunch 9am-3pm Sat.-Sun., $around $10) serves Lowcountry and Gullah-inspired soul food, with special homestyle fried chicken, cornbread, shrimp and grits, greens, and other country delicacies.

Penguin Drive-In (1921 Commonwealth Ave., 704/375-1925, www.penguindrive-in. com, 11am-11pm Sun.-Thurs., 11am-2am Fri.-Sat., under $10) is a Charlotte icon. Its status and its killer burgers, served on toast, and fried pickles brought stars from the Food Network and the Travel Channel to shoot segments here. This restaurant is done in the spirit of the original drive-in but with innovative sandwiches, chopped salads, and burgers. You can order the Penguin, a pimento cheeseburger; the Freak Flag, with *queso*, bacon, slaw, lettuce, and tomato; or the Billy Goat, with bacon, pimento cheese, onion rings, slaw, tomato, and Penguin sauce. Sandwiches and hot dogs are equally interesting, with the Dr. Evil, a blackened bologna sandwich on Texas toast, or the I Can Hear You Getting Fatter hot dog, piled high with bacon, chili and *queso*. You can grab a root beer or adult beer, and for dessert, try the Cup of Dirt; it'll surprise you.

Dish (1220 Thomas Ave., 704/344-0343, www.eatdish.com, 11am-10pm Mon.-Thurs., 11am-11pm Fri.-Sat., bar open later, $7-15) has also appeared on the Food Network because of their quality take on country cookin'. The chicken and dumplings are particularly noteworthy, as are the salmon patties, something I remember my mom making but that I rarely see on a menu. Burgers, meatloaf, and other comfort food rounds out the menu.

Jake's Good Eats (12721 Albemarle Rd., 704/545-4741, http://jakesgoodeats.com, 11am-9pm Tues.-Sat., lunch $4-10, dinner $9-24) serves new Southern dishes in a 1930s gas station they converted into a fine restaurant. The Food Network was here too, sampling their renowned blackened flounder with crawfish sauce and a country-ham grit cake, but that's not the only thing they do well; try the oyster po'boy for lunch, a pit-cooked barbecue sandwich, or an overstuffed BLT.

Asian

Charlotte is a city of immigrants, with more arriving every year, and among the many benefits of such diversity is an amazingly rich culinary environment. Asian cuisines are especially prominent, with Vietnamese, Thai, Malaysian, and Japanese restaurants.

Pisces Sushi (1100 E. Metropolitan Ave., Suite 120, 704/334-0009, http://piscessushi.com, 11:30am-10:30pm Mon.-Wed., 11:30am-2am Thurs.-Sat., $14-50) is the perpetual *Charlotte* magazine winner for Best Sushi Restaurant, and given their reputation for high-quality fish and a large menu of traditional and innovative rolls, it's no wonder. Lunch features by-the-piece or all-you-can-eat sushi; the remainder of the entrées are served hibachi-style.

The Cowfish Sushi Burger Bar (4310 Sharon Rd., 704/365-1922, www.thecowfish.com, 11am-11pm Mon.-Thurs., 11am-midnight Fri. and Sat., 11am-10pm Sun., $8-16) dishes up a mix of juicy burgers and fresh sushi. Be ready for a creative take on hand-held food, as Cowfish has a reputation for interesting toppings and fillings. Try The Deliverance Roll, a sushi roll featuring pulled pork; they call it Bar-B-Q-shi.

Thai Taste (324 East Blvd., 704/332-0001, www.thaitastecharlotte.com, 4pm-9:30pm Mon.-Thurs., 5pm-10:30pm Fri.-Sat., 5pm-9:30pm Sun., $11-18) has been a favorite for more than 20 years. The menu includes a variety of curries, noodle dishes, and stir-fries, including many vegetarian options. **Monsoon Thai Cuisine Restaurant** (2801 South Blvd., 704/523-6778, www.thaimonsoon.com, lunch 11am-2:30pm daily, dinner 5pm-10pm daily, $10-15), serves many classic Thai dishes and has a good reputation among locals for value in the Thai food arena.

Charlotte has quite a few Vietnamese restaurants, which are great fun to sample. Perhaps the best known is **Lang Van** (3019 Shamrock Dr., 704/531-9525, www.langvanrestaurant.com, 11am-10pm Tues.-Thurs., 11am-11pm Fri.-Sat., under $10). Lang Van has an incredibly long menu, with many varieties of *pho*, noodle soup, and vermicelli dishes. Like many Vietnamese restaurants, this is an ideal eatery for vegetarians. *Charlotte Observer* readers have voted Lang Van the area's top Asian restaurant multiple times.

The readers of *Creative Loafing*, on the other hand, have given that honor to **Cuisine Malaya** (1411 Elizabeth Ave., 704/372-0766, www.cuisinemalaya.com, noon-11pm Sat., noon-10pm Sun., lunch 11am-4pm Mon.-Fri., dinner 4pm-10pm Mon.-Thurs., 4pm-10pm Fri., $10-16). Although it is based in Malay cuisine, this restaurant has a pan-Asian menu featuring sushi, hibachi specialties, and Thai, Singaporean, and other dishes.

Pizza

Among the many exotic foreigners arriving in Charlotte by the thousands every year, few have so difficult a time adjusting to the culture of the Southern United States as do Yankees. They have to become accustomed to a new language, a new climate, a new structure of social mores, and a new cuisine. Like so many immigrants, Northerners in Charlotte spend a lot of time trying to recreate aspects of their home culture in their new surroundings, often starting with native food ways—specifically New York-style pizza.

Everyone seems to like **Brooklyn South Pizza** (7725 Colony Rd., 704/542-5439, www.brooklynsouthpizzeria.com, 11am-9pm Mon.-Sat., noon-9pm Sun., $6-23), which makes a mighty fine pie at each of their area locations (19400 Jetton Rd., Cornelius, 704/896-2925; 119 Market Place Dr., Mooresville, 704/696-2694; 6400 Weddington Rd., Wesley Chapel,

704/821-0974). They have a number of gourmet pizzas, by-the-slice pies, and Sicilian-style pizzas, along with some great pasta, peppers and onions, fried zucchini sticks, and hero sandwiches.

With two locations in the city and several more elsewhere in the state, **Tony's Pizza** (14027 Conlan Circle, 704/541-8225; 1530 Overland Park, 704/688-6880, http://tonys-bigpizza.com, 11am-8pm Mon.-Fri., noon-8pm Sun., $5-25), founded by two Italian-born, Brooklyn-raised friends, is another favorite among natives and Yankee transplants alike.

The loudly lauded **Hawthorne's Pizza** (1701 E. 7th St., 704/358-9339; 5814 Prosperity Church Rd., 704/875-8502; 4100 Carmel Rd., Suite A, 704/544-0299, www.hawthornespizza.com, 11am-midnight Sun.-Thurs., 11am-2am Fri.-Sat., $6-14) has pizzas, calzones, stromboli, baked and fresh pasta dishes, and a cannoli tray for dessert. There are other kinds of top-notch pizza around Charlotte; **Luisa's Brick Oven** (1730 Abbey Place, 704/522-8782, http://louisasbrickovenpizza.com, lunch 11am-2pm Mon.-Fri., dinner 5pm-9pm Sun.-Thurs., under $20) has, among other extremely tempting choices of topping, a muffuletta pie.

You won't drive far in Charlotte without passing a **C Fuel Pizza** (14145 Rivergate Pkwy., 704/588-5333; 500 S. College St., 704/370-2755; 214 N. Tryon St., 704/350-1680; 1801 South Blvd., 704/335-7375; 1501 Central Ave., 704/376-3835; 4267 Park Rd., 704/525-3220, www.fuelpizza.com, hours vary, under $20). This regional chain was founded in Charlotte by New Yorkers and has grown to include nine locations in both Carolinas and even a couple in Washington DC.

Latin American

Charlotte has a large Latino population of people from many countries, and their imprint on the culinary landscape adds a welcome dimension to the diversity of restaurants in the city. Many venues can be found along Central Avenue. Try **Taquería Mexico** (7001 South Blvd., 704/552-2461, 10am-9pm Mon.-Thurs., 10am-10pm Fri.-Sat., 10am-8pm Sun., under

$10) and **Taquería Allende** (4801 N. Tryon St., 704/598-6666, under $10) for an authentic Mexican taquería experience.

Vida Mexican Kitchen y Cantina (210 E. Trade St., 704/971-8432, http://charlotte.vida-cantina.com, 11am-11pm Mon.-Thurs., 11am-midnight Fri.-Sat., 11am-10pm Sun., lunch $8-14, dinner $10-26, brunch $7-13) provides an upscale take on traditional Mexican food. Tacos include surf-and-turf, with chipotle rubbed filet mignon and butter-poached lobster tail; spice-crusted ahi tuna; and shredded short ribs. Other dishes include equally upscale ingredients, such as goat-cheese, spinach, and mushroom enchiladas, enchiladas stuffed with crab and shrimp, and *barbacoa* and filet mignon dishes covered in sauces that go beyond run-of-the-mill *queso* and guacamole.

Lenpira (5906 South Blvd., 704/552-1515, 8am-midnight daily, around $10) is an especially good Central American restaurant on South Boulevard. Delicious Latin American bakeries also are popping up all over, like **Panadería Salvadoreña** (5724-G E. W. T. Harris Blvd., 704/537-1615, $11-25) and **Delicias Colombianas** (212 N. Polk St., 704/889-5328, under $10).

Chima Brazilian Steakhouse (139 S. Tryon St., 704/601-4141, http://chima.cc, 5:30pm-9:30pm Mon.-Thurs., 5:30pm-10pm Fri., 5pm-10pm Sat., 4pm-9pm Sun., from $30) is a meat bonanza. Servers carry around swords and forks filled with succulent cuts of meat, chicken, and sausages, serving you slice after slice until you can't take any more. But don't just eat the meat; hit the superb salad bar.

European

The Plaza-Midwood neighborhood has lots of appealing eateries, and among the most popular is **Lulu's** (1911 Central Ave., 704/376-2242, www.luludinewine.com, lunch 11am-2pm, dinner 5pm-10pm Mon.-Thurs., 5pm-11pm Fri.-Sat., 5pm-9pm Sun., brunch 11am-3pm Sat., 10am-3pm Sun., $11-36). The American and pan-European fare ranges from burgers and Reuben sandwiches to roasted rabbit and fine steaks.

Fiamma (2418 Park Rd., 704/333-3062, www.fiamma-restaurant.com, lunch 11:30am-3pm Mon.-Sat., dinner 5pm-10pm Sun.-Thurs., 5pm-11pm Fri.-Sat., under $30), an Italian restaurant in the Dilworth neighborhood, was named one of "The Top 10 Restaurants in Charlotte" by Zagats a couple of years ago. For their spectacular menu, Fiamma has fresh fish flown in every day from Italy, and they make their pasta and pizza crust dough twice every day from scratch. Such dedication to quality can be tasted at first bite.

Ilios Noche (11508 Providence Rd., Suite 1, 704/814-9882, http://xeniahospitality.com, lunch 11am-4pm Mon.-Sat. and 10am-4pm Sun., dinner 4pm-10pm Mon.-Wed., 4pm-11pm Thurs., 4pm-midnight Fri.-Sat., 4pm-9pm Sun., $11-30), just outside the Beltline on Providence Road, is an excellent restaurant that combines Greek and Italian cuisines. The menu is endless, with dozens of mezes (small plates) choices, as well as sandwiches, pasta, and hearty entrées. Vegetarians can easily cobble together a good meal from the many vegetable mezes. Ilios Noche also offers many choices of beer, wine, and cocktails.

Miro Spanish Grill (7804 Rea Rd., 704/540-7374, www.mirospanishgrill.com, lunch 11:30am-2pm Mon.-Fri., dinner 5pm-10pm Sun.-Thurs., 5pm-11pm Fri.-Sat., $10-29) is primarily a Spanish restaurant, with such dishes as paella valenciana and zarzuela de mariscos. It also brings in elements of Latin American cuisine such as black beans and fried plantains.

If you're looking for oysters and an incredible raw bar, Georges Brasserie (4620 Piedmont Row Dr., 980/219-7409, www.georgesbrasserie.com, lunch 11:30am-2:30pm Mon.-Fri., light fare 2:50pm-5pm Mon.-Fri., dinner 5pm-10pm Mon.-Thurs., 5pm-11pm Fri. and Sat., 5pm-9pm Sun., lounge open Fri. and Sat. until 1am, brunch 11am-2:30pm, lunch $8-95, dinner $16-95, brunch $8-95) is your stop. Their selection of oysters is out of this world, but that's just the beginning. The menu is packed with fine French comfort food

made with the highest quality ingredients and is worth the wait and the splurge.

Indian

Woodlands (7128-A Albemarle Rd., 704/569-9193, http://woodlandsusa.com, 11:30am-10pm Wed.-Mon., lunch buffet 11:30am-3pm Sat.-Sun., lunch specials from $4, entrées $7-21) serves absolutely wonderful vegetarian southern Indian cuisine, offering nearly 20 different curries, utthapam (rice and lentil pancakes), Chinese-influenced rice and noodle dishes, and dozens of other components with which to assemble one of the best Indian meals you'll find in North Carolina.

Nirvana II Indian Fusion (401 S. Tryon St., 704/919-0502, www.nirvana-2.net, 11am-3:30pm Mon-Fri, around $12) serves dishes from both northern and southern India. With a menu that varies every day, the selection of vegetarian and nonvegetarian items is hard to predict, but expect paneer and chicken tikka masala, dal, chana sag, various curries with chicken, fish, and shrimp, as well as tandoori specialties.

Eclectic American

Among Charlotte's fanciest places to dine is Bonterra Dining and Wine Room (1829 Cleveland Ave., at E. Worthington Ave., 704/333-9463, http://bonterradining.com, dinner from 5:30pm Mon.-Sat., bar from 4:30pm Mon.-Sat., $21-39), which has received both the Four Diamond Award from AAA and Wine Spectator magazine's Award of Excellence. It is housed in an old Methodist church, and house specialties include New York strip steak, veal chop, and fried lobster tail. Really, though, it's as much about wine as food; the wine list features dozens of fine wines from California, France, Australia, and even North Carolina. There are also many choices of single-malt scotch, port, and cognac.

Fern (1323 Central Ave., 704/377-1825, www.fernflavors.com, 11am-9pm Tues.-Thurs., 11am-10pm Fri.-Sat., 10:30am-3pm Sun., lunch $5-13, dinner $11-18, brunch $6-12) is a vegetarian and vegan eatery that does their food so well that meat-eaters flock here to see what high-end vegetarian food is all about. They're creative and bold, taking on traditional meaty dishes like burgers, cioppino, po'boys, and even biscuits and gravy, in addition to their crafty veg-only dishes. The food is good, filling, and reasonably priced, and the cocktails are equally good. While you're here, check out the fern wall, a giant wall-hanging planter filled with dozens of different kinds of ferns; it's pretty cool.

Driving out Independence Boulevard away from Uptown, you'll pass a classic 1950s drive-in, **South 21** (3101 E. Independence Blvd., 704/377-4509, www.south21drivein.com, 11am-3pm Tues., 11am-9pm Wed.-Thurs., 11am-10pm Fri.-Sat., $3-13). South 21 has been serving fast food to Charlotteans since 1955. Today, the menu includes drive-in classics like burgers, fish sandwiches, and barbecue as well as several kinds of pies and sundaes. Their burgers are so good that the Travel Channel came to do a segment on these tasty creations.

The Peculiar Rabbit (1212 Pecan Ave., 704/333-9197, www.thepeculiarrabbit.com, 5pm-midnight Mon., 11am-midnight Tues.-Wed., 11am-2am Thurs.-Fri., 10am-2am Sat., 10am-midnight Sun., lunch $9-16, dinner $9-27, late night $4-12, brunch $8-16) has not only one of the best names I've come across, but their gastropub menu is one of the best I've seen in the South. Their take on burgers is creative enough to be distinct, but recognizable enough to be anything but intimidating. For dinner, their fish-and-chips comes with a Granny Smith apple tartar sauce, and their roast duck, grouper, and Peculiar Pork (juniper-rubbed pork belly) are all outstanding. They serve a late-night menu that features their burgers, sweet tea-brined wings, Disco Fries (fries with oxtail *poutine* gravy), and more snacks. Brunch is hearty and creative, again with burgers but also blueberry-peach pancakes and Eggs Oscar. This is a pub and so has a great list of beers in bottles and on tap; the bartenders can help you find one you'll love.

At **Cowbell Burger & Bar** (201 N. Tryon St., Suite 1010, 704/332-4141, www.eatmorecowbell.com, 11am-2am, $8-20) they serve a selection of burgers that is unparalleled in Charlotte. Toppings from the exotic to the expected, sides from onion rings to sweet potato tots, and an incredible bar make this a popular spot for late night dining. Try the Umami Burger, a thick burger topped with shitake mushrooms, a parmesan crisp, and a roasted tomato, but before you dig in for dinner, start with some fried pickles or the Southern classic, Deviled Eggs.

The King's Kitchen (129 W. Trade St., 704/375-1990, www.kingskitchen.org, lunch 11am-2:30pm Mon.-Fri., dinner 5pm-late Mon.-Sat., lunch $7-17, dinner $8-24) operates on an interesting concept: they're a not-for-profit establishment. The King's Kitchen provides employment opportunities to Charlotteans in need of a hand, and returns 100 percent of profits to hungry people in the area. All this while serving upscale Southern comfort food in an elegant setting.

Eclectic International

Chef Bernard Brunet learned to cook in his native France, and he worked in fine restaurants in England and Russia before coming to Charlotte and founding his own. **Global Restaurant** (3520 Toringdon Way, 704/248-0866, www.global-restaurant.com, bar and patio 3pm-late Mon.-Sat., dining room 6pm-11pm Mon.-Sat., $19-29), located in the Ballantyne neighborhood, blends cuisines of Europe, Asia, the Middle East, and the Americas to create signature dishes like seared lamb and eggplant in a tomato-cumin sauce and a Spanish paella made with Prince Edward Island mussels.

Soul Gastrolounge (1500-B Central Ave., 704/348-1848, http://soulgastrolounge.com, 5pm-2am daily, full menu 5pm-midnight, late-night menu midnight-2am, brunch 11am-3pm Sun., $5-18) also blends global cuisines, with a dinner menu of traditional and original sushi dishes as well as Mediterranean tapas. On Sunday the menu features classic brunch fare, with special items like *loukoumades* (Greek deep-fried doughnuts) and Southern-fried chicken with waffles; Disco Drag Brunch is the second Sunday of the month.

The Blue Taj (14815 Ballantyne Village Way, 704/369-5777, www.thebluetaj.com, lunch 11:30am-2:30pm Mon.-Fri., buffet 11:30am-2:45pm Sat., dinner 5pm-10pm Mon.-Thurs., 5pm-10pm Fri.-Sat., 5pm-9pm Sun., $13-25), in the Ballantyne area, builds its menu from a foundation of tandoori cooking but explores many other cuisines, creating dishes such as trout marinated in a Goan *xec-xec* rub and innumerable specials.

INFORMATION AND SERVICES

Two Uptown (Charlotte's name for its downtown) locations serve as **visitors centers** (330 S. Tryon St., 800/231-4636, www.charlottesgotalot.com, 8:30am-5pm Mon.-Fri., 9am-5pm Sat., noon-4pm Sun.; lobby of the Levine Museum of the New South, 200 E. 7th St., 704/333-1887, ext. 235, www.museumofthenewsouth.org, 10am-5pm Mon.-Sat., noon-5pm Sun.). There is also a visitors center at the Charlotte Douglas International Airport (5501 Josh Birmingham Pkwy., 704/359-4910, www.charmeck.org, 7:45am-11pm daily). The *Charlotte Observer* (www.charlotteobserver.com) publishes an excellent annual guide to the region called *Living Here*. Pick up a print copy at many major destinations, or read it on the website.

Carolinas Medical Center (1000 Blythe Blvd., 704/355-2000, www.carolinashealthcare.org) is one of the largest hospitals in the Carolinas. Emergency vet clinics include **Carolina Veterinary Specialists** (2225 Township Rd., 704/588-7015 or 704/504-9608, www.carolinavet.com) and **Emergency Veterinary Clinic** (2440 Plantation Ctr. Dr., Matthews, 704/844-6440 or 704/907-0326, www.c-vets.com).

GETTING THERE AND AROUND

Charlotte Douglas International Airport (CLT, 5501 Josh Birmingham Pkwy., 704/359-4910, www.charmeck.org) is the 10th-largest hub in the United States, with nonstop flights to over 120 destinations worldwide and nearly 30 million passengers each year. A short cab ride from major Uptown hotels and attractions, Charlotte's **Amtrak Station** (1914 N. Tryon St., 704/376-4416, www.amtrak.com) is served by the New York-New Orleans *Crescent*, the *Carolinian* to New York City, and the *Piedmont* line to Raleigh.

Charlotte's extensive and ever-expanding **public transportation** system provides routes around the city. Some routes around the Center City and Uptown area are free. The city has inaugurated an ambitious light rail system, called LYNX that will eventually provide rapid access to far-flung neighborhoods and suburbs. Routes and fares are posted at www.charmeck.org, or call 704/336-7433.

Vicinity of Charlotte

There are far too many NASCAR-related attractions and racing sites of interest to name, but you'll find a selection of the best listed below. This region's love of stock cars is part of a general devotion to things with wheels. Within an easy drive of Charlotte are a museum honoring a fleet of red trucks, an old roundhouse that shelters beautiful restored locomotives, and even a paddle-wheel steamboat.

Several of the state's special food traditions intersect in this region. The fumes of Lexington barbecue waft over the entire Piedmont, and serious aficionados of fried fish scout out inland fish camps on the back roads of Gaston and neighboring counties. Folks in country kitchens radiating out from Shelby and the foothills know that the best thing to do with those spare pig heads and organs is to mash them up with cornmeal and serve them as livermush.

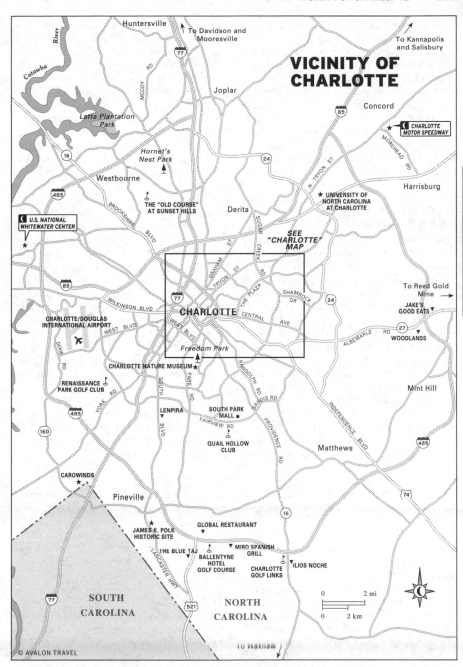

CHARLOTTE

You'll see livermush sandwiches on the menus of many little cafés in this region.

The rocky rivers that cross what is now the I-85 corridor once powered hundreds of textile mills, brick fortresses around which sprouted little towns with a culture all their own. As international trade becomes more and more globalized, the ramifications are still being felt as the last generation of these mill villages is vanishing, scattering residents to the wind and leaving unwieldy but sometimes beautiful structures to puzzle the developers tasked with demolishing or repurposing them.

MOORESVILLE AND LAKE NORMAN

Downtown Mooresville is an attractive historic area filled with appealing turn-of-the-20th-century small-town commercial architecture. There are several antiques shops and galleries as well as **DeLuxe Ice Cream** (186 N. Broad St., 704/664-5456, www.deluxe1924.com, noon-7pm Mon.-Thurs., noon-8pm Fri.-Sat., noon-6pm Sun. Mar.-Apr., 11am-9pm Mon.-Thurs., 11am-10pm Fri.-Sat., noon-6pm Sun. June-Sept., around $5), which has been in operation since 1924. Today, they have many more flavors than when they started, with around four dozen to choose from.

Racing Sights

Mooresville is home to some of the nation's most important racing facilities and attractions, as well as the home base of more than 60 individual teams. There are several racing museums, including the **North Carolina Auto Racing Hall of Fame** (Mooresville Visitor Center, 119 Knob Hill Rd., 704/663-5331, www.ncarhof.com, 10am-5pm Mon.-Fri., 10am-3pm Sat., $6 adults, $4 ages 6-12 and over age 54). The **Memory Lane Motorsports Museum** (769 River Hwy., 704/662-3673, www.memorylaneautomuseum.com, 10am-5pm Mon.-Sat. Mar.-mid-Nov., Sun. during race weeks, 10am-5pm Mon.-Tues. and Thurs.-Sat. mid-Nov.-Feb., $10 adults, $6 ages 6-10, free under age 6) features the largest private collection of retired NASCAR automobiles

and the world's largest collection of go-karts. There are more than 150 automotive exhibits and some very cool, very rare cars.

Some of the major teams and racing companies based here operate public facilities and gift shops. **Dale Earnhardt Inc.** (1675 Dale Earnhardt Hwy./Hwy. 3, 704/334-9663, www.daleearnhardtinc.com, 11am-2pm Thurs.-Sat.) has a showroom and a museum about the career of legendary Dale Sr. Other team complexes scattered throughout the area include Dale Earnhardt Jr.'s **JR Motorsports** (349 Cayuga Dr., 704/799-4800, www.jrmracing.com, 8:30am-5:30pm Mon.-Fri., 10am-4pm Sat., shop tours 9am-4:30pm Thurs.-Fri., reservations required), **Penske Racing** (200 Penske Way, 704/664-2300, www.penskeracing.com, gift shop 704/799-7178, 9am-5pm Mon.-Fri., Fan Walk 9am-5pm Mon.-Fri.), and **Michael Waltrip Racing** (20310 Chartwell Center Dr., 704/897-5555, www.michaelwaltripracing.com, 9am-5pm Mon.-Fri.), where you can tour the shop from the catwalks above and see the pit road practice area. If you're lucky, the pit crew will be there practicing their act.

One site not many race fans know about is the **Sam Bass Gallery** (6104 Performance Dr., 800/556-5464, http://sambass.com, 10am-5pm Tues.-Fri.). Bass is the first officially licensed artist of NASCAR, and his gallery is chock-full of original art, prints, paintings, and more of your favorite NASCAR drivers and venues through the sport's history.

Racing Schools

Not to be missed are the **NASCAR Technical Institute** (220 Byers Creek Rd., 704/658-1950, www.uti.edu), a formal training school for motorsports automotive technology, and **PIT Instruction and Training** (156 Byers Creek Rd., 704/799-3869, www.pit-now.com), a pit-crew training school.

Entertainment

Queens Landing (1459 River Hwy., 704/663-2628, www.queenslanding.com, 9am-5pm Mon.-Sat., 9am-3pm Sun.) is a huge lakeside entertainment complex that offers sightseeing

© JONATHAN WELCH/123RF.COM

Lake Norman

and dinner cruises on the paddleboat *Catawba Queen* and the yacht *Lady of the Lake.* There is also a lakeside restaurant, two bars, a water park, bumper boats, and miniature golf.

Sports and Recreation

If it's too hot to be around all that asphalt, there's plenty to do on the water. **Lake Norman State Park** (159 Inland Sea Lane, Troutman, 704/528-6350, http://ncparks.gov, 8am-6pm daily Nov.-Feb., 8am-8pm daily Mar.-Apr. and Sept.-Oct., 8am-9pm daily May-Aug., paddleboat and canoe rental $5 first hour, $3 per additional hour, camping with picnic table $20, seniors $15, primitive camping $13, swimming area $5 over age 12, $4 under age 13) is home to the state's largest artificial lake, with boating, swimming, camping, and more than six miles of cycling and hiking trails. Fishing is good for striped and largemouth bass, perch, and crappie. On the five-mile Lake Shore Trail you'll pass several spots to fish from the shore, dip your toes in the water, or just take in the scenery.

If you're interested in getting out on the water, **Premier Boat Rentals** (18919 W. Catawba Ave., Cornelius, 704/743-4184, www. thelakecalls.clickforward.com) rents pontoon boats ($165 for 4 hours, $205 for 6 hours, $250 for 8 hours) and well as Jet Skis ($75 for 1 hour, $100 for 2 hours, $150 for 3 hours), so whether you like your lake adventure speedy or relaxing, you can get your fix. If you want to get out onto the lake and into the coves and spots where the big ones congregate, **Pro-Am Guide Service** (704/491-8719, www.proamguideservice.com, half-day $165 for 2 people, full-day $200) can get you there. Guide Drew Montgomery meets you at the boat ramp with all the rods, reels, and tackle you need, but you have to get your own fishing license. He has a no fish, no pay policy, so even if you don't catch anything, you will have spent a nice day on the lake.

CONCORD AND KANNAPOLIS

Cabarrus County, which wraps around the northeastern corner of Charlotte, is one of the linguistic zones that tends to cause stress among newcomers and longtime North Carolinians alike. The place-names tend not to be pronounced as the standard rules of Carolinian speech would dictate. The county's name is stressed on the middle syllable, breaking one of the cardinal Carolinian rules of front-loading multisyllabic words: It's "cuh-BAH-russ," with the "a" pronounced as in "hat." Similarly, Kannapolis is stressed on the second syllable to rhyme with Annapolis. Even more vexing are the two-syllable place-names. The stress in the words Concord and Midland is weighted equally on the two syllables—"con cord" and "mid land."

(Charlotte Motor Speedway

Charlotte Motor Speedway (704/455-3200 or 800/455-3267, www.charlottemotorspeedway.com, tours 9:30am-3:30pm Mon.-Sat., 1:30pm-3:30pm Sun.), on Highway 29, is Concord's best-known attraction. The 167,000-seat arena with a 1.5-mile track hosts the NASCAR Sprint Cup as well as other NASCAR, Busch, and Craftsman Truck Series events. Two tours take you through the facility and even onto the track for a close look at this sporting marvel. In the Feel the Thrill Speedway Tour (hourly 9:30am-3:30pm Mon.-Sat., 1:30pm-3:30pm Sun., $12, $10 over age 55, under age 10, military, police, fire, and EMS) you'll see areas that are off-limits on race days, like the NASCAR Sprint Cup Series Garage, two infield race tracks, and a pit road, and you'll stop for a photo in Victory Lane. Oh, and you'll also drive on the track in your tour van, getting to experience the 24-degree pitch of the track. The Over the Wall Tour (10:30am and 1:30pm Mon.-Sat., groups only Sun., $20, $18 over age 55, under age 10, military, police, fire, and EMS) was designed with the hard-core NASCAR fan in mind. In addition to visiting the zMax Dragway and the Dirt Track, you'll get to visit the Speedway Club (which has a stellar view of the track), one of the private suites, the Performance Racing Network studio, and do a lap on the track before cruising down the pit road.

The Speedway is also home to the **Richard Petty Driving Experience,** where you can ride—or even drive—a 600-hp stock car at speeds up to 165 mph, as well as the **Xtreme Measures Teen Driving School,** where teenage drivers can spend two days learning safe driving skills in an exhilarating environment. Oddly enough, the Speedway's Smith Tower, on the second floor, inexplicably hosts the **Carolinas Boxing Hall of Fame** (www.carolinasboxinghalloffame.com).

Racing Sights and Racing Schools

Not to be outdone by its neighbor Concord, Kannapolis honors racing and the life of its hometown star Dale Earnhardt Sr. with the **Dale Trail.** Dale Sr. died at the age of 50 in a famous last-lap crash at the Daytona 500 race in 2001, one of the tragedies in racing history that have most starkly illustrated the great danger to which drivers subject themselves. Dale Sr. is honored by a nine-foot bronze statue, fan-financed granite monument, and huge murals at the **Dale Earnhardt Tribute** (Main St. and B St.) in the middle of Cannon Village, a historic shopping district in Kannapolis. The Dale Trail also goes by **Mike Curb's Motorsports Museum** (600 Dale Earnhardt Blvd., 704/938-6121, www.mikecurb.com), which displays more than 20 race cars driven by Curb Motorsports drivers, a star roster that includes Richard Petty, Dale Jarrett, and many others.

The **Jeff Gordon Racing School** (5555 Concord Pkwy., Concord, 877/722-3527, http://home.877racelap.com, $129-3,000) gives you some amazing NASCAR experiences, such as riding along with a professional racing-instructor driver, allowing you to drive the car on the track solo, and 1.5-day ultimate race experience that puts you on the track with five other professional drivers, giving you the nearest experience to a live race as you can get. The **Backing Up Classics Museum** (4545 Concord Pkwy., 704/788-9500, www.morrisonmotorco.com, 10am-5pm Mon.-Tues. and Thurs.-Sat., $5) is just north of the Speedway and houses more than 50 classic cars, muscle cars, and rides form the 1950s and 1960s.

THE ORIGINAL GOLDEN STATE

California's 1848 gold rush wasn't the nation's first; it was merely the shiniest. The first gold rush in the United States started in North Carolina, not far from Charlotte.

In 1799 young Conrad Reed was playing in Little Meadows Creek on his family's Cabarrus County farm when he found an intriguing shiny yellow rock. He took the 17-pound specimen to his father, who, unable to identify it, promptly put it to use as a doorstop. It sat in that utilitarian role for three years until the elder Reed took it to a jeweler in Fayetteville, who identified it as gold and bought it for $3.50, about a week's wages for a farmer, even though it was worth at least 1,000 times that amount.

Now knowing that Conrad's find was valuable, the Reed family began exploring their stretch of creek, looking for more gold. In 1804, just few years after the discovery of the 17-pound rock, a slave unearthed a 28-pound nugget from the creek bed. The Reeds built the nation's first gold mine, which produced more than $1 million over its lifetime (around $19 million in today's dollars). The boom was officially on.

After the discoveries on the Reed farm, prospectors, land-grabbers, miners, and anyone with the thought of quick riches flocked to the area. Hundreds and thousands of acres of land was bought in hopes of even bigger nuggets. Soon more than 300 mines were opened across North Carolina's Piedmont, and they were profitable and productive; President Andrew Jackson ordered the construction of a new U.S. Mint and our first national bank, both headquartered in Charlotte, the nation's first boomtown.

From 1804 to 1828, all domestic gold in the United States came from North Carolina, giving it the nickname "The Golden State" until being eclipsed by the California discovery of gold at Sutter's Mill.

CHARLOTTE

Historic Sights

In all the racing excitement, don't miss the sights of downtown Concord. The **Union Street Historic District** preserves some of the area's most spectacular homes, built with turn-of-the-20th-century textile dollars. Also along Union Street are the **Cabarrus Creamery** (21 Union St. S., 704/784-1923, www.cabarruscreamery.com, 10am-9pm Mon.-Thurs., 10am-10pm Sat., 1pm-9pm Sun.), an old-time ice cream shop.

Bost Grist Mill (4701 Hwy. 200, 704/782-1600, www.bostgristmill.com, free) is a beautiful and interesting building, home to a working grist mill where, in the 1800s, a water wheel created 15 hp and allowed the mill to produce around 150 bushels of meal per day. Today it's still in operation and still uses the same French Buhr millstones as it did two centuries ago. In addition to a number of varying events (check the calendar on the website), you can arrange for a group tour by prior arrangement.

While in Cabarrus County, pay a visit to the

Reed Gold Mine National Historic Landmark (9621 Reed Mine Rd., 704/721-4653, www.nchistoricsites.org, 9am-5pm Tues.-Sat., free, gold panning $3) in Midland to find out about a bonanza that hit this area long before the heyday of the textile mills and before stock cars were even imagined. In 1799 a local 12-year-old discovered—but didn't recognize the value of—a 17-pound gold nugget. Three years later, a sharp-eyed visitor noticed the huge lump of gold that the family was using as a doorstop and bought it for $3.50. This was the beginning of the first gold rush in the United States.

Concord Mills Mall

You might be surprised to learn that North Carolina's single most visited attraction is a shopping mall, the **Concord Mills Mall** (8111 Concord Mills Blvd., 704/979-3000, office 704/979-5000, www.simon.com, 10am-9pm Mon.-Sat., noon-7pm Sun.). I was puzzled as to how this could be the state's most-visited place, but then it hit me: It's right across from

Charlotte Motor Speedway, which draws hundreds of thousands of people at a time. The mall has a humongous Bass Pro Shops store anchoring one end, which brings anglers, hunters, and outdoor enthusiasts of all types; there's also a movie theater, a couple of outlets, and a Lego store, but otherwise it's just a typical mall.

Great Wolf Lodge

Great Wolf Lodge (10175 Weddington Rd., 704/549-8206, www.greatwolf.com, from $279) is a resort that is filled with children and families frolicking in the 80,000-square-foot 84°F indoor water park. There are slides, splash areas, and a giant bucket that dumps an unbelievable amount of water on the people below. There are racing water slides, tube slides, and a waterslide called the Howlin' Tornado that shoots you and three others into a six-story funnel where you swirl and twist and splash your way up and down the 30-foot walls until you're spit out the bottom. You can go bowling at a kid-size bowling alley, play mini golf, and take part in dozens of daily activities. There's a restaurant on-site and the guest rooms are sizable, so even if it's two adults and a couple of kids, there's plenty of space for everyone.

SALISBURY AND POINTS NORTH

Well north of Charlotte and well worth a day trip are the Salisbury and Mocksville areas. This is another area where place-names have unusual pronunciations. Salisbury is easy enough as "SAWLS-bree," with the first syllable rhyming with Paul. More unusual is Rowan, the county of which Salisbury is the seat. In the Carolinas, Rowan, both as a place-name or a person's name, is pronounced with stress on the second syllable, "row-ANN," which makes it sound like a girl's name. Oddest of all is Cooleemee, a tiny mill village in Davie County, pronounced "COOL-uh-mee."

Sights

Salisbury has a very pretty downtown, girded all around by attractive historic residential and commercial neighborhoods. The **Confederate**

Monument (W. Innes St. and Church St.), dedicated in a 1909 ceremony attended by Stonewall Jackson's widow, is surely one of the South's most beautiful war memorial statues. There are many historically significant buildings downtown, including **Kluttz Drug Store** (101 Main St.), which was the tallest commercial building in North Carolina at the time of its construction in 1858; **The Plaza,** directly across the street, an early seven-story "skyscraper"; the 1819 **Utzman-Chambers House** (116 S. Jackson St.); the 1820 **Josephus Hall House;** and hundreds more. Many of these places are open to the public, and a walking tour brochure can be found at the local **Visitors Bureau** (204 E. Innes St., 800/332-2343, 9am-5pm Mon.-Sat.).

In Spencer, just north of Salisbury, the **North Carolina Transportation Museum** (Spencer Shops, 411 S. Salisbury Ave., 704/636-2889, http://nctrans.org, 9am-5pm Tues.-Sat., 1pm-5pm Sun., $6, $5 seniors and military, $4 ages 3-12, free under age 3, with train ride $12, $10 seniors and military, $8 ages 3-12, free under age 3) occupies the old Spencer Shops, a 100-year-old Southern Railroad complex. The museum includes a restored 1890s passenger station, a mechanics office, a boiler flue repair shop, and a 37-bay roundhouse where more than 25 restored locomotives and train cars are on display. Extensive exhibits about railroad history and a gift shop full of transportation books and ephemera are great fun for any train spotter.

◖ Textile Heritage Center

Northwest of Salisbury on Highway 801 is the small town of Cooleemee, home of the **Textile Heritage Center** (Old 14 Church St., 336/284-6040, www.textileheritage.org, 10am-4pm Wed.-Sat. and by appointment, $4 adults, $3 seniors, free under 12). This very interesting little museum tells the story of the village that was built here at the turn of the 20th century around a large cotton mill on the banks of the Yadkin River. More than 20 years of oral history research have been conducted among Cooleemee's old-timers, resulting in an extremely rich portrait not only of this village but of "mill hill" life throughout the South. Just down the block from Zachary House, which houses the Textile Heritage Center, is the **Mill House Museum,** an authentic mill house restored and furnished to reflect life in Cooleemee around 1934.

Shopping

Downtown Salisbury is home to many restaurants, antiques shops, and boutiques. Stop in at the **Literary Book Post** (110 S. Main St., 704/630-9788, www.literarybookpost.com, 10am-5:30pm Mon.-Sat.), a small bookshop with a good array of titles in many genres, including a well-chosen selection of books about North Carolina. Be warned: The more than 40,000 titles on their shelves are guarded by a trio of black cats.

In nearby Gold Hill, a former mining town, you'll find the **E. H. Montgomery General Store** (770 St. Stephens Church Rd., Gold Hill, 704/267-9439, www.themontgomerystore.com, 11am-5pm Thurs. and Sat.-Sun., 11am-9pm Fri.), an 1840s general store that once supplied the town with just about everything it needed. Today, you'll find a little gift shop that sells old-fashioned candies, hand-dipped ice cream, glass-bottled sodas, jams, jellies, and other canned goods from nearby Amish communities, and coffee. On Friday evening starting at 7pm there's an open bluegrass jam session with acoustic instruments.

Accommodations

Salisbury has a pair of beautiful downtown bed-and-breakfasts. [**Rowan Oak House** (208 S. Fulton St., 800/786-0437, www.rowanoakbb.com, from $130) is an ornate, turreted 1901 house with four plush guest rooms. Breakfast might include such treats as crab grits or an egg and tortilla casserole. Race fans should inquire about the three-night NASCAR packages, a special rate available during some of the top events at Charlotte Motor Speedway.

The **Turn of the Century Victorian Bed and Breakfast** (529 S. Fulton St., 704/642-1660, www.turnofthecenturybb.com, from $120, no

pets or children under age 12) has four lovely guest rooms and is only a short walk to historic downtown Salisbury. The home dates to 1905, and the delicate preservation efforts undertaken to turn it around in the mid-1990s garnered attention and official recognition from the state and the town of Salisbury.

Food

Coopers: The Gathering Place (122 E. Fisher St., 704/754-4907, www.coopersofsalisbury.com, from 5pm Tues.-Sat., $8-21) features an interesting menu. For starters, they offer a Southern "BreadBasket" which consists of fried green tomatoes, onion-battered green beans, and a rémoulade dipping sauce; sunflower seed and chickpea falafel served with baked mozzarella; and nachos stopped with northern beans and grilled chicken. Then they have a fabulous little mac-and-cheese menu, with interesting toppings and cheeses, and even a celiac disease-friendly menu. For mains, they offer an assortment of pastas, steaks, and seafood. All in all this is a surprising restaurant to find in a town this size.

WEST OF CHARLOTTE
Sights

You'll have noticed by now that North Carolinians really like things with wheels and like to enshrine in museums those that aren't on the road. Cherryville's **C. Grier Beam Truck Museum** (111 N. Mountain St., Cherryville, 704/435-3072, www.beamtruckmuseum.com, 10am-3pm Thurs.-Sat., free) houses a fleet of beautiful cherry-red Carolina Freight Carriers trucks dating from the 1930s. There's also a great restored 1927 filling station.

The **International Lineman's Museum** (529 Caleb Rd., Shelby, 704/482-7638, ext. 3119, www.linemanmuseum.com, 8am-5pm Mon.-Thurs., free) evokes Glen Campbell's "Wichita Lineman," a song that will get stuck in your head until you listen to it at least five times. The museum contains thousands of artifacts from the early electrical industry, fascinating historical photos of linemen at work in generations past, and the International Lineman's

Hall of Fame. Cherryville, by the way, is pronounced like the herb: "chervil."

Sports and Recreation

Crowders Mountain State Park (522 Park Office Lane, 704/853-5375, http://ncparks. gov, 8am-6pm daily Nov.-Feb., 8am-8pm daily Mar.-Apr. and Sept.-Oct., 8am-9pm daily May-Aug.) embraces a small mountain range where Crowders Mountain and King's Pinnacle tower dramatically over the upper Piedmont landscape. Ten trails, ranging from short and easy to long, steep, and extremely strenuous, scale the ridges and explore the woods below. The high sheer cliffs are frequented by experienced rock climbers (who must obtain permits and observe strict rules, laid out on the website). Primitive campsites ($13) are located about one mile from the visitors center.

Food

One might not expect to find a generations-old seafood tradition up here in the Piedmont, but in fact this region is dotted with old-time eating places called fish camps. Today's fish camps evolved from riverside and lakeside shacks, where a day's catch would be fried up and served to local mill workers and neighbors. While most of the fish served in these joints nowadays is not locally caught, the tradition of waterfront fried-fish eateries persists. Presentation is often plain, a heap of fried stuff on a paper plate, but folks don't come to these places for aperitifs and tapas. Some favorite area fish camps include **Love's Fish Box** (1104 Shelby Rd., Kings Mountain, 704/739-4036, www.lovesfishbox.com, under $15), **Twin Tops Fish Camp** (4574 S. New Hope Rd., Gastonia, 704/825-2490, http://twintopsfish-camp.com, $8-16), **Graham's Fish Fry** (4539 S. New Hope Rd., Gastonia, 704/825-8391), and **Fisherman's Feast** (1215 E. Marion St., Shelby, 704/487-6000). Fish camp hours are unpredictable, so call ahead.

Red Bridges Barbecue Lodge (2000 E. Dixon Rd., 704/482-8567, www.bridges-bbq.com, 11am-8pm Wed.-Sun., under $11) opened in 1946 and has been cooking with the same traditions ever since. You're not limited to barbecue here; you can also get burgers, chicken tenders, a deviled-egg sandwich, and grilled cheese, but whatever you get, order up some sweet tea and hush puppies.

Tony's Ice Cream (604 E. Franklin Blvd., Gastonia, 704/853-0018, www.tonysicecream. com, 7am-10pm Mon.-Sat., 10am-10pm Sun., under $5) has been serving homemade ice cream in its present location since 1947, but the business started a generation earlier in 1911, when Carmine Coletta, Tony's father, began selling snacks from a pushcart. Today, it's run by Tony's sons, who serve 25 flavors done up in cones, sundaes, shakes, and splits. You can also choose from a list of diner-style sandwiches or stop in for breakfast (where, presumably, you could have your grits à la mode).

GETTING THERE AND AROUND

Two major interstate arteries lead north out of Charlotte. I-77, the more westerly route, leads north towards Mooresville. I-85 leads into racing country to Concord and Kannapolis.

NORTHERN BLUE RIDGE AND FOOTHILLS

Once upon a time, this region of rolling mountains and foothills was the immigration frontier of the New World, calling to the brave and foolhardy to carve out a place among the hollows and hills. In 1752 one of the first written impressions of the area was recorded by Bishop Augustus Spangenberg, traveling from Pennsylvania on the Great Wagon Road and looking for a suitable tract of land for his Moravian Church and community. He eventually found a welcoming spot in the city of Salem, but his first sight of the Blue Ridge filled him with dread. Cresting a ridge, Spangenberg, who had crossed the Atlantic and braved thousands of miles of the frontier, wrote, "We have reached here after a hard journey over very high, terrible mountains and cliffs.... When we reached the top we saw mountains to the right, to the left, before and behind us, rising like great waves in a storm."

This corner of the state wasn't just the frontier in Spangenberg's time; until the 20th century the farthest northwestern counties of North Carolina were known as the "Lost Provinces" because they were so remote and difficult to reach. As automobiles and improved roads, including the Blue Ridge Parkway, found their way to this area, so too did the flatlanders. Since then, the region has evolved into a popular destination for vacationers throughout the year. The mountains around Boone feel subtly different from the ranges closer to Asheville and the Smokes farther south and west; they're more spread out and softened. The northern Blue Ridge is no less beautiful, and the valleys become even wider and the peaks less craggy.

HIGHLIGHTS

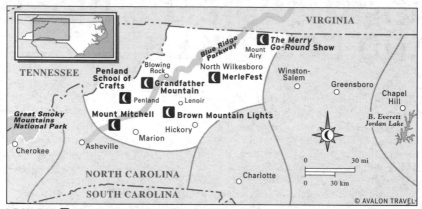

LOOK FOR ◖ TO FIND RECOMMENDED SIGHTS, ACTIVITIES, DINING, AND LODGING.

◖ **Grandfather Mountain:** Grandfather Mountain is smaller than Mount Mitchell but still fully a mile high and no less beautiful (page 286).

◖ **Penland School of Crafts:** One of the venerable centers of art in the mountains, Penland offers residential classes in dozens of media. The innovative studio creations of many of the artists are exhibited and sold in the elegant gallery (page 288).

◖ **Mount Mitchell:** You'd have to travel west until you hit the Black Hills of South Dakota before you could find a higher mountain. The East's tallest peak was the subject of a scholarly feud in the mid-1800s, and one of the feuders, Mitchell himself, is buried at the summit (page 288).

◖ **Brown Mountain Lights:** The mysterious lights that hover over Brown Mountain have been seen by Carolinians since at least 1833. Whether they're vapors, reflections, or a supernatural phenomenon has never been settled. If you're in the right place at the right time, you may see them for yourself (page 289).

◖ **MerleFest:** For one long weekend in April, many of the best artists in American roots music are in North Wilkesboro, along with thousands of their fans (page 294).

◖ *The Merry-Go-Round* **Show:** Mount Airy has a rich musical tradition and a great small-town radio station, WPAQ. The weekly *Merry-Go-Round* show is broadcast in front of a live audience from the old movie theater downtown (page 298).

Although the wilderness is a little less wild now, it's still isolated. Stands of virgin forest, or at least forest that hasn't been logged in more than a century, still stand in remote coves, and spots like Linville Gorge challenge the most intrepid outdoor enthusiasts. Getting lost in the tangle of winding mountain roads is easy, especially as you move closer to the Tennessee state line, where the mountains get taller and the valleys more narrow. Here you'll find back roads and hollows (pronounced "hollers" in much of these parts) where only the noonday sun reaches the valley floor, and in winter, some are lucky to see an hour or two of true daylight. The trees are gnarled and mossy and cling to the edge of windy ridges and cliffs. You'll find

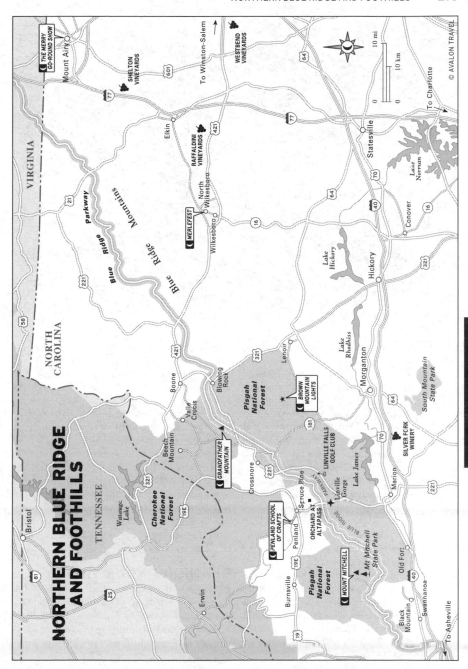

NORTHERN BLUE RIDGE AND FOOTHILLS

THE MERRY GO-ROUND SHOW

Mount Airy

SHELTON VINEYARDS

WESTBEND VINEYARDS

To Winston-Salem

To Charlotte

© AVALON TRAVEL

10 mi

10 km

VIRGINIA

Elkin

RAFFALDINI VINEYARDS

Statesville

North Wilkesboro

MERLEFEST

Wilkesboro

Lake Norman

Conover

NORTH CAROLINA

Lake Hickory

Hickory

Blue Ridge Parkway

Blue Ridge Mountains

Lake Rhodhiss

Lenoir

Lake Hickory

Blue Ridge

Boone

Blowing Rock

Pisgah National Forest

BROWN MOUNTAIN LIGHTS

Morganton

South Mountain State Park

NORTHERN BLUE RIDGE

Valle Crucis

Beech Mountain

GRANDFATHER MOUNTAIN

Crossnore

LINVILLE FALLS GOLF CLUB

Lake James

Marion

SILVER FORK WINERY

NORTHERN BLUE RIDGE AND FOOTHILLS

TENNESSEE

Cherokee National Forest

Watauga Lake

Bristol

Spruce Pine

Linville Gorge

BLUE RIDGE PARKWAY

PENLAND SCHOOL OF CRAFTS

Penland

ORCHARD AT ALTAPASS

Mt Mitchell State Park

Old Fort

Erwin

Burnsville

Pisgah National Forest

MOUNT MITCHELL

Mt Mitchell

Black Mountain

Swannanoa

To Asheville

© JASON FRYE

the rolling pastures of the Northern Blue Ridge

waterfalls and wide rivers perfect for wading, floating, or fishing.

Much of the Appalachian folklore collected and popularized in the last 100 to 150 years has come out of this section of North Carolina. It was here that the young Confederate Army veteran known as Tom Dooley—who was a real person and whose actual identity is still debated around these parts—killed his girlfriend, Laurie Foster, a ghastly crime immortalized in legend and song. In Wilkesboro, you can see the jail cell where he waited to go to the gallows in Statesville. Another crime immortalized in legend is the 1831 murder of Charlie Silver, apparently in self-defense, by his young wife, Frankie. She too was carried down the mountain to hang, and was executed in Morganton. It's not all ghost stories, though. Many of the "Jack Tales," which became a sort of signature of Appalachian storytelling, were recorded around Beech Mountain and have been told by the Harmon and Hicks families for generations. Head into Mount Airy or any other mountain town on any weekend and you'll find

old-time musicians singing traditional songs the way their daddy (and their daddy's daddy, and their daddy's daddy's daddy) taught them, or old-timers telling Jack Tales old and new on some front porch or park bench.

When you visit, leave room in your luggage for some cheese; Ashe County is known for it, along with homemade jam or preserves. Take home a piece by area potters or weavers, eat dinner at a barbecue joint and get a feel for western North Carolina style 'cue, and visit a winery and carry a bottle back with you. Go skiing, rafting, caving, and gallery hopping; just remember to leave time to explore the back roads at your own pace, windows down, soaking it all in.

PLANNING YOUR TIME

Be aware of the weather when traveling in the region. Thick mountain fog in spring and fall, even in summer, can form out of nowhere, making driving on twisting unfamiliar roads dangerous. Pop-up thunderstorms in summer can put a damper on hiking, especially in high or exposed places, and can slow your drive to a crawl as your windshield wipers struggle to keep up. Snow squalls and even black ice in winter and cold days in spring and fall will slow you down too. When unexpected weather descends, slow to a comfortable, safe pace or find a good spot to pull over and wait it out; most of the time, you won't be there long. With a little foresight, seasonal planning, and weather updates, you'll have no trouble discovering the beauty of this part of North Carolina. Know too that the mountain roads can be confusing, so bring a good paper map, gazetteer, or road atlas with you.

Three days will give you a general overview of the area and let you experience parts of what these mountain towns have to offer, but five days will provide ample time to explore by car, on foot, and by raft. If you're planning on spending most of your time in the deep mountains near Tennessee or around Mount Mitchell and Grandfather Mountain, Linville Gorge, Banner Elk, or Beech Mountain, Boone offers the convenience of bigger-town

amenities (a wider selection of restaurants and shopping for day-trip supplies), but Blowing Rock offers picturesque mountain-town digs. Both towns are not far from the Blue Ridge Parkway, and most destinations are 30 to 60 minutes' drive from either one. Mount Airy and Wilkesboro are both at the edge of the mountains and easily accessible to the junction of I-77 and U.S. 421, a jumping-off point for most foothills locations.

INFORMATION AND SERVICES

The state Department of Transportation operates a real-time **Road Conditions Map** (http://apps.dot.state.nc.us/tims). For current conditions along the Blue Ridge Parkway, you can check the recorded message at 828/298-0398. Hospitals are located in most of the major towns in this region, but in case of an emergency, help might be delayed by weather, road conditions, or distance. In many areas—not just deep in the woods, but in populated areas as well—there may be no cell phone signal.

© JASON FRYE

enjoying the view from Grandfather Mountain

Deep Mountains

Something about ascending into the high country gives visitors a sense of anticipation. I think it's the cinematic buildup to the drama of the landscape. As the roads move through gently rolling hills, you catch your first glimpse of high peaks on the horizon, clouds following the lines of the Blue Ridge Mountains, forming a second mountain range of vapor above the earth. Soon the terrain becomes rockier and you see cows grazing in steep fields, their barn in the valley below and the homestead on the mountain opposite. Hairpin turns appear, the elevation sweeps up to meet you, and you see how high and exposed you are; the mountains march off into the distance, gaining their namesake blue tinge as they retreat. Your ears pop, the road levels out, and the trees open; across the valley, you see the road where you were, that hairpin turn, clinging to the mountain.

Most travelers experience this part of North Carolina via the Blue Ridge Parkway (BRP), making side trips into the mountains and peering off across the Piedmont below. This section of the parkway, from roughly Asheville to the Virginia state line, is widely regarded as the most beautiful section of the 469-mile road. This road connects the bluffs and coves along the Virginia state line to the canoe launches and Christmas tree farms around Jefferson, and the college town of Boone and the resort town of Blowing Rock, with the natural wonders of Grandfather Mountain and Linville Gorge.

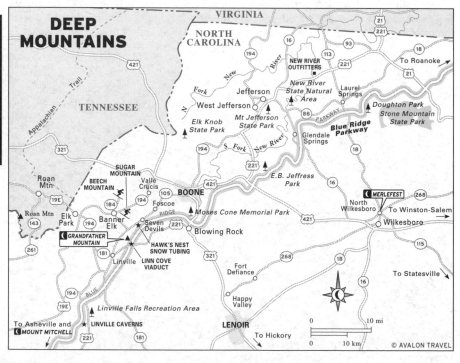

Boone is a fun mountain town, with its own counterculture flair based at Appalachian State University and its 15,000 students. There are good organic markets, plenty of restaurants, good antiques shops, and outdoor activities in every season. Blowing Rock and Linville were tony summertime roosts for wealthy folks in the early 20th century, and much of that elegance remains, both in the stylish bungalows, shopping and dining selections, and modern spas and resorts that populate the area. Venturing off the Parkway and into the mountains, artistic communities like Penland, Crossnore, and other towns in the Toe River Valley await your visit. Many artists came to the area to be part of the folk school in Penland, which has exerted a great deal of influence on the modern American craft movement; there is a dense concentration of artists working in folk and studio pottery and glasswork, hand-wrought ironwork, delicately crafted jewelry, and unusual textile arts.

BLOWING ROCK

Blowing Rock, named for a nearby geological oddity, is an old resort town filled with beautiful homes that once belonged to wealthy early-20th-century industrialists. It's a small town, but the surprising array of restaurants, cafés, and galleries make it pleasant to stroll, window-shop, and sit to enjoy an ice cream. The Blue Ridge Parkway is nearby, providing easy access to Moses Cone Manor and other notable landmarks.

Sights
BLOWING ROCK

Many of western North Carolina's best-known attractions are geological: Chimney Rock, Linville Caverns, Mount Mitchell, and stately Grandfather Mountain. The **Blowing Rock** (U.S. 321 S., 828/295-7111, www.theblowingrock.com, hours vary, $6 adults, $1 ages 4-11, free under age 4) is a strange rock outcropping purported by *Ripley's Believe It or Not* to be the only place in the world where snow falls upward. Indeed, light objects

(think handkerchiefs, leaves, hats) thrown off Blowing Rock—not allowed, by the way, to prevent the valley from filling up with litter—do tend to come floating back up. Adding to its otherworldly draw, there's a Native American legend associated with Blowing Rock. The story goes that a Chickasaw chieftain, fearful of the admiration his beautiful daughter was receiving, journeyed far to Blowing Rock, where he hoped to hide her away in the woods and keep her safe and pure. One day, the maiden spied a Cherokee warrior wandering in the valley below. Smitten by his looks, she shot an arrow in his direction, hoping he would seek her out. Soon he appeared at her home, courting her with songs of his land. They became lovers, and one day, a strange reddening sky brought the pair to Blowing Rock. He took it as a sign that he was to return to his people in their coming time of trouble; to her it spelled the end of their love. She begged him not to go, but he was torn between staying loyal to his duties and following his heart; in his desperation he leapt from their perch into the gorge below. The young maiden prayed for him to be spared death, but it didn't work. She remained at the site, and one day the sky reddened and the now-famous winds of the John's River Gorge shifted, blowing her lover back into her arms. Since that day, a perpetual wind has blown up onto the Rock from the valley below.

MOSES CONE MANOR

The **Moses Cone Manor,** more commonly called **Flat Top Manor** (BRP milepost 294, 828/295-7938, 9am-5pm daily Mar. 15-Nov., free), is a wonderfully crafted house, a huge white and ornate mountain palace built in 1901 that was the country home of North Carolina textile baron Moses Cone. He became a leading philanthropist, and as you drive around the state, especially in the northern Piedmont, you'll notice his name on quite a few institutions. Today, the manor is the centerpiece of the Moses Cone Memorial Park. Appropriately, it is home to one of the

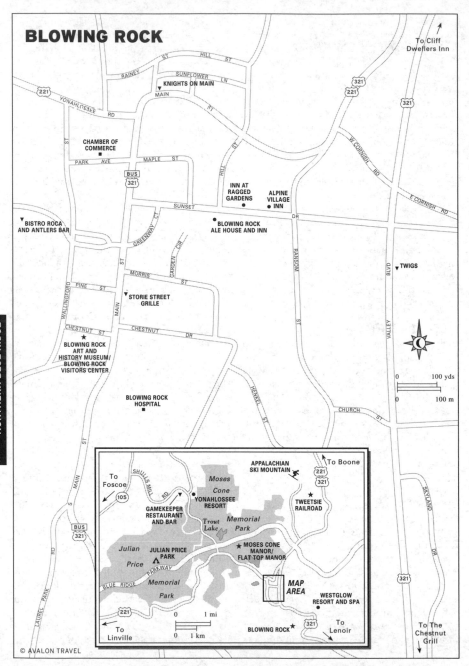

BLOWING ROCK

To Cliff
Dwellers Inn

KNIGHTS ON MAIN

CHAMBER OF
COMMERCE

INN AT
RAGGED
GARDENS

ALPINE
VILLAGE
INN

BISTRO ROCA
AND ANTLERS BAR

BLOWING ROCK
ALE HOUSE AND INN

TWIGS

STORIE STREET
GRILLE

BLOWING ROCK
ART AND
HISTORY MUSEUM/
BLOWING ROCK
VISITORS CENTER

BLOWING ROCK
HOSPITAL

0   100 yds

0   100 m

To Boone

APPALACHIAN
SKI MOUNTAIN

To
Foscoe

Moses
Cone

YONAHLOSSEE
RESORT

TWEETSIE
RAILROAD

GAMEKEEPER
RESTAURANT
AND BAR

Trout
Lake

Memorial
Park

Julian

JULIAN PRICE
PARK

Price

MOSES CONE
MANOR/
FLAT TOP MANOR

Memorial

MAP
AREA

Park

WESTGLOW
RESORT AND SPA

To Linville

1 mi

1 km

BLOWING ROCK

To
Lenoir

To The
Chestnut
Grill

© JASON FRYE

the namesake Blowing Rock

Southern Highland Craft Guild (828/295-7938, www.southernhighlandguild.org, 9am-5pm daily mid-Mar.-Nov.) stores, a place to buy beautiful textiles, pottery, jewelry, furniture, and dolls handmade by some of the best craftspeople of the Appalachian Mountains. There are also extensive hiking and riding trails on the estate.

BLOWING ROCK ART AND HISTORY MUSEUM

The **Blowing Rock Art and History Museum** (159 Chestnut St., 828/295-9099, www.blowingrockmuseum.org, 10am-5pm Tues.-Wed., 10am-7pm Thurs., 10am-5pm Fri.-Sat., 1pm-5pm Sun., $8 adults, $5 over age 5, students, and military) opened in October 2011 after more than a decade of work. In addition to rotating exhibits of fine art from private collections, gallery shows by local and regional artists, and traveling exhibitions, BRAHM also has galleries with rotating exhibits displaying artifacts of historical value to the area. It's small, but the art displayed is carefully curated and excellent. It's easy to spend a couple of hours here admiring the collections.

TWEETSIE RAILROAD

Between Blowing Rock and Boone, **Tweetsie Railroad** (300 Tweetsie Railroad Rd., 828/264-9061, http://tweetsie.com, 9am-6pm Fri.-Sun. mid-Apr.-late May, 9am-6pm daily late May-mid-Aug., 9am-6pm Fri.-Sun. late Aug.-Nov., Ghost Train 7:30pm Fri. late Sept.-early Nov., $37 over age 12, $23 ages 3-12, free under age 3) is a veritable gold mine for kids who are into trains (which, in my experience, is most of them). There's opportunities to pan for gold and gems in one section of the park, a Country Fair-themed area, a Western store and Cowboy Cantina in another, the Tweetsie Junction area where you'll find a saloon, a blacksmith, and an antique photo parlor. And, of course, the train: The Tweetsie Railroad's steam engines, number 12 or *Tweetsie,* and number 190, *Yukon Queen,* encircle the amusement park on a narrow-gauge track as part of a Wild West show featuring a frontier outpost and Indian attacks. The railroad isn't all fun and games; it's also partly a history lesson, as the *Tweetsie* was an actual working train in the early part of the 20th century, until washed-out tracks and the advent of reliable automobiles and roads rendered it obsolete.

Accommodations

The lavish 1916 Greek Revival mansion of painter Elliot Daingerfield is now home to the ◖ **Westglow Resort and Spa** (224 Westglow Crescent, 828/295-4463 or 800/562-0807, www.westglow.com, from $325, spa packages from $425). In addition to the cushy guest rooms, many of which have whirlpool tubs, private decks, and views of Grandfather Mountain, the menu of spa treatments and health services befits the elegance of the surroundings. All kinds of massage and body therapy are available, as well as fitness classes, cooking and makeup lessons, and a variety of seminars in emotional well-being. Taking advantage of the spa's wonderful location, visitors can also sign up for hiking, cycling, snowshoeing, and camping trips.

The **Inn at Ragged Gardens** (203 Sunset Dr., 828/295-9703, www.ragged-gardens.com, from $145) is a stone-walled and chestnut-paneled manor, a handsome and stylish turn-of-the-20th-century vacation home. The plush guest rooms feature goose-down bedding, fireplaces, and in most rooms, balconies and whirlpool tubs. A sister property to the Inn at Ragged Gardens, the **Blowing Rock Ale House and Inn** (152 Sunset Dr., 828/414-9254, www.blowingrockalehouseandinn.com, $125-160) is an eight-room bed-and-breakfast and full pub. It has been in operation as a B&B since the late 1940s, once heralded as a fancy place to stay because most guest rooms had private baths. Today, the addition of the Blowing Rock Brewing Co. restaurant and tavern (828/414-9600, http://blowingrockbrewing.com, 11am-6pm daily, around $14) has helped keep this long-running institution going in a new era.

Alpine Village Inn (297 Sunset Dr., 828/295-7206, www.alpine-village-inn.com, from $60), in downtown Blowing Rock, has comfortable accommodations at good rates. The guest rooms are located in the main inn and in a motel-style wing. It's a convenient location for checking out the shops and restaurants in town. Another good value is the **Cliff Dwellers Inn** (116 Lakeview Trail, 828/295-3098, www.cliffdwellers.com, from $90), with clean, simple guest rooms and a beautiful lakefront view.

CAMPING

The campground at **Julian Price Park** (BRP milepost 297, near Blowing Rock, 828/963-5911, www.recreation.gov, $16-19) is the largest on the Parkway, with a good selection of standard and tent-only nonelectric campsites. Pets are allowed, flush toilets and a telephone are accessible, and there's good hiking and boating nearby, with boat rentals available.

Food

◖ **The Chestnut Grille** (9239 Valley Blvd., 828/414-9230, www.greenparkinn.com, from 6pm Tues.-Sun., $17-25) is in the Green Park Inn on the edge of town. Chef James Welch, a James Beard Award nominee and winner of a number of state food awards, directs the kitchen. The food draws inspiration from across the globe; Cuban spice-rubbed scallops, seared tuna with wasabi and soy-ginger sauce, rigatoni with chicken, lamb, steaks, pulled pork, and even tempeh grace the menu. The Divide Tavern (from 5pm daily, $8-11), also in the Green Park Inn, serves a smaller menu of pub food such as wings and other handhelds.

Storie Street Grille (1167 Main St., 828/295-7075, www.storiestreetgrille.com, 11am-3pm and 5pm-9pm Mon.-Sat., lunch $5-13, dinner $10-30) has a long lunch menu of sandwiches and main-course salads. Try the ever-elusive monte cristo, the salmon cake, or the bacon, brie, and apple panini. For dinner they serve a few Italian choices, grilled steak, and seafood. The Vegetarian Sauté, a mix of mushrooms, spinach, roasted garlic, almonds, and shallots served with smoky adobo sauce and fingerling potatoes, will satisfy even a hungry carnivore.

Bistro Roca and Antlers Bar (143 Wonderland Trail, 828/295-4008, http://bistroroca.com, 11:30am-3pm and 5pm-10pm Wed.-Mon., bar 11am-midnight Wed.-Mon., $10-30) serves hearty and creative dishes like lobster mac-and-cheese, their take on coq au vin (made with riesling instead of red wine), and a pork rib eye with goat cheese "butter" and a peach *gastrique*. An interesting note is that the Antlers Bar has been open since 1932, making it the oldest continuously serving bar in the state.

Twigs (7956 Valley Blvd., 828/295-5050, http://twigsbr.com, 5:30pm-9:30pm Tues.-Thurs. and Sun., 5:30pm-10pm Fri.-Sat., bar until 11pm Sun. and Tues.-Thurs., until 1:30am Fri.-Sat., $10-35), is popular with locals and visitors alike. It has both a casual bar and a fancier dining room, and serves popular regional dishes like shrimp and grits and mountain trout alongside more unusual fare like venison. About 18 wines available by the glass and another 200 by the bottle, featuring a wide selection of California wines as well as Australian, European, and Argentine choices.

For a comfy small-town ambience, visit **Knights on Main** (870 Main St., 828/295-3869, www.knightsonmainrestaurant.com, breakfast and lunch 6:30am-2:30pm Mon.-Thurs., 6:30am-3pm Fri.-Sun., breakfast $2-8, lunch $3-12), serves down-home cooking, including homemade soups, fried oysters, and barbecue ribs. At breakfast you can get your livermush fix, go with something a little milder like fried bologna, or stick to the french toast.

BOONE

Boone is the quintessential western North Carolina city, a blend of old and new, where proponents of homesteading and holistic living find a congenial habitat in the culture of rural Appalachia. It's also a college town, the home of Appalachian State University, lending the city an invigorating youthful verve. Boone continues to grow as more people discover how amenable this part of the state is for year-round living.

Shopping

Several antiques shops in Boone make the downtown a great place for browsing. **Appalachian Antique Mall** (631 W. King St., 828/268-9988, www.appalachianantiquemall.com, 10am-6pm Mon.-Sat. and 11am-6pm Sun. summer, 10am-5pm Mon.-Sat., noon-5pm Sun. winter) is one of the best and biggest in the area. You'll find everything from farm implements to paintings and furniture from far and wide. **Footsloggers** (139 S. Depot St., 828/262-5111, www.footsloggers.com, 9:30am-5:30pm Mon.-Thurs., 9:30am-6pm Fri.-Sat., noon-5pm Sun.) has been selling gear for climbing, hiking, and camping for 40 years. They have a 40-foot climbing tower that simulates many conditions you might find climbing the real rock faces that attract so many climbers and outdoor enthusiasts to this area.

There are several branches of the **Mast General Store** (630 W. King St., 828/262-0000, www.mastgeneralstore.com, 10am-6pm Mon.-Sat., noon-6pm Sun.) in the Carolina High Country, but the original is in Valle Crucis (Hwy. 194, 828/963-6511, www.mastgeneralstore.com, 7am-6:30pm Mon.-Sat., noon-6pm Sun. summer, hours vary in winter), about 20 minutes west of Boone. It has been a visitor attraction for about 30 years, but its history as a community institution goes back before the 1880s. When the Mast family owned it the store had the reputation of carrying everything "from cradles to caskets," and today it still has a varied inventory, with specialties in outdoor wear (Carhartt, Columbia, Mountain Hardware, Patagonia, Teva), camping gear, and more penny candy than a modern-day store should have.

Sports and Recreation
ROCK CLIMBING
Rock Dimensions (139 Depot St., 828/265-3544, www.rockdimensions.com, from $65)

is a guide service that leads rock climbs at gorgeous locations throughout western North Carolina and parts of Tennessee and Virginia. Guides teach proper multipitch, top-rope anchoring, and rappelling techniques, and they lead caving expeditions ($330 for 4 people).

If you're an experienced climber, take a look at the **Boone Adventure Guide** (http://advguides.com/boone), a website that will lead you to some nice pitches and help you find places for other outdoor activities such as fly-fishing, hiking, and dog-friendly adventures.

WINTER SPORTS

The Banner Elk area has some of the state's best ski slopes. **Sugar Mountain** (1009 Sugar Mountain Dr., 828/898-4521, www.skisugar.com, lift tickets $41-68 adults, $32-45 children, rentals $21-36 adults, $15-28 children) is North Carolina's largest winter resort, with 115 acres of ski slopes and 20 trails. In addition to skiing, activities on the 5,300-foot-high mountain include snow-tubing, skating, snowshoeing, and in summer, the Showdown at Sugar National Mountain Bike Series. They offer lessons in skiing and snowboarding for adults and children.

Ski Beech Mountain Resort (1007 Beech Mountain Pkwy., Beech Mountain, 800/438-2093, www.skibeech.com, lift tickets $30, rentals $9-26) peaks 300 feet higher than Sugar Mountain and has 15 slopes and 10 lifts, as well as skating and snowboarding areas. In summer they shift focus to mountain bikes and disc golf, with a beautiful disc course as well as challenging downhill biking trails that range from beginner-friendly to expert.

Hawksnest Snow Tubing (2058 Skyland Dr., Seven Devils, 828/963-6561, www.hawksnesttubing.com, 1.5 hours $25-30, zip-lining $75-85) is on a 4,800-foot mountain in Seven Devils. It has 12 slopes all dedicated to the family-friendly art of tubing, making it one of the largest snow-tubing parks on the East Coast. Throughout the year you can experience the thrill of zip-lining on more than four miles of zip lines, including two longer than 2,000 feet, at speeds up to 50 mph.

HIKING, RAFTING, AND CAVE TRIPS

Down the road from the Mast General Store in Valle Crucis, **River and Earth Adventures** (1655 Hwy. 105, 866/411-7238, www.raftcavehike.com) leads all sorts of exciting trips on the water, in the woods, and in the area's deep caves. Rafting expeditions ($45-85 adults, $35-75 children) ride the French Broad River (Class III-IV) and Watauga River (Class II-III), or, for big white water, try the Watuga Gorge Ex-Stream Whitewater trip ($125, 4-person minimum), which gives you more than five miles of Class III, IV, and V rapids. This trip runs spring through fall, using rafts during high water and inflatable kayaks during low water. Participants must be at least age 18. Cave trips (daily year-round, $45-75 pp) meet at their Elizabethton, Tennessee, outpost, about an hour away, for a day's spelunking in Worley's Cave. Guided hiking trips are available that include all-day kids-only hikes with adult guides to free up parents who'd like a day on their own. If you're looking to hike or go rock climbing or bouldering, they offer guide services; inquire about routes and rates.

High Mountain Expeditions (1380 Hwy. 105 S., Banner Elk, 800/262-9036, www.highmountainexpeditions.com), which also has a Boone location, leads rafting trips on the Watauga River (Class I-III) and the much more challenging Nolichucky River (Class III-IV). They also lead caving expeditions for adults and children, for which no experience is necessary.

GEM MINING

Many people don't know that North Carolina is rich in gems and gold. Around Boone and the more heavily visited places in the mountains you'll find businesses that offer gem "mining." You don't need a pick and a shovel, just a keen eye and a few bucks. To "mine," you buy a bucket of material, graded and priced according to the likelihood of it having a valuable gem in it, and then sort, sift, and pan it yourself. You get to keep what you find, and you really can come across some beautiful specimens, some even worthy of jewelry. **River and Earth**

Adventures (1655 Hwy. 105, 866/411-7238, www.raftcavehike.com) offers gem mining ($15-100), as does **Foggy Mountain Gem Mine** (4416 Hwy. 105, 828/263-4367, www.foggymountaingems.com, $17-120), where you can get gemstones cut and polished in-house, and **The Greater Foscoe Gem Mining Co.** (8998 Hwy. 105, 828/963-5928, www.foscoeminingco.com, $16-212), where 24 kinds of gemstones can be found and the owner, a master goldsmith and stone cutter, will cut and polish the larger gems you find.

GOLF

Around Boone are a number of private golf courses; among the few public courses is **Boone Golf Club** (433 Fairway Dr., 828/264-8760, www.boonegolfclub.com, 18 holes, par 71, Apr.-Nov., greens fees $41-57) has wide, forgiving fairways that are playable for all skill levels and from any tee set. Designed by Ellis Maples in the late 1950s, the course is picturesque and enjoyable to play.

Accommodations

The **Lovill House Inn** (404 Old Bristol Rd., 800/849-9466, www.lovillhouseinn.com, $129-219) is close to the Appalachian State University campus, and it was in the parlor of this 1875 farmhouse that the papers were drawn up that led to the founding of the university. The inn sits on 11 evergreen-shaded acres and is a lovely place to relax and read. The **Smoketree Lodge** (11914 Hwy. 105 S., 800/422-1880, www.smoketree-lodge.com, from $75 summer, from $55 off-season) is another good choice; it's a large hotel with basic but comfortable guest rooms and efficiencies, a large rustic lobby, a nice indoor pool, and saunas.

The **Yonahlossee Resort** (Shulls Mill Rd., 800/962-1986, www.yonahlossee.com, from $129), between Boone and Blowing Rock, is a former girls camp built in the 1920s. The resort has a big stone inn and studio cottages, a fitness center and sauna, tennis courts with a pro shop, and a 75-foot indoor heated pool. **Parkway Cabins** (599 Bamboo Heights, 828/262-3560 or 866/679-3002, www.parkwaycabins.com, $150-350) is just 5 minutes from downtown Boone and 10 minutes from Blowing Rock; it sits at 4,000 feet in elevation, providing a panoramic view of Grandfather Mountain, Beech Mountain, Seven Devils, and other peaks. Most of the cabins sleep four or more, making them perfect for mountain excursions with a group.

Among area chain motels, some good bets are **Fairfield Inn and Suites** (2060 Blowing Rock Rd., 828/268-0677, www.marriott.com, from $79), **Comfort Suites** (1184 Hwy. 105, 828/268-0099, www.choicehotels.com, from $55), **Holiday Inn Express** (1943 Blowing Rock Rd./Hwy. 321 S., 828/264-2451, www.hiexpress.com, from $90), and **Best Western Blue Ridge Plaza** (840 E. King St., 828/266-1100, www.bestwestern.com, from $65).

Food

Boone is a college town and has dining that suits both students and their visiting parents. That means three things must be done well: pizza, breakfast, and moderately priced bistro or steakhouse fare. This town delivers on all counts.

Sunrise Grill (1675 Hwy. 105, 828/262-5400, 6:30am-2pm Mon.-Fri., 7am-3pm Sat.-Sun., around $8) is widely considered the best breakfast place in Boone. It's a regular bacon-and-eggs sort of place with some interesting omelets, tasty grits, and hot coffee, but everything's done well and the staff are friendly. The menu at **Our Daily Bread** (627 W. King St., 828/264-0173, www.ourdailybreadboone.com, 11am-8pm Mon.-Thurs., 11am-10pm Fri.-Sat., noon-6pm Sun., about $10) includes no fewer than 30 specialty sandwiches, from their best-selling Jamaican Turkey Sub to the Fruity Chicken Sammy—chicken salad with shredded apples, red grapes, and walnuts on a fresh croissant. Try their tempeh reuben, a daring mixture of flavors that features marinated tempeh, sauerkraut, swiss cheese, and mustard on rye. It sounds outrageous but it works. Our Daily Bread also makes a variety of fresh soups and meat and veggie chilies every day.

Melanie's Food Fantasy (664 W. King St., 828/263-0300, www.melaniesfoodfantasy. com, 8am-2pm Mon.-Sat., 8:30am-2:30pm Sun.) is worth a special trip to Boone. The breakfast menu is nothing short of spectacular, with a variety of whole-grain waffles, pancakes, and french toast ($6-9), all sorts of fancy omelets (try the spinach, garlic, provolone, and swiss, $7), and enough options to keep both carnivores and vegetarians full. Lunch at Melanie's is every bit as good.

The **Dan'l Boone Inn** (130 Hardin St., 828/264-8657, http://danlbooneinn.com, hours vary, dinner $17 adults, $10 ages 9-11, $8 ages 6-8, $6 ages 4-5, free under age 4, breakfast $10 adults, $7 ages 9-11, $6 ages 6-8, $5 ages 4-5, free under age 4) serves old-time country food family style. Despite the complicated pricing system, the food is straightforward good. At breakfast you can feast on country ham and red-eye gravy, stewed apples, and grits; at dinner, there's fried chicken, country-style steak, ham biscuits, and lots of vegetable sides.

For good college-town pizza, **Capone's Pizza** (454 W. King St., 828/265-1886, http:// caponesboone.com, 11am-10:30pm Mon.-Thurs., 11am-11pm Fri.-Sat., noon-10:30pm Sun., $8-22) hits the spot. The staff is funny and friendly and make a good pie. You can go with the standard peperoni and cheese or go off the rails with some odd pizza topping combinations. Try Big Joe's Buffalo Pizza, with spicy sauce, blue cheese, buffalo chicken, crumbled bacon, and red onion; it's different and delicious.

The **Gamekeeper Restaurant and Bar** (3005 Shull's Mill Rd., 828/963-7400, www.gamekeeper-nc.com, bar from 5pm daily, dinner from 5pm Wed.-Sun., $24-41) is tucked away between Boone and Blowing Rock at the Yonahlossee Resort. Since opening, this restaurant has built and maintained a reputation for high-quality meals using exotic meats. It's common to see ostrich, venison, bison, boar, and the like on the frequently changing menu. Don't miss the bourbon bread pudding and white Russian cheesecake—or the seemingly endless wine list ($20-215 per bottle).

Joy Bistro (115 New Market Centre, 828/265-0500, www.joybistroboone.com, dinner from 5:30pm Tues.-Sun., $12-35) is Southern-French cuisine—not from the south of France but rather a fusion of French techniques and Southern flavors. You'll find a lot of ingredients from local and regional food producers, such as in the baby beet salad, which uses beets from a local farmer, and the ravioli, made fresh by a local pasta maker. Standards like the filet mignon (served with Boursin cheese mashed potatoes and finished with a roasted garlic and chive compound butter) are fantastic, and dishes like the scallops au poivre or lamb loin chop deliver big flavor.

NORTH OF BOONE
Sports and Recreation

The small scenic New River town of Todd is a slow, winding 12 miles north of Boone. Brand-new **Elk Knob State Park** (5564 Meat Camp Rd., Todd, 828/297-7261, http:// ncparks.gov, office 8am-5pm Mon.-Fri., park 8am-6pm daily Nov.-Feb., 8am-8pm daily Mar.-May and Sept.-Oct., 8am-9pm daily June-Aug.) is one of the newest parks in the North Carolina State Park system, and some areas are still under development. Elk Knob is the second-highest peak in Watauga County at 5,520 feet; a 1.9-mile hike takes you to the summit. Nature photographers love it here as wildflowers carpet the forest floor in spring and summer, providing breathtaking photo opportunities. Backcountry campers love it too, as a handful of primitive campsites, including a nice backcountry spot, accommodate only a few campers ($10-13/night, reservations required at improved campsite). The sites are a short hike in: The closest is about one mile and the farthest about two miles.

Mount Jefferson State Natural Area (1481 Mt. Jefferson State Park Rd., Jefferson, 336/246-9653, http://ncparks.gov, 9am-5pm Nov.-Feb., 9am-7pm Mar.-Apr. and Sept.-Oct., 9am-8pm May-Aug.) preserves a peak that was known long ago as Panther Mountain, the result of a legend about a panther that killed a child here. Mount Jefferson has a forbidding countenance, with outcroppings of black volcanic rock, and on the north slope is a stunted forest of wind-daunted aspen and maple, perhaps giving credence to another legend about caves under the mountain that were once stopovers for enslaved people on their way to freedom. Hiking trails, ranging from gentle to strenuous, wend along the crests and up to the peak, through laurel thickets and virgin red oak forests.

New River State Park (park office on Wagoner Access Rd./Hwy. 1590, east of Jefferson, 336/982-2587, http://ncparks.gov, visitors center 8am-5pm Mon.-Fri., 10am-4pm Sat.-Sun., park 8am-6pm daily Nov.-Feb., 8am-8pm daily Mar.-Apr. and Sept.-Oct., 8am-9pm daily May-Aug.) threads along what is, despite the name, one of the oldest rivers in the world. The beautiful New River is popular for canoeing along the North Carolina stretch; farther north in West Virginia, it narrows and becomes a white-water paradise. Here it's a gentle ride through some stunning countryside. Water is highest in May-June, lowest in August-September. Access points are located all along the river. There are also many campsites, both canoe-in and drive-in; some have access to hot showers and restrooms ($25) while others have no facilities ($13).

New River Outfitters (10725 U.S. 221 N., Jefferson, 800/982-9190, www.canoethenew.com) offers canoe runs ranging from one hour to six days as well as tubing trips along the New. They operate from the old New River General Store, where you can buy mountain honey, hoop cheese, and local crafts. **Zaloo's Canoes** (3874 Hwy. 16 S., Jefferson, 800/535-4027, www.zaloos.com) is another long-established area outfitter that also offers canoe and raft trips.

GOLF

At **Jefferson Landing** (148 E. Landing Dr., Jefferson, 336/982-7767, www.visitjeffersonlanding.com, 18 holes, par 72, greens fees $59 Mon.-Thurs., $69 Fri.-Sun.

mid-May-mid-Oct., $39 Mon.-Thurs., $49 Fri.-Sun. mid-May-mid-Oct.) you'll find a course designed to challenge golfers. Deceptively easy holes, like Number 16, can coax you into hitting your tee shot too long or too short and put you in a bad position for your second shot. The possibility of year-round play, when the weather cooperates, makes it appealing in shoulder seasons.

Mountain Aire (1396 Fairway Ridge Dr., West Jefferson, 336/877-4716, www.mountainaire.com, 18 holes, par 72, greens fees $31-37 Apr.-May 19, $32-49 May 20-Oct., $25-30 Nov.-Dec.) uses the natural terrain to create a course that plays longer than it measures (5,900 yards, give or take). The course opens with a par 3, but Number 2 takes you straight uphill. You'll fight your way uphill on Number 4, a long par 5 that plays even longer. On Number 5, you get a little break, so take in the mountain views.

Accommodations

There aren't a whole lot of choices in the area north of Boone, but a solid option is **Doughton-Hall Bed and Breakfast** (12668 Hwy. 18, Laurel Springs, 336/359-2341, http://doughtonhall.webs.com), named in part for an important but often forgotten member of the U.S. House of Representatives, Robert Doughton. He was responsible for ensuring the Blue Ridge Parkway ran through North Carolina rather than an alternate route through Tennessee. The Queen Anne-style home itself dates to the 1890s, and it has been a B&B since the early 1990s. Guest rooms are filled with antiques, but don't be afraid to make use of what you find.

At the **Cabins on Laurel Creek** (BRP milepost 250, 2900 S. Laurel Fork Rd., 336/207-7677, www.cabinsonlaurelcreek.com, $115-650) you'll find a number of quaint but nicely appointed cabins as well as The Lodge, a larger home with multiple bedrooms, a game room, private balconies, and more. Fire pits, outside grills, and porch swings at the standard cabins make it easy to create a cozy base for Parkway exploration.

SOUTH OF BOONE

The **Blue Ridge Parkway** (828/298-0398, www.blueridgeparkway.org) is a stunning bit of roadway, especially south of Boone. There are a number of sights on and near this stretch of the Parkway, including plenty of places to pull off for pictures or exploration, and marked trails meandering up and down the mountain and into thick woods, rocky coves, and waterfalls. Stop at the wide spots in the road to photograph a tree in a field, a herd of cows grazing, a trail wandering into the shadows of the trees, or the mountains marching off into the distance.

◖ Grandfather Mountain

Grandfather Mountain (U.S. 221, 2 miles north of Linville, 828/733-4337, www.grandfather.com, $18 adults, $15 over age 60, $8 ages 6-12, free under age 5, 8am-7pm daily summer, 9am-6pm daily spring and fall, 9am-5pm daily winter, weather permitting), at a lofty 5,964 feet, is not the highest mountain in North Carolina, but it is one of the most beautiful. The highest peak in the Blue Ridge

Mountains (the higher Mount Mitchell is in the Black Mountains), Grandfather is a United Nations-designated Biosphere Reserve. Privately owned for decades though open to the public, Grandfather Mountain has remained a great expanse of deep forests and wildlife with many hiking trails. The main attraction is the summit and the **Mile High Swinging Bridge.** It is indeed a mile high, and it swings a little in the breeze, but it should be called the "Singing Bridge" because of the somewhat unnerving sound of the constant wind through the steel cables holding it in place. The view from Grandfather Mountain is stunning, and the peak is easily accessible via the scenic road that traces the skyward mile. From the parking lot just below the summit, you can access a number of trails (open during park hours only) that lead to nearby peaks, under the crest of Grandfather, and along nearby ridgelines.

Linn Cove Viaduct

One of the most iconic spots along the Blue Ridge Parkway, the **Linn Cove Viaduct** (BRP

© JASON FRYE

the Mile High Swinging Bridge at Grandfather Mountain

© JASON FRYE

The Blue Ridge Parkway twists across the Linn Cove Viaduct.

milepost 304.4, a couple of miles from the entrance to Grandfather Mountain) is a bridge-like structure hanging from the side of the mountain in a dizzying S-curve. At nearly 1,300 feet long, this amazing feat of engineering makes you feel like you might just fly off into space if you lose focus. A pair of viewing areas about 0.25 miles from either end of the viaduct give you the chance to stretch your legs and snap a few pictures of this amazing part of the road.

Grandfather Mountain looming above offers great photo opportunities, as does the road itself when it ducks back into one deep cove and emerges on the side of the mountain opposite, snaking away into the trees; the sight of it, this lifelike concrete and asphalt peeking out from the trees and following the contours of the mountains, is enough to take your breath away.

Linville Gorge

The deepest gorge in the United States, **Linville Gorge** is located near Blue Ridge Parkway milepost 316 in a 12,000-acre federally designated

Wilderness Area. It's genuine wilderness, and some of the hollers in this preserve are so remote that they still shelter virgin forests—a rarity even in these wild mountains. **Linville Falls** (BRP milepost 316) is one of the most photographed places in North Carolina, a spectacular series of cataracts that fall crashing into the gorge. It can be seen from several short trails that depart from the **Linville Falls Visitors Center** (BRP milepost 316, 828/765-1045, 10am-5pm daily Apr. 25-Nov. 2). The National Park Service operates the **Linville Falls Campground** (BRP milepost 316.3, 828/765-2681, www.linevillefalls.com, $20) near the falls. Tent and RV sites are interspersed, and water and flush toilets are available May-October.

Linville Gorge has some great climbing spots, including Table Rock, parts of which are popular with beginning climbers and other parts of which should only be attempted by experts. Other extremely strenuous options are the Hawksbill cliff face and Sitting Bear rock pillar. Speak to the folks at the visitors center or at **Fox Mountain Guides** (3228 Asheville Hwy., Pisgah Forest, 888/284-8433, www.foxmountainguides), a Hendersonville-area service that leads climbs in the gorge, to determine which of Linville Gorge's many climbing faces would be best suited to your skill level.

Orchard at Altapass

At milepost 328 on the Blue Ridge Parkway, the **Orchard at Altapass** (1025 Orchard Rd., Spruce Pine, 888/765-9531, www.altapassorchard.org, 10am-6pm Wed.-Mon. Nov.-Sept., 10am-6pm daily Oct.) is much more than an orchard, although it does produce apples in abundance. The land on which the orchard grows has been settled since the 1790s, when Charlie "Cove" McKinney and his large family lived here. McKinney had four wives—at the same time—who bore him 30 sons and a dozen daughters. An early chronicler of local history wrote that the four wives "never had no words bout his havin so many womin. If it ware these times thar would be har pulled." Many of the McKinneys are buried on the mountain. Around the turn of the 20th century, the land became an orchard, and in its best years produced 125,000 bushels of apples. To get a sense of how many apples that would have been, consider that today's standard for a bushel of apples is 48 pounds.

Today, the Orchard at Altapass continues to turn out wonderful apples. It is also a favorite music venue in this region. Country, bluegrass, old-time, and gospel musicians as well as artists in a variety of other styles perform at the orchard on the weekend. There is a staggering amount of musical talent in these mountains, and the Orchard at Altapass is a showcase of local treasures.

Penland School of Crafts

In the 1920s, Lucy Morgan, a teacher at a local Episcopal school, and her brother embarked on a mission to help the women of the North Carolina mountains gain some hand in their own economic well-being. Equipping several households in the Penland area with looms, they touched off a local cottage industry in weaving, which quickly centralized and grew into the Penland School, a center for craft instruction and production. Several "folk schools" sprouted in the southern Appalachians in that era, most of them the projects of idealistic Northerners wanting to aid the benighted mountaineers. The Penland School, however, has the distinction of being one of the few such institutions that was truly home-grown, as Miss Lucy was herself a child of the rural Carolina highlands. Today, the **Penland School of Crafts** (off Penland Rd., Penland, 828/765-2359, www.penland.org) is an arts instruction center of international renown. More than 1,000 people, from beginners to professionals, enroll in Penland's one-, two-, and eight-week courses every year to learn about crafts in many different media. Tours of the workshops (Tues. and Thurs. Apr.-Dec., reservations required) are available, and the school operates a beautiful shop, the **Penland Gallery** (Conley Ridge Rd., 828/765-6211, www.penland.org, 10am-5pm Tues.-Sat., noon-5pm Sun.), where the work of many of the school's instructors and students can be purchased.

◖ Mount Mitchell

At 6,684 feet, **Mount Mitchell** (accessible from BRP milepost 355, near Burnsville, 828/675-4611, http://ncparks.gov) is the highest mountain east of South Dakota. It is the pinnacle of the Black Mountain range, a 15-mile-long J-shaped ridge that was formerly considered one mountain. Now that the various peaks are designated as separate mountains, 6 of them are among the 10 highest in the eastern United States. Elisha Mitchell, for whom the mountain is named, is buried at the summit. He was one of North Carolina's first great scholars, a geologist and botanist who taught at the University of North Carolina in Chapel Hill. His skill as a scientist is demonstrated by his 1830s calculation of the height of the peak that now bears his name; using the technology of the day, the height that he estimated was within 12 feet of today's measurement. In the 1850s he became embroiled in a controversy when Senator Thomas Clingman, one of his former students, disputed the calculation. On a return trip to remeasure Mount Mitchell, Elisha Mitchell fell from the top of a waterfall (now Mitchell Falls) and drowned in the water below. The rivalry recalls the climactic moment when Sherlock Holmes and his nemesis, Dr. Moriarty, fall to their deaths from the top of a waterfall—although in this case, Senator Clingman went on to live another 40 years. He also has a mountain named for him, Clingmans Dome, a mere 41 feet shorter, that glares up at Mount Mitchell from the Tennessee state line.

Mount Mitchell State Park (http://ncparks. gov) is not only a place to get an amazing panoramic view—up to 85 miles in clear weather—it also has an education center, a restaurant, a gift shop, and nine campsites (late Apr.-late Oct. $20, $15 seniors, off-season $12).

(Brown Mountain Lights

One of North Carolina's most enduring mysteries are the **Brown Mountain Lights.** These mysterious orbs are seen floating in the air on some evenings around Brown Mountain, along the Burke County-Caldwell County line. A number of official agencies have studied the phenomenon, and the U.S. Geological Survey determined the orbs may be the reflection of the headlights of cars and trains in the valley below, completely ignoring the fact that the lights have been seen since at least 1833. The Brown Mountain Lights are believed by many to be supernatural. One legend, related in the song "Brown Mountain Lights," says the lights are the lanterns of a hunter lost in these woods and the dutiful slave who lost his life searching for his master. Ghost fanciers will be delighted to know that the Brown Mountain Lights can be observed by visitors from the Lost Cove overlook on the southeast side of the Blue Ridge Parkway near milepost 310. Try a clear evening in the summer, right around dusk, and you might see them.

Other Sights

Since the early 1920s, the master weavers of

© JASON FRYE

This is a great place to watch for the Brown Mountain Lights.

the **Crossnore Weaving Room** (Crossnore School, 100 DAR Dr., Crossnore, 828/733-4660, www.crossnoreweavers.org, gallery hours 9am-5pm Mon.-Sat.) have produced beautiful textiles—afghans, rugs and runners, baby blankets, and scarves—that they've sold to benefit the Crossnore School. Founded in the 1910s for orphaned and disadvantaged children, the Crossnore School is today an actively operating children's home for western North Carolina kids who have no guardians, and for some local children who live with their families but whose educational needs are best served by the structure that the school offers. The fame of the weaving room is much more than a fund-raising program. The skills of the Crossnore Weavers are highly regarded, and the sales gallery is an essential stop for anyone interested in North Carolina's fine crafts.

The **Mountain Gateway Museum** (102 Water St., Old Fort, 828/668-9259, http://mountaingatewaymuseum.org, noon-5pm Mon., 9am-5pm Tues.-Sat., 2pm-5pm Sun., free) presents the cultural history of the North Carolina mountains from the arrival of the first Europeans, through the time before the Revolution when Old Fort was the wild frontier, to the present day. The museum hosts events throughout the year, showcasing all manner of traditional arts from this region.

A complete visit to the Blue Ridge Mountains includes more than looking at their outsides: **Linville Caverns** (U.S. 221, between Linville and Marion, south of BRP milepost 317, 800/419-0540, www.linville-caverns.com, 9am-4:30pm daily Mar. and Nov., 9am-5pm daily Apr.-May and Sept.-Oct., 9am-6pm daily June-Aug., 9am-4:30pm Sat.-Sun. Dec.-Feb., $7.50 adults, $6.50 over age 61, $5.50 ages 5-12) is one of the venerable underground attractions of the Southern mountains. The natural limestone caverns feature all sorts of strange rock formations, underground trout streams, and, of course, a gift shop. Don't worry if you're mildly claustrophobic; the caverns are much bigger than you might think.

Sports and Recreation

Lake James State Park (Hwy. 126, 5 miles northeast of Marion, 828/584-7728, http://ncparks.gov) comprises 6,500-acre Lake James and its 150 miles of shoreline. Created around 1920, the artificial lake is in a graceful mountain setting among hemlocks and rhododendrons. Canoes ($5 per hour) can be rented, and there are campsites (Mar. 15-Nov. 30, $20) with restrooms, showers, and drinking water nearby.

GOLF

Linville Falls Golf Club (17677 U.S. 221, Marion, 828/756-4653, 18 holes, par 71, greens fees $35 Mon.-Thurs., $38 Fri.-Sun.) features a few water hazards, but none like its namesake waterfall. Golf legend Lee Trevino designed this course, which opened for play in 1995, to have firm, fast fairways that make the course play shorter than it actually is, a rarity for mountain courses. The placement of water hazards on some holes make aggressive play both risky and very rewarding if your ball placement is extremely accurate.

The **Linville Golf Club** (83 Club Lane, Linville, 828/733-9493, www.eseeola.com, 18 holes, par 72, greens fees $125, same-day replay $63) has been challenging golfers in these parts since 1924. Donald Ross designed the course, which was contoured and graded originally with a mule-and-pan system, and any maintenance done over the years has made concerted efforts to keep the integrity of the original design. The greens here are small and difficult, requiring excellent approach play and patience. *Golfweek* magazine called the par-4 number 3 one of the "Greatest 100 Holes in Golf," and named Linville one of the best courses you can play in North Carolina.

Accommodations

Linville's **Eseeola Lodge** (175 Linville Ave., 800/742-6717, www.eseeola.com, from $269) has been in the business of luxury mountain vacations for more than 100 years. The first lodge was built in the 1890s, along with a nine-hole golf course. The original lodge burned down and was replaced by the present lodge; in 1924, Donald Ross was engaged to build the championship golf course now known as the Linville Golf Club. Eseeola Lodge offers a complex but splendid array of lodging packages, with breakfast and dinner at the Lodge's restaurant included, and depending on your predilections, tee times at the Linville Golf Club, spa services, and even croquet lessons.

Scattered around a 92-acre private nature preserve in Marion, the six **Cottages at Spring House Farm** (219 Haynes Rd., Marion, 877/738-9798, www.springhousefarm.com, from $245) are quiet hideaways with eco-conscious comforts. The proprietors, who live in a historic farmhouse on the property, stock the cabin kitchens with fresh bread, eggs, and local honey. Each cottage has an outdoor hot tub and access to pond-side gazebos and hiking trails.

Food

Famous Louise's Rockhouse Restaurant (23175 Rockhouse Lane, Linville Falls, near BRP milepost 321, 828/765-2702, 6am-8pm daily), built in 1936 with stones taken from the Linville River, is not a large restaurant, but the dining room is spread out over three counties: The lines of Burke, McDowell, and Avery Counties meet on this exact spot, and customers, for reasons of loyalty or legality, often have preferences about where to take their repast. Famous Louise's is owned by a mother and daughter, and Louise, the mom, is a cook of some renown. The fare is traditional and homemade—the pimento cheese is mixed here, the cornbread and biscuits are whipped up from scratch, and the pot roast stewed at a leisurely simmer. On your way out, pick up a jar or two of Louise's homemade berry jams, probably the best $3 souvenirs to be found in the mountains. You'll find them in the Avery County part of the restaurant.

MORGANTON

Morganton, a charming but often overlooked town on I-40, is actually a vibrant little community with an active arts scene, a handful of good restaurants, and a budding wine scene.

Downtown, stop in at **Kalā** (100 W. Union St., 828/437-1806, http://kalagallery.com, 10am-6pm Mon.-Fri., 10am-5pm Sat.), pronounced "kal-AY," a gallery of local and regional artists. The beautiful work here includes functional pieces like cutting boards and turned-wood pens as well as fun folk art like bugs made from old electronic and mechanical components, and some fantastic blown and fused glass pieces. **Signature Studio and Gallery** (106 W. Union St., 828/437-6095, 10am-4pm Tues.-Sat.) is an active art studio and gallery dedicated to serving the creative-expression needs and learning opportunities for adults with intellectual and developmental disabilities. The work is incredible, and many of the resident artists have shown nationally and internationally.

Along a 30-mile stretch of I-40 east and west of Morganton is the **Catawba Valley Wine Trail.** A recent and growing addition to North Carolina's vineyard and winery population, there are six wineries to visit, each making wine in different styles and geared toward different palates. I found **Silver Fork Winery** (5000 Patton Rd., off I-40 exit 94, 828/391-8783, www.silverforkwinery.com) to have a beautiful tasting room and some good wine. Their cabernet sauvignon was especially nice, as was their rosé. Taste a few and pick your favorite bottle, then enjoy it on their shaded patio or stick around for a movie or some live music in the summer months.

Golf

Quaker Meadows (826 N. Green St., 828/437-2677, www.qmgolf.com, 18 holes, par 71, greens fees $38, includes cart) has been challenging golfers with numerous water hazards and sloping greens since the 1960s. It is a pretty course, and its history is quite interesting: The "Over Mountain Boys" met here in 1780 before marching to Kings Mountain, a key battle in the Revolutionary War.

Food

For such a small town, dining in Morganton is surprisingly good. **Wisteria Southern Gastropub** (108 E. Meeting St., 828/475-6200,

© JASON FRYE

The tasting room at Silver Fork Winery boasts an incredible view.

http://wisteriagastropub.com, lunch 11:30am-2:30pm Tues.-Fri., dinner 5pm-9pm Tues.-Sun., brunch 11:30am-4:30pm Sun., pub 5pm-2am Wed.-Sat., 5pm-midnight Sun., lunch $5-13, dinner and pub fare $6-19, brunch $5-24) has been making waves with their seasonal menus and quality preparations. It's a cozy place, serving familiar dishes that have been turned up a notch. The trout cakes and deviled eggs three ways are twists on classics, as are the scotch eggs and the chicken and waffles.

Root and Vine (139 W. Union St., 828/433-1540, http://rootandvinerestaurant.com, lunch 11am-2:30pm Tues.-Fri., dinner 5pm-9:30pm Tues.-Sat., lunch $8-10, dinner $17-25) is a hip, slightly more upscale place than other venues in Morganton. The menu changes with some frequency, but entrées are grilled on a wood fire and draw on all sorts of culinary inspiration: vindaloo curry with shrimp, scallops, mussels, or organic tofu; grilled North Carolina mountain trout served with tasso ham gravy and collard greens; and

the seared duck breast with pork belly and an orange-raspberry coulis. The cocktails are good, and their wine list is well done for a restaurant this size. When the weather is mild, take your dinner on the patio and dine alfresco.

GETTING THERE AND AROUND

There are no major airports in this region, but two are reasonably close: **Asheville Regional Airport** (AVL, 61 Terminal Dr., Asheville, 828/684-2226, www.flyavl.com), with regularly scheduled domestic flights, and the larger **Piedmont Triad International Airport** (GSO, 1000 Ted Johnson Pkwy., 336/665-5600, www.flyfrompti.com) in Greensboro. The major highway, I-77, runs north-south along the edge of the mountains west of Mount Airy. Two other major interstate highways run just beyond the boundaries of the northern mountains: I-40, to the east and south, runs from Winston-Salem to Asheville, and I-26, to the south and west, runs from Asheville to Johnson City, Tennessee. U.S. 321 and U.S. 421 are the main roads, and U.S. 19 winds through the southwest edge of the area covered in this chapter.

The **Blue Ridge Parkway** follows some of its most beautiful miles in the northern mountains and connects several important towns. While it's probably the most fun and scenic route, it is not the most efficient if you're trying to cover a lot of ground quickly. The maximum speed limit is 45 mph, and because of weather, traffic, and twists and turns, you can count on driving slower than that most of the time.

Watauga County, which includes the towns of Blowing Rock, Boone, Deep Gap, and Zionville, is covered by **AppalCart Bus Routes** (828/264-2278, www.appalcart.

com). Riders must make reservations to ride, and the service is only available Monday-Friday, but the fares, which vary by route, are much cheaper than driving. AppalCart also runs routes to Charlotte, Winston-Salem, Hickory, Lenoir, and Wilkesboro, with fares ranging $10-50 round-trip. Another way to get to and from the area is via the **Mountaineer Express Bus** (336/662-0002 or 800/588-7787, www.horizoncoachnc.org), with routes among Greensboro, Winston-Salem, Yadkinville, Wilkesboro, and Boone. The highest-price one-way trip, Greensboro to Boone, is only $13, and fares are half-price for students, wheelchair users, and passengers over age 60.

In the Shadow of the Blue Ridge

The foothills of the Blue Ridge are among the most beautiful stretches of countryside in North Carolina. You'll find the iconic Pilot Mountain, a mesa-like monolith standing alone in a wide valley, drawing the eye as soon as you come down off the mountain from Virginia. This is also home to part of the Yadkin Valley Wine Trail, an American Viticultural Area comprising 1.4 million acres of land, includes three dozen local vineyards and wineries and is the center of viticulture in North Carolina.

The land is incredibly rich: Just as the mountain streams bring nutrient-laden water to the valley floors, the valley fosters what we think of today as "mountain music." Several major festivals are held here in the spring and summer, most famously North Wilkesboro's annual MerleFest, which has become one the country's most important music festivals, drawing major bluegrass, country, old-time, and Americana artists for a weekend of outdoor performances. Mount Airy is a community of many charms, but it's best known for music and *The Andy Griffith Show*. Since the 1920s, old-time and bluegrass musicians from the countryside between Mount Airy and Galax, Virginia (which has an incredible festival of its

own, the Old Fiddlers Convention), have been known as some of the greatest string-band artists. Aficionados of the genre who can recognize the cadences of string-band and bluegrass music can pick out a fiddler or banjo player from this region almost immediately, and the best can tell you which side of the Blue Ridge—Virginia or North Carolina—they're from. From Mount Airy west to Wilkesboro, north to Galax, Virginia, and east to Floyd, Virginia, you'll find that 20-something old-time and bluegrass musicians number almost as many as musicians in their 70s. In the world of folk and traditional music, this is something of an anomaly, but it speaks to the genre's deep and strong roots.

Mount Airy is also a friendly, comfortable town, and its annual Fiddlers Convention is one of the best events on the old-time music summer festival circuit. To the south, in the town of Union Grove, another important fiddlers convention, known as Fiddlers Grove, happens every year a week or two before the Mount Airy festival.

Hanging Rock State Park, near Danbury, is one of the state's favorite climbing spots. For outdoor adventurers, the foothills conceal

© JOHN HAYES/COURTESY WILKES COMMUNITY COLLEGE

Mando Mania performs in front of a large audience at MerleFest.

environments as wild and challenging as any you'll find in the deep mountains.

WILKESBORO AND NORTH WILKESBORO
◖ MerleFest

It began as a small folk festival more than 20 years ago, but **MerleFest** (www.merlefest.org, late Apr., $40 per day, multiday packages $135-260) has grown into one of the premier roots-music events in the country. It was founded in honor of Merle Watson, the son of legendary guitarist Doc Watson. Merle, also a guitarist, died unexpectedly in 1985 in a tractor accident, cutting short an influential career. Doc Watson, who grew up in the nearby community of Deep Gap, was the festival's ceremonial host until his death in 2012, and though his absence is deeply felt by musicians and fans alike, MerleFest is as strong and successful as ever, speaking to his lasting legacy in bluegrass, roots, and Appalachian music. MerleFest draws thousands of visitors every year for many of the top-name performers in folk, country,

and bluegrass music. Recent headliners have included Steep Canyon Rangers, Chatham County Line, Sam Bush, Jim Avett, The Avett Brothers (Jim's sons), and Tift Merritt. With multiple stages and dozens of artists, there's a great deal of musical variety to sample.

Springtime in the mountains can be changeful; some years it's boiling hot and sunny at MerleFest, other times as damp and raw as winter, and sometimes it's both by turns. If you're traveling through the northern mountains during MerleFest, keep in mind that all the motels within an hour's drive of North Wilkesboro, and probably farther, will be booked solid, so be sure to reserve a room well in advance. Tenting and RV camping are available on the festival grounds. Before you pack a cooler full of adult refreshments that may be common at other music festivals, note that tobacco, alcohol, and pets are not allowed at MerleFest.

Other Entertainment and Events
Follow Highway 901 southeast out of Wilkesboro to the little town of Union Grove,

NORTHERN BLUE RIDGE

SIAMESE TWINS CHANG AND ENG

Andy Griffith may have put Mount Airy on the map and became its favorite son, but he's not the only famous person to call this small town in the Blue Ridge foothills home. In the middle of the 19th century, two of the most famous men in the world lived on a bucolic farm in rural Surry County, just outside Mount Airy. Chang and Eng were both born in Siam (now Thailand) in 1811, joined at the sternum by a cartilaginous band of flesh. Today, it would have been a relatively simple operation to separate these so-called "Siamese twins," but in 1811 they were lucky not to have been killed in the birthing bed. When they were teenagers, they began to tour the world, eventually becoming one of the top draws at P. T. Barnum's shows.

During their extensive travels across the United States, they took a liking to North Carolina, and when they got burned out on show business, around the age of 30, they decided to settle in Wilkesboro. Once in North Carolina, they adopted the last name Bunker. Chang fell in love with local woman, Addie Yates, and soon Eng began courting her older sister, Sally. The four married and moved in together, raising a very large, very close family—Eng and Sally had 11 children, Chang and Addie had 10. A good number of their descendants live in the area today.

In many ways, Chang and Eng were like one person. On learning English, they immediately referred to themselves as "I," and they were rarely observed to speak to each other, as if it were unnecessary. In one of countless medical experiments they underwent, the examining doctor tickled one brother, causing the other brother not to laugh but to become angry. In other ways they were very different, and as differences between siblings often do, it caused some degree of unpleasantness between them. Chang was temperamental and vivid while Eng was reticent and contemplative. More dangerously, Chang enjoyed a drink and Eng found joy in gambling. Sometimes they had bitter arguments, which escalated into fistfights on more than one occasion. Perhaps it's best not to dwell on each couple's conjugal relations, but their domestic life required plenty of compromise. They divided their time between Chang and Addie's and Eng and Sally's houses, each brother living as the other's houseguest half the time.

Despite the limitations that biology saddled them with, the Bunkers became fairly conventional upper-middle-class farmers, owning a few slaves and sending two sons to fight in the Confederate Army. The Civil War left them in dire financial straits, and in 1870 they took to touring again, heading this time to Europe. On the voyage home, Chang suffered a severe stroke, which didn't kill him but left his health in a bad state. After that, he began to drink heavily, and his health declined rapidly. One January night in 1874, Eng awoke to find his brother dead. Within a few hours, Eng, who had been in excellent health, was also dead. An autopsy showed that Chang died of a cerebral hemorrhage, but Eng's cause of death is, to this day, unknown. Some say he may have died of fright, and others say it was a broken heart.

Chang and Eng Bunker, to whom we owe the existence of the phrase "Siamese twins," are buried at White Plains Baptist Church (506 Old Hwy. 601), just south of Mount Airy.

home of two great local music institutions, one a year-round venue and one an annual festival. The **Cook Shack** (Hwy. 901, 2 miles west of I-77, Union Grove, 704/539-4353) is a little country store and grill that has been hosting live bluegrass, old-time, and country music for more than 40 years. Owners Myles and Pal Ireland open the Cook Shack early Saturday morning for a community jam session that begins at 8am—and for musicians to get up that early on a Saturday, you know this place has to be special. There are also concerts throughout the year, including evenings midweek, so this is a great place to catch touring bands between stops in Asheville and the Triangle. Come to listen or to play, and have a burger or a livermush sandwich between tunes.

Union Grove is also one of the most

important festival sites on both the old-time and bluegrass summer festival circuit. The **Fiddler's Grove Ole Time Fiddlers and Bluegrass Convention** (late May, Fiddlers Grove Campground, Union Grove, 828/478-3735, www.fiddlersgrove.com, $5 per day, camping $15) has taken place every year since 1924. Hundreds of musicians and fans come every year, camping at the festival or staying nearby, to jam with friends and hear some of the best old-time and bluegrass music you'll find anywhere.

Food

North Wilkesboro's **Brushy Mountain Smokehouse and Creamery** (201 Wilkesboro Blvd., 336/667-9464, www.brushymtnsmokehouse.com, 11am-9pm Mon. and Wed.-Sat., 11am-2pm Sun., around $15) is famous for its pulled pork barbecue and country sides (biscuits, fried okra, baked apples), but it's also a great ice cream shop. The ice cream is made here, and they bake their own waffle cones, so it's as fresh as it can be. Fried apple pie, cobbler, and ice cream pie are all available by the slice.

YADKIN VALLEY WINE TRAIL

The Yadkin Valley stretches from the Virginia state line down past Winston-Salem and includes stretches of both the Blue Ridge foothills and the Piedmont. The terrain, climates, and microclimates are remarkably similar to that of France's Burgundy and Italy's Piedmont, two areas where viticulture has thrived for centuries. Winemakers discovered that North Carolina's soil was ideal for a number of familiar varietals, including the sweeter native muscadine and scuppernong grapes. There are three dozen vineyards in this 1.4-million-acre American Viticultural Area, most within an easy drive of Elkin, Mount Airy, and Winston-Salem.

Raffaldini Vineyards and Winery (450 Groce Rd., Ronda, 336/835-9463, www.raffaldini.com, tours 1 and 4pm Wed.-Sun., tasting room 11am-5pm Mon. and Wed.-Sat., noon-5pm Sun.) has a stunning Tuscan villa-style tasting room that overlooks 27 acres of

Raffaldini Winery's tasting room

vines. There are 10 wines to sample and purchase in the tasting room. The Vermentino Riserva 2011 is particularly good, as is their Montepulciano, which sells out quickly. After a tasting and tour, grab your favorite bottle and a bite to eat—they have a nice selection of antipasti on hand—and enjoy it on the terrace overlooking the vines and the valley.

McRitchie Winery and Ciderworks (315 Thurmond Post Office Rd., Thurmond, 336/874-3003, www.mcritchiewine.com, noon-5pm Thurs.-Sun.) has nine wines, including one blackberry wine that's sweet but interesting, and a pair of ciders. Their wines are fair, but their cider, which comes in semisweet and dry, is intriguing because it's sparkling, and they use heirloom apples that have been grown in the area for many years. The vineyard and kitchen garden is operated as sustainably as possible using low-impact methods that other wineries have yet to adopt.

Shelton Vineyards (286 Cabernet Lane, Dobson, 336/366-4724, www.sheltonvineyards.com, tasting room 10am-6pm Mon.-Sat., noon-6pm Sun. Mar.-Oct., 10am-5pm Mon.-Sat., noon-5pm Sun. Nov.-Feb.) is a perennial North Carolina favorite, available at most grocery stores across the state. They offer tours and tastings ($5 pp) on the half hour, or elevate your tasting to the Reserve Tasting (noon, 2pm, and 4pm Fri., 2pm and 4pm Sat.-Sun., $20), which includes a tasting of Shelton's Reserve wines and a souvenir crystal wine glass. Be sure to try their dry riesling and port; they're one of the only vineyards that makes port.

While you're at Shelton Vineyards, grab a meal, not just a snack, at **Harvest Grill** (336/366-3590, 11am-9pm Mon.-Thurs., 11am-10pm Fri.-Sat. year-round, 11am-6pm Sun. Mar.-Oct., 11am-5pm Sun. Nov.-Feb., $14-35). This bistro serves what the chef calls "sophisticated comfort food," featuring many North Carolina ingredients. Try the Cornmeal Dusted Rainbow Trout, the Crispy Cornbread Crab Cakes with Texas Pete Tartar Sauce, or the Citrus Grille North Carolina Black Grouper. They serve a number of vegetarian and gluten-free options.

Round Peak Vineyards (765 Round Peak Church Rd., Mount Airy, 336/352-5595, www.roundpeak.com, noon-5pm Sun.-Thurs., noon-8pm Fri., 11am-6pm Sat. mid-Mar.-May and Sept.-mid-Jan., noon-5pm Sun.-Thurs., noon-8pm Fri., 11am-sunset Sat. June-Aug., noon-8pm Fri., 11am-6pm Sat., noon-5pm Sun. mid-Jan.-mid-Mar.) has 13 acres of vineyards producing 10 French and Italian varietals. Unlike some of the larger vineyards in the Yadkin Valley, Round Peak makes wine using only grapes grown in its own vineyards. On Saturday during summer there are concerts and tastings, lawn games, and a number of special events. Round Peak is dog-friendly, and they have an area set aside for your four-legged traveling companion to stretch out and play while you taste wine.

Accommodations and Food

To really tour the wine country, you'll need to spend a night or two. **The Rockford Bed and Breakfast** (4872 Rockford Rd., Dobson, 800/561-6652, www.rockfordbedandbreakfast.com, $119-139) is a beautiful mid-19th-century farmhouse south of Mount Airy in Dobson, convenient to many of the Yadkin Valley wineries.

At **Frog Holler Cabins** (564 E. Walker Rd., Elkin, 336/526-2661, www.froghollercabins.com, $95-145) you can stay in a well-appointed cabin with a fireplace and a hot tub overlooking Big Elkin Creek. Three cabins, The Cottage, Hawks Nest, and Mill House, are around 400 square feet and suitable for a couple; Deer Run is a bit bigger and sleeps four. There's plenty of peace and quiet, and they're within 30 minutes of more than two dozen vineyards and wineries. On the property are miles of hiking trails and a fishing pond, but one of the big draws is the fact that you can park and take a tour ($60) of wineries and let Frog Holler be your guide so that everyone can enjoy tasting.

In downtown Elkin, **Twenty One & Main Restaurant and Wine Bar** (102 E. Main St., Elkin, 336/835-6246, www.twentyoneandmain.com, dinner from 5:30pm Tues.-Sat., $10-27, 3-course tasting menu $36, 5-course

$60, wine pairings $4 per course) serves an eclectic menu that changes biweekly. Dishes are meat-heavy, with steaks, lamb, pork, and seafood often taking center stage. Twenty One & Main is an upscale restaurant but unpretentious and quite comfortable. The staff is quick with reliable food recommendations and drink pairings.

MOUNT AIRY AND VICINITY
Sights
In downtown Mount Airy you'll notice 1960s police squad cars, business names that may seem oddly familiar, and cardboard cutouts of Barney Fife peering out from shop windows. Mount Airy is the hometown of Andy Griffith and a mecca for fans of *The Andy Griffith Show*. People who grew up in small towns in the Carolinas and probably in small towns elsewhere recognize their families and neighbors in the fictional residents of Mayberry. The show's inspired writing and acting are a deep well of nostalgia, and its fans are legion. **TAGSRWC** (www.imayberry.com) is an intentionally obtuse acronym for *The Andy Griffith Show* Rerun Watchers Club, the show's international fan club whose hundreds of chapters have names that reference the series, such as "Her First Husband Got Runned Over by a Team of Hogs" (Texas) and "Anxiety Magnifies Fearsome Objects" (Alabama). The Surry Arts Council hosts the citywide **Mayberry Days,** an annual fall festival entering its second decade in which TAGSRWC members, other fans, some of the remaining cast members, and impersonators of Mayberry characters come to town and have a big-eyed time getting haircuts at Floyd's Barbershop, riding in squad cars, and arresting each other.

For a one-of-a-kind view of Mount Airy, hop into a Mayberry squad car to tour all the major sights in town. **Mayberry Squad Car Tours** (625 S. Main St., 336/789-6743, www.tourmayberry.com) leave from "Wally's Service Station" and cost "$35 for a carload."

Finally, two roadside oddities in Mount Airy are not to be missed. At 594 North Andy Griffith Parkway/U.S. 52 stands the **Giant Milk Carton.** This 12-foot-tall metal sculpture now advertises Pet Milk, but since its creation in the 1940s it has also stood as an advertisement for Coble Dairy and Flavo-Rich Milk. At the intersection of U.S. 52 and Starlite Drive stands a **Great Big Man,** a very tall metal service station attendant. He is an old friend to out-of-towners who come to Mount Airy for the fiddlers convention every year, who remember to turn off the highway to get to Veterans Park when they see "the big man."

A little more than 20 miles away in Pinnacle is **Horne Creek Living Historical Farm** (308 Horne Creek Farm Rd., Pinnacle, 336/325-2298, www.nchistoricsites.org, 9am-5pm Tues.-Sat., free). The farm life of the Hauser family—an ancient clan in this area—is recreated as Thomas and Charlotte Hauser, and their lone daughter and 11 sons, would have experienced it around 1900. Costumed interpreters demonstrate the old ways of farm work while livestock of historic breeds go about their own work, probably not realizing that they're museum docents. The Hausers had an orchard, of which only a single superannuated pear tree remains, but today a new orchard has taken its place. The Southern Heritage Apple Orchard preserves old Southern heirloom species, trees grown from seeds that have been passed down in families for generations.

The Merry-Go-Round Show
Teamed up with WPAQ 740 AM, the Surry Arts Council hosts *The Merry-Go-Round,* the country's third-longest-running live bluegrass and old-time music radio show. Come to the **Earle Theater** (142 N. Main St., Mount Airy, 336/786-2222, www.surryarts.org) for the show (11am-1:30pm Sat.), or show up as early as 9am toting an instrument if you'd like to join in the preshow jam session. It's one of the state's great small-town treats.

Other Entertainment and Events
When you're in the area, tune in to **WPAQ** (AM 740, www.wpaq740.com). For over 60 years WPAQ has provided a venue for live local talent to perform old-time, bluegrass, and gospel

music. To get a really good idea of this community's life, tune in for the live Saturday-morning *The Merry-Go-Round* show, or any other day of the week when you'll hear local call-in shows, old-style country preaching, and more music.

Along with WPAQ, another local institution that has a great deal to do with the vitality of Mount Airy's musical traditions is the **Bluegrass and Old-Time Fiddlers Convention** (631 W. Lebanon St., 336/345-7388, www. mtairyfiddlersconvention.com), held for almost 40 years during the first full weekend in June at Veterans Memorial Park. Thousands of people come to the festival from around the world to play old-time and bluegrass music with their friends and compete in what is a very prestigious competition in this genre. The heart of the action takes place at the hundreds of individual campsites that spring up all over the park in informal jam sessions among old and new friends. It's some of the best old-time music to be heard anywhere.

The **Surry Arts Council** is one of the hubs of artistic activity in the Mount Airy-Surry County area. They sponsor and host many events throughout the year that showcase local talent in drama, visual arts, and especially music. At 7:30pm on the third Saturday of the month, local and regional old-time and bluegrass bands perform in the **Voice of the Blue Ridge Series** ($10 adults, free under age 6) at the Earle Theatre (142 N. Main St., Mount Airy, 336/786-2222).

Across the Virginia state line at Blue Ridge Parkway milepost 213 is the **Blue Ridge Music Center** (276/236-5309, www.blueridgemusic-center.org, museum 10am-5pm daily May-Oct., free, concerts $10, daily midday music free), a museum dedicated to the roots music of the hills in this part of North Carolina and Virginia. Midday Mountain Music concerts (noon-4pm daily, free) give area musicians opportunities to play for a crowd, and regular evening concerts by more established acts draw crowds from all over.

Sports and Recreation

Mount Airy and its neighbors are foothills towns, and you have to drive a little farther west before you start to climb the Blue Ridge. This is why the geographical anomaly of Pilot Mountain is so startling. The 1,400-foot mountain, with a prominent rocky knob at the top, looks like a giant dog's head, or the UHF knob of an old TV set that you could use to tune in *The Andy Griffith Show*. The surrounding **Pilot Mountain State Park** (1792 Pilot Knob Park Rd., Pinnacle, 336/325-2355, http://ncparks.gov) is a beautiful place for hiking, swimming, rock climbing, and rappelling (in designated areas), canoeing on the Yadkin River, and camping (Mar. 15-Nov. 30, $20, $15 over age 61) at one of the 49 designated tent and trailer sites. Each site has a tent pad, a picnic table, and a grill, as well as access to drinking water and hot showers.

A series of 400-foot rock faces extending for two miles are the most striking feature of **Hanging Rock State Park** (Hwy. 2015, 4 miles northwest of Danbury, 336/593-8480, http:// ncparks.gov, 8am-6pm daily Nov.-Feb., 8am-8pm daily Mar.-Apr. and Sept.-Oct., 8am-9pm daily May-Aug.). It's a great place for rock climbing and rappelling (which requires a permit and registration with park staff; climbers must also be finished and out of the park by closing time). You can also hike to waterfalls and beautiful overlooks, and swim in a nearby lake. Hanging Rock State Park has 73 tent and trailer campsites ($13-20), one of which is wheelchair-accessible. Each site has a tent pad, a picnic table, a grill, access to drinking water, and access to a washhouse (mid-Mar.-Nov.) with hot showers and laundry sinks. There are also two-bedroom, four-bed vacation cabins (around $450 weekly summer, $88 daily off-season) for rent. Reserve camping or cabins at least a month in advance with the park office.

Yadkin River Adventures (104 Old Rockford Rd., Rockford, 336/374-5318, www. yadkinriveradventures.com, canoe trips $50/2 hours, $60/4 hours, and $70/6 hours; kayak trips $30/2 hours, $40/4 hours, $50/6 hours) offers rentals of canoes, kayaks, and sit-on-tops, along with shuttle service for full- and half-day paddling adventures. The Class I

Yadkin River is great for paddlers of all ages and experience levels, and it has some beautiful views of Pilot Mountain. Balloon pilots Tony and Claire Colburn lead tours of the Yadkin Valley by hot-air balloon any time of year, weather permitting. **Yadkin Valley Hot Air Balloon Adventures** (336/922-7207, www.balloonadventure.net) requires advance reservations—contact the Colburns for rates and availability; it's an amazing way to see the Carolina foothills.

The centerpiece of **Stone Mountain State Park** (3042 Frank Pkwy., Roaring Gap, 336/957-8185, http://ncparks.gov, office 8am-5pm daily, park 8am-6pm daily Nov.-Feb., 8am-8pm daily Mar.-Apr. and Sept.-Oct., 8am-9pm daily May-Aug.), is the spectacular 600-foot smooth rock face of **Stone Mountain,** This is, of course, a popular spot for rock climbing and rappelling. The park recommends that only experienced climbers attempt the faces in this park. Be sure to register with the park office, and carefully read all park literature about climbing before setting out. Both primitive backpack camping ($12) and family camping in sites that are near a washhouse with hot showers ($25) are available.

Much like the rest of the Blue Ridge Parkway, the section between Boone and the Virginia state line is stunning in any season. In addition to the scenic overlooks with photo opportunities of panoramic views of the valleys and mountains, there are a number of trails and sights. At milepost 238.5 the **Cedar Ridge Trail** is 4.2 miles that are part of a larger trail complex at Doughton Park. Here you can wander trails one to five miles in length, or string together several trails for a challenging 14-mile day hike. Farther north, at milepost 217.5, the **Cumberland Knob Trail** is an easy 0.5 miles that's the perfect way to stretch your legs after a couple of hours in the car. Also at milepost 217.5, the two-mile **Gully Creek Trail** leads across a stream to a small picturesque waterfall.

GOLF

A rare golf course among the pastures and hay fields is the beautiful **Cross Creek Country Club** (1129 Greenhill Rd., 336/789-5131, www.crosscreekcc.com, 18 holes, par 72, greens fees $41 Mon.-Fri., $46 Sat.-Sun. and holidays, 9 holes $23 Mon.-Fri., $25 Sat.-Sun. and holidays, includes cart) in Mount Airy. Course conditions are always fantastic, and the course presents quandaries to golfers of all levels. If you want a fun little par-3 course, head to **Hardy's Custom Golf** (2003 W. Pine St., 336/789-7888, www.hardrockgolf.net, 18 holes, par 54, greens fees $8, with cart $10, 9 holes $5, with cart $8). The course is lighted for play day or night. If the weather isn't cooperating, try the golf simulator (18 holes $25, 9 holes $15) where you can play 40 different world-famous courses, including St. Andrews and Pinehurst.

Accommodations

In Mount Airy, try **Quality Inn** (2136 Rockford St., 336/789-2000, www.qualityinn.com, from $70), **Holiday Inn Express** (1320 Ems Dr., 336/719-1731, www.hiexpress.com, from $80, pets allowed), and **Hampton Inn** (2029 Rockford St., 336/789-5999, www.hamptoninn.com, from $100).

Pilot Knob Inn Bed and Breakfast (361 New Pilot Knob Lane, Pinnacle, 336/325-2502, www.pilotknobinn.com, $129-249) is an unusual B&B in that guests can stay in suites in the main lodge or in one of several restored century-old tobacco barns on the property. Each one-bedroom barn-turned-cabin is well equipped with modern conveniences, including two-person hot tubs and stone wood-burning fireplaces. Children and pets are not allowed, but horses can occupy a stall on the property for an additional $50 per night.

West of Mount Airy on the Blue Ridge Parkway, the **Glade Valley Bed and Breakfast** (330 Shaw Lane, BRP milepost 229, 336/657-8811 or 800/538-3508, www.gladevalley.com, $120-170) has six bedrooms and a private cabin built to look like a classic frontier cabin. This bed-and-breakfast sits on 29 acres of mountainside with miles of walking trails and tremendous views, making it a relaxing place to rest for a night or two. In addition to breakfast, they provide guests with complimentary bottled water, making the hikes a little easier.

Food

While you're in Mount Airy, you have to eat at **The Snappy Lunch** (125 N. Main St., 336/786-4931, www.thesnappylunch.com, 5:45am-1:45pm Mon., Wed., and Fri., 5:45am Tues., Thurs., and Sat., $1-5), a diner whose claims to fame include being mentioned on *The Andy Griffith Show* and the "World Famous Pork Chop Sandwich," which is notoriously sloppy, delicious, and cheap. Eating here is like stepping back in time; The Snappy Lunch has been in the community since 1923.

There's only one source for good strong coffee in Mount Airy, the **Good Life Café** (Main-Oak Emporium, 248 N Main St., 336/789-2404, www.mainoakemporium. com, 10am-6pm Mon.-Sat., 1pm-5pm Sun. Jan.-Aug., 10am-6pm Mon.-Thurs. and Sat., 10am-8pm Fri., 1pm-5pm Sun. Sept.-Dec.). **The Copper Pot Restaurant** (123 Scenic Outlet Lane, Suite 4, 336/352-4108, www. copperpotrestaurant.com, 6am-8pm Mon.-Thurs., 6am-9pm Fri.-Sat., around $10) is a down-home restaurant specializing in dishes of the "meat and two" or "meat and three" variety. It's country cooking all the way, so prepare for fried okra, pinto beans, and inexpensive food.

SOUTH ALONG U.S. 321
Sights

Traditions Pottery (4443 Bolick Rd., 3 miles south of Blowing Rock, 828/295-5099, www. traditionspottery.com, 10am-6pm Mon.-Fri., 9am-8pm Sat., 10am-6pm Sun.) is a hotbed of Piedmont and Appalachian folk traditions. The Owen-Bolick-Calhoun families trace their roots as potters back through six generations in the Sandhills community of Seagrove and here in Caldwell County. They have also become renowned old-time musicians and storytellers. In addition to ceramics with an impeccable folk pedigree, Traditions Pottery is the location of numerous music jams and kiln openings throughout the year as well as the Jack Tales Festival in August; Glenn Bolick learned

storytelling from the great Ray Hicks of Beech Mountain, a National Heritage Award winner.

The seat of Caldwell County, Lenoir (pronounced "luh-NORE," not "len-WAR"), was named for General William Lenoir, a Revolutionary War hero and chronicler of the Battle of King's Mountain. **Fort Defiance** (1792 Fort Defiance Dr./Hwy. 268, Happy Valley, 828/758-1671, www.fortdefiancenc.org, 10am-5pm Thurs.-Sat., 1pm-5pm Sun. Apr.-Oct., 10am-5pm Sat., 1pm-5pm Sun. and by appointment Nov.-Mar., $6 adults, $4 under 14), his 1792 plantation house in Happy Valley, is beautifully restored and open to visitors. Among its unusual charms are a 200-year-old oriental chestnut tree, an English boxwood garden of the same vintage, and the largest beech tree in the state.

The **Hickory Museum of Art** (243 3rd Ave. NE, Hickory, 828/327-8576, www.hickorymuseumofart.org, 10am-4pm Tues.-Sat., 1pm-4pm Sun., free) was established in the early 1950s and was the first major museum of American art in the Southeast. Its early partnership with the National Academy of Design in New York gained it the nickname the "Southern Outpost of the National Academy." The museum has an impressive permanent collection, with special emphases on American painting, outsider and folk art, North Carolina folk pottery, and American studio pottery and glass.

One part spectacle, one part shopping experience, one part North Carolina heritage, the **Hickory Furniture Mart** (2220 U.S. 70, Hickory, 800/462-6278, www.hickoryfurniture.com, 9am-6pm Mon.-Sat.) houses more than 100 factory outlets, stores, and galleries representing more than 1,000 furniture and home accessories manufacturers. It's a draw for designers, shop owners, and those looking for a serious redecoration project; the spectacle of the four-level showroom is amazing.

Festivals

Every year on Labor Day weekend in early September, Caldwell County is home to the **Historic Happy Valley Old-Time Fiddlers**

NORTHERN BLUE RIDGE

THE REAL TOM DOOLEY

Probably North Carolina's most famous murder case, the 1867 murder of a young Wilkes County woman named Laura Foster by her lover, Tom Dula, is known around the world because of a 1950s recording by the Kingston Trio of "The Ballad of Tom Dooley," as it has come to be known. The song was sung in the North Carolina mountains long before its emergence as a folk revival standard; most notably, the Watauga County banjo player and balladeer Frank Profitt kept the story alive through song. Even today, almost 150 years later, the intricacies of the Dula case are debated in this area by descendants of the principal players and by neighbors who have grown up with the legend.

The story is sordid. Tom Dula was 18 years old when he enlisted in the Confederate Army, and by that time he had already been involved for several years in a romantic relationship with a woman named Ann Melton. Following the Civil War, much of which he spent as a prisoner at the notoriously ghastly Point Lookout prison in Maryland, Dula came home to Wilkes County, older but apparently no wiser. He picked up where he left off with Ann Melton, by then married to another man, and at the same time started living with another local woman, Laura

Foster. In one version of the story, he was seeing yet a third woman, another Melton.

The subtleties of the motives and means that led to Laura Foster's death are still subjects of hot debate, but the facts are that on May 25, 1866, Laura Foster set off from home riding her father's horse. The next day, the horse returned without her. After searchers had combed the woods and riverbanks for nearly a month, Laura Foster's body was finally discovered; she had been stabbed to death and buried in a shallow grave. When news got out that the body had been found, Dula disappeared.

He was caught a few weeks later in Tennessee. Back in Wilkes County, Tom Dula and Ann Melton were indicted for murder. Officials moved the trial down the mountain to nearby Iredell County, where a jury found Dula guilty; Ann Melton was acquitted. After a series of appeals and the eventual overturning of the verdict by the state supreme court, a new trial was convened, and Dula was again convicted. He was hanged on May 1, 1868, in Statesville. Historians write that even before the hanging, people in the area were singing a song with the verse, "Hang your head, Tom Dula / Hang your head and cry / You killed poor Laura Foster / And now you're bound to die."

Convention (828/758-9448, www.happyvalleyfiddlers.com), a laid-back event in a gorgeous location, the Jones Farm. The festival includes music competitions and concerts, drawing some great traditional artists from all over the hills. Other events include a rubber duck race, demonstrations by instrument makers, tours of Fort Defiance, and visits to the grave of Laura Foster, the 1867 victim of North Carolina's most famous murderer, Tom Dooley, who happened to be a fiddler. The crime is a common theme in bluegrass and roots music death ballads. Participants and visitors can camp ($10) along the Yadkin River on the Jones Farm during the festival. No alcohol is allowed; pets are permitted as long as they're leashed.

The Catawba Valley is an important place for North Carolina folk pottery, with a tradition all its own dating back to the early-19th-century potter Daniel Seagle and exemplified in modern times by the late Burlon Craig, one of the giants of Southern folk art, and contemporary master Kim Ellington. Hickory's annual Catawba Valley Pottery and Antiques Festival (Hickory Convention Center, 828/324-7294, www.catawbavalley-potteryfestival.org, late Mar., $6 adults, $2 children) brings together more than 100 potters and dealers in pottery and antiques. It's a great introduction to Southern folk pottery, and the covetable wares are dangerous if you're on a budget.

Sports and Recreation

Between Hickory and Morganton, outside the town of Connelly Springs, is one of the state's most rugged recreational areas, **South Mountain State Park** (3001 South Mountain Park Ave., Connelly Springs, 828/433-4772, http://ncparks.gov, office 8am-5pm Mon.-Fri., park 8am-6pm daily Nov.-Feb., 8am-8pm daily Mar.-Apr. and Sept.-Oct., 8am-9pm daily May-Aug.), rising to elevations of 3,000 feet. One trail follows the Jacob Fork River to the top of 80-foot-tall High Shoals Falls. Another 0.75-mile trail travels along the lower reaches of Jacob Fork and is wheelchair-accessible. There are 17 miles of strenuous mountain-biking trails. Hike-in campsites ($13) are located in various spots throughout the park, from 0.5 miles to 5.5 miles away the Jacob Fork parking area. Pit toilets are located near campsites, but all supplies and water must be packed in. Watch out for bears!

The **Hickory Crawdads** (828/322-3000, www.hickorycrawdads.com) baseball team is a Single-A affiliate of the Pittsburgh Pirates. They were the 2002 and 2004 South Atlantic League Champions, and they play at the modern Frans Stadium (2500 Clement Blvd. NW, Hickory), where you may meet the mascot, Conrad the Crawdad.

Golfers may want to stop at **Hampton Heights Golf Course** (1700 5th St. NE, Hickory, 828/328-5010, 18 holes, par 72, greens fees 18 holes $15 walking, $23 riding Mon.-Fri., $20 walking, $29 riding Sat.-Sun., 9 holes $10 walking, $16.50 riding Mon.-Fri., $15 walking, $16.50 riding Sat.-Sun.) for a round. The fairways aren't judiciously wide, but they are forgiving enough to help you keep a shanked shot or two in play. The greens can vary from hole to hole, so judging putting speed can be difficult at times.

Food

If you're traveling between Lenoir and Hickory on a weekend, take a detour to the little community of Dudley Shoals, where you'll find **Sims Country BBQ** (6160 Petra Mill Rd., Dudley Shoals, 828/396-5811, www.simscountrybbq.com, from 5pm Fri.-Sat., all-you-can-eat buffet $11). Sims is known not only for its all-you-can-eat Texas-style barbecue, which they pit-cook all day, but for live bluegrass music and clogging (starts at 7pm). It also hosts the annual Molasses Festival on the second Saturday in October, with bluegrass, dancing, and harvest-time activities.

(**Highland Avenue** (883 Highland Ave. SE, Hickory, 828/267-9800, www.highlandavenuerestaurant.com, $12-23) serves the best food in Hickory. The philosophy of the restaurant revolves around using the freshest ingredients available from local sources. The menu does change, but the staples—shrimp and grits, pork shoulder, and the burger—are consistently delicious. The Butchers Block with Select Cheeses charcuterie appetizer is a knockout, and many of the meats are cured in-house.

GETTING THERE AND AROUND

The towns in this chapter are all an easy drive from Winston-Salem, Boone, and, slightly farther away, Charlotte. Wilkesboro is on U.S. 421, between Winston-Salem and Boone. U.S. 321, a pretty road, winds through Happy Valley to Lenoir and Hickory. I-77 runs from Charlotte to the Virginia state line, passing just west of Mount Airy.

NORTHERN BLUE RIDGE

ASHEVILLE AND THE SOUTHERN BLUE RIDGE

There's an energy in the mountain town of Asheville that you don't find in many other places in North Carolina. For more than a century Asheville has been a hive of progressive thinking and a surprisingly cosmopolitan level of living. With all the writers, artists, musicians, dancers, wealthy industrialists, and eclectic personalities that have inhabited this town, it's easy to understand how it earned the nickname "Paris of the South." Built on a series of hills around the confluence of the Swannanoa ("swan-uh-NO-uh") and French Broad Rivers, commerce found its way here in the 18th and 19th centuries via water routes and a mountain stagecoach road. In the late 1800s the town experienced a boom as railroad lines began to bring vacationers by the tens of thousands. It was around that time that George Vanderbilt,

scion of the massively wealthy Vanderbilt dynasty, began building his mountain home, the Biltmore, just south of downtown. From the 1880s to the 1930s the mountain town underwent a long and rapid expansion, eventually becoming a small city in its own right.

Surrounding Asheville are mountains and hundreds of years of folk traditions, with folk art, music, dancing, and customs that survive today. Old-time Appalachian string-band music (not to be confused with bluegrass, although bluegrass is alive and well here too) thrives in the hills and hollows among the descendants of the region's early settlers, among whom songs, instruments, and techniques have been passed down over many generations. Four- and five-string banjo pickers, guitarists, fiddlers, and other musicians have migrated here from all

HIGHLIGHTS

LOOK FOR **◖** TO FIND RECOMMENDED SIGHTS, ACTIVITIES, DINING, AND LODGING.

◖ Downtown Architecture: In the early 20th century wealthy summer vacationers, industrialists, and stock market investors left their mark in Asheville's downtown, a district packed with art deco and beaux arts masterpieces (page 307).

◖ Biltmore Estate: Asheville's most popular attraction is not only an awe-inspiring palace and symbol of the Gilded Age; it's also a collection of great little restaurants, shops, and a popular winery, all in a beautiful riverside setting (page 308).

◖ Folk Art Center: Learn about the master craftspeople of the southern Appalachians and purchase gorgeous handmade items such as traditional weaving, woodcarving, fine-art furniture, paintings, and photographs depicting the area in all its natural glory (page 314).

◖ Pisgah Ranger District: This 150,000-acre section of the Pisgah Forest encompasses the Cradle of Forestry Museum, Shining Rock Wilderness, Sliding Rock, Cold Mountain, and many other favorite outdoor destinations (page 336).

◖ Chimney Rock: A natural tower of stone growing out of a mountainside like a rhino's horn, Chimney Rock is the centerpiece of a large park with amazing hiking trails (page 339).

across the globe to be part of the music traditions and the thriving music scene. Asheville is one of the best places in the world to hear old-time and bluegrass music as well as a sidetrack genre known as mountain swing (similar to how western swing is a child of country music and up-tempo jazz). The Mountain Dance and Folk Festival, founded in 1928 by banjo-playing folklorist and Buncome County native Bascom Lamar Lunsford, is the longest-running folk festival in the United States and draws audiences and participants from far and wide every year.

One of the epicenters of the visual arts in the Southeast, Asheville and the surrounding artsy towns draw from centuries-old traditions of folk carving, weaving, and other arts, merging them with elements of the modern craft movement and fine arts and forming a pressure cooker of studios and galleries. A regional infrastructure of arts organizations such as the Southern Highland Craft Guild (www.southernhighlandguild.org) and dozens of local galleries and studios make Asheville an exciting place for lovers of fine art and craft, and an energy source for artists looking for inspiration

ASHEVILLE

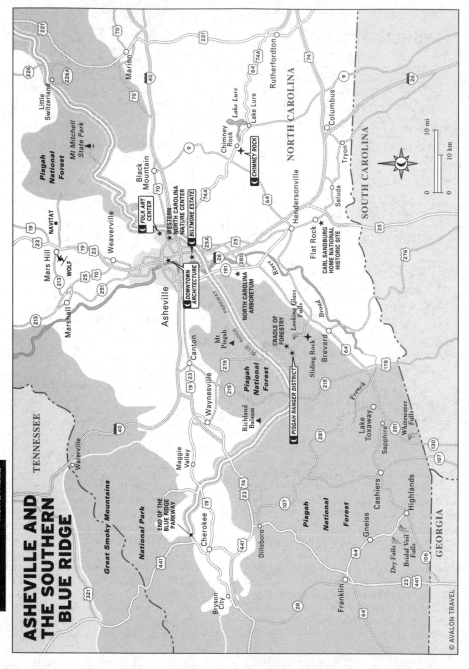

ASHEVILLE

ASHEVILLE AND THE SOUTHERN BLUE RIDGE

© AVALON TRAVEL

Asheville is North Carolina's countercul-ture mecca, with elements of Haight-Ashbury circa 1968, Woodstock, the Grand Ole Opry, Beatnik enclave, and Andy Warhol's Factory; there's a palpable energy here that says "some-thing's about to happen." It's a town where you're liable to find a 90-year-old local and a dreadlocked organic farmer talking weather, a suit-and-tie banker talking banjo picking with a busker, a soccer mom at a drum circle, or you rubbing elbows with all of them at one of the town's top-notch restaurants.

PLANNING YOUR TIME

Many mountain towns shut down for visi-tors once the last beautiful leaf falls from the trees, but not Asheville; it stays vibrant year-round, although the pace does slow a bit when the snow falls. Visiting Asheville in the winter is less expensive than when trav-elers compete for hotel rooms and restaurant reservations in summer and fall. Tables are easy to come by, most of the tours operate on a regular but limited schedule, live music doesn't slow down at all, and there are plenty of craft cocktails and coffee shops to keep you warm. Driving up into the mountains around Asheville, winter weather is more likely to be problematic than it is in the city, although between the snow and year-round potential for fog, the weather in the high-lands always calls for caution. As such, this is the place where all-wheel-drive station wag-ons come to die (count them as you drive around town), or perhaps they're given away with every home purchase.

Summer, of course, is a great time to be in Asheville as the elevation brings cooler air on the same day it will be sweltering across the Piedmont and Sandhills. Summer also brings a number of festivals and special events, and it's the time when the greens and blues of the Blue Ridge are most vivid. Fall colors arrive at slightly different times each year, so you'll want to keep an eye on leaf forecasts for ideal getaway times. You can plan to see leaves start to turn in mid-late September, peaking in mid-October, and finished by the second week of November. Fall is prime season to visit Asheville, so make lodging reservations early and expect some delays on scenic routes like the Blue Ridge Parkway.

The **Blue Ridge National Heritage Area** (www.blueridgeheritage.com) has a number of valuable trip-planning resources, but a pre-ferred resource is **Explore Asheville** (www.ex-ploreasheville.com), the Asheville Convention and Visitors Bureau's website. The site's cre-ators and the people at the **Asheville Visitors Center** (36 Montford Ave., 828/258-6129, www.exploreasheville.com, 8:30am-5:30pm Mon.-Fri., 9am-5pm Sat.-Sun.), take a lot of pride in their town and can help steer you to-ward new and old favorites in the area.

Asheville

SIGHTS
ⓒ Downtown Architecture

As beautiful as Asheville's natural environ-ment may be, the striking architecture is just as attractive. The Montford neighborhood, a contemporary of the Biltmore, is a mixture of ornate Queen Anne houses and craftsman-style bungalows. The Grove Park Inn, a huge luxury hotel, was built in 1913 and is decked out with rustic architectural devices intended to make vacationing New Yorkers and wealthy

people feel like they were roughing it. In down-town Asheville is a large concentration of art deco buildings on the scale of Miami Beach. Significant structures dating to the boom before the Great Depression include the **Buncombe County Courthouse** (60 Court Plaza, built in 1927-1929), the **First Baptist Church** (Oak St. and Woodfin St., 1925), the **S&W Cafeteria** (56 Patton Ave., 1929), the **Public Service Building** (89-93 Patton Ave., 1929) and the **Grove Arcade** (37 Battery Park Ave., 1926-1929).

Asheville's First Baptist Church

© ROBERT HAINER/123RF.COM

The **Jackson Building** (22 S. Pack Square, built in 1923-1924) is a fine example of neo-Gothic architecture with a disturbing backstory. According to legend, on the day of the stock market crash in 1929 that started the Great Depression, one of the wealthiest men in Asheville lost it all and leaped to his death from the building. Three or four (depending on who's telling the story) more of Asheville's wealthiest followed suit. What is known to be true is that there's a bull's-eye built into the sidewalk in front of the building as a morbid monument to the story.

(Biltmore Estate

Much of downtown Asheville dates to the 1920s, but the architectural crown jewel is the **Biltmore Estate** (1 Approach Rd., 800/411-3812, www.biltmore.com, 9:30am-3:30pm daily Jan.-mid-Mar., 9am-4:30pm daily mid-Mar.-Dec., open late for special events, check the website or call, $44-69 adults, $22-34 ages 10-16, free under age 10, additional fees

for activities), built in the late 1800s for owner George Vanderbilt, grandson of Gilded Age robber baron Cornelius Vanderbilt. Like many of his wealthy Northern contemporaries, George Vanderbilt was first introduced to North Carolina when he traveled to Asheville for the mountain air and nearby hot springs. He found himself so awestruck by the land that he amassed a 125,000-acre tract south of Asheville where he would build his "country home" and enjoy the area's restive and healthful benefits. He engaged celebrity architect Richard Morris Hunt to build the home, and because the land and the views reminded them of the Loire Valley, they planned to build the home in the style of a 16th-century French château. The Biltmore Estate was once the largest privately owned home in the country. Vanderbilt also hired the esteemed Fredrick Law Olmstead, creator of New York City's Central Park, to design the landscape for the grounds, gardens, and surrounding forest, a project nine times the size of the New York project for which he is famous.

A three-mile-long approach road leads through manicured forests, revealing bits of the landscape and hiding the house until you are upon it, creating a sense of drama and wonder for arriving visitors. While the Biltmore Estate's original 125,000 acres are now greatly diminished—the estate comprises a little more than 8,000 acres today—it's easy to see just how big it was; standing on the South Terrace and looking south and west, everything in view was once part of the estate. A large tract of the land was donated to the federal government and has become part of the Pisgah National Forest; what remains is immaculately manicured.

Primary construction of the home was done between 1888 and 1895, although construction continued through World War II, when part of the home was used as a bunker to store treasures from the National Gallery of Art. More than 250 rooms were built, and there are more than three acres of open floor space here, most of which is open to visitors on a self-guided tour or a behind-the-scenes tour into seldom-seen corners of the home, even onto the roof. The art and decoration are as grand as the architecture, with paintings by Renoir, James Abbott Whistler, and John Singer Sargent; a stunning collection of European antiques, among them Napoleon's chess set; and room upon room of masterwork in tiling, woodworking and carving, masonry, and stone carving. For its time, the Biltmore was a technological marvel, with electricity, elevators, central heat, and hot water. In the basement, an indoor pool that could be filled with heated water, a gymnasium, and a bowling alley seem over-the-top by today's standards, which may be one reason the 1994 film *Richie Rich* was filmed here.

George Vanderbilt found the concept of a self-sustaining estate appealing, and he included a working farm with crops, herds of cattle, a dairy, and all the farmers and workers required for such an operation. The Asheville neighborhood known as **Biltmore Village** was part of this mountain empire.

If he could see it today, George Vanderbilt might be happy to find that the estate is ogled by 500,000 people every year and that his vision of a self-sustaining estate endures. A vineyard (not open to the public) produces grapes that are processed at the estate's winery; a livestock breeding program produces fine stock; and a farm supplies more than 70 percent of seasonal and specialty vegetables to the estate's restaurants. Visitors can eat, shop, tour, explore, relax, and unwind without leaving the grounds, and there's easily enough here to fill a weekend.

The **Biltmore Winery** in **Antler Hill Village,** which is part of the estate, operates in what was formerly the estate's dairy; check out the industrial-farm rafters in the tasting room. Daily tours and tastings allow visitors to sample some award-winning wines and see how they're

ASHEVILLE'S "BUNK" HISTORY

This story starts in 1820 as Congress hotly debated the issue of Missouri's statehood: Would it enter the union as a free state or a slave-holding state? The debate ground on for a month. Then, moments before the vote was to be called, Felix Walker, the Representative from Asheville's district, brought the whole thing to a standstill with a long-winded, elaborate, hyperbolic speech. When his fellow members of Congress attempted to stop this seemingly interminable production, Walker refused, stating that he was speaking for his constituents, not for the benefit of his colleagues in the House. He was, he said, "speaking for Buncombe," referring to the county, pronounced "bunkum," of which Asheville is the seat.

"Speaking for Buncombe," and ultimately the words "bunkum" and "bunk," came to mean hollow political grandstanding. Today, nearly 200 years after Walker's verbose speech, you'll still hear news anchors, political pundits, bloggers, and talking heads refer to empty political rhetoric as "bunk."

ASHEVILLE

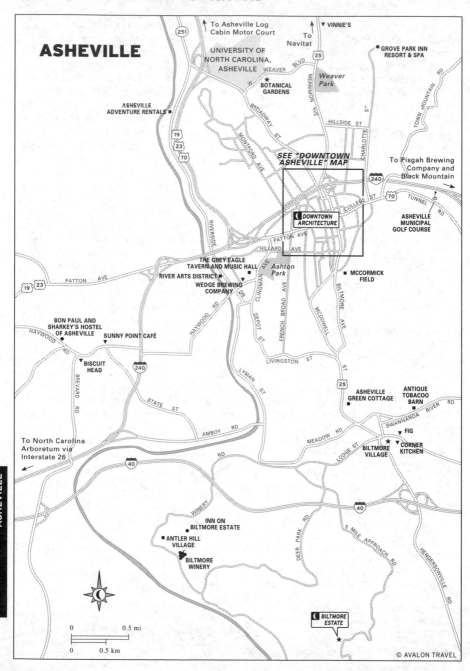

ASHEVILLE

To Asheville Log Cabin Motor Court

251

VINNIE'S

To Navitat

UNIVERSITY OF NORTH CAROLINA, ASHEVILLE

25

GROVE PARK INN RESORT & SPA

WEAVER BLVD

Weaver Park

★ BOTANICAL GARDENS

ASHEVILLE ADVENTURE RENTALS

BROADWAY ST

HILLSIDE ST

19
23
70

MONTFORD AVE

SEE "DOWNTOWN ASHEVILLE" MAP

240

To Pisgah Brewing Company and Black Mountain

COLLEGE ST

70

TUNNEL RD

DOWNTOWN ARCHITECTURE

ASHEVILLE MUNICIPAL GOLF COURSE

RIVERSIDE

PATTON AVE

HILLARD AVE

THE GREY EAGLE TAVERN AND MUSIC HALL

Ashton Park

19 23

PATTON AVE

RIVER ARTS DISTRICT

CLINGMAN AVE

MCCORMICK FIELD

WEDGE BREWING COMPANY

BILTMORE AVE

FRENCH BROAD AVE

DEPOT ST

MCDOWELL

BON PAUL AND SHARKEY'S HOSTEL OF ASHEVILLE

HAYWOOD RD

HAYWOOD RD

SUNNY POINT CAFÉ

240

BISCUIT HEAD

BREVARD RD

LIVINGSTON ST

LYMAN ST

STATE ST

25

ASHEVILLE GREEN COTTAGE

ANTIQUE TOBACOO BARN

SWANNANOA RIVER RD

AMBOY RD

To North Carolina Arboretum via Interstate 26

MEADOW RD

LODGE ST

FIG

40

BILTMORE VILLAGE

CORNER KITCHEN

WINERY

INN ON BILTMORE ESTATE

DEER PARK RD

3 MILE APPROACH RD

40

ANTLER HILL VILLAGE

BILTMORE WINERY

HENDERSONVILLE RD

BILTMORE ESTATE ★

0   0.5 mi

0   0.5 km

the Biltmore Estate

© ROLLIE/123RF.COM

made. More than 500,000 people visit the tasting room annually, so expect a wait if you're here in high season.

Antler Hill Village is also home to **Cedric's,** a brewery named after a beloved family dog, as well as a small museum, a souvenir shop, and a green to relax on. **River Bend Farm** is a beautiful compound that was once the hub of the estate's farming operation but now stands as a showpiece for traditional period crafts like woodworking and blacksmithing. Be sure to stop by the blacksmith's shop and watch master blacksmith Doc Cudd speak with considerable eloquence about the art of smithing as he hammers out everything from common nails to decorative leaves, flowers, and other pieces. Ask him to make the anvil sing and he'll happily oblige; he's one of a handful of smiths who know how to play the anvil as a musical instrument in the 18th- and 19th-century fashion. It's a beautiful, almost haunting, sound you won't soon forget.

The **Equestrian Center** gives lessons and the opportunity to ride more than 80 miles of equestrian trails, many with sweeping views of the estate and glimpses of the main house that will take your breath away. Other ways to tour the estate include carriage rides, paved bike trails and mountain bike trails, canoes, kayaks, and rafts (the French Broad River bisects the estate), Segways, and, of course, on foot. You can even challenge your driving skills at the **Land Rover Experience Driving School.**

Admission cost for the Biltmore Estate varies by season and includes the house, gardens, and winery; activities such as horseback riding, rafting, and behind-the-scenes tours cost extra. Special events, like the Christmas Candlelight Tour (Nov.-Dec.) also have additional fees. Parking is free, and a complimentary shuttle takes you from parking lots to the house.

Asheville Art Museum

The **Asheville Art Mueseum** (2 S. Pack Square, 828/253-3227, www.ashevilleart.org, 10am-5pm Tues.-Sat., 1pm-5pm Sun., $8 adults, $7 students with ID, $7 over 60, free 5 and under) has been around since 1948, and

THOMAS WOLFE, NATIVE SON

A native son of Asheville, author Thomas Wolfe (*You Can't Go Home Again; Look Homeward, Angel*) grew up in a boardinghouse run by his mother and operated today as the **Thomas Wolfe Memorial** (52 N. Market St., Asheville, 828/253-8304, www.wolfememorial.com, 9am-5pm Tues.-Sat., $5, $2 students). He described the town of "Altamont" (Asheville), his mother's boarding house as "Dixieland," and its people so vividly in *Look Homeward, Angel* that the Asheville library refused to own it, and Wolfe himself avoided the town for almost eight years. Even then, he only came back after his mother published an article titled "Return" in the Asheville newspaper.

In this passage from *Look Homeward, Angel*, Wolfe describes the excitement of approaching Asheville as a traveler.

The next morning he resumed his journey by coach. His destination was the little town of Altamont, twenty-four miles away beyond the rim of the great outer wall of the hills. As the horses strained slowly up the mountain road Oliver's spirit lifted a little. It was a gray-golden day in late October, bright and windy. There was a sharp bite and sparkle in the mountain air: the range soared above him, close, immense, clean, and barren. The trees rose gaunt and stark: they were almost leafless. The sky was full of windy white rags of cloud; a thick blade of mist washed slowly around the rampart of a mountain.

Below him a mountain stream foamed down its rocky bed, and he could see little dots of men laying the track that would coil across the hill toward Altamont. Then the sweating team lipped the gulch of the mountain, and, among soaring and lordly ranges that melted away in purple mist, they began the slow descent toward the high plateau on which the town of Altamont was built.

In the haunting eternity of these mountains, rimmed in their enormous cup, he found sprawled out on its hundred hills and hollows a town of four thousand people.

There were lands. His heart lifted.

in the intervening decades has enriched the art community of Asheville by displaying works by some of the most important, influential, and up-and-coming artists of the 20th century. The permanent collection includes a wide array of mediums and styles, ranging from photo portraits to ceramics to statuary to beautiful modern pieces. A large collection from the nearby experimental school, Black Mountain College, shows the highlights of works created by faculty and students.

North Carolina Arboretum

The enormous **North Carolina Arboretum** (100 Frederick Law Olmstead Way, 828/665-2492, www.ncarboretum.org, 8am-9pm daily Apr.-Oct., 8am-7pm daily Nov.-Mar., greenhouse 8am-2pm Mon.-Fri., parking $8) is considered by many to be one of the most beautiful in the country. The 434 natural and landscaped acres back into the Pisgah National Forest, just off the Blue Ridge Parkway. Major collections include the National Native Azalea Repository, where you can see almost every species of azalea native to the United States as well as several hybrids, and the very special Bonsai Collection, where staff horticulturists care for over 200 bonsai plants, many of their own creation.

Bicycles and leashed dogs are permitted on

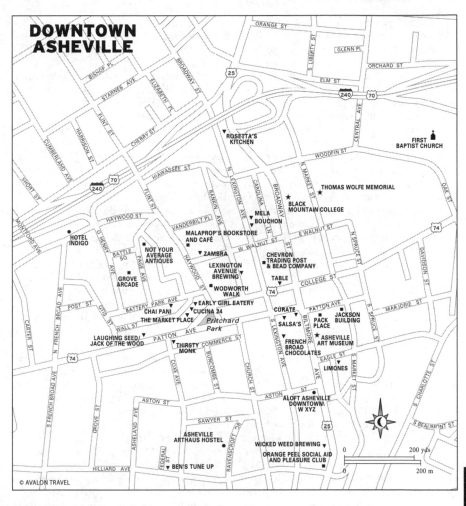

DOWNTOWN ASHEVILLE

© AVALON TRAVEL

many of the trails. Walking areas range from easy to fairly rugged, but with 10 miles of hiking and biking trails, you will find one that suits your skill level. To learn a more about the history of the Arboretum, the plants themselves, and the natural history of the region, join one of the guided tours (1pm Tues. and Sat.). These two-mile walk-and-talk tours happen rain or shine, so dress for the weather. The Arboretum also has a very nice café, the **Savory Thyme Café** (11am-4pm Tues.-Sat., noon-4pm

Sun.), and a gift shop, the **Connections Gallery** (11am-4pm daily).

Botanical Gardens

The **Botanical Gardens** (151 W. T. Weaver Blvd., adjacent to UNC-Asheville campus, 828/252-5190, www.ashevillebotanicalgardens.org, dawn-dusk daily year-round, donation) is a 10-acre preserve for the region's increasingly threatened native plant species. Laid out in 1960 by landscape architect Doan

Ogden, the gardens are an ecological haven. The many "rooms" are planted to reflect different environments of the mountains, including the Wildflower Trail, the Heath Cove, and the Fern and Moss Trail. Spring blooms peak in mid-April, but the Gardens are an absolutely lovely and visually rich place to visit any time of year. Because of its serious mission of plant preservation, neither pets nor bicycles are allowed. Admission is free, but as the Gardens are entirely supported by donations, your contribution will have a real impact. On the first Saturday in May, the **Day in the Gardens** brings food and music to this normally placid park, and garden and nature enthusiasts from all around come to tour and to buy native plants for their home gardens. There is also a gift shop (10am-4pm Mon.-Sat., 1pm-4pm Sun. Apr.-Oct., noon-4pm daily Nov.-Dec.).

Western North Carolina Nature Center

Asheville, and western North Carolina generally, tend to be very ecologically conscious, as reflected in the **Western North Carolina Nature Center** (75 Gashes Creek Rd., 828/259-8080, www.wildwnc.org, 10am-5pm daily, $8 adults, $7 seniors, $4 ages 3-15, free under age 3, under age 16 must be accompanied by an adult). On the grounds of an old zoo—don't worry, it's not depressing—wild animals that are unable to survive in the wild due to injury or having been raised as pets live in wooded habitats on public display. This is the place to see some of the mountains' rarest species—those that even most lifelong mountain residents have never seen: cougars, wolves, coyotes, bobcats, and even the elusive hellbender. What's a hellbender, you ask? Come to the Nature Center to find out.

Black Mountain College

Considering the history of Black Mountain College from a purely numerical standpoint, one might get the false impression that this little institution's brief odd life was a flash in the pan. In its 23 years of operation, Black Mountain College had only 1,200 students, 55

of whom actually completed their degrees. But between 1933 and 1956, the unconventional school demonstrated an innovative model of education and community life.

The educational program was almost devoid of structure. Students had no set course schedule or requirements, lived and farmed with the faculty, and no sense of hierarchy was permitted to separate students and teachers. Most distinguished as a school of the arts, Black Mountain College hired Josef Albers as its first art director when the Bauhaus icon fled Nazi Germany. Willem de Kooning taught here for a time, as did Buckminster Fuller, who began his design of the geodesic dome while he was in residence. Albert Einstein and William Carlos Williams were among the roster of guest lecturers. I had the honor of working with and befriending poet Robert Creeley, one of the few people to get a degree here, and who taught here briefly before the school shut down in 1956, partly due to the prevailing antileft climate of that decade.

The **Black Mountain College Museum and Arts Center** (56 Broadway, 828/350-8484, www.blackmountaincollege.org, noon-4pm Tues.-Wed., 11am-5pm Thurs.-Sat.) is located in downtown Asheville rather than in the town of Black Mountain. It's both an exhibition space and a resource center dedicated to the history and spirit of the college.

◖ Folk Art Center

The **Folk Art Center** (BRP milepost 382, 828/298-7928, 9am-5pm daily Jan.-Mar., 9am-6pm daily Apr.-Dec.) is a must-see for anyone interested in traditional Appalachian handicrafts and fine art. At this beautiful gallery, coupled with the oldest continuously operating craft shop in the United States, **Allanstand Craft Shop,** you'll find the work of members of the prestigious Southern Highland Craft Guild, a juried-membership organization that brings together many of the best artists in Appalachia. Although the folk arts are well represented in beautiful pottery, baskets, weaving, and quilts, you'll also find the work of contemporary studio artists in an array of media, including gorgeous handcrafted furniture, clothing, jewelry, and toys. Bring your Christmas shopping list even if it's April.

ENTERTAINMENT AND EVENTS

Great live music is the rule rather than the exception in Asheville, in the form of national touring acts as well as regional and local bands that give them stiff competition for audiences on any given night. It seems that everywhere you turn in this town, you'll find live musicians—buskers playing on street corners, solo guitarists in cafés, or a bluegrass trio set up on a restaurant deck. Follow the sound of drums to **Pritchard Park** (Patton Ave. at Haywood St., and College St.), where a huge drum circle forms every Friday night. There are also formal music venues where you can hear rock, jam bands, bluegrass, funk, blues, country, rockabilly, alt-country, mountain swing, old-time music, and electronica.

Nightlife
LIVE MUSIC
A favorite spot for live music is the **Orange Peel Social Aid and Pleasure Club** (101 Biltmore Ave., 828/398-1837, www.theorangepeel.net, noon-midnight or later daily). They're billed as "the nation's premier live music hall and concert venue," and they can back that up with some powerful acts taking the stage, including Bob Dylan, Smashing Pumpkins, Bruce Hornsby, Mickey Hart of Grateful Dead fame, Mike Gordon from Phish, Chvrches, Beastie Boys, Flaming Lips, and My Morning Jacket. The Orange Peel is a cool concert hall with a big dance floor, great sound, and great history.

One of the best venues in town for roots music and eclectic small bands is the **Grey Eagle Tavern and Music Hall** (185 Clingman Ave., 828/232-5800, www.thegreyeagle.com). It's a small space set up more like a listening-room than a bar or club, meaning folks come to listen to the music and interact with the performer rather than grab a beer and hop to the next bar. Don't underestimate their local beer selection, though. **Taqueria con Cuida** serves up some inexpensive and tasty Latin American

cuisine on-site. Performers include smaller acts along with influential roots, folk, and bluegrass musicians such as Dr. Ralph Stanley.

Another local favorite is **Jack of the Wood** (95 Patton Ave., 828/252-5445, www.jackofthewood.com, 3pm-1am Mon.-Thurs., noon-2am Fri.-Sun.), where the music tends toward progressive approaches to traditional music; it's interesting and always somewhat familiar. Throughout the week are themed jam sessions that bring in local musicians, including the Irish Session (from 5pm Sun.), singer-songwriters in the round (1st and 3rd Tues.), an old-time music jam (from 6pm Wed.), bluegrass (from 6pm Thurs.), and touring bands (Fri.-Sat. and some weeknights).

COCKTAILS
Asheville is growing a reputation as a craft-cocktail destination to match its food renown, and one big contributor to that movement is **The Imperial Life** (48 College St., 828/254-8980, http://imperialbarasheville.com, 4:30pm-late Wed.-Mon.), specializing in pre-Prohibition cocktails, a wine list that showcases lesser-known varietals, and small batch spirits. They serve a limited menu of small plates made downstairs at Table, a much-lauded restaurant under the same ownership.

For a mix of music and crazy-good craft cocktails, head to **W Xyz bar** (Aloft Asheville Downtown, 2nd Fl., 51 Biltmore Ave., 828/232-2838, www.aloftashevilledowntown.com, 5pm-midnight Sun.-Thurs., 3pm-2am Fri.-Sat.), a trendy bar that feels like Asheville five years in the future; the bartenders are some of the most innovative in the city. They specialize in cocktails that use North Carolina-distilled spirits in flavorful drinks that let the spirits shine without becoming overpowering. Weekends feature music, ranging from DJs to small local live acts, all in keeping with the bar's hip vibe.

BEER
Asheville's reign as Beer City USA and subsequent years as a contender for the title demands discussion of the city's finest tap rooms,

© JASON FRYE

the Thirsty Monk, one of Asheville's top watering holes

breweries, and specialty beer bars. I can attest to the quality of brews you'll find in Asheville, and every time I visit, I find a new place to try. Beer is serious business here, but don't be intimidated; there's something for everyone.

My go-to specialty beer bar in Asheville is the **Thirsty Monk** (92 Patton Ave., 828/254-5470, http://monkpub.com, 4pm-midnight Mon.-Thurs., noon-2am Fri.-Sat., noon-10pm Sun.). This unusual bar in a purple building serves American craft beer upstairs and Belgian brews downstairs in a cozy basement. If you find the menu overwhelming, the knowledgeable barkeeps can point you to a beer you'll like. Ask for a tasting pour of their drafts, or just order a flight of beer and sample a range; it's a great way to find your favorite. As much as I love American craft beer, I'm always drawn to the Belgian basement where I find some unusual, and awesome, beers.

If you tend to prefer hoppier beers or sours (sometimes called "wild ales"), **Wicked Weed Brewing** (91 Biltmore Ave., 828/575-9599, www.wickedweedbrewing.com, tasting room

3pm-11pm Mon.-Tues., 3pm-midnight Wed.-Thurs., 3pm-2am Fri.-Sat., 3pm-11pm Sun., restaurant 11am-11pm Mon.-Tues., 11am-midnight Wed.-Thurs., 11am-2am Fri.-Sat., noon-11pm Sun.) is a place to stop for a drink. A relative newcomer that opened in 2011, Wicked Weed is gaining fans across the state for their hops-forward brews. They feature some two dozen beers in their tasting room, with Belgian red ales, fruit-forward sours, IPAs, and even a handful of porters and stouts.

Lexington Avenue Brewery (39 N. Lexington Ave., 828/252-0212, www.lexavebrew.com, 11:30am-midnight Mon.-Tues., 11:30am-2am Wed.-Sat., noon-midnight Sun.), or LAB, is a brewery and pub in the heart of downtown. With seating areas that open to the street and a 92-foot-long custom-built curved bar to sit at, it's a great place to spend an afternoon people-watching and enjoying a pint of Belgian White Ale or Nitro Chocolate Stout.

Another good microbrewery is **Wedge Brewing Company** (125B Roberts St., 828/505-2792, www.wedgebrewing.com, 4pm-10pm

Mon.-Thurs., 3pm-10pm Fri., 2pm-10pm Sat.-Sun.), located in an old warehouse in the River Arts District. Wedge has more than a dozen brews on tap, including pale ales, pilsners, and a Russian imperial stout flavored with raspberries. Their strong relationship with area food trucks makes this a great hangout for local beer and local grub with local beer enthusiasts any evening.

How can you go wrong with pizza and beer? At **Barley's Taproom and Pizzeria** (42 Biltmore Ave., 828/255-0504, http://barleystaproom.com, 11:30am-2am Mon.-Fri., 11:03am-midnight Sat., noon-1am Sun., $2-21) you'll find piping hot pies and a plethora of pints. Barley's has 29 beers on draft downstairs and a full suite of 29 different beers on tap upstairs. They also have around 40 brews available in bottles. They pour everything from local brews to the top craft beers from across the nation. You'll need some pizza, a calzone, a burger, or even a tofu sandwich to go with your beer, and they serve a small but tight menu that satisfies your hunger for some first-stop or last-stop grub.

To sample a variety of Asheville's great microbreweries, join a tour from **Asheville Brews Cruise** (828/545-5181, www.brewscruise.com, from $50). The enthusiastic beer experts will shuttle you from brewery to brewery in the Brews Cruise van to sample some beer, learn about the growth of Asheville's beer scene, and gain some insight in the art and craft of brewing. On the tour, you'll visit **Asheville Pizza and Brewing Company** (675 Merrimon Ave., 828/254-1281, http://ashevillebrewing.com, 11am-midnight or later daily), where you can start off the evening with one of this pizzeria, microbrewery, and movie house's tasty beers and fortify yourself for the evening by filling up on good pizza. The **French Broad Brewing Company** (828/277-0222, www.frenchbroadbrewery.com, 1pm-8pm daily) is another popular local nightspot that's grown up around a first-rate beer-making operation, where you can choose from a varied menu that includes signature pilsners, lagers, and ales while listening to some good live music. The

third destination on the cruise is the **Highland Brewing Company** (12 Old Charlotte Hwy., Suite H, 828/299-3370, www.highlandbrewing.com, tasting room 2pm-8pm Mon.-Sat., tours 4pm and 4:45pm Mon.-Fri., 2:45pm, 3:30pm, 4pm, and 4:45pm Sat.), Asheville's first microbrewery. They've been making beer and raking in awards for well over a decade, and on first sip you'll understand why they're one of the Southeast's favorite breweries.

Ballet

Asheville's noteworthy ballet company, **Terpsicorps** (2 South Pack Square, 828/252-4530, http://terpsicorps.org) performs for two brief but brilliant runs in the summer. Under the direction of North Carolinian dancer and choreographer Heather Malloy, Terpsicorps takes advantage of what is normally a slow season for other companies and hires some of the country's best dancers for a brief stint in Asheville. They have two productions each summer, and each usually has only a three-night run, so tickets sell out fast.

Comedy Tour

Around Asheville you may have noticed a giant purple bus zipping through the streets, laughter and bubbles (yes, bubbles) emanating from the windows. That's the **LaZoom Comedy Tour** (1½ Battery Park Ave., departing from 90 Biltmore Ave., 828/225-6932, www.lazoomtours.com, $24 adults, $18 ages 13-18, $22 seniors), delivering tours big in history and hilarity. The tour guides are outrageous—they're some of Asheville's weirdest (in a good way) people—and I guarantee you'll learn a thing or two (some history, a joke you may or may not want to tell your mom). They also offer the Haunted Comedy Tour (departing from 92 Patton Ave., $21), which adds in a supernatural note and tales of some of Asheville's spectral denizens.

Festivals

Twice yearly, in late July and late October, the Southern Highland Craft Guild hosts the **Craft Fair of the Southern Highlands** (U.S. Cellular

BABE RUTH IN ASHEVILLE

One day in 1925, the New York Yankees baseball team were on their way to Asheville to play an exhibition game at **McCormick Field** (30 Buchanan Place, 828/258-0428). Babe Ruth was on the train, and he didn't feel well—a touch of flu, perhaps, or indigestion, but the bumpy rails of western North Carolina did him no good. Stepping off the train at Asheville, greeted by a rush of fans, he fainted and fell. Luckily, Ruth passed out next to the catcher, Steve O'Neill, who did his job and caught his bulky teammate before the famous mug hit the station's marble floor. Ruth was rushed off to the Battery Park Hotel, where apparently he made a full recovery. The newspapers failed to note that fact, though, and it was briefly reported that Ruth had died in Asheville—a story that caused no small amount of grief. All was well a few years later when, on April 8, 1931, Ruth returned to Asheville, and both he and Lou Gehrig hit home runs at McCormick Field. This august ground is now the home field of the **Asheville Tourists** (30 Buchanan Place, 828/258-0428, www.milb.com), the Class A farm team of the Colorado Rockies.

Center, 87 Haywood St., 828/298-7928, www.southernhighlandguild.org, 10am-6pm Thurs.-Sat., 10am-5pm Sun., $8 adults, under age 12 free). Since 1948 this event has brought much-deserved attention to the Guild's more than 900 members, who live and work throughout the Appalachian Mountains. Hundreds of craftspeople participate in the event, selling all sorts of handmade items.

Asheville's **Mountain Dance and Folk Festival** (www.folkheritage.org, 828/258-6101, ext. 345, $20 adults, $10 under age 12 per day, $54 adults, $24 under age 12 for 3 days) is the nation's longest-running folk festival, an event founded in the 1920s by musician and folklorist Bascom Lamar Lunsford to celebrate the heritage of his native Carolina mountains. Musicians and dancers from western North Carolina perform at the downtown Diana Wortham Theater at Pack Place for three nights each summer. Also downtown, many of the same artists can be heard on Saturday evening at the city's **Shindig on the Green** concert series (Martin Luther King Jr. Park, 50 Martin Luther King Jr. Dr.).

In October, a series of creepy and offbeat happenings take place in the monthlong festival called **Ashtoberfest** (www.ashtoberfest.com). Among the events are a horror film festival, a summit of horror writers, and—the pinnacle of Ashtoberfest—the Zombie Walk. Ashevillians and a surprising number of out-of-towners prepare for the Zombie Walk months in advance by planning their makeup, practicing their zombie lurch, and burying clothes in the yard. When they dig them back up and don their zombie garb, they give off a properly fetid, sepulchral funk. On the appointed date, the zombies, in their grubby duds and nasty makeup, gather at a city cemetery, and all at once begin to lurch, in the top-heavy fashion of the zombies in the 1968 film *Night of the Living Dead,* in an undead shamble along the sidewalks of Asheville. The Zombie Walk ends as the ghouls gradually disappear into various pubs and parties downtown. Event dates and locations vary each year; check the website for details.

Moog Fest (www.moogfest.com) is an annual electronic music festival that honors the legacy of Robert Arthur "Bob" Moog, godfather of electronic music and inventor of the iconic Moog synthesizer. Huge national and international acts and influential DJs descend on Asheville for a two- or three-day party at music venues across the city.

Foodies looking for a festival should attend the **Asheville Wine and Food Festival** (U.S. Cellular Center, 87 Haywood St., and venues around town, www.exploreasheville.com), an annual event held over three days each August. Palate-pleasing events include competitive dining, dessert-centric parties, mixology demonstrations, and the Grand Tasting.

SHOPPING
Antiques and Secondhand Goods

For lovers of vintage, retro, and aged things, the **Antique Tobacco Barn** (75 Swannanoa River Rd., 828/252-7291, www.atbarn.com, 10am-6pm Mon.-Thurs., 9am-6pm Fri.-Sat., 1pm-6pm Sun.) has more than 77,000 square feet of goodies to plunder through. This perpetual winner of the *Mountain XPress* "Best Antiques Store in Western North Carolina" has toys, art, tools, furniture, radios, sporting equipment, folk art, farm relics, oddball bric-a-brac, mid-century furniture, and all those great weird things you can only find in a collection this large. It takes a while to explore this humongous shop, so carve out some time.

One of the best stores in Asheville is the tiny curiosity shop **Not Your Average Antiques** (21 Page Ave., across from the Grove Arcade, 828/252-1333, www.notyouraverageantiques.com, hours vary). This folk art and antiques shop is like some madcap fantasyland of vintage toys. Trading almost exclusively in toys coveted between 1900 and 1960, the cases are packed with tin robots, spacefarers, ray guns, flying saucers, posters for magicians and circuses, everything you'd need to play cowboys and Indians, and some fantastic folk art. It's quite the shop and quite the find in Asheville.

As Asheville is surrounded by the great outdoors, it's no surprise there's a busy market for secondhand outdoor goods. **Second Gear** (415-A Haywood Rd., 828/258-0757, 10am-6pm Mon.-Sat., 11am-5pm Sun.; 15 W. Walnut St., downtown, 828/505-8160, 11am-7pm Mon.-Thurs., 10am-8pm Fri.-Sat., 11am-7pm Sun., www.secondgearwnc.com) carries just about everything the outdoor adventurer needs: mountain bikes, kayaks, canoes, clothing, guidebooks, boots, backpacks, tents, and climbing gear.

Galleries

One of Asheville's shopping highlights is the 1929 **Grove Arcade** (1 Page Ave., 828/252-7799, www.grovearcade.com), a beautiful and storied piece of architecture that is now a chic shopping and dining destination in the heart of downtown. The expansive Tudor Revival building, ornately filigreed inside and out in ivory-glazed terra-cotta, was initially planned as the base of a 14-story building, a skyscraper by that day's standard. There are some fantastic galleries and boutiques, including **Mountain Made** (828/350-0307, www.mtnmade.com, 10am-6pm Mon.-Sat., noon-5pm Sun.), a gallery celebrating contemporary art created in and inspired by the mountains around Asheville. Another favorite is **Alexander & Lehnert** (828/254-2010, www.alexanderandlehnert.com, 10am-6pm Mon.-Sat.), a gallery showcasing the work of two talented jewelers with different styles—Lehnert takes an architectural approach to designs, and Alexander chooses organic forms as inspiration. Not all stores in the Grove Arcade sell fine art and jewelry; at **Asheville Home Crafts** (828/350-7556, www.ashevillehomecrafts.com, 10am-6pm Mon.-Sat., noon-6pm Sun.) you can buy specialty yarn, patterns, hooks, and needles for all sorts of knitting, weaving, and crocheting projects. Or you can buy a piece made by local artists. At the Grove Arcade you'll also find a number of restaurants, a wine bar, home-goods shops, and places to relax and primp.

There are a number of galleries in downtown Asheville, and while most exhibit works from multiple artists, none can match the size of the **Woolworth Walk** (25 Haywood St., 828/254-9235, www.woolworthwalk.com, 11am-6pm Mon.-Thurs., 11am-7pm Fri., 10am-7pm Sat., 11am-5pm Sun., soda fountain closes 1 hour before the gallery), a two-story, 20,000-square-foot gallery featuring more than 160 local artists. Nearly every conceivable medium is represented, including digitally designed graphic prints, oil paintings, watercolors, jewelry, and woodworking. This gallery is a favorite not just because it has a soda fountain but because

The Grove Arcade is a hub of downtown life.

© JASON FRYE

the work on display is affordable as well as stunning.

American Folk Art and Framing (64 Biltmore Ave., 828/281-2134, www.amerifolk. com, 10am-6pm Mon.-Sat., noon-5pm Sun.) does a wonderful job of displaying contemporary Southern folk artists, including potters, painters, and woodcarvers, as well as helping the art-appreciating public learn more about local folk-art traditions and styles. They host six openings a year in the gallery, so work changes frequently, keeping the place bubbling with energy.

Books, Toys, and Crafts

One of the social hubs of this city is **Malaprop's Bookstore and Café** (55 Haywood St., 828/254-6734, www.malaprops.com, 9am-9pm Mon.-Sat., 9am-7pm Sun.). This fun and progressive bookstore carries a deep selection of books that includes tomes by North Carolina authors and a particularly fine collection of regional authors. You'll find the requisite coffee bar and café with wireless Internet access,

making it a particularly good spot to hang out. It's bright, comfortable, and the staff are well versed in all sorts of literature, so they can help you find a local author you'll enjoy reading. People in all walks of Asheville life come to Malaprop's, so expect to see creative dressers, the tattooed, business types, artists, students, and grannies.

Dancing Bear Toys (518 Kenilworth Rd., 800/659-8697, www.dancingbeartoys.com, 10am-7pm Mon.-Sat., noon-5pm Sun.) is located among the motels and chain restaurants out on U.S. 70 (Tunnel Rd.), but inside it has the ambience of a cozy village toy shop. Dancing Bear has toys for everyone from babies to silly grown-ups: a fabulous selection of Playmobil figures and accessories, Lego, Brio, and other favorite lines of European toys; beautiful stuffed animals of all sizes; all sorts of educational kits and games; and comical doodads.

There are a lot of jewelry makers in North Carolina, and in Asheville they come to **Chevron Trading Post & Bead Company** (40 N. Lexington Ave., 828/236-2323, www.

chevronbeads.com, 10am-6pm Mon.-Sat., noon-5pm Sun.). Millions of beads in bowls and tubes and strands on every surface in the shop are so irresistibly twinkly and colorful that even if you're not crafty, you'll want to buy them by the basket just to hoard. Best of all, there's Rosie, a rotund orange-and-white cat known to help shoppers with their selection.

The **Mast General Store** (15 Biltmore Ave., 828/232-1883, www.mastgeneralstore.com, 10am-6pm Mon.-Thurs., 10am-9pm Fri.-Sat., noon-6pm Sun.) is an institution in western North Carolina and beyond. They call themselves a general store, but they mean it in a very contemporary way. Cast-iron cookware, penny candies, and Mast logo shirts and jackets sit alongside baskets and handmade crafts. A good selection of top-shelf outdoor clothing and equipment can get you outfitted for some time in the woods.

River Arts District

Along the Swannanoa River, a number of Asheville's old warehouses and industrial buildings are being transformed into studio spaces, galleries, restaurants, and breweries in an area known as the **River Arts District** (www.riverartsdistrict.com). More than 160 artists have working studios here, and twice a year, during the first weekend of June and November, nearly every artist in the district opens their studios to the public for a two-day **Studio Stroll**. On the second Saturday of each month some of the studios (they rotate based on medium, so one month may be photography, the next clay, the next painting and drawing) are open for **A Closer Look**, a day of artist demonstrations, classes, workshops, and creative activities.

Some studios are open daily, among them **Jonas Gerald Fine Art** (240 Clingman Ave., daily 10am-6pm), where the namesake artist specializes in abstract art that uses vivid colors and unusual composition to draw the viewer in. He works across many media, so there's a lot to see. **Odyssee Center for Ceramic Arts** (236-238 Clingman Ave, www.odysseyceramicarts.com, 9am-5pm Mon.-Sat., 1pm-5pm Sun.) is full of sculptors and teachers. Part of their mission is to promote artistic appreciation and advancement of ceramic arts; they hold regular classes, workshops, and talks led by master ceramic artists.

At the 1910 **Cotton Mill Studios** (122 Riverside Dr., at W. Haywood St., www.cottonmillstudiosnc.com, hours vary), several painters work alongside potters and jewelers. **Riverview Station** (191 Lyman St., http://riverviewartists.com, hours vary) is a circa-1896 building that houses the studios of a wonderful array of jewelers, ceramicists, furniture designers, painters, and photographers. Another favorite gallery is **CURVE Studios & Garden** (6, 9, and 12 Riverside Dr., 828/388-3526, www.curvestudiosnc.com, 11am-4pm daily). A fun, funky studio that has been around since before the River Arts District was a thing, and once a punk rock club called Squashpile—you can't make up stuff like that—CURVE is home to encaustic painters, ceramic workers, jewelry designers, glass artists, fiber artists, and more. This is just a sampling of what's happening in the River Arts District; visit the website for detailed listings of the artists and their studios.

SPORTS AND RECREATION

Asheville is a "go out and do it" kind of town. It's not unusual to see mountain bikers, road riders, runners, hikers, flat-water kayakers, and their daredevil white water-loving cousins all on the streets in town. A number of gear shops call Asheville home, and access to trails, rivers, and mountain roads are all right here.

Asheville Adventure Rentals (704 Riverside Dr., 828/505-7371, http://ashevilleadventurerentals.com, 10am-6pm Mon.-Thurs., 10am-6:30pm Fri.-Sun., rentals from $30 per day) specializes in sports that get you wet, namely stand-up paddleboards, kayaks, and bellyaks—a cross between a kayak and an ergonomically designed surfboard. You lie down on it and paddle like you're swimming, and take the river's rapids head on. It's a fun ride on the small but exciting rapids of the French Broad River when it's at normal levels, and it's a thrilling ride when the river is running a little high. If you've come to Asheville equipped with your own paddleboard or kayak, Adventure Rentals can rent you helmets, dry suits, PFDs, kayak skirts, and more.

For a different perspective on the Asheville area, head north a few miles and spend the day at **Navitat** (242 Poverty Branch Rd., Barnardsville, 855/628-4828 or 828/626-3700, www.navitat.com, 8am-5pm daily, Mon.-Fri. $89, Sat.-Sun. $99). You can streak through the forest canopy on 10 zip lines like an overgrown flying squirrel. The tallest zip line here is an incredible 200 feet high—they say "don't look down," but do, it's amazing. The longest is more than 1,000 feet; that's a long ride. Two rappels, a pair of sky bridges, and three short hikes provide interludes from all the zipping and flying, and there are plenty of opportunities for photos and action-camera videos.

In town, take a tour by bicycle. I know what you're thinking; "It's too hilly, I'll never be able to climb that." With **Electro Bike Tours** (departing from Weaver Park's Merrimon Ave. entrance, 828/513-3960, http://electrobiketours. com, tours 10am daily, $45 with 2-hour rental) they provide you with pedal-assisted bikes that make the hills easier and the flats seem like nothing at all. To show off how well the pedal-assist system works, your first shot is straight up the hill to the Grove Park Inn, the first stop on a two-hour tour around Asheville's historic and cultural sites. The bikes really are ingenious because rather than rely on a throttle like a moped or electric scooter, they use their power to make pedaling easier, meaning you still have to work, just not as hard, to get where you're going.

The French Broad and Swannanoa Rivers offer a lot of opportunities to try your hand a stand-up paddleboarding on the river. It's much different than on a lake, marsh creek, or even the ocean, and you have to know how to read the river for underwater hazards and how to fall off correctly. **Asheville Outdoor Center** (521 Amboy Rd., 828/232-1970, www. paddlewithus.com, introductory lessons $65 for 1.5 hours, tours $40-65) provides lessons to make sure you're safe on the river and rentals to make sure you keep having fun. They offer tours ranging from a few to many miles, but it's all scenic and mostly downstream.

Ready for mountain air? Join **Blue Ridge Hiking Co.** (15 Hildebrand St., 828/713-5451, http://blueridgehikingco.com, half-day and full-day hikes $35-185) on a half-day, full-day, or overnight hike in the Pisgah National Forest. Founder Jennifer Pharr Davis has hiked more than 11,000 miles of long-distance trails and became the first woman to be the overall record holder for fastest through-hike of the Appalachian Trail: She hiked its 2,181 miles in 46.5 days. Don't worry, she and her guides don't go that fast on the trail; they like to slow down, enjoy the moment, and make sure everyone gets a look and feel for what they love about hiking.

On the Biltmore Estate

The Biltmore Estate really is an all-in-one vacation compound. You can spend a few days here and not exhaust the activities, and I'm not even talking about touring the house or visiting the winery; there are a variety of outdoor recreational opportunities offered in this 8,000-acre backyard. For starters, there are countless miles of **bicycle trails** on the estate, and you can bring your bike or rent one in Antler Hill Village from the **Bike Barn** (800/411-3812, single speed beach cruiser $15 per hour, mountain and hybrid bikes half-day and full-day $30-60 adults, $20-40 children, $50 tandem bikes, estate admission not included). Riding on paved roads is not allowed (they're too narrow to share with cars), so stick to the marked paths, which will take you past prime photo spots and some of the most beautiful land on the estate.

The Biltmore is an Orvis-endorsed **fly-fishing school,** and it's an excellent place to learn or hone your technique. Outings include two-hour introductory lessons ($125), half-day lessons ($225), kid's fishing outings ($125), full-day guided fishing float trips on the French Broad River, wading trips on a private trout stream ($350-450 for 1-2 people), and no fishing license is required.

Hiking on the Biltmore Estate can mean anything from walking the 2.5 miles of mulched paths in the manicured gardens to exploring the hills, meadows, streams, and riverbank on more than 22 miles of trails. None are rugged, so you don't need any special equipment, just water, your camera, and maybe a walking stick. The Outdoor Adventure Center in Antler Hill Village has maps and can help you identify the right hike. For a more placid outing, try a **river float trip** (800/411-3812, raft trips $35 adults, $25 under age 13, kayaks $25 pp) on a raft or kayak down the French Broad River. Raft trips feature a guide who knows the land and its history who will regale you with stories; kayak trips are more private, self-guided affairs, but either way it makes for a relaxing afternoon.

Finally, for a loud, blood-pumping good time, try **clay target shooting** ($100-450). If you've never handled a shotgun before or have never shot clay targets, the introductory sporting clays lesson will have you on target in no time. For more experienced shooters, two-hour advanced lessons, a sporting clay course, and even full-day shotgun sports clinics will challenge your skills and help you refine them. All equipment is provided for activities on the Biltmore Estate (except your hiking shoes). The **Outdoor Adventure Center** (800/411-3812) in Antler Hill Village has full information on these activities and can make reservations and recommendations.

Golf

Golf in the mountains can be a challenge, with course layouts big on blind approaches and hard doglegs, but it pays off with beautiful views and long downhill shots that can make you feel like you hit it like a pro.

The **Asheville Municipal Golf Course** (226 Fairway Dr., 828/298-1867, www.ashevillenc. gov, 18 holes, par 72, greens fees $31-36, includes cart, tee-time reservation required) opened in 1927 and is one of the oldest in the western part of the state. This Donald Ross-designed course is nearly 6,500 yards long from the championship tees and features a good mix of forgiving and narrow fairways, par-5 fairways begging for a birdie, and par-3 fairways that will challenge your ball placement.

Play a round at the **Grove Park Inn Golf Club** (290 Macon Ave., 828/252-2711, ext. 1012, www.groveparkinn.com, 18 holes, par 70, greens fees 9 holes $50-85, 18 holes $85-149, includes cart, discounts for juniors, late play, and off-season), where President Obama played a round during his 2010 stay. *Golf Digest* named this course one of the top 10 courses that are at least 100 years old, and it plays beautifully. This is a must-play course for serious golfers, and not just because the views are spectacular but also because the course contains so much history.

The **Black Mountain Golf Course** (18 Ross Dr., Black Mountain, 828/669-2710, www. blackmountaingolf.org, 18 holes, par 71, greens fees 9 holes $18-21, 18 holes $34-39, includes cart, discounts for seniors, walking, and late play) was once home to the world's longest fairway, number 17, a 747-yard par 6. Although the record no longer stands, the hole is still here, ready to challenge even the longest drivers. Originally designed as a nine-hole course in 1929, the back nine opened in 1962. Even though its age is starting to show around the edges, this is a fun course to play, even if you have to pull out your driver a few times on number 17.

ACCOMMODATIONS
Hotels
Hotel Indigo (151 Haywood St., 828/239-0239, www.boutiquehotel-asheville.com, $217-399 peak season, $152-315 off-season) is shiny, modern, and steps away from downtown. The staff are attentive and courteous, and the concierges know the ins, outs, shortcuts, best restaurants and bars, and top townie things to see and do. As one of the tallest buildings in Asheville, the mountain views are spectacular from upper floors; keep that in mind when making a reservation.

If you've spent the day touring Biltmore House, viewing the incredible splendor in which a robber baron of the Gilded Age basked, it may be jarring to return to real life, unless you're Richard Branson or European royalty. You can soften the transition with a stay at the

the Inn on Biltmore Estate

© JASON FRYE

luxurious **Inn on Biltmore Estate** (866/336-1245, www.biltmore.com, $499-599 peak season, $259-399 off-season, suites up to $2,000). It's everything you'd wish for from a hotel in this location. The suites are beautifully furnished and luxurious, the views are magnificent, and the lobby, dining room, and library have the deluxe coziness of a turn-of-the-20th-century lodge. On the other hand, if you do happen to be Richard Branson or Queen Elizabeth and simply need a mountain getaway, consider the Inn's **Cottage on Biltmore Estate.** This historic two-room cottage was designed by Richard Howland Hunt, son of the mansion's designer, Richard Morris Hunt. Your own personal butler and chef come with the digs; call for rates.

In the heart of downtown, **C Aloft Asheville Downtown** (51 Biltmore Ave., 828/232-2838 or 866/716-8143, www.aloftashevilledowntown.com, $290-459 peak season, $169-459 off-season) offers a hip spot to rest your head. There is a trendy bar serving rock-star cocktails, plush modern guest rooms,

and fantastic city and mountain views from most rooms (others are poolside). Some of the best restaurants in Asheville are a few minutes' walk away, and the best live music in town is just a couple of blocks south.

Resorts

The **Grove Park Inn Resort & Spa** (290 Macon Ave., 800/438-5800, www.groveparkinn.com, $349-942 peak season, $177-755 off-season, spa and golf packages available) is the sort of place Asheville residents bring their out-of-town houseguests when giving them a grand tour of the city, simply to walk into the lobby to ooh and aah. The massive stone building—constructed by a crew of 400 who had only mule teams and a single steam shovel to aid them—was erected in 1912 and 1913, the project of St. Louis millionaire E. W. Grove, the name behind Grove's Tasteless Chill Tonic, a medicinal syrup that outsold Coca-Cola in the 1890s. You may have seen it in antiques shops; on the label was a picture of a wincing baby who looks more like he's just been given a dose of the stuff than that he needs one.

The opening of the Grove Park Inn was cause for such fanfare that William Jennings Bryan addressed the celebratory dinner party. In the coming years, at least eight U.S. presidents would stay here, as would a glittering parade of early 20th-century big shots, among them Henry Ford, Thomas Edison, Eleanor Roosevelt, Harry Houdini, F. Scott Fitzgerald, Will Rogers, and George Gershwin. Even if you don't stay at the Grove Park while you are visiting Asheville, swing by just to see it. You can drive right up to the front door, and if you tell the valets that you just want to go in and see the lobby, they'll probably be willing to watch your car for five minutes (don't forget to tip them). The lobby is quite amazing, a cross between a Gilded Age hunting lodge and the great hall of a medieval castle. There are 14-foot fireplaces at each end, and the elevators, believe it or not, are inside the chimneys. It's easy to imagine flappers, foreign dignitaries, mobsters, and literati milling about the lobby with their martinis when this hotel was young.

Being a guest at the Grove Park is quite an experience. In addition to the spectacle of the lodge and its multiple restaurants, cafés, bars, and shops, for an additional charge guests have access to its world-famous spa (Mon.-Fri. $65, $90 Sat.-Sun.). Nonguests can purchase day passes Monday-Thursday ($90). The pass gives access to the lounges, pools, waterfall, steam room, inhalation room, and outdoor whirlpool tub. The indoor pool is a fantastic place, a subterranean stone room with vaulted skylights and tropical plants. For extra fees ($109-500, mostly $200-300), guests can choose from a long menu of spa treatments: massages, facials, manicures, aromatherapy, and body wraps. For $70 you can have your aura photographed before and after the treatment to gauge the depth of your relaxation.

Bed-and-Breakfasts

One of the most charming and hospitable bed-and-breakfasts in Asheville is ⚑ **Asheville Green Cottage** (25 St. Dunstans Circle,

828/707-6563 or 828/707-2919, www.ashevillegreencottage.com, $125-165 peak season, $95-135 off-season). This 1920s arts-and-crafts-style home is built of huge granite blocks and is simply decorated but cozy. Guest rooms are big enough, but breakfast is outstanding, and they can cater to special dietary needs. Asheville Green Cottage is a "healthy and green" bed-and-breakfast, meaning they're smoke-free, fragrance-free, and use natural products for cleaning. It's a great place to come home to after a day of exploring Asheville.

An artsy little inn just a few minutes outside Asheville is the **Fox & Fiddle** (31 Toms Rd., Candler, 828/665-9830, www.foxandfiddle.net, $45-60, 7th night free), where breakfast is only available on weekends ($15 per room). Guest rooms here are simply appointed but comfortable, and in addition to free Wi-Fi, there are also stupendous mountain views, seven acres to explore, an organic farm, and a fire pit. They roast their own coffee in-house and give a portion of their sales toward programs that support human rights.

Hostels

With so many neo-hippie types, college kids, dirt bags (it's not an insult, it's what rock climbers often call themselves), kayakers, hikers, and bikers coming through, it's no surprise to find a nice hostel nestled in among the hotels and bed-and-breakfasts. At the **Asheville ArtHaus Hostel** (16 Ravenscroft Dr., 828/423-0256, http://aahostel.com, $60, bungalow with private bath $88) you'll find only private guest rooms and even a private bungalow. Reservations are available up to five months in advance, so it's easy to get a room if you know when you're traveling. At the hostel you'll find free waffles, coffee, and tea at make-your-own stations; free Wi-Fi; free parking; and downtown within walking distance.

Bon Paul and Sharky's Hostel of Asheville (816 Haywood Rd., 828/350-9929, www.bonpaulandsharkys.com, cash only) is a pleasant old white house with a porch and a porch swing, high-speed Internet access, and dorm-style bunks in women-only or coed shared rooms ($25) as well as camping ($18) in the yard. If you want a little more of a retreat, a private room with a TV and a queen bed ($68) and a cottage are available. Dogs must stay in the outdoor kennels. And Bon Paul and Sharky, because I know you were wondering, were goldfish.

Motor Courts

In the days of yore, before budget hotels became the norm, the motor court or cottage court was the stay-over of choice for middle-class travelers. In one of the greatest road-trip movies ever, *It Happened One Night*, unmarried and feuding Clark Gable and Claudette Colbert build a "Wall of Jericho" between their beds with a rope and a blanket as a means to keep themselves in check while staying in a cottage court somewhere between Miami and New York. I like to think it was Asheville. Today, these motor courts and cottage courts are relics of the past and few remain, but the mountains of North Carolina still contain a handful of fine examples; in the Asheville area at least two are still operating today, providing travelers with retro accommodations. **Asheville Log Cabin Motor Court** (330 Weaverville Hwy., 828/645-6546, www.cabinlodging.com, 2-night minimum stay weekends, $75-250, pets allowed for a fee) was constructed around 1930 and appears in the fantastic 1958 Robert Mitchum movie *Thunder Road*. The cabins have cable TV and wireless Internet access but no phones. Some are air-conditioned, but that's not usually a necessity at this elevation. Another great cabin court is the **Pines Cottages** (346 Weaverville Hwy., 828/645-9661, http://ashevillepines. com, $115-175, $15 per pet, up to 2 pets allowed). Billed as "A nice place for nice people," how could you resist staying here?

FOOD

No matter what you're craving, from Mediterranean to vegetarian, four-star to down-home, Asheville has the eateries that both embrace the Southern traditions of its mountain home and explore well beyond its borders. This is a town that clearly loves its food, with 13 active farmers markets, more than 250 independent restaurants, and 12 microbreweries in a city of fewer than 100,000 residents. Farmers work with restaurants to provide the highest-quality produce and meats, and artisanal bakers and cheese makers supply their tasty foodstuffs to restaurants high and low.

With such a robust food scene, it can be hard to pick out where you want to go. For a sampling of the best of what Asheville has to offer the gastronome, take a walking tour with **Eating Asheville** (tours begin at the Grove Arcade, 1 Page Ave., Suite 101, 828/489-3266, http://eatingasheville.com, daily tour $47, high-roller tour $54). Tours stop in at six of Asheville's best farm-to-table restaurants for a taste of what they're cooking and provide two or three drink pairings as well as a talk about their food philosophy; sometimes tours meet the chef. Held on Saturday only, the deluxe high-roller tour visits six of the top restaurants and includes four or five beverage pairings (wine, beer, and craft cocktails); for just a few bucks more, it's the way to go.

Eclectic American

A new arrival on Asheville's culinary scene is **Biscuit Head** (733 Haywood Rd., 828/333-5154, www.biscuitheads.com, 7am-2pm Tues.-Fri., 8am-3pm Sat.-Sun., around $8) in West Asheville. They serve up an Appalachian specialty, cat-head biscuits, so named because they're huge—the size of a cat's head. These biscuits are dynamite. Order the fried green tomato biscuit and you'll get more than you can eat: a cat-head biscuit, split and topped with a fried green tomato, brie, a sliced tomato, poached eggs, and smoked tomato hollandaise. Or just get the "Biscuit And," which comes with a biscuit and your choice of crazy butters, jams, hot sauces, infused honeys, and toppings from the biscuit bar, featuring all house-made spreadables. Or make a go of breakfast sans biscuit (blasphemy, I know) and order a number of side dishes, including Sriracha maple sausage, seitan vegetarian "sausage," smoked chèvre grits, fried chicken, and flavored bacon. The chef, his wife, and their crew did all of the work

ASHEVILLE

to make the interior of the place reflect their funky outlook on food, and it does that quite well; it's a little weird, a little bit like home, and a cool spot for breakfast. If you eat outside, check out the wild terrarium tables made from salvaged windows.

Tupelo Honey Café (12 College St., 828/255-4863, http://tupelohoneycafe.com, 9am-10am daily, breakfast and lunch around $10, dinner around $18) is a well-known downtown eatery serving breakfast all day (the sweet potato pancake is their claim to fame, and for good reason), but lunch and dinner are where it's at. At lunch it's hard to go wrong with the Shoo Grill Cheese, Have Mercy, which is served with a big hearty mug of tomato soup. The name is crazy, as is the meal—the sandwich has havarti and pimento cheeses, caramelized onions, maple peppered bacon, city ham (like country ham, but more sophisticated), fried green tomatoes, and fresh basil; the soup is thick, rich, and begging for a corner of the sandwich to be dunked in it. When dinnertime rolls around, try the Sunburst Mountain Trout, fresh from not too far outside Asheville and served with a spinach beurre blanc over goat cheese grits.

◖ **Early Girl Eatery** (8 Wall St., 828/259-9292, www.earlygirleatery.com, 7:30am-3pm Mon., 7:30am-9pm Tues.-Fri., 9am-9pm Sat.-Sun., $10-15) has caused a stir among area locavores and is gaining a following among visitors. More than half of the vegetables, meat, and fish used at Early Girl was raised or caught within 20 miles of the restaurant. The menu is accommodating of Asheville's large vegetarian and vegan contingent, but nonveg diners can feast on pan-fried trout with pecan butter, pan-fried free-range chicken, or a cheeseburger made from hormone-free beef and topped with farmstead cheese, basil mayo, and all the fixings, among many other delicious New Southern creations. Breakfast is among the best in Asheville, in part because it's served all day and in part because their multigrain pancakes are out of this world.

When you've been at the Grey Eagle or the Orange Peel, the show has just let out, it's the middle of the night, and you need to refuel with some good food, the lights are on at **Rosetta's Kitchen** (111 Broadway Ave., 828/232-0738, www.rosettaskitchen.com, 11am-11pm Mon.-Thurs., 11am-3am Fri.-Sat., brunch 11am-3pm Sun., around $10). There's so much to recommend about this place: The food is good, it's all vegetarian and mostly vegan, and it's made with local produce in season. Best of all, it's open late on weekends. They compost everything that makes its way back to the kitchen, recycle all their trash, and make sure their used vegetable oil goes to power biodiesel cars—it's Asheville's signature countercultural reinterpretation of the South.

The **Laughing Seed** (40 Wall St., 828/252-3445, http://laughingseed.jackofthewood.com, 11:30am-9pm Mon. and Wed.-Thurs., 11:30am-10pm Fri.-Sat., 10am-9pm Sun., under $20) achieves what vegetarian restaurants always aim for but are seldom able to achieve—their food is so good and so widely praised that a legion of nonvegetarians become loyal fans and customers. The restaurant describes its style as "international vegetarian cuisine" and it draws on Latin American, Thai, Indian, and other world cuisines to create hearty and addictively flavorful dishes. The Laughing Seed also has a great cocktail menu, and their Bloody Mary is especially good.

In 2005, ◖ **Table** (48 College St., 828/254-8980, http://tableasheville.com, lunch 11am-2:30pm Mon. and Wed.-Sat., dinner 5:30pm-10pm Mon. and Wed.-Sat., brunch 10:30am-2pm Sun., $19-34) opened to much local fanfare, and not long after the critical acclaim, including becoming a James Beard Award semifinalist, began to roll in. This restaurant is the realization of a plan by husband and wife Jacob and Alicia Sessoms and their friend Matthew Dawes, who met as students at Warren Wilson College in nearby Swannanoa, to found a restaurant that's upscale, interesting, innovative, and above all, good. They use ingredients like locally caught bass and mountain-raised pork and lamb, creating a menu that takes full advantage to the culinary riches of western North Carolina. You can find some unusual ingredients on their menu, like sweetbreads and quail, and they're renowned for their charcuterie, much of which is made in-house. The chef takes a minimalist approach to food, choosing to do as little as possible to coax out the maximum flavor, which is why this tiny restaurant is always packed. Call for reservations, and if you're feeling bold, go with the chef's tasting menu, a selection of dishes that showcase the best this miniscule kitchen (you'll see it on your way in) has to offer.

The Market Place (20 Wall St., 828/252-4162, www.marketplace-restaurant.com, dinner 5:30pm Mon.-Sat., entrées $16-30) has been serving great food in downtown Asheville for more than 30 years. This local favorite constructs an elegant menu from ingredients raised or caught within 100 miles of the restaurant. Try the sweet pea and goat cheese ravioli, or whatever their seasonal ravioli happens to be, the locally caught trout with smoked bacon and a tomato confit vinaigrette, or the buttermilk fried chicken.

West Asheville's **Sunny Point Café** (626 Haywood Rd., 828/252-0055, www.sunnypointcafe.com, 8:30am-9pm Tues.-Sat., 8:30am-2:30pm Sun.-Mon., $10-17) serves three meals most days, but is so famous for its brunch that a line sometimes forms out the door. The breakfast menu is popular and served any time of day, even though the lunch and dinner menus are also well worth a trip. This is a great bet for vegetarians—the meatless options are imaginative and beautifully created.

HomeGrown (371 Merrimon Ave., 828/232-4340, www.slowfoodrightquick.com, 8am-9pm Sun.-Fri., 5pm-9pm Sat., around $10) is a down-home eatery that serves "slow food right quick," meaning they take time and care with their ingredients (as did the farmers, ranchers, artisans, and foragers who supplied them) but bring it to the table as soon as they can. Their selection of "Samiches," soups, and specialties caters to vegetarians and omnivores alike, and they draw on both traditional and contemporary Southern influences in their menu.

BILTMORE VILLAGE

In one of the historic cottages of Biltmore Village is the **Corner Kitchen** (3 Boston Way, 828/274-2439, www.thecornerkitchen.com, breakfast 7:30am-11am Mon.-Fri., brunch 9am-3pm Sat.-Sun., lunch 11:30am-3pm Mon.-Fri., dinner 5pm daily, starters around $10, entrées $18-28). Head chef Joe Scully, first in his class at the Culinary Institute of America, counts among his illustrious former gigs New York's Waldorf Astoria and the United Nations, where he served as executive chef. He is joined in the Corner Kitchen by Josh Weeks, a young Carolina-born chef with an impressive résumé and expertise in Southern, French, and Pacific cuisines. Chefs Joe and Josh have put together an elegant menu that combines homestyle and haute cuisines quite harmoniously. The Obamas ate at Corner Kitchen when they were in Asheville in 2010, and if you want to recreate their meal, you're out of luck—the menu changes frequently. They had corn and crab chowder, mahimahi (there's always a fresh North Carolina fish on the menu), baby arugula salad, corn-fried oysters, lobster tacos, pork chops, and soufflé. They have a long wine list that features many Napa Valley, French, and Italian wines, including several fine champagnes and sparkling whites and rosés. Prices range $20-275 by the bottle, and a number of wines are available by the glass ($6-12); no word on what the first couple paired with their meal. The cozy, cheerful dining room of this Victorian cottage opens into the kitchen, where guests can see every step of their meal's preparation while chatting with the staff.

Also excellent in Biltmore Village is **Fig** (18 Brook St., 828/277-0889, www.figbistro.com, lunch 11:30am-3pm daily, dinner 5:30pm-9pm Mon.-Sat., $12-27). Chef William Klein worked at fine restaurants in France and San Francisco before returning to western North Carolina, where he feels his career began. Here at Fig he has created an elegant bistro menu that includes classic French desserts.

BILTMORE ESTATE

There are no fewer than nine places to eat (plus snacks, ice cream, and coffee) on the Biltmore Estate (800/411-3812, www.biltmore.com, estate admission required to visit restaurants). The **Dining Room** (5:30pm-9:30pm daily, reservations required, $9-24, 5-course tasting menu $80) is an elegant restaurant, led by chef David Ryba, featuring estate-raised Angus beef, mountain trout, Biltmore wines, and vegetables grown on estate gardens. The food is spectacular, and tables with a mountain view make the meal all that much better. Evening dress and reservations are recommended.

The **Biltmore Bistro** (11am-9pm daily, lunch $15-21, dinner $19-45) in Antler Hill Village, adjacent to the winery, has a well-rounded gourmet menu sourced from the Biltmore's own kitchen garden, locally raised heirloom crops, meat and seafood delicacies, and artisanal cheeses and breads. Lunch and dinner are dramatically different (wood-fired pizza at lunch, braised veal cheeks at dinner), but each menu features something from the wood-fired oven.

The dining room of the **Deerpark Restaurant** (11am-3pm Sat., 10am-2pm Sun., Sat. buffet $18, Sun. buffet $28) is a former barn designed by architect Richard Morris Hunt, now renovated to airy splendor with walls of windows. Expect hearty and homey meals based on Appalachian cuisine. Like the Deerpark, the **Stable Café** (lunch 11am-4pm daily, dinner from 5pm daily) was once livestock housing, and guests can sit in booths that were once horse stalls. This is a meat eater's paradise, where you can order estate-raised Angus beef, and pork barbecue with the house special sauce, among others.

In the stable area near the house, both the **Bake Shop** (8:30am-5:30pm daily) and the **Ice Cream Café** (noon-5pm daily) serve fresh treats. The **Creamery** (11am-7pm Sun.-Thurs., 10am-8pm Fri.-Sat.) is the place for sandwiches and hand-dipped ice cream in Antler Hill Village, and **Chauncey's Corner** (from 1pm daily), adjacent to the gardens, will keep you fed after a day admiring the roses. If you have a hankering for barbecue, a quick sandwich, some snacks, or a cold drink, the **Smokehouse** (noon-5pm daily) in Antler Hill Village serves just what you need.

While you're in Antler Hill Village, check out the newest addition to the Biltmore's food offerings, **Cedric's Tavern** (11am-9pm daily, lunch $15-21, dinner $17-30). Named for George Vanderbilt's beloved Saint Bernard (you can see his huge collar on display at the entrance), Cedric's pays homage to pubs and taverns found in Britain, with a Southern twist. The fish-and-chips and scotch egg are both delicious. You can also grab a pint of Cedric's Pale or Brown Ale, both brewed by the Biltmore Brewing Company.

Indian

Mela (70 Lexington Ave., 828/225-8880, www.melaasheville.com, 11:30am-2:30pm daily, 5:30pm-9:30pm Sun.-Thurs., 5:30pm-10:pm Fri. and Sat., entrées $10-15) is one of the best Indian restaurants in North Carolina. The elaborate menu offers dozens of choices, combining cuisines of both northern and southern India with great meat, seafood, and vegetable dishes. The restaurant is dark and elegant, but the prices are surprisingly low; you can put together a great patchwork meal of appetizers, which start at $2, along with soup and roti. Don't miss the samosas.

Local favorite **Chai Pani** (22 Battery Park Ave., 828/254-4003, www.chaipani.net, 11:30am-4pm Mon.-Sat., noon-4pm Sun., 5pm-9:30pm Sun.-Thurs., 5:30pm-10:pm Fri. and Sat., under $10), continues to win fans because of its cool atmosphere and great food. The restaurant's name means "tea and water," a phrase that refers to a snack or a small gift. This restaurant is inspired by Indian street-food vendors and serves casual and affordable specialties from all over India.

Asian

Asheville's well-known chef Elliott Moss's new restaurant, **Ben's Tune Up** (195 Hilliard Ave., 828/424-7580, http://benstuneup.com, 5pm-2am daily, around $12) is an odd but tasty

FOODTOPIA AND BEER CITY USA

From writers to musicians to artists, those with a creative streak have always found something inspiring in Asheville. In recent years, a new set of artists has emerged: **chefs, mixologists,** and **brewers** who are putting Asheville on the map for their creativity on the plate and in the glass.

Asheville's status as a "foodtopia" started in earnest in 2009, when the town won the coveted title of "Beer City USA" (a title it held until 2013), was named "Best Craft Beer City in America," and was included in the Huffington Post's Top 10 Undiscovered Local Food Cities. With more than a dozen breweries downtown, some 50-odd local beers on tap at any given moment, and 250 independent restaurants, it's surprising that Asheville's food scene remained a secret as long as it did.

Once the word was out, the James Beard Award nominations included chefs and restaurants from Asheville, and more chefs wanted to come here to cook. Asheville now boasts a number of James Beard nominees, including Jacob Sessoms of **Table,** Katie Button of **Cúrate,** and Elliott Moss of **Ben's Tune Up.**

Award-winners and nominees aren't the only foodies drawing attention to Asheville. A local character known as the Mushroom Man forages the surrounding forests for mushrooms, ramps, ferns, greens, berries, and roots, then sells his loot to restaurants in town. Stephen Steidle of **Eating Asheville** (828/489-3266, www.eatingasheville.com) leads walking tours of the town's best spots for food and drink, and the guys at **Asheville Brewery Tours** (828/233-5006, http://ashevillebrewerytours.com) help visitors find the tastiest brews in town.

addition to the food and craft cocktail scene. An American sake brewery and Japanese-inspired restaurant, you'll find sake made on-site and dishes that stand up to time-tested Japanese food traditions but geared toward the Southern palate and using local ingredients.

Latin American

Ask an Asheville resident for restaurant recommendations, and chances are **Salsa's** (6 Patton Ave., 828/252-9805, www.salsas-asheville.com, 11:30am-4pm and 5pm-9:30pm Mon.-Fri., noon-4pm and 5pm-10pm Sat., noon-4pm and 5pm-9:30pm Sun., $10-20) will be one of the first names mentioned. Salsa's pan-Latin concoctions, from their famous fish burritos to exquisite cocktails, keep this tiny café jam-packed with locals and visitors. When the weather's good, it's fun to eat on their little street-side patio and watch the people go by.

Also delicious is **Limones** (13 Eagle St., 828/252-2327, http://limonesrestaurant.com, daily 5pm-10pm daily, brunch 10:30am-2:30pm Sat.-Sun., $10-14). Chef Hugo Ramírez, a native of Mexico City, combines his backgrounds in Mexican and French-inspired California cuisine to create a menu unlike any other in Asheville.

European

◖ **Cúrate** (11 Biltmore Ave., 828/239-2946, www.curatetapasbar.com, 11:20am-10:30pm Tues.-Thurs., 11:30am-11pm Fri.-Sat., 11:30am-10pm Sun., small plates from $5-20) features the food of chef Katie Button, a James Beard Award semifinalist who cooked at the world's best restaurant, elBulli, in Spain. She serves a Spanish tapas style menu, so you'll be making a meal of a bunch of small plates and get to try a variety of flavors and textures. The *table de jamón* (a selection of three delicious and very different Spanish hams), and the *pulpo a'la gallega* (octopus and paprika with potatoes) are good dishes to share. There are also a number of vegan and gluten-free selections on the menu. The can't-miss street dish that people rave about is the *berenjenas la taberna*—fried eggplant drizzled in wild mountain honey and garnished with rosemary. This dish is incredible and can even serve as a component to a dessert course if you like a savory-sweet dessert. There's a lot of energy in this restaurant, partially because a long bar faces the kitchen, putting everyone from chef Button to her expert kitchen brigade on display.

Chef Michael Baudouin grew up in France's Rhône Valley, the son of a winemaker and an excellent cook. He brings his culinary heritage to Asheville at his restaurant **Bouchon** (62 N. Lexington Ave., 828/350-1140, http://ashevillebouchon.com, from 5pm daily, small plates $6-16, entrées $12-25). Bouchon's "French comfort food" includes classics such as mussels frites, French-style trout, and roasted half-duck rubbed with cocoa nibs, sea salt, coriander, and black pepper. Delicious vegetarian options are available.

Zambra (85 Walnut St., 828/232-1060, www.zambratapas.com, dinner from 5pm daily, $10-20) combines cuisines of the western Mediterranean—Spanish, Rom, and North African—with fresh North Carolina ingredients. Specials change nightly and often feature North Carolina seafood. The long tapas menu has many choices for vegetarians. **Vinnie's** (641 Merrimon Ave., 828/253-1077, www.vinniesitalian.com, 5pm-9pm Sun.-Wed., 5pm-9:30pm Thurs.-Sat., $11-24), on Merrimon Avenue downtown, is a good and reasonably priced Italian eatery. Pasta, pizza, heroes, and calzone are offered in abundance, along with heartier veal and chicken dishes, lasagna, and eggplant parmigiana.

C Cucina 24 (24 Wall St., 828/254-6170, http://cucina24restaurant.com, dinner from 5:30pm Tues.-Fri., from 5pm Sat.-Sun., $10-26) is, as executive chef Brian Canipelli says, "not a fettuccine alfredo and lasagna kind of place; we do cooking like it's done in Italy, but with North Carolina ingredients." That's a strong statement, but his food backs it up. With a menu that changes completely just about weekly, there's always something new on the plates coming out of the kitchen, often inspired by a farmer that morning when Canipelli was out buying for the day. A recent example is rabbit meatballs with dandelion greens, stinging nettles, and house-made gnocchi with a spicy red sauce, using foraged greens and house-made pasta.

Chocolate

French Broad Chocolates (10 S. Lexington Ave., 828/252-4181, http://frenchbroadchocolates.com, 11am-11pm Sun.-Thurs., 11am-midnight Fri.-Sat.) describes itself as "a sacred space for chocophiles." This mellow café serves a menu that celebrates chocolate, featuring French Broad Chocolates' own artisanal truffles, brownies, and pastries as well as sipping chocolates and floats. If, by some freakish chance, you don't care for chocolate, you can sample Pisgah Brewing Company beers and nonchocolate desserts like pecan tart and butter cake. This is a true "bean to bar" chocolatier, as they roast their own cacao in a rooftop solar roaster at their nearby factory and tasting room (21 Buxton Ave., 828/504-4996, noon-6pm Mon.-Sat., tours 2pm Sat.).

At **The Chocolate Fetish** (36 Haywood St., 828/258-2353, http://chocolatefetish.com, 11am-7pm Mon. and Thurs., 11am-6pm Tues.-Wed., 11am-9pm Fri.-Sat., noon-6pm Sun.) has been making handmade chocolates since 1986 and winning awards for them for years. From traditional truffles to truffle bars and assorted boxes and more, the chocolate is long on flavor.

INFORMATION AND SERVICES

The **Asheville Visitors Center** (36 Montford Ave., near I-240 exit 4C, 828/258-6129), can set you up with all the maps, brochures, and recommendations you could need. Other sources are **Explore Asheville** (www.exploreasheville.com) and the **Asheville Area Chamber of Commerce** (www.ashevillechamber.org). **Mission Hospital** (509 Biltmore Ave.; 428 Biltmore Ave., 828/213-1111, www.missionhospitals.org) in Asheville has two campuses and two emergency departments.

GETTING THERE AND AROUND

Asheville is spread around the junction of I-40, North Carolina's primary east-west highway, and I-26, a roughly north-south artery through the Southern highlands. U.S. 19 runs at a diagonal, deep into the Smokies in one direction and into the northern Blue Ridge in the other. Asheville has an extensive public bus system called **ART** (www.ashevillenc.gov, 6am-11:30pm Mon.-Sat., $1, $0.50 seniors), connecting most major points in the metropolitan area, including the airport, with downtown. See the website for routes and schedules. **Asheville Regional Airport** (AVL, 61 Terminal Dr., 828/684-2226, www.flyavl.com) is a 20-minute drive on I-26 south of the city in Fletcher. Several airlines have flights to Atlanta, Charlotte, and other U.S. cities.

BLACK MOUNTAIN
Sights
Black Mountain is a beautiful little town just a short distance from Asheville. Step into the **Swannanoa Valley Museum** (223 W. State St., 828/669-9566, www.swannanoavalleymuseum.org, 10am-5pm Tues.-Sat. Apr.-Oct., $2) to learn about the history of this area, including settlement by the Cherokee people, early industrialization, and the shutdown of the all-important Beacon Blanket Factory. A lot has happened in this neck of the woods. While you're here, stop in next door at the **Black Mountain Center for the Arts** (225 W. State St., 828/669-0930, http://blackmountainarts.org, 10am-5pm Mon.-Fri.) to get a feel for what some of this region's many artists are up to.

Entertainment and Events
Twice yearly, in the spring and fall, Black Mountain is the scene of the **Lake Eden Arts Festival** (377 Lake Eden Rd., 828/686-8742, www.theleaf.com), better known as LEAF. Based around roots music—and there are some amazing performers here every year—LEAF is also a festival of visual arts, poetry, food, and even the healing arts. It's an amazing scene, and it takes place, appropriately, at Camp Rockmont, once the campus of Black Mountain College, the short-lived but historically important avant-garde institution that was

home to a number of influential American artists and writers.

NIGHTLIFE
Pisgah Brewing Company (150 Eastside Dr., 828/669-0190, www.pisgahbrewing.com, 4pm-9pm Mon.-Wed., 2pm-midnight Thurs.-Fri., noon-midnight Sat., 2pm-9pm Sun., cash only) is both a brewpub and a music venue, featuring an eclectic mix of bands from roots music to rock. Pisgah was the Southeast's first certified organic brewery, and several beers are on tap all year, including their pale ale, porter, and stout; a long list of seasonal brews rotates through the year. You can tour the brewery (2pm and 3pm Sat.).

Shopping
Black Mountain Books (103 Cherry St., 828/669-8149, 11am-5pm Mon.-Sat., 11am-3pm Sun.) specializes in rare and out-of-print titles and is a great place to find unusual volumes on North Carolina, Black Mountain College, the Southern Appalachians, and even 18th- and 19th-century England and Scotland. Down the road, stop in at **Sourwood Gallery** (110 Broadway, 828/669-4975, www.sourwoodgallery.com, 11am-3pm Mon.-Tues., 10am-5pm Wed.-Sat., 1pm-4pm Sun.), a little co-op gallery featuring paintings, jewelry, wood carving and turned wood, photography, and other fine art by local artists. Styles and skill levels vary from artist to artist, but there's solid and reasonably priced work.

Accommodations
The **Inn Around the Corner** (109 Church St., 800/393-6005, www.innaroundthecorner.com, $135-195, cash only) is a classic bed-and-breakfast in a lovely 1915 wooden house with a big front porch. **Arbor House of Black Mountain** (207 Rhododendron Ave., 828/669-9302, www.arborhousenc.com, $159-199), a four-room bed-and-breakfast, hosts travelers year-round, but like most places in the area, peak season coincides with the turning of the leaves every fall. Views from the inn are wide and

beautiful, especially when the leaves are out, but book early for leaf season.

Food

Berliner Kindl German Restaurant (121 Broadway, 828/669-5255, http://berlinerkindl.homestead.com, 11am-8pm Mon.-Sat., 11:30am-3pm Sun., $9-28) serves traditional German food like schnitzel, a variety of sausages, and the sides you'd expect: fried potatoes, German potato salad, sauerkraut, and red cabbage. They make their own sauerkraut in-house. Over on Church Street you'll find the **Black Mountain Bakery** (102 Church St., 828/669-1626, 8am-4pm Tues.-Sat.), a little café where you can order a quick soup and sandwich as well as a dessert or a cookie for the road.

WEAVERVILLE

Shopping

There are a lot of great potters in western North Carolina, but Rob and Beth Mangum of **Mangum Pottery** (16 N. Main St., Weaverville, 828/645-4929, www.mangumpottery.com, 9am-5pm Mon.-Fri., 10am-4pm Sat.) are two of the most innovative. They make beautiful earthy-colored dinnerware and mugs to satisfy the practical side of life, and they also build the most unexpected things out of pottery—ceramic clocks, ceramic furniture, ceramic musical instruments that really play—all in the most Seussian shapes and colors. If Salvador Dalí and the Cat in the Hat were on vacation together in the mountains, Mangum Pottery would be their first stop, and even they would be shocked at how cool this stuff is.

Food

A few doors down from Mangum Pottery you'll find **Well Bred Bakery & Café** (26 N. Main St., Weaverville, 828/645-9300, www.wellbredbakery.com, 7:30am-7pm Mon.-Thurs., 7:30am-9pm Fri., 8am-9pm Sat., 8am-7pm Sun.), which sells soups, sandwiches, quiche, and salads as well as a dazzling array of artisanal breads and elaborate desserts. They promise "karma-free coffee" (I think that means

fair-trade), and even sell the *New York Times,* so you don't have to go into crossword-puzzle withdrawal on your trip.

If you're in Weaverville and you have a hankering for pizza, **Blue Mountain Pizza and Brew Pub** (55 N. Main St., 828/658-8777, 11am-9pm Tues.-Thurs. and Sun., 11am-10pm Fri.-Sat., $7-24) is your spot. The building dates to the 1820s and now houses a two-barrel brewing system, meaning the brewmasters get to experiment a lot; they've had a positive reception. Blue Mountain Pizza serves specialty pizzas, calzones, stromboli, subs, and salads. Their Henny Penny Pizza is a barbecued chicken pizza with red onion and bacon, and the Marge is simply olive oil, Roma tomatoes, fresh mozzarella, and basil.

MADISON COUNTY

North of Asheville, Madison County is a world unto itself: wild mountain terrain with a handful of small, peculiar towns whose reputation in the rest of the state is that of tough independence. Madison is revered by lovers of traditional balladry because a group of families—including Chandlers, Wallins, Nortons, and their kin—have committed to disc and tape over the course of the last 50 years some of the finest and most powerful renditions of the ancient ballads brought to the mountains by the early English and Celtic settlers. These ballads are not archaic oddities from a forgotten past but are lovingly cared for and taught by family elders to their children and grandchildren. A new generation of singers is emerging today, with a core group of young women reared in the tradition who have inherited the remarkable voices, memories, and sense of stewardship.

Entertainment and Events

Mars Hill, a tiny college town, is a center of mountain culture thanks to Mars Hill College. The **Bascom Lamar Lunsford "Minstrel of the Appalachians" Festival** (early fall, 828/689-1571, www.lunsfordfestival.com, $10 adults, $5 children) is a nearly 50-year-old annual gathering of some of the best mountain musicians, dancers, and craftspeople from this hotbed of folk traditions. Mars Hill College is also the home of the **Southern Appalachian Repertory Theatre** (Owen Theater, 44 College St., 828/689-1239, http://sartplays.org), a highly regarded ensemble presenting a range of contemporary drama, musicals, and family productions. SART's stage is in the Owen Theater, a great-looking old Baptist Church on the Mars Hill College campus.

Sports and Recreation

On a 4,700-foot mountaintop above Mars Hill, the **Wolf Ski Resort** (578 Valley View Circle, 800/817-4111, www.skiwolfridgenc. com, 9am-4:30pm and 6pm-10pm Tues.-Sat., 9am-4:30pm Sun.-Mon. Dec.-Mar., $39-54 adults, $34-49 students and ages 9-18, $24-34 ages 5-8, free under age 4, rentals $19-34) has more than 80 acres of prime skiing and snowboarding slopes. It is also the home of the Snow Sports School, which offers private and group lessons for all ages of beginning and intermediate winter sports enthusiasts. There are multiple lifts, two lodges to relax in, and multiple hearty dining options. The attached **Scenic Wolf Resort** offers year-round cabin accommodations ($300-550 in season), a huge indoor heated pool, and numerous recreational activities.

Sandy Bottom Trail Rides (1459 Caney Fork Rd., Marshall, 800/959-3513, www. sandybottomtrailrides.net, 10am, noon, and 2pm daily, 1 hour $35, 2 hours $65, 3 hours $85), based at a 100-year-old family farm, leads horseback treks deep into the forest to an early-19th-century garnet mine. They'll also carry you in style in a horse-drawn buggy, if you prefer.

There are plenty of white-water rafting opportunities in the area, with several guide companies to choose from. **Huck Finn Rafting Adventures** (158 Bridge St., Hot Springs, 800/303-7238, www.huckfinnrafting.com, rafting $48-58 adults, $43-53 children, unguided floats $35 adults, $30 ages 8-15, $10 under age 8, river tubing $15) runs guided and unguided white-water rafting

and float trips, allowing to customize your thrills and get the level of adrenaline you want from gnarly white water or flat-water floating. **French Broad Rafting and Ziplining** (U.S. 25/70, Marshall, 800/570-7238, www. frenchbroadrafting.com, white-water rafting $51-75, flat-water rafting $30-46, zip-lining $75) can get you equipped and ready for a guided or unguided rafting trip on the French Broad River, which has both white-water and calm sections. Or get your adrenaline rush in the trees on a zip-line course that mixes zip lines, rappels, and short hikes to make a unique mountain experience.

Accommodations

Defying that worn-out stereotype of mountain isolation, Madison County has for centuries been a destination for vacationers because of its natural hot springs. Going back at least to the mid-18th century—and, according to tradition, long before the first European settlers arrived—the springs have had a reputation for curative powers. A succession of grand hotels operated at Hot Springs, all long since burned down. In one of the area's odder historical moments, the resort served as an internment camp for German prisoners during World War I, mainly commercial sailors and members of an orchestra who had the misfortune of being in the United States when the war broke out. This in itself was not an uncommon arrangement, but the oddity of the camp at Hot Springs is that the prisoners constructed for themselves a miniature German village, an almost Disneyesque collection of tiny picturesque *fachwerk* (post-and-beam) cottages, alpine lodges, and rustic churches. The village is long gone, but you can see pictures of the internees' astonishing project at www. ibiblio.org/ww1gd.

Modern visitors can still take a dip in the mineral springs. **Hot Springs Resort and Spa** (U.S. 25/70, at the entrance to the town of Hot Springs, 828/622-7676, www.nchotsprings. com, suites $145-200, cabins $50-75, camping $24-60) is a much simpler affair than the old hotels; it's not a luxury destination but a place where you can lodge or camp for the night and soak in the famous 100°F water.

The **Mountain Magnolia Inn** (204 Lawson St., Mars Hill, 828/622-3543 or 800/914-9306, www.mountainmagnoliainn.com, $100-230) provides lodging in an ornate 1868 home and in nearby creek-side cabins. The inn's dining room is a nice gourmet restaurant (breakfast for guests daily, dinner for guests and non-guests 5:30pm-9pm Thurs.-Mon., $18-45) that features locally raised organic produce, meats, cheeses, and wines. Massages and limited spa treatments are available in-room if the hot springs aren't relaxing enough for you. This is a lovely place where it's easy to find private moments on your balcony, patio, or one of the private cabins.

Food

French Broad Deli and Café (798 Walnut Creek Rd., Marshall, 828/649-8177, www. frenchbroaddeli.com, 7am-9pm Tues.-Sat., 11:30am-3pm Sun., around $8, buffet $12 adults, $6 ages 6-11, free under age 6) serves up country cooking with many a plate piled high with meat, two veggies, cornbread, and dessert. On Sunday, they do it like supper at Granny's house: a buffet. The spread is filled with the expected comfort foods—mashed potatoes and gravy, fried chicken—and some surprises, such as popcorn shrimp.

For burgers in Marshall, it's hard to beat **Blue Flame Grill** (1650 Hwy. 213, 828/649-8201, 7am-8pm Mon.-Fri., 7am-3pm Sat.-Sun., around $12). They serve burgers, barbecue, breakfast, and brunch. The onion rings are solid, and the cupcakes they sell make the perfect snack after a recreational outing, so grab one for the road.

Southern Blue Ridge and Foothills

The mountains of Polk, Rutherford, and Henderson Counties, south of Asheville, have an air of enchantment to them—meaning that the area gives the impalpable sense of having had a spell cast on it. No doubt a parapsychologist could assign a name to this atmosphere; it has a weird energy where it seems as likely that you'll encounter a fairy or an alien as a postal worker. There are some quantifiable symptoms of this peculiarity. For one, Polk County has its own climate; called the Thermal Belt, the meteorological pocket formed on this sheltered slope of the Blue Ridge has distinctly milder summers and winters than the surrounding areas. In the 19th century it became a favorite summering spot for the Charleston elite and other Southerners of the plantation class. Some old houses and inns remain as vestiges of this genteel past.

In January 1874, Bald Mountain, north of Chimney Rock, began to rumble; it grew louder until, by the spring of that year, the mountain shook with such force that windows and crockery in valley homes shattered. A smoking, hissing crack opened in the side of the mountain, causing residents to fear a volcanic eruption. Many moved away or found religion. The shaking and rumbling eventually settled down. A crew of spelunkers a generation later concluded that the mountain was hollow and that enormous boulders sometimes became dislodged inside, showering into the caves below and causing the enormous booms. At least that's one theory.

Chimney Rock itself was the scene of bizarre phenomena in the first decade of the 1800s. Locals and visitors began to report witnessing spectral gatherings, crowds of people gathered on top of the rock and rising together into the sky. In the fall of 1811 multiple witnesses saw, on different occasions, two armed cavalries mounted on winged horses battling in the air over Chimney Rock, their gleaming swords clashing audibly. Whichever phantom cavalry triumphed in that battle, the rock is now maintained by the state of North Carolina and

ASHEVILLE

climbed daily by hundreds of visitors, none of whom have reported sightings of any spectral cavalry, horse droppings, or flashing sabers.

BREVARD

Brevard is the pleasant seat of the improbably named Transylvania County (unlike in vampire stories, it's not creepy, but beautiful in a Gothic forest way). As you might expect, Halloween is a big deal in this town. Brevard is also known for sheltering a population of rather startling and odd-looking white squirrels. The local legend about their origins is that their ancestors escaped from an overturned circus truck in Florida in 1940 and made their way to Brevard as pets. More likely, say researchers, they came from an exotic pet breeder in Florida and were acquired by a Brevard area family. In any case, the white squirrels escaped into the wild of Transylvania County, and you'll probably see their descendants in the area when you visit.

Entertainment and Events

The **Brevard Music Center** (349 Andante

© MARC PARSONS/123RF.COM

ASHEVILLE

one of Brevard's white squirrels

Lane, 828/862-2100, www.brevardmusic. org) has attracted the highest-caliber young musicians for more than 70 years for intensive summer-long classical music instruction. Throughout the summer, Brevard Music Center students, as well as visiting soloists of international fame, put on world-class concerts, performing works from Tchaikovsky to Gilbert and Sullivan.

Shopping

A center for a very different sort of music is **Celestial Mountain Music** (16 W. Main St., 828/884-3575, www.celestialmtnmusic.com, 10am-5:30pm Mon.-Fri., 10am-4pm Sat.). Among more usual musical items, this nice little shop carries two lines of locally made instruments. Cedar Mountain Banjos, of the open-backed, old-time variety, are beautifully crafted and ring clear and pretty. The work of local fiddle builder Lyle Reedy is also sold at Celestial Mountain Music. His fiddles are handmade of a variety of fine woods and have a deep, biting sound loved by fiddlers. Musicians and woodworkers alike will enjoy a stop at this Main Street shop.

Sports and Recreation

About 10 miles south of Brevard, **Dupont State Forest** (U.S. 276, 828/877-6527, www.dupontforest.com) has more than 90 miles of hiking trails covering 10,000 acres. Some of Transylvania County's beautiful waterfalls are located within the forest and accessible on foot via moderate or strenuous forest trails or, with special permits and advance reservation for people with disabilities only, by vehicle. Visitors should use caution, wear brightly colored clothing, and leave that bearskin cape at home from September through December, when hikers share the woods with hunters.

◪ PISGAH RANGER DISTRICT

Just north of Brevard in the town of Pisgah Forest is the main entrance to the **Pisgah Ranger District** (U.S. 276, Pisgah Forest, 828/877-3265, www.cfaia.org, 9am-5pm daily mid-Apr.-mid-Nov., 8:30am-4:30pm daily mid-Nov.-mid-Apr.) of the Pisgah National Forest. The forest covers 500,000 acres, which is a large swath of western North Carolina, but this 157,000-acre ranger district has many of the forest's favorite attractions. A good topographic map of the ranger district is available from National Geographic (www.natgeomaps.com/ti_780). In the ranger district are more than 275 miles of hiking trails and several campgrounds; the most easily accessible is **Davidson River Campground** (828/877-3265, reservations at www.recreation.gov, year-round, $10), which is 1.5 miles from the Brevard entrance. It has showers and toilets.

The **Shining Rock Wilderness** and the **Middle Prong Wilderness,** which adjoins Shining Rock to the southwest, are a rugged terrain that rises from 3,200 feet at its lowest point, along the West Pigeon River, to a towering 6,400 feet at Richmond Balsam. **Cold Mountain,** made famous by the book and movie of the same name, is a real peak located within the Shining Rock Wilderness, and seeing it helps make the struggles of the fictional characters more real. These mountains are steep and the forests dense, and what trails there are have no signage. This is a popular area among experienced backwoods trekkers, but it is not recommended for casual visitors because it is exceedingly easy to get lost. At a minimum, hikers should be adept at using both a compass and a topographic map before venturing into these wilderness areas.

Not to be confused with Shining Rock, **Sliding Rock** is an easily accessible waterfall and swimming spot with a parking lot ($1), bathhouse, and lifeguards (10:30am-6pm daily late May-early Sept.). You can actually ride down the 60-foot waterfall, a smooth rock face (not so smooth that you shouldn't wear sturdy britches) over which 11,000 gallons of water rush every minute into the chilly swimming hole below.

The **Cradle of Forestry** (U.S. 276, Pisgah Forest, 828/877-3130, www.cradleofforestry.com, 9am-5pm daily mid-Apr.-early Nov., $5 adults, free under age 16) is a museum and activity complex commemorating the rise of the forestry profession in the United States, which originated here at a turn-of-the-century training school in the forests once owned by George Washington Vanderbilt, lord of Asheville's Biltmore Estate. Plow days and living history days throughout the year give an interesting glimpse into this region's old-time methods of farming and frontier living. Self-guided trails lead through the woods to many interesting locations of this campus of the country's first school of forestry.

HENDERSONVILLE

An easy drive from Asheville, Hendersonville is a comfortable small city with a walkable downtown filled with boutiques and cafés. It's also the heart of North Carolina's apple industry. Hundreds of orchards cover the hillsides of Henderson County, and all along the highway, long packinghouses bustle in late summer as they process more than three million tons of apples. There are also many shops and produce stands run by members of old orchard-owning families, where you can buy apples singly or by the bushel, along with cider, preserves, and many other apple products.

Sights

One of North Carolina's cool small transportation museums is located at the Hendersonville Airport. The **Western North Carolina Air Museum** (Hendersonville Airport, Brooklyn Ave. and Gilbert St., off U.S. 176/Spartanburg Hwy., 828/698-2482, www.wncairmuseum.com, 10am-5pm Sat., noon-5pm Wed. and Sun. Apr.-Oct., noon-5pm Sat.-Sun. and Wed. Nov.-Mar., free) houses a collection of more than a dozen historic small aircraft, both originals and reproductions. Most are from the 1930s and 1940s, though some are even older; all are wonderfully fun contraptions to visit.

Shopping

Hendersonville's downtown **Curb Market** (221 N. Church St., at 2nd Ave., 828/692-8012, www.curbmarket.com, 8am-2pm Tues., Thurs., and Sat.) has been in operation since

1924. Here you can buy fresh locally grown fruits, vegetables, and flowers; fresh-baked cakes, pies, and breads; jams, jellies, and pickles made in local home kitchens; and the work of local woodcarvers, weavers, and other craftspeople.

While in the Hendersonville area, keep an eye out for brightly colored folk painting-adorned packages of **Immaculate Baking Company** (www.immaculatebaking.com) cookies. Besides making totally delicious cookies, this Hendersonville-based company helps support the work of visionary outsider artists throughout the South; they're "cookies with a cause."

FLAT ROCK
Sights
Just south of Hendersonville is the historic village of Flat Rock. Founded in the early 19th century as a vacation spot for the Charleston plantation gentry, Flat Rock retains a delicate, cultured ambience created many years ago. Many artists and writers have lived in this area, most famously Carl Sandburg, whose house, Connemara, is preserved as the **Carl Sandburg Home National Historic Site** (81 Carl Sandburg Lane, Flat Rock, 828/693-4178, www.nps.gov/carl, 9am-5pm daily, house tour $5 adults, $3 over age 61, free under age 16). Sandburg and his family lived here for more than 20 years, during which time he wrote and won the Pulitzer Prize for *Complete Poems,* no doubt observed bemusedly as his wife and daughters raised champion dairy goats (a herd of goats lives on the grounds today). Half-hour tours take visitors through the house to see many of the Sandburgs' belongings. There is a bookstore in the house, and more than five miles of trails through the property. As a poet whose first steps were in the mountain clay, I have a soft spot for this place, and it's easy for me to see what Sandburg found so inspiring and appealing about the quiet, the air, and the space; take a moment to sit and reflect while you're here, let your poet-mind take over, and try your hand at a couple of lines of your own.

Entertainment and Events
Another literary landmark in the village is the **Flat Rock Playhouse** (2661 Greenville Hwy., Flat Rock, 866/732-8008, www.flatrockplayhouse.org). Now the state theater of North Carolina, the Flat Rock Playhouse's history dates to 1940, when a roving theater company called the Vagabonds wandered down from New York and converted an old gristmill in the village into a stage. They returned every summer for the next few years, entertaining the locals with plays held in a succession of locations, from the old mill to a circus tent, eventually constructing a permanent theater. They now have a 10-month season, drawing more than 90,000 patrons each year.

Shopping
You'll find quite a few nice galleries and studios in Flat Rock, and one place that jumps out is **The Wrinkled Egg** (2710 Hwy. 225, 828/696-3998, www.thewrinkledegg.com, 9:30am-5:30pm Mon.-Sat., noon-5:30pm Sun.). This weird little store sells custom care packages for kids heading off to Scout camp, equestrian camp, religious camp, and whatever summer camps kids go to these days. It's a fun place to stop to get a little something for the kids in your life.

SALUDA AND VICINITY
Just east and south of Hendersonville, bordering South Carolina, Polk County is home to several interesting little towns, most notably Tryon and Saluda, along with a lot of beautiful mountain countryside. In Saluda you'll find a tiny downtown laid out along the old Norfolk Southern Railway tracks. The tracks at Saluda are the top of the steepest standard-gauge mainline railroad grade in the United States. This county's history abounds with exciting stories of runaway trains that derailed at spots like "Slaughterhouse Curve," and more than two dozen railroad workers have been killed on this grade.

Entertainment and Events
For one weekend every July, Saluda busts at

the seams with visitors to the **Coon Dog Day Festival** (800/440-7848, www.saluda.com). Hundreds of beautifully trained dogs from all over the region come to town to show off in a parade and trials, while the humans have a street fair and a 5K race.

Shopping

Six miles southeast of Columbus, potters Claude and Elaine Graves have been making distinctive pottery for 35 years at **Little Mountain Pottery** (6372 Peniel Rd., www.crowsounds.com). The Graves' work draws on North Carolina's folk traditions in ceramics, but it's quite different from much of the pottery made in this area in that it also draws inspiration from the ceramics of North Africa, the Canary Islands, Spain, and Mexico. The tones of Little Mountain's glazes reflect the many colors, by turns earthy and airy, of the North Carolina mountains. A showroom and sales shop is attached to the kiln room, and the pottery is surprisingly affordable. Don't miss Claude's wonderful portraits of influential North Carolina potters, arranged in an outdoor gallery along the walls of his barns and kiln.

Sports and Recreation

Equestrian life plays a growing role in Polk and the surrounding counties of North Carolina's southern mountains. The **Foothills Equestrian Nature Center** (3381 Hunting Country Rd., Tryon, 828/859-9021, www.fence.org), known as FENCE, occupies 380 beautiful acres along the border with South Carolina. The equestrian center has stables for 200 horses and two lighted show rings. FENCE hosts cross-country, three-day, A-rated hunter and jumper, dressage, and many other equestrian events throughout the year. The annual Block House Steeplechase has been held in Tryon for 60 years, and FENCE has hosted the event for 20 of those years. FENCE also offers regular hikes and bird-watching excursions on its beautiful property.

Food

For such a tiny town, there are an awful lot of eating places in Saluda. Just stand in the middle of Main Street and look around; there are several choices, and you won't go wrong at any of them. The **Saluda Grade Café** (40 Main St., 828/749-5854, http://saludagradecafe.com, lunch 11am-3pm Tues.-Sat., dinner 5pm-9pm Wed.-Sat., 11am-7pm Sun., $11-25) serves food representing a variety of cuisines, including comfort food meatloaf and Low Country shrimp and grits; the menu has a little bit of everything on it, although it is a small menu. Finding something to eat isn't hard, but steer toward the pasta, as it's house-made.

Wildflour Bakery (173 E. Main St., 828/749-9224, http://wildflourbakerync.com, 8am-3pm Mon.-Sat., 10am-2pm Sun., Pizza Night 5pm-8pm Fri., breakfast and lunch $2-8, pizza night $6-22) stone-grinds wheat every morning to make absolutely delicious breads. Breakfast and lunch are served, making this a great place to fill up before a day of kayaking or hiking. Don't miss Friday Pizza Night, where they serve up regular or thin-crust (and even gluten-free) pies with your choice of toppings, along with 10 specialty pizzas. You can bring your own wine or beer on pizza night, so order a pie or two, crack open a local brew, and settle in for a little while.

CHIMNEY ROCK AND LAKE LURE

◗ **Chimney Rock**

Chimney Rock Park (U.S. 64/74A, Chimney Rock, 800/277-9611, www.chimneyrockpark.com, 8:30am-5:30pm daily Apr.-Oct., 8:30am-4:30pm daily Nov., 10am-4:30pm Fri.-Tues. early Dec.-Dec. 24, 10am-4:30pm daily Dec. 26-31, 10am-4:30pm Fri.-Tues. Jan.-Mar., $15 adults, $7 ages 5-15, free under age 5) is home to some amazing rock formations. The star of the show, of course, is the Chimney Rock itself. Whether you climb the long series of steps to the top of this 315-foot tower of rock or take the elevator, the view is great. Also dazzling are the Needle's Eye, the Opera Box, and other formations that visitors can explore.

The 400-foot **Hickory Nut Falls** can be reached on the Hickory Nut Falls trail, a fairly

ASHEVILLE

© ALEX GRICHENKO/123RF.COM

The view is amazing from the top of the Chimney Rock.

leisurely 0.75-mile walk. An easy walk for children, the 0.6-mile Woodland Walk is dotted with animal sculptures and "journal entries" by Grady the Groundhog. The Skyline-Cliff Trail Loop is a good deal more strenuous, but this two-hour hike will take you to some spectacular sights. You may also recognize it from the 1992 film *The Last of the Mohicans*. Chimney Rock's website has a nifty interactive trail map that will show you the lay of the land. Needless to say, Chimney Rock Park is a desirable location for rock climbing. To rock-climb in this park, you must arrange your climb with **Fox Mountain Guides** (888/284-8433, www.foxmountainguides.com, $160-350), which offer all sorts of instruction and guide services for climbers of all levels.

Sports and Recreation

Lake Lure, a 720-acre artificial highland lake, was created in the 1920s. Several local outfitters will guide you on set you up for a day on the lake or on area rivers. Try **Lake Lure**

Adventure Company (442 Memorial Hwy., 828/625-8066, www.lakelureadventurecompany.com, 9am-7pm daily) for ski trips ($140 per hour), fishing (half-day $250), to ride around (from $65 per hour), or kayaking and stand-up paddleboarding (rentals from $19 per hour, tours $34 adults, $29 children). For a relaxed sightseeing tour on the lake, **Lake Lure Tours** (next to Lake Lure Town Marina, 877/386-4255, www.lakelure.com, tours depart hourly from 11am daily Apr.-May and Sept.-Oct., from 10am June-Aug., call for times Mar. and Nov., $15-30 adults, $7-10 under age 12), which offers dinner and sunset cruises as well as daytime jaunts.

Accommodations

The 1927 **Lake Lure Inn and Spa** (2771 Memorial Hwy., 888/434-4970, www.lakelure.com, from $109) is a grand old hotel that was one of the fashionable Southern resorts of its day. Franklin Roosevelt and Calvin Coolidge stayed here, as did F. Scott Fitzgerald. The lobby is full of strange antiques that are the picture of obsolete opulence—a Baccarat chandelier much older than the hotel and a collection of upright disc music boxes, up to eight feet tall, that were all the rage before the invention of the phonograph. The Lake Lure Inn has been restored beautifully and equipped with two restaurants, a bar, and a spa.

HIGHLANDS AND VICINITY
Waterfalls
This part of the country is blessed with some beautiful waterfalls, some of which are easily visited. **Whitewater Falls** (Hwy. 281, at the state line, south of Highlands, $2 per vehicle), at over 400 feet, is reported to be the highest waterfall east of the Rockies. An upper-level viewing spot is located at the end of a wheelchair-accessible paved trail, while a flight of more than 150 steps leads to the base of the falls. The falls are a fabulous sight, but remember to stay on the trails; several visitors have fallen to their deaths when they left the trail to get a different perspective. A much smaller but still very beautiful waterfall is **Silver Run Falls** (Hwy. 107, 4 miles south of Cashiers), reached by a short trail from a roadside pullout. **Bridal Veil Falls** (U.S. 64, 2.5 miles west of Highlands) flows over a little track of road right off U.S. 64. You'll see a sign from the main road where you can turn off and actually drive behind the waterfall, or park and walk behind it. Another falls that you can walk through is **Dry Falls** (U.S. 64, between Highlands and Franklin, $2 per vehicle), reached by a small trail off the highway, curving right into and behind the 75-foot waterfall.

Sports and Recreation
North Carolina's newest state park, **Gorges State Park** (Hwy. 281 S., Sapphire, 828/966-9099, http://ncparks.gov) is a lush mountain rainforest that receives 80 inches of precipitation annually. The steep terrain rises 2,000 vertical feet in four miles, creating a series of rocky waterfalls and challenging trails. This 7,500-acre park is the only state park west of

Asheville, and it's a sight, with a collection of waterfalls and a fantastic concentration of rare and unique plant and animal species. You'll find a number of rugged trails for hiking, mountain biking, and horseback riding, and there are streams filled with rainbow and brown trout as well as smallmouth bass. Primitive camping (free) is permitted in designated areas.

Accommodations and Food
The 3,500-foot-high town of Cashiers ("CASH-ers") is home to the **High Hampton Inn and Country Club** (1525 Hwy. 107 S., 800/334-2551, www.highhamptoninn.com, 2-night minimum, from $203), a popular resort for generations of North Carolinians. This was originally the home of Confederate General Wade Hampton, the dashing Charlestonian cavalryman. The lodge, a big old 1930s wooden chalet with huge cozy fireplaces in the lobby, is surrounded by 1,400 acres of lakeside woodlands, with an 18-hole golf course, a good buffet-style restaurant (dinner jacket requested in the evening), clay tennis courts, and a fitness center that features a climbing tower.

INFORMATION AND SERVICES
In addition to Asheville's **Mission Hospital** (509 Biltmore Ave., 428 Biltmore Ave., Asheville, 828/213-1948 or 828/213-4063, www.missionhospitals.org), there are several regional hospitals with emergency or urgent care departments. In Hendersonville, the primary hospital is **Pardee Hospital** (800 N. Justice St., Hendersonville, 866/790-9355, www.pardeehospital.org). In Brevard, the main hospital is **Transylvania Community Hospital** (90 Hospital Dr., Brevard, 828/884-9111, www.trhospital.org), and in Rutherfordton is **Rutherford Hospital** (288 S. Ridgecrest Ave., Rutherfordton, 828/286-5000, www.rutherfordhosp.org).

Maps and guides are available at the **Hendersonville and Flat Rock Visitors**

ASHEVILLE

Information Center (201 S. Main St., Hendersonville, 800/828-4244, www.historichendersonville.com) and at the **Transylvania County Tourism Development Authority** (35 W. Main St., Brevard, 800/648-4523, www.visitwaterfalls.com).

GETTING THERE AND AROUND

The Brevard-Hendersonville area is an easy drive from Asheville, with Hendersonville less than 30 minutes down I-26, and Brevard a short jog west from it on U.S. 64. To reach Tryon and Rutherfordton, follow U.S. 74 south and east from Hendersonville. **Asheville Regional Airport** (AVL, 61 Terminal Dr., 828/684-2226, www.flyavl.com), south of Asheville, is very convenient to this region; several airlines have flights to Atlanta, Charlotte, and other U.S. cities.

GREAT SMOKY MOUNTAINS

If you started your exploration of North Carolina along the coast and have driven, rafted, hiked, eaten, toured, biked, and ridden your way across the cities, countryside, Piedmont, and hills, you can understand how the state's vast wingspan and all it encompasses can be summed up in the phrase "from Manteo to Murphy." It's a long ride from the seaside town of Manteo to the mountain enclave of Murphy—right around 600 miles if you take U.S. 64, and 544 miles if you take the interstate—and in terms of landscape, barbecue styles, and dialects, it may as well be from the earth to the moon. From Asheville, which many people mistakenly regard as the end of the state, you can drive for another two or three hours on 100 mountain miles and still be in North Carolina. Murphy, which lays claim

to a patch of land in the narrow western end of the state, is actually closer to Atlanta than Asheville. Distance notwithstanding, there's a cultural kinship between the folks who live in the deep mountains and those on the Outer Banks, born of the natural beauty and isolation of their respective communities.

The mountains here are so rugged and the forests so wild that they have been featured in a number of feature films, including *The Hunger Games* and *The Last of the Mohicans*. It has been home to outlaws and runaway rebels dating from the Revolutionary War up to the 1996 Atlanta Olympic Park bomber; after Eric Rudolph bombed the Olympics, he fled here to evade capture. While people watching the news were scratching their heads, wondering how one man could escape in such a relatively

HIGHLIGHTS

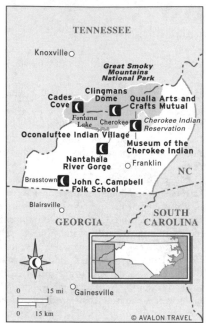

TENNESSEE

Knoxville○

Great Smoky
Mountains
National Park

Clingmans
Cades   Dome   Qualla Arts and
Cove   Crafts Mutual

Fontana
Lake   Cherokee   Cherokee Indian
                  Reservation
Oconaluftee Indian Village

Museum of the
Cherokee Indian

Nantahala
River Gorge   ○ Franklin

Brasstown   John C. Campbell   NC
            Folk School

Blairsville○

GEORGIA   SOUTH
          CAROLINA

0   15 mi   ○
            Gainesville
0   15 km
                  © AVALON TRAVEL

LOOK FOR ◖ TO FIND RECOMMENDED SIGHTS, ACTIVITIES, DINING, AND LODGING.

◖ **Cades Cove:** The most visited spot in Great Smoky Mountains National Park is a formerly bustling mountain village that is witness to the depth of history in the Southern highlands (page 351).

◖ **Clingmans Dome:** From this third-highest peak in the eastern United States, set in a dramatic alpine environment, you'll find an astounding view of up to 100 miles on a clear day (page 351).

◖ **Museum of the Cherokee Indian:** The Cherokee people have lived in the Smoky Mountains for thousands of years. This excellent museum tells unforgettable tales of their history (page 363).

◖ **Qualla Arts and Crafts Mutual:** Ancient craft traditions still thrive among Cherokee artists in western North Carolina. At the Qualla Mutual, visitors to the Eastern Band's seat of government can learn about and purchase the work of today's masters (page 363).

◖ **Oconaluftee Indian Village:** Demonstrations in traditional cooking, flint knapping for arrowheads and spear points, and ritual dance give visitors a glimpse into 18th-century tribal life at this recreated Cherokee Indian Village (page 364).

◖ **Nantahala River Gorge:** So steep that in some places the water is only brushed by sunlight at high noon, this gorge is an unbeatable place for white-water rafting (page 368).

◖ **John C. Campbell Folk School:** For nearly a century the Folk School has been a leading light in promoting American craft heritage, nurturing new generations of artists, and securing the future of Appalachian artistic traditions (page 379).

small geographical area, folks in these parts had their doubts he'd ever be found. After driving a little ways into the high country southwest of Asheville, it's easy to imagine how fugitives and hermits could hide here unnoticed.

The thought of a large group disappearing here may sound far-fetched, but think of the Lost Colony on the Outer Banks, who managed to disappear from a small island, and

look at the story of the indigenous Cherokee people. After President Van Buren gave the final go-ahead in the 1830s to fulfill the Indian Removal Act and send the Cherokee Nation west on the Trail of Tears, several Cherokee families fled into the caves and hills here and refused to leave their homeland. They lived as refugees and outlaws, hunted and hated and hiding, surviving the elements and death by squads of soldiers who searched

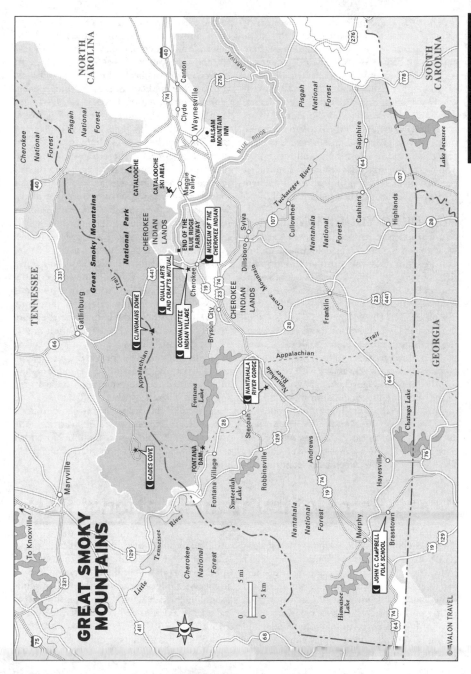

for them. These families are the ancestors of today's Eastern Band of the Cherokee.

The Cherokee people have deep roots here going back centuries, from the early days described in their mythology, when the Anigituhwa-gi shared these mountains with witches, fairies, and birds the size of bears. The early 19th century and the Trail of Tears were the darkest hour for them, when they were split into two groups—those forced into exile and those forced into hiding and resistance. Today, the Cherokee Nation is still split, but the Eastern Band's seat of government is here in the land known as the Qualla Boundary.

PLANNING YOUR TIME

Many people plan visits to the Smokies around what's blooming or turning color on the mountainsides, but it's a wonderful area to visit any time of year. Spring wildflowers begin to appear in late March, peaking in mid-late-April. Azaleas, mountain laurels, and rhododendrons put on the best show during summer, blooming first at lower elevations and then creeping up the mountains. Flame azalea is a funny plant, peaking in different areas as the microclimates dictate; they're ablaze with color April to July. Mountain laurel overlaps with blooms in May-June, and rhododendron shows its color in June-July. Fall colors appear in the opposite order, with the mountaintops the first to show autumn's arrival in early October, with colors then bleeding down until mid-late October and early November, when trees from the foot

to the crest of the mountains are aflame with color. Summer heat can throw the schedule for blooms and fall colors off, as can rainfall levels, but if you call the Great Smoky Mountains National Park or check with regional websites, you can find out how the season is progressing.

Bisecting the national park is the Newfound Gap Road, striking northwest from Cherokee, where it meets with the southern end of the Blue Ridge Parkway, to Gatlinburg and Pigeon Forge, Tennessee. On the Tennessee side of the park, the valleys spread out a little and mountain coves form, making that the side to visit for side-road exploration and short loop roads. Cherokee is a great place to stay as it's not as touristy as Gatlinburg, Tennessee, which is good to visit for a day. There are campsites available on both sides of the park if you're roughing it, or find a rustic cozy cabin for a taste of country living. While you can certainly get from Cherokee to Gatlinburg in an hour and see a sight or two in a day, the more time you can spend here, the better, and the more it will grow on you. This is the nation's most visited National Park for a reason, so spend at least three days; a week provides enough time for a touristy day in Tennessee, a couple of days for trail and side-road exploration, a day learning about Cherokee culture in Cherokee, and some time in the casino. Many campgrounds here limit stays to one week from May 15 to the end of October, and two weeks from November to May 14, so plan accordingly if you're packing your tent.

Great Smoky Mountains National Park

The Great Smoky Mountains National Park (GSMNP) is like no other, and it's very close to my heart. My family would vacation here for weekend and weeklong getaways, and I remember taking my first bite of trout here, riding my first roller coaster at Silver Dollar City in Pigeon Forge (now Dollywood), and seeing R2-D2 outside of Ripley's Believe It or Not in Gatlinburg. GSMNP comprises over

800 square miles of cloud-ringed high peaks and rainforest. There are tens of thousands of species of plants and animals that call the park home, with 80 species of reptiles and amphibians alone, which is why the park is sometimes called the Salamander Capital of the World. More than 200 species of birds nest here, and 50-plus mammals, from mice to mountain lions, roam these hills. The nonprofit

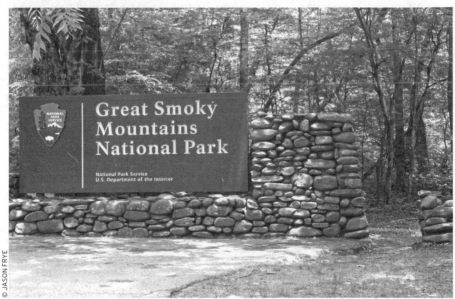

© JASON FRYE

It's the most visited national park — and for good reason.

organization Discover Life in America (www. dlia.org) has been conducting an All-Taxa Biodiversity Inventory, a census of all nonmicrobial life forms in the GSMNP; as of 2012 they had discovered over 900 species of plants and animals previously unknown to science. The deep wilderness is an awesome refuge for today's outdoor enthusiasts, and the accessibility of absolutely ravishing scenery makes it ideal for visitors of all ability levels and nearly all interests.

VISITING THE PARK
Weather Considerations
To get a sense of the variability of the weather in the GSMNP, keep in mind that the elevation ranges from under 1,000 to over 6,600 feet. Low-lying areas like the one around Gatlinburg, Tennessee, are not much cooler than Raleigh in the summer, with an average high of 88°F in July. Gatlinburg's average lows drop just a few degrees below freezing during only three months of the year (Dec.-Feb.). The opposite extreme is illustrated by Clingmans

Dome, the highest elevation in the park, where the average high temperature is only 65°F in July, and only in June-August can you be sure that it won't snow. If ever there were a place for wearing layers of clothing, this is it. No matter what season the calendar tells you it is, be on the safe side and pack clothing for the other three as well. Keep these extremes in mind in terms of safety as well; a snowstorm can bring two feet of snow at high elevations, and it's not at all unusual for the weather will be balmy at the foot of the mountain and icy at the top. At times the temperature has fallen to -20°F. Roads can be closed in the winter if the weather gets bad or restricted to vehicles with snow chains or four-wheel drive. Drive super-slowly when it's icy. Leave plenty of room between you and the next car, and shift to a lower gear when going down slippery slopes. You can find out current conditions by calling the park's weather information line (865/436-1200, ext. 630).

Seasonal Considerations
The most crowded times in the park are from

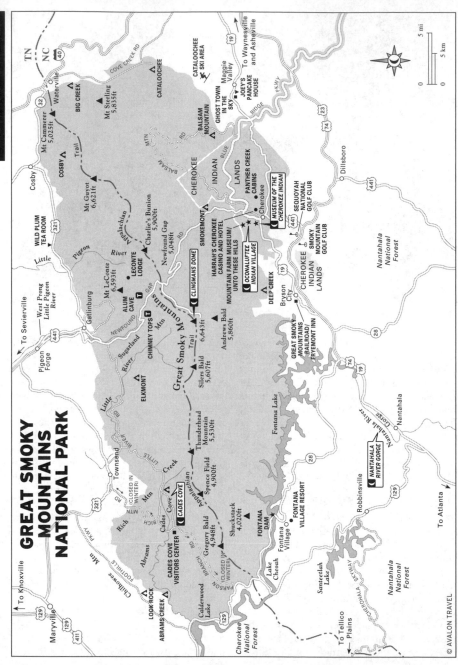

GREAT SMOKY MOUNTAINS NATIONAL PARK

© AVALON TRAVEL

mid-June to mid-August and all of October. Traffic is most likely to be heavy on the Cades Cove Loop Road and Newfound Gap Road. Several roads in the park are closed in the winter, but closing dates vary. Among these are Balsam Mountain, Clingmans Dome, Little Greenbrier, Rich Mountain, and Round Bottom Roads and the Roaring Fork Motor Nature Trail.

Safety

Sometimes even the most experienced outdoorspeople have emergencies. Whether you're going into the backcountry alone or with others, make sure that someone you trust knows where you're going, what your likely route is, and when to expect you back. The National Park Service recommends leaving their phone number (865/436-1230) with someone at home to call if you're not back when expected.

Some of the basic safety rules may seem obvious, but it's good to review them. Climbing on rocks and waterfalls is always dangerous, and crossing a deep or flooded stream can be treacherous as well. If you have to cross a stream that's more than ankle-deep, it's recommended that you unbuckle the waist strap on your backpack (so you don't get pinned underwater if you fall), that you use a hiking stick to steady yourself, and that you wear nonslippery shoes.

Cold is a concern, even in summer. Wear layers, pack additional warm duds (warmer than you think you'll need), and try to stay dry. It may be shorts-and-T-shirt weather when you set out, but even in the summer it can be very cold at night. Plan well, double check before setting out that you have everything you could possibly need on your trek, and, says the National Park Service, "eat before you're hungry, and rest before you're tired" (it's good advice; trust me, I'm an Eagle Scout). Water from streams must be boiled or filtered to make it potable.

Wildlife can pose hazards. Despite assurances to the contrary, there are still panthers (mountain lions) in these mountains. Ignore what the officials say in this (and only this) regard, locals see and hear them throughout

Appalachia. But panthers are rare and reclusive, as are coyotes, wild hogs, and other resident tough guys. On a grim note, several years back there was a series of murders of hikers in the highlands of North Carolina and Georgia. The apparent perpetrator is now behind bars, but it bears remembering that human beings are the most dangerous animals in the woods. You might know how to protect yourself from wild animals and the elements, but dangerous people are another matter. It's always better to hike or camp with at least one companion. A sturdy walking stick can be a lifesaver, and bear spray, cheap and readily available in many different kinds of stores, is good for deterring more than bears.

Permits and Regulations

Permits are required for camping in the national park but are quite easy to obtain. You can register at any of the 12 visitors centers and ranger stations. This must be done in person, not online or over the phone. Fishing requires a permit as well, which can be bought at outfitters and bait shops in nearby towns. Strict rules governing fishing apply; these can be found on the park website (www.nps.gov/grsm). Other rules apply to interaction with wildlife. Don't feed animals, and make sure to seal up your foodstuffs to discourage night visitors. Firearms are forbidden in the park, as is hunting.

Your dog is welcome in the park, but only in certain areas. To prevent transmission of diseases to or from the wildlife, and to avoid disrupting or frightening the resident fauna, dogs are not permitted on hiking trails. They are allowed to accompany you at campgrounds and picnic sites.

WILDLIFE IN THE PARK

The largest animals in the park are also the most recent arrivals. In the spring of 2001, the National Park Service reintroduced **elk** to the Great Smoky Mountains, a species that used to live here but was hunted to regional extinction in the 18th century. In the years since their reintroduction, the herd has reproduced steadily, boding well for a successful future. If you hear a strange bellowing in the early autumn, it may be a male elk showing off for his beloved. One of the best places to see the elk is in the Cataloochee Valley, particularly in fields at dawn and dusk. Be sure to keep your distance; these animals can weigh up to 700 pounds, and the males have some formidable headgear.

An estimated 1,600 **black bears** live in the GSMNP—two per square mile—so it's quite possible that you'll encounter one. They are a wonder to see, but the 100-400-pound creatures pose a real risk to humans, so it's important to be aware of how we interact with them. It is illegal to come within 150 feet of a bear or elk, and those who knowingly get closer can be arrested. If you see a bear, the recommended procedure is to back away slowly. The National Park Service recommends that if the bear follows you, you should stand your ground. If it keeps coming toward you persistently and looks menacing, make yourself big and scary. Stand on a rock to look taller, or get close to anyone else present, to show the bear that it's outnumbered. Make a lot of noise (bear bells or bear whistles are handy for this) and throw rocks or sticks. Should a bear actually attack you, the National Park Service recommends that you "fight back aggressively with any available object." Don't try to run, because they're much faster than you, and don't climb a tree, as black bears are avid climbers.

The best course of action is simply to avoid them and hope that any sightings you have will be from a safe distance. When camping, lock your food in the trunk of your car, or hoist it into a tree too high off the ground for a bear to reach it, and suspended far enough from the nearest branch that it can't be reached by climbing the tree. Bears may approach picnic areas. Don't feed them, no matter how sweet they look. "Habitual panhandler bears" (this is a real term, Scout's honor) die younger than those afraid of humans, as they are more likely to be hit by cars, swallow indigestible food packaging, become easy targets for hunters, or, if they are too problematic, be captured and euthanized.

Bears are not the only huge ferocious animals in the park. Believe it or not, there are hundreds of snorting, tusky **wild hogs** here, descendants of a herd that escaped from a hunting preserve in Murphy in the 1910s. There are **coyotes, wolves,** and **bobcats,** and extremely rare **mountain lions,** often called panthers or painters in this region.

Of the many natural miracles in this park, one of the most astonishing is the light show put on for a couple of weeks each year by synchronous **fireflies.** Of the park's 14 species, only one, *Photinus carolinus,* flashes in this manner. While the average backyard's worth of fireflies twinkles like Christmas lights, synchronous fireflies, as their name implies, are capable of flashing in unison, by the hundreds or thousands. The sight is so amazing that, during the peak flashing period in June, the park organizes nighttime expeditions to the best viewing spots.

If you go hiking in the backcountry, you might well see a **snake.** It's unlikely that you'll encounter a poisonous one, as there are only two kinds of vipers here—rattlesnakes and copperheads—that pose a danger to humans. There has never been a death from snakebite in the park, as far as anyone knows, and snakes are shy, but to be on the safe side, watch where you step or put your hands; you don't want to be the first on that list.

SIGHTS
Mountain Farm Museum
The area that is now the Great Smoky Mountains National Park was once dotted with towns and farms, communities that were displaced for the establishment of the park. The **Mountain Farm Museum** (U.S. 441, 2 miles north of Cherokee, 828/497-1900), next to the Oconaluftee Visitors Center, recreates a mountain fastness of the late 19th and early 20th centuries. On the site of what was the Enloe family's farm, on the banks of the Oconaluftee River, a collection of historic buildings is preserved, some original to the site and others moved from elsewhere in the Smokies. The Davis House, a circa-1900 log house, is

remarkable in that it is constructed from enormous chestnut timbers, a wood not available in this region since the chestnut blight of the 1930s. A large cantilevered barn is constructed to allow wagons to be driven straight through, with stalls and haylofts to the sides. A variety of other dependencies—a meat house, a chicken house, an apple house, a corncrib, a gear shed, a blacksmith shop, and a springhouse—highlight the homesteading skills necessary for a mountain farm like this to prosper. Demonstrations are held here throughout the year, along with two festivals, one at harvest and the other a commemoration of women's work in mountain farm life.

◖ Cades Cove

On the Tennessee side of the park, an 11-mile one-way loop road traverses Cades Cove, a historic settlement dating to the late 18th century. Originally part of the Cherokee Nation, the land was ceded to the United States in 1819. The population grew throughout the 19th century until it was a busy town of several hundred. The village is preserved today as it appeared around 1900, with homes, churches, barns, and a working gristmill, but without the people—a mountain counterpart to Cape Lookout National Seashore's Portsmouth Village. Because of the cove's scenic beauty and abundance of wildlife, this is the most popular part of the nation's most visited national park. The loop road through Cades Cove takes about an hour to drive when visitors are sparse; on crowded days—peak summer and fall seasons and most weekends—it can take several hours to cover the 11 miles.

The **Cades Cove Visitors Center** (9am-4:30pm daily Dec.-Jan., 9am-5pm daily Feb. and Nov., 9am-6pm daily Mar. and Sept.-Oct., 9am-7pm daily Apr.-Aug.) is located at about the halfway point on the Cades Cove Loop. It has a bookstore, exhibits on Southern mountain culture, and seasonal ranger programs. At the southwestern side of the park, Cades Cove is most easily reached from Laurel Creek Road inside the park, which links up to Highway 73 near Townsend, Tennessee. Cades Cove Loop

road begins and ends at Laurel Creek Road, but there are two outlets toward the western end—Forge Creek Road and Rich Mountain Road—which both lead out of the park, one-way; both are closed in winter.

Cataloochee

Cataloochee in North Carolina was an even larger village than Cades Cove. Several important historic buildings from this extremely remote apple-growing town are still standing and can be toured, including Palmer Chapel, the settlement's only church, which was served by once-monthly visits by circuit-riding Methodist preachers. Cataloochee is also a prime spot for watching the park's elk, reintroduced in 2001 and prospering. Look for them in the open fields around sunrise and twilight. The Cataloochee area is at the far northeastern edge of the park, and a reasonably direct drive from I-40 via the Cove Creek Road. The National Park Service recommends a more adventurous route as well for those with plenty of time and immunity to car sickness (it's a twisty road): Highway 32 from Cosby, Tennessee. Whichever way you go, part of the route will be on a gravel road. The park sells an auto tour booklet at the visitors centers, which will help guide you through Cataloochee. Several houses, a school, churches, and barns are open to the public.

◖ Clingmans Dome

At 6,643 feet, Clingmans Dome is the third-highest mountain in the eastern United States, and the highest in the Great Smoky Mountains. A flying saucer-like observation tower at the end of a long, steep walkway gives 360-degree views of the surrounding mountains, and on a clear day, that view can be as far as a hundred miles. More often, though, it's misty up here in the clouds, and Clingmans Dome receives so much precipitation that its woods are actually a coniferous rainforest. The road to the summit is closed December 1-March 31, but the observation tower remains open for those willing to make the hike. To get to Clingmans Dome, turn off Newfound Gap Road 0.1 miles south

Elk are often seen in the Cataloochee area.

© DAVEALLENPHOTO/123RF.COM

of Newfound Gap, and then take Clingmans Dome Road (closed in winter), which leads seven miles to the parking lot. The peak is near the center of the park, due north from Bryson City.

Fontana Dam

At the southeastern edge of the park, Fontana Dam, with 11,000 surface acres, is an artificial impoundment of the Little Tennessee River. This largest dam east of the Rockies was built in the 1940s, a stupendous wall of concrete the height of a 50-story skyscraper. It caused the river to flood back through little mountain towns, vestiges of which can be seen every five years when the water level is lowered for dam inspection. The **visitors center** (Hwy. 28, Fontana Dam, 828/498-2234 or 800/467-1388, 9am-6pm daily May-Oct., free) is worth a visit, and the Appalachian Trail goes right along the top of the dam.

Newfound Gap Road

While many visitors use this 32-mile road that bisects Great Smoky Mountains National Park as a mere throughway, it's actually one of the prettiest drives you'll find anywhere. This curvy road alternates between exposed and tree-enclosed, and a number of scenic overlooks provide spectacular views of the Smokies. Stop at one that has a trail (more than half of them do) and take a short walk into the woods, or eat a picnic lunch on one of the mountainside overlooks. Whatever you do on this road between Cherokee and Gatlinburg, take your time and enjoy the ride.

SPORTS AND RECREATION

The Great Smoky Mountains National Park covers over 500,000 acres, and within that expanse are more than 800 miles of hiking trails, ranging from easy walks around major attractions to strenuous wilderness paths suited to the most experienced backpackers. A section of the Appalachian Trail goes through the park, crossing the Fontana Dam. There are dozens of books available about hiking in the Smokies, available at bookstores and outfitters

© JASON FRYE

Sharp turns? How about spirals?

throughout the region as well as online. The park staffs a **Backcountry Information Office** (865/436-1297, 8am-5pm daily), and the knowledgeable folks who work there are a good first resource when planning a hiking trip. The park website (www.nps.gov/grsm) has some downloadable maps to give you a general sense of the lay of the land. The Great Smoky Mountains Association website (www.smokiesinformation.org) has a good online bookstore where you can find many books about hiking in the park.

Hiking

The Great Smoky Mountains National Park contains hundreds of miles of hiking trails, ranging from family-friendly loop trails to strenuous wilderness treks. Below are a sampling of hikes in the park. Before embarking on any of these trails, obtain a park map, and talk to a park ranger to ascertain trail conditions and gauge whether it's suited to your hiking skills.

A quick and easy foray into the woods is the

Spruce-Fir Trail, off Clingmans Dome Road, a walk of just over 0.3 miles. Almost flat, and mostly following a wooden boardwalk, this is the ideal trail if you've been traveling in the car all day and simply want to stretch your legs and experience a bit of easily accessible forest atmosphere.

A longer but also fairly easy walk is the **Oconaluftee River Trail,** which begins behind the Oconaluftee Visitors Center. This path, which is gravel-covered, follows the river and goes through part of the Mountain Farm Museum grounds. Unlike all the other trails in the GSMNP, dogs and bicycles are allowed. It's about three miles round-trip, popular with families, and absolutely littered with wildflowers in the spring. An added bonus is that one end is adjacent to the GSMNP "Welcome" sign, and the National Park Service has conveniently installed a post and platform to hold your camera for selfies in front of it.

At many of the pullouts deeper into the park, you'll find **Quiet Walkways.** These short, easy trails pull you into the woods just off the road, but far enough that the road noise is drowned out by bird calls, rustling leaves, flowing streams, and mountain breezes that build a cocoon around you. Signs at the trailhead encourage you to take your time, sit and lose yourself in the sounds of nature, the aroma of the leaves, water, flowers, and mountain air, and the textures of the wild woodlands.

At the **Alum Cave Trail** trailhead, off Newfound Gap Road, you'll find a trio of hikes ranging from easy to rugged. Hiking to **Arch Rock** is an easy 2.8-mile round-trip. Arch Rock has eroded into a giant arch. A moist, winding set of stairs goes under, up, and through the arch, and the trail continues to **Alum Cave,** another mile in, making for a 4.6-mile round-trip. Just before you get here you'll reach Inspiration Point, with a commanding view of the valley below, including the interesting Eye of the Needle rock formation on an adjacent ridge. Shortly after Inspiration Point, you'll come to Alum Cave, where Epsom salts and saltpeter (used in the manufacture of gunpowder) were mined starting in the 1850s. To get

Surround yourself with nature's sounds on a Quiet Walkway in the Great Smoky Mountains National Park.

to Alum Cave, the path transitions from easy to moderate, but if you want to push on another 3.7 miles to the peak of Mount LeConte for a hike that's a little over 10 miles round-trip, you'll be in for a much more difficult trail. For around two miles you'll encounter many exposed ledges, some with waterfalls to negotiate, all with a cable handhold you'll want to use, especially if the rocky path is slick. When you get to the top, you'll find yourself at the LeConte Lodge, but not the actual summit. To reach the highest point at the summit of Mount LeConte, follow a short trail to High Top. The views from High Top are nice, but not fantastic; for the best views, try Myrtle Point (a great spot to photograph the sunrise) or Cliff Top, near the lodge.

The **Boogerman Trail** is a loop trail off the Cove Creek Road in the Cataloochee section of the park. This is a moderate 7.5-mile round-trip that takes between 2-3 hours to complete. You'll pass old-growth trees, streams and cascades, and several old homesites, including that of "Boogerman" himself, an early resident named Robert Palmer.

Another popular hike on the Newfound Gap Road is the **Chimney Tops Trail.** This four-mile round-trip starts out easy enough, but in the last mile gains more than 830 vertical feet. Severe weather in 2012 turned parts of the trail into an obstacle course of rocks, roots, and mud, and at times the trail may be closed for ongoing rehabilitation. If the trail is open, the effort is worth the reward, as the views of Mount LeConte and Mount Kephart to the east and Sugarland Mountain to the west are amazing. This is one of the few mountains in the Smokies with a bare-rock top, and although the trail here is steep, it doesn't require any technical gear, just caution and the ability to scramble up steep rocks.

As if the mountains and valleys, flora and fauna, and close-enough-to-touch clouds weren't wonder enough, the GSMNP has literally hundreds of waterfalls. Several of the most popular and most beautiful are

THE APPALACHIAN TRAIL

The 2,184-mile Appalachian Trail runs from Georgia to Maine, with 95.5 miles within North Carolina and another 200 straddling the border of North Carolina and Tennessee. It's a high climb, with many peaks over 5,000 feet and gaps brushing 4,000 feet, but the fantastic balds (natural and agricultural areas devoid of trees) along the trail here—like Cheoa Bald and Max Patch—are big draws for day hikers and segment hikers, and having vistas this beautiful this early on in the long journey helps through-hikers retain their focus and determination to reach their goal.

The Appalachian Trail cuts a path through the Nantahala Forest, regarded by many as one of the best sections of the southern portion of the trail, before crossing the rills of the southern Blue Ridge and following the crest of the Smokies along the Tennessee border. This section of the trail is rated between a 3 and a 6

on the AT's 10-point scale, which means the trail varies from moderate elevation changes on well graded trails, to strenuous and short but steep climbs, to extended climbs that last hours, as well as short sections with difficult footing. For through-hikers, who often have years of trail experience, the path here isn't as difficult as it may be for some day- or even overnight-hikers.

Finding a day hike isn't hard west of Asheville, especially in the deeper mountains along Great Smoky Mountain National Park. Driving the Newfound Gap Road from the town of Cherokee into Tennessee, go about 16 miles from the Oconaluftee Visitors Center to the Newfound Gap parking lot. The trailhead is to the left of the overlook. Take the moderate four-mile hike to Charles Bunion, a peak along the trail with a very odd name. You'll gradually gain around 1,600 feet in elevation, but if you bring a picnic lunch, you'll have a lovely dining spot.

accessible from major trails. Close to Bryson City, 25-foot **Indian Creek Falls** is a moderate hike of less than two miles round-trip; it's a two-for-one deal as the path also goes by Tom Branch Falls. Crossing Deep Creek on bridges and logs and going by old homesites, this is an especially interesting hike. The Deep Creek-Indian Creek Trailhead is at the end of Deep Creek Road in Bryson City. It gets very crowded in nice weather, particularly because this is a popular area for tubing, which makes parking quite difficult. Restrooms are available at the picnic area. Also accessible from the Indian Creek Trailhead is the path to 90-foot **Juney Whank Falls.** This hike is shorter but more difficult than to Indian Creek Falls. Since it shares the same trailhead, you can expect to find the same crowds and parking difficulties.

Mingo Falls, a beautiful 120-foot plume, is just outside the park, on the Qualla Boundary (Cherokee land). It can be seen from the Pigeon Creek Trail, which begins in the Mingo Falls Campground, off Big Cove Road south

of Cherokee. The hike is very short, less than 0.5 miles round-trip, but it's fairly strenuous.

Some longer hikes on the Tennessee side of the park lead to equally beautiful falls. **Rainbow Falls** is 80 feet high and produces such a cloud of mist that when the sun hits it right, you can see a rainbow. In winter it sometimes freezes solid, which is an amazing sight. The Rainbow Falls Trail near Gatlinburg is a difficult 5.5 miles round-trip. It ascends about 1,500 vertical feet and is rocky most of the way, but it provides some great views of the falls and of Gatlinburg. Parking is available on Cherokee Orchard Road in Gatlinburg, but it fills up quickly, and you may need to pay to park a little farther from the trailhead.

The tallest waterfall, 100-foot **Ramsey Cascades,** is also the most difficult to reach. Those able to make a strenuous eight-mile round-trip hike are richly rewarded with a journey through old-growth hardwood forests and along fast-moving rivers. The pool at the bottom of the falls is a great place to glimpse some of the creatures that make GSMNP the

© JASON FRYE

Many trailheads lead to easy, moderate, and strenuous hikes in the National Park.

Salamander Capital of the World. The parking area for the Ramsey Cascades Trail is off Greenbrier Road, a few miles southeast of Gatlinburg. The nearest portable toilets are at the picnic area on Greenbrier Road.

As tempting as it may be, and as fun as it may appear, don't try to climb the waterfalls; it's never a good idea. Over the years quite a few people have died in the park trying to climb up, so be safe and admire the cascading water from the trails. Because of its height, Ramsey Cascades is particularly dangerous. Maps and guides to the waterfalls are available at many locations in the park and at bookstores and outdoors shops nearby.

Horseback Riding

Three commercial stables in the park offer "rental" horses on a by-the-hour basis (about $30 per hour). **Smokemont** (828/497-2373) is located in North Carolina near Cherokee. Two are in Tennessee: **Smoky Mountain** (865/436-5634, www.smokymountainridingstables.com) and at **Cades Cove** (10018 Campground Dr.,

Townsend, TN, 865/448-9009, http://cadescovestables.com).

In North Carolina, near Cherokee, an equestrian-friendly campground at **Round Bottom Horse Camp** (Straight Fork-Round Bottom Rd., 865/436-1261, www.nps.gov/grsm, $20) has five campsites, stalls, and bedding for horses. Its location, just inside the park and far up a narrow riverside road, makes it perfect for long rides with larger groups.

Bike Rentals

The **Cades Cove Store** (near Cades Cove Campground, 865/448-9034) rents bicycles in summer and fall (adult geared bikes $6/hour, single gear $4/hour, kids' single gear $4/hour). From the second week in May to the second-to-last Saturday in September, the park closes off the loop road through Caves Cove on Wednesday and Saturday mornings, sunrise-10am, so that cyclists and hikers can enjoy the cove without having to worry about automobile traffic.

Field Schools

Two Tennessee-based organizations affiliated with the GSMNP offer ways to get to know the park even better. The **Smoky Mountain Field School** (865/974-0150, www.outreach.utk.edu) teaches workshops and leads excursions to educate participants in a wide array of fields related to the Smokies. One-day classes focus on the history and cultural heritage of the park, the lives of some of the park's most interesting animals, folk medicine and cooking of the southern Appalachians, and much more. Instructors also lead one-day and overnight hikes into the heart of the park. This is a great way to discover the park far beyond what you would be able to do on your own, so check their schedule and sign up for a class that interests you.

The **Great Smoky Mountains Institute at Tremont** (9275 Tremont Rd., Townsend, TN, 865/448-6709, www.gsmit.org) teaches students of all ages about the ecology of the region, wilderness rescue and survival skills, and even nature photography. Many of the classes and guided trips are part of Elderhostels, kids camps, or teacher-training institutes; however, there are also rich opportunities for unaffiliated learners.

ACCOMMODATIONS

There is only one inn in the entire 500,000-acre park, and it's an unusual one. The **C LeConte Lodge** (250 Apple Valley Rd., Sevierville, TN, 865/429-5704, www.lecontelodge.com, cabins with dinner and breakfast $126 adults, $85 ages 4-12, 2-bedroom lodges $676 for up to 8 people, dinner and breakfast $41.50 adults, $25 ages 4-12, 3-bedroom lodge $1,014 for up to 12 people, dinner and breakfast $41.50 adults, $25 ages 4-12, cash or check only, no pets) was built in the 1920s and sits at an elevation of nearly 6,600 feet. It's only accessible on foot after a hike of several hours. A thrice-weekly llama train delivers supplies, and there are flush toilets but no showers. There is no electricity at the lodge, and kerosene heaters will keep you toasty; even in summer, temperatures can fall into the 30s at night. It's an amazing place, and enough people are willing to make the necessary trek to stay here that reservations are usually required far in advance.

For those who don't want to camp or hike to a rustic lodge, there are countless motels just outside the GSMNP. Reservations are always a good idea, especially in summer and in leaf season. There are many choices in Cherokee, Maggie Valley, Bryson City, Pigeon Forge, Gatlinburg, Sevierville, and other neighboring communities. In addition to the many chain motels, affordable mom-and-pop motels also dot this landscape in abundance. Two homey choices in Gatlinburg are the **River House Motor Lodge** (610 River Rd., Gatlinburg, 865/436-7821, www.riverhouse-motels.com, around $179 in season, from $69 off-season), and **Johnson's Inn** (242 Bishop Lane, Gatlinburg, 800/842-1930, www.johnsonsinn.com, $49-104). In Cherokee, on the North Carolina side of the park, go with a hotel like **Cherokee Grand Hotel** (196 Painttown Rd., 828/497-0050, www.cherokeegrandhotel.com, $109-159), located only five minutes from the park entrance, or cabin accommodations with **Panther Creek Cabins** (Wrights Creek Rd., Cherokee, 828/497-2461, www.panthercreekresort.com, cabins $100-175), a quiet, quaint, comfortable set of cabins just outside downtown Cherokee.

Camping

The GSMNP has many locations for camping, fees for which range $14-23. Campers can stay up to 14 consecutive nights at car-accessible campsites, but no more than three consecutive nights at backcountry campsites, and only nonconsecutive nights in shelters and at campsite 113. There are 10 car-accessible campgrounds, each of which has cold running water and flush toilets but no showers or power and water hookups. Most of these sites are first come, first served, but May 15-October 15 sites at the Elkmont, Smokemont, Cades Cove, Catalloochee, and Cosby campgrounds can be reserved (877/444-6777, www.nps.gov/grsm).

In North Carolina, from northeast to southwest, the first campground is **Big Creek,** near I-40, at an elevation of 1,700 feet. This walk-in,

© JASON FRYE

Mountain cabins offer solitude after a day of play.

tent-only campsite features the beautifully soporific sound of rushing water from the nearby creek. It's open from spring to the beginning of November. The **Cataloochee** campground, also reasonably close to I-40, is at 2,610 feet and is also open from spring to the beginning of November. You must have a reservation for Cataloochee, and make it early, as this place fills up.

Smokemont, open year-round, has a whopping 142 campsites for tents and RVs, and is the closest to Cherokee; it sits at 2,198 feet elevation. **Deep Creek,** at 1,800 feet, is closest to Bryson City, and is open spring through early November.

In Tennessee, from northeast to southwest, **Cosby** campground, at 2,459 feet elevation and open spring through early November, is closest to Cosby, Tennessee, and is not far from I-40. **Elkmont,** at 2,150 feet on the Little River, open spring through the end of November, is the closest campsite to the Gatlinburg entrance to the park. This site is near Cades Cove, but is notable as a popular sight for

June's synchronized firefly shows. The **Cades Cove** campground, located off the loop road at Cades Cove, at an elevation of 1,807 feet, is open year-round.

Another car-accessible camping option is the **Mile High Campground** (828/269-2945, http://campmilehigh.azurewebsites.net, $20 tent or RV, $30 primitive cabin, $50 group site) located on the Cherokee Reservation and owned by a member of the Eastern Band of the Cherokee. It is near Blue Ridge Parkway milepost 458; turn onto Wolf Laurel Gap, and the campground entrance is one mile along, on the left, after the "Molly's Gap Road" sign. This campground is indeed a little over a mile high in elevation and has around 50 sites in tent and RV areas along with primitive cabins. A beautiful campground near a number of hikes, the Blue Ridge Parkway, Cherokee, and the Great Smoky Mountains National Park, it's a great spot to set up for a few days. All campsites have fire rings and are fairly private. Bears and elk are common sights, so take pictures, but use caution.

Backcountry camping is abundant. It is only permitted at designated sites and shelters, and a permit is required, but the permits are free and can be obtained at any of 15 different visitors centers and campground offices throughout the park or online (https://smokiespermits.nps.gov). The Appalachian Trail runs through, hugging the ridgeline and the border between North Carolina and Tennessee, and shelters on the trail fill up fast with through-hikers and day hikers, but other shelters and campsites on side trails are ideal for out-and-back camping trips. The Kephart shelter and the shelter at Laurel Gap are on two beautiful trails, and a number of campsites—numbers 52-57—are on the Mountains-to-Sea Trail that traverses North Carolina. There are also five drive-in horse camps ($20-25) and seven group campgrounds ($35-65). A map of the available campsites can be found on the park's website (www.nps.gov/grsm). Before camping at the GSMNP, be sure to familiarize yourself with the park's backcountry regulations and etiquette, available online and at locations in the park.

FOOD

Unless you're staying at the LeConte Lodge, you'll have to leave the park for meals. The easiest way is simply to drive into Bryson City or Cherokee, or in Tennessee, Gatlinburg or Pigeon Forge, which are all right on the edge of the park. In Gatlinburg, try the **Smoky Mountain Brewery** (1004 Parkway, Suite 501, Gatlinburg, 865/436-4200, www.smoky-mtn-brewery.com, 11:30am-1am daily, under $20), a popular brewpub and restaurant. The menu is about what you'd expect—burgers, wings, and cheesesteaks—but they also have some pretty good pizzas and even barbecue ribs. Their beer selection includes porters, wheat beers, red ales, and hoppy pale ales, so they hit practically every color on the beer spectrum for almost any palates.

The **Wild Plum Tea Room** (555 Buckhorn Rd., Gatlinburg, 865/436-3808, www.wildplumtearoom.com, 11am-3pm Mon.-Sat. Mar. mid Dec., under $15) is a nice spot for soup and sandwiches, homemade desserts, and the signature wild-plum muffins served with every entrée. You can get a wide range of things to eat, including salmon burgers, lobster pies, chicken salad, and even stratas (like a quiche), and wild plums make an appearance again in the hot or cold wild-plum tea. They also offer vegetarian and vegan dishes, and dogs are welcome on their patio.

The formal restaurant of the **Buckhorn Inn** (2140 Tudor Mountain Rd., Gatlinburg, 866/941-0460, www.buckhorninn.com, prix fixe $35, reservations required) has a different beautiful multicourse set menu every day of the week. Typical meals are French-inspired, but other cuisines show up from time to time, and every meal includes soup, often a salad, and always dessert. Vegetarian meals can be prepared with advance notice.

In Pigeon Forge, try the kitschy but endearing **J. T. Hannah's Kitchen** (3214 Parkway, Pigeon Forge, 865/428-4200, http://jthannahs.com, 10am-10pm daily, $9-19), a restaurant that serves up a good list of burgers and deluxe sandwiches such as the Tennessee Pulled Pork Sandwich and their signature Prime French Dip.

INFORMATION AND SERVICES

The official website of **Great Smoky Mountains National Park** (www.nps.gov/grsm) has much information to help you plan your trip, as do the websites of **Smoky Mountain Host** (www.visitsmokies.org) and the **Blue Ridge National Heritage Area** (www.blueridgeheritage.com). Detailed touring suggestions for sites associated with Cherokee history and heritage can be found at the websites of **Cherokee Heritage Trails** (www.cherokeeheritagetrail.org) and the **North Carolina Folklife Institute** (www.ncfolk.org), and in *Cherokee Heritage Trails,* an excellent guidebook that can be purchased at either website.

Area hospitals include those in Bryson City, Sylva, and Clyde, as well as a little farther afield in Asheville as well as in Knoxville and Maryville, Tennessee.

GETTING THERE AND AROUND

The closest airports to the Smokies are **Asheville Regional Airport** (AVL, 61 Terminal Dr., 828/684-2226, www.fly-avl.com) in Fletcher, which has commercial scheduled flights, and the **Gatlinburg-Pigeon Forge Airport** (GKT, 134 Air Museum Way, Sevierville, 865/453-8393), over the state line in Tennessee, which has no scheduled flights but can handle private aircraft. Amtrak doesn't run trains in this area. Unless you're hiking through on the Appalachian Trail, the best way to get around the Smokies is by car. U.S. 19 and U.S. 23 stretch down from Asheville to the Georgia state line, while U.S. 64, which literally stretches from Murphy to Manteo, snakes along the southern edge of the Smokies. Cresting the northern edge is I-40, running between Asheville and Knoxville.

Maggie Valley

Maggie Valley is a vacation town from the bygone era of long family road trips in wood-paneled station wagons. Coming down the mountain toward Maggie Valley you'll pass an overlook that, on a morning when the mountains around Soco Gap are looped with fog, is surely one of the most beautiful vistas in the state.

SIGHTS AND ENTERTAINMENT

Maggie Valley's best-known attraction is the **Ghost Town in the Sky** (16 Fie Top Rd., 828/926-1130, www.ghosttowninthesky.com, 10am-6pm daily June-Oct., weather permitting, $25 adults, $16 ages 3-12), an Old West theme park where the good guys and bad guys shoot it out daily for your viewing pleasure. There are rides—zip lines, carousels, roller coasters, a free-fall tower—as well as regular bluegrass and gospel concerts. A renovation project is partially completed, with Phase Three, a religious section intended to be a model of Jerusalem to draw religious travelers, slated for completion in 2014.

Bluegrass music and clogging are a big deal in this town. The great bluegrass banjo player Raymond Fairchild is a Maggie native, and after his 50-year touring and recording career, he and his wife, Shirley, are now the hosts of the **Maggie Valley Opry House** (3605 Soco Rd., 828/648-7941, www.raymondfairchild.com, 8pm daily June-Oct.). In season, you can find bluegrass and country music concerts and clogging exhibitions most every night.

In a state with countless attractions for automotive enthusiasts, Maggie Valley's **Wheels Through Time Museum** (62 Vintage Lane, 828/926-6266, www.wheelsthroughtime.com, 9am-5pm Thurs.-Mon. late Mar.-late Nov., $12 adults, $10 over age 65, $6 ages 5-12, free under age 4) stands out as one of the most fun. A dazzling collection of nearly 300 vintage motorcycles and a fair number of cars are on display, including rarities like a 1908 Indian, a 1914 Harley-Davidson, military motorcycles from both World Wars, and some gorgeous postwar bikes. This collection, which dates mostly to before 1950, is maintained in working order—almost every one of the bikes is revved up from time to time, and the museum's founder has been known to take a spin on one of the treasures.

SPORTS AND RECREATION
Skiing and Winter Sports

Maggie Valley's **Cataloochee Ski Area** (1080 Ski Lodge Rd., off U.S. 19, 800/768-0285, snow conditions 800/768-3588, www.cataloochee.com, lift tickets $20-60, rentals $21-30) has slopes geared to every level of skier and snowboarder. Classes and private lessons are taught for all ages. At Cataloochee's sister snow-sports area, **Tube World** (U.S. 19, next

© JASON FRYE

a hiking trail in Maggie Valley

to Ski Area, 800/768-0285, www.cataloochee. com, $25, must be over 42 inches tall, late Nov.-mid-Mar.), you can zip down the mountain on inner tubes, and there's a "Wee Bowl" area for children (call ahead, $5).

Hiking

The Blue Ridge Parkway (BRP) is not far from Maggie Valley, which means there are a number of hiking trails to explore. Easy trails include the **Buck Springs Trail** (BRP milepost 407.6), just over one mile long, and the 0.25-mile **Bear Pen Gap Trail** (BRP milepost 427.6) that connects to the Mountains-to-Sea Trail; additionally, you can go for a stroll around **Lake Junaluska** in the town of Maggie Valley. Moderate trails are longer and usually involve some elevation gain and loss; a couple of the best are **Graveyard Fields Loop Trail** (BRP milepost 418.8), a 3.2-mile loop through alpine-like meadows. Extend your hike here by following one of the spur trails that lead to some fantastic waterfalls. Another moderate option is the **Richland**

Balsam Trail (BRP milepost 431), a loop through a spruce and fir forest. Tougher trails often pay off with the best views, and **Waterrock Knob Trail** (BRP milepost 451.2) does that on a 1.18-mile trail that's steep and a little rocky but manageable. It leads to a summit where views await. Another option is the **Devil's Courthouse Trail** (BRP milepost 422.4), a short but strenuous hike of just under 0.5 miles leading to another panoramic summit view.

ACCOMMODATIONS

The main drag through Maggie Valley (Soco Rd./U.S. 19) is lined with motels, including some of the familiar national chains. Among the pleasant independent motels are the **Valley Inn** (236 Soco Rd., 800/948-6880, www.thevalleyinn.com, in-season rates vary, call for specifics, from $39 off-season) and **Jonathan Creek Inn and Villas** (4324 Soco Rd., 800/577-7812, www.jonathancreekinn. com, from $60), which has creek-side rooms with screened porches.

FOOD

J. Arthurs Restaurant (2843 Soco Rd., 828/926-1817, www.jarthurs.com, lunch noon-2:30pm Fri.-Sun., early bird dinner 4:30pm-6pm daily, dinner from 4:30pm daily, $15-25) is a popular spot locally for steaks, which are the house specialty; they've been serving them up for more than 25 years. The restaurant also has a variety of seafood and pasta dishes, but few vegetarian options. The **Mountaineer Restaurant** (6490 Soco Rd., 828/926-1730, breakfast, lunch, and dinner daily, $6-20) is a typical mountain café serving barbecue, steaks, catfish, trout, and country-cooking specialties.

A Maggie Valley dining institution—this place has been around since 1952—is **Maggie Valley Restaurant** (2804 Soco Rd., 828/926-0425, www.maggievalleyrestaurant.net, 7am-9pm daily May-Oct., breakfast $1-10, lunch and dinner $5-12). Expect comfort-food the classics—meatloaf, meatloaf sandwiches, something called a chuck wagon, pork chops, biscuit sandwiches, grits, bottomless coffee, and even buttermilk—along with one of the best pieces of fresh fried trout you'll find in these mountains.

Joey's Pancake House (4309 Soco Rd., 828/926-0212, www.joeyspancake.com, 7am-noon Fri.-Wed., about $8) has been flipping flapjacks for travelers and locals alike since 1966. The pancakes, waffles, and country ham are so good that lines form on the weekends—get here early.

GETTING THERE AND AROUND

U.S. 19 is the main thoroughfare in these parts, leading from Asheville to the Great Smoky Mountains National Park. If you're taking your time between Asheville, Boone, or parts north, the Blue Ridge Parkway is a beautiful, but slow, drive to this part of the state. Maggie Valley is also a reasonably short jog off I-40 via exits 20, 24, and 27.

Cherokee and the Qualla Boundary

The town of Cherokee is a study in juxtapositions: the cultural traditions of the Cherokee people, the region's natural beauty, a 24-hour casino, and community-wide preparation for the future. Cherokee is the seat of government of the Eastern Band of the Cherokee, who have lived in these mountains for centuries. Today, their traditional arts and crafts, government, and cultural heritage are very much alive, although their language seems to be disappearing. The Qualla ("KWA-lah") Boundary is not a reservation but is a large tract of land owned and governed by the Cherokee people. Institutions like the Museum of the Cherokee Indian and the Qualla Arts and Crafts Mutual provide a solid base for the Eastern Band's cultural life. As you drive around, take a look at the road signs: Below each English road name is that same name in Cherokee, a beautiful script created by Sequoyah, a 19th-century Cherokee silversmith. This language, once nearly extinct, is being taught to the community's youth now, and there is a Cherokee language immersion school on the Qualla Boundary. This doesn't mean the language is not in danger; few Cherokee people speak it fluently.

The main street in Cherokee is a classic cheesy tourist district where you'll find "Indian" souvenirs—factory-made moccasins, plastic tomahawks, peace pipes, faux bearskins, the works. In a retro way, this part of Cherokee, with its predictable trinket shops and fudgeries, is charming; check out the garish 1950s motel signs with comic-book Indians outlined in neon, blinking in the night.

Aside from its proximity to the Great Smoky Mountains National Park and the Blue Ridge Parkway, the biggest draw in town is Harrah's Cherokee Casino, one of the largest casino hotels in the state and home to a world-class spa. The 24-hour entertainment opportunities attract visitors from far and wide, some of whom stay on the property the whole time, while others take a break from the slap of cards and the flash of slot machines to experience the natural and cultural wonders of Cherokee.

Take all of this that you see—the casino, the tacky tourist shops, and the stereotyping signs—with a grain of salt, as they don't represent the true nature of the Cherokee people and their long history.

SIGHTS
【 Museum of the Cherokee Indian

The **Museum of the Cherokee Indian** (589 Tsali Blvd., 828/497-3481, www.cherokeemuseum.org, 9am-7pm Mon.-Fri., 9am-5pm Sat.-Sun. late May-early Sept., 9am-5pm daily early Sept.-late May, $10, $6 ages 6-12, free under age 6) was founded in 1948 and was originally housed in a log cabin. Today, it is a well-regarded modern museum and locus of community culture. In the exhibits that trace the long history of the Cherokee people, you may notice the disconcertingly realistic mannequins. Local community members volunteered to be models for these mannequins, allowing casts to be made of their faces and bodies so that the figures would not reflect an outsider's notion of what Native Americans should look like; the mannequins depict real people. The Museum of the Cherokee Indian traces their history from the Paleo-Indian people of the Pleistocene, when the ancestral Cherokees were hunter-gatherers, through the ancient days of Cherokee civilization, and into contact with European settlers.

A great deal of this exhibit focuses on the 18th and 19th centuries, when a series of tragedies befell the Cherokee as a result of the invasion of their homeland. It was also a time of great cultural advancement, including Sequoyah's development of the script to write the Cherokee language. The forced relocation of Native Americans called the Trail of Tears began near here, along the North Carolina-Georgia border, in the early 19th century. A small contingent of Cherokees remained in the Smokies at the time of the Trail of Tears, successfully eluding, and then negotiating with, the U.S. military, who were trying to force most of the Native Americans in the Southeast to move to Oklahoma. Those who stayed out in the woods, along with a few others who were able to return from Oklahoma, are the ancestors of today's Eastern Band, and their history is truly remarkable.

A favorite part of the museum are the stories, legends, and myths described on placards throughout the museum. There's the story of a boy who became a bear and convinced his entire clan to become bears also. There's one about Spearfinger, a frightening creature that some say still lives in these woods today. And there are tales about Selu, the corn mother, and Kanati, the lucky hunter. Cherokee member and contemporary writer Marilou Awiakta has written widely about Selu, tying the past and present together with taut lines of thought that challenge our views on culture and technology.

【 Qualla Arts and Crafts Mutual

Across the street from the museum is the **Qualla Arts and Crafts Mutual** (645 Tsali Blvd., 828/497-3103, http://quallaartsandcrafts.com, 8am-5pm Mon.-Sat., 9am-5pm Sun.), a community arts co-op where local artists sell their work. The gallery's high standards and the community's thousands of years of artistry make for a collection of very special pottery, baskets, masks, and other traditional art. As hard as it is to survive as an artist in a place like New York City, artists in rural areas such as this have an exponentially more difficult time supporting themselves through the sale of their art while maintaining the integrity of their vision and creativity. The Qualla co-op does a great service to this community in providing a year-round market for the work of traditional Cherokee artists, whose stewardship of and innovation in the arts are so important. The double-woven baskets are especially beautiful, as are the carvings of the masks representing each of the seven clans of the Cherokee people (the Bird, Deer, Longhair, Blue, Wolf, Paint, and Wild Potato).

© JASON FRYE

Cherokee clan masks at Qualla Arts and Crafts Mutual

Oconaluftee Indian Village

Oconaluftee Indian Village (778 Drama Rd., 828/497-3481, http://cherokeehistorical.org, open May-Mid-March, Mon.-Sat., gates open and tours begin at 10am, tours run every 15 minutes until 4pm when the box office closes, village closes after final tour, usually around 5pm, $19 adults, $11 children, free 5 and under) is a recreated Cherokee Indian Village tucked into the hills above the town. Here, you'll see how the tribe lived in the 18th century. Tour guides in period costumes lead groups on walking lectures with stops at stations where you can see Cherokee cultural, artistic, and daily-life activities performed as authentically as possible. From cooking demos to flint knapping (for arrowheads and spear points) to wood carving and clay work, you'll get a look at how the Cherokee lived centuries ago. The highlight of the tour is the ritual dance demonstration showing half a dozen dances and explaining their cultural significance.

ENTERTAINMENT AND EVENTS

Of the several outdoor dramas for which North Carolina is known, among the longest running is Cherokee's **Unto These Hills** (Mountainside Theater, 688 Drama Rd., adjacent to Oconaluftee Village, 866/554-4557, www.cherokeesmokies.com, 8pm Mon.-Sat. June-Aug., $18-22 adults, $8-12 ages 6-12, free under age 6). For more than 60 summers, Cherokee actors have told the story of their nation's history, from ancient times through the Trail of Tears. Every seat in the house is a good seat at the Mountainside Theater, and the play is certainly enlightening. Be warned: If you're gun-shy or easily startled, there is some cannon fire and gunfire in the play.

Hear stories, learn dances, and interact with Cherokee storytellers at the **Cherokee Bonfire** (Oconaluftee Islands Park, Tsalagi Rd. and Tsali Blvd., where U.S. 19 and U.S. 441 intersect, 800/438-1601, http://visitcherokee.com, 7pm and 9pm Thurs.-Sat., free, including marshmallows). Bring your bathing suit and

© JASON FRYE

mountain golf at the stunning Sequoyah National Golf Club

some water shoes to the bonfire; afterward, you may want to go for a wade or a quick dip in the Oconaluftee River, which is wide, rocky, and fun.

SPORTS AND RECREATION

Cherokee has more than 30 miles of streams, rivers, and creeks ideal for fishing. Add to that the fact that the Eastern Band owns and operates a fish hatchery that releases around 250,000 trout into these waters every year and you have the perfect mix for fantastic fishing. Unlike the rest of North Carolina, you don't need a North Carolina fishing license; you need a **Tribal Fishing Permit** ($10 per day, 2 days $17, 3 days $27, 5 days $47), sold at a number of outlets in Cherokee. You'll find brook, brown, golden, and rainbow trout, and it's fly-rod only, so you have to have your cast down pat if you want to bring in a big one. There are both catch-and-release and catch-and-keep waters in the Qualla Boundary, but if you want to fish outside the boundary, where several streams and the Oconaluftee River have

great fishing, you need a North Carolina or Tennessee fishing permit. Tennessee permits are only valid inside the Great Smoky National Park boundaries in North Carolina.

The **Sequoyah National Golf Club** (79 Cahons Rd., Whittier, 828/497-3000, www.sequoyahnational.com, 18 holes, par 72, greens fees from $40) is a stunning mountain golf course. Making the most of the contours and elevation, the course offers tee boxes with breathtaking views of the fairway and the Smoky Mountains. The course record is 62, an impressive feat on a normal course, but here it's something else. Holes like number 12, a par 5 that plays uphill the whole way, present the usual par-5 difficulties combined with steep elevation gain, and number 15, a par 4 that entices golfers to play overly aggressively and drop a ball short of the fairway and into the woods, test a golfer's club knowledge and course IQ. This is a tough course for first-timers because so many of the holes have blind approaches, doglegs, or both, but it's enjoyable enough

For fun on the water, try **Smoky Mountain**

Tubing (1847 Tsali Blvd., 828/497-4545, http://cherokeetubeandraft.com, 10am-6pm daily, weather permitting, $10). They do only one thing: rent tubes on which you'll drift down the river and splash your friends. Smoky Mountain Tubing has mountains of tubes, so rent one and float down the Oconaluftee River for two or three hours. They have a fleet of shuttle buses to pick you up a few miles downstream to bring you back.

I'd be in trouble with my dad if I didn't mention that you can ride go-karts at **Cherokee Fun Park** (1897 Tsali Blvd., 828/497-5877, www.cherokeefunparknc.com, 10am-10pm Sun.-Thurs., 10am-11pm Fri.-Sat., single rider $8, doubles $12). A family tradition for as long as I remember, we love to strap ourselves into a go-kart and hurtle around a track—and, boy, do they have a track at Cherokee Fun Park. You can't miss it as you're driving to or from the Great Smoky Mountains National Park; there's an insane three-level corkscrew turn on one track and a pro track inside where you can drive faster-than-usual carts. And there's mini golf ($8).

ACCOMMODATIONS

The Eastern Band of the Cherokee operates **Harrah's Cherokee Casino and Hotel** (777 Casino Dr., 828/497-7777, www.harrahscherokee.com, from $109). This full-bore Vegas-style casino has more than 3,800 digital games and slot machines along with around 150 table games such as baccarat, blackjack, roulette, and a poker-only room. Inside the casino complex is a 3,000 seat concert venue where acts like Alicia Keys and the Black Crows have performed, a huge buffet, and a grab-and-go food court next to the casino floor. Unlike in the rest of the state, smoking is allowed on the casino floor, though certain areas have been designated as nonsmoking. If you're a nonsmoker, it may take some patience.

The casino is separate from the two towers housing more than 1,100 hotel rooms and suites, with sky bridges joining the hotel to the casino. In the hotel you'll find a country-buffet restaurant and a Starbucks. If you want to

relax, the **Mandara Spa** is an 18,000-square-foot oasis in the heart of the hotel that offers all sorts of luxurious treatments for individuals and couples. From basic massages (from $129) to body treatments like the Balinese Body Polish ($125), the Juniper Berry and Algae Detox ($165), and the Elemis Aroma Spa Seaweed Massage ($165) to rejuvenating spa experience packages (from $260), you can create the relaxing experience you need. They also provide an array of salon services, including blowouts, beard trims, facials, and manis and pedis.

Cherokee has many motels, including a **Holiday Inn** (376 Painttown Rd., 828/497-3113, www.ihg.com, from $80) and an **Econo Lodge** (20 River Rd./U.S. 19, 828/497-4575, www.econolodge.com, from $80, pets allowed). There's something about visiting a place and living where the residents live: **Panther Creek Cabins** (Wrights Creek Rd., 828/497-2461, www.panthercreekresort.com, cabins $100-175) gives you that chance with your choice of eight cabins, ranging from private two-person affairs to larger lodges that would easily sleep you and seven others in four beds. These quaint cabins are quiet, just outside of downtown Cherokee, and comfortable.

FOOD

The arrival and expansion of Harrah's Cherokee Casino brought with it a bevy of restaurants. **Ruth's Chris Steak House** (Harrah's Cherokee Casino, 828/497-8577, www.harrahscherokee.com, dinner 5pm-10pm Mon.-Thurs., 5pm-11pm Fri.-Sat., lounge 4pm-11pm Mon.-Thurs., 4pm-midnight Fri.-Sat., lounge and dinner 4pm-9pm Sun., around $40) is here, and like its other locations, serves a variety of steaks and chops, a handful of seafood dishes, and more than 200 wines.

Also in Harrah's is **Brio Tuscan Grille** (828/497-8233, 11:30am-10pm Sun.-Thurs., 11:30am-11pm Fri.-Sat., $14-30), a fine Italian restaurant specializing in dishes from Northern Italy. This isn't a spaghetti-and-meatballs kind of place; it's more refined, with dishes like lasagna Bolognese al forno, lobster and shrimp ravioli with crab insalata, Tuscan grilled pork chops, and bistecca alla Fiorentina. The ambience is nice, the wine list is nicer, and the food is great.

Downstairs in Harrah's, just off the casino floor, is an airport-style food court that includes the **Winning Streaks Deli** (11am-11pm daily, $10), a deli serving hot and cold sandwiches and paninis made with Boars Head meats and cheeses; grab-and-go sandwiches are available 24 hours daily. There is also **Pizzeria Uno Express** (11am-11pm Sun.-Thurs., 11am-2am Fri.-Sat., around $10) serving thin-crust pizza, calzones, and pasta dishes; **Johnny Rockets** (24 hours daily, around $10), serving burgers, sandwiches, fries, milk shakes, and breakfast; and a **Dunkin' Donuts Express** (24 hours daily, around $5) that has doughnuts and coffee. The food court also has a variety of snacks and drinks available 24 hours daily.

Just outside of the town of Cherokee is

Granny's Kitchen (1098 Painttown Rd., 828/497-5010, www.grannyskitchencherokee. com, breakfast 7am-11am Tues.-Sun. June-Oct., 7am-11am Fri.-Sun. Apr.-May and Nov., lunch and dinner 11am-8pm Sun.-Thurs. Apr.-Nov., breakfast $8, lunch $8.50, dinner $12), a country-buffet restaurant where you can get some of the best fried chicken in North Carolina (and I don't say that lightly). You won't find Granny here; Granny is actually a man who likes to joke, "no one wants to eat a grandpa's, so I became granny."

GETTING THERE AND AROUND

Cherokee is located on a particularly pretty winding section of U.S. 19 between Maggie Valley and Bryson City. U.S. 441 leads here from Tennessee to the north. Just north of Cherokee is the southern terminus of the Blue Ridge Parkway.

Bryson City and the Nantahala Forest

To look at the mountains here, you'd think that the defining feature in this part of North Carolina would be the surrounding peaks, but you're only partly right. This is a land dominated by water: Smoke-thick fog crowds valleys in the pre-dawn hours. The peaks stand ringed in clouds. Moss, ferns, and dense forests crowd the edge of rivers and streams. When you're in the Nantahala Gorge, it feels like you've stepped into a fairy tale. According to Cherokee legends, a formidable witch called Spearfinger lived here, as did a monstrous snake and even an inchworm so large it could span the gorge. Spearfinger and her cohorts haven't been seen in years, and the Nantahala River, which runs through the narrow gorge, attracts white-water enthusiasts.

Nearby Bryson City is a river town whose proximity to white water makes it a favorite haunt for rafters, kayakers, and other white-water thrill seekers. If you approach Bryson City from the north on U.S. 19, you're in for

a strange sight: The banks of the Tuckasegee River are shored up with crushed cars.

SIGHTS

The **Great Smoky Mountains Railroad** (GSMR, depots in Bryson City and Dillsboro, 800/872-4681, www.gsmr.com, from $50 adults, $29 children) is one of the best and most fun ways to see the Smokies. On historic trains, the GSMR carries sightseers on excursions from two to several hours long, through some of the most beautiful scenery in the region. Trips between Dillsboro and Bryson City, with a layover at each end for shopping and dining, follow the banks of the Tuckasegee River, while round-trips from Bryson City follow the Little Tennessee and Nantahala Rivers deep into the Nantahala Gorge. Many other excursions are offered, including gourmet dining and wine- and beer-tasting trips. There are Thomas the Tank Engine and the Little Engine That Could trips for kids, and runs to and from river rafting outfitters.

SPORTS AND RECREATION
◖ Nantahala River Gorge

The stunningly beautiful Nantahala River Gorge, just outside Bryson City in the Nantahala National Forest, supports scores of river guide companies, many clustered along U.S. 19 west. Nantahala is said to mean "land of the noonday sun," and there are indeed parts of this gorge where the sheer rock walls above the river are so steep that sunlight only hits the water at the noon hour. Eight miles of the Nantahala River flow through the gorge over Class II-III rapids. The nearby Ocoee River is also a favorite of rafters, and the Cheoah River, when there are controlled water releases, has some of the South's most famous and difficult Class III-IV runs.

Outfitters and Tours

Because some of these rapids can be quite dangerous, be sure to call ahead and speak to a guide if you have any doubts as to your readiness. If rafting with children, check the company's weight and age restrictions beforehand. **Endless River Adventures** (14157 U.S. 19 W., near Bryson City, 800/224-7238, www.endlessriveradventures.com) gives white-water and flat-water kayaking instruction, rentals, and guided trips on the Nantahala, Ocoee, and Cheoah Rivers. They'll be able to suggest a run suited to your skill level. **Carolina Outfitters** (715 U.S. 19, Topton, 800/468-7238, www.carolinaoutfitters.com) has several package outings that combine river trips with horseback riding, bicycling, panning for gems, and riding on the Great Smoky Mountains Railroad. In addition to river guide services, **Wildwater Rafting** (10345 U.S. 19 W., 12 miles west of Bryson City, 828/488-2384, www.wildwaterrafting.com) leads **Wildwater Jeep Tours** ($46-99 adults, $36-74 children), half- and full-day jeep excursions through back roads and wilderness to waterfalls and old mountain settlements.

You can explore the mountains around Bryson City with the **Nantahala Outdoor Center** (13077 U.S. 19 W., Bryson City, 800/232-7238, www.noc.com, 9am-5pm daily, from $33), which offers a variety of adventure options that include white-water rafting, stand-up paddleboarding on the flat-water sections of the river, hiking, mountain biking, and zip-lining. Half-day, full-day, and overnight trips are possible, and excursions like the Rapid Transit combine a relaxing morning train ride with an afternoon rafting trip.

Fly-Fishing

The mountain streams around Bryson City are teeming with fish; a few outfitters can help you catch them. **Fly Fishing the Smokies** (Bryson City, 828/488-7665, www.flyfishingthesmokies.net) has a number of guides and options for a day or more of fishing. Wade the streams with them for a half-day (1 person $150, 2 people $175) or full-day (1 person $200, 2 people $250) outing, try a float trip (half-day $225 per boat, full-day $300 per boat), or go backcountry camping and fly-fishing in the Great Smoky Mountains National Park. They also go bass fishing on nearby Fontana Lake (half-day $225, full-day $300).

Another top fishing guide in the Bryson City area is **Steve Claxton's Smoky Mountain Adventures** (Bryson City, 828/736-7501, http://steveclaxton.com), who specializes in leaving civilization behind in favor of camping, catching wild mountain trout, and getting a true taste of the wilderness. Three-day, two-night camping trips for 5-7 people run around $400 pp, and four-day, three-night trips are $450-500 pp. They also offer day-long fishing trips (1 person $225, 2 people $250, 3 people $300). **Nantahala Fly Fishing Co.** (Robbinsville, 828/479-8850, www.flyfishnorthcarolina.com, guided trips and private lessons half-day $150 pp, $75 per additional person, full-day $225 pp, $75 per additional person) provides guided trips for fly-rod fishing, but if you've never held one of these odd fishing rods in your hand, they also provide a fly-fishing

© JASON FRYE

Streams in the Smoky Mountains are ideal for trout fishing.

school ($250 for 2 days) and private instruction. Best of all, they have a "No Fish, No Pay" guarantee.

For fly-fishers who don't need a guide, a number of streams around are packed with fish, but be sure to inquire about regulations for individual streams; some are catch-and-release while a neighboring stream is catch-and-keep, and some have regulations about the types of hooks you can use. Once you're ready to put your line in the water, try **Hazel Creek** on the north shore of Fontana Lake, where you'll find pristine waters and a good number of fish. Other nearby creeks, like **Eagle Creek** and any of the feeder creeks that empty into the lake, are prime spots as well.

Hiking

The Great Smoky Mountains National Park has more than 800 miles of wilderness trails, and with around 40 percent of the park located in Swain County, more trails than you could hike in a week are within striking distance from Bryson City. **Deep Creek Loop** is a four-mile loop that passes two waterfalls on it's easy, mostly flat, track. You can also take the strenuous **Deep Creek Trail** to Newfound Gap Road, a 14.2-mile one-way hike that will require a return ride. The **Noland Creek Trail** is a fairly easy six-mile trail near the end of the Road to Nowhere (a failed road-building project from the 1930s and 1940s). At the end of the Road to Nowhere, just past the tunnel, is the **Goldmine Loop Trail,** a three-mile track that's beautiful and enjoyable.

Golf

Smoky Mountain Country Club (1300 Conleys Creek Rd., Whittier, 828/497-7622, www.carolinamountaingolf.com, 18 holes, par 71, greens fees 18 holes $49, 9 holes $30, includes cart, discounts for students, seniors, and off-peak play) is a mountain golf course where nearly every hole here has views that will distract you from the sport; an aggressive player will find rewards on several holes. While some of the greens are open, many are well guarded by bunkers and contours that make greenside chipping tricky, especially if you haven't played much in the mountains.

ACCOMMODATIONS

The **((Folkestone Inn** (101 Folkestone Rd., 888/812-3385, www.folkestoneinn. com, from $100) is one of the region's outstanding bed-and-breakfasts, a roomy 1920s farmhouse expanded and renovated into a charming and tranquil inn. Each room has a balcony or porch. Baked treats at breakfast include shortcake, kuchen, cobblers, and other delicacies. An 85-year-old hotel on the National Register of Historic Places, the **Fryemont Inn** (245 Fryemont St., Bryson City, 800/845-4879, www.fryemontinn. com, mid-Apr.-Nov., from $110 with meals, $90 without meals) has a cozy, rustic feel with chestnut-paneled guest rooms and an inviting lobby with an enormous stone fireplace.

Some river outfitters offer lodging, which can be a cheap way to pass the night if you don't mind roughing it. The **Rolling Thunder River Company** (10160 U.S. 19 W., near Bryson City, 800/408-7238, www.rollingthunderriverco.com, no alcohol permitted) operates a large bunkhouse with beds ($10-12) for its rafting customers. **Carolina Outfitters** (715 U.S. 19, Topton, 800/468-7238, www. carolinaoutfitters.com) has a number of accommodations available (from $50), including two-room cabins, two-bedroom apartments, and three-bedroom cabins suitable for a large group. Many of the outfitters also offer camping on their properties.

Way back in the forest by Fontana Lake, the **Fontana Village Resort** (Hwy. 28, Fontana Dam, 800/849-2258, www.fontanavillage. com, from $79) was originally built as housing for the workers building the dam, a massive wartime undertaking that created a whole town out in the woods. Renovated into a comfortable resort, Fontana Village features a lodge, cabins, camping (from $15), and a variety of boat rentals, including pontoon boats and fishing charters.

Camping

Among the nicest camping options available in the Nantahala Forest is **Standing Indian Campground** (90 Sloan Rd., Franklin, 877/444-6777, www.fs.usda.gov, Apr.-Nov., $16). Standing Indian has a nice diversity of campsites, from flat grassy areas to cozy mountainside nooks. Drinking water, hot showers, flush toilets, and a phone are all available on-site, and leashed pets are permitted. At 3,400 feet in elevation, the campground is close to the Appalachian Trail.

Another nice campground is the **Deep Creek Tube Center and Campground** (1090 W. Deep Creek Rd., Bryson City, 828/488-6055, www.deepcreekcamping.com, camping $22-43, cabins $69-195). They have more than 50 campsites, 18 cabins, and access to Deep Creek, which runs right by many campsites, where you can go tubing (tube rentals $3-6 per day). The best part is that they are within walking distance of the Great Smoky Mountains National Park.

GETTING THERE AND AROUND

Bryson City can be reached via U.S. 19, if you're coming south from Maggie Valley and Cherokee. U.S. 74 also passes close by for easy access from the east or the west.

Waynesville and Vicinity

Toward the Balsam Range is the town of Waynesville, an artistic little community where crafts galleries and studios line the downtown. In nearby Cullowhee, Western Carolina University is one of the mountain region's leading academic institutions as well as the location of the Mountain Heritage Center museum and Mountain Heritage Day festival.

WAYNESVILLE

Waynesville's downtown can keep a gallery-hopper or shopper happy for hours. Main Street is packed with studio artists' galleries, cafés and coffee shops, and a variety of boutiques.

Shopping

Blue Ridge Books & News (152 S. Main St., 828/456-6000, www.blueridgebooksnc.com, 8am-7pm Mon.-Thurs., 8am-8pm Fri.-Sat., 8am-6pm Sun.) is a nice bookstore with specialties of regional interest and good coffee.

Good Ol' Days Cigars (46 N. Main St./145 Wall St., 828/456-2898, www.goodoldayscigars.com, 11am-6pm Mon.-Sat.) offers a large selection of fine tobacco and smoking products—cigars as well as pipes, loose tobacco, and rolling papers—and a lounge to enjoy them.

One of the several locations of **Mast General Store** (63 N. Main St., 828/452-2101, www.mastgeneralstore.com, 10am-6pm Mon.-Sat., noon-6pm Sun. spring-fall, hours vary in winter) is here in Waynesville. While the stores are perhaps best known among vacationers for making children clamor for the candy kept in big wooden barrels, old-time dry-goods-store style, they have an even larger selection of merchandise for adults, including camping gear such as top-brand tents, cookware, and maps and outdoors-oriented upscale clothing and shoes by Columbia, Teva, Patagonia, and Mountain Hardwear.

Galleries

Waynesville's galleries are many and varied, although the overarching aesthetic is one of studio art with inspiration in the environment and folk arts. **Twigs and Leaves** (98 N. Main St., 828/456-1940, www.twigsandleaves.com, 10am-5:30pm Mon.-Sat., 1pm-4pm Sun.) carries splendid art furniture that is both fanciful and functional, pottery of many hand-thrown and hand-built varieties, jewelry, paintings, fabric hangings, mobiles, and many other beautiful and unusual items inspired by nature.

Studio Thirty Three (822 Balsam Ridge Rd., 828/452-4264, www.studio33jewelry.com, by appointment) carries the work of a very small and select group of fine jewelers from western North Carolina. Their retail and custom inventory consists of spectacular handcrafted pieces in a variety of styles and an array of precious stones and metals. This is a must-see gallery if you have a special occasion coming up. The gallery describes its stock as ranging in price from "$65 to $16,000," and most items cost upward of $2,000. Even if you're not about to mark a major life event or spend that kind of money just for fun, it's worth stopping in to gaze at all that sparkle.

Art on Depot (250 Depot St., 828/246-0218, www.artondepot.com, 10am-5pm Mon.-Sat.) is a working pottery studio and gallery where local and regional artists exhibit and sell their work. Artistic creations for sale include decorative and functional pottery by the resident potter and many of her contemporaries as well as paintings, jewelry, sculpture, and a few pieces by area fiber artists.

Accommodations

In the nearby community of Balsam, the **Balsam Mountain Inn** (68 Seven Springs Dr., Balsam, 800/224-9498, www.balsaminn.com, $145-225, no pets) has stood watch for a century in a haunting location—an imposing old wooden hotel with huge double porches overlooking a rather spooky little railroad platform and the beautiful ridges of Jackson and

Haywood Counties beyond. The interior has barely changed since its earliest days, paneled in white horizontal bead board throughout with 10-foot-wide hallways said to have been designed to accommodate steamer trunks. The one telephone is at the front desk, and there are no TVs, so plan to go hiking or to sit on the porch before dining in the downstairs restaurant, and then curl up and read in the library. There is, incongruously, fast Wi-Fi. Among the inn's reported ghosts is a woman in a blue dress, said to originate in room 205 but to come and go elsewhere on the second floor. This inn has a few rough edges, but the atmosphere can be found nowhere else.

Up on the Blue Ridge Parkway above Waynesville and quite close to Asheville is the fantastic **(Pisgah Inn** (BRP milepost 408.6, 828/235-8228, www.pisgahinn.com, Apr.-Oct., from $128) is much like Skyland and Big Meadows on Virginia's Skyline Drive, with motel-style accommodations surrounding an old lodge with a large family-style dining room and a Parkway gift shop. The inn is on a nearly 5,000-foot-high mountaintop, so the view is sensational. Trails lead from the inn to short pretty strolls and challenging daylong hikes. The restaurant (7:30am-10:30am, 11:30am-4pm, and 5pm-9pm daily) has a mesmerizing view and an appetizing and varied menu ($5-25) of both country cooking and upscale meals. The guest rooms are simple but comfortable, each with its own balcony and rocking chairs overlooking the valley, and with a TV but no telephone. The Pisgah is a perfect spot for resting, reading, and porch-sitting.

Waynesville also has quite a selection of luxury inns. The **Andon-Reid Inn** (92 Daisey Ave., 800/293-6190, www.andonreidinn.com, $149-239, no pets or children) is a handsome turn-of-the-century house close to downtown with five tranquil guest rooms, each with its own fireplace, and a sumptuous breakfast menu that might include sweet-potato pecan pancakes and pork tenderloin, homemade cornbread with honey butter, or the intriguing baked lemon eggs. With advance notice they can cater to special dietary needs. The **Inn**

at Iris Meadows (304 Love Lane, 888/466-4747, www.irismeadows.com, from $225, dogs permitted with advance notice, no children) is another splendid house on a hillside surrounded by lush trees and gardens. Shepherd-mix Scratch and gray tabby cat Zephyrus help run the place.

For absolute tip-top luxury, try **The Swag** (2300 Swag Rd., 800/789-7672, www.theswag. com, $495-800). Superb guest rooms and cabins of rustic wood and stone each have a steam shower, and several have saunas, wet bars, and cathedral ceilings. The menu is decidedly country and upscale, two things you wouldn't think go together, but they do, and quite nicely, at The Swag. The inn is at 5,000 feet elevation in a stunning location at the very edge of the Great Smoky Mountains National Park.

Food

Waynesville's **Frogs Leap Public House** (44 Church St., 828/456-1930, http://frogsleap-publichouse.com, 4pm-9pm Tues.-Thurs., 4pm-10pm Fri.-Sat., $8-26) serves an interesting menu that's quite sophisticated but not afraid of its Southern roots. The fried green tomato and pimento cheese napoleon combines two Southern favorites with a treasured French technique, and the foie gras torchon glazed with local peaches and served with Amish butter again brings these two disparate elements together.

The ever-popular **Bogart's** (303 S. Main St., 828/452-1313, www.bogartswaynesville.com, 11am-9pm Sun.-Thurs., 11am-10pm Fri.-Sat., $7-20), is locally famous for its filet mignon, though their local trout also has a good reputation. The menu is huge but very steak-housey; vegetarians will have a tough time, although a few dishes, like the chipotle black bean burger and the grilled portobello salad, are options.

If you're just passing through town and need a jolt of good strong coffee, visit **Panacea** (66 Commerce St., 303 S. Main St., 828/452-6200, http://panaceacoffee.com, 7am-5pm Mon.-Fri., 8am-5pm Sat., under $5) in the funky Frog Level neighborhood downhill from downtown.

The proprietors give back to their community, and trade fairly with the communities that supply their coffee. They stock beans, blends, and brews from all around the world.

SYLVA

The small town of Sylva, southwest of Waynesville, is crowned by the pretty Jackson County Courthouse, an Italianate building with an ornate cupola, kept under wistful watch by the requisite courthouse-square Confederate monument.

Sights

South of Sylva, the mysterious **Judaculla Rock** (off Caney Fork Rd., www.judacullarock.com) has puzzled folks for centuries. The soapstone boulder is covered in petroglyphs, estimated to be at least 500 years old. The figures and symbols and squiggles are clearly significant, but as of yet are not understood. I'm fascinated with petroglyphs, and these are some of the most mysterious I've encountered. The soft rock has eroded and the pictures are not as clear as they were in generations past, but many of them can still be discerned. To reach the rock, drive south on Highway 107 eight miles past the intersection with Sylva's Business U.S. 23. Make a left on Caney Fork Road/County Road 1737 and drive 2.5 miles to a gravel road. Turn left, and just under 0.5 miles you'll see the rock on the right, and a parking area on the left.

Shopping

Sylva's City Lights Bookstore (3 E. Jackson St., 828/586-9499, www.citylightsnc.com, 9am-9pm Mon.-Sat., 10am-3pm Sun.) is hardly a knockoff of the monumental Beat establishment in San Francisco with which it shares a name. Instead, it's a first-rate small-town bookstore with stock that has the novelty sought by vacationers and the depth to make regulars of the local patrons. In addition to the sections you'll find in any good bookstore, at City Lights there is an excellent selection of books of regional interest, including folklore, nature, recreation guides, history, and fiction and poetry by Appalachian and Southern authors.

Food

The North Carolina mountains are experiencing a booming organic foods movement, and you'll find eco-aware eateries throughout the area. **(Lulu's Café** (612 W. Main St., 828/586-8989, www.lulusonmain.com, 11:30am-late Mon.-Sat., $11-19) is one of the most acclaimed restaurants in the area. The menu is American gourmet at heart with splashes of Mediterranean and Nuevo Latino specialties. Try the walnut-spinach ravioli or the raspberry rum pork loin. There are plenty of vegetarian options. A more casual option is **Nick and Nate's Pizza** (38 The Village Overlook, 828/586-3000, 11am-9pm Mon. and Wed.-Thurs., 11am-9:30pm Fri.-Sat., noon-9pm Sun., lunch $6-8, dinner $8-15), where the dough is handmade, the toppings are fresh, and the beer is from fine microbreweries far and wide.

Try **Annie's Naturally** (506 W. Main St., 828/586-9096, 11am-3pm Tues.-Sat., $4-7), a bakery and sandwich shop owned by Joe and Annie Ritota. Joe is a fourth-generation professional baker from an old Italian American family known for its skill in the kitchen. The breads, cookies, and pastries are baked on-site in the Ritotas' old-time way. **Soul Infusion** (628 E. Main St., 828/586-1717, www.soulinfusion.com, 11am-10pm Tues.-Fri., noon-late Sun., $5-10) is a cozy hippie-gourmet teahouse in an old house on Main Street, between Sylva Tire and UPS. You can get very good burritos, sandwiches, pizza, wraps, several dozen kinds of loose-leaf tea, and even more selections of bottled beer. On weekends and some weeknights, local blues, folk, reggae, and experimental musicians put on a show. Seize the opportunity to hear some of the talent in this musical region.

DILLSBORO

Next door to Sylva is Dillsboro, a river town of rafters and crafters. **Dogwood Crafters** (90 Webster St., 828/586-2248, www.dogwoodcrafters.com, 10am-6pm daily Mar.-Dec., 11am-4pm Fri.-Sat. Jan.-Feb.), in operation for more than 30 years, is a gallery and co-op

WESTERN NORTH CAROLINA FLY-FISHING TRAIL

Jackson County is the home of the first and only Fly-Fishing Trail in the country; it includes 15 spots on some of the best trout waters in the Smokies where you can catch rainbow, brook, and brown trout, and even the occasional golden trout. Because of the close proximity of many mountain communities, the Fly-Fishing Trail has become an epicenter for fly-fishing in the region. Easy access to these waters, convenient complimentary **maps** (available at www.flyfishingtrail.com and http://mountainlovers.com), and the excellent support the trail receives make it a choice spot for trout fishing no matter which community you're visiting.

Top spots include **Panthertown Creek,** where a two-mile walk from the end of Breedlove Road (Hwy. 1121) leads you to what some have called the "Yosemite of the East" because of its picturesque rocky bluffs. You'll catch more brook trout than you may have thought possible on this three-mile stream, which is catch-and-release only.

For an "urban" fishing experience, try the **Tuckasegee River** as it passes through Dillsboro. You can park and fish at a number of places between Dillsboro Park and the Best Western River Escape Inn, and you run a good chance of catching a large rainbow or brown trout.

The **Lower Tuckasegee River,** running from Bakers Creek Bridge to Whittier along U.S. 19/74, is around 10 miles of excellent fishing for rainbow and brown trout as well as smallmouth bass.

Fly Fishing Trail co-founder Alex Bell, who knows the waters of Western North Carolina intimately, operates **AB's Fly Fishing Guide Service** (828/226-3833, www.abfish.org, half day wading trips $150/1 person, $225/2 people, $300/3 people, full day with lunch, $225/1 person, $300/2 people, and $375/3 people; float trips half day $275 one or two people, full day with lunch $350 one or two people). AB's supplies tackle and waders if you need them, as well as extensive lessons in proper casting, water reading, and fly selection, but you're responsible for securing your own North Carolina fishing license and trout stamp.

---

that represents around 100 local artists and artisans. While the shop carries some of the ubiquitous country-whimsical stuff, mixed in is the work of some very traditional Blue Ridge weavers, potters, carvers, and other expert artisans, making the shop well worth a visit.

Sports and Recreation

Dillsboro River Company (18 Macktown Rd., 866/586-3797, www.northcarolinarafting.com, 10am-6pm daily May-Sept., rentals $12-30, guided trips $15-40), across the river from downtown Dillsboro, will set you afloat on the Tuckaseegee River, a comparatively warm river with areas of Class II rapids. It's pronounced "tuck-a-SEE-jee" but is often referred to simply as "the Tuck." Dillsboro River Company rents rafts, "ducks," and inflatable and sit-on-top kayaks. If you'd like to hire a

river rat, guides will be happy to lead you on tours twice daily, and for an extra fee you can share a boat with the guide. There are minimum weight restrictions for these watercraft, so if you are traveling with children, call ahead to ask if the guides think your young ones are ready for the Tuckaseegee.

Accommodations

Of the many historic inns in this region, one of the oldest is Dillsboro's **Jarrett House** (100 Haywood St., 800/972-5623, www.jarretthouse.com, $85 for 2 people, full country breakfast $5). The three-story 1880s lodge was built to serve passengers on the railroad, and today it's once again a busy rail stop, now for the Great Smoky Mountains Railroad's excursion trains. The guest rooms have old-fashioned furniture, air-conditioning, and private baths, but the only TV is in the lobby. The Hartbarger family, keepers of this inn for over 30 years, are serious about giving their guests a chance for what they call "real loafing"—truly recuperative peace and quiet.

Food

The **ⓒ Jarrett House** (100 Haywood St., 800/972-5623, www.jarretthouse.com, 11:30am-2:30pm and 4:30pm-7:30pm Tues.-Sun., under $15), is also famous for its dining room, an extravaganza of country cooking based on the staples of country ham and red-eye gravy. You can order many other mountain specialties, including fried catfish, fried chicken, sweet tea, biscuits, and for dessert the daily cobbler or vinegar pie (a strange but tasty pie that's similar to a pecan pie without the pecans and with vinegar). There are few options for vegetarians, but if you like heavy Southern fare, you'll think you're in heaven.

Dillsboro Smokehouse (403 Haywood St., 828/586-9556, www.dillsborosmokehouse. com, lunch and dinner 11am-7pm Tues. and Fri.-Sat., 11am-5pm Wed.-Thurs., around $8) is a funky little barbecue shack serving some fine western North Carolina 'cue, craft beers, and house-made smoked barbecue sauces. The menu's small, but if it's pork or chicken and it's barbecuable, it's here. The Dillsboro Smokehouse is biker-friendly, so don't be surprised if you see a line of Harleys outside.

CULLOWHEE

The unincorporated village of Cullowhee ("CULL-uh-wee"), located on Highway 107 between Sylva and Cashiers, is the home of Western Carolina University (WCU). The university's **Mountain Heritage Center** (in the lobby of the H. F. Robinson Administration Building, WCU campus, 828/227-7129, www. wcu.edu, 8am-5pm Fri.-Mon., 8am-7pm Tues. year-round) is a small museum with a great collection that will fascinate anyone interested in Appalachian history. The permanent exhibit *Migration of the Scotch-Irish People* is full of artifacts like a 19th-century covered wagon, wonderful photographs, homemade quilts, linens, and musical instruments. The Mountain Heritage Center also hosts two traveling exhibits in addition to the permanent installation as well as the annual **Mountain Heritage Day** festival (late Sept.), which brings together many of western North Carolina's best and most authentic traditional musicians and artisans in a free festival that draws up to 25,000 visitors.

GETTING THERE AND AROUND

Waynesville is easily reached from Asheville by heading west on I-40, and then taking either U.S. 23 or U.S. 74. The Blue Ridge Parkway also passes a little to the south of the town, near Balsam. Sylva is to the southwest of Waynesville on U.S. 23, and from there, Cullowhee is an easy drive down Highway 107.

Robbinsville and the Valley Towns

Between Robbinsville and the Georgia state line is another region at the heart of Cherokee life. Snowbird, not far from Robbinsville, is one of the most traditional Cherokee communities, where it's common to hear the Cherokee language and the arts, crafts, and folkways are flourishing. The burial site of Junaluska, one of the Eastern Band's most prominent leaders, is here.

As moving as it is to see the memorial to one of the Cherokee heroes, the town of Murphy is forever linked with tragedy for the Cherokee people and a dark incident in American history—the Trail of Tears. Around 16,000 Cherokee people, including warriors and clan leaders, men, women, children, the elderly, and the infirm, were forced to leave their homes in North Carolina, Tennessee, and Georgia; they were arrested and marched under guard to Fort Butler, here in Murphy, and from Fort Butler

© JASON FRYE

Motorcyclists come hundreds of miles to ride the Cherohala Skyway.

they were forced to walk to Oklahoma. You'll find the names of these people, many of whom died along the way, inscribed in Cherokee on a memorial at the L&N Depot in Murphy.

In addition to places of historic significance in Cherokee culture, this farthest southwestern corner of North Carolina has other compelling sights. Brasstown, a tiny village on the Georgia state line, is the home of the John C. Campbell Folk School, an artists' colony nearly a century old, where visitors can stroll among studios and along trails and stop in to a gallery shop with some of the most beautiful crafts you'll find in the region. Back up toward Robbinsville, the relentlessly scenic Cherohala Skyway crosses 43 miles of the Cherokee and Nantahala Forests. This road is a major destination for motorcyclists and sports-car drivers as well as day-trippers and vacationers.

ROBBINSVILLE

The whole southwestern corner of North Carolina is rich with Cherokee history and culture, and the Robbinsville area has some of the deepest roots of great significance to the Cherokee people. In little towns and crossroads a few miles outside Robbinsville, several hundred people known as the Snowbird community keep alive some of the oldest Cherokee ways. The Cherokee language is spoken here, and it's a place where some of the Eastern Band's most admired basket makers, potters, and other artists continue to make and teach their ancient arts. If you're visiting and want to enjoy an adult beverage, you'd better bring your own, as Graham County is North Carolina's one and only dry county.

Sights

Outside Robbinsville in the ancient Stecoah Valley, an imposing old rock schoolhouse built in 1930 and used as a school until the mid-1990s. It has been reborn as the **Stecoah Valley Center** (121 Schoolhouse Rd., Stecoah, 828/479-3364, www.stecoahvalleycenter.com), home of a weaver's guild, a native plants preservation group, a concert series, several festivals, and a great **Gallery Shop** (828/497-3098, 10am-5pm Mon.-Sat. year-round) of local artisans' work. Concerts in the Appalachian Evening summer series, featuring area musicians, are preceded by community suppers of traditional mountain cuisine.

On Robbinsville's Main Street is the **Junaluska Memorial** (Main St., 0.5 miles north of the Graham County Courthouse, 828/479-4727, 9am-5pm Mon.-Sat. Apr.-Oct., call for hours Nov.-Mar.), where Junaluska, a 19th-century leader of the Eastern Band of the Cherokee, and his third wife, Nicie, are buried. The marker was dedicated in 1910 by the Daughters of the American Revolution, and the gravesite is maintained by the Friends of Junaluska, who also operate the **Junaluska Museum** (828/479-4727, 9am-5pm Mon.-Sat. Apr.-Oct., call for hours Nov.-Mar., free) on the same site. At the museum you'll find ancient artifacts from life in Cheoah thousands of years ago. There are also contemporary Cherokee crafts on display, and outside you can walk a path that highlights the medicinal plants used for generations in this area.

Down a winding country road 14 miles outside Robbinsville, **Yellow Branch Pottery and Cheese** (136 Yellow Branch Circle, Robbinsville, 828/479-6710, www.yellowbranch.com, noon-5pm Tues.-Sat. Apr.-Dec. or by appointment) is a beautifully rustic spot for an afternoon's excursion. Bruce DeGroot, Karen Mickler, and their herd of Jersey cows produce prizewinning artisanal cheeses and graceful, functional pottery. Visitors are welcome at their farm and shop.

Entertainment and Events

Every year on the Saturday of Memorial Day weekend in late May, the Snowbird Cherokee host the **Fading Voices Festival** in Robbinsville. The festival features a mound-building ceremony along with typical festival attractions—music, dancing, storytelling, crafts, and lots of food—but in the deeply traditional forms carried on by the Snowbird community. Contact the Junaluska Museum (828/479-4727) for more information.

Sports and Recreation

The **Joyce Kilmer Memorial Forest** (Joyce Kilmer Rd., off Hwy. 143 west of Robbinsville, 828/479-6431) is one of the largest remaining tracts of virgin forest in the eastern United States, where 450-year-old tulip poplar trees have grown to 100 feet tall and 20 feet around. The forest stands in honor of Joyce Kilmer, a soldier killed in action in France during World War I. His poem, "Trees," inspired this living memorial. The only way to see the forest is on foot, and a two-mile loop or two one-mile loops make for an easy hike through a remarkable forest.

The Joyce Kilmer Memorial Forest abuts the Slickrock Wilderness Area, and **Slickrock Creek Trail** is one of its longest trails. This 13.5-mile (one-way) trail starts out easy, but the final 5 to 5.5 miles are fairly strenuous. *Backpacker* magazine named this one of the toughest trails in the country several years ago, in part because the hike can be a 21.7-mile loop by connecting with the **Haoe Lead, Hangover Lead,** and **Ike Branch** trails. Be forewarned that this is a big trip, but it's rewarding, with views of waterfalls (the first is only a few miles in, on the easy part) and rhododendron thickets. Its name is apt: The rocks here can be incredibly slick.

On the **Hangover Lead South Trail,** the trailhead is adjacent to the parking area at Big Fat Gap (off Slick Rock Rd., about 7 miles from U.S. 129). The trail is only 2.8 miles long but it's strenuous. The payoff is the view from the Haoe summit at 5,249 feet. There are backcountry campsites here, and the rule is to keep campsites 100 yards from streams and practice Leave No Trace guidelines.

A handy collection of trail maps for Joyce Kilmer Memorial Forest, Slickrock Creek, Snowbird Back Country, and Tsali Recreation Area are available from the Graham Chamber (http://grahamchamber.com). The maps provide a rough idea of the locations and routes of these trails, but they are not a replacement for topographic maps, which you should have with you while on any of these rugged or isolated trails.

JUNALUSKA

One of the most important figures in the history of the Eastern Band of the Cherokee is Junaluska, who was born near Dillard, Georgia, in 1776. During the wars against the Creek Indians from 1812 to 1814, the Cherokee people fought beside U.S. forces, and it's said that the fierce young Junaluska saved the life of Andrew Jackson at the battle of Horse Shoe Bend in Alabama.

Twenty years later, Jackson, by then president, repaid Junaluska's bravery and the loyalty of the Cherokee people by signing the Indian Removal Act, which ordered that they, along with four other major Southern nations, be forced from their homelands and marched to the new Indian Territory of Oklahoma. Junaluska traveled to Washington and met with Jackson to plead for mercy for the Cherokee nation; his pleas were ignored, and in 1838, Junaluska joined 16,000 members of the Cherokee nation who were force-marched close to 1,000 miles to Oklahoma. Midway across Tennessee, he led a failed escape attempt and was captured and chained; he completed the march in leg irons and manacles. It was during this time that Junaluska supposedly said, "If I had known what Andrew Jackson would do to the Cherokees, I would have killed him myself that day at Horse Shoe Bend." In 1841 he was finally able to leave Oklahoma and made the 17-day trip to North Carolina on horseback.

He spent his final years in Cherokee County, on land granted to him by the state of North Carolina. He and his third wife, Nicie, are buried at Robbinsville, at what is now the Junaluska Memorial and Museum. His grave was originally marked according to Cherokee tradition—with a pile of stones—but in 1910 the Daughters of the American Revolution commissioned a marker for his gravesite. During the dedication ceremony, Reverend Armstrong Cornsilk delivered a eulogy in the Cherokee language:

He was a good man. He was a good friend. He was a good friend in his home and everywhere. He would ask the hungry man to eat. He would ask the cold one to warm by his fire. He would ask the tired one to rest, and he would give a good place to sleep. Juno's home was a good home for others. He was a smart man. He made his mind think well. He was very brave. He was not afraid.

Juno at this time has been dead about 50 years. I am glad he is up above [pointing upward]. I am glad we have this beautiful monument. It shows Junaluska did good, and it shows we all appreciate him together—having a pleasant time together. I hope we shall all meet Junaluska in heaven [pointing upward] and all be happy there together.

Accommodations

The **Snowbird Mountain Lodge** (4633 Santeetlah Rd., 11 miles west of Robbinsville, 800/941-9290, http://snowbirdlodge.com, $165-455) was built in the early 1940s, a rustic chestnut-and-stone inn atop a 3,000-foot mountain. The view is exquisite, and the lodge is perfectly situated among the Cherohala Skyway, Lake Santeetlah, and the Joyce Kilmer Forest. Guests enjoy a full breakfast, picnic lunch, and four-course supper created from seasonal local specialties. Another

pleasant place to stay near Robbinsville is the **Tapoco Lodge Resort** (14981 Tapoco Rd., 15 miles north of Robbinsville, 828/498-2325, www.tapocolodge.com, Thurs.-Sat. Nov.-Sept., daily Oct., suites $249-339, cabins $229-249). Built in 1930, the lodge is on the National Register of Historic Places, and it has the feel of an old-time hotel. Guest rooms in the main lodge and surrounding cabins are simple but comfortable, and the resort overlooks the Cheoah River, a legendary run for rafters several times each year when controlled releases of water form crazy-fast rapids.

Mountain Ivy Rentals (56 Airport Rd., 2.5 miles east of Robbinsville, 8258/735-9180, www.mountainivy.com, 2-night minimum, $163) has one log-sided cabin that sleeps six and is steps away from great trout fishing in the stream that runs alongside the cabin. An indoor fireplace and a space outside for a campfire help make it cozy in any season. The garage is handy for motorcycle travelers as it gives them a place to secure trailers, bikes, and other gear.

At the **Simple Life Campground** (88 Lower Mountain Creek Rd., 828/788-1099, www.thesimplelifecampground.com, Mar.-Nov., cabins $27-85, RVs $22-38, tents $14) the cabins, RV sites, and tent sites have access to hot showers, and Wi-Fi. This campground is near the Cherohala Skyway, Joyce Kilmer National Forest, and Lake Santeelah.

If you're RVing your way through the Smokies, the six-acre **Teaberry Hill RV Campground** (77 Upper Sawyers Creek Rd., 828/479-3953, http://teaberryhill.com, $45) is one of the nicest campgrounds you'll find, with large pull-through sites to accommodate any size RV. Amenities include 50-amp electrical hookups, water and sewer, and Wi-Fi access.

HAYESVILLE, BRASSTOWN, AND MURPHY

Between Hayesville and Brasstown, you can get a really good sense of the art that has come out of this region over the years. These three small towns are along the Georgia border on U.S. 64.

Murphy River Walk

The Murphy River Walk is a three-mile trail along the Hiwassee River and Valley River, winding from Konehete Park to the Old L&N Depot. A beautiful walk (and a great way to stretch your legs after a long ride) through this charming, tiny town, the Riverwalk gives you the chance to see Murphy up close and personal.

After your walk along the river, take a look at some of the antique stores in Murphy. A popular stop is **Linger Awhile Antiques and**

Collectibles (46 Valley River Ave., 321/267-2777, 10am-5pm Tues.-Sat.).

🄲 John C. Campbell Folk School

One of North Carolina's most remarkable cultural institutions, the **John C. Campbell Folk School** (1 Folk School Rd., Brasstown, 800/365-5724, www.folkschool.org) was created by Northern honeymooners who traveled through Appalachia 100 years ago to educate themselves about Southern highland culture. John C. and Olive Dame Campbell, like other high-profile Northern liberals of their day, directed their humanitarian impulses toward the education and economic betterment of Southern mountain dwellers. John Campbell died a decade later, but Olive, joining forces with her friend Marguerite Butler, set out to establish a "folk school" in the Southern mountains that she and John had visited. She was inspired by the model of the Danish *folkehøjskole*, workshops that preserved and taught traditional arts as a means of fostering economic self-determination and personal pride in rural communities. Brasstown was chosen as the site for this grand experiment, and in 1925, the John C. Campbell Folk School opened its doors.

Today, thousands of artists travel every year to this uncommonly lovely remote valley, the site of an ancient Cherokee village. In week-long and weekend classes, students of all ages and skill levels learn about the traditional arts of this region, such as pottery, weaving, dyeing, storytelling, and chair caning, as well as contemporary and exotic crafts such as photography, kaleidoscope making, bookmaking, and paper marbling. The website outlines the hundreds of courses offered every year, but even if you're passing through the area on a shorter visit, you can explore the school's campus. Visitors are asked to preserve the quiet atmosphere of learning and concentration when viewing the artist studios, but you can have an up-close look at some of their marvelous wares in the school's **Craft Shop** (bottom floor of Olive Dame Campbell Dining Hall, 8am-5pm Mon.-Wed. and Fri.-Sat., 8am-6pm Thurs.,

1pm-5pm Sun.), one of the nicest craft shops in western North Carolina. Exhibits about the school's history and historic examples of the work of local artists of past generations are on display at the **History Center** (8am-5pm Mon.-Sat., 1pm-5pm Sun.), next to Keith House.

There are several nature trails on campus that thread through this lovely valley. Be sure to visit the 0.25-mile **Rivercane Walk,** which features outdoor sculpture by some of the greatest living artists of the Eastern Band of the Cherokee. In the evenings you'll often find concerts by traditional musicians, or community square, contra, and English country dances. A visit to the John C. Campbell Folk School, whether as a student or a traveler, is an exceptional opportunity to immerse yourself in a great creative tradition.

Clay County Historical and Arts Council Museum

Hayesville's Old Clay County Jail, built in 1912, is now home to the **Clay County Historical and Arts Council Museum** (21 Davis Loop, Hayesville, 828/389-6814, 10am-4pm Tues.-Sat. late May-early Sept., call for hours early Sept.-late May). This is a small and extremely interesting museum with varied collections, including the medical instruments of an early country doctor; an original jail cell complete with a file hidden by a long-ago prisoner, discovered during renovations; an old moonshine still; a collection of beautiful Cherokee masks; and a remarkable crazy quilt embroidered with strange and charming illustrations.

Food

Herb's Pit Bar-B-Que (15896 W. US Hwy. 64, Murphy, 828/494-5367, www.herbspitbarbque.com, 11am-8pm Wed., Thurs., and Sun., 11am-9pm Fri. and Sat., closed Mon. and Tues, $2-24) is the western terminus of the North Carolina Barbecue Trail and should be your first (or last) stop on it. Here you can sample more than the 'cue that pitmasters in the deep mountains make—you can also order plates of tasty fried trout and chicken, and even thick steaks off the grill.

Café Touche (82 Main St., Hayesville, 828/361-9475, 7am-5pm Mon.-Fri., 8am-noon Sat., 9am-2pm Sun., breakfast under $10, brunch around $10, cash only) is a spot to stop for a good cup of coffee and a pastry as you set off on a mountain adventure. On Sunday, they're open for brunch, meaning you can sleep in after a couple of days of hiking, grab a bite to eat, and set off before it gets too late.

The Copper Door (2 Sullivan St., Hayesville, 828/389-8460, http://thecopperdoor.com, 5pm-10pm Mon.-Sat., $16-38) is an upscale joint serving a nice selection of seafood, steaks, and other meat-centric dishes, but they can accommodate vegetarians and vegans. This elegant restaurant is run by a chef from New Orleans, and his influence is all over the menu, from crawfish to mussels to other French- and creole-inspired creations. In 2011 they received *Wine Spectator* magazine's Award of Excellence.

GETTING THERE AND AROUND

This is the southwestern-most corner of North Carolina, in some places as close to Atlanta as to Asheville. Robbinsville is remotest destination in this chapter, located on U.S. 129 southwest of Bryson City. Hayesville and Brasstown are easily reached via U.S. 64, which closely parallels the Georgia border.

BACKGROUND

The Land

GEOGRAPHY

North Carolina encompasses more than 50,000 square miles of land and water; within that space are three distinct geographic regions. The **Mountain Region** forms the western border of the state, with the ridges of the Blue Ridge and Great Smoky Mountains, both subranges of the long Appalachian Mountain Range, undulating like the folds of a great quilt, running northeast to southwest from Virginia along the border with Tennessee and into the southwestern corner where the inland tip of North Carolina meets Georgia. This is a land of waterfalls, rivers and fast-flowing creeks, and rugged, beautiful peaks of smaller mountain configurations. Hemmed in among the peaks and hollows of the Blue Ridge and the Smokies are the Black Mountains, the Pisgah Range, and the Unka Range. The Black Mountains are only about 15 miles wide and are confined mostly to Yancey County, but they're the highest in the state, and 6 of the 10 highest peaks in the eastern United States are here, including Mount Mitchell, the highest at 6,684 feet.

Since the mid-19th century, the **Piedmont** has been the center of the state's population and industry. Most of North Carolina's major cities are in the Piedmont, including Charlotte,

© JASON FRYE

Winston-Salem, Greensboro, and the Raleigh-Durham metro area. In the late 19th century and most of the 20th century the textile mills, furniture factories, and tobacco fields of the Piedmont ruled the state's economy. Today, most of the textile mills have been shuttered and the furniture factories have mostly vanished thanks to economic globalization. The earliest mills were generally water-powered, harnessing the power of swift rivers as they charge toward the coast. Changes in the tobacco industry have led farmers to give up the former cash crop in favor of more savory crops, and the fields that were once thick with tobacco are now growing corn and soybeans.

The **Coastal Plain** is the third region, and though I-95 is commonly regarded as its western boundary, geologically the Sandhills section of the state is part of the Coastal Plain. Wedged between the Piedmont and the wetlands-rich Cape Fear Valley (the delta stretching from Fayetteville to Wilmington), the Sandhills are a zone of transition between the rich soil and rolling topography of the Piedmont and the sandy soil and dune systems of the Coastal Plain. The Sandhills are a range of sand dunes that mark where the coast was several million years ago. Since then the ocean has retreated a hundred miles or so to the coastline we know today.

The sandy soil, immense freshwater and saltwater wetlands, deep rivers, wide shallow sounds on the northern coast, and the chain of barrier islands stretching from Virginia to South Carolina make eastern North Carolina's landscape distinct. Among the wetlands are pocosins and Carolina bays, two distinct types of wetlands. Pocosins are wet, peaty expanses of moist ground that are slightly elevated in the center. Carolina bays are ovoid bodies of water on diagonal axes, and are unexplained but beautiful; they dot the landscape across the southeastern corner of the state.

The **Outer Banks** make a giant, sweeping arc from Virginia to the north out to the point at Cape Hatteras; they then turn almost due west, forming the Bogue Banks, also known as the Crystal Coast. Along this northerly half of the North Carolina coast, the barrier islands work with wide complexes of sounds and marshes to protect the mainland from hurricanes and smaller storms. To the south, barrier islands are closer to the mainland, but also work with marshes, creeks, and rivers to absorb the brunt of a storm's strength. At all points along the coast, from the Outer Banks to the southern border, hurricanes can change the shape and structure of the protective islands in an instant, although the northerly barrier islands, which tend to be longer and thinner than those in the south, are often impacted more dramatically when wind and water join forces to rearrange geography.

CLIMATE

Generalizing about North Carolina's climate is difficult. It's not as hot as at the equator and not as cold as at the poles, but beyond that, each region has its own range of variables and has to be examined separately.

The mountains are much cooler than either the Piedmont or the coast, and winter lasts longer. Towns like Asheville and Boone can be blanketed in snow while less than 100 miles away the trees in Piedmont towns aren't even showing their fall colors. The coldest temperature ever recorded in North Carolina, -34°F, was recorded in 1985 on Mount Mitchell. Spring and fall can bring cool to temperate days and chilly nights, while summer days can hit the 80s, and the evenings bring a welcome relief.

The Piedmont, on the other hand, can be brutally hot during the summer and quite warm on spring and fall days. Cities like Charlotte and Fayetteville can feel like the hottest places on earth in high summer; the hottest temperature recorded in the state—110°F—was at Fayetteville in 1983. Add to that the stifling humidity of the summer months, which is more intense than along the coast because there the ocean breezes mitigate its effects, and you have some uncomfortable heat. Winter afternoon temperatures often peak in the 50s, although there are many nights when the temperature stays below freezing. It snows, but not

GEOGRAPHICAL VOCABULARY

North Carolina has some unusual landscapes and environments, and some unusual vocabulary to describe them. As you explore the state, you may encounter the following terms.

POCOSIN

Pronounced "puh-COH-sin," the word is said to come from the Algonquin for "swamp on a hill." A pocosin is a moist peat bog of a sort unique to the Southeast and particularly associated with eastern North Carolina. The peat layer is thinnest around the edges and usually supports communities of pine trees. Moving toward the center of the bog, the ground becomes slightly higher, the peat thicker, more acidic, and less welcoming to plant species. Because the soil is so poor and leached of nutrients, carnivorous plants, which have their meals delivered rather than depending on the soil's bounty, are particularly well suited to life in pocosins.

CAROLINA BAY

The word bay here refers not to an inlet on the coast but to another kind of upland swamp. The bays' origins are mysterious, and their regularity of form and commonness in this region is uncanny. If you look down at eastern North and South Carolina from an airplane, or in a satellite image, the bays are unmistakable. They're oval-shaped depressions, varying in size from Lake Waccamaw to mere puddles, and are always aligned in a northeast-to-southwest configuration. Unlike ponds and regular swamps, Carolina bays are usually unconnected to any groundwater source but are fed solely by rainwater. Like pocosins, bays attract colonies of carnivorous plants, which love to establish their dens of iniquity in such unwholesome soil.

SANDHILLS

If you're in Wilmington or Southport, or somewhere else along the southeastern coast, take note of what the soil beneath your feet looks like. Now, turn your back to the ocean and head inland. Travel 100 miles west and then look down again. What you'll see is very similar—sandy, light-colored ground, wiry vegetation (and a few carnivorous plants), maybe even some scattered shells. About 20 million years ago, during the Miocene Epoch, the areas of present-day Fayetteville, Southern Pines, and Sanford were sand dunes on the shores of an ocean that covered what is now North Carolina's coastal plain. Imagine the landscape millions of years ago, when the Uwharrie Mountains, just west of the Sandhills, towered 20,000 feet over an ocean that swirled at their feet.

HOLLER

Here's a term that's really more of a regional pronunciation than a unique word. A holler is what is on paper termed a "hollow"—a mountain cove; it's just that in the South we aren't much for rounding words that end in "ow." If you don't believe me, just beller out the winda to that feller wallering in yonder meada.

BALD

An ecological mystery, the Appalachian bald is a mountaintop area on which there are no trees, even though surrounding mountaintops of the same elevation may be forested. Typically a bald is either grassy or a heath. Heaths are more easily explained, as they are caused by soil conditions that don't support forest. Grassy balds, though, occur on land where logically trees should be found. Some theories hold that grassy balds were caused by generations of livestock grazing, but soil studies show that they were grassy meadows before the first cattle or sheep arrived. Grazing may still be the answer, though; the balds may originally have been chomped and trampled down by prehistoric megafauna—ancient bison, mastodons, and mammoths. Today, in the absence of mammoths or free-ranging cattle, some balds are gradually becoming woodland, except where deliberately maintained.

as heavily or as frequently as in the mountains, and the counties east of this area are more likely to see rain during winter storms.

Along the coast, temperatures are more moderate than in the Piedmont. The warm Gulf Stream washes past not far off shore, influencing air temperatures in all seasons: keeping temperatures from getting too frigid in winter, bringing spring early, keeping water warm near shore and pushing storms farther inland in summer, and extending the fall season, making it a pleasant time to be here. It's windy along the coast, and these breezes help mitigate summer's heat and make the humidity more bearable.

North Carolina gets its fair share of hazardous weather to go along with beautiful summer days and crisp fall nights. Along the Outer Banks, which jut far out into the Atlantic, **hurricanes** are a particular threat. It's not just the Outer Banks that are vulnerable to these powerful storms; the coastline south of the Banks suffers plenty of hits, and even inland, hurricanes that make landfall in South Carolina can curve up through the Lowcountry and into North Carolina's Piedmont, bringing high winds and heavy rains to inland cities and dangerous floodwaters to coastal towns. Hurricane season is June to November, but it's toward the end of summer and the start of fall that the risk becomes greatest. Normally there is plenty of warning before a storm hits, and by the time they hit people have had time to prepare and stock up. Wind and rain are the first effects of a hurricane, but the storm surge and high waves can cause massive damage to barrier islands, dune systems, and sensitive estuarine complexes. Flooding from inland rains as well as the coastal deluge can spell disaster.

In 1999, Hurricane Floyd killed 35 people in North Carolina, caused billions of dollars of property damage, and permanently altered the landscape in places. During this storm, rivers in eastern North Carolina reached 500-year flood levels, leaving one-third of Rocky Mount under water and causing devastating damage to Tarboro, Kinston, and other towns in the region. Princeville, the oldest African American town in the United States, was nearly destroyed. Today, many towns in eastern North Carolina still carry scars to their infrastructure and economies due to Floyd.

Tornadoes, most common in the spring, can cause trouble any time of year. A rare November twister touched down in 2006, smashing the Columbus County community of Riegelwood, killing eight people and leaving a seven-mile swath of destruction. Even plain old **thunderstorms** can be dangerous, bringing lightning, flash flooding, difficult driving conditions, and even hail. **Snowstorms** are rare, and usually occur in the mountains. The Piedmont sees more snow than the Coast, which sees flurries once or twice each winter and the occasional dusting of snow. Outside the mountains, most North Carolinians are woefully inexperienced snow drivers, and the state Department of Transportation doesn't have the equipment in coastal counties to handle much more than a little snow. Along the coast, the humorous rule of thumb is that for every inch of snow that is predicted, banks, schools, and government offices shut down for a day, and for every inch of snow that actually falls, it's two days. As soon as the meteorologists mention flurries, there's a run on the most valuable snowstorm essentials: milk, bread, peanut butter, toilet paper, and magazines.

Flora

In the early 1700s, John Lawson, an English explorer who would soon be one of the first victims of the Tuscarora War, wrote of a magnificent tree house somewhere in the very young colony of North Carolina. "I have been informed of a Tulip-Tree," he wrote, "that was ten Foot Diameter; and another, wherein a lusty Man had his Bed and Household Furniture, and liv'd in it, till his Labour got him a more fashionable Mansion. He afterwards became a noted Man, in his Country, for Wealth and Conduct." Whether or not there was ever a tulip poplar large enough to serve as a furnished bachelor pad, colonial North Carolina's forests must have seemed miraculous to the first Europeans to see them.

FORESTS

Today, after generations of logging and farming across the state, few old-growth forests exist. In the Smoky Mountains, stands of old-growth timber, like the Joyce Kilmer Forest, are a sight to behold, and some of the trees almost validate Lawson's anecdote. Across the state, scores of specialized ecosystems support a marvelous diversity of plant and animal life. In the east, cypress swamps and a few patches of maritime forest still stand; across the Sandhills are longleaf pine forests; in the mountains are fragrant balsam forests and stands of hardwoods.

Because the state is so geographically and climatically varied, there's a greater diversity in tree species than anywhere in the eastern United States. In terms of land area, more than half of the land is still forested in the Piedmont and eastern North Carolina. Coastal forests are dominated by hardwoods—**oaks** of many varieties, **gum, cypress,** and **cedar**—and the barrier islands have a few remaining patches of maritime forest where the branches of **live oak** trees intertwine to shed storm wind and their roots sink deep to keep islands stable. The best and largest remaining example of a pristine maritime forest is on Bald Head Island,

where the Bald Head Island Conservancy provides education and studies the form, function, and future of barrier islands, including these important maritime forest ecosystems. In the Piedmont, oak and **hickory** dominate the hardwoods alongside bands of piney woods. In the mountains oak and hickory are also the rule, but a number of conifers, including **pine** and **balsam,** appear.

The science and profession of forestry were born in North Carolina: In the 1880s and 1890s, George W. Vanderbilt, lord of the manner at Biltmore, engaged Fredrick Law Olmstead, who designed New York City's Central Park, to plan a managed forest of the finest, healthiest, and most hardy trees. Vanderbilt hired Gifford Pinchot and later Carl Shenck to be the stewards of the thousands of wooded acres he owned in the Pisgah Forest south of Asheville. The contributions these men made to the nascent field are still felt today and are commemorated at the Cradle of Forestry Museum near Brevard.

Longleaf Pine

Arguably, the most important plant in North Carolina's history is the longleaf pine, sometimes called the pitch pine. This beautiful tree is something of a rare sight today as the vast stands of longleaf pines that formerly blanketed the eastern part of the state were used extensively in the naval stores industry in the 18th and 19th centuries, providing valuable turpentine, pitch, tar, and lumber. The overharvesting of this tree has a lot to do with the disappearance of North Carolina's once-legendary pine barrens, but an unanticipated ancillary cause is the efficiency of modern firefighting. Longleaf pines depend on periodic forest fires to clear out competition from the underbrush and provide layers of nutrient-rich singed earth. In the 20th century the rule was to put out forest fires, cutting down on smoke but disturbing the natural growth cycles of these trees. In some longleaf-harboring nature preserves today, controlled burns keep the longleaf piney woods alive and healthy as crucial habitats for several endangered species, including the red cockaded woodpecker and the pine barrens tree frog.

A great place to get a feel for this ecosystem that once covered so much of the Southeast is Weyouth Woods-Sandhills Preserve, near Southern Pines. Some of the longleaf pines here are believed to be almost 500 years old. Many of these centuries-old trees bear scars from the days of the naval stores bonanza, when turpentine makers carved deep gashes in the bark to collect the resin that bled out. The tallest and oldest longleaf pine in the state is here, and at over 130 feet tall, it's a sight.

FLOWERS

Some of North Carolina's flora puts on great annual shows, drawing flocks of admirers—the gaudy **azaleas** of springtime in Wilmington, the **wildflowers** of the first warm weather in the hills, the **rhododendrons** and **mountain laurel** of the Appalachian summer. The Ericaceae family, a race of great woody bushes with star-shaped blossoms that includes azaleas, rhododendrons, and laurel, is the headliner in North Carolina's floral fashion show. Spring comes earliest to the southeastern corner of the state, and the Wilmington area is explosively beautiful when the azaleas are in bloom. The **Azalea Festival,** held annually for more than 50 years, draws hundreds of thousands of people to the city in early to mid-April, around the time that public gardens and private yards are spangled with azaleas.

The flame azalea makes a late-spring appearance on the mountainsides of the Blue Ridge and Great Smokies, joined by its cousins the mountain laurel and Catawba rhododendron in May and June. The ways of the rhododendron are a little mysterious; not every plant blooms every year, and there's no surefire way of predicting when they'll put on big shows. The area's widely varying elevation also figures into bloom times. If you're interested in timing your trip to coincide with some of these flowering seasons, your best bet is to call ahead

© JASON FRYE

azaleas in bloom

and speak with a ranger from the Great Smoky Mountains National Park or the Blue Ridge Parkway to find out how the season is coming along.

Around the end of April and into May, when spring finally arrives in the mountains but the forest floor is not yet sequestered in leafy shade, a profusion of delicate flowers emerges. **Violets** and **chickweed** emerge early on, as do the quintessentially mountainous white **trillium** blossoms and the Wake Robin, also a trillium, which looks something like a small poinsettia. Every year since 1950, around the end of April, the Great Smoky Mountains National Park has hosted the **Spring Wildflower Pilgrimage,** a weeklong festival featuring scores of nature walks that also reveal salamanders, birds, and wild hogs, along with workshops and art exhibits. Visit www.springwildflowerpilgrimage.org for upcoming events.

Surprisingly, one of the best places in North Carolina to view displays of wildflowers is along the major highways. For more than 20 years the state Department of Transportation has carried out a highway beautification project that involves planting large banks of wildflowers along highways and in wide medians. The displays are not landscaped but are allowed to grow up in unkempt profusion, often planted in inspired combinations of wildly contrasting colors that make the flowerbeds a genuinely beautiful addition to the environment. The website of the state's **Department of Transportation** (www.ncdot.org) offers a guide to the locations and seasons of the wildflower beds.·

FALL FOLIAGE

Arriving as early as mid-September at the highest elevations and gradually sliding down the mountains through late October, autumn colors bring a late-season wave of visitors to western North Carolina. Dropping temperatures change trees' sugar production, resulting in a palette of colors, while simple fatigue causes the green to fade in others, exposing underlying hues. Countless climatic factors can alter the onset and progress of leaf season, so the mountains blush at slightly different times every year. The latter weeks of October tend to be the peak; during those weeks it can be difficult to find lodging in the mountains, so be sure to plan ahead. Some of the best places for leaf peeping are along the Blue Ridge Parkway and in the Great Smoky Mountains National Park.

CARNIVOROUS PLANTS

You've probably seen **Venus flytraps** for sale in nurseries, and maybe you've even bought one and brought it home to stuff with kitchen bugs. Venus flytraps grow in the wild only in one tiny corner of the world, a narrow band of counties between Wilmington and Myrtle Beach, South Carolina. The flytraps and their dozens of carnivorous Tar Heel kin, including Seussian sundews and pitcher plants, the abattoirs of the bug world, are fondest of living in places with nutrient-starved soil, like pine savannas and pocosins, where they have little competition for space and sunlight and can feed handsomely on meals that come right to them.

There are many species of **pitcher plants,** a familiar predator of the plant world. Shaped like tubular vases with a graceful elfin flap shading the mouth, pitcher plants attract insects with an irresistible brew. Unsuspecting bugs pile in, thinking they've found a keg party, but instead find themselves paddling in a sticky mess from which they're unable to escape, pinned down by spiny hairs that line the inside of the pitcher. Enterprising frogs and spiders that are either strong or clever enough to come and go safely from inside the pitcher will often set up shop inside a plant and help themselves to stragglers. Another local character is the **sundew,** perhaps the creepiest of the carnivorous plants. Sundews extend their paddle-shaped leaf-hands up into the air, hairy palms baited with a sticky mess that bugs can't resist. When a fly lands among the hairs, the sundew closes on it like a fist and gorges on it until it's ready for more.

There are several places where you can see wild carnivorous plants in North Carolina. Among the best are the Bluethenthal

HORTICULTURAL HAVENS

North Carolina's natural scenery provides inspiration for man-made landscapes of almost equal beauty. Wilmington, the Triangle, and Asheville are home to great botanical gardens, touchstones of the state's horticultural heritage.

WILMINGTON AND ENVIRONS

It's hard to imagine anywhere more beautiful than Wilmington in the springtime. The old port city is a year-round knockout, but the floral fireworks of spring are really special. **Airlie Gardens** is a century-old formal garden with a stunning azalea collection, a 500-year-old oak tree, and a sculpture garden dedicated to longtime gatekeeper Minnie Evans, a renowned visionary artist. **Halyburton Park** comprises almost 60 acres of native ecosystems of the southern coast, including sandhills and Carolina bays, some of this region's most distinctive features.

The **Cape Fear Botanical Gardens** in Fayetteville are simply gorgeous. On a 78-acre strip of land between the Cape Fear River and Cross Creek, more than 2,000 varieties of ornamental plants flower and fruit throughout the year, and miles of walking trails provide a chance to stretch your legs.

THE TRIANGLE

The urban Raleigh-Durham region might not be an obvious destination for garden lovers, but if you look in the right places you'll find a horticultural heaven. First, there are the formal gardens: Chapel Hill's **North Carolina Botanical Gardens,** the Southeast's largest botanical garden, with plants ranging from herbs to carnivorous species; Raleigh's **J. C. Raulston Arboretum,** devoted to the development of ornamental plants that thrive in Southern climates; and the **Sarah P. Duke Gardens** in Durham.

All around the Triangle are small **organic farms and dairies.** Visit the Carolina Farm Stewardship Association's website (www.carolinafarmstewards.org) for a list operations

that welcome visitors. If you're here on the right weekends in April, you'll love their annual Piedmont Farm Tour. Several local farmers markets give you chances to sample produce. The **Carrboro Farmers Market** is small but overflowing with treasures—fruits and vegetables in season, heaps of herbs, live plants for your own garden, and fabulous cut flowers. The **State Farmers Market** in Raleigh is a larger affair, where farmers from central North Carolina and beyond peddle a wonderful variety of seasonal produce, along with preserves and pickles, baked goods, and candies.

AROUND ASHEVILLE

Asheville is the home of the **North Carolina Arboretum,** a garden of more than 400 acres that borders the Pisgah National Forest and the Blue Ridge Parkway. Special collections include the National Native Azalea Repository and more than 200 bonsai. You can tour the arboretum on foot, by Segway, or on your bike, and you can even bring your dog on some of the trails.

At the **Biltmore Estate,** Frederick Law Olmstead created formal gardens of beauty to match the opulent mansion, and architect Richard Morris Hunt designed the conservatory where young plants are still raised for the gardens. Self-guided tours of the conservatory—and the walled, shrub, Italian, vernal, and azalea gardens—are all included in admission to the estate.

Asheville is also an excellent home base for excursions to other garden spots in the mountains. Don't miss the **Rivercane Walk** at the John C. Campbell Folk School in Brasstown, where modern Cherokee sculpture lines a path along Little Brasstown Creek. The **Mountain Farm Museum** at the edge of Great Smoky Mountains National Park demonstrates gardening methods used on the early mountain homesteads. The **Cradle of Forestry** in Pisgah National Forest explains how the science of modern forestry was born here in western North Carolina.

Wildflower Preserve at the University of North Carolina Wilmington, Carolina Beach State Park, and the Green Swamp Preserve and Ev-Henwood Nature Preserve in Brunswick County. There's also a good collection of them on display at Chapel Hill's North Carolina Botanical Garden.

Fauna

Among the familiar wildlife most commonly seen in the state, **white-tailed deer** are out in force in the countryside and in the woods; they populate suburban areas in large numbers as well. **Raccoons** and **opossums** prowl at night, happy to scavenge from trash cans and the forest floor. **Skunks** are common, particularly in the mountains, and are often smelled rather than seen. They leave an odor something like a cross between grape soda and Sharpie markers. There are also a fair number of **black bears,** not only in the mountains but in swamps and deep woods across the state.

In woods and yards alike, **gray squirrels** and a host of familiar **songbirds** are a daily presence. Different species of **tree frogs** produce beautiful choruses on spring and summer nights, while **fireflies** mount sparkly shows in the trees and grass in the upper Piedmont and mountains. Down along the southeast coast, **alligators** and **turtles** sun themselves on many a golf course and creek-side backyard.

The town of Brevard, in the Blue Ridge south of Asheville, is famous for its population of ghostly **white squirrels.** They're regular old gray squirrels that live all over North America, but their fur ranges from speckled gray and white to pure bone-white. They're not albinos; it's thought that Brevard's white squirrels are cousins of a clan that lives in Florida and that their ancestors may have found their way to the Blue Ridge in a circus or with a dealer of exotic pets in the early 20th century.

The Carolina woods harbor colonies of **Southern flying squirrels.** It's very unlikely that you'll see one unless it's at a nature center or wildlife rehabilitation clinic because flying squirrels are both nocturnal and shy. They're also almost unspeakably cute. Fully extended, they're about nine inches long snout to tail, weigh about four ounces, and have super-silky fur and pink noses, and like many nocturnal animals have comically long whiskers and huge, wide-set eyes that suggest amphetamine use. When they're flying—gliding, really—they spread their limbs to extend the patagium, a membrane that stretches between their front and hind legs, and glide along like little magic carpets.

Also deep in the Smokies are some herds of **wild hogs,** game boar brought to the area about 100 years ago and allowed to go feral. The official line among wildlife officials is that **mountain lions**—in this region called panthers—have been extinct in North Carolina for some time. But mountain dwellers claim there are still panthers in the Blue Ridge and Smokies, and most people here have seen or heard one—their cry sounds like a terror-filled scream. There are even tales of a panther in the inland woods of Brunswick and Columbus Counties on the southeast coast.

WILD PONIES

Small herds of wild ponies have called several barrier islands in the Outer Banks home for more than 400 years. Locally known as "Banker ponies," but more properly as feral horses, they're descendants of Spanish horses, a fact established by extensive DNA testing. No one's quite sure how they arrived here, but the consensus is that they've been here since the 1500s. They may have arrived with early English colonists, who may have bought Spanish horses at a Caribbean port, or with even earlier Spanish explorers. Stories passed down here for hundreds of years say they swam ashore from long-ago shipwrecks. Today, the

BEST SPOTS TO SNEAK UP ON WILDLIFE

In every region of North Carolina, there are compelling opportunities for close-up animal observation, in areas where wild animals live in their own habitats and in and humane facilities designed for captive breeding and rehabilitation.

Great Smoky Mountains National Park is home to a reintroduced population of **elk.** They're most likely to be seen in the Cataloochee section of the park, grazing and meditating in the misty fields early in the morning. On summer evenings, synchronous **fireflies** put on baffling and beautiful displays of coordinated self-illumination. This unusual sight is so popular that the National Park Service leads guided nighttime hikes to the best viewing spots.

Red wolves have also been reintroduced to North Carolina in recent years, and the **Alligator River National Wildlife Refuge** in Eastern Sound country is wolf central. Highly elusive animals, the wolves are likelier to be heard than seen.

To view hundreds of **exotic species** from around the world, your best bet is the **North Carolina Zoo in Asheboro.** Some species, including **elephants, rhinos,** and other huge African mammals, live in multiple-acre enclosures where they roam entire fields and hillsides.

In nearby Pittsboro, **Carolina Tiger Rescue,** also known as the Carnivore Preservation Trust, is a rescue facility for **big cats,** including **leopards, ocelots, jaguars,** and their lesser-known cousins such as binturongs, caracals, and kinkajous. Visitors can meet the cats up close on guided tours.

Bird lovers must visit the **Carolina Raptor Center** north of Charlotte, where **hawks, eagles, owls,** and dozens of other birds of prey are rehabilitated from injury and illness. Many birds permanently in residence are on display for visitors to observe.

In the extreme northeastern corner of the state, the **Sylvan Heights Waterfowl Park** is a world-renowned breeding facility for **rare and endangered waterbirds.** You can get amazingly close to some of the world's rarest waterfowl at the park's outdoor aviaries. There are also three excellent branches of the **North Carolina Aquarium** along the coast, on Roanoke Island, at Pine Knoll Shores near Morehead City, and at Fort Fisher near Wilmington.

Parks, refuges, and captive facilities are hardly the only places to see wildlife in North Carolina. Drive along just about any country road at dawn or dusk and you're likely to see **white-tailed deer** grazing. Campers in the mountains or deep swamps should be prepared for the real possibility of visits from **black bears.** When canoeing or kayaking in the southeastern part of the state, you may well spot basking **alligators.** And most anywhere in the state, even in the cities, leave your window open to be serenaded by chirping **tree frogs,** hooting **owls,** and warbling **mockingbirds.**

---

primary herds are on Shackleford Banks in the Cape Lookout National Seashore and in Corolla, at the extreme north end of the Outer Banks, near the Virginia border. Since they roam freely in areas open to public visitation, you may find one staring you down from behind a sand dune or a stand of scrubby cedar trees. Remember to use caution around the Banker ponies; they may resemble domestic horses, but they are wild animals. Feeding them or approaching them only ends up hurting the herd in the long run. They also pose some physical danger; all it takes for them to show you who's boss is one swift kick. You can learn more about the horses and their history at http://shacklefordhorses.org and www.corollawildhorses.com.

REINTRODUCED SPECIES

In the 1990s and early 2000s a federal program to reestablish **red wolf** colonies in the Southeast focused its efforts on parkland in North Carolina. Red wolves, thought to have existed in North Carolina in past centuries,

A pony walks along the Outer Banks.

were first reintroduced to the Great Smoky Mountains National Park. They did not thrive, and the colony was moved to the Alligator River National Wildlife Refuge on the northeast coast. The packs have fared better in this corner of the state and now roam several wilderness areas in the sound country.

The Smokies proved a more hospitable place for the reintroduction of **elk.** Now the largest animals in the Great Smoky Mountains National Park, elk, which can grow up to 700 pounds, are most often observed in the Cataloochee section of the park, grazing happily and lounging in the mist in the early morning and at twilight.

BIRDS
Bird-watchers flock to North Carolina because of the great diversity of songbirds, raptors, and even hummingbirds across the state—a 2013 count put the number of species at 473—but the state is best known for waterfowl. In the sounds of eastern North Carolina, waterfowl descend en masse as they migrate. Hundreds of thousands of birds crowd the lakes, ponds, trees, marshes, and waterways as they move to and from their winter homes. Many hunters take birds during hunting season, but they're outnumbered by bird-watchers. Birders say that one of the best spots for birding in the state is around large, shallow Lake Mattamuskeet on the central coast, with 40,000 acres of water to attract incredible numbers of snow geese and tundra swans, Canada geese, and ducks. Just a few miles away, Swan Quarter National Wildlife Refuge is also a haven for ducks, wading birds, shorebirds, and their admirers.

While in eastern North Carolina, bird fanciers should visit the Sylvan Heights Waterfowl Park and Eco-Center, a remarkable park in the small town of Scotland Neck that's a conservation center and breeding facility for rare waterfowl from across the globe. Visitors can walk through the grounds, where large aviaries house bird species that, unless you're a world-traveler and a very lucky birder, you're unlikely to see elsewhere. There are more than 170 species, and you can get quite close to most of them.

Bring your camera; you'll have the chance to take shots you could never get in the field.

Another place not to miss is the Carolina Raptor Center, on the grounds of the Latta Plantation Nature Preserve in Huntersville, north of Charlotte. The center is primarily a rehabilitation facility—they've treated and released thousands of birds over the years—but there is also a 0.75-mile nature trail through the park, where you can see many of the facility's resident raptors, including owls, hawks, eagles, kites, kestrels, and merlins that were found to be too profoundly injured to survive in the wild.

There are many books and websites about birding in North Carolina. One of the most helpful is the North Carolina Birding Trail, both a website (www.ncbirdingtrail.org) and a series of print guidebooks. Organized by region (mountains, Piedmont, and coast), these resources list dozens of top sites for bird-watching and favorite bird-watching events throughout the state. Another good resource is the **Carolina Bird Club** (www.carolinabirdclub.org).

AMPHIBIANS

Dozens of species of **salamanders** and their close kin, including **mudpuppies, sirens,** and **amphiumas,** call North Carolina home, and Great Smoky Mountains National Park harbors so many of them that it's known as the Salamander Capital of the World. Throughout the state, **frogs** and **toads** are numerous and vociferous, especially the many species of dainty **tree frogs.** Two species, the gray tree frog and the spring peeper, are found in every part of North Carolina, and beginning in late winter they create the impression that the trees are filled with ringing cell phones.

Hellbenders are quite possibly the strangest animal in North Carolina. They are enormous salamanders—not the slick little pencil-thin five-inch salamanders easily spotted along creeks, but hulking brutes that grow to more than two feet long and can weigh five pounds. Rare and hermetic, they live in rocky mountain streams, venturing out from under rocks at night to gobble up crayfish and minnows.

They're hard to see even if they do emerge in the daytime because they're lumpy and mud-colored, camouflaged against streambeds. Aggressive with each other, the males often sport battle scars on their stumpy legs. They've been known to bite humans, but as rare as it is to spot a hellbender, it's an exponentially rarer occurrence to be bitten by one.

REPTILES

Turtles and **snakes** are the state's most common reptiles. **Box turtles,** found everywhere, and **bog turtles,** found in the Smokies, are the only land terrapins. A great many freshwater turtles inhabit the swamps and ponds, and on a sunny day every log or branch sticking out of fresh water will become a sunbathing terrace for as many turtles as it can hold. Common water turtles include **cooters, sliders,** and **painted turtles. Snapping turtles** can be found in fresh water throughout the state, so mind your toes. They grow up to a couple of feet long and can weigh more than 50 pounds. Not only will they bite—hard!—if provoked, they will actually initiate hostilities, lunging for you if they so much as disapprove of the fashion of your shoes. Even the tiny hatchlings are vicious, so give them a wide berth. Finally, we are visited often by **sea turtles,** a gentle and painfully dwindling race of seafarers. The most frequent visitor is the **loggerhead,** a reddish-tan living coracle that can weigh up to 500 pounds and nests as far north as Ocracoke. Occasional visitors include the **leatherback,** a 1,500-pound goliath at its largest, **hawksbills, greens,** and **olive ridleys.** The Bald Head Island Conservancy on Bald Head Island has been protecting the turtles and their nests since the mid-1980s, gathering data on birth rates, nest numbers, and the mother turtles. During the nesting season, conservancy members can tag turtles along with ecologists and interns and watch them lay their eggs.

There are not many kinds of **lizards** native to North Carolina, but those that are present make up for their homogeneity with ubiquity. **Anoles,** tiny, scaly dragons that dart along almost any outdoor surface, are found in great

Gators look docile, but it's best to admire them from a distance.

numbers in the southeastern part of the state, up the coast, and along the South Carolina state line to west of Charlotte. They put on great shows by puffing their ruby-red dewlaps and by vacillating between drab brown and gray or lime-Slurpee green, depending on the color of the background they hide on. The ranks of lizard kind are rounded out by several varieties of **skinks** and **glass lizards,** also called glass snakes because they look like snakes, although they're not, and **fence lizards.**

There are plenty of real **snakes** in North Carolina. The vast majority are shy, gentle, and totally harmless to anything larger than a rat. There are a few species of venomous snakes that are very dangerous. These include three kinds of **rattlesnake:** the huge diamondback, whose diet of rabbits testifies to its size and strength; the pigmy; and the timber or canebrake rattler. Other venomous species are the beautiful mottled **copperhead** and the **cottonmouth or water moccasin,** famous for flinging its mouth open in hostility and flashing its brilliant white palate. The **coral**

snake is a fantastically beautiful and venomous species.

Most Carolina snakes are entirely benign to humans, including old familiars such as **black racers** and **king snakes** as well as **milk, corn,** and **rat snakes.** One particularly endearing character is the **hognose snake,** which can be found throughout North Carolina but is most common in the east. Colloquially known as a spreading adder, the hognose snake compensates for its total harmlessness with amazing displays of histrionics. If you startle one, it will first flatten and greatly widen its head and neck and hiss most passionately. If it sees that you're not frightened by plan A, it will panic and go straight to plan B: playing dead. The hognose snake won't simply lay inert until you go away, though; it goes to the dramatic lengths of flipping onto its back, exposing its pitiably vulnerable belly, opening its mouth, throwing its head back limply, and sticking out its tongue as if it had just been poisoned. It is such a devoted method actor that should you call its bluff and poke it back onto its belly, it will fling itself

© JASON FRYE

like the sign says...

energetically back into the mortuary pose and resume being deceased.

Alligators make their reptilian kin look tiny. Tar Heel gators are most abundant in the area south of Wilmington, but they've been seen the full length of the state's coast—note how far north the Alligator River is—and as far inland as Merchants Millpond State Park near the Virginia state line. The biggest ones can reach 1,000 pounds and measure 10-15 feet long. Smaller gators are more common, and the six- and eight-foot females are small in comparison to the massive bull gators. They have approximately a mouthful of sharp teeth, and even hatchlings can pack a nasty bite. These amazing prehistoric-looking amphibious assault machines appear to spend most of their waking hours splayed out in the sun with their eyes closed, or floating motionless in the water. Don't fall for it; it's their fiendishly clever, or perhaps primitively simple, ploy to make you come closer. They can launch themselves at prey as if spring-loaded and are more than capable of catching and eating a dog, cat, or small child. It happens very rarely, but given the chance, large gators can and will eat an adult human. The best course of action, as with most wildlife, is to admire them from a distance.

History

ANCIENT CIVILIZATION

By the time the first colonists arrived and called this place Carolina, the land had already sustained some 20,000 years of human history. We know that Paleo-Indians hunted these lands during the last ice age, when there were probably more mammoths and saber-toothed tigers in North Carolina than people. Civilization came around 4000 BC, when the first inhabitants settled down to farm, make art, and trade goods. By the first century, Southern Woodland and Mississippian Indians were also living in advanced societies with complex religious systems, economic interaction among communities, advanced farming methods, and the creation of art and architecture.

When the Europeans arrived, there were more than a dozen major Native American groups within what is now North Carolina. The Cherokee people ruled the mountains

Native Americans fishing with spears and nets (sketch by John White, 1585)

while the Catawba, Pee Dees, Tutelo, and Saura, among others, were their neighbors in the Piedmont. In the east, the Cheraw, Waccamaw, and Tuscarora were some of the larger communities, while many bands occupied land along the Outer Banks and sounds.

CONQUEST

The first Europeans to land here were Spanish. We know conquistador Hernando de Soto and his troops marched around western North Carolina in 1539, but they were just passing through. In 1566, another band of Spanish explorers, led by conquistador Juan Pardo, came for a longer visit. They were making a circuitous trek in the general direction of Mexico, and along the way they established several forts in what are now the Carolinas and Tennessee. One of these forts, called San Juan, has been identified by archaeologists outside present-day Morganton in a community called Worry Crossroads. Although the troops who were garrisoned for a year and a half at Fort San Juan eventually disappeared into the woods or were killed, it's theorized that they may have had a profound impact on the course of history, possibly spreading European diseases among the Native Americans and weakening them so much that, a couple of decades later, the indigenous people would be unable to repel the invasion of English colonists.

The next episode in the European settlement of North Carolina is one of the strangest mysteries in American history, the Lost Colonists of Roanoke. After two previous failed attempts to establish an English stronghold on the island of Roanoke, fraught by poor planning and disastrous diplomacy, a third group of English colonists tried their luck. Sometime between being dropped off in the New World in 1587 and one of their leaders returning three years later to resupply them, all of the colonists—including Virginia Dare, the first English person born in the Americas—had vanished into the

RAISED FROM THE DEAD

In 1587, Thomas Hariot, an English man of science, visited Roanoke Island and the surrounding area. Acting in effect as an early ethnographer, he learned Algonquin during his time in the New World and recorded social customs of Native Americans, along with observations of the region's natural resources, in his 1587 *An Account of the Inhabitants and Commodities of Virginia*. From conversing with religious leaders, he learned the following about the religious beliefs of the area's indigenous inhabitants.

They believe also the immortality of the soul, that after this life as soon as the soul is departed from the body, according to the work it has done, it is either carried to heaven the habitat of the gods, there to enjoy perpetual bliss and happiness, or else to a great pit or hole, which they think to be in the furtherest parts of their part of the world toward the sunset, there to burn continually. The place they call Popogusso.

For the confirmation of this opinion, they told me two stories of two men that had been lately dead and revived again, the one happened but a few years before our coming into the country of a wicked man, which having been dead and buried, the next day the earth of the grave being seen to move, was taken up again, who made declaration where his soul had been, that is to say, very near entering into Popogusso, had not one of the gods saved him, and given him leave to return again, and teach his friends what they should do to avoid that terrible place of torment. The other happened in the same year we were there, but in a town that was 60 miles from us, and it was told me for strange news, that one being dead, buried, and taken up again as the first, showed that although his body had lain dead in the grave, yet his soul was alive, and had traveled far in a long broad way, on both sides whereof grew most delicate and pleasant trees, bearing more rare and excellent fruits, than he had seen before, or was able to express, and at length came to most brave and fair houses, near which he met his father that had been dead before, who gave him great charge to go back again, and show his friends what good they were to do to enjoy the pleasures of that place, which when he had done he should after come again.

woods. To this day, their fate is unknown, although a host of fascinating theories are still debated and probably always will be.

The disappearance of the Roanoke colonists did little to slow the process of the European conquest of North America. After the establishment of the Virginia colony in 1607, new English settlers began to trickle southward into Carolina, while Barbadians and Europeans from Charles Town (in present-day South Carolina) gradually began to populate the area around Wilmington. The town of Bath was established in 1706, and New Bern was settled shortly thereafter. The bloody Tuscarora War followed, and after a crushing defeat near present-day Snow Hill, in which hundreds were killed, the Tuscarora people retreated, opening the land along the Neuse River to European colonization.

COLONIALISM

The conflict between Europeans and Native Americans wasn't the only world-changing cultural encounter going on in the Southern colonies. By the middle of the 18th century, nearly 100,000 enslaved people had been brought to North Carolina from West Africa. By the end of the 18th century, many areas, especially those around Wilmington, had populations where enslaved African Americans outnumbered whites. Although North Carolina did not experience slavery on as vast a scale as South Carolina, there were a handful of plantations with more than 100 slaves, and many smaller plantations and town homes of wealthy planters, merchants, and politicians with smaller numbers of slaves. Africans and African Americans were an early and potent cultural force in the South, influencing the economy, politics, language, religion, music, architecture, and cuisine in ways still seen today.

In the 1730s the Great Wagon Road connected Pennsylvania with Georgia by cutting through the Mid-Atlantic and Southern backcountry of Virginia and North Carolina. Many travelers migrated south from Pennsylvania, among them a good number of German and Scottish-Irish settlers who found the mountains and Piedmont of North Carolina to their liking. Meanwhile, the port of Wilmington, growing into one of the most important in the state, saw a number of Gaelic-speaking Scots move through, following the river north and putting down roots around what is now Fayetteville. Shortly before the American Revolution, a group of German-speaking religious settlers known as the Moravians constructed a beautiful and industrious town, Salem, in the heart of the Piedmont, later to become Winston-Salem. Their pacifist beliefs, Germanic heritage, and artistry set them apart from other communities in colonial North Carolina, and they left an indelible mark on the state's history.

The 18th century brought one conflict after another to the colony, from fights over the Vestry Act in the early 1700s, which attempted to establish the Anglican church as the one official faith of the colony, through various regional conflicts with Native Americans, and events that played out at a global level during the French and Indian War. At mid-century the population and economic importance of the Piedmont was growing exponentially, but colonial representation continued to be focused along the coast. Protesting local corruption and lack of governmental concern for the western region, a group of backcountry farmers organized themselves into an armed posse in resistance to colonial corruption. Calling themselves the Regulators, they eventually numbered more than 6,000. Mounting frustrations led to an attack by the Regulators on the Orange County courthouse in Hillsborough. Finally, a colonial militia was dispatched to crush the movement, which it did at the Battle of Alamance in 1771. Six Regulators were captured and hanged at Hillsborough.

REVOLUTION AND STATEHOOD

Many believe the seeds of the American Revolution were sewn, tended, and reaped in New England, but the southern colonies, particularly North Carolina, played important roles before and during the rebellion. In 1765, as the War of the Regulation was heating up, the residents of Brunswick Town, the colonial capital and the only deep-water port in the southern half of the colony, revolted in protest of the Stamp Act. They placed the royal governor under house arrest and put an end to taxation in the Cape Fear region, sending a strong message to the crown and to fellow patriots hungry to shake off the yoke of British rule. In the ensuing years, well-documented events like the Boston Tea Party, the Battles of Lexington and Concord, and the signing of the Declaration of Independence occurred, but North Carolina's role in leading the rebellion was far from over.

After the Battles of Lexington and Concord, the colonies were aflame with patriotic fervor, and Mecklenburg County (around Charlotte) passed the first colonial declaration rejecting the crown's authority. By this time, North Carolina, like the other colonies, had formed a provincial government, and it was busy in the tavern at Halifax writing the Halifax Resolves, the first official action in the colonies calling for independence from Britain. On April 12, 1776, the resolves were ratified and delegates carried them to the Second Continental

North Carolinians played a very important role in the American Revolution.

Congress in Philadelphia. Other delegates were so inspired that more such resolves appeared, ultimately the Declaration of Independence was written and ratified, and the revolution was on in earnest.

Although North Carolina may have been the first to call for independence, the state was divided in its loyalties. Among the most noteworthy Loyalists was the community of Highland Scots living in and around modern-day Fayetteville. Men from this community were marching to join General Cornwallis near Brunswick Town and Southport (then Smithville) when Patriots ambushed them at the bloody battle of Moore's Creek, killing 30 Scots and routing the Loyalist force.

North Carolinians fought all over the eastern seaboard during the Revolution, including about 1,000 who were with Washington at Valley Forge. The year 1780 brought fighting back home, particularly in the area around Charlotte, which a daunted General Cornwallis referred to as "the hornets' nest." The battle

of Kings Mountain, west of Charlotte, was a pivotal moment in the war, and one that was particularly costly to the Loyalist forces. Cornwallis received another blow at the Battle of Guilford Courthouse; although technically a British victory, it weakened his forces considerably. By the time the war ended, thousands of North Carolinians were dead and the treasury was far in debt. But North Carolina was now a state with the business of statehood to attend to. The capital was moved inland to Raleigh, and 20 miles away at Chapel Hill, ground was broken for the establishment of the University of North Carolina, the first state university in the country.

THE FEDERAL ERA

The early 19th century in North Carolina was a good deal more peaceful than the previous hundred years had been. The first decade of the 1800s saw a religious awakening in which thousands of North Carolinians became devout Christians. At the same time, the introduction of the cotton gin and bright-leaf tobacco were economic boons in the state, particularly the eastern counties. Railroads and plank roads made trade immeasurably more efficient, bringing new prosperity to the Piedmont.

There was also conflict, of course, in the early 19th century. Andrew Jackson's administration presided over the passage of the Indian Removal Act in 1830, which assigned reservations in the Indian Territory of present-day Oklahoma to the "Five Civilized Tribes" of the southeastern United States—the Cherokee, Choctaw, Creek, Chickasaw, and Seminole. Thousands of Cherokee people were forced out of western North Carolina, northern Georgia, eastern Tennessee, and Alabama and marched west on the Trail of Tears. About 4,000 died along the way. Another 1,000 or so Cherokee people, through hiding, fighting, and negotiation, managed to win the right to stay in North Carolina—an act of resistance that was the birth of the modern Eastern Band of the Cherokee, still centered around the town of Cherokee on the Qualla Boundary in North Carolina's Great Smoky Mountains. The

Eastern Band of the Cherokee tell the story of their relocation in the enlightening outdoor drama *Unto These Hills*.

THE CIVIL WAR

Compared to South Carolina and a few other Southern states, North Carolina was considered politically moderate in the mid-19th century because it was less invested economically and politically in slavery. Combined with the knowledge that if secession became a reality, war would follow and North Carolina's tobacco and cotton fields would quickly become battlefields, secession was on the lips of everyone across the South. As some states voted to remove themselves from the Union, North Carolina's voters rejected a ballot measure authorizing a secession convention. As grand a gesture as that victory may have been, when fighting erupted at Fort Sumpter in Charleston Harbor, North Carolina's hand was forced and its secession was a reality. Secessionist governor John Ellis rejected Lincoln's call to federalize state militias, instead seizing control of the state and all federal military installations within its boundaries as well as the Charlotte Mint. North Carolina officially seceded on May 20, 1861, and a few weeks later Union ships began to blockade the coast. Roanoke Island in the Outer Banks fell, and a freedmen's colony (a home for enslaved people who had been freed or escaped) sprung up. New Bern, which fell in the spring of 1862, became a major focal point of Union military strategy and a thriving political base for freed and escaped African Americans. To the south, Fort Fisher, on the Cape Fear River just south of Wilmington, guarded the river's inlet and was crucial to the success of the blockade runners—smugglers whose speedy boats eluded the Union blockade. Fort Fisher kept Wilmington in Confederate hands until nearly the end of the war. When it finally did fall to Union forces in February 1865, it required what would be the largest amphibious assault in American military history until World War II. Wilmington was the last major port on the Confederacy's eastern seaboard,

and its fall severed supply lines and crippled what remained of the Confederate army in the area.

The varying opinions felt by Southerners about the Civil War, in the South also called the War between the States, was particularly strong in North Carolina, where today you'll still hear whites refer to it as the War of Northern Aggression or the War of Yankee Aggression. More than 5,000 African Americans from North Carolina joined and fought in the Union Army, and there were pockets of strong Union sentiment and support among white North Carolinians, especially in the mountains. Some 10,000 North Carolinians fought for the Union. Zebulon Vance, who won the 1862 gubernatorial election and served as governor through the duration of the war, was a native of Weaverville, near Asheville, and felt acutely the state's ambivalence toward the Confederacy. Much to the consternation of Richmond (the Confederate capital), Governor Vance was adamant in his refusal to put the interests of the Confederacy over those of his own state. Mountain communities suffered tremendously during the war from acts of terrorism by deserters and rogues from both armies.

The latter years of the Civil War were particularly difficult for North Carolina and the rest of the South. Approximately 4,000 North Carolina men died at the Battle of Gettysburg alone. After laying waste to Georgia and South Carolina, General William T. Sherman's army entered North Carolina in the spring of 1865, destroying homes and farms. His march of fire and pillage spared Wilmington, which is one reason the town contains such an incredible collection of Federal architecture. The last major battle of the war was fought in North Carolina, when General Sherman and Confederate General Joseph Johnston engaged at Bentonville. Johnston surrendered to Sherman in Durham in April 1865.

By the end of the war more than 40,000 North Carolina soldiers were dead—a number equivalent to the entire present-day population of the city of Hickory, Apex, or Kannapolis.

RECONSTRUCTION AND THE NEW SOUTH

The years immediately after the war were painful as well, as a vast population of newly free African Americans tried to make new lives for themselves economically and politically in the face of tremendous opposition and violence from whites. The Ku Klux Klan was set up during this time, inaugurating an era of horror for African Americans throughout the country. Federal occupation and domination of the Southern states' political and legal systems also exacerbated resentment toward the North. The state's ratification of the 14th Amendment on July 4, 1868, brought North Carolina back into the Union.

The late 1800s saw large-scale investment in North Carolina's railroad system, launching the industrial boom of the New South. Agriculture changed in this era as the rise of tenancy created a new form of enslavement for many farmers—black, white, and Native American. R. J. Reynolds, Washington Duke, and other entrepreneurs built a massively lucrative empire of tobacco production from field to factory. Textile and furniture mills sprouted throughout the Piedmont, creating a new cultural landscape as rural Southerners migrated to mill towns.

THE 20TH CENTURY AND TODAY

The early decades of the 1900s brought an expanded global perspective to North Carolina, not only through the expanded economy and the coming of radio, but as natives of the state scattered across the globe. About 80,000 North Carolinians served in World War I, many of them young men who had never before left the state or perhaps even their home counties. Hundreds of thousands of African Americans migrated north during what became known as the Great Migration. The communities created by black North Carolinians in the Mid-Atlantic and the Northeast are still closely connected by culture and kinship to their cousins whose ancestors remained in the South. The invasion of the boll weevil, an insect that devastated the cotton industry, hastened the departure of Southerners of all races who had farmed cotton. The Great Depression hit hard across all economic sectors of the state in the 1930s, but New Deal employment programs were a boon to North Carolina's infrastructure, with the construction of hydroelectric dams, the Blue Ridge Parkway, and other public works.

North Carolina's modern-day military importance largely dates to the World War II era. Installations at Fort Bragg, Camp Lejeune, and other still-vital bases were constructed or expanded. About 350,000 North Carolinians fought in World War II, and 7,000 of them died.

A few old-timers remember World War II quite vividly because they witnessed it firsthand: German U-Boats prowled the waters off the coast, torpedoing ships and sinking them with frightening regularity. These German submarines were often visible from the beach, but more often the evidence of their mission of terror and supply-chain disruption—corpses, wounded sailors, and the flotsam of exploded ships—washed up on the shore. More than 10,000 German prisoners were interned in prisoner-of-war camps, in some parts of the state becoming forced farm laborers. In Wilmington, just a few blocks from downtown, is an apartment complex that was part of a large prisoner-of-war compound for U-boat officers.

In the 1950s and 1960s, African Americans in North Carolina and throughout the United States struggled against the monolithic system of segregation and racism enshrined in the nation's Jim Crow laws. The Ku Klux Klan stepped up its pro-segregation efforts with political and physical violence against Native Americans as well as African Americans; in the famous 1958 Battle of Maxton, 500 armed Lumbee people foiled a Klan rally and sent the Knights running for their lives. Change arrived slowly. The University of North Carolina accepted its first African American graduate student in 1951 and the first black undergraduates four years later. Sit-ins in 1960 at the Woolworth's lunch counter in Greensboro began with four African American men, students at North Carolina A&T. On the second day of their protest they were joined by 23 other demonstrators; on the third day there were 300, and by day four about 1,000. This was a pivotal moment in the national civil rights movement, sparking sit-ins across the country in which an estimated 50,000 people participated. You can see the counter today at the International Civil Rights Center and Museum in Greensboro. Even as victories were won at the level of Congress and in the federal courts, as in *Brown v. the Board of Education* and the 1964 Civil Rights Act, actual change on the ground was inexorably slow and hardwon. North Carolina's contribution to the civil rights movement continues to be invaluable for the whole nation.

North Carolina continues to adapt and contribute to the global community. It is now a place of ethnic diversity, growing especially in Latino residents. In 2011 an estimated 8.6 percent of North Carolinians were Latino, and that number is still climbing. There are also significant communities of Dega and Hmong people from Southeast Asia as well as Eastern Europeans, among many others.

Government and Economy

POLITICAL LIFE
Liberal Enclaves
Although historically a red state, North Carolina's large population of college students, professors, and artists has created several boisterous enclaves of progressive politics. The outspoken archconservative U.S. Senator Jesse Helms supposedly questioned the need to spend public money on a state zoo in North Carolina "when we can just put up a fence around Chapel Hill." The Chapel Hill area is indeed the epicenter of North Carolina's liberalism, with its smaller neighboring town of Carrboro at its heart. Would-be Democratic presidential candidates and politicians on the campaign trail regularly stop here to bolster support in the state.

Although you'll find a mixture of political views statewide, the Triangle is not the only famously liberal community. In Asheville, lefty politics are part of the community's devotion to all things organic and DIY. Significant pockets of liberalism also exist in Boone, the cities of the Triad, and Wilmington.

Famous Figures
Several major players in modern American politics are from North Carolina. The best-known politician in recent years is former U.S. Senator John Edwards, who made two runs for the White House, the first leading to a vice presidential spot on the Democratic ticket. Edwards was born in South Carolina but grew up here in the Sandhills. At the other end of the political spectrum, Monroe native Jesse Helms spent 30 years in the U.S. Senate, becoming one of the most prominent and outspoken conservative Republicans of our times. Upon his retirement, Helms was succeeded in the Senate by Salisbury-born Duke University graduate Elizabeth Dole, who had previously served in Ronald Reagan's cabinet and George H. W. Bush's cabinet. She was also president of the American Red Cross and had a close brush with the White House when her husband, Kansas Senator Bob Dole, ran for president in 1996.

MAJOR INDUSTRIES
Over the last 20 years, North Carolina has experienced tremendous shifts in its economy as the industries that once dominated the landscape and brought wealth and development declined. The **tobacco** industry ruled the state's economy for generations, employing innumerable North Carolinians from field to factory and funding a colossal portion of the state's physical and cultural infrastructure. The slow decline of the tobacco industry worldwide from the 1980s changed the state dramatically, especially the rural east, where tobacco fields

once went from green to gold every fall. Other agricultural industries, especially **livestock**— chickens and hogs—are still important in the east. The **textile** industry, a giant for most of the 20th century, suffered the same decline as manufacturers sought cheaper labor overseas. Likewise, the **furniture** industry slipped into obscurity. Today, the once-thriving **fishing** industry is in steep decline, largely due to globalization and overfishing.

While these staple industries have fallen off, new industries and fields have sprouted across the state. **Pharmaceutical** and **biotech** companies have set up in the Research Triangle, formed by Raleigh, Durham, and Chapel Hill. The **film industry** has made Wilmington a hub of feature film production, Charlotte is a major production center for television programming and commercials, and Raleigh is home to a number of visual-effects studios that contribute to films and TV. **High-tech** leaders like Apple have set up in North Carolina, and other tech giants have followed, locating database and network centers here. Charlotte is second only to New York City among the country's largest **banking** centers. **Tourism** continues to grow and contribute in a major way to the state's economy. **Agriculture** continues to remain relevant, though it is increasingly becoming more specialized, especially as the demand for organic products and locally and regionally sourced products continues to be a trend.

Tourism

North Carolina has always drawn visitors to its mountains, waters, beaches, and cities. As the economy evolves, the tourism sector has become even more important. Mountain and beach landscapes sell themselves, but competition is strong to be the town visitors think of first. The Yadkin Valley's **wine industry** and **wine trail** and the boom in **NASCAR** tourism are well-established examples of niche destinations, but the niche tourism trend continues to evolve. As **culinary tourism** gains momentum so too do foodie destinations like **Asheville,** which was named "Beer City USA" from 2009 to 2012 and boasts some two dozen breweries

and specialty beer shops along with more than 250 independently owned restaurants. **Raleigh** and **Durham** continue to build foodie credentials as chefs and breweries rack up impressive awards and prestigious nominations. It seems that every city large or small celebrates some sort of "Taste of the Town" or restaurant week. **Heritage tourism** is also enormously important, with a number of guidebooks and driving trails established or under development to promote history, traditional music, folk arts, and literary achievements. The state's Department of Commerce estimates that nearly 46 million people visit North Carolina every year, bringing in more than $19 billion, and that close to 200,000 state residents work in industries directly related to and dependent on tourism.

DISTRIBUTION OF WEALTH

For the most part, North Carolina is basically working-class. Pockets of significant wealth exist in urban areas, and as more and more retirees relocate to North Carolina, there are moneyed people in the mountains and coastal counties. Extensive white-collar job availability makes the Triangle a comparatively prosperous region, with average household incomes in 2010 exceeding $60,000, much higher than the state's average of just over $40,000.

The state also experiences significant **poverty.** The proportion of people living in poverty has been rising since 2000, partly due to the ongoing worldwide economic slowdown but also due to the derailment of many of North Carolina's backbone industries. As recently as 15 years ago, a high school graduate in small-town North Carolina could count on making a living wage in a mill or factory; nowadays those opportunities have dried up, and the poverty rate in 2011 was just over 16 percent. Even more distressing, the number of children living in poverty is just over 24 percent, and for children under age 6 climbing to 28 percent.

The northeastern quadrant of North Carolina is the most critically impoverished, which points to **financial inequality** correlating to race, as the region has a significant African American population. Broken down by ethnicity, the data reveal that 10 percent of urban and rural whites live in poverty, while 20-30 percent of rural and urban Latinos, African Americans, and Native Americans live in poverty.

Several hardworking organizations and activists are trying to alleviate the economic hardship found in North Carolina. National organizations like **Habitat for Humanity** (www.habitat.org) and regional groups like the **Southern Coalition for Social Justice** (http://southerncoalition.org) and the **Institute for Southern Studies** (www.southernstudies. org) bring community activism and research to the state. There are also excellent North Carolina-based advocates in groups such as the **North Carolina Rural Economic Development Center** (www.ncruralcenter.org), the **North Carolina Justice Center** (www.ncjustice. org), the **Black Family Land Trust** (www.bflt. org), and **Student Action with Farmworkers** (http://saf-unite.org).

People and Culture

DEMOGRAPHICS

The 10th most populous state in the union, North Carolina's population of 9.75 million residents is slightly larger than New Jersey and slightly smaller than Georgia. More than two-thirds of North Carolinians are white, primarily of German and Scottish-Irish descent, and not quite one-quarter are African American. The state's population is about 8.6 percent Latino, and has the seventh-largest Native American population of any state after California, Arizona, Oklahoma, New Mexico, Washington, and Alaska.

More than 40 percent of North Carolinians are between the ages of 25 and 59, but the older population is steadily rising, due in large part to the state's popularity with retirees. The majority—about 70 percent—of North Carolinians live in family groups, with married couples constituting about half of those, and married couples with children (not mutually exclusive data sets) making up almost one-quarter of households. Of the remaining one-third of the state's population who live in "nonfamily households"—that is, not with blood relatives or a legally recognized spouse—the vast majority are individuals living on their own. Unmarried couples, both straight and gay, have a much lower rate of cohabitation here than in more urban parts of the United States, but such households are common and accepted in the Triangle, Asheville, Charlotte, and other urban areas.

Native Americans

Many Americans have never heard of the **Lumbee people** despite the fact that they claim to be the largest Native American nation east of the Mississippi. This is in part due to the federal government's refusal to grant them official recognition, although the state of North Carolina does recognize them. The Lumbee are primarily based in and around Robeson County in the swampy southeastern corner of the state, their traditional home. In the Great Smoky Mountains, the town of Cherokee on the Qualla Boundary, which is Cherokee-administered land, is the governmental seat of the **Eastern Band of the Cherokee.** The Eastern Band are largely descended from those Cherokee people who escaped arrest during the deportation of the Southeast's Native Americans on the Trail of Tears in the 19th century, or who made the forced march to Oklahoma but survived and walked home to the mountains again. The Lumbee people and Cherokee people are both important cultural groups in North Carolina. Several other Native American communities are indigenous to the state as well; those recognized by the state are the **Waccamaw-Siouan, Occaneechi Band of the Saponi Nation, Haliwa-Saponi, Coharie, Sappony,** and **Meherrin.**

Latinos

North Carolina has one of the fastest-growing

HOW CAN YOU TELL A TAR HEEL?

the front page of the first issue of UNC's *The Tar Heel*

What manner of man is a North Carolinian? How can you tell a Tar Heel? What ingredients went into his making? Is he different, and if so, how and why? There is no slide-rule answer to these questions, but it may be interesting to explore them. The Tar Heel is not a distinct species, but he may have some distinguishing marks. [We are] independent, courageous, resourceful, democratic, gregarious and individualistic, although we would use plainer words than these Latin terms to describe ourselves.... There is a progressive strain in this Tar Heel, a realistic and resourceful determination to get ahead with the work for a better way of life for himself and his fellows.... There is often a kindness in the voice which covers a lot of humanity in its acceptance of all sorts and conditions of men.... But there is no pouring Tar Heels into a mold. The point is that we are by preference and habit individualists, or what we call "characters."

So much for our good side. Generally, we are liable to be pretty good folks, but we have a bad side too, and the truth is that we can be, when we take a notion or for no reason at all, as violent, ornery, cantankerous, stubborn, narrow and lazy as any people anywhere on earth, civilized or uncivilized. We cut and shoot one another at a rate not even equaled in the centers of urban civilization. True, we consider our violence too valuable to waste on outsiders and so confine it to ourselves.... Tar Heels hardly ever kill or maim anybody unless he is either an old friend or a close relative.

Blackwell P. Robinson, ed., *The North Carolina Guide*, UNC Press, 1955.

Latino populations in the United States, a community whose ranks have swelled since the 1990s, in particular as hundreds of thousands of **Mexican and Central American laborers** came to work in the agricultural, industrial, and formerly booming construction trades. Their presence in such large numbers makes for some unexpectedly quirky cultural juxtapositions, as in small rural towns that are now majority Latino, or in Charlotte, where the Latino population has made Roman Catholicism the most common religion.

Other Immigrants
Significant numbers of non-Latino immigrants also live in North Carolina. Charlotte

is a dizzying hodgepodge of ethnicities, where native Southerners live and work alongside **Asians, Africans,** and **Middle Easterners,** where mosques and synagogues and *wats* welcome worshipers just down the street from Baptist churches and Houses of Prayer. Many **Hmong** and other **Southeast Asian** immigrants have settled in the northern foothills and the Piedmont Triad, and the dense thicket of universities in the Triangle attracts academics from around the world.

RELIGION

As early as the 17th century, North Carolina's religious landscape foreshadowed the diversity we enjoy today. The first Christians in North Carolina were Quakers, soon followed by Anglicans, Presbyterians, Baptists, Moravians, Methodists, and Roman Catholics. Native American and African religions, present in the early colonial days, were never totally quashed by European influence, and Barbadian Sephardic Jews were here early on as well. All of these religions remain today, with enrichment by the presence of Muslims, Buddhists, and an amazing mosaic of other Christian groups.

North Carolina claims as its own one of the world's most influential modern religious figures, Billy Graham, who was raised on a dairy farm outside Charlotte and experienced his Christian religious awakening in 1934. After preaching in person to more people around the world than anyone in human history, and being involved with every U.S. president since Harry Truman, Billy Graham is now home in his native state, where he divides his time between Charlotte and Montreat, outside Asheville.

LANGUAGE

Few states can boast the linguistic diversity of North Carolina. North Carolina speech varies widely by region and even from county to county. These variations have to do with the historical patterns of settlement in a given area—whether Scots-Irish or German ancestry is common, how long Native American

languages survived after the arrival of the Europeans, the presence or lack of African influence—as well as other historical patterns of trade and communication.

Of our distinct regional accents, the **Outer Banks brogue** is probably the best known. Much like the residents of the Chesapeake islands in Maryland and Virginia, "Hoi Toiders," as Outer Bankers are jokingly called, because of how they pronounce the phrase "high tide," have a striking dialect that resembles certain dialects in the north of England. "I" is rounded into "oi," the *r* sound is often hard, and many distinctive words survive from long-ago English, Scottish, and Irish dialects. Not dissimilar is the Appalachian dialect heard through much of the mountains. The effect is more subtle than in the Outer Banks, but "oi" replaces "I" in Appalachian English too, and *r*'s are emphasized. A telltale sign of upcountry origins is the pronunciation of the vowel in words like bear and hair, which in the mountains is flattened almost inside-out so that the words are pronounced something like "barr" and "harr." This is similar to mountain accents in Tennessee, West Virginia, Virginia, and Kentucky.

Piedmont Carolinians, both white and black, have a wide spectrum of linguistic influences. The heart of the state has been a cultural and commercial crossroads since the days of the Great Wagon Road, which brought 18th-century white settlers into the Southern backcountry; the magnetic influence of jobs in cigarette factories and textile mills drew rural Southerners from all over the region. The product of this linguistic mix-and-match is probably the closest thing in North Carolina to the generic Hollywood version of "the Southern accent," but Piedmont speech is far from homogenous within the region. For example, native central Carolinians are equally likely to call the Queen City "CHAR-lit" or "SHOLL-utt."

There are a great many smaller linguistic zones peppered throughout the state. Folks from up around the **Virginia border** in eastern North Carolina may have a distinctively

UNDERSTANDING LOCAL LINGO

North Carolina speech features delightful and sometimes perplexing regional vocabulary and grammar. Following are some of the common Carolinianisms most likely to stump travelers:

- **Bless your/his/her heart:** A complex declaration with infinitely varied intentions, interpreted depending on context or tone. In its most basic use, "Bless your heart," is a sincere thank-you for a favor or a kindness paid. It's also an exclamation of affection, usually applied to children and the elderly, as in, "You're *not* 92 years old! You are? Well, bless your heart." Frequently, though, hearts are blessed to frame criticism in a charitable light, as in, "Bless his heart; that man from New York don't know not to shout."

- **buggy:** a shopping cart, as at a grocery store.

- **carry:** convey, escort, give a ride to. "I carried my mother up to the mountains for her birthday."

- **cattywompus:** topsy-turvy, mixed up. Used especially in the Piedmont and farther west.

- **Coke:** any soft drink; may be called "pop" in the mountains.

- **Come back:** often uttered by shopkeepers as a customer leaves, not to ask them to return immediately, but simply an invitation to patronize the establishment again someday.

- **dinner:** the midday meal.

- **evening:** not just the twilight hours, but all the hours between about 3pm and nightfall.

- **ever-how:** however; similarly, "ever-when," "ever-what," and "ever-who."

- **fair to middling:** so-so, in response to "How you?"; a holdover term from North Carolina's moonshining days, the term originally applied to grading 'shine by examining bubbles in a shaken mason jar.

- **fixing:** about to or preparing to do something. "She's fixing to have a baby any day now."

- **holler:** hollow, a mountain cove.

- **Kakalak:** Carolina. (Also Kakalaky, Cakalack)

- **mash:** press, as a button. "I keep mashing the button, but the elevator won't come."

- **mess:** discombobulated, in a rut, not living right. "I was a mess until I joined the church."

- **might could/should/would:** could/should/would perhaps. "Looks like it's fixing to rain. You might should go roll up your car windows."

- **mommocked:** see *cattywompus*. Used especially on the Outer Banks and in rural southeastern North Carolina.

- **piece:** a vague measure of distance, as in, "down the road a piece" (a little ways down the road) or "a fair piece" (a long way).

- **poke:** a bag, such as a paper shopping bag. Used especially in the mountains.

- **reckon:** believe, think. Often used in interrogative statements that end in a falling tone, as in, "Reckon what we're having for dinner." (That is, "What do you suppose is for lunch?")

- **right:** quite, very. Variations include "right quick" (soon, hurriedly), "right much" (often), and "a right many" or "a right smart of" (a great quantity).

- **sorry:** worthless, lame, shoddy. "I wanted to play basketball in college, but I was too sorry of an athlete."

- **speck so:** "I expect so," or, "Yes, I guess that's correct."

- **supper:** the evening meal (as opposed to "dinner," the midday meal).

- **sy-goggling:** see *cattywompus, mommocked*. Used especially in the mountains.

- **ugly:** mean or unfriendly, spiteful. Sometimes referred to as "acting ugly." "Hateful" is a common synonym. The favorite Southern injunction that "God don't like ugly" does not mean that God wants us to be pretty, but rather that we should be nice.

- **wait on:** to wait for.

- **Y'all:** pronoun used to address any group of two or more people.

- **yonder:** over there.

- **Y'uns:** mountain variation of y'all.

Virginian accent. Listen for the classic telltale word *house.* Southside Virginians and their neighbors south of the state line will pronounce it "heause," with a flat vowel. **Cherokee English,** heard in the Smokies, combines the Appalachian sound with a distinctively Cherokee rhythm, while **Lumbee English,** spoken in and around Robeson County in the southeast, combines sounds somewhat like those of the Outer Banks or deep mountains with a wealth of unusual grammatical structures and vocabulary of unknown origin. Oft-cited examples are the Lumbee construction "be's," a present-tense form of "to be," and words like *ellick* for coffee and *juvember* for slingshot: "Get me some more ellick, please, if you be's going to the market." Residents of the **Sandhills** area, bounded by the Uwharries to the west, Sanford to the north, and Southern Pines to the southeast, have a highly unusual rhythm to their speech—a rapid, soft, almost filigreed way of talking, delivered in bursts between halting pauses. Down around Wilmington and south to the South Carolina state line, African American English, and to a lesser extent white English, have some of the inflections of the **Gullah language** of the Lowcountry. These are only a few of the state's dialects, and even these have subvariations. Old-timers can pinpoint geographical differences within these categories—whether a Lumbee speaker is from Prospect or Drowning Creek, for example, or whether a Banker is from Ocracoke or Hatteras.

Of course, English is hardly the only language spoken here. If you visit Cherokee, you'll see that many street and commercial signs bear pretty, twisty symbols in a script that looks like a cross between Khmer or Sanskrit and Cyrillic; **written Cherokee** uses the script famously devised by **Sequoyah** in the early 19th century. Cherokee also survives as a spoken language, mostly among the elders in traditional communities such as Snowbird, near Robbinsville, and many younger Cherokee people are determined to learn and pass on their ancestral tongue, but the small pool of speakers points to the slow death of the language. **Spanish** is widely spoken throughout the state as the Latino population continues to grow rapidly, and within Latino communities here are many national and regional dialects of Spanish. Some Central American immigrants who speak indigenous languages arrive unable to understand English or Spanish. Anyone who doubts that newcomers to this country are dedicated to the task of integrating into American society need only consider the incredibly difficult task faced by such immigrants, who must first learn Spanish before they can enroll in ESL programs to learn English.

The Arts

As much as North Carolinians like to brag about the beaches and mountains and college sports teams, it's the artists across the state who help North Carolina distinguish itself. There is an incredibly rich and complex cultural heritage here that has strong support from the North Carolina Arts Council and a vast network of local and regional arts organizations. These groups have supplied inspiration, financial and emotional support, and sustenance for generations of remarkable musicians, writers, actors, and other artists.

LITERATURE

Storytelling seems to come naturally to Southerners. From the master storytellers of Jack Tales in the Blue Ridge to the distinguished journalists we see every night on television, North Carolinians have a singular gift for communication. Thomas Wolfe was an Asheville native, and O. Henry, whose real name was William Sidney Porter, was born and raised in Greensboro. Tom Robbins (*Even Cowgirls Get the Blues*) was born in Blowing Rock. Charles Frazier (*Cold Mountain*) is from Asheville. Sarah Dessen (*Just Listen*) is from Chapel Hill. Kaye Gibbons, Lee Smith, Fred Chappell, Randal Kenan, and Clyde Edgerton, leading lights in Southern fiction, are all natives or residents of North Carolina. Also closely associated with the state are Carl Sandburg, David Sedaris, Armistead Maupin, and Betsy Byars, who have all lived here at some point in their lives. Arts programs focused on creative writing have sprung up across the state, imbuing the literary scenes in towns like Wilmington, Greensboro, Asheville, and Chapel Hill with talented undergraduate and graduate students and their professors. Notable writers teaching creative writing programs include poet A. Van Jordan, essayist David Gessner, and novelist and short story writer Jill McCorkle.

North Carolina has also given the world some of the giants of 20th-century journalism. Edward R. Murrow, Charles Kuralt, David Brinkley, and Howard Cosell were all sons of Carolina, and Charlie Rose carries their torch today.

MUSIC

It's hard to know where to begin in describing the importance of music to North Carolinians. With fiddlers conventions, renowned symphony orchestras, busy indie-rock scenes, and a thriving gospel-music industry, there is no escaping good music here. Since the earliest days of recorded country music, North Carolinians have shared their songs with the world. Charlie Poole and Wade Mainer were among the first to record, and became influential artists in the 1930s. By 1945 a banjo player named Earl Scruggs was helping create what would become the quintessential sound of **bluegrass** music, particularly his three-fingered picking style. Bluegrass greats like Del McCoury helped further define the sound. Today, bluegrass is alive and well in North Carolina; Steve Martin's collaboration with the Steep Canyon Rangers sells out concerts around the world and garners awards at every turn, and the late Doc Watson's annual **MerleFest** is still going strong. **Country** musicians like Ronnie Milsap, Donna

Fargo, Charlie Daniels, and Randy Travis made big names for themselves from the 1970s to the 1990s; more recently, Kellie Pickler and Scottie McCreery (of *American Idol* fame) and Eric Church have made waves on the country charts.

The growth of **jazz** and **funk** would be unimaginably different if not for a number of notable innovators that make North Carolina nearly as important as New Orleans to the development of these genres. John Coltrane was raised in High Point, Thelonious Monk was a native of Rocky Mount, Nina Simone hails from Tryon, and Dizzy Gillespie grew up just over the South Carolina state line but contributed greatly when he studied music in Laurinburg. On the funk side of the coin, what would the genre be without George Clinton, founder of Parliament and Parliament-Funkadelic? Saxophonist Maceo Parker and his brother, drummer Melvin Parker, played with Clinton and with South Carolina's favorite son and the Godfather of Soul, James Brown, to help develop the classic funk sound and influence the groove-driven side of **soul** music.

In North Carolina, you're never far from some good **gospel** music. On the coast, African American choirs blend spirituality and faith with showmanship and serious talent to perform beautiful inspired sets. In the mountains, you're more likely to find gospel quartets and old-time gospel music, which is more inspired by bluegrass and traditional music, at camp meetings and gospel sings on weekend nights. The state's Native American communities also have thriving gospel traditions of their own.

Artists that include James Taylor, Tori Amos, Clay Aiken, the Squirrel Nut Zippers, the Avett Brothers, Fred Durst (from Limp Bizkit), rapper and producer Jermaine Dupri, Corrosion of Conformity, Ben Folds Five, Daughtry, Southern Culture on the Skids, and Megafaun have all had a hand in shaping the state's musical legacy.

THEATER

Regional theater companies such as the venerable Flat Rock Playhouse near Hendersonville

© BILLY POTTER/COURTESY WILKES COMMUNITY COLLEGE

the Snyder Family Band performing at MerleFest

make great theater accessible in small towns and rural areas. Wilmington is home to Thalian Hall and the Thalian Association, a group founded in 1788 that was named the Official Community Theatre of North Carolina thanks to their long-running commitment to the arts in Wilmington. The North Carolina School for the Arts in Winston-Salem mints great actors and filmmakers, among other artists. The film and television industries have long recognized North Carolina as a hotbed of talent as well as a place with amazing locations to film at.

For some reason, **outdoor historical dramas** have long flourished in North Carolina. The most famous is North Carolina playwright Paul Green's *Lost Colony,* which has been performed every summer since 1937 on Roanoke Island, except during World War II when German U-boats lurked nearby. The Cherokee people depict emblematic episodes in their history in the outdoor drama *Unto These Hills,* in production since 1950. The community of Boone has presented *Horn in the West* since 1952 and it is joined by Valdese and several other communities in North Carolina in turning to performance tableaux to commemorate their heritage. It's especially important to note that among the characteristics of outdoor drama in North Carolina is the fact that the cast, crew, and often the producers and playwrights are members of the communities whose stories the plays tell.

ARTS AND CRAFTS

Folk art and studio craft show vitality in North Carolina. Several communities are known worldwide for their local traditions, and countless individual artists, studios, and galleries can be found across the state.

Seagrove, a miniscule town at the geographical center of the state, has been the home of hundreds of **potters** since the 18th century. What began as a commercial enterprise to turn out utilitarian products made for trade on the Great Wagon Road became an increasingly artistic form in the early 20th century. Skilled potters still work in Seagrove today; many of them descendants of founding members of

© JASON FRYE

Modern-day blacksmiths carry on this centuries-old tradition in North Carolina.

the community. Wilson, between Raleigh and Wilmington, was home to Vollis Simpson, a folk artists and maker of internationally admired whirligigs that were named the Official Folk Art of North Carolina.

Cherokee craft is an important aesthetic school comprising a wide range of techniques and media such as wood- and stone-carving, fiber arts, traditional weaponry, and avant-garde sculpture and painting. **Qualla Arts and Crafts Mutual,** located in the town of Cherokee, has a wonderful sales gallery that will dazzle lovers of fine craft.

Asheville is an epicenter of the arts, the heart of a vast community of artists that stretches throughout western North Carolina and includes such major folk schools as **John C. Campbell** in Brasstown, near the Georgia state line, and **Penland,** close to Tennessee in the northeastern mountains. In Asheville you can see and purchase an infinite variety of crafts that include handmade baskets, quilts, furniture, clothing, jewelry, and iron architectural elements. The **Southern Highland Craft Guild**

(www.southernhighlandguild.org), an old and accomplished organization, deserves a lot of the credit for the thriving health of the craft movement in western North Carolina. Its website has a great deal of information about contemporary master crafters and their work. On the coast, Wilmington, New Bern, Hatteras, and other towns have folk-art and fine-art artists and galleries.

As people become more accustomed to a world where almost every object we see and use was mass-produced far away, we develop an ever deeper appreciation for the depth of skill and aesthetic complexity that went into the production of everyday objects in past generations. North Carolinians have always been great crafters of utilitarian and occupational necessities. As you travel through the state, keep an eye out for objects that you might not immediately recognize as art—barns, fishing nets, woven chair bottoms—but that were made with the skill and artistry of generations-old traditions. In North Carolina, art is everywhere.

Food

You'll probably have heard of North Carolina's most famous specialties—**barbecue, Brunswick stew,** and **hush puppies**—but are you brave enough to venture deeper into the hinterlands of Carolina cooking? Few snacks are more viscerally craved by locals, and more revolting to non-Southerners, than **boiled peanuts.** The recipe is simple: Green peanuts are boiled in their shells in bulk in water as salty as the chef deems necessary. Once they're soft and slimy, the peanuts are dumped into a strainer and are ready to eat. All you need to make them is a big kettle and a fire, so boiled peanuts are often made and sold in small bags at roadside stands, primarily in the Lowcountry and coastal plain, but increasingly in the mountains as well. Often these roadside stands are themselves folk art, with handmade signs reading "Bolit P-Nuts Here," with a collection of carvings or sculptures for sale in the bed of a truck nearby. To eat a boiled peanut, pick it up by the ends with your thumb and forefinger and place it lengthwise between your front teeth. Gently crack open the shell—don't bite through it—and detach the halves. Pry off half of the shell, and nip or slurp the peanuts out as if you're eating an oyster (boiled peanuts often show up at Lowcountry oyster roasts). Toss the shell out the window—chances are you're driving as you eat—and have another. Be sure you have a lot of something to drink close at hand, because you'll soon get thirsty.

Many cultures have a recipe that makes thrifty use of the leftover meat scraps that are too small or too few or too disgusting to be served alone. For upper Piedmont Carolinians, particularly those of German ancestry raised in the wavy ribbon of towns between Charlotte and Winston-Salem, that delicacy is **livermush.** Some folks say that if you're from the Mid-Atlantic and are familiar with scrapple, you'll have a pretty good idea of what livermush is like; that's not true—livermush is much worse and tastes like some bitter combination

of burning hair and pepper. Under North Carolina law (really), livermush must contain at least 30 percent hog liver, which is supplemented with sundry scraps from hog heads, sometimes some skin, and cornmeal. At the factory, it's mashed up and cooked in loaves. In the kitchen, it's sliced and fried. You can eat it at breakfast like sausage, in a sandwich, or even on a stick if you go to the annual livermush festivals in Drexel and Shelby. Should you try it? Yes, at least a bite; plenty of people like it.

In the eastern part of the state, a similar aesthetic underlies the creation of **hog hash,** best made directly after an old-time hog killing, when the animal's organs are pulled steaming hot out of the carcass in the frosty fall morning. The liver, lungs, and a variety of other organs and appendages are dumped in a kettle with potatoes, a liquid base (broth, milk, or just water), and some vegetables and seasonings. Unlike livermush, hog hash is served in bowls or tubs as a dark, musky stew; it's not common.

Another food that you have to look pretty hard for is **dandoodle,** also called **tom thumbs,** seen in far northeastern North Carolina and the bordering Virginia counties. At hog-killing time, the animal's stomach is removed and stuffed with sausage and flavorings. It's then tied shut and hung in the smokehouse for seasoning with hickory smoke. Like livermush, dandoodle comes out in a sort of loaf shape, held together by the stomach membrane. Some people toss their tom thumbs in a pot to boil, either alone or with greens, while others slice them and lay them out with sliced boiled eggs.

Up in the Great Smoky Mountains, the early spring is the season for **ramps,** sometimes called skunk cabbage—very pungent wild onions that grow along creek beds in the deep mountains. They're another of those foods passionately defended by those who grew up eating them but are greeted with trepidation by outsiders. The reason they're feared by the uninitiated is their atomically powerful taste, which will emanate from every part of your body for days if the ramps are too strong or not prepared correctly. Ramps taste like a cross between regular onions, garlic, leeks, shallots, and kryptonite. When they're young, they're perfectly pungent—not too overwhelming, but still powerful enough to let you know they're in the dish. Folks skillet-cook them, fry them up in grease, boil them with fatback, or just chomp on them raw. For a special treat and a gentle introduction to ramps, stop in at the Stecoah Valley Center near Robbinsville and pick up a bag of the Smoky Mountain Native Plants Association's special cornmeal mix with dried ramps, and make yourself a skillet of deliciously tangy cornbread. You can also try them at the local ramps festivals held in Robbinsville and Cherokee in spring. A growing number of restaurants from Asheville to Wilmington are buying ramps and **morel mushrooms** from mountain foragers and preparing them every way from skillet fried to pickled, so ramp lovers can get a taste of this springtime mountain delicacy even on the coast.

You can read all about these and other acquired tastes at **NCFOOD** (www.ncfolk.org) or **Our State Eats** by *Our State* magazine (www.ourstate.com), two food blogs devoted to Carolina cooking, or on the **Southern Foodways Alliance** (www.southernfoodways. com) and **Dixie Dining** (www.dixiedining.com) websites.

Vegetarians and devotees of organic food, fear not; North Carolina is an unusually progressive state when it comes to healthy and homegrown grub. Nevertheless, if you want to avoid meat, you have to be cautious when ordering at a restaurant: Make sure the beans are made with vegetable oil rather than lard, ask if the salad dressing contains anchovies, beware of hidden fish and oyster sauce. Traditional Southern cooking makes liberal use of fatback (cured pork fat) and other animal products; greens are often boiled with a strip of fatback or a hambone, as are most soups and stews. Even pie crusts are still made with lard in many old-time kitchens.

In the major cities, you'll find organic grocery stores. Earth Fare and Whole Foods are the most common chains, but there are also plenty of small independent markets. Farmers markets and roadside stands are so plentiful that they almost have to fight for space. Visit the state Department of Agriculture's **North Carolina Farm Fresh** (www.ncfarmfresh.com) for directories of farmers markets and pick-your-own farms and orchards.

ESSENTIALS

Getting There

BY AIR

The state where air travel began has over 70 public airports, almost 300 privately owned airfields, and about 20 "fly-in" communities where residents share an airstrip and have their own hangar space. Nine airports have regularly scheduled passenger service, and two of them host international flights. The state's Department of Transportation estimates that more than 35 million people fly in and out of North Carolina every year. The main hubs are North Carolina's international airports in Charlotte, Greensboro, and Raleigh-Durham; Wilmington has more limited service.

The 8th busiest airport in the country, **Charlotte Douglas International Airport** (CLT, 5501 Josh Birmingham Pkwy., Charlotte, 800/359-2342, http://charmeck. org) has more than 730 daily departures and is served by dozens of airlines. There are non-stop flights to 140 U.S. cities as well as international flights to Latin America and the Caribbean, London, Frankfurt, Munich, and Toronto. Parking is abundant and inexpensive, with parking shuttle buses operating from 5am. **Raleigh-Durham International Airport** (RDU, 2400 W. Terminal Blvd., Morrisville, 919/840-2123, www.rdu.com),

located in Wake County about midway between Raleigh and Durham, has flights to most domestic hubs as well as London, Toronto, and Cancún, Mexico. Hourly and daily parking is available for reasonable rates within walking distance of the terminals and in satellite lots linked by shuttle buses. **Piedmont Triad Airport** (GSO, 1000 A Ted Johnston Pkwy., Greensboro, 336/665-5600, www.flyfrompti.com) serves the Greensboro and Winston-Salem area with flights to domestic destinations in the South, Midwest, and Mid-Atlantic.

There are several smaller airports around the state with regularly scheduled domestic passenger service, including **Wilmington International Airport** (ILM, 1740 Airport Blvd., Wilmington, 910/341-4125, www.flyilm.com), **Asheville Regional Airport** (AVL, 61 Terminal Dr., Fletcher, 828/684-2226, www.flyavl.com), and **Fayetteville Regional Airport** (FAY, 400 Airport Rd., Fayetteville, 910/433-1160, www.flyfay.com). **Pitt-Greenville Airport** (PGV, 400 Airport Rd., Greenville, 252/902-2025) has flights to Charlotte, and New Bern's **Coastal Carolina Regional Airport** (EWN, 200 Terminal Dr., New Bern, 252/638-8591) has flights to Atlanta and Charlotte. **Albert J. Ellis Airport** (OAJ, 264 Albert Ellis Airport Rd., Richlands, 910/324-1100), near Jacksonville and Richlands, has flights to Atlanta, Charlotte, and Washington DC.

Private aircraft can fly into any of over 75 regional, county, and municipal air strips statewide; **NC Airports Association** (www.ncairports.org) has a full list with phone numbers, website links, navigational information, airstrip specifications, and aerial photos. For historical reasons there are more municipal airports in the central and western parts of the state. When the state government started handing out grants for small public airstrips in the 1950s, there were already many surplus military airfields in the eastern part of the state, a legacy of World War II.

BY CAR

Several major interstate highways run through North Carolina, so if you're driving and would prefer that your trip be efficient rather than scenic, you've got several choices. From anywhere along the eastern seaboard, I-95 slices through the eastern third of the state, providing easy access to the beaches, which are mostly one or two hours east of I-95, and to the Triangle area, under an hour west of I-95 via U.S. 64, U.S. 70, or I-40. From the north, you might choose to veer southwest at Richmond, Virginia, on I-85; this is an efficient route to Durham and Chapel Hill as well as to the Triad and Charlotte regions.

I-40 starts in California and runs east to Wilmington. It's a fast road all the way through North Carolina, although weather—ice in the fall, winter, and spring, and fog any time of year—might slow you down considerably between Knoxville, Tennessee, and Asheville. U.S. 64 and I-77 connect North Carolina to the Midwest. I-77 cuts through the toe of Virginia, in the mountains, straight to Charlotte, while U.S. 64 meanders east through the Triangle all the way to Roanoke Island and the Outer Banks. From the Deep South or Texas, the best bet is probably I-20 to Atlanta, and from there I-85 to Charlotte, or U.S. 19 or U.S. 23 if you're going to the mountains.

There are no checkpoints at the state line to inspect vehicles for produce or animals, but sobriety checkpoints are established and staffed throughout the year.

BY BUS

Travel around North Carolina can be accomplished easily and cheaply by bus. **Greyhound** (800/231-2222, www.greyhound.com) offers daily service to many towns and cities, with the exception of the Outer Banks and mountain towns other than Asheville, but you can access that region via the Tennessee cities close to the state line, including Knoxville and Johnson City. Before you reserve bus tickets, be sure to check out special discounts on the Greyhound website. There are often regional promotions as well as special "Go Anywhere" fares as low as $29 each way with 14-day advance booking, for example, as well as regular discounts for students and seniors.

These days, the large buses used by Greyhound and its local subsidiaries are clean and comfortable, and if you make a reservation ahead of time, you can choose your seat. One word of caution is that some bus stations are located in seedy parts of town, so make sure taxi service is available at your destination station after dark.

BY TRAIN

Although it does not currently serve the mountains or the coast, **Amtrak** (800/872-7245, www.amtrak.com) is a great way to get to and around central North Carolina. The main New York-Miami *Silver Service* and *Palmetto* trains pass through North Carolina following the I-95 corridor. The New York-New Orleans *Crescent* stops at both Winston-Salem and Charlotte. The *Carolinian* runs from New York to Charlotte by way of Raleigh.

Getting Around

BY CAR

North Carolina's highway system, with the largest network of state-maintained roads in the country and a good interstate grid, provides access to the whole state. I-95 crosses north-south, demarcating the eastern third of the state, and I-85 runs northeast-southwest from north of the Triangle area through Charlotte. I-40 is the primary east-west route, from Wilmington through the Smoky Mountains to Knoxville, Tennessee. The highest speed limit, which applies to some rural interstates and four-lane roads, is 70 mph. Highways in developed areas have much lower speed limits, and in residential areas it's a good idea to keep it under 25 mph.

You can take your pick of car-rental agencies at the major airports at Charlotte, Winston-Salem, and Raleigh-Durham; there are fewer choices at smaller regional airports. There are also car-rental pickup and drop-off offices in many towns. Rental car companies in North Carolina include Alamo (800/462-5266, www.alamo.com), Avis (877/222-9075, www.avis.com), Budget (800/218-7992, www.budget.com), Dollar (800/800-4000, www.dollar.com), Enterprise (800/261-7331, www.enterprise.com), Hertz (800/654-3131, www.hertz.com), National (877/222-9058, www.nationalcar.com), Thrifty (800/847-4389, www.thrifty.com), and Triangle Rent-A-Car (800/643-7368, www.trianglerentacar.com). To rent a

car you must be at least 25 years old, and have both a valid driver's license and a credit card, although some companies will accept a cash security deposit in lieu of credit.

Driving to and through the Outer Banks can be a bit complicated, depending on your destination, because there are not many bridges. The northern banks are linked to the mainland by bridges between Point Harbor and Kitty Hawk, and from Manns Harbor over Roanoke Island to just south of Nags Head. There are no bridges to Hatteras, and none until you get all the way to the southern end of the banks, where bridges link Morehead City and Cedar Point to the towns along Bogue Banks. The state's excellent ferry system connects the Outer Banks to the mainland; it's a fun way to travel. Detailed information is available from the state Department of Transportation (www.ncdot.gov/ferry). Several ferries link mainland points across sounds and rivers, while ferries from Currituck to Knotts Island, and from both Swan Quarter and Cedar Island to Ocracoke, will carry you to the Outer Banks.

On the other side of the state, driving in the Great Smoky Mountains and Blue Ridge can be difficult in bad weather, and roads can be icy in winter. The major interstates that cross the mountains are fast, and if you're traveling from one major town to another, U.S. 19, U.S. 74, and U.S. 421 are also fast. On smaller highways, count on much slower traveling. The

DRIVING TRAILS

The state of North Carolina and a variety of regional organizations have created a wonderful network of automobile "trails"– thematic itineraries showcasing North Carolina's treasures. Check out the destinations on this sampling of trails.

- **Asheville Ale Trail:** http://asheville-aletrail.com
- **Blue Ridge Music Trails:** www.blueridgemusic.org
- **Cherokee Heritage Itinerary:** www.ncfolk.org
- **Cherokee Heritage Trails:** www.cherokeeheritagetrail.org
- **Civil War Traveler:** www.civilwartraveler.com
- **Core Sound Itinerary:** www.ncfolk.org
- **Discover Craft North Carolina:** www.discovercraftnc.org
- **Family Frolic in Winston-Salem:** http://visitwinstonsalem.com/Family
- **Haw River Wine Trail:** www.hawriverwinetrail.com
- **Historic Albemarle Tour** (northeast coast): www.historicalbemarletour.org
- **Homegrown Handmade Art Roads and Farm Trails:** www.homegrownhandmade.com
- **North Carolina Scenic Byways:** www.ncdot.gov/travel/scenic
- **North Carolina Wine Country:** www.visitncwinecountry.com
- **Pottery Itinerary for the Seagrove Area:** www.ncfolk.org
- **Quilt Trails of Western North Carolina:** www.quilttrailswnc.org
- **Trail of Tears National Historic Trail, North Carolina Chapter:** www.arch.dcr.state.nc.us/tears
- **Western North Carolina Cheese Trail:** http://wnccheesetrail.org
- **Yadkin Valley Wine Country:** www.yadkinvalleywinecountry.com

Blue Ridge Parkway, while geographically direct, is very slow. The maximum speed is 45 mph, but there are few stretches of the Parkway where it's safe to drive that fast; add to that the frequent braking of sightseers and traffic can crawl. Numbered roads in the mountains are often similar, with surprise hairpin turns or narrow cliff-side shoulders. Allow plenty of time to get from point to point; on some roads it'll take you an hour to cover 20 miles. In the mountains you have to take it slow and be alert to weather and wildlife. If you find a local driver tailgating you, find a place to pull over and allow the faster drivers to pass.

Highway Safety

Write "*HP" (*47) on a sticky note and affix it to your dashboard. That's the direct free hotline to the North Carolina Highway Patrol, which will send help if you're trouble. North Carolinians don't hesitate to report aggressive, reckless, or drunk motorists to the highway patrol, and you might be reported by another driver if you're tailgating, speeding, weaving, or driving aggressively. What passes for normal driving in many parts of the United States is regarded as aggressive driving in the South.

Pull well off the road and turn on your hazard lights if you have an accident. If you can't safely pull your vehicle out of traffic, at least get away from the roadway. A distressing number of motorists with disabled vehicles as well as pedestrians are struck and killed by cars every year.

Some rules to remember while driving in North Carolina: Wearing your seat belt is required by law; child safety seats are mandatory for anyone under age 8 or weighing less than 80 pounds; and if it's raining hard enough to need windshield wipers, you must also turn your headlights on.

Weather Considerations

If you're driving in the mountains in the morning or at night, you may run into heavy **fog.** Because the clouds perch on and around mountaintops, you may find yourself in clear weather one moment and only seconds later in a fog with little visibility. It can be dangerous and frightening, but if this happens, slow down, keep an eye on the lines on the road, watch for other cars, and put on your low beams. As in any kind of bad weather, it's always best to find a safe place to pull off the road and wait for the weather to improve. Fog can dissipate as quickly as it appears.

In the winter you might encounter icy roads in any part of the state, and up in the mountains you might hit **ice and snow** three seasons of the year. Many Southerners on the coast and in the Piedmont tend to panic when snow is forecast; folks in the mountains manage to keep their wits about them no matter the weather. In anticipation of a half-inch dusting of snow, schools and businesses may close, fleets of sand and salt trucks hit the highway, and residents mob the grocery stores. This overreaction to snow makes the roads a little safer because many folks are more likely to stay home, but those who do drive in winter weather are less likely to know how to drive on ice than the average Yankee or Midwesterner. That can make the roads hazardous, so even if you are an experienced snow driver, stay alert.

While North Carolinians from the mountains are more experienced at driving in snowy or icy weather, the roads themselves can be dangerous. The safest plan is to avoid driving in the mountains in bad weather. If you must go, keep in mind that mountain roads, even highways, may close—especially those maintained by the National Park Service, including the Blue Ridge Parkway and the roads in Great Smoky Mountains National Park. The National Park Service offers the following advice: "When driving downhill on slippery mountain roads, shift to a lower gear (2, 1, or L on automatic transmissions) to avoid using brakes more than necessary. Leave extra room between you and the vehicle in front of you. Be aware that icy sections persist on mountain roads even when the weather is warm in the lowlands."

Wildlife on the Road

A final note about highway travel: Be conscious of wildlife. Deer, rabbits, turtles, foxes, coyotes, raccoons, and opossums litter the highways. Head-on collisions with deer can be fatal to both species, and smaller animals die because drivers are going too fast to avoid them. If you see an injured animal and are able to help it without putting yourself in danger, you'll find a phalanx of wildlife rehabilitators throughout the state to give it the care it needs.

The large number of deer in urban and rural areas makes them frequent victims of highway accidents. In clear weather when there's not much oncoming traffic, use your high beams so that you'll see them from farther away. If you see a deer cross the road in front of you, remember that they usually travel in small herds, and there may be several more waiting to jump out.

Road Etiquette

Certain informal rules of road etiquette apply in North Carolina, and they help make driving less stressful. North Carolina drivers willingly let others vehicles get in front of them, whether merging onto the highway or exiting a parking lot. Wave to say thanks when someone lets you in; positive reinforcement helps keep these habits alive. Folks will often wave at drivers in oncoming traffic on two-lane country roads, and there is an expectation of a quick wave from drivers and pedestrians as well. It's not a big production; simply lift two or three fingers off the steering wheel. A general rule of thumb is that if you're able to discern the facial features of someone outside your car, waving to that person is appropriate.

Drivers are legally obligated to pull over to let emergency vehicles pass. There's also an old tradition of pulling over to allow funeral processions to pass. Very few drivers are willing to merge into or cross a train of cars headed for a funeral, but in rural areas you will still see drivers pulling all the way off the road and waiting for a procession to pass before resuming driving. It's meant as a gesture of respect to the deceased and the mourners.

In all of these situations, safety should be the top priority. You don't need to wave or make eye contact with someone you feel is threatening, and don't pull off the road if there's no safe place to do so. But if you show courtesy to other drivers when you're able, you'll find that traffic karma will work its way back around to you when it's needed.

BY BUS

Municipal bus services operate in larger towns and some of the more popular tourist areas. In Asheville, **Riverfront Bus Tours** (828/252-8474 www.riverlink.org) offers historical tours along the French Broad and Swannanoa Rivers. **Hatteras Tours** (www.hattarastours. com, 252/986-2995) offers narrated tours of the islands of the Outer Banks, with a focus on the region's colorful history. There are ghost tours, Christian tours, farm tours, home and garden tours, Civil War history tours, ecology tours, and many other specialized tours, as well as tours of historic sites within many cities and towns; see www.visitnc.com to search for bus tours by town, region, or keyword. The state **Department of Transportation** (www. ncdot.gov/nctransit) maintains an index of information on the state's 99 public transportation systems, including those that serve rural counties.

BY BICYCLE

Before the Wright brothers made history as the first aviators, they were bicycle men. With its temperate climates, abundance of scenic roads, and full spectrum of terrain, North Carolina is bicycling heaven. There are hundreds of organized bicycling events every year, many of them in support of charities, and they welcome participants from all over. The most popular bike events are held spring to fall, including a six-day Ocracoke Vacation Tour from New Bern to the tip of the Outer Banks, regular scenic rides through wine country, and rides along the Blue Ridge that include a five-day bicycling vacation starting in Blowing Rock.

Each month except December has as many as a dozen public cycling events, including January's New Year's Day Breakfast Ride in Jacksonville, February's Frostbite Tour in Raleigh, and March's Rumba on the Lumber

5K Run and Bike Ride in Lumberton. In April there's the annual Circle-the-Bald Bike Ride, starting in Hayesville, and in May, Wilkesboro's Burn 24 Hour Challenge, a team relay endurance challenge. June has bicycling events as part of the North Carolina Blueberry Festival in Burgaw; July has North Wilkesboro's Hurt, Pain, and Agony Century Race; and August has a Beginner Skills Bicycling Camp in Asheville. In late September is the state-spanning Annual Mountains to the Coast Ride that even goes to the islands of the Outer Banks by ferry; approximately 1,000 cyclists take part. In October there's Rutherfordton's Tour de Pumpkin, and in November, the North Carolina Horse Country Tour. For a full roster of events, see the official **Calendar of Bicycling Events** (www.ncdot.gov/bikeped/bicycle/events).

Baggage cars on **Amtrak**'s *Piedmont* trains are equipped with bicycle racks; call 800/872-7245 to reserve bike space on a train. You can also take your bicycle on any of the seven **North Carolina Ferries** (800/293-3779, www.ncdot. gov/ferry).

BY TRAIN

North Carolina has good rail connections among the major cities in the central part of the state. **Amtrak** (800/872-7245, www.am-trak.com) serves North Carolina with its *Silver, Carolinian, Crescent,* and *Palmetto* trains; cities served include Raleigh and Durham, High Point, Winston-Salem, Gastonia, Kannapolis, and Charlotte. *Piedmont* trains connect Raleigh to Charlotte twice daily with stops in several Piedmont towns in between.

BY FERRY

For hundreds of years, ferries were a crucial link between points on North Carolina's coast, and they still provide an essential service today. The **North Carolina Department of Transportation's Ferry Division** (877/293-3779, www.ncdot.gov/ferry) operates seven primary ferry routes along the coast. All ferries have restrooms, and some can accommodate cars and allow pets. Commercial ferries also operate throughout the coastal region.

Conduct and Customs

GREETINGS

Common courtesy, such as saying "please" and "thank you," being deferential to the elderly, and demonstrating concern for others, is hardly proprietary to the South. No matter where you're from, chances are your parents raised you to "act like folks," as people say here. The difference is that in North Carolina and elsewhere in the South, manners are somewhat more ritualized.

If you're unfamiliar with Southern ways, the thing you may find strangest is the friendliness of strangers. When passing a stranger on the sidewalk or in a corridor, riding together in an elevator, or even washing hands in the restroom, eye contact and a quick greeting are usually in order. Most common greetings are "Hey," "How you doing," and "How you," spoken as a statement rather than a question. The reply is usually equally casual: "Doing good, how about you," pronounced with just four syllables, "Doin' good, 'bout you," again spoken as a statement rather than a question. Often that's the end of the conversation, although passengers on elevators sometimes wish each other a good day when one gets out. In these encounters, eye contact needn't be lingering, there's no expectation of false pleasantries, and there is certainly no obligation to engage someone who makes you uncomfortable.

It's standard courtesy in a retail or similarly casual transaction to inquire as to the well-being of the person serving you. It takes little time, especially when delivered in the spoken shorthand most Southerners use. For instance, a cashier at McDonalds in another part of the country might greet you with "What would you like?" or simply wait for your order and not speak until asking for your money. The transaction here would more likely start with the "How you," "Doin' good, 'bout you," exchange. With that two- or three-second dialogue, a bit of human warmth and mutual respect is shared.

It's expected that people hold doors open for each other and thank each other for doing so. In addressing someone elderly that you don't know well, the standard courtesy is to use a title, Mr. or Ms. with the last name, or in friendlier situations, Mr. or Ms. the first name. The South was way ahead of the curve in adopting the "Ms." designation; Southerners have always pronounced both "Mrs." and "Miss" as "miz." North Carolinians will likely address you as ma'am or sir regardless of your age; it doesn't mean they think you're old.

TIPPING

Besides restaurant servers, tip motel and hotel housekeeping staff, bartenders, cab drivers, bellhops, redcaps, valet parking staff, and other service workers. Standard tipping rates are 20 percent for meals, 15 percent for a taxi ride, and $1 per piece of luggage for a redcap or porter, although tipping extra for good service is always gracious and appropriate.

Tips for Travelers

GAY AND LESBIAN TRAVELERS

North Carolina offers no legal protection against discrimination based on sexual orientation or gender identity. The effects of the landmark 2013 Supreme Court decision on the Defense of Marriage Act have yet to play out. The state's sodomy law, which applied to straights and gays alike, was struck down in 2003, but there hasn't been much progress since. Hate-crimes statutes do not address violence targeting victims because of their sexual orientation or gender identity. Despite all this, don't close the book on North Carolina. While the laws may be retrogressive, the people are not; much of North Carolina is gay-friendly.

Despite being a red state, North Carolina has a strong purple streak. Metropolitan areas have active and open queer communities with numerous organizations and social groups, publications, human rights advocacy services, and community centers. Like anywhere in the United States, smaller and more rural communities are less likely to be gay-friendly, although there are exceptions and pleasant surprises. As a general rule, a same-sex couple will attract little attention holding hands on Durham's 9th Street, Asheville's Patton Avenue, or Weaver Street in Carrboro, but they may not be received warmly at the Big Al's Shuckin' Shack in Bay Creek Waters (not a real place, but you get the idea).

Gay, lesbian, bisexual, and transgendered travelers planning to visit North Carolina can learn a great deal about community resources and activities at **QNotes** (www.q-notes.com), **Carolina Purple Pages** (www.carolinapurplep-ages.com) which serves Charlotte, Asheville, and the Triangle, **North Carolina Pride** (www.ncpride.org), and **NC Gay Travel** (http://ncgaytravel.com).

SENIOR TRAVELERS

North Carolina has attracted a tremendous number of retirees in recent years, especially in the mountains and coast. It's also an increasingly popular destination for older travelers. For those who want to visit the state through organized programs, **Elderhostel** (www.roadscholar.org) is a great choice. Tours and classes are available throughout the state; the offerings in the mountains are particularly rich, with a great variety of courses and hands-on workshops about Appalachian culture and crafts. The North Carolina chapter of the **AARP** (866/389-5650, www.aarp.org/nc) is a good resource for senior issues and information. **VisitNC** (800/847-4862, www.visitnc.com) can also answer questions about activities and accessibility.

WOMEN TRAVELERS

Women from other parts of the country might find male strangers' friendliness a little disconcerting, but keep in mind that while some of them may be flirting with you, it's just as likely that they are simply being courteous. When a Southern man holds a door open for you, offers to help you carry something, or even calls you "honey," "darlin'," or "dear heart," it usually implies no ulterior motives and isn't intended to be condescending; he's probably just showing that he was raised up right. Again, manners should never preclude safety, so if some sketchy character is coming on to you in a way that gives you the creeps, trust your instincts.

TRAVELERS WITH DISABILITIES

Access North Carolina (800/689-9090, TDD 919/733-5924, www.ncdhhs.gov) is an excellent up-to-date guide on the accessibility of hundreds of cultural, recreational, historical, environmental, and commercial sites of interest and a goldmine for travel planning. Download a copy or phone to ask for the current edition, published by the state Department of Health and Human Services. The guide is set up by region and county, and sites and venues are described and rated in terms of accessibility.

Health and Safety

CRIME

As nice a place as North Carolina is, it's not immune to crime. Common sense about safety applies, particularly for women. Lock your doors immediately when you get into the car, park in well-lit areas as close as possible to your destination, and don't hesitate to ask a security guard or other trustworthy type to see you to your car. Don't carry too much cash on you. Pepper spray might save your life if you're attacked, whether by a person or by a bear.

Note that 911 emergency phone service is available everywhere in the state, but cell phone signals are not dependable everywhere. The deep mountains and more remote parts of western North Carolina and isolated stretches of the coast are more likely to have cell-phone dead zones.

SPECIAL WEATHER CONCERNS
Hurricanes

Hurricanes are a perennial danger, but luckily there tends to be plenty of warning when one is approaching. Evacuation orders should always be heeded, even if they are voluntary. It's also a good idea to leave sooner rather than later to avoid being trapped in traffic when the storm hits. The state **Department of Crime Control and Public Safety** (www.nccrimecontrol.org) posts a map online every year showing evacuation routes. You'll also see evacuation routes marked along the highways.

Tornadoes

Tornadoes can happen in any season and have killed people here in recent years. Pay close attention to tornado watches and warnings, and don't take chances: Find a safe place to shelter until the danger is over.

Rip Currents

More than 100 people die every year on U.S. beaches because of rip currents. Also called riptides, these dangerous currents can occur on any beach and can be very difficult to identify by sight. In rip current conditions, channels of water flow swiftly out toward deep water, and even if you are standing in relatively shallow water, you can suddenly be swept under and out into deep water. Rip current safety tips are available on the National Oceanic and Atmospheric Administration's National Weather Service website (www.ripcurrents. noaa.gov). Among their advice: "Don't fight the current. Swim out of the current, and then to shore. If you can't escape, float or tread water. If you need help, call or wave for assistance." Heed riptide warnings, and try to swim within sight of a lifeguard. Even good swimmers can drown in a rip current, so if you have any doubts about your swimming abilities or water conditions, play it safe and stay close to shore.

ANIMAL THREATS

There are a handful of dangerous creatures across the state, ranging in size from microscopic to monstrous, that can pose risks to health and safety. Be on the lookout for mean bugs: **Ticks** can carry Lyme disease and Rocky Mountain spotted fever, both serious and lingering conditions. Most likely to climb on you if you are walking through brush or bushes but liable to be lurking about anywhere, ticks come in many sizes and shapes, from barely visible pinpoint-size to that thing that looks like a grape hanging off your dog's neck. Wear insect repellent if you're going to be tramping around outside, and check your body and your travel companions thoroughly—your clothing as well as your skin—for stowaways. They'll attach themselves to any soft surface on your body, but they particularly like people's heads, often latching on to the scalp an inch or so behind the ears. If you find a tick on you or a human or canine companion, don't remove it roughly, no matter how freaked out you are. Yanking can leave the tick's head buried in your skin, increasing the risk of infection. Grasp the tick in a pinching motion, and pull slowly but firmly. You may have to hang on for several moments, but eventually it will decide to let go. Dab the bite with antiseptic, and over the next several weeks be alert for a bull's-eye-shaped irritation around the bite and for flu-like symptoms such as fever, achiness, malaise, and fatigue. If you have any of these signs, visit your doctor for a blood test.

Mosquitoes can carry West Nile virus, La Crosse encephalitis, and eastern equine encephalitis. Wear insect repellent and clothing that covers your arms and legs to avoid bites. Although not disease vectors, **fire ants** are among the state's most feared insects. It's easy to stumble onto one of their nests, and before you realize what you've stepped in, they can be swarming up your legs and biting you. Certainly this is a painful and frightening experience, but it's also potentially dangerous if you're allergic to bees. There have been documented cases in recent years of adult humans being swarmed and killed by fire ants. Watch where you step, and keep an eye out for areas of disturbed ground and turned-up soil. Sometimes their nests look like conventional anthills, sometimes like messy piles of dirt, and other times just soft spots on the ground.

Another reason to mind where you tread: snakes. The vast majority of snakes in North Carolina are harmless and shy, but we do have a few pit vipers. **Copperheads** are quite common in every part of the state and in wooded or semiwooded terrain—even in backyards, where they can lurk in bushes and leaf piles,

under porches and in storage sheds, and even in the walls of a house. They have a gorgeous pattern of light and dark brown splotches, which makes them incredibly difficult to spot against the ground in fall. Copperheads are usually less than three feet long. Their bite is poisonous but usually not fatal.

Found in the eastern half of the state and up into the Sandhills, **cottonmouths**—also called water moccasins—are very dangerous. They range in color from reddish brown to black, can grow up to 5.5 feet long, and are easily mistaken for harmless water snakes (and vice versa). They sometimes venture into the woods and fields, but cottonmouths are most commonly seen on or near water. Be especially careful walking along creek beds or in riverside brush. When threatened, they display the inside of their mouths, a startling and beautiful cottony white. Their bite is potentially lethal.

Coral snakes are endangered in North Carolina, but if you're going to be in the woods in the southeastern quarter of the state, keep an eye out. These jewel-toned snakes are generally small and slim, rarely more than a couple of feet long. Like the harmless scarlet king snake and scarlet snake, coral snakes have alternating bands of red, yellow, and black. The way to tell coral snakes from their harmless kin is to note the order of colors. On coral snakes, the yellow bands separate the black and the red, whereas on their imitators, red and black touch. An adage advises, "Red and black, friend of Jack; red and yellow, kill a fellow." Coral snakes can also be identified by their sinister black snouts, making them look like cartoon burglars, whereas scarlet snakes and scarlet king snakes have red clown noses. That's a lot to remember in that instant of panic when you notice a coil of red and yellow and black stripes at your feet looking up at you testily. Rather than stopping to figure out if the snake is friend or foe, it's better just to step away fast. Coral snakes' venom works on its prey's respiratory system, and it can kill humans. They're cousins of cobras and are some of the most beautiful snakes in these parts, but locals fear them more intensely than the huge, lumpy-headed, tusky-fanged vipers that appear more threatening.

There are also three poisonous native rattlesnakes: The **eastern diamondback rattlesnake** is the largest of rattlesnakes and can grow to nearly six feet long and as fat around as an adult human's arm. They are extremely dangerous—powerful enough to catch and eat rabbits, and willing, to kill a person. Eastern diamondbacks are rare but can be found in the southeastern sandy swamp counties. Also large are **canebrake rattlers,** more formally known as timber rattlers. They are found throughout the state, including the mountains. Their bite can be fatal to humans. To make them even scarier, they too can grow to nearly six feet in length, and in cold weather they like to congregate in large numbers to hibernate. **Pygmy rattlesnakes** are found along the state's coastline, up into the Sandhills, and around Crowder's Mountain. Generally up to about a 1.5 feet long, pygmies are also venomous.

Alligators are incredible creatures, scaly submarines that can exceed 15 feet snout to tail (females generally mature at around 10 feet) and can weigh 1,000 pounds, with a steel-trap maw of 75-80 fangs. They are found through much of eastern North Carolina, as far north as Merchants Millpond State Park near the Virginia border, but they are most common from Wilmington south. You don't have to trek into the depths of a swamp to see gators; they like to sun themselves on golf courses, next to roadside drainage ditches, even in yards that adjoin fresh water. Their behavior is deceptive, because they seem to spend 90 percent of their time in a motionless stupor; but they can awaken and whirl around to grab you before you have time to back away. They also spend much of their time submerged, sometimes entirely underwater, and more often drifting just below the surface with only their nostrils and brow ridges visible. Be aware of floating logs as they may have teeth attached. Alligators will gladly eat dogs that venture too close, so it goes without saying that small children should never be allowed to wander alone

near potential alligator habitats. An adult alligator can kill an adult human, and even the cute little ones will be only too happy to help themselves to your foot, so don't tempt fate for the sake of a photo or a closer look. If you're determined to get a close-up picture, visit one of the state's aquariums.

Bear attacks are rare and usually defensive, but considering that the creatures can weigh up to 800 pounds, caution would seem to be indicated. They are present in the woods in various parts of the state, especially up in the mountains and in the deep swamps and pocosins along the coast. They're quite shy and apt to gallop into the brush if they see a human coming. They will investigate potential meals, though, so securing your food when camping is crucial. If your car is nearby, lock the food in it; otherwise, hoist it into a tree with a rope, too high to reach from the ground and out of reach from the tree trunk. The National Park Service recommends the following course of action if a bear approaches you. First, try backing away slowly. If the bear follows, stand your ground. If it continues to menace you, try to scare it: Make yourself look bigger and more threatening by standing on a rock or next to your companions. Try waving sticks and throwing rocks. In the extremely unlikely event that you actually find yourself in hand-to-hand combat with a bear, remember the Park Service's advice to "fight back aggressively with any available object." Your chances of seeing a bear in North Carolina, much less being threatened by one, are pretty slim.

DISEASES AND NATURAL THREATS

Among the invisible villains here is **giardia,** a single-celled protozoan parasite that can be contracted by drinking untreated water. Hikers and campers should avoid drinking from streams unless they first boil the water vigorously for at least one minute. Filtering water with a filter of 0.1 to 1 micron absolute pore size or chemically treating it with iodine or chlorine is less reliable than thorough boiling.

There's a fairly high incidence of **rabies** in

North Carolina's raccoons, bats, foxes, groundhogs, and skunks. If you're bringing a pet into the state, be sure that its vaccinations, including rabies, are up-to-date. If you plan to go hiking with your dog, it may even be wise to bring a copy of its rabies vaccination certificate in case you have to prove its immunity. If you are bitten by a wild animal, seek medical help immediately, even if you're out in the woods. Rabies is deadly to humans and it's extremely important to start treatment immediately.

HEALTH PRECAUTIONS
Emergencies
As elsewhere the United States, calling 911 in North Carolina will summon medical help, police, or fire fighters. On the highway, blue road signs marked with an "H" point the way to hospitals, but if you're experiencing a potentially critical emergency, it's best to call 911 and let the ambulance come to you. There are plenty of rural places in the state where cellphone coverage is spotty to nonexistent, so if you have a medical condition from which an emergency could arise, keep this in mind.

Summer Weather
Heat, humidity, and air pollution often combine in the summer to create dangerous conditions for children, the elderly, and people with severe heart and lung conditions. Even if you're young and healthy, don't take chances in the heat. Carry drinking water with you, avoid exertion and being outside in the hottest part of the day, and stay in the shade. Even young healthy people can die from the heat. Remember that even if it doesn't feel very warm outside, children and pets are in grave danger when left in cars. Temperatures can rise to fatal levels very quickly inside closed vehicles, even when it's not terribly hot outside.

Information and Services

MONEY
For international travelers, currency-exchange services can be found in the big cities at some major banks and at currency-exchange businesses. Numerous money-transfer services, from old familiars like Western Union to a multitude of overseas companies, are easily accessible. The easiest place to wire or receive money is at a grocery store—most have Western Union or a proprietary wiring service—or at a bank. Banking hours vary by location and chain, but most are closed on Sunday and federal holidays. ATMs are located at most bank branches as well as in many grocery stores and convenience stores.

COMMUNICATIONS AND MEDIA
Newspapers and Radio
North Carolina has several major newspapers, the largest of which is the Pulitzer Prize-winning *Charlotte Observer* (www. charlotteobserver.com). In addition to the print edition, the *Observer* has extensive online-only content for travelers. The Raleigh *News & Observer* (www.newsobserver.com) serves the Triangle area and much of central Carolina. Other prominent newspapers include the Wilmington *Star-News* (www.starnewsonline. com) and the Asheville *Citizen-Times* (www. citizen-times.com). Alternative papers like the *Mountain Xpress* (www.mountainx.com) and the Triangle-area *Independent Weekly* (www. indyweek.com), available in print and online, cover the state's counterculture. Among the many local and regional radio stations is a number of NPR affiliates. There are few parts of the state where you won't be able to tune in to a clear NPR signal.

Magazines
Our State magazine (www.ourstate.com) is a widely distributed monthly that tells the stories of the people, places, and history across North

Carolina. As a travel resource, it will give you a feel for the people you're likely to encounter, but it will give you an even better idea of places to eat and towns you may not have thought to visit. Their website has an extensive collection of archived stories arranged by topic. In most larger cities in North Carolina it isn't hard to find magazines covering the local arts scene or guiding area parents to the best the town has to offer for kids. Look at news racks outside grocery stores and on street corners to pick up free publications like **North Brunswick Magazine** in and around Brunswick County; **Salt, Wilma!** and **Encore** in Wilmington; and **O.Henry Magazine** in Greensboro.

Internet Access

Internet access is widespread. Coffee shops are always a good place to find Wi-Fi, usually free but sometimes for a fee. A few small towns have free municipal wireless access. Most chain motels and major hotels offer free wireless access, and smaller hotels and bed-and-breakfasts often do too. This is true for some remote areas as well The deep mountains are the most difficult place to get a reliable Internet connection, but you'll probably be able to get online at your place of lodging or the coffee shop in town.

Cell Phones

Cell phone coverage is not consistent across North Carolina. You'll get a signal in all of the cities and most areas in between. You may hit dropout spots in central North Carolina, but there aren't many. On the other hand, service can be spotty in the eastern and western parts of the state. Up in the mountains, you may have a good signal on one side of a ridge and none on the other. Driving along the Blue Ridge Parkway, you'll find that signals come and go. This is also true on the coast and in rural eastern North Carolina. Along the sounds, and

certainly on the Outer Banks, there are plenty of areas where you could drive 20 miles before finding any reception. Spotty cell-phone coverage is a safety issue; if you're treed by a bear or run out of gas on a backwoods track, 911 may be unreachable.

MAPS AND VISITOR INFORMATION

Among the best sources for travel information in North Carolina is the state's tourism website, **VisitNC** (www.visitnc.com). They maintain an up-to-date list of festivals and events, tours and trails, and almost anything else you might want to know. Also excellent is the magazine **Our State** (www.ourstate.com), available at grocery stores, drugstores, and bookshops. Their website monitors upcoming events as well.

North Carolina Welcome Centers, located at several major highway entry points to the state, are sources for more free brochures and maps than one person could carry. They are located at the Virginia state line on I-77 near Mount Airy, on I-85 in Warren County, and on I-95 in Northampton County; at the Tennessee state line on I-26 in Madison County and on I-40 in Haywood County; and along the South Carolina state line on I-26 in Polk County, I-85 in Cleveland County, I-77 just outside Charlotte, and I-95 in Robeson County.

For basic planning, the maps on the VisitNC website will give you a good sense of the layout of the state and its major destinations. Many areas are experiencing rapid growth, particularly around Charlotte and the Triangle, so if your map is even a little out of date, you may not know about the newest bypass. For features like mountains, rivers, back roads, and small towns that don't change, atlas-style books of state maps are useful. My own favorite is DeLorme's *North Carolina Atlas & Gazetteer;* I live here and find it indispensable.

RESOURCES

Suggested Reading

TRAVEL

Daniels, Diane. *Farm Fresh North Carolina.* Chapel Hill: UNC Press, 2011. This guidebook will help you find the perfect place to pick apples, cut Christmas trees, visit a pumpkin patch, pick a bushel of blueberries, and shop at every farmers market across the state. You'll find recipes from chefs and farmers as well.

Duncan, Barbara, and Brett Riggs. *Cherokee Heritage Trails.* Chapel Hill: UNC Press, 2003; online companion at www.cherokeeheritage.org. A fascinating guide to both the historic and present-day home of the Eastern Band of the Cherokee in North Carolina, Tennessee, and Georgia, from ancient mounds and petroglyphs to modern-day arts co-ops and sporting events.

Eubanks, Georgann. *Literary Trails of the North Carolina Mountains: A Guidebook.* Chapel Hill: UNC Press, 2007. This book and its companion books *Literary Trails of the North Carolina Piedmont: A Guidebook,* 2010, and *Literary Trails of Eastern North Carolina: A Guidebook,* 2013, introduce fans of Southern literature to the places that produced and inspired various scribes. Also included are the best bookstores and book events across the state.

Fussell, Fred, and Steve Kruger. *Blue Ridge Music Trails of North Carolina: A Guide to Music Sites, Artists, and Traditions of the Mountains and Foothills.* Chapel Hill: UNC Press, 2013. A guide to destinations—festivals, restaurants, oprys, church singings—in the North Carolina mountains where authentic bluegrass, old-time, and sacred music can be experienced by visitors. An accompanying audio CD allows you to continue to hear the music. The exceptional photography by Cedric N. Chatterley in this book and in *Cherokee Heritage Trails*—reproduced in full color—and the depth of context conveyed make these two guides worth buying even if you're not touring the region.

North Carolina Atlas and Gazetteer. Yarmouth, ME: DeLorme, 2012. Since I was in Boy Scouts, I have always been partial to DeLorme's state atlases. This series represents in great detail the topography and other natural features of an area, giving far more useful and comprehensive information than the standard highway map.

Our State. www.ourstate.com. For a lively and informative look at North Carolina destinations and the cultural quirks and treasures you may find in your travels, *Our State* magazine is one of the best resources around. The magazine is easy to find, sold at most bookstores and even on grocery store and drugstore magazine racks. It covers arts, nature, folklore, history, scenery, sports, and lots of food, all from a traveler's perspective.

HISTORY AND CULTURE

Cecelski, David. *The Waterman's Song: Slavery and Freedom in Maritime North Carolina.* Chapel Hill: UNC Press, 2001. A marvelous treatment of the African American heritage of resistance in eastern North Carolina, and how the region's rivers and sounds were passages to freedom for many enslaved people.

Powell, William S. *North Carolina: A History.* Chapel Hill: UNC Press, 1988. A readable, concise account of our fascinating and varied past.

Powell, William S., and Jay Mazzocchi, editors. *Encyclopedia of North Carolina.* Chapel Hill: UNC Press, 2006. A fantastic compendium of all sorts of North Carolina history, letters, and politics. If you can lift this mammoth book, you'll learn about everything from Carolina basketball to presidential elections to ghosts.

Setzer, Lynn. *Tar Heel History on Foot: Great Walks through 400 Years of North Carolina's Fascinating Past.* Chapel Hill: UNC Press, 2013. This book sends you on a series of short walks in all parts of the state—coastal and mountain, city and country, historic sites and state parks—to discover the history of the state. The walks are arranged by theme and location, making it simple to find one near you.

Wright, David, and David Zoby. *Fire on the Beach: Recovering the Lost Story of Richard Etheridge and the Pea Island Lifesavers.* New York: Oxford University Press, 2002. The riveting tale of the first African American captain of a U.S. Life Saving Station and his all-African American crew. Spanning the time from just before the Civil War to the turn of the 20th century, it's a fascinating look at life for enslaved people and former slaves on the Outer Banks.

SPORTS

Blythe, Will. *To Hate Like This Is to Be Happy Forever: A Thoroughly Obsessive, Intermittently Uplifting, and Occasionally Unbiased Account of the Duke-North Carolina Basketball Rivalry.* New York: Harper, 2007. A highly entertaining book about the hatred that exists between partisans of UNC and Duke, and how the famous basketball rivalry brings out the best and worst in the fans.

Thompson, Neal. *Driving with the Devil: Southern Moonshine, Detroit Wheels, and the Birth of NASCAR.* New York: Broadway Books, 2008. The creation story of a great sport, the rise of stock-car racing from moonshiners' getaway wheels to a multibillion-dollar industry.

Internet Resources

NEWSPAPERS

North Carolina newspapers have unusually rich online content, and are great resources for travel planning.

Charlotte Observer
www.charlotteobserver.com
This website is packed with information about the arts, food, newcomer issues, and more.

Raleigh News & Observer
www.newsobserver.com
Raleigh's paper of record.

Asheville Citizen-Times
www.citizen-times.com
A good online edition for this Ashville-based paper.

Mountain Xpress
www.mountainx.com
Also covering the Asheville area, with a politically progressive and artistically countercultural bent—much like Asheville itself.

Mountain Times
http://mountaintimes.com
Weekly newspaper covering Boone and the High Country.

Independent Weekly
www.indyweek.com
A great source for the Triangle on the local music scene, politics, food, and more.

Fayetteville Observer
http://fayobserver.com/
News and culture from Fayetteville and the surrounding towns.

StarNews
www.starnewsonline.com
Providing daily news coverage of Wilmington and neighboring towns.

Outer Banks Sentinel
www.womacknewspapers.com/obsentinel
News and events pertinent to Outer Banks towns.

ARTS AND CULTURE

North Carolina's arts and history have an ever-growing online dimension, telling the story of the state in ways that paper and ink simply can't.

North Carolina Folklife Institute
www.ncfolk.org
The website will fill you in on the many organizations across the state that promote traditional music, crafts, and folkways. You'll also find a calendar of folk life-related events in North Carolina, and travel itineraries for weekends exploring Core Sound, the Seagrove potteries, and Cherokee heritage in the Smokies.

NCFOOD
www.ncfolk.org/category/food
This wonderful food blog, maintained by the Folklife Institute, features articles about the culinary back roads of the state.

North Carolina Arts Council
www.ncarts.org
The Arts Council provides information about performing arts, literature, cultural trails, galleries, and fun happenings.

North Carolina ECHO
www.ncecho.org
ECHO stands for "Exploring Cultural Heritage Online," and this great site has links to hundreds of online exhibits and brick-and-mortar museums.

Carolina Music Ways
www.carolinamusicways.org
A lively guide to the extremely varied musical traditions of the North Carolina Piedmont.

Blue Ridge Heritage Area
www.blueridgeheritage.com
This resource has a huge amount of mountain-area travel information and an ever-growing directory of traditional artists of all kinds in the Carolina mountains.

Southern Highland Craft Guild
www.southernhighlandguild.org
An Asheville-based regional arts giant with an extensive online guide to craftspeople throughout the region.

Creative Loafing Charlotte
http://clclt.com
A creative, enlightening, and sometimes irreverent look at Charlotte life, art, culture, news, and events.

Our State
www.ourstate.com
The online companion to this print publication provides expanded coverage of the history,

people, food, and arts across North Carolina. An extensive archive of stories lets you look back several years for the best the state has to offer.

OUTDOORS

Great online resources exist for planning outdoor adventures in North Carolina, where rich arts and blockbuster sports are matched by natural resources.

North Carolina Sierra Club
http://nc2.sierraclub.org

Find information about upcoming hikes and excursions as well as an overview of the state's natural areas and environmental issues.

North Carolina Birding Trail
www.ncbirdingtrail.org

Covering bird-watching across the state, this site contains information about dozens of pristine locations and active flyways along the coast, in the Piedmont, and in the mountains.

Carolina Canoe Club
www.carolinacanoeclub.com

A clearinghouse of statewide canoeing resources.

Carolina Kayak Club
www.carolinakayakclub.org

A repository for flat-water kayaking information, resources, trails, and activities across the state.

CanoeNC
www.canoenc.org

A nice starting point for planning a flat-water paddling trip in eastern North Carolina.

North Carolina Sportsman
www.northcarolinasportsman.com

Covering hunting and fishing news, destinations, and seasonal trends across the state.

North Carolina Outdoors
www.northcarolinaoutdoors.com

This privately operated site is full of excellent information and cross-referenced sources for state and national parklands and wilderness throughout the state.

Friends of the Mountains to Sea Trail
www.ncmst.org

Find details, hike-planning tools, and resources for a day or longer on the 1,000-mile-long Mountains to Sea Trail that crosses North Carolina.

NC Hikes
www.nchikes.com

All things hiking-related, including trails in every corner of the state, books, and trip recommendations.

Index

List of Maps

Acknowledgments

Without the following people helping, pushing, prodding, editing, traveling, and working with me, this book would not have been possible.

To Lauren, the best cheerleader, travel companion, research assistant, and wife I could ask for. You make every day fun, even the rainy ones when you have a long drive ahead.

To Billy and Tammy for taking me to North Carolina for the first time.

To Bob and K.D. for teaching me to see and appreciate this state from a new perspective.

To Dodie, Ryan, Craig, Aaron, and all the other folks who helped me put trips together and introduced me to the characters in your corner of North Carolina.

To the North Carolina Division of Tourism for the introductions, tips, and contacts.

To my editors at Avalon Travel, without your help, this book wouldn't be nearly as good.

To you, North Carolina, for being awesome, beautiful, and fun.

And finally, to the travelers, adventure seekers, foodies, and explorers who will pick up this book and discover new favorite places.

www.moon.com

DESTINATIONS | ACTIVITIES | BLOGS | MAPS | BOOKS

MOON.COM is ready to help plan your next trip! Filled with fresh trip ideas and strategies, author interviews, informative travel blogs, a detailed map library, and descriptions of all the Moon guidebooks, Moon.com is all you need to get out and explore the world—or even places in your own backyard. While at Moon.com, sign up for our monthly e-newsletter for updates on new releases, travel tips, and expert advice from our on-the-go Moon authors. As always, when you travel with Moon, expect an experience that is uncommon and truly unique.